Mao's Last Revolution

Mao's Last Revolution

RODERICK MACFARQUHAR
MICHAEL SCHOENHALS

The Belknap Press of Harvard University Press
Cambridge, Massachusetts, and London, England

First Harvard University Press paperback edition, 2008.

Library of Congress Cataloging-in-Publication Data

MacFarquhar, Roderick.
  Mao's last revolution / Roderick MacFarquhar and Michael Schoenhals.
    p.   cm.
  Includes bibliographical references and index.
  ISBN 978-0-674-02332-1 (cloth : alk. paper)
  ISBN 978-0-674-02748-0 (pbk.)
  1. China—History—Cultural Revolution, 1966–1976.
  I. Schoenhals, Michael.   II. Title.

DS778.7.M33 2006
951.05′6—dc22   2006042707

This work is dedicated to all Chinese whose works and words on the Cultural Revolution have enlightened us

And to future generations of Chinese historians, who may be able to research and write on these events with greater freedom

Contents

Illustrations follow pages 144 and 336

Preface

This book has had a long gestation. I started chronicling China's Cultural Revolution (1966–1976) while it was taking place, for a variety of mainly British newspapers, magazines, and scholarly journals as well as BBC TV and Radio. In 1968, I began researching the origins of this political convulsion. Three decades later I published the last volume in what had turned into a trilogy on the subject. In the meanwhile I had joined the Harvard faculty, and shortly after I arrived there, in the mid-1980s, a very distinguished historian asked me to give a course on the Cultural Revolution in a section of Harvard College's Core Program called Historical Study B. The formal remit of this section is to "focus closely on the documented details of some central historical event or transformation . . . sufficiently delimited in time to allow concentrated study of primary source materials." My colleague explained that the assumption was that all the documentation was in and all emotion had been spent, thus providing the possibility of greater objectivity. I explained that very few reliable primary materials were available, and that in China, and even among some Western China scholars, emotions still ran deep over the events of the tumultuous Cultural Revolution decade. However, by this time I had taken on the co-editorship with John K. Fairbank of the final two volumes of the *Cambridge History of China,* covering the People's Republic of China, and had undertaken to write a chapter covering most of the Cultural Revolution period, and eventually I decided I might as well teach the course anyway. The course was unexpectedly popular and required a sourcebook of readings for the students. Preparing it, I found that most of the English-language materials had been written in the 1970s and early 1980s, mainly on the basis of the materials issued during the Cultural Revolution by Mao and his victorious leftist coalition. Significant materials were finally beginning to emerge in Chinese to permit presentation of a more balanced picture of events, steering between the Scylla of the Maoist radicals and the Charybdis of the Deng-era survivors.

These materials informed the participants at a 1987 conference at Harvard's John K. Fairbank Center for East Asian Research, whose findings were published in *New Perspectives on the Cultural Revolution,* edited by William A. Joseph, Christine P. W. Wong, and David Zweig (Cambridge, Mass.: Council on East Asian Studies, Harvard University, 1991). But the new materials were of no use to the vast majority of undergraduates in my course who did not know Chinese.

From 1991 to 1997, sociologist Andrew Walder (now at Stanford), anthropologist James L. Watson, and I ran a project on the Cultural Revolution with a generous grant from the Luce Foundation. This enabled us to bring to the Fairbank Center a number of Western scholars and Chinese who had lived through the Cultural Revolution. The project included a conference on "The Cultural Revolution in Retrospect" convened by Andrew Walder at the Hong Kong University of Science and Technology in July 1996.

Among the Western scholars who joined the project at the Fairbank Center was Michael Schoenhals, whose earlier work on pre–Cultural Revolution politics had greatly impressed us when he was one of our postdoctoral fellows. Michael, who had been a student in China during the final year of the Cultural Revolution, combines superb language skills and meticulous scholarship with a bloodhound ability to find obscure but fascinating materials in the flea markets of urban China.

Michael and I discussed what we might do with the rapidly increasing Chinese documentation. We decided that we could best serve the wider scholarly and student community as well as a more general readership by writing a history of the Cultural Revolution. This book is the product of that decision. Michael prepared the first versions of the great majority of the chapters, which then went through a number of drafts. Administrative responsibilities in Cambridge, Stockholm—where Michael convened an international Cultural Revolution conference—and Lund dragged the process out. But we were encouraged by signs of renewed academic interest in the Cultural Revolution at other institutions; each of us gave a lecture in a year-long seminar course on the subject at the University of California, San Diego.

In the spring of 2003, Michael and I took advantage of the Radcliffe Institute's innovative Exploratory Seminar program, presided over by Katherine Newman, then its Dean of Social Science, and run by Phyllis Strimling. We presented a complete if not quite final draft to Merle Goldman, Nancy Hearst, Dwight Perkins, Elizabeth Perry, Lucian Pye, Anthony Saich, Stuart Schram, Ross Terrill, and Andrew Walder, and this work owes much to their informed and insightful comments. Nancy Hearst, with the unrivaled contacts she has built up as Fairbank Center Librarian and on her annual book-hunting visits to Beijing, provided me with the latest books and magazines; later she did truly yeoman service in questioning the text, regularizing the notes, compiling the bibliography, and transforming English usage into American usage. Victor Shih read through a lot of recent issues of Chinese party history journals and provided me with excellent and useful synopses of relevant articles. On visits to China, I was fortunate to be able to have discussions with the few Chinese historians who have written about the Cultural Revolution and whose works are mentioned in our notes, and even with one or two significant participants in the events themselves.

When I finally handed our manuscript to Kathleen McDermott, the editor for History and the Social Sciences at Harvard University Press, she seemed pleased, tactfully concealing any surprise or relief she might have felt. After receiving positive feedback and suggestions from two anonymous reviewers—to whom we are most grateful—she put the impressive HUP machine into gear. Elizabeth Gilbert supervised the project with loving care, Ann Hawthorne edited the manuscript with speedy and patient efficiency, deadlines were met. Indexing was in the familiar and expert hands of Anne Holmes. On behalf of Michael and myself, I extend our warmest thanks to them and to other members of the HUP staff whom we expect to meet as the manuscript turns into a book looking for readers. At this point, over to Michael . . .

. . . who, when Rod started researching the origins of the Cultural Revolution, was still in high school, dreaming of one day becoming the beatnik translator of Tang poetry in Jack Kerouac's novel *Dharma Bums*. Eight years later, in what our campus loudspeakers in Shanghai told us was the "tenth spring of the Great Proletarian Cultural Revolution," I found myself at Fudan University, learning by observing what mass politics Maoist style was all about. Nothing was further from my mind than one day coauthoring a history of the Cultural Revolution. Throughout the 1980s, engaged in research in Europe and North America, first on the Great Leap Forward, then on CCP rhetoric and propaganda, my Shanghai experience was simply a reservoir of more or less outrageous stories with which at parties I was able to one-up fellow students from the United States who had arrived in China only *after* the Chairman was dead and gone.

When Rod invited me to join him in the venture that has resulted in this book, I became very excited, relishing the idea of promotion to comrade-in-pens with someone whose scholarship I so deeply admired. And after so many years, I was finally ready to return to the Cultural Revolution "as history." What I did not realize was that with both of us being perfectionists, there was no way we would be able to meet our own deadlines, nor that set for us by Harvard University Press. But if this book is much behind schedule, it is certainly enriched by much more material, and, we hope, far better than it would have been had it appeared earlier.

My thanks to the Swedish Research Council (VR) and its predecessor, the Swedish Research Council for the Humanities and Social Sciences (HSFR), for generously funding my research. A special word of thanks to my colleagues on the VR Program for Research on Communist Regimes, a source of great inspiration and intellectual stimulus. And an immense debt of gratitude to the many Chinese—participants, victims, perpetrators, brilliant analytical minds, storytellers, obvious liars, patient relatives, kind strangers—who have shared with me their own experiences and insights and from whom I have learned so much.

We are conscious that, however much reading and interviewing we have done, there will continue to be a constant flow of newer materials some of which may overtake our judgments. Even when all the archives are opened, mysteries will remain. But by then, possibly Chinese historians will be free not merely to recount the events of the Cultural Revolution—as a few have brilliantly done—but even to assess and debate those events untrammeled by the procrustean bed of the party line.

Roderick MacFarquhar
Michael Schoenhals

Abbreviations

CC	Central Committee
CCEG	Central Case Examination Group
CCP	Chinese Communist Party
CCRG	Central Cultural Revolution Group
CPSU	Communist Party of the Soviet Union
CYL	Communist Youth League
Fairbank Center	John K. Fairbank Center for East Asian Research, Harvard University
FYP	Five-Year Plan
GLF	Great Leap Forward
HQ	Headquarters
KMT	Guomindang (Kuomintang)
MAC	Military Affairs Commission
MD	Military District
MR	Military Region
NPC	National People's Congress
PLA	People's Liberation Army
PRC	People's Republic of China
PSC	Politburo Standing Committee
RC	Revolutionary Committee
SEM	Socialist Education Movement
WGHQ	Workers' Revolutionary Rebels General Headquarters

Mao's Last Revolution

Introduction

They will begin by taking the State and the manners of men, from which, as from a tablet, they will rub out the picture, and leave a clean surface. This is no easy task. But whether easy or not, herein will lie the difference between them and every other legislator,—they will have nothing to do either with individual or State, and will inscribe no laws, until they have either found, or themselves made, a clean surface . . .

. . . let there be one man who has a city obedient to his will, and he might bring into existence the ideal polity about which the world is so incredulous.
—Plato, *The Republic*, book VI

China's 600 million people have two remarkable peculiarities; they are, first of all, poor, and secondly, blank. That may seem like a bad thing, but it is really a good thing. Poor people want change, want to do things, want revolution. A clean sheet of paper has no blotches, and so the newest and most beautiful pictures can be painted on it.
—Mao Zedong, 1958

The Cultural Revolution was a watershed, the defining decade of half a century of Communist rule in China. To understand the "why" of China today, one has to understand the "what" of the Cultural Revolution. To understand what happened during the Cultural Revolution, one has to understand how it came to be launched. This introduction seeks to explain the origins of the "Great Proletarian Cultural Revolution." The rest of the book chronicles what happened during its terrible decade, 1966–1976.

Before the Cultural Revolution started, in May 1966, China was by and large a standard Communist state, if more effective than most. The Chinese Communist Party (CCP) ruled unchallenged. Its writ ran throughout the nation. Its leader, Mao Zedong, "Chairman Mao," was held in a reverence that even Stalin would have envied. Its 19 million members ensured that the Chairman's directives were heard and heeded at all levels of society. And when those directives led to widespread famine and tens of millions of deaths, as they did during the Great Leap Forward (GLF) and its aftermath (1958–1961), the cadres held the country together and enabled the CCP to weather the calamity. By 1966, the Chinese economy had recovered sufficiently for a Soviet-style third Five-Year Plan (FYP) to be scheduled. But the Cultural Revolution overwhelmed careful plans and policies. For a decade, the Chinese political system was first thrown into chaos and then paralyzed.

Two years after the Cultural Revolution ended in October 1976, the principal survivor of that cataclysm, onetime CCP General Secretary Deng Xiaoping, initiated China's reform era. The enormity of the challenge facing him and his colleagues was visible throughout East Asia. When the CCP had come to power in 1949, its morale high, determined to transform China economically and socially, Japan was under foreign occupation, still demoralized by defeat and the nuclear coup de grâce. Taiwan was a rural backwater to which the defeated remnants of Chiang Kai-shek's Nationalist Party (KMT) and army had fled. Within a year, South Korea would be devastated by invasion from the north, and soon afterward Chinese troops were contributing to its destruction. As late as the eve of the Cultural Revolution seventeen years later, not much seemed to have changed in East Asia. Only a few observant foreigners had noted the signs of dynamic growth in the Japanese economy.[1]

But by the time that Deng returned to power, the Japanese miracle had been emulated in South Korea and Taiwan. The sleepy entrepôts of Singapore and Hong Kong had become flourishing industrial centers. The rampant East Asian tigers had proved that being part of the old Chinese cultural area, let alone Chinese, need not condemn one to poverty. Yet at the historic heart of the area, China itself now lay spread-eagled, this time by its own hand, not as a result of foreign invasion or conventional civil war.

For the Chinese leaders, the message was clear: they had to embark upon a policy of rapid economic growth to make up for lost time and to relegitimize CCP rule. They had to abandon Maoist utopianism in favor of building the strong and prosperous nation of which they had dreamed when they joined the nascent CCP in the 1920s. Otherwise the CCP itself might not last. So "practice," not ideology—not Marxism-Leninism, not Mao Zedong Thought—became the "sole criterion of truth." If it worked, it would be done.

Since that decision, China's quarter-century of rapid economic growth, fueled in part by enormous quantities of foreign direct investment, has amazed the world. Though some point to very significant weaknesses in China's economic and financial structures, most Westerners see the PRC as a future global superpower. Individual Chinese have become prosperous once getting rich was officially declared to be glorious. Private ownership was finally accepted and enshrined in the constitution. The new order was called "socialism with Chinese characteristics" by its progenitors, "market Leninism" and other neologisms by Western observers. Perceived threats to the dominance of the CCP would not be tolerated, as shown by the brutal suppression of the student movement in 1989 and the Falungong in 1999, along with the regular arrests of political dissidents. But concomitant social changes freed Chinese from the most egregious terrors of the 1950s, 1960s, and 1970s.

China scholars who have followed PRC developments for decades are more amazed than most, for they understand how great these changes are. A common verdict is: no Cultural Revolution, no economic reform. The Cultural Revolution was so great a disaster that it provoked an even more profound cultural revolution, precisely the one that Mao intended to forestall. For it was indeed Mao who was responsible for the Cultural Revolution, as the CCP's Central Committee (CC) formally admitted in its 1981 *Resolution on Party History:*

> The "cultural revolution," which lasted from May 1966 to October 1976, was responsible for the most severe setback and the heaviest losses suffered by the Party, the state and the people since the founding of the People's Republic. It was initiated and led by Comrade Mao Zedong.[2]

Why did China's supreme leader decide to tear down what he had done so much to create?

The Evolution of Mao's Thinking

The origins of the Cultural Revolution demand an understanding of Mao's reactions to a complex mix of domestic and foreign developments over the decade preceding its launch.[3] In his major speeches, Mao often started with a global *tour d'horizon,* giving his colleagues an appraisal of the progress of revolution throughout the world and locating Chinese policies and problems within that context. Central to that global context in the decade before the Cultural

Revolution was the burgeoning split between Moscow and Beijing over the appropriate international policies of the Communist bloc and internal politics of Communist nations. From the Chinese point of view, that split began with the two speeches delivered by First Secretary Nikita Khrushchev at the Twentieth Congress of the Communist Party of the Soviet Union (CPSU) in February 1956.[4] The first of these, his official report on the work of the Central Committee, provided the basis for subsequent disagreements on bloc policy; and the second, his notorious "secret speech," immediately angered the Chinese.

The CCP delegation was neither given advance warning nor allowed to attend the session on February 25 when the secret speech was delivered, being informed of it only immediately afterward.[5] Chinese anger had two sources. First of all, the attack on Stalin and his "cult of personality" had obvious implications for the cult of Mao, and CCP propaganda quickly differentiated the roles of the two dictators.

The other reason for Chinese anger was the likely impact on the world Communist movement. Suddenly to destroy the image of the man who had been the unquestioned leader and the paragon of all virtue for Communists everywhere was seen in Beijing as the height of irresponsibility, a verdict that was amply demonstrated later in the year by the Hungarian revolt and the defection of thousands of Communists from parties in the West. In an unsuccessful effort to preempt such repercussions, the CCP issued a measured analysis of Stalin, describing him as an "outstanding Marxist-Leninist fighter," stressing that his achievements far outweighed his faults, serious though they were.[6]

But it was the ideological innovations in Khrushchev's public report that were the main grounds for the subsequent polemics between the CCP and the CPSU. Khrushchev revised Leninist doctrine in two ways: he proclaimed that war between communism and imperialism was not fatally inevitable; and he foresaw the possibility of peaceful, rather than revolutionary, transitions to socialism to enable Communists to come to power. At the time, Chinese propaganda supported his doctrine on war and voiced no objection on the issue of peaceful transition. This position was in line with China's current adherence to the doctrine of peaceful coexistence, its opening of ambassadorial talks with the United States, and its cultivation of friendly relations with the "bourgeois nationalist" governments of Asia, whose leaders would not have liked to hear that their regimes were ripe for revolution, together with a domestic thaw after years of class struggle.[7]

But after Mao turned left in domestic and foreign affairs in mid-1957, the CCP began to chivvy the CPSU on these issues. In Moscow later that year for the celebration of the fortieth anniversary of the Bolshevik revolution, Mao was emboldened by the launch of the first Soviet Sputnik, and the implication of Soviet missile superiority, to proclaim that the East Wind was prevailing over the West Wind. He argued with the Soviet leadership against the Khrushchev innovations on war and peace and on peaceful transition, and managed to insert some codicils into the joint declaration issued by the ruling Communist parties present, though the Soviet views still predominated.[8] In one of his speeches, Mao struck a chill among his fellow Communist leaders when he seemed to contemplate with equanimity a third world war in which perhaps half of humanity might perish, but after which there would be global socialism.[9]

From the Soviet viewpoint, Mao seemed increasingly bent on bringing about such a conflagration by inciting a Soviet-American nuclear exchange. On July 13, 1958, when the Western-oriented Iraqi regime was toppled by a left-wing general, American and British troops were sent to Lebanon and Jordan respectively to shore up those pro-Western regimes, with a view also, it was widely speculated, to invading Iraq and overthrowing the new regime. The Chinese reaction was far more bellicose than the Soviet one. Apparently fearing a Soviet-American confrontation on the USSR's southern border, Khrushchev twice called for an urgent summit meeting with the Western permanent members of the United Nations Security Council—the United States, the United Kingdom, and France—plus India and the UN secretary general "in order that immediate steps may be taken to put an end to the conflict that has broken out."[10] Since in reality no conflict had broken out, the Soviet leader's anxiety was clearly about possible Western action against the new Iraqi regime. His son later claimed that Khrushchev was nervous at first, but in "the heat of battle, Father felt like a fish in the sea."[11]

It did not seem that way to Mao and his colleagues. In their view, the Soviet reaction was pusillanimous and uncomradely: uncomradely because Khrushchev wanted India to attend but did not mention the People's Republic of China (PRC), and because he was prepared to hold the conference under the auspices of the United Nations, of which China was not a member; pusillanimous because, as the official CCP newspaper, the *People's Daily*, argued, this was no time for appeasement. Rather, volunteer armies, implicitly from the Soviet Union, should be sent to the Middle East, presumably to defend the Iraqi revolution. As it became clear that the West was not going to interfere in Iraq, Khrushchev's tone began to resemble China's. With the crisis diminishing, Khrushchev flew secretly to Beijing to try to repair the damage and settle another troubling issue in Sino-Soviet relations, his proposals for joint military facilities, including what the Chinese indignantly termed a "joint fleet in China to dominate the coastal area, and to blockade us."[12]

Relations were superficially patched up in talks between the two leaders beside Mao's swimming pool, and so it was possible to reveal that the visit had taken place. The Soviet proposals were effectively withdrawn, but the Chairman was still determined to demonstrate to Khrushchev how he should behave toward the United States now that the East Wind was prevailing over the West. The lesson would be the Taiwan Straits crisis of August–September 1958.[13]

On August 23, three weeks after Khrushchev had returned to Moscow, the Chinese started shelling the Nationalist-held offshore island of Jinmen (Quemoy) and disrupting Nationalist attempts to resupply it. The object seems to have been to force either the withdrawal or the surrender of the garrison, thus demonstrating the powerlessness of the Americans to aid their allies. The gamble failed as Secretary of State John Foster Dulles indicated U.S. willingness to convoy Nationalist relief vessels and a direct Sino-American clash seemed imminent. In fact, the crisis demonstrated rather the unwillingness of the Soviets to aid *their* allies, despite the Sino-Soviet treaty of 1950, if there were the slightest danger of being dragged into a Soviet-American nuclear exchange. Only after the Chinese had clearly backed away from a direct confrontation with the United States did Khrushchev write to President Eisenhower stating that an attack on China would be regarded as an attack on the Soviet Union.[14]

Mao's unhappiness with Soviet caution was compounded in 1959 by Khrushchev's decision to renege on the secret agreement to give the Chinese a sample atomic bomb with details of nuclear technology. This was quickly followed by the unfraternal Soviet decision to assume a neutral stance on the border clashes between China and India. To Chinese eyes, Khrushchev was sacrificing the national interests of his principal ally in his efforts to promote peaceful coexistence with the United States and to cultivate the friendship of bourgeois nationalist leaders of the Third World like India's Premier Nehru. Both of these aims were seen by Mao as reflections of the unpalatable revisions of Leninist doctrine by Khrushchev in his public report to the CPSU's Twentieth Congress.[15] Khrushchev rubbed salt in the wounds to the Chinese psyche when he went almost directly from a barnstorming tour of America to China for the tenth anniversary of the Communist revolution on October 1, 1959, and publicly informed his angry hosts that Eisenhower was a man of peace.

Mao's Obsession with Revisionism

Mao chose the ninetieth anniversary of Lenin's birth, April 22, 1960, to launch four major polemics against revisionism, albeit without pointing the finger directly at Moscow. "Long Live Leninism!" raised the argument to the ideological level, thus indicating that these were issues of principle on which the Chairman would not back down.[16] The year witnessed a series of heated Sino-Soviet clashes at Communist gatherings, in the end so infuriating Khrushchev that in July he ordered the withdrawal of the almost 1,400 Soviet specialists then working in China to help its development program. Despite the subsequent dispatch of a high-level Chinese delegation headed by Liu Shaoqi, No. 2 in the Chinese Politburo and already Mao's successor as head of state, to Moscow in November 1960, only a cosmetic truce resulted. The statement patched together by the eighty-one Communist parties present at the deliberations was the now familiar combination of Soviet positions and Chinese codicils.[17]

For much of the next eighteen months, the Chinese leaders were desperately concerned with trying to alleviate the terrible GLF famine. The Sino-Soviet dispute continued to smolder, however, despite the efforts of other Communist parties to bring the two sides together. A superficial civility was maintained by the avoidance of direct attacks on the other, with the Chinese blasting the Yugoslav Communists instead of the CPSU, and the Soviets denouncing Beijing's ally Albania as a surrogate for the CCP.

Even this transparent device was abandoned in 1963. The Chinese decided that the partial test-ban treaty, initialed by the Soviet Union, the United States, and Britain on July 25, was an attempt by Khrushchev to freeze the Chinese out of the nuclear club. From September 1963 to July 1964, in a series of nine polemics, the Chinese spelled out their reasons for breaking with the CPSU. They included expositions on the issues of Stalin, war and peace, peaceful coexistence, peaceful transitions to socialism, and Khrushchev's revisionism. The most important of the polemics was the ninth, "On Khrushchev's Phoney Communism and Historical Lessons for the World," published on July 14, 1964.[18] It contained the justification for what would turn out to be the Cultural Revolution.

Domestic Dilemmas

It would be a travesty to suggest that the turmoil of the Cultural Revolution was the result solely of Mao's assessment of what was happening in the Soviet Union.[19] His thinking was shaped equally by what was happening at home. But with his global outlook, no revolution was an island. In his darkening vision, the Chinese slogan of the 1950s, "The Soviet Union's today is our tomorrow," was increasingly a foreboding rather than a promise. The reason for his gloom was the behavior of his colleagues in response to the travail of the GLF famine.

In 1961, the last of the "three bitter years" of dearth and death, Mao presided over a wide range of innovative policy-making—for agriculture, industry, commerce, education, and intellectual life—designed to jump-start the economy. In particular, he sanctioned the abolition of the unpopular and wasteful collective mess halls in the rural people's communes. Even more importantly, he agreed that in the countryside, the accounting unit should be the production team, the lowest level organization within the commune, corresponding most closely to the natural village. This strategy increased incentives by diminishing the equalization of incomes across a commune composed of a large number of villages of differing prosperity.

By the end of the year there was little to show for the plethora of plans. Officials were all too aware that in 1959 sensible retrenchment of GLF excesses had been abruptly reversed after Mao had dismissed Defense Minister Peng Dehuai for what the Chairman characterized as a challenge to the fundamental philosophy of the GLF. Cadres who had revised GLF policies in good faith found themselves attacked and purged like Peng as "right opportunists." In 1961, no official would make the same mistake.

Under the circumstances, only Mao could breathe life into the new policies. He did so by offering a tepid but uncharacteristic self-criticism at an unprecedentedly large conference of 7,000 cadres in January–February 1962, and then absenting himself from policy-making for a few months. At the time, nobody could tell whether the size of the harvest would presage a fourth bitter year. Food was still the major problem. Left in charge, Mao's colleagues espoused radical policies for the countryside which would have effectively restored family farming. But once it became clear that the economy had turned the corner, Mao reclaimed the agenda and insisted on holding the line on collectivist agriculture.

The Chairman was well aware that his colleagues had been responding to peasant unhappiness with the communes. Maintaining collectivism was not enough; the peasants had to be convinced that it was good for them. Mao called for a Socialist Education Movement (SEM) to restore the faith. But party leaders soon realized that peasants were unresponsive to the arguments of rural cadres who in many places had become as corrupt as the KMT officials they had replaced. The SEM was transformed into intensive investigations and purging of rural cadres by massive teams of central officials under the aegis of Liu Shaoqi. Supportive, even admiring at first, Mao turned against the policy in late 1964. There appear to have been two main reasons.

The Dismissal of Khrushchev

Nikita Khrushchev fell on October 14, 1964, as a result of a coup by his colleagues. They had tired of his abuse and his "harebrained scheming, half-baked conclusions and hasty decisions and actions divorced from reality . . . attraction to rule by fiat, [and] unwillingness to take into account what science and practical experience have already worked out."[20] Since the Chinese had tended to personalize the Sino-Soviet dispute, putting most of the blame on Khrushchev, they quickly sent a delegation to Moscow under Premier Zhou Enlai, the leader least involved in the anti-Soviet confrontations. But Zhou's conversations with Leonid Brezhnev and Khrushchev's other successors led the Chinese to conclude that they would continue to practice what the *People's Daily* termed "Khrushchevism without Khrushchev."

Worse from Mao's point of view was that the Soviets, too, had personalized the dispute. An allegedly drunken Soviet defense minister told a member of Zhou's delegation, Marshal He Long: "We've already got rid of Khrushchev; you ought to follow our example and get rid of Mao Zedong. That way we'll get on better." In 1956, Mao had worried that he, like Stalin, might be denounced after his death; in 1964, he had reason to wonder if he, like Khrushchev, might be toppled *before* his death. After all, the indictment of the Soviet leader could have been applied with even more force to Mao.

For by this time Mao seemed very different from when he had become party chairman twenty years earlier. Back then, he had been a welcome unifier after years of internecine struggle: the leadership lineup formed at the Seventh Congress in Yan'an in 1945 basically lasted through the Eighth Congress in 1956 and to the eve of the Cultural Revolution in 1965. Up till the mid-1950s, Mao seemed tolerant of debate in the Politburo, even accepting defeat on economic policy issues. But then his attitude and behavior toward his colleagues changed. He thrust aside the cautious planners at the outset of the tragically misconceived GLF and forced Premier Zhou Enlai into a humiliating self-criticism. Eighteen months later, Mao flew into a rage at Defense Minister Marshal Peng Dehuai and dismissed this hero of the revolution and the Korean War. In 1962, when he judged that the GLF catastrophe was ending, he disrupted the ongoing national recovery effort by forcing his colleagues to accept renewed class struggle, unquestionably rule by fiat. Whatever camaraderie had been forged among the veterans of the revolution had given way to trepidation in the face of a headstrong Chairman who would brook no opposition. Mao may well have sensed, probably welcomed, his comrades' fear. But the fall of Khrushchev would have alerted him to the possibility that fear might unite them against him. From this point on, loyalty to his *person* rather than his *policies* became the touchstone for the Chairman.[21]

From that viewpoint, the loyalty of a "rightist" like Zhou Enlai was to be preferred to the questioning of a "leftist" like Liu Shaoqi. Those different attitudes toward the Chairman date back to the revolutionary period, and since official Chinese historians do not explore such topics, their origins can only be deduced from an examination of the record.

In the 1920s and early 1930s, Zhou was Mao's superior. His enormous abilities, considerable charm, and apparently inexhaustible energy were recognized early, and he was drafted into the Politburo in 1927, when he was twenty-nine. That year, he played major roles in the abortive Shanghai and Nanchang uprisings, the latter commemorated in the PRC as the birth of the People's Liberation Army (PLA).[22] Forced to flee to the countryside as Chiang Kai-shek's Nationalist forces hunted down their erstwhile Communist allies in the cities, Zhou arrived in the soviet that Mao had set up in the wilds of Jiangxi province. There he eventually sidelined Mao, and it was Zhou who gave the order for the Long March in October 1934.

Despite his prominence during these years, Zhou seems never to have sought the supreme position within the party. Instead he worked as the trusted lieutenant of successive general secretaries, nimbly managing, as each was disgraced, to enlist with the next one, readily self-criticizing if necessary for supporting previous policies. Possibly Zhou saw his strength as lying in the execution rather than the conception of policy, or possibly he was simply risk-averse. Or possibly, when Mao began his rise to supreme leadership from January 1935, Zhou recognized that here finally was a man with the vision for the party and country that he himself lacked. Thereafter, he attempted to follow Mao's line, and if he discovered that he had deviated, as at the beginning of the GLF, he abased himself.

Early on in the Cultural Revolution, Zhou revealed that he was fully aware of Mao's overriding demand when he stated: "With a single stroke of the pen, all your past achievements will be canceled out, should you fail the final test of loyalty."[23] The premier might disagree profoundly with Mao's policies, but he would never oppose or even question them. Mao's doctor characterized the relationship between the two men as that of "master and slave."[24]

Liu Shaoqi, on the other hand, "accepted a position as Mao's subordinate, but clearly had no intention of abandoning his critical faculties."[25] Liu had an independent status within the party, having risen by a different route from Mao. The latter had early on seen the peasantry as the engine of a Chinese revolution,[26] whereas Liu had taken the more conventional Leninist route as an organizer of the nascent proletariat in the cities. The two men were also very different personalities, Mao the romantic revolutionary, reveling in struggle and martial action, Liu "somewhat bookish, thoughtful, rather taciturn, but clearly persevering," stoic by temperament, a man who ascended step by step "not by obvious talents, but by solid hard work." Truly gray in his eminence, Liu seemed to have totally internalized the principle of the primacy of the organization over the individual,[27] a principle of which the Cultural Revolution was a total negation.

This odd couple, Liu and Mao, came together in the late 1930s when they found themselves on the same side against leaders preferred by Moscow. Mao must have recognized the organizational talents of his new ally, for Liu played a major role in the rectification campaign of the early 1940s, which reeducated the CCP to accept Mao's leadership. And at the party's Seventh Congress in 1945, Liu's political report was a paean of praise to Mao's thought, marking the beginning of the Mao cult that the Chairman would use to such devastating effect against Liu and others during the Cultural Revolution.

Like Zhou, Liu was not always successful in divining Mao's line. During the early 1960s he espoused Mao's SEM enthusiastically, but had been prepared to argue with the Chairman over its goals and its implementation.[28] With a strong base in the party machine that he had done so much to create, Liu must have loomed in Mao's imagination as a potential Brezhnev, able to topple him if he turned his back.

The Ninth Polemic

The second reason for the Chairman's dissatisfaction with Liu was that Mao had become uninterested in the SEM purge of rural cadres for what he considered petty peculation. It was the ideological backsliding of party members and the consequent danger of a capitalist restoration that concerned him more. Mao's views were spelled out in the ninth anti-Soviet polemic. In this document, items were quoted from the Soviet press to prove that the proletariat was under attack by the bourgeoisie in the Soviet Union. This development was held to be unsurprising and would have been unworrying had the Soviet leadership been true Marxist-Leninists. But their exaltation of material incentives, tolerance for high income differentials, defamation of the proletarian dictatorship by attacking Stalin's cult of personality, and substitution of capitalist management for socialist planning demonstrated that the "revisionist Khrushchev clique are the political representatives of the Soviet bourgeoisie, and particularly of its privileged stratum."[29] The unprecedented danger of a "capitalist restoration" in the Soviet Union should sound the tocsin throughout the Communist world, where parties like the CCP were struggling to prevent a similar "peaceful evolution."

The polemic listed fifteen principles based on conventional Marxism-Leninism and Maoist ideas to avert this danger, but these were deemed insufficient. In addition, it was absolutely vital to rear revolutionary successors:

> In the final analysis, the question of training successors for the revolutionary cause of the proletariat is one of whether or not there will be people who can carry on the Marxist-Leninist revolutionary cause started by the older generation of proletarian revolutionaries, whether or not the leadership of our Party and state will remain in the hands of proletarian revolutionaries, whether or not our descendants will continue to march along the correct road laid down by Marxism-Leninism, or, in other words, whether or not we can successfully prevent the emergence of Khrushchev's revisionism in China. *In short, it is an extremely important question, a matter of life or death for our Party and our country.* It is a question of fundamental importance to the proletarian revolutionary cause for a hundred, a thousand, nay ten thousand years. (Emphasis added)

Here was the black vision of a possible liquidation of communism that would justify a Cultural Revolution. Even the process by which succeeding generations would be imbued with Maoist principles was hinted at: "Successors to the revolutionary cause of the proletariat come forward in mass struggles and are tempered in great storms of revolution. It is essential to test and know cadres and choose and train successors in the long course of mass struggle."[30]

Storm Warning

There is no way to know if Mao's colleagues perceived this polemic as potentially a threat to themselves. Possibly they saw it simply as propaganda hype designed to please Mao. But by the end of 1964, the Chairman's dissatisfaction with some of them became clearly visible. At a top-level conference, Mao challenged Liu's handling of the SEM, and accused Liu and Deng Xiaoping of trying to prevent him from speaking by excluding him from the conference. In an absurdly theatrical but not untypical gesture, Mao produced his party card and a copy of the constitution to prove his right to be there and be heard.

And of course, he was not merely heard; he got his way. In an unusual development for the well-organized party Secretariat, a CC directive on the next stages of the SEM had to be rescinded because the Chairman had had second thoughts. The new directive, issued in January 1965, contained a passage that clearly presaged that the Chairman had in mind a movement far more significant than just the elimination of corrupt rural accounting:

> The key point of this movement is to rectify those people in positions of authority within the Party who take the capitalist road . . . Of those people in positions of authority who take the capitalist road, some are out in the open and some are concealed . . . Among those at higher levels, there are some people in the communes, districts, counties [*xian*], special districts, and even in the work of provincial and Central Committee departments, who oppose socialism.[31]

At this point, there should have been no doubt in his colleagues' minds that Mao's target was high-level "capitalist roaders." Who were they? How would Mao seek to remove them? The Chairman was too experienced a guerrilla fighter to tip his hand, but he soon launched a covert operation to begin his purification of the party.

1

The First Salvos

On February 24, 1965, Mao Zedong sent his wife Jiang Qing to Shanghai on an undercover mission to light the first spark of the Cultural Revolution. She knew the city well, having been a minor actress on stage and screen there in the 1930s, before moving to Yan'an during the anti-Japanese war and marrying Mao. By the 1960s, Shanghai's prewar bohemian demimonde had long since disappeared, and the city had become a Maoist bastion.[1] The Chairman relied on its leftist party leader, Ke Qingshi, for total support for his more extravagant schemes. It was the obvious place to send his wife to launch his most extravagant scheme yet.

Jiang Qing had been frustrated for years by her inability to influence cultural policy. When she married Mao in Yan'an in 1939, she bore the stigma of causing his divorce from an admired revolutionary heroine, Mao's comrade on the Long March. Mao's senior colleagues insisted that she devote herself to caring for the Chairman and stay out of politics for twenty-five to thirty years. By the mid-1960s that prohibition was nearing its term, and Jiang Qing was making increasing efforts to play a role in the cultural sphere. She was not content to be just the consort of a great man. In her acting days, her favorite part had been Nora in Ibsen's *A Doll's House*, the drama of a woman who broke free from her stifling conventional role as a housewife. Unlike Nora, Jiang Qing could not leave her husband because she wanted power, but she was determined not to be stifled by the party bureaucracy.[2]

Jiang Qing's growing desire for a political role may have been inversely related to the Chairman's diminishing desire for her; they were often apart, and Mao had long enjoyed dancing and dalliance with a bevy of attractive young women, often from cultural troupes, some of whom became members of his household.[3] What is clearer is that, though Jiang Qing could legitimately claim experience and expertise, the relevant officials regarded her as an interloper and ignored her suggestions. After the Chairman called for a revolution in the cultural field in 1964, it was senior party cadres who formed the Group of Five to carry out his wishes. Even Mao had been unsupportive of her wishes, agreeing to let the group be led by Peng Zhen, the powerful No. 2 on the CCP Central Committee Secretariat, who most recently had provoked Jiang Qing's ire by dismissing a pet opera project of hers as "politically pointless." But now, finally, Mao needed her for a guerrilla campaign that could not be conducted through party channels. He permitted her to solicit help in Shanghai for an attack on a prolific Beijing intellectual who had long been her bête noire.

The Campaign against Wu Han

Wu Han, blacklisted by the Nationalist government for his left-leaning views while a professor of history at Tsinghua University in the 1940s, was China's leading historian of the Ming dynasty.[4] During the Great Leap Forward, frustrated by dishonest reporting of output figures, Mao had called on party cadres to emulate a forthright Ming official called Hai Rui and tell the truth. One of Mao's secretaries called on Wu Han to write articles explaining just who Hai Rui was and what he had done. Among Wu's writings on the subject was a play commissioned by a Beijing Opera company, performed in early 1961 under the title *Hai Rui Dismissed from Office.* Mao expressed approval of the play at the time and later that year honored the author with an autographed copy of the latest volume of his *Selected Works.* But Jiang Qing had always argued that the play was in fact an attack on the Chairman's policies. Now at last, Mao had unleashed her to arrange a counterattack on Wu Han.

Had Wu Han been a run-of-the-mill academic, a public campaign to attack him would have been a step with which intellectuals were by now all too familiar. But two factors led Jiang Qing to prepare the campaign in the utmost secrecy. All attacks by name on intellectuals as senior as Wu Han were supposed to be officially sanctioned by Peng Zhen's Group of Five. Since Peng Zhen was also the party first secretary and mayor of the capital, Wu Han as a vice mayor was doubly under his protection. Unsurprisingly, Jiang Qing had failed to find any polemicist in Beijing who dared to provoke Peng Zhen's anger. Hence her four-month visit to Shanghai.[5]

Knowing that Jiang Qing had to be acting with the Chairman's approval, Ke Qingshi had no qualms about assigning two of his propagandists, Zhang Chunqiao and Yao Wenyuan, to help her. Unfortunately for Mao as he prepared for the Cultural Revolution, this would be the last act of political significance his longtime ally performed for him; Ke died suddenly and unexpectedly on April 9, 1965, while convalescing in Chengdu after lung cancer surgery.[6]

Zhang Chunqiao and Yao Wenyuan had long been in Mao's good books: the senior, Zhang, for his radical views on the subject of Communist egalitarianism, which clearly resonated with the CCP Chairman's own. Zhang also made an extraordinary impression on American radical Communists who journeyed secretly to China during the 1960s and met him before he reached his Cultural Revolution prominence:

> In large measure our attitude toward the Cultural Revolution resulted from a meeting several comrades and I had with Zhang Chunqiao in Shanghai in late 1965 or early 1966 . . . There was none of this by-now familiar CCP form of pontificating. The meeting took place in a small room in our hotel, not in any official reception hall. Here was a guy who was a member of a revolutionary communist group, as we were . . . His whole point at our meeting was that the CCP had been wrong in the past and might very well be wrong now or in the future. There was a struggle in the CCP now and there always had been. Chairman Mao was prepared to go back to the mountains to start the revolution again if necessary. It was our duty, as fellow communists, to sharply criticize the CCP whenever we felt it was wrong. National sovereignty didn't apply. That is what comradely relations were all about. Otherwise revisionism would develop and triumph in China and throughout the world. We talked for hours. We had a real give-and-take for the first time ever with a CCP representative. At this moment I don't remember any of the details. But I remember my impression, which was overpowering. Here was an honest revolutionary, an antibureaucrat, a real human no different from me, concerned about the development of the world revolution. We were impressed, but we didn't know what to make of our discussion.[7]

Zhang's junior partner, Yao Wenyuan, then only thirty-three, had won the Chairman's respect for his razor-sharp pen and what Mao called the "convincing" quality of his anti-bourgeois polemics in the Shanghai press. Yao was told by Jiang Qing to write a polemic against Wu Han's play. Zhang supervised the project. Unversed in Ming history, Yao sought advice on appropriate literature and gave himself a crash reading course in the field. In the resulting essay, Yao alleged that Hai Rui's defense of Ming peasants in Wu Han's play was an oblique criticism of GLF agrarian policies and the peasant unrest they had provoked. It thus reflected class struggle. Whether Wu Han was prepared to admit it or not was, in Yao's view, irrelevant; his play was a poisonous weed and a reactionary intervention in the great class struggle between the bourgeoisie and the proletariat.[8]

Mao personally revised Yao's ninth draft three times before publication. The Chairman had always taken a close interest in class struggle in the cultural sphere, but in the past his interventions had been known to his colleagues. Over the next few months, such was the premium he put on absolute secrecy that intermediate drafts of Yao's polemic were couriered back and forth between Shanghai and Beijing concealed in boxes of tape recordings of Beijing Opera performances—the explanation for the steady stream of boxes being Jiang Qing and Zhang Chunqiao's shared involvement in what was to become known as the production of "revolutionary model operas." Zhang later recalled that "I ended up spending 90 percent of my time on two operas and Yao Wenyuan's 'On the New Historical Play *Hai Rui Dismissed from Office.*'"

Mao's secretiveness suggested that he had bigger fish to fry than Wu Han. The Chairman had sanctioned and participated in an undercover Shanghai operation that would be seen as directed against the Beijing party establishment and especially Peng Zhen. If Peng ignored Yao's article, he could be accused of failing to protect the nation's capital against the greatest danger of all—revisionism, the slow sinister almost imperceptible perversion of the revolution by the forces of "peaceful evolution"; if he endorsed the article, he would have exposed himself as derelict in failing to spot Wu Han's heresy himself; whereas if he counterattacked, he would be defending the indefensible, not to mention defying Chairman Mao.

And yet, the article might never have been published. Had party discipline been maintained in the aftermath of Ke Qingshi's death, Jiang Qing's activities in Shanghai could have been disrupted. Ke's successor as the city's first secretary was Chen Pixian, a respected local party official who had not been made privy to what was going on, probably because Ke had not trusted him.[9] Zhang and Yao were uneasy about concealing their activities from their new boss, and so Jiang Qing sought Chen's consent. The two were well acquainted, for in 1950, when Jiang Qing was suffering from depression, Mao had sent her to Wuxi to be under Chen's supervisory care. Possibly this factor weighed with Chen as Jiang Qing explained the background to her activities, requested his permission for Zhang Chunqiao and Yao Wenyuan to continue to assist her, and urged him to maintain secrecy, particularly with the Beijing party. More likely it was her revelation of Mao's commitment to the project that decided Chen to ignore party requirements about informing higher authorities. He thought it all sounded very suspicious and worried about the impact that the affair might have on relations between the Shanghai and Beijing parties, but apparently reassured himself by thinking that a mere article could not be a big deal. Chen did not steel himself to defy Jiang Qing and to ensure that Premier Zhou Enlai—the third-ranking member of the Politburo after Mao and head of state Liu Shaoqi—was informed of the article's genesis until after it had been published. Chen's dereliction of duty left his superiors caught off guard by Mao's plot.[10]

Initially Peng Zhen ignored the attack, published in the Shanghai *Wenhui bao* on November 10 and reprinted the next day in the Shanghai Party Committee's official organ, the *Liberation Daily*. When the chief correspondent for the *Wenhui bao* in the capital called the editor-in-chief of Peng's own mouthpiece, the *Beijing Daily*, to elicit some reactions, the editor-in-chief asked her immediate superior and Peng's right-hand man in charge of propaganda, "What do I tell him?" "Just tell him what the weather is like today, ha-ha-ha!" was the reply.[11] The only other newspapers to have reprinted Yao's polemic by November 28 were six provincial party organs in eastern China, apparently because Shanghai had by then shared with them the crucial secret that Yao enjoyed Mao's personal backing.[12]

Peng Zhen, however, had forbidden the party's chief newspaper, the *People's Daily*, as well as other national, provincial, and municipal papers, to reprint the article.[13] When Zhou Enlai learned on November 26 of Mao's role in the genesis of the article, he telephoned Peng Zhen urging publication.[14] Peng must now have known that Mao was behind the unauthorized polemic, and he allowed the *Beijing Daily* to reprint it on November 29. The next day the *People's Daily* followed suit.

Peng was still not prepared to admit defeat, nailing his colors to the mast with the challenging comment that "people are all equal before the truth."[15] The *People's Daily* treated Yao's article as an academic rather than a political polemic and, under Zhou Enlai's supervision, editorialized in favor of the "freedom to criticize, as well as the freedom to counter-criticize." The *Beijing Daily* reprint was accompanied by an editorial note written by Deng Tuo, the municipal secretary in charge of culture and education, calling for an open academic debate on the nature of Wu Han's play. In December, Peng Zhen instructed Deng Tuo to organize a group to write articles to prove that Wu Han's errors were academic, not political. Peng was encouraged in this maneuver when he met Zhang Chunqiao in Shanghai. Zhang deceived him with an assertion that it was all just a scholarly discussion and with a proposal as to how the discussion should proceed. Peng Zhen approved Zhang's proposal and even promised him a Peking duck dinner in the capital when the debate had run its course.[16]

Heads Begin to Roll

Immediately after the publication of Yao's article, Mao left Beijing for Shanghai. "Mao in attack was Mao on the move," his personal physician concluded many years later. Traveling in his East German custom-built, air-conditioned luxury train with an entourage of security guards, confidential aides, his personal chef, photographers, and young female attendants, Mao was to spend the next eight months alternating between Shanghai and a handful of other cities in the lower Yangtze region. In Hangzhou, he stayed in Liuzhuang, on the shore of West Lake, in a Qing dynasty villa renovated and expanded for him during the GLF on a 130-acre piece of land that had once been the home of a fabulously wealthy tea merchant.[17] In Wuhan, the most important industrial city in central China, he stayed in a secluded villa on the shore of East Lake. Mao would not set foot in Beijing again until mid-July. This was the first of seven southern tours he made during the Cultural Revolution decade; in all he spent two years and eight months away from the capital.[18] But Mao continued to mastermind events there from afar.

On November 10, simultaneously with the publication of Yao Wenyuan's attack on Wu Han, Mao had dismissed Yang Shangkun as the director of the party center's General Office, the organ that among other activities controlled the paper flow of the Central Committee.[19] The rest of the CCP was informed of the dismissal by a so-called Central Document *(Zhongfa)*—numbered [1965] 644 and bearing the second-highest level of classification in use at the time— which did, however, not explain the reasons for dismissal. Central Documents (*Zhongfa*, meaning literally "issued by the center") would throughout the Cultural Revolution remain the most authoritative bureaucratic means whereby Mao, in his capacity as CCP Chairman, informed the rest of the CCP of major policies and policy decisions. In 1966, about a dozen such documents appeared each week; ten years later, toward the end of the Cultural Revolution, the number had declined to a mere two a month, a reflection of Mao's failing health and possibly a leadership incapacitated by profound factional disagreements. Only when Mao had explicitly authorized it, for example, when he was himself traveling or chose to remain incommunicado, might a deputy like Liu Shaoqi be authorized to issue a *Zhongfa* document.[20]

Yang Shangkun, who had joined the party almost forty years earlier, having studied in Moscow and later participated in the Long March, was demoted to membership of the party secretariat in Guangdong province, some 1,200 miles away from the national capital, a banishment amounting to internal exile.[21] At Yang's request, Mao granted him an hour-and-a-half interview, and instructed him to investigate whether CC and State Council policies jibed with local conditions, and to let him know personally if not. After two or three years in the Pearl River area, Mao consoled him, he would transfer him for another two or three years to the Yellow River area![22]

To replace Yang, Mao chose Major General Wang Dongxing, the director of the Central Bureau of Guards, which controlled the division-strength central guard unit (PLA Unit 8341), the "security detail" of the Politburo. Wang would occupy both these sensitive posts throughout the Cultural Revolution.[23] He was a Long March veteran who had joined the revolution as a thirteen-year-old; he had since advanced in the ranks on Mao's security detail and accompanied him on his journey to Moscow in 1949. A probable reason for Mao's trust in Wang—who was to serve him loyally until his death in September 1976, but would then help arrest his widow a few weeks later in what became known as the "smashing" of the "Gang of Four"—was the discretion and dedication with which he kept unwanted callers at bay. Many years later, Wang himself recalled that at the height of the Cultural Revolution, "No matter who wanted to see the Chairman, they all had to be vetted and approved by me first. Even Jiang Qing, when she wanted to see him, was no exception. First I would go in and ask if the Chairman approved her entering. There were times when he said no."[24] In addition to turning away the company Mao did not want, Wang also discreetly provided Mao with the kind of company that he craved increasingly in his later years. It was one of Wang's duties as director of the Central Bureau of Guards to organize and maintain the so-called Zhongnanhai "Cultural Work Troupe." Years after Mao's death, his personal physician remembered: "The troupe contained a pool of young women, selected for their good looks, their artistic talent, and their political reliability. Over time, the role of these . . . young women . . . became too obvious for me to ignore."[25]

The Purge of the PLA Chief of Staff

The fall of Yang Shangkun probably precipitated the next political upheaval, Defense Minister Marshal Lin Biao's move against the chief of staff of the People's Liberation Army, General Luo Ruiqing.[26] Luo, a longtime political commissar, and like Yang a Long March veteran, had been minister of public security until 1959, and in that role accompanied Mao on many of his trips. When Mao chose Lin Biao to be defense minister, replacing the disgraced Marshal Peng Dehuai in 1959, Luo was Lin's choice to replace Chief of Staff Huang Kecheng, who was dismissed for siding with Peng. Luo had served under Lin in a number of posts during the revolution. In his new role, Luo became a member of the party's CC and was the secretary general of the party's Military Affairs Commission (MAC), of which Mao was chairman and through which he controlled the military.[27] Lin Biao was executive vice chairman of the MAC, but because of poor health left much of its day-to-day business to Luo.

By the winter of 1964–65, however, Lin Biao was disenchanted with Luo. Luo, he later alleged, had failed to "give prominence to politics," instead putting too much emphasis on military training. Lin Biao, arguably the PLA's most brilliant commander during the anti-Japanese and civil wars, accepted the importance of training, but he derided drill by numbers as "formalism" and said it was "unreasonable" to transfer a company commander simply because he failed an obstacle course. In his instructions on PLA work circulated in January 1965, Lin argued: "If [our army] is in a total mess politically, and retreats once the enemy comes, then even the best military and technical skills will be of no use!" When shown the instructions, Mao wrote on them: "I agree entirely," while Liu Shaoqi's annotation was "I approve entirely."[28]

Despite this endorsement of Lin's views at the highest level, Luo attempted to mitigate the impact of his instructions when editing them for circulation. Lin had written: "While a definite amount of time must be set aside for military training, production, etc., these activities should not be permitted to assault politics. Politics, on the other hand, may be permitted to assault other activities." In an attempt to strike a more even balance between politics and professionalism— the constant tension in Maoist politics between "red and expert"—Luo added the words: "Of course, even when necessary there must not be any indiscriminate assaults." According to one biographer, to the extent possible within the rules of the organization, Luo did everything possible to resist the thrust of Lin's instructions, and altered them in seventy-eight places.[29] Luo was supported by General Xiao Xiangrong, a MAC deputy secretary general and head of its General Office, who apparently "stopped employing the expression 'Give prominence to politics' in his professional capacity" because he found Lin Biao's interpretation of it disruptive of professional military activities.[30]

In mid-1965, Lin began putting together a secret dossier on Luo Ruiqing to document his allegedly "sinister designs" and "arrogant and imperious" attitude toward the policy of "giving prominence to politics."[31] A few senior officers, including Vice Admiral Li Zuopeng, the navy's political commissar, were prepared to testify to Luo's "erroneous opinions on 'giving prominence to politics.'"[32] Emulating Mao's strategy of moving against a major figure by first attacking a deputy—Wu Han in the case of Peng Zhen—Lin first targeted Xiao Xiangrong.

On November 15, while Luo Ruiqing was in southern China inspecting defense installations along the Sino-Vietnamese frontier, Xiao was brought before an enlarged meeting of the PLA General Staff Party Committee and accused of being anti-Mao, of opposing "giving prominence to politics," of "singing from a different libretto than Vice Chairman Lin's," and of being a "member-in-hiding of the Peng [Dehuai]-Huang [Kecheng] anti-party clique." But a few days into the struggle meeting, Luo Ruiqing arrived back in the capital to defend Xiao, asserting that "although Xiao Xiangrong may have committed this or that mistake," he was not a member of the Peng-Huang clique. The meeting broke up in total confusion,[33] but like Peng Zhen's defense of Wu Han, Luo's defense of his deputy gave his enemies their opening.

On November 18, while the anti-Xiao struggle was still in progress in Beijing, Lin Biao, wintering in Suzhou, reaffirmed his position by issuing five new principles for giving prominence to politics in PLA work in 1966. The first was that the works of Chairman Mao had to be the supreme instructions for every item of work for the whole PLA.[34] When he heard of Luo's intervention, Lin ordered the meeting reconvened, arguing that: "To have someone who opposes Mao Zedong Thought and who opposes 'giving prominence to politics' entrenched in an important military position will have evil consequences for the future. He must be thoroughly exposed and criticized. A chicken should be killed to scare the monkey."[35]

Lin's real intention, however, was to "kill" the monkey too. When, during a brief stopover in Shanghai and Suzhou on his way back to the Sino-Vietnamese frontier, Luo suggested to him on November 27 that the case against Xiao had been overblown, Lin Biao was noncommittal,[36] a tactic that Mao also employed during the Cultural Revolution when talking to people he proposed to purge. On November 30 Lin sent his wife, Ye Qun, to Hangzhou to enlist Mao's support against the chief of staff.

As director of her husband's office, Ye Qun had been very active in the collection of material against Luo. Herself a colonel in the PLA, she nourished personal grudges against both Xiao Xiangrong, who had refused her promotion in the late 1950s,[37] and Luo Ruiqing. Characterized by her private tutor in world history as something of a scatterbrain ("She had great difficulty concentrating!"), widely disliked by her husband's staff ("Everybody thought she was malicious," according to one secretary), politically ambitious, and regarded by those who had known her in Yan'an before she married Lin as a woman of easy virtue, Ye at the same time was genuinely loved by her husband, to whom she had borne a son and a daughter.[38] Ye carried with her the anti-Luo dossier and a cover note from Lin to the Chairman in which he explained that these "important matters" were ones that "already some time ago, a number of senior comrades suggested I share with you; but only now, after seeing how they relate to the Yang Shangkun issue (about which I've just been told by [Marshal] Ye Jianying), I feel I must report them to you."[39] Lin Biao was indicating to Mao that the removal of Luo was as important to him as the dismissal of Yang Shangkun was to the Chairman and simultaneously hinting that the two cases might be linked with advantage.

In seven hours of one-on-one conversation with Mao, Ye Qun raised two "important matters" in addition to Luo's alleged failure to give prominence to politics: his unwillingness to report to Lin on a regular basis and his attempts to supplant Lin by getting him to resign. On the first issue, Luo Ruiqing's daughter proffered a very different explanation after the Cultural Revolution:

> [My father's] biggest problem was when and how to report on his work to Lin Biao. If he didn't phone first, but just took the car [over], he would be stopped at the door and told Lin wasn't feeling well and couldn't see him. If he phoned first, the reply would be "How many times do I have to tell you that you don't have to make an appointment to report on your work but can come at any time." Then if [my father] really just went there, [Lin] would say it was an ambush, and that he hadn't time to mentally prepare himself, and that because he was ill it made him all apprehensive and made him break out in a sweat. The next time, if [my father] phoned he'd be told later that because of the phone call Lin hadn't been able to get to sleep but had been awake all night.[40]

Lin Biao's secretaries have provided ample confirmation of the late defense minister's erratic behavior. On the occasion of their last encounter, Luo did not phone first; however, Lin Biao learned that he was planning to come and had his secretary tell him to come over immediately.[41]

Lin Biao's second complaint was more serious from Mao's point of view. If Luo Ruiqing were really trying to unseat Lin, the Chairman was in danger of losing a crucial ally in charge of the key institution whose backing he needed for his imminent attack on the party in the Cultural Revolution. The evidence for Lin's charge was principally a conversation between Luo Ruiqing and the PLA air force commander, Liu Yalou, in which Luo had supposedly asked Liu to relay to Ye Qun that Lin should step down and allow him (Luo) to run the PLA.[42] Since Liu Yalou had conveniently died shortly thereafter, there was no third party to contradict this allegation.

The actual weight accorded by Mao to Ye Qun's farrago of allegations and half-truths may never be known, but the Chairman's consciousness that he had to maintain Lin Biao as a loyal and powerful ally is underlined by the speed with which he acted.[43] Moreover, Mao probably realized that this was the way to sever the organizational link between the PLA and the CCP, a necessary step, as he was about to use the former as his base for attacking the latter. Luo had become that link since entering the Central Committee Secretariat in 1962.[44] Concluding that Luo was indeed another "revisionist at the party center," Mao wrote briefly to Lin on December 2 stating that people who did not believe in giving prominence to politics were "practicing eclecticism (that is, opportunism)." He explained this point to a small group of senior officers of the Nanjing Military Region (MR) the same day. Those who openly advocated professionalism taking precedence over politics were not a threat, because they were few in number. But those who argued eclectically that the two were equally important had to be dealt with resolutely:

> I am of the opinion that the struggle between giving prominence to politics and opposing giving prominence to politics has now become intensified and entered a new stage . . . If political and professional matters are seen as equally important, then this amounts to eclecticism . . . Eclecticism does not distinguish between the enemy and us, or between classes, or between what's right and what's wrong . . . It really is revisionism. Revisionism is not wanting struggle, and not wanting revolution.[45]

Mao took seriously Luo's practice of emasculating Lin Biao's directives on politics by the use of "however" or "on the other hand" clauses, with their implication that Lin was sabotaging the military preparedness of the PLA.

> Ideologically, there's a distance between Luo and us. Comrade Lin Biao has been commanding soldiers for decades; how could he possibly not know what military matters are about? . . . In fact, Luo treats comrade Lin Biao as if he were an enemy. Since becoming chief of staff, Luo has never once on his own come to me to ask for instructions or report on this work. Luo does not respect

the marshals . . . acts dictatorially, and is a careerist. He is always in contact with people who engage in conspiracies.[46]

With his attack on the Beijing party approaching its most decisive phase, Mao could not afford simultaneously to be fighting a second major campaign. He quickly decided to hold an enlarged meeting of the Politburo Standing Committee (PSC) to resolve the issue. Convened in Shanghai on December 8, the session was attended by sixty-one people, including thirty-four senior PLA officers. The most notable absentee was Luo Ruiqing himself, still on his inspection tour of the "Third Front"—Mao's scheme for the massive transfer to, and construction of industry in, inland China for protection in case of war[47]—and about to leave Guangxi for the province of Yunnan on the day the session began. Luo heard that a meeting was being called but was kept in ignorance about its purpose.[48]

The case against Luo was deployed principally by Ye Qun, who spoke three times for a total of ten hours. Supporting speeches were made by Lin Biao himself and by Li Zuopeng and Lieutenant General Wu Faxian, both Long March veterans. Li and Wu had steadily moved up the ranks under Lin's patronage and were blindly loyal to him: after Lin's death and disgrace in 1971, Li—the political commissar of the navy—admitted, "In life and in death, I would have stood by Vice Chairman Lin's side!" Wu—the commander of the air force—said of his relationship with Lin, "I was prepared to do whatever he told me to do . . . I was Lin Biao's running dog!"[49] The materials that Ye had shown Mao were circulated to the conferees. Senior Politburo members were not impressed. Liu Shaoqi pronounced Ye's tale "difficult to believe," and Deng Xiaoping felt that without an affidavit from the deceased Liu Yalou it was difficult to make the most serious charge stick. Peng Zhen expressed his doubts to the conference.[50]

But Mao and Lin Biao were determined to have their way, and Luo was summoned from Kunming, the provincial capital of Yunnan, from where Claire Chennault's legendary "Flying Tigers" had once helped defend the China-Burma-India theater from the invading Japanese and where much of the Third Front construction was now concentrated. Zhou Enlai telephoned Luo without telling him that he was the subject of the conference, just that he had to get on a plane on December 11. After his arrival in Shanghai, Luo was confronted by Zhou and Deng Xiaoping, who informed him of the charges against him.[51] Luo tried to deny everything, but Zhou coldly cut him short. Luo was warned not to contact Mao or Lin.[52]

Meanwhile Luo's deputy, General Xiao Xiangrong, had been escorted down from Beijing to Shanghai, where two of his superiors—their identities have never been revealed—did everything they could to pressure him into denouncing Luo: "The time has come for you to surrender your heart to the party," they announced. "This is the moment when you should wake up; it's an opportunity not to be missed!" Luo's deputy flatly refused to denounce the man who had protected him so very recently, and was sent back to Beijing on December 15. Within a week, he had been sent into internal exile beyond the Great Wall in northwest China, where he quickly found himself deprived of his freedom and subject to an MAC inquiry into his own "serious errors."[53]

The enlarged PSC reached no conclusion about what to do about Luo. This hesitation may have reflected general uneasiness about a case against a four-star Long March veteran, based on flimsy evidence presented by a mere colonel, and—since this was the patriarchal CCP—a woman to boot, who was not a member of the CC and probably owed her military rank to being a marshal's wife.[54] If ever there was an ideal occasion for the uninvolved members of the PSC present—Liu Shaoqi; Zhou Enlai; Marshal Zhu De, chairman of the National People's Congress (NPC); and Deng Xiaoping—to have got together, along with Peng Zhen (whose clout if not rank was equivalent), to tell Mao that they could not go along with this travesty, this was it. None of them was personally implicated, and the few supporting speeches made by the military representatives indicates that backing for Lin Biao by that contingent was marginal. But they let the opportunity slip. It turned out to be the last chance for this powerful group of men to act together to restrain the Chairman before themselves being divided and denounced during the Cultural Revolution.

Instead, the enlarged PSC agreed to create a special team to work on the case and report directly to Zhou, Deng, and Peng Zhen. On December 17 Luo was flown to Beijing, where he asked to be relieved of his posts. General Yang Chengwu was appointed acting chief of staff on December 29, and Marshal Ye Jianying replaced Luo as MAC secretary general in January 1966. Luo produced a first written self-criticism on January 9. On February 1, he denied ever having called for Lin's resignation: "I have no recollection whatever of saying those things. I swear I never meant to imply that Vice Chairman Lin should make way for someone better qualified. I'm not so wicked, so arrogant, so foolish!"[55]

Between March 4 and April 8, Luo was attacked at a meeting of forty-two senior cadres from various branches of the military establishment under the joint chairmanship of Deng Xiaoping, Peng Zhen, and Ye Jianying. Devastated by the ferocity of the attacks upon his character and actions—his erstwhile brothers-in-arms would by now have realized what was expected of them—Luo attempted suicide on March 18. The following is a report of the cold-blooded account given to non-party notables three months later by Liu Shaoqi:

> [Luo] jumped off the three-story building in which he lives in an attempt to commit suicide. He suffered a few injuries, but didn't die. He's now in hospital. First of all, if you're going to commit suicide, you have to have some technique, that is, heavy head and light feet, but he arrived feet first and did not injure his head. At this point Deng Xiaoping interjected: He jumped like a female athlete diver [feet first], resembling an ice lolly. Liu continues: This kind of act on his part is one of . . . resistance to the party. . .[56]

Mao's immediate response when given the news over the telephone in the midst of a PSC meeting in Hangzhou was to ask, "Why?" and then to remark, "How pathetic! [*mei chuxi*]."[57]

During the remaining sessions, Luo's critics belabored an empty chair. Luo had played into the hands of his enemies; by attempting suicide he enabled even those who doubted his guilt to square their consciences with the argument that since Luo had proved capable of betraying the party by trying to kill himself, he could have betrayed it in other ways too.[58]

On April 12, Zhou, Deng, and Peng Zhen wrote to Mao to tell him that the struggle against Luo had been concluded and that a report on his "errors" had been drafted. It was one of the last official acts performed by Peng Zhen before he met a fate similar to Luo's. When the report was approved and circulated by the PSC on May 16, an added paragraph described the doubts about the charges against him expressed by Peng Zhen in Shanghai as "trying to minimize, cover up, apologize for, and support" Luo's mistakes.[59]

The February Outline

As the Luo Ruiqing affair unfolded in December and January, Peng Zhen clung to his strategy of defense by definition. Wu Han's case was an academic not a political affair. But on December 22 Mao had raised the ante, telling Peng Zhen, who was visiting him in Hangzhou, that Yao Wenyuan had missed the point in his critique: the crucial word in the title of *Hai Rui Dismissed from Office* was "dismissed." The play had been written not long after Marshal Peng Dehuai had been dismissed and was really an allegorical defense of the disgraced minister of defense.[60] He did not explain why he had failed to point this out to Yao when he was revising his text. Mao's omission was later taken by some as proof of just how close to his chest the Chairman played his hand: "When the time wasn't yet ripe, he would not reveal as much as half a word, in case the rustling of the grass alerted the snakes."[61] For the Chairman, the Wu Han case was very definitely political. Peng Zhen argued, however, that there were no organizational links between Peng Dehuai and Wu Han, and indeed had told the latter, "Where you're wrong, criticize yourself, and where you're right, persist."[62] Zhang Chunqiao expressed surprise at Peng Zhen's steadfastness: "I had not realized [he] would be so stirred up and so deeply shaken. Even less had I realized that he would put up such determined resistance."[63]

Meanwhile, prompted by Yao's original polemic and the editorial note in the *People's Daily*, an open debate had begun to unfold. Contributions appearing in China's major academic journals and newspapers were carefully vetted at the highest level of the party's propaganda apparatus. A number of pseudonymous pieces by his senior colleagues in the Beijing party establishment, which in effect defended Wu Han, were easily cleared by the CC's Propaganda Department, whose director, Lu Dingyi, was a member of the Group of Five. Lu's department also chose to "sit on" some of the most outrageously polemical political attacks on Wu Han.

In January, two particularly harsh pieces concerned solely with the supposedly "reactionary essence" and "anti-party, anti-socialist" nature of Wu Han's "poisonous weeds" were held up and not cleared for immediate publication. As it turned out, their authors were on Mao's private list of favorite "young leftists" worth "fostering," and the fact that they had been, in Mao's words, "suppressed" by the Propaganda Department was to give the careers of the two men a remarkable boost, for they were invited to join the Chairman's inner circle. Guan Feng, the older of the two, had first come to Mao's attention during the Anti-Rightist Campaign in 1957 with a harshly worded pseudonymous critique of the British-educated anthropologist Fei Xiaotong, well known outside China for such classic works as *Peasant Life in China* and *Earthbound China*. Years later, Mao still remembered Guan's critique of Fei as very good. Guan was an alumnus of the group recruited to write the anti-Soviet polemics, but his forte was analysis of China's ancient sages from a Marxist/materialist viewpoint. Qi Benyu, Guan's junior by thirteen years, was a section chief in the clerical office of the CC General Office when, in 1963, his Marxist critique of the established orthodoxy surrounding the nineteenth-century Taiping Rebellion had, to Mao's delight, provoked an uproar in Chinese historical circles. Mao liked the way Qi reasoned ("black and white, mountains of irrefutable evidence" was how he characterized it), and in December 1965 he had endorsed Qi's most recent work in print by claiming to have "read it three times."[64] At the beginning of 1966, both Guan and Qi were affiliated with *Red Flag,* the official CC theoretical journal, Guan as a deputy editor-in-chief and Qi as the head of the journal's history group.

After hunkering down for two months behind his prepared positions, Peng Zhen suddenly sallied forth. On February 3 he convened the Group of Five and proposed that it should draw up a programmatic document defining the parameters of debate, to be issued in the name of the party center. This "Outline of a Report of the Group of Five to the Center," which became known as the "February Outline," was drafted on February 4, mainly by two deputy directors of Lu Dingyi's Propaganda Department, and a third draft was presented the next day by Peng to the only members of the PSC currently in Beijing, Liu Shaoqi, Zhou Enlai, and Deng Xiaoping. Peng Zhen obtained his colleagues' formal approval, incorporated their views into a fourth draft, and sent it in the form of an urgent telegram to Mao in Wuhan on February 7. At dawn on the following day, Peng flew to Wuhan with three other members of the Group of Five—Lu Dingyi, Kang Sheng, both alternate members of the Politburo, and Wu Lengxi, chief editor of the *People's Daily* and the Xinhua News Agency—and formally presented the document to the Chairman. The document spoke of the need to "adhere to such principles as seeking truth from facts and everyone is equal before the truth" and emphasized that "we must not only prevail over our opponents politically, but also truly prevail over them and greatly surpass them in as far as our academic and professional qualities are concerned."[65]

According to differing accounts, Mao asked whether Wu Han was "antiparty and anti-socialist" and/or had links to Peng Dehuai. Peng Zhen repeated his assertion that there were no organizational links between Wu and Peng Dehuai, and Mao said that Wu could stay on as a vice mayor after criticism. The Chairman raised only two formal objections to the text of the February Outline, and agreed to its circulation in the name of the center. Sources fail to indicate what form this authorization took. What seems beyond doubt is that it was far from explicit and certainly not enthusiastic. Zhou Enlai had concluded from being around Mao for decades that when the Chairman really agreed with something he was likely to sign it off with "Excellent! Act accordingly," or words to that effect. Slightly less enthusiastic endorsement might prompt a simple "Circulate accordingly." When he merely circled his name on the preprinted cover letter of a document draft, it meant simply that Mao had read it and was not about to veto it.[66] In the case of the February Outline, no *written* endorsement by Mao in any form has ever surfaced. Peng Zhen and his colleagues finalized the document on February 11 and on February 12 sent the printed text plus a short preamble (the only part of the document not shown to Mao) back to Beijing, where their PSC colleagues again endorsed it. On February 13, the Confidential Office of the CC General Office in Zhongnanhai, the nerve center of the Chinese party and state in Beijing, distributed the February Outline in the form of *Zhongfa* [1966] 105, classified "top secret."[67]

A possible explanation for Peng Zhen's sudden flurry of activity is that he got wind of a Jiang Qing cultural initiative, agreed on during a visit she paid on January 21 to Lin Biao and Ye Qun in Suzhou. Like Mao, Lin liked to get away from Beijing when possible and had a number of villas kept ready for his temporary use across the country: one in the northeastern seaside port of Dalian; another an hour by train from Shanghai in the city of Suzhou, famous for its many parks and canals and described by an American visitor in 1852 as "the Chinaman's counterpart of heaven—his terrestrial paradise."[68] In Suzhou on this the first day of the new year according to the traditional Chinese calendar (the Spring Festival), she had suggested to Lin and Ye that she might hold a cultural forum in the PLA. Lin readily agreed, possibly as a quid pro quo for Mao's backing in the Luo Ruiqing affair, and from February 2 a group of senior officers under a lieutenant general, a deputy director of the PLA General Political Department, spent almost three weeks listening to Jiang Qing's leftist views on the arts and watching more than thirty movies and plays most of which, she explained to them, were ideologically and artistically flawed, some seriously, some less so. Finally, she had a docile and respectful audience.

The proceedings were published on April 10 as *Zhongfa* [1966] 211, the "Summary of the Army Forum on Literature and Art Work called by Jiang Qing at the Behest of Lin Biao," after editing by Chen Boda, the editor of *Red Flag* and an alternate member of the Politburo, by Zhang Chunqiao and Yao Wenyuan, and on no less than three occasions by Mao himself. The document took a radically different line from the February Outline, claiming in one particularly noteworthy passage that "since the founding of our People's Republic . . . we have been under the dictatorship of a sinister anti-party and anti-socialist line which is diametrically opposed to Chairman Mao's Thought." It also made a point of repeatedly underscoring the importance of and desperate need in China for what it called a "socialist cultural revolution," something the February Outline had not.[69] If Peng Zhen had planned the latter as a preemptive maneuver, it was a failure. By the time Jiang Qing's "Summary" came out, Peng Zhen's disgrace was well advanced, and his "Outline" was history.

Yet in Wuhan in February, Peng thought he had been successful. A junior aide recalled many years later that after the meeting with Mao, "Nobody worried any more about the criticism of *Hai Rui Dismissed from Office*. We made our way to the antiquarian bookshops."[70] On the way back to Beijing, Peng stopped off in Shanghai, and he and his colleagues told local party leaders that Mao supported the proposition that Wu Han's case was not political.[71] Why did the Chairman give Peng that impression? With hindsight, it seems clear that the Chairman was deceiving Peng Zhen, playing him along until he was ready to deliver the coup de grâce.

2

The Siege of Beijing

In mid-March 1966, Mao began his final assault on the party organization in the capital. At an expanded PSC meeting in Hangzhou, Peng Zhen heard the Chairman describe Wu Han and another distinguished Marxist intellectual as anti-party and no better than members of Chiang Kai-shek's Nationalist Party. He criticized the *People's Daily* as semi-Marxist and warned the Central Propaganda Department not to suppress young revolutionary intellectuals— among whom he evidently included Guan Feng and Qi Benyu—hinting that it might be dissolved like the Rural Work Department in 1962. When Mao lashed out at the editor-in-chief of the *People's Daily* by describing his paper as no more than 30 percent Marxist, one member of his audience later claimed to have sensed that Mao was unhappy with far more than simply one or two highly placed propaganda officials.[1] Mao also attacked Peng Zhen for running an "independent kingdom" because a certain Shanghai opera could not be staged in Beijing; in fact, arrangements for its staging were already in hand, but Peng said nothing because, he later explained to Zhou Enlai, he did not want to contradict the Chairman to his face.[2]

On March 31, Peng Zhen got worse news. Kang Sheng informed him and Zhou Enlai that Mao had told him (Kang), Jiang Qing, Zhang Chunqiao, and others in three conversations between March 28 and 30 that Peng Zhen, the Propaganda Department, and the Beijing Party Committee had shielded bad people while suppressing leftists. If this continued, these organizations should all be dissolved. Peng defended himself by insisting that he had not "shielded" Wu Han but only wanted to allow a hundred flowers to bloom, a Maoist policy that the February Outline had mentioned but the Forum Summary had not. Peng finally began to retreat, offering to revise the February Outline. Zhou Enlai, seeing the way the wind was blowing, telephoned the Chairman to express his "total agreement" with his instructions and began preparations for a meeting of the Central Committee Secretariat to criticize Peng.[3]

The Secretariat met in Beijing under General Secretary Deng Xiaoping's chairmanship from April 9 to 12. The main charges against Peng Zhen were leveled by Mao's trusties, Kang Sheng and Chen Boda. Kang, who had been promoted to the CC Secretariat in 1962, was an enigmatic figure widely feared for what those who worked under him called his paranormal sixth sense for who was and who wasn't an "anti-party element," and for his ruthlessness, which bordered on the perverse after a lifetime—Kang had joined the CCP in 1925—in counterintelligence and covert operations of the most unsavory kind. Sometimes likened to Stalin's notorious secret police chief Lavrenti Beria, Kang was characterized by someone who knew him well as a man "with a heart of stone, who did not know how to cry." Yet he was also genuinely respected for his erudition—Marxist and classical Chinese—his antiquarian connoisseurship, and, more than anything else, for his calligraphy. Mao's private relations with Kang Sheng were excellent, and the letters they exchanged were always written with a brush. The bookish Chen Boda, like Kang an alternate member of the Politburo, had few of Kang Sheng's personality traits: when under pressure he was known to be prone to nervous breakdowns, weeping, and contemplating suicide. Afflicted with a stammer and never able to rid himself of a heavy Fujian accent, his speeches were all but totally unintelligible to his audiences. Educated at Sun Yat-sen University in Moscow in the late 1920s, he had upon his return to China become Mao's political secretary and ghostwriter, and as such helped the future CCP Chairman formulate what was to become "Mao Zedong Thought."[4] Kang and Chen did not get along in private, yet on this occasion, as on many similar ones as the Cultural Revolution unfolded, they operated in perfect tandem as Mao's political henchmen.

Peng desperately defended himself against their one-two punch, insisting that he neither had nor would "oppose Chairman Mao," but Zhou and Deng Xiaoping were unmoved, declaring that Peng's errors amounted to carrying out a line that "contravened Mao Zedong Thought" and "opposed Chairman Mao." They decided to propose to Mao and the PSC that a new circular be drafted to annul and criticize the February Outline. On April 16, the PSC—with Liu Shaoqi absent abroad during these events—duly annulled the document, dissolved the Group of Five, and set up in its place a "cultural revolution document-drafting group," which eventually morphed into the Central Cultural Revolution Group (CCRG).[5]

On April 19, Mao called an enlarged PSC meeting in Hangzhou that would follow up on these proposals and further denounce Peng's alleged errors. Ordered to attend in person, Peng Zhen asked upon arrival to be granted a twenty-minute audience in private with the Chairman, but Mao would not have it. Liu Shaoqi arrived at the meeting two days late after an extended four-week tour of Pakistan, Afghanistan, and Burma; it was probably not coincidental that Mao moved against Liu's ally Peng Zhen while Liu was out of the country.[6] Because Liu was unfamiliar with much of what had transpired in his absence, it was Zhou Enlai who in Liu's stead ended up chairing most of the meetings that were not presided over by Mao.[7] On April 24, the draft of a Central Document annulling the February Outline was approved by the PSC. The meeting concluded on April 26, and from the moment he stepped off the plane in Beijing the following day, Peng Zhen found himself under constant guard and no longer able to move about freely.[8] Foreign diplomats in the capital duly noted his conspicuous absence from the May 1 celebrations, which took place in a torrential downpour, the likes of which had not been seen for years and which the resident Agence France-Presse correspondent described as "presaging a bumper harvest."[9] But unlike in previous years, the size of the harvest was not the subject uppermost in the minds of Mao's colleagues.

Poison Pen Letters

The Chairman's assault on the cultural establishment and his warning to the Propaganda Department sealed the fate of Lu Dingyi, the department's director and Peng Zhen's senior colleague in the Group of Five. Yet the exact reasons for Lu's dismissal are not known. Liu Shaoqi described him as the kind of person "who opposes dogmatism but not revisionism, factionalism but not capitulationism, and the left but not the right."[10] Zhou Enlai agreed that "he attacked leftists and shielded rightists."[11] "All he has," Zhou said on another occasion, "is individualist thinking. No party spirit, and no class struggle,"[12] though Zhou's complaints formed no part of the official record of what contributed to Lu's downfall. Lin Biao insisted that among many other things, he "vilified Mao Zedong Thought."[13] Certainly, some of Lu's "vilification" took an irreverent form: "So you say that it was Mao Zedong Thought that taught you to win at table tennis! How are you going to explain losing?"[14] But complaints relating to ideology and to "isms" of one kind or another took no prominence in the official record of what contributed to Lu's downfall. The matter that occupied most of the document was a catalytic event known as "Special Case, No. 502," centered on a remarkable string of anonymous letters from Lu's wife, Yan Weibing, to members of Lin Biao's family.

Yan Weibing, who had worked for many years as a deputy section chief in her husband's department, began to write anonymous letters to Ye Qun in 1960 after the latter became director of her husband's office. In the letters, Yan referred to Ye (whom she had known in the 1940s in Yan'an) as a woman of easy virtue and to Lin as a cuckold. By chance, Ye Qun discovered the identity of the author of these scurrilous letters in early 1966 and decided to make a case of it.[15] In March, Lu Dingyi was exiled from Beijing "for his own good" while his wife's conduct was investigated. On April 28, Lu's wife was arrested and accused of being a "counterrevolutionary element." On May 6, Lu was recalled to Beijing, where he was immediately put under house arrest. Summoned to appear at an enlarged session of the Politburo, he was accused of having colluded with his wife to frame Lin Biao and his family. On the day the session met to hear Lu's self-criticism, each participant found a copy of a note in Lin Biao's handwriting on his or her chair. In what must count as one of the most bizarre statements ever submitted to a meeting of the Politburo, symptomatic of the low level to which "political struggle" within the leadership had sunk by this time, the note read in full:

> I certify that (1) when she and I got married, Ye Qun was a pure virgin, and she has remained faithful ever since; (2) Ye Qun and Wang Shiwei [a writer executed in Yan'an] had never been lovers; (3) Laohu and Doudou are Ye Qun's and my own flesh and blood; and (4) Yan Weibing's counterrevolutionary letters contain nothing but rumors. Lin Biao, May 14, 1966.[16]

The note was to become legendary among those who lived through the Cultural Revolution. As the years passed, its precise wording was slowly forgotten, and alternative versions began to circulate. In 1981, an intoxicated public security officer in Beijing insisted in conversation with one of the authors that according to a private diary he had seen, belonging to a PLA marshal who had been present at the Politburo session, it had actually ended with the words "the Chairman can testify to Ye Qun's virginity"! Regardless of exactly what the note may actually have said (photographs of it have never been published, and the original copies were all withdrawn at the end of the day by the Politburo session secretariat), Lu Dingyi emphatically denied any previous knowledge of his wife's letters, but to no avail. When Lin Biao asked how this could be the case, Lu responded pointedly by asking: "Aren't there quite a few husbands who don't really know what their wives are up to?" An outraged Lin Biao threatened to kill Lu right there and then.[17]

Bugging Mao

The altercation between Lin Biao and Lu Dingyi in connection with Ye Qun's virginity took place at an expanded session of the Politburo held in Beijing from May 4 to 26. The guidelines for the meeting had been laid down by Mao to the PSC at a meeting in Hangzhou two weeks earlier, but he allowed Liu Shaoqi—who had been abroad while the attack on his ally Peng Zhen was mounted—to preside over the political demise of Peng, as well as those of Luo Ruiqing, Lu Dingyi, and Yang Shangkun.

Yang Shangkun, former head of the CC General Office, was summoned back to Beijing and finally provided with grounds for his dismissal: bugging Chairman Mao's quarters, leaking party secrets, maintaining "extremely suspect links" with Luo Ruiqing and others, and committing "additional grave errors." No proof of any kind was provided.[18]

The first charge was undoubtedly the most remarkable, even though it was in a sense history by the time Yang was relieved of his directorship of the General Office. The circumstances surrounding the bugging incident appear to have been as follows. At around the time of the Eighth Party Congress, in the second half of 1956, confidential clerks from the CC General Office had begun using tape recorders to preserve accurate records of speeches and discussions at major party conferences. The reason for this was simple, Mao's confidential secretary explained many years later: to augment and improve on the undoubtedly less-than-perfect stenographer's records also kept on such occasions.[19]

By late 1958, the scope of meetings at which tape recorders were being used had expanded to include even such lesser events as Mao's meetings with local leaders during his provincial travels. In that year, the Chinese leadership imported ten tape recorders from Switzerland. Two were passed directly to Mao's confidential secretary, while the other eight were given to Yang Shangkun.[20] For a time the eight tape recorders were used to record what was said during meetings of the Politburo. Mao apparently was none too happy with the use of such equipment to make verbatim records of high-level conversations. In the winter of 1959–60, he for the first time grumbled about the General Office's "excessive" use of tape recorders. In 1960 a set of formal regulations was put in place, with Mao's approval, specifying under what circumstances recordings were to be made and when not. In 1961, Mao became livid upon discovering that his flirtations with a female attendant had been caught on tape. Although Yang Shangkun was spared at the time, several of his subordinates were implicated, assigned the blame, and demoted and/or transferred away from the General Office. At Mao's insistence all the existing tapes were destroyed after part of their contents had been transcribed by a team of secretaries supervised by Deng Xiaoping.[21]

In 1968, Deng Xiaoping was willing to admit in a letter to the CC "political responsibility for handling the matter of the bugging devices installed by Yang Shangkun in an untimely and sloppy fashion."[22] But twelve years later, the CC General Office insisted that no "bugging" had ever been carried out in the first place. "The recordings carried out by the Confidential Office were part of normal work routine," a special investigation report concluded, "and therefore the so-called 'bugging,' 'secret recording,' 'private' recording of Chairman Mao's conversations, or 'theft of party secrets' has no basis in fact, and was nothing but a political frame-up."[23] The second charge of leaking party secrets was repeated later by Red Guards, but well-informed party historians insist that Yang "never caused the leak of any core party secrets."[24]

Since it hardly seems coincidental that on the eve of the Cultural Revolution, Mao and Lin between them contrived to remove simultaneously the powerful party boss of the capital, the chief of staff of the PLA, and the director of propaganda, it is reasonable to assume that Yang, too, was sacked for none of the ostensible reasons, but because Mao wanted someone he could trust totally to control the CC's paper flow.

A "Time Bomb" Removed

At the enlarged Politburo meeting attended by close to eighty people, the principal prosecutors were again Kang Sheng, who spoke for eight hours on May 5 and 6, and Chen Boda, supported by Zhang Chunqiao. The latter briefed the session on the circumstances surrounding the publication of "On the New Historical Play *Hai Rui Dismissed from Office*" and illustrated the controversy it had stirred up by revealing that in the wake of its publication, "we" received over 10,000 readers' letters from all over the Chinese mainland "with the exception of Tibet." Chen Boda, speaking on May 7, delved among the records of Peng Zhen's past in an effort to show that signs of his "opposition to Chairman Mao" had been accumulating for a long time. But criticism of the four men who were about to become the Peng-Luo-Lu-Yang "anti-party clique" was not confined to Mao's trusties. Zhou Enlai declared on May 21:

> In less than half a year, the true faces of the "four big families" have been fully exposed. This has not been a simple matter. The struggle had only just begun when they took our positions away one by one. Now we must take them back

37

one by one. They wave the red banner to oppose the red banner, and have spread plenty of toxin . . . Now that this time bomb has been removed, the center is even more united.[25]

The odd label—"four big families" *(si da jiazu)*—that Zhou used to refer to the four purged leaders was not a precursor of the "Gang of Four," but was the one used by the CCP in pre-Liberation days to refer to Nationalist leaders: Chiang (Kai-shek), (T. V.) Soong, (H. H.) K'ung, and the brothers Ch'en (Kuo-fu and Li-fu). It was Zhou's way of adding insult to injury; neither Zhou nor Liu Shaoqi realized, it was later asserted, that there would be a fifth "family," Liu himself.[26] On May 23, the four men were formally dismissed by decision of the meeting. Yet "these are all my friends," Mao hypocritically told Ho Chi Minh later when explaining the purge of the revisionists.[27]

"A victory for Mao Zedong Thought, to be celebrated," was how Zhou in May 1966 described the purge that Mao had felt coming "a long time ago."[28] A "*great* victory for Mao Zedong Thought," is how Liu Shaoqi referred to it a month later.[29] This carefully orchestrated and protracted affair was a hinge event, serving as both the last of the CCP's great pre–Cultural Revolution purges and the first of the Cultural Revolution itself.

"From the very beginning to the end of the session," according to the subsequent recollections of one participant, "everything happened in an atmosphere of extreme political tension."[30] Mao, still absent from the capital after six months, used Kang Sheng as his personal conduit of information and "instructions." Addressing a plenary session on May 18, Lin Biao, using speaking notes prepared for him under Kang Sheng's supervision, charged the four with attempting a "revisionist power-seizure" and of plotting a counterrevolutionary coup d'état:

> In the [seventeenth-century anthology of ancient-style prose] *Gems of Chinese Literature (Guwen guanzhi)*, the piece entitled "On Discerning Traitors" speaks of how to "clearly predict the ultimate consequences on the basis of the very first symptoms" and notes that "when a halo of color surrounds the moon, there will be wind; and when the stone in which a pillar is set is damp, there will be rain." Bad things are preceded by omens. Anything essential will always express itself by way of phenomena. Recently a number of weird things and weird signs have drawn our attention to the possibility of a counterrevolutionary coup, one in which people will be killed, political power will be usurped, capitalism will be restored, and the whole of socialism will be done away with. [We have] plenty of signs, plenty of material [to prove it], and I won't go into detail here . . .
>
> [Peng, Luo, Lu, and Yang] flaunted the signboard of the Communist

Party—in reality they are a bunch of anti-Communist elements. Their exposure was a great victory for the party: it would have been highly dangerous not to expose them. Had they been allowed to go on, it might all have ended up not with the party exposing them but with *them* putting the party "on trial."[31]

The reason Lin did not "go into detail here" was almost certainly that the "material" he hinted at was not plentiful. Occasionally departing from his speaking notes, he made up for weak substance with obscenities, edited out of the final official transcript released to a wider audience in September 1966.[32]

Indictments

While in session, the Politburo issued six Central Documents that dealt directly with the purge of Peng, Luo, Lu, and Yang and the launching of a "Great Cultural Revolution"—the latter event one that intrigued foreign observers were slowly beginning to take notice of. A domestic Chinese audience was told by the official Xinhua News Agency that "experts" in the United States were "carefully monitoring events" and that one unnamed Washington official had admitted, "It may be five years before we really know what is happening today."[33]

The extensive report on Luo Ruiqing's "errors," dated April 30, had been prepared by a special task group under the MAC. Together with Luo's self-criticism, extended denunciations of him by four of his most senior colleagues—Marshal Ye Jianying and generals Xie Fuzhi, Xiao Hua, and Yang Chengwu—and a letter to Mao in which the "disgusting performance of comrade Peng Zhen during the meetings held to denounce Luo" was condemned, the report was circulated on May 16 as *Zhongfa* [1966] 268.[34]

No similarly detailed reports concerning Lu Dingyi's and Yang Shangkun's "errors" were released, only a brief statement in which the Politburo purported to "explain" the character of those errors and announced that a special Central Case Examination Committee had been set up to "further investigate" the "anti-party activities and irregular relationships" linking the two men to Luo Ruiqing and Peng Zhen.[35]

Peng's "errors" and the Cultural Revolution were the subject of Central Document *Zhongfa* [1966] 267, clearly the most important document of them all. It contained a Notification *(Tongzhi)* prepared under Mao's personal supervision, well in advance of the Politburo session, to which were attached six appendices. The latter included not only texts documenting Peng's alleged "errors" in general terms, but also a document concerned with his "Wang Ming line in international affairs";[36] the full text of the February Outline, allegedly the conclusive evidence of Peng's "revisionism"; and a chronology prepared in Beijing under the supervision of Liu Shaoqi and Deng Xiaoping tracing the "struggle between the two roads on the cultural front" since September 1965.

The Notification was then put to the vote. In the words of one participant, "everyone was in favor, and nobody voiced any dissenting opinion. [Liu] Shaoqi announced that since it was an enlarged session, everyone present had the right to vote. The Notification was approved unanimously by a show of hands, without any alterations whatever to the text."[37]

The text contained not only ordinary typos—easily corrected, should anyone present have dared to point them out—but also major inconsistencies in political terminology. Given the hypersensitivity with which CCP leaders normally approached matters of language, the fact that the Notification referred to the Cultural Revolution with two quite different formulations *(tifa)* was highly noteworthy. In calmer times, people like Mao's longtime ghostwriter and political secretary Hu Qiaomu, Kang Sheng—a prominent "Marxist theoretician," according to the obituary published in the *People's Daily* when he died in 1975—and others had waged proxy battles in the party press about the supposedly essential differences between "bourgeois rights" and "rights of a bourgeois kind," between "class societies" and "societies containing classes," and between other near-synonymous formulations, the consistently "correct" use of which supposedly distinguished a socialist from a revisionist.

But on this occasion, it was as if nobody noticed that the Notification did not even indicate clearly whether what was to follow next was to be a "socialist" or a "proletarian" Cultural Revolution. The Notification contained both formulations. Furthermore, its occasional characterization of the Cultural Revolution as not merely a revolution, but a *"great ... revolution,"* echoed Liu Shaoqi's characterization of the earlier Socialist Education Movement (today regarded by many historians as a dress rehearsal for the Cultural Revolution) as a "great revolution, more profound, more complex, and more arduous" than anything the CCP had ever previously been engaged in.[38] And on this point, at least, it seemed as if the drafters of the Notification had a carefully considered motive for doing what they did. The Cultural Revolution was to be by far the most ambitious attempt at dealing with revisionism ever attempted by the CCP: "far from being a minor issue, the struggle against this *revisionist line* is an issue of prime importance having a vital bearing on the destiny and future of our party and state, on the future complexion of our party and state, and on the world revolution."[39]

Losers

The May 16 Notification, like the report on Luo Ruiqing's "errors," was given the second-highest level of classification then in use within the CCP, so only cadres of rank 17 and above were allowed to begin studying it on May 17 while the Politburo was still in session. When it was finally declassified and reprinted in the *People's Daily* a year later, on May 17, 1967, it was described as having "sounded the Great Proletarian Cultural Revolutionary bugle to advance" and marked the "mighty beginning" of the movement. Senior cadres across the country began poring over it while the Politburo was still in session; ordinary party members and cadres with the Communist Youth League (CYL) often had to wait an extra week or so before the spirit of it was transmitted "down" to them orally during "political study," those dreary afternoon rituals that were such an inescapable part of political life in Mao's China. Helping them to divine the direction of the movement were Zhou Enlai's remarks on May 21, when he told the Politburo session that it would "target the center, rather than the localities, the domestic scene rather than the international one, inside rather than outside the party, and higher levels rather than lower levels." Quoting Mao, he reiterated: "The stress will be on the inside and at the top [of the CCP]."[40]

But it is doubtful that his audience really understood Mao's message. After the session, the minister of education, who had been present during the latter half of it, said to his colleagues, "Now I am very confused."[41] Another minister in Zhou Enlai's State Council who was also present instructed party branch secretaries in the ministry to "do a good job of lining up targets and checking up on people, so that you know what you're doing when you begin dragging them out." The designated targets of the movement were first of all to be sought among people who "normally express revisionist opinions and views; who have expressed dissatisfaction with the organization for a long time and who show signs of sectarian behavior; who are deeply influenced by bourgeois thinking, severely individualistic, and have a strikingly erroneous stand and viewpoints"[42]—in short, the usual suspects; perhaps a chance to settle scores and advance one's career. Yet the minister should have realized from the stature of the leaders already indicted that the Cultural Revolution was about "dragging out" people not "normally" associated with revisionist views.

In June, the first in what was to become an endless series of rallies to denounce the four big families was held in Zhongnanhai. At the same time, across Beijing mass rallies to celebrate their ouster and pledge support were organized. A Western diplomat was there to witness one such rally—occasioned by the reorganization of the Beijing Party Committee—in front of the Beijing party office:

> Appointment of new Peking party secretaries became public on afternoon of 3 June. By nightfall excited Peking citizens were queuing up to buy copies of the *Peking Evening News* . . . Main focus was at Peking Municipal Party Headquarters. Portrait of Mao flanked by two red flags bearing the hammer and sickle had been quickly stuck above main entrance. Arc lamps and a loudspeaker system were erected. From early evening trucks were seen conveying groups representing different sections of Peking life to the Headquarters. Group leaders in turn read out protestations of welcome for and loyalty to new party committee and uttered slogans expressing confidence in the thought of Mao Tse-tung and the Central Committee, and the need to maintain purity of Marxist/Leninist revolution, by smashing all "monsters and freaks." Demonstration was tightly controlled and minutely organised. Except for cheer-leading activists, many in the crowd appeared either apathetic or enjoying the excitement. Firecrackers and the roll of pedicab-mounted drums completed picture.[43]

Behind the vermilion wall which had once enclosed the Forbidden City but which now protected the residences of the party elite and the offices of the CC and State Council from the prying eyes of the public, the actual members of the four big families were denounced and humiliated at meetings attended by the staffs of central organs.[44] These early rallies were organized under the aegis of the central party apparat; later the rallies became public affairs, and much of the practical work of organizing them was delegated to Red Guards.

Luo Ruiqing, hospitalized after his suicide attempt, which cost him the use of his legs, was at first attacked in absentia; his wife, herself a PLA officer, was designated a proxy target and made to appear in his stead.[45] Before the end of the year she was herself imprisoned, while her crippled husband—in a testimony to the "revolutionary ingenuity" of the "masses"—would be carried onto the stage of one rally after the other in a crude basket of the kind normally used to store cabbages. Lu Dingyi's wife was "struggled" repeatedly in public with her husband in the autumn and winter of 1966.[46] Lu's son was imprisoned for six years, his sisters-in-law for six, eight, and nine years respectively, and his mother-in-law died in prison. Yang Shangkun's wife was dismissed and repeatedly subjected to public "struggle sessions" beginning in the summer of 1966.

The purge of Peng Zhen in particular resulted in the further dismissal from office and persecution of countless minor officials accused of being his "sworn followers" and "sinister henchmen." Purged with him in May were his two ranking deputies, Liu Ren and Zheng Tianxiang. In June, all of Peng's ten vice mayors (including Wu Han) lost their jobs. In July, municipal party secretary Zhao Fan was purged, and the director of the municipal propaganda department, Li Qi, committed suicide after being publicly denounced as an "ultra-vanguard opponent of Mao Zedong Thought." In October, the only two remaining members of Peng Zhen's original party secretariat, Wan Li and Chen Kehan, were also purged, and in addition to Peng some 81 officials—including Liu Ren, 42 department and bureau directors, and 34 section chiefs—were rounded up in great secrecy and imprisoned. Had they but known, their conditions there were humane in comparison to what would later befall them.[47]

One other senior leader was under fire as Peng Zhen's apparat was being dismantled, though his case was not tied in with that of the four families. Vice Premier Ulanfu, an ethnic Mongol, was an alternate member of the Politburo, first party secretary of the Inner Mongolian Autonomous Region, commander and political commissar of the Inner Mongolian MR, and second secretary of the CC's North China Region. Already in the winter of 1965, Ulanfu had been criticized within the CCP for supposedly being "soft" on Mongol "class enemies." In the increasingly harsher political climate that was prevailing by May 1966, the charges against him were rewritten to include opposing the CCP, socialism, and Mao Zedong Thought and threatening to "destroy national unity by creating ethnic division."[48] In July, Liu Shaoqi told Ulanfu that he had failed to "carry out the class struggle, in particular among the Mongol population," and Deng Xiaoping argued that Ulanfu had been grasping the wrong "key link"; instead of concentrating on economic development he should have been grasping "the key link of class struggle." On August 16, 1966, Ulanfu was dismissed from his party posts and accused of being the "biggest party power-holder taking the capitalist road in the Inner Mongolian Autonomous Region."[49] By 1967, he had lost his PLA and State Council posts as well.

Among those who refused to accept such fates, suicides became increasingly common. On the night of May 17, Deng Tuo—Peng Zhen's party secretary for culture and education, former editor-in-chief of the *People's Daily* (demoted in 1957 by Mao personally for failing to spread his ideas in editorials), the disgraced

Wu Han's longtime prolific fellow-columnist in the Beijing papers, a loyal Communist if ever there was one—was, in the words of his Western biographer, "driven to ritual suicide by those he served."[50] Mao's political secretary, Tian Jiaying, who had lost the Chairman's confidence for advocating partial decollectivization during the GLF famine, took the same way out, committing suicide on May 23 after being accused of obstructing the campaign against Wu Han by "falsifying" the Chairman's words. On June 25, the director of Peng's municipal foreign affairs office committed suicide amid accusations of having maintained "illicit contacts with foreign countries." On July 10, the head of propaganda on the Beijing Party Committee—who had clashed repeatedly with Jiang Qing over her efforts to "revolutionize Beijing Opera"—committed suicide. On July 23, one of the two principal drafters of the February Outline hanged himself after a secretary of Kang Sheng accused him of being a "mole" used by Peng Zhen to spy on Kang. Families suffered in silent agony. After Deng Tuo's suicide, "his children were expelled from school, his wife was paraded through the streets of Beijing, and 'revolutionary successors' occupied his traditional-style home."[51]

But these personal tragedies were merely footnotes in the far greater political upheaval by then well under way.

Winners

Dead or disgraced leaders had to be replaced. One of the most macabre but universal political rules of thumb is "While there's death, there's hope." In a major promotion, Tao Zhu, first secretary of the party's Central-South Bureau, took over Peng Zhen's job as permanent secretary of the CC Secretariat and also stepped into Lu Dingyi's shoes as head of propaganda. A onetime student in Chiang Kai-shek's Whampoa Military Academy turned Communist agitator and organizer, the feisty Tao was known to be blunt and outspoken: a collection put out by university students in 1967 under the title *Tao Zhu on Tao Zhu* contained quotes like "I'm prepared to say that I've always been revolutionary, but I haven't always been right" and "Leftist errors, rightist errors—I've committed them all. But I've not committed errors in line!" Tao's equivalent on the CC's North China Region, Li Xuefeng, replaced Peng Zhen as first secretary of the Beijing Party Committee;[52] but presumably he failed in the herculean task of controlling the capital to Mao's full satisfaction, for by the end of the year he was serving only as the party boss of the decidedly less glamorous port city of Tianjin. Ye Jianying, vice chairman of the MAC, replaced Luo Ruiqing as its secretary general and member of the Central Committee Secretariat. As noted above, Wang Dongxing, director of the Central Bureau of Guards, had already taken over Yang Shangkun's job at the CC's General Office.

Once promoted, Tao, Li, and Ye were in turn able to reward their cronies with promotions and/or much-sought-after transfers. Tao Zhu's case was the perfect illustration of a popular Chinese proverb, in use since at least as far back as the Han dynasty: "When a man attains the Dao, even his pets ascend to heaven!" meaning that when an official gets to the top, all his friends and relatives get to go there with him. Tao was able to bring numerous colleagues from southern and central China with him to Beijing, including no less than fifty-four county-level officials who took over from fallen members of Peng Zhen's municipal government, as well as the first party secretary of his native Hunan, whom he appointed permanent deputy director of the Central Propaganda Department, and a onetime secretary general on the Central-South Region whom he got placed as secretary in charge of culture and education on Li Xuefeng's new Beijing party secretariat.[53]

But the even bigger winners were the key members of the ad hoc group that had drafted the May 16 Notification under the leadership of Chen Boda and Kang Sheng: Jiang Qing, Zhang Chunqiao, Yao Wenyuan, Guan Feng, Qi Benyu, Wang Li, and Mu Xin. Wang, the offspring of a long line of scholars, was a holdover from the group that had written the CCP's anti-Soviet polemics. Mu was editor-in-chief of *Guangming Daily,* China's most prominent national newspaper for an educated elite readership. After the enlarged Politburo session, this team was renamed the "Central Cultural Revolution Group" (CCRG), a body that in theory reported to the PSC but in reality was Mao's personal instrument in what followed. It was no coincidence that its founding meeting took place on his temporary turf in Shanghai rather than under the watchful eyes of Liu Shaoqi and Deng Xiaoping in Beijing. Chen Boda, who claimed to have tried to decline the leadership of the CCRG on the grounds that he was a mere scholar only to be told by Zhou Enlai to submit to party discipline,[54] later observed that of all the many impressively labeled party bodies he had ever led, none had enjoyed greater de facto powers than this "group" *(xiaozu).* Initially, it functioned primarily as a high-level ghostwriting team, its first task being to put the key elements of Mao's evolving great Cultural Revolutionary design on paper. The attempt started out in June as a twelve-point directive, quickly grew into a twenty-three-point document "On the Situation in the Great Proletarian Cultural Revolution and Some of the Party's Long-Term Policies," and finally, after no less than thirty-one consecutive drafts became the "Decision concerning the Great Proletarian Cultural Revolution" (the "Sixteen Points") that would be passed by the CC on August 8. Thereafter, the CCRG became the preeminent organ for promoting the Cultural Revolution.[55]

Reactions

Party cadres found the accusation made by the drafters of the May 16 Notification that Peng, Luo, Lu, and Yang "opposed the party" hard to believe. Some immediately began to worry about who might be next in line. The party secretary of the Beijing No. 2 Language Institute, who got word of the purge of his "old friend" (as he liked to call him) Peng Zhen while traveling abroad, reacted by saying, "We're not safe either."[56] Others asked anyone with a solid grasp of Marxism-Leninism to provide credible explanations. Yet even in the CCP Central Party School, attended by senior party cadres from all over China eager to improve their grasp of Marxist-Leninist theory, there were those who found the accusations against such exalted party leaders literally incomprehensible. They were told by the president of the school, Lin Feng, "It is a class issue that you cannot explain by focusing on the individual. It has a class impetus that is *independent of man's will.*"[57]

While party cadres voiced incredulity, intellectuals and non-party luminaries panicked. On May 5, a speech by Guo Moruo, president of the Academy of Sciences and China's cultural Pooh-Bah, was published in the *People's Daily*, in which he declared that the "many millions of words" that he had written and translated should "in the light of present day standards . . . all be burned."[58] Later in May, Deng Xiaoping was informed by the CC's United Front Work Department that among non-party intellectuals and members of the eight non-Communist "democratic parties," there were widespread signs of "shock, tension, and terror."[59] Deng arranged for Liu Shaoqi to brief senior "democratic personages" in the Great Hall of the People in late June, to help them overcome their anxieties about the Cultural Revolution and the purge of the big four party revisionists, a purge that Deng insisted on calling a "normal sign, a sign of health" from the CCP's point of view.[60]

Ironically, in view of his later fate, Liu Shaoqi echoed Lin Feng's argument, portraying the fallen four almost as zombies: "Seen as individuals, they would have been capable of not acting. But from a class struggle point of view, their action appears normal, not strange. Class struggle is independent of man's will.

Why they should act the way they did is because their class made them do it."[61] How reassuring Liu himself, let alone the intellectuals, found this Marxist-Leninist gobbledygook is unclear, but at least it could be peddled as an *ex post facto* explanation. Far more difficult to explain was how to detect revisionists in advance, given that they "wave a red flag to oppose the red flag, and speak of Marxism-Leninism and Mao Zedong Thought—speak of socialism—while doing all that capitalist stuff."[62] Liu's tortured account made revisionists into invisible men, even though the media claimed that no matter how skillfully they disguised themselves, revisionists could be detected by grasping the "telescope and microscope of Mao Zedong Thought."[63]

"Working toward" the Chairman

Indeed, the May Notification had not been merely, or even primarily, a document that summed up a struggle already won, but in actuality pointed forward in time, as was hinted at in key passages added by Mao himself. As Mao told Chen Boda and Kang Sheng at the time, he specifically *intended* these passages to be "inflammatory."[64] Hints about how to interpret them were given by Kang to the participants at the enlarged Politburo session. The "really soul-stirring" passage, Kang observed on one of the first days of the session, claiming to be speaking also on behalf of Lin Biao, occurred in the very last section of the Notification.[65] Penned by Mao, it read in full:

> Those representatives of the bourgeoisie who have sneaked into the party, the government, the army, and various spheres of culture are a bunch of counter-revolutionary revisionists. Once conditions are ripe, they will seize political power and turn the dictatorship of the proletariat into a dictatorship of the bourgeoisie. Some of them we have already seen through; others we have not. Some are still trusted by us and are being trained as our successors, persons like Khrushchev, for example, who are still nestling beside us. Party committees at all levels must pay full attention to this matter.[66]

Whom did Mao have in mind? Amazingly, it would seem as if the identity of the person or persons "like Khrushchev" to whom the Chairman was alluding escaped even members of Mao's inner circle. "When the Chairman mentioned Khrushchev-type persons nestling beside us still being trained as our successors last year, we had a very poor understanding [of whom he was talking about]," Qi Benyu maintained in April 1967.[67] According to Zhang Chunqiao in May 1967,

"When the movement began, quite a few people had a very poor understanding of—and responded very ineffectively to—the Chairman's words, in particular the passage about 'persons like Khrushchev, for example, who are still nestling beside us . . .' At the time, I did not really understand this passage. I could only think of Peng Zhen and did not fully anticipate Liu Shaoqi."[68] In October 1968, even Kang Sheng insisted that "at the time, I did not sense that the reference was to Liu Shaoqi, but had only a very superficial understanding of this important instruction from Chairman Mao."[69]

In fact, only Mao himself could "detect" revisionists, or, more accurately, decide who they were. The purge of the four big families was a major coup for the Chairman, but until he named them nobody could be certain that they were the real targets. Mao was playing his cards very close to his chest. To have confided his longer-range aims to even his trusties risked disclosure. Had a hint of his plans leaked, his intended victims might have attempted preemptive counter-measures.

The more profound result of Mao's secretiveness was that during the Cultural Revolution his ardent supporters had to try to intuit what he wanted and to fulfill what they believed to be his aims. They had to "work toward" the Chairman, sometimes conceivably exceeding what even he might have contemplated. On those grounds, the survivors of the Cultural Revolution would have some justification for blaming Mao's radical allies for the worst excesses of the movement. But it was the Chairman's deliberate opaqueness that was ultimately the cause.[70]

Securing the Capital

A prime example of Mao's carefulness, perhaps paranoia, is provided by the measures he took to consolidate the control of the capital that he had secured by the purge of Peng Zhen.[71] In great secrecy, troop movements in and around Beijing proceeded simultaneously with the demotions of officials and denunciation meetings behind closed doors in party and government organizations. There is no way of knowing whether Mao believed in the threat of a coup d'état to which he had alluded in conversation off and on since the autumn of 1965 and which was emphasized by Lin Biao as well as Zhou Enlai in the May Politburo session—"As far as the threat of a coup d'état is concerned," Zhou said, "I agree with what comrade Lin Biao said in his speech"—though curtly dismissed by Peng Zhen.[72] But the Chairman had always taught that political power grew out of the barrel of a gun, and even with Lin Biao in firmer control of the MAC, he was taking no chances.[73]

A special task force, known as the Capital Work Team, was set up under the PSC to respond comprehensively to Mao's concerns about security in the capital.[74] The Capital Work Team was led by Marshal Ye Jianying in his role as the new secretary general of the Central Military Affairs Commission. Ye's deputies were acting Chief of Staff General Yang Chengwu and Minister of Public Security General Xie Fuzhi. The members of the team included the deputy director of the PLA General Political Department, two deputy commanders of the Beijing Military Region, and the respective directors of the general offices of the CCP CC, the State Council, and the CCP's North China Region.[75] Yang Chengwu's performance during the "launch phase" of the Cultural Revolution was clearly to Mao's satisfaction, according to Qi Benyu's comments in January 1967: "Yang Chengwu has made a special contribution to this Great Cultural Revolution. His service has been especially meritorious. Had the military forces under his command not stood firm, Luo would already have carried out a coup a long time ago."[76]

Though the Capital Work Team's offices were located inside the MAC, of which Lin Biao was the highest-ranking vice chairman, Lin had no personal representative on it. The member of the PSC to whom Ye Jianying reported directly was Zhou Enlai. The first plenary meeting of the team, held on May 26, authorized Ye to mobilize garrison troops in an emergency situation with the prior consent of Zhou Enlai or, in Zhou's absence, Deng Xiaoping.[77]

In June 1966, the Capital Work Team oversaw the transfer of command of two armed police divisions based in Beijing from the Chinese Public Security Force to the Beijing Garrison.[78] This transfer of command coincided with the implementation of an earlier decision, taken on Mao's instructions by the CCP Central Committee Secretariat in February 1966, to abolish the Chinese Public Security Force as a unique national institution subject to joint control by the MAC and the Ministry of Public Security.[79] The team furthermore oversaw a massive reinforcement of the Beijing Garrison. It expanded from one division and one regiment to three divisions and a regiment, but soon became four divisions, each consisting of six regiments, plus the independent regiment and various other units. Two of the additional PLA main force divisions, the 70th and the 189th, transferred in from Hebei province, had historical links to Yang Chengwu. The garrison commander had the right to call upon three neighboring divisions in case of emergency.[80] He was responsible directly to the MAC, that is, ultimately to Mao and Lin Biao, and not to the commander of the surrounding Beijing MR.

At this point, the garrison command was changed. Major General Li Jiayi was replaced by Major General Fu Chongbi, one of the two deputy commanders of the Beijing MR on the Capital Work Team. Both men were Long March veterans who had commanded significant forces in Korea (Li as a deputy division commander and Fu as a division commander), but unlike Li, Fu was able to boast of a long-standing and close relationship with Yang Chengwu, under whom he had served in the 1940s.[81] Yang is alleged to have told Fu later: "You, Fu Chongbi, if it wasn't for me, you would never have made garrison commander!"[82]

An offhand remark by the Chairman to a visiting Albanian delegation in 1967 seemed to imply that Mao truly believed that it would have been "unsafe" for him and his guests to walk the streets of Beijing prior to May 1966. Indeed, an incident not reported in the media at the time had occurred in the morning of February 2, 1966, when a single 5.6-millimeter rifle bullet had suddenly shattered a window on the northern side of the Great Hall of the People. An accident? An assassination attempt? The work of a madman? A high-powered investigation under the leadership of a vice minister of public security quickly concluded that the culprit was the teenage son of a vice director of the National Physical Culture and Sports Commission who, from the roof of his home across the street, had been shooting sparrows that morning and whose aim had been less than perfect.[83] Rather more significantly from a political point of view, also in February 1966, the Beijing Municipal Intermediate Court had sentenced two men to three-year sentences for spreading "counterrevolutionary leaflets" and allegedly plotting to blow up Tiananmen Gate.[84] Mao told his Albanian guests that he was, on the whole, satisfied with the steps of a military nature taken by the Capital Work Team. "At the time when we announced the reorganization of the Beijing Party Committee," Mao declared, "we added another two divisions to the garrison . . . Now you are able to go wherever you want, and I am able to go wherever I want too."[85] Zhou Enlai recalled the redeployments less dramatically a year later when he insisted that the changes were "really no big deal."[86]

The troops that made up the new reinforced Beijing Garrison were crack units described by Zhou to an unruly gathering of students in January 1967 as highly "capable and vigorous." They would not permit themselves to be provoked by people "cursing them" or "hitting them with their fists," and they would certainly "not shoot at people." "If you curse them, hit them, you should know that they are Chairman Mao's fighters," Zhou Enlai explained.[87] According to Fu Chongbi, at the height of the Cultural Revolution the Beijing Garrison was home to in excess of 100,000 officers, men, and dependents. "At that time, a greater number of copies of Central Documents were being distributed to the garrison than to the [entire] Beijing Military Region," he recalled some thirty years later.[88]

In addition to taking steps intended to ensure that the greater Beijing area was "safe," the Capital Work Team set out in even greater secrecy to enhance security behind the walls of Zhongnanhai. According to Zhou Enlai, speaking in June 1967, since Zhongnanhai for so many years had in effect been "ruled" by Yang Shangkun, it was littered with people "with complicated backgrounds." In order to make it "safe" for the CCP Chairman, whose worries at this point even included being "assassinated by a counterrevolutionary clique on the party Central Committee,"[89] a major shakeup of the CC General Office was carried out by Yang's successor, Wang Dongxing. "If we hadn't chased those people away, the Chairman would not have been able to move back to Zhongnanhai," Zhou explained.[90]

Not only was the part of Zhongnanhai where Mao Zedong and his colleagues lived cleansed of staff possibly having "illicit links" to Yang Shangkun; a number of prominent party figures who had lived there for years simply by virtue of their seniority were "chased away" too. In early July, Vice Premier Li Fuchun and Wang Dongxing informed them that the center had "recently decided" that only those senior officials who were involved directly in the work of the PSC would henceforth be allowed to live inside Zhongnanhai. All others were to be relocated to other parts of Beijing.[91]

"By June," Zhou recalled almost a year later, "Beijing was stable."[92] Stable it may have been, but it was by no means calm. In fact, this was the month when the Cultural Revolution turned public, noisy, and boisterous.[93]

3

Confusion on Campuses

In a letter to his wife on July 8, 1966, Mao expressed his determination to create "great disorder under heaven" for the purpose of ultimately achieving "great order under heaven."[1] To achieve this extraordinary end, Mao chose to employ extraordinary means. He had started the Cultural Revolution by letting Jiang Qing secretly supervise the production of a newspaper article attacking an intellectual in order to topple the boss of Beijing. Now, in phase two, he would manipulate a mass movement at China's educational institutions to unseat the head of state.

But while the first battles of Mao's Cultural Revolution raged out of public view in the Politburo and the criticism of Wu Han and his colleagues had yet to fully engage the intellectual elite on university campuses, ordinary Chinese still managed to lead ordinary lives. Politics was never completely absent, as evidenced in the diaries the CCP and CYL encouraged the young to keep. Pledges to emulate Lin Biao's self-sacrificing soldiers, the paragons of proletarian virtue; outrage directed at the latest atrocities of the American imperialists in Vietnam; disgust with Fidel Castro in Havana, who had recently compared the Chinese people's love for Chairman Mao to "superstitious idol worship"—a week if not a day never seemed to pass without an entry on such subjects, copied, one suspects, verbatim from the party media.[2] Yet much of the time, the concerns of 745 million Chinese were with more mundane, private everyday matters, often of precisely the kind that would soon be denounced as insufficiently focused on class struggle.

Left to their own devices, students described a life and echoed sentiments that did not seem all that far removed from the May 4 era and its concerns with saving the nation and making it wealthy and powerful. At the end of a wet, dreary Friday in March, a Nanjing college student returning to campus after a day of semaphore flag practice on Lake Xuanwu recorded in his diary that "on the way home I entered a grocer's, and just as I was about to pay for a fried donut an old man walked up to me saying, 'Young friend, please help me! Give me a few coins for a bowl of noodles!' . . . After giving him two cents and three liang [about 113 grams] of grain coupons, I thought to myself, our country still hasn't quite made it as far as grain and the economy are concerned, and I promised myself to master science and give my all to the people of China and the world still living in misery!"[3] Even the diaries of young soldiers conjured up images of a China far more concerned with escaping poverty and leading a better life than with a "class struggle" that, in any case, as Liu Shaoqi put it, proceeded "independently of man's will." After spending a sunny Friday morning in April on his motorcycle delivering report forms to a neighboring armored corps, a young soldier billeted at the foot of Jiuhuashan—one of the four sacred mountains of Chinese Buddhism—wrote in his diary: "From the Sun Yat-sen Bridge I could see so many people collecting river silt: workers, students, ordinary locals, cadres, women, teenagers, old people, and children. What an atmosphere of true prosperity! That jet-black river-bottom silt is the finest fertilizer of all!"[4]

There were of course reasons why such youths were not afire with the Cultural Revolution. For the first few months of 1966, the Xinhua News Agency imposed what critics later called a "news blackout" on the criticism of people such as Wu Han, but which in reality amounted to consigning occasional criticisms to the inner pages or academic supplements of the newspapers that received them. Not until April 15 did this practice change;[5] three days later a powerful editorial in the *Liberation Army Daily* "leaked" the main points of Jiang Qing's Forum Summary, urging all the Chinese people to throw themselves heart and mind into the "Great Socialist Cultural Revolution," and attempted to overcome any inhibitions about this project by asserting that "a socialist cultural revolution demands that there be destruction as well as creativity. Without thorough destruction, there can be no real construction."[6] By the end of April, *Red Flag* had weighed in with an authoritative "commentator" article, the title of which proclaimed that "The Participation of the Worker-Peasant-Soldier Masses in Academic Criticism is a Major Epoch-Making Event!"[7] The Cultural Revolution was about to become a mass movement.

But could the "worker-peasant-soldier masses" be trusted to emerge victorious in what the media called "the battle on the cultural front to foster that which is proletarian and to liquidate that which is bourgeois"? *Red Flag*, of course, left no doubt about the final outcome, but contemporary diaries suggest that in China's usual political environment it was by no means a given. A frustrated research student from a humble background, a CCP member of four years' standing, recorded in mid-May what happened at his institute at a meeting to debate the primacy of proletarian politics over vocational work: "One guy said, 'In research, the real goal is to complete the assignments, and in this context politics is a means,' and he expressed himself very dialectically and all . . . Those guys use a lot of fancy words to confound us students from worker-peasant backgrounds. But they'd better not imagine we're here for them to manipulate at will. We're armed with Mao Zedong Thought." Later the same week, in an entry that hinted between the lines at where he himself saw a possible solution to the problem, he wrote: "This morning I went to have it out with [one of them], but he is very articulate and has a sharper tongue than mine. Moreover, we still don't have enough real dirt on him. I didn't get very far."[8]

Fortunately for such inarticulate youngsters, Mao Zedong had no intention of maintaining the normal poltical environment. Though the process by which Mao translated high-level political intrigue into mass mobilization remains one of the many obscure issues of the Cultural Revolution, we do know that it all started at Peking University (Beida).[9]

China's First Marxist-Leninist Big-Character Poster

On May 14, like Mao before him, Kang Sheng sent his wife on a secret mission on behalf of the Cultural Revolution. Cao Yiou went to Beida at the head of a close-knit seven-person "central investigation team," supposedly to check up on the progress of "academic criticism" at this most prestigious of Chinese universities. Cao's position was that the "orientation of the academic criticism at Beida is wrong" and that the university president, Lu Ping, must be held responsible. She had to determine, in her husband's words, the extent to which "academic criticism" at Beida was "genuine or bogus."[10] It was "bogus," according to Kang, if it followed the line of the February Outline. Since the outline had not yet been publicly repudiated, and the May 16 Notification that would introduce Mao's alternative to it was only just becoming available to an as yet highly restricted inner party circle, it was inevitable that Peking University would be awash in "bogus" criticism. Cao's true mission, in fact, was to stir up grassroots opposition to the school's party leadership. As Kang Sheng put it, "If the masses don't rise in rebellion [by themselves], we will mobilize them to rise up in rebellion."[11]

But had Kang received a direct order from Mao or was he "working toward the Chairman," intuiting that he would want this done? Was this just another way of spreading great disorder under heaven, or had Mao, mindful of campus criticism of the party during the Hundred Flowers Campaign of 1957, already decided to recruit students as the shock troops of the Cultural Revolution?

Cao Yiou was certainly in possession of information of great importance to campus leftists. As head of her husband's private office, Cao knew of the denunciation of Peng Zhen made by Kang on behalf of Mao at the expanded Politburo meeting earlier in the month. She also knew that Beida leftists resented Peng Zhen. The faculty had been badly split during the Socialist Education Movement the year before. Leftists, espoused by Kang Sheng, had attacked the school's party leaders as "capitalist roaders," only to see the latter exonerated after Peng Zhen had intervened personally and a work team that included Deng Tuo had been sent to Beida to restore order. Thus the imminent fall of Peng Zhen would have been heartwarming news to Nie Yuanzi, a forty-five-year-old party branch secretary in the Philosophy Department and one of the leftists most criticized in 1965 as a result of her vendetta against university president Lu Ping.[12] Nie Yuanzi was about to lose her job—her successor had already been selected— and had been told to await a "downward" assignment to a small branch of the university in mountainous Huairou county, 30 miles north of central Beijing.[13] Cao's visit could not have come at a better time.

Cao sought out Nie, whom she and her husband had known slightly in Yan'an. Nie was very well connected, having joined the CCP in 1938 at the age of seventeen and spent most of the Sino-Japanese War years in Yan'an. The day the first big-character poster appeared, with Nie's name prominently upon it, one of Deng Xiaoping's daughters, a Beida student, phoned home and told her mother about it. Her mother's immediate concern was less with the political content of the poster than with the moral qualities of its most senior signatory: "Nie Yuanzi is a bad person . . . she behaved badly in Yan'an. Don't tell anybody I said so!"[14] Kang Sheng held a similar view of Nie but did not really care about her morals: "I've known since back in Yan'an that Nie Yuanzi is not a very good person. But now we will support her, even if she is a fucking turtle's egg [*hundan wangbadan*]."[15]

Nie and her leftist friends had realized just from reading the *People's Daily* that the widening of the anti–Wu Han campaign to include Deng Tuo meant that the Beijing party propaganda establishment which had quashed them in 1965 was in bad trouble. With the intra-party sources available to a branch secretary and whatever inside information about the struggle against Peng Zhen that Cao passed on, Nie knew that Lu Ping had lost his high-level protection and was therefore vulnerable.[16] As it happened, six of Nie's colleagues in the Philosophy Department who also had inside information about the wholesale destruction of the Beijing party apparat were already planning a move of some kind against the university party committee. Emboldened by Cao, Nie teamed up with them. One of them told a member of Cao's team that they were contemplating writing a letter to Mao about the matter, but he was told that such a move would be pointless: the letter would not reach the CCP Chairman.[17] Given the Cao team's agenda, the real reason was probably that a letter would hardly serve the purpose of "mobilizing the masses to rise up in rebellion."

Yet Cao did not know of, and Nie was only marginally involved in, the gestation of the big-character poster, which the seven leftists finally decided would be the best way of attacking the school's party leadership.[18] Nie later claimed, however, that she was the one who arranged for a last-minute meeting with Cao Yiou. Though Cao had not seen the text of the poster herself, in her capacity as "someone higher up in the party organization" she gave Nie the green light to put it up.[19] When a third draft was completed in the early hours of May 25, the other members of the group were summoned to sign off on it, which they did later that morning after only minor changes. Nie's most significant contribution was to add three slogans at the last minute at the end of the text: "Defend the party center! Defend Mao Zedong Thought! Defend the dictatorship of the proletariat!" As the senior faculty member in the group, Nie signed first, and to her accrued all the credit and blame that the poster attracted.[20]

Entitled "What are Song Shuo, Lu Ping, and Peng Peiyun up to in the Cultural Revolution?" the poster was put up at two in the afternoon of May 25 on the eastern wall of the building housing the university's main canteen. The answer to the rhetorical question in the title was provided by the authors, who said that Song (the deputy head of the Universities' Work Department of the Beijing Municipal Party Committee), Lu (the school's party secretary and president), and Peng Peiyun (the school's deputy party secretary)[21] were up to a "cunning scheme."[22] This scheme had been presented in a speech made by Song at an urgent meeting of senior party officials from Beijing's major universities on May 14. Song had cited the plans of the CC's North China Region for the conduct of the Cultural Revolution in Beijing, a very palpable indication that the Beijing Party Committee was no longer functioning. These plans were far removed from Mao's preference for "great disorder under heaven":

> [In the movement at present] stronger leadership is urgently needed, and we
> ask of the party organization within the school that it strengthen leadership

and [have party members] stand fast at their posts . . . The masses, having
stood up, must be led onto the correct road . . . If the indignant masses demand
that mass rallies be held, they should not be pressured [into withdrawing such
demands], but be persuaded [instead] to convene meetings in small groups, to
study documents, and to write small-character posters.[23]

According to Nie and her colleagues, any leadership that attempted to direct the
Cultural Revolution onto this "correct road" was really "revisionist." Song, Lu,
and Peng were afraid of big-character posters, mass rallies, and the "total mobilization of the masses." They did not want a "noisy and spectacular" movement,
but one over which they could retain their "sinister" control. They were, in other
words, a "bunch of Khrushchev-type revisionist elements."

The poster had the desired effect. Chaos ensued. A contemporary account
by Nie's supporters claimed that within a few hours of the poster's going up,
"hundreds if not thousands more revolutionary big-character posters appeared
striking at Lu Ping and Peng Peiyun's black gang like furious artillery shells."[24] A
post–Cultural Revolution account sympathetic to the poster's targets claimed
that "within just half a day, more than 1,500 big-character posters appeared spontaneously all over the campus, and by far the greatest number refuted and exposed the poster by Nie Yuanzi et al."[25]

While Kang Sheng was, as Nie put it, "fanning the flames of revolution" behind the scenes, Zhou Enlai was out front dispatching firefighters who would
ensure a "controlled burn."[26] When he got word of the poster, the premier sent
Zhang Yan, deputy director of the State Council's Foreign Affairs Office, to the
campus to remind everyone there that the presence of foreign students on campus imposed certain restrictions on the right to put up big-character posters in
public places.[27] At midnight on May 25, on instructions from a panicky Chen
Boda, who feared street demonstrations, the newly appointed Beijing first secretary, Li Xuefeng, visited Beida and, to an audience of 800 CCP and CYL members summoned by the university's leaders, stressed the importance of "struggling
in an orderly fashion, and not making a total mess of things."[28] The next morning, a member of the university party committee tried unsuccessfully to pressure
Nie into taking down the poster.[29] A senior party secretary from neighboring
Tsinghua University said that what Nie had done was inexcusable and to prove
his point added, "The rightists are delighted, as are Soviet revisionist students
taking pictures."[30]

However, Jiang Nanxiang, the minister of higher education and concurrently president of Tsinghua, who had accompanied Li Xuefeng to Beida, con-

sidered the publication of such posters useful tools to lure "the snakes out of their pits and to vaccinate [the masses] against smallpox." In a phone message to Tsinghua University, he ordered: "Create the conditions that will make them speak up. [Then] grab hold of the main points, grab hold of the problems, and mobilize the masses in discussion [against them]."[31] Jiang evidently thought that the Cultural Revolution would be no more than a rerun of the blooming of the Hundred Flowers on campuses in 1957, when outspoken students and faculty had voiced criticisms and had later been punished for their temerity.[32] He, too, did not get it.

Meanwhile Cao Yiou had received a copy of the poster, which she quickly passed on to her husband. After a private briefing from Nie Yuanzi on the circumstances leading up to its publication, Kang Sheng printed the text of the poster in an ad hoc "intelligence watch" set up by the CCRG a few days earlier to keep Mao and the PSC informed about the Cultural Revolution and sent it to Mao in Hangzhou.[33] After Mao read it at noon on June 1, he wrote on it: "It is very important that this text be broadcast in its entirety by the Xinhua News Agency and published in all the nation's newspapers. Now the smashing of the reactionary stronghold that is Peking University can begin." That afternoon, Mao phoned Kang Sheng and Chen Boda in Beijing and told them that the poster was the manifesto of the Beijing commune of the 1960s and was "even more significant than the Paris Commune." It had to be broadcast that evening.[34] A surprised Zhou Enlai was informed of the broadcast by Kang Sheng only a few hours before it aired at 8:30.[35] Li Xuefeng, alerted by a handwritten note from Kang Sheng while addressing a conference of North China cadres, immediately passed on the information to his audience.[36] Yet Liu Shaoqi, formally superior to both Zhou and Li, had no advance warning of either the broadcast of the poster or its publication in the *People's Daily* on June 2.[37]

Alongside the text in the *People's Daily* was a laudatory essay written under the direction of Chen Boda entitled "Hail Beida's Big-Character Poster." It described Lu Ping and his colleagues as representatives of a "fake" and "revisionist" Communist Party, about to be swept aside "by the raging tide of the Great Cultural Revolution surging forward."[38] On November 1, Nie Yuanzi was to look back at the publication of the big-character poster with the words: "Five months ago today, our most dearly beloved great leader Chairman Mao . . . by making [our] revolutionary big-character poster known to the entire country and the entire world, lit the blazing fire of the Great Proletarian Cultural Revolution!"[39]

A "Noisy and Spectacular" Movement

Even allowing for Nie's self-congratulatory hype, June 2 was a turning point for Cultural Revolution activity in colleges. As Mao put it a few months later, "I really caused a huge uproar by having that Peking University poster by Nie Yuanzi broadcast."[40] At the center of the storm, a French woman studying at Beida recalled, "university and secondary school students, cadres, workers, and even some suburban peasants . . . came [to our campus] to bring posters and make speeches supporting the revolutionaries of Beida."[41] One of those who visited Beida was an Englishman teaching at the newly established Foreign Languages School. He remembers things' unfolding at a "frustratingly slow pace":

> The dismissals in the Beijing Party were at first intriguing and then unsettling (when it reached to Peng Zhen). We all had to go to the football field to hear the radio announcement of that one, and the semihysterical announcer spoke only three or four factual sentences. Nobody had a clue as to what was coming next. After classes were stopped I bicycled with some of my grad students in the evenings to Beida to read Nie Yuanzi and other wall posters. It hardly made things clearer. When the first work groups came into the school I asked my most intelligent grad student (from Shanghai) what was going on; "I haven't a clue," he said. "Can't you sit on the fence until things are clearer?" I asked him. "No," he said; "you have to choose one line or the other." "But surely you can sense which is going to win?" I asked him. "No, it is quite impossible. You just have to jump." By July the uncertainty was palpable, but everybody shouted and criticized the institute's first secretary (actually a splendid and much-liked man). The accusations were not convincing, but the noise was horrific (just outside my dorm window). So the slow lead into the Cultural Revolution was very upsetting for kids used to being fed certainties. When at last in mid-July things seemed to be getting clearer, it must have come with a huge sense of relief to be told that Mao (the only real hero in China at that time they must have felt) was under attack and they should defend him. This was clear enough (at least by comparison with the months of Aesopian talk and murky events preceding).[42]

In Beijing, as a direct result of the purge of Peng Zhen and the ripples it sent through the municipal administration, quite a few middle and elementary school principals had already suspended ordinary teaching activities. After the publication of Nie Yuanzi's poster, all schools in the capital suspended classes. Even kindergarten staff, while continuing to care for the "little successors of the revolution," became embroiled in the Cultural Revolution. The "revisionist leadership" of the municipal Bureau of Education was charged specifically with attempting to train preschool children "not to get into fights, not swear at people, be polite, and be clean and tidy." "See for yourselves, comrades," the staff of one Beijing kindergarten maintained, "how hostile they are, and how fearful they are of giving our infants a class education!"[43] But some professional educators took more conventional views; they were especially unable to comprehend the suspension of classes in primary schools. What could taking part in class struggle possibly mean to a seven-year-old boy or girl? The president of one of Beijing's finest elementary schools complained bitterly: "Class struggle this and class struggle that; even chicken feathers and garlic skins have become a matter of class struggle!"[44]

Nevertheless, on June 13 the CCP center and State Council issued a decision to suspend classes "temporarily" in universities and schools nationwide. Suddenly 103 million primary school students, 13 million secondary school students, and 534,000 university students all over the country were "free" to leave their classrooms and to devote themselves full-time to the Cultural Revolution and what Mao called the "main subject" of "class struggle."[45]

Outside schools and cultural institutions, the public announcement on June 3 of the dismissal of the Beijing Party Committee—the kind of news that normally was never publicized—was the more significant "explosion," particularly for foreigners.[46] Diplomats talked about little else for the next couple of days. Asked at a garden party to mark Sweden's National Day on June 6 what would happen to the purged officials, Foreign Minister Chen Yi responded by pointing at the Soviet ambassador a few feet away: "We're not barbarians like those guys. We don't slit people's throats; we pay them a proper pension."[47]

At this time few foreigners were living in Beijing, and so far most of them had been only vaguely aware of something going on. A newly arrived Dutch scholar-diplomat wrote that "during the first weeks we did not take much notice of the Cultural Revolution and looked at remnants of the old China."[48]

But by the beginning of June, the movement became impossible to ignore even off campus. The handful of foreign journalists in Beijing, laboring under the watchful eyes of the public security authorities twenty-four hours a day, found their movements further curtailed. Some of the best reporting was that of Japanese journalists, whose impeccable command of Chinese enabled them to read the student posters, and who now and then succeeded in melting away into the crowd as they crisscrossed the city on bicycles, dressed in Chinese clothes, and wearing face masks ostensibly to protect them from the elements.

Diplomats, too, were reporting. The Swedish ambassador, whose earlier posting had been in Africa, wrote to his foreign minister on June 16:

> Beijing has been in a state of feverish activity since the end of May, and demonstrations in support of Mao Zedong and the new municipal party leadership have been taking place day and night since June 3. Many of us are kept awake until the early morning hours by the monotonous beating of drums and clashing of gongs by groups marching or riding past our building on the back of trucks. The tom-tom of the Africans strikes me in retrospect as full of harmony compared with this noise.[49]

A British diplomat confirmed that "noise in fact was the hallmark of the revolution and before long earplugs became standard embassy issue."[50] But a Dutch colleague commented on the unserious, unthreatening, even festive nature of the open-air demonstrators:

> In no other world capital would one take the car to have a look at such demonstrations. One would drive one's car into the garage as fast as possible, stay at home and lock the door. In those days demonstrations were still quite orderly in Peking. The International Club, with its swimming pool and tennis courts, was situated in front of the headquarters of the Peking party organization. By the end of the afternoon the Austins, Chevrolets and Citroëns were driving to and fro. They had to park just in front of the flight of steps where the new party committee stood and listened to vociferous expressions of loyalty. The traffic police often had to break up the long rows of demonstrators in order to enable a foreign diplomat to arrive or leave. In this, the police were politeness itself, and no one seemed disturbed by the incongruity of this civility and the meaning of the slogans that were chanted to the deafening accompaniment of drums and cymbals. The active young organizers even made arrangements for foreigners who wanted to take pictures. They were willing to halt a procession, and told the demonstrators to straighten their backs and to raise higher the framed portrait of Chairman Mao, carried in front of each of the groups.[51]

But the noisy fairground atmosphere that gave foreigners the illusion of good humor and organization was achieved only by considerable behind-the-scenes activity by the Beijing Garrison.

Keeping the Peace, Picking Up the Pieces

In the confusion engendered by the dismissal of Peng Zhen and many of his close colleagues in the Beijing administration, Premier Zhou Enlai seems to have assumed many of their responsibilities. His instrument was the reinforced Beijing Garrison, which was charged with ensuring the security of the central authorities and their units. Under the leadership of Zhou and Marshal Ye Jianying, the garrison was also made responsible for maintaining the supply of food, fuel (including bringing coal from Shanxi), and electricity to the capital, and protecting foreign embassies. Later in the year, it would be necessary to restore order at the Beijing Hotel when militants began to refuse to serve the foreigners staying there.

Even with the additional troops, garrison commander Fu Chongbi's task was virtually impossible. Sections of the capital were paralyzed by militants denouncing whoever or whatever was the target *du jour*, but Lin Biao ordered the PLA: "Don't strike back if hit, don't talk back if abused." Often at his wits' end, Fu had to call in Zhou and Ye to solve disputes or raise the morale of the garrison forces.[52] Though foreigners trying to get a meal at the Beijing Hotel may have experienced periodic inconveniences, many of Fu's problems and solutions were invisible to them. As the correspondent of Japan's *Asahi Shimbun* reported on June 16, "Foreigners are not permitted to become involved in these internal matters, but the big-character posters denouncing people by name that foreigners have been able to see have allowed them to judge the impact of the movement."[53] One better-placed foreigner was a British Communist working as a translator for the Foreign Languages Press, but even he remarked that most intense activity at this stage was still behind the scenes:

> The city carried on living and breathing as if nothing untoward was happening . . . And yet one knew that behind the walls of every office, factory, college and school in the city dramas were being enacted similar to the one at [my] office. For if one could not *see* the revolution one could *hear* it in the evenings, carried across the Peking sky. The sound was the angry, shrill shouting of slogans, often accompanied by the beating of drums and the clashing of cymbals. It poured out of the hundreds of meetings that were being held throughout the city, meetings that began late at night and carried on until the early hours. You could not escape from the roar of the meetings; it was like the moaning of a gigantic animal crouching over the city.
>
> The continuous evening din only added to the mystery. What was going on at the meetings? Who was being criticized and why? I was utterly bewildered.[54]

In actuality, the Cultural Revolution was equally bewildering to many Chinese. The people of Beijing, so the *People's Daily* claimed, were unanimous in their support of the decision to dismiss the municipal party committee and regarded it as "extremely wise and extremely correct."[55] Whether they did or didn't, the reason for the dismissal was still a closely guarded secret. As one perceptive middle school student noted in his diary on June 4, "Everybody is of course expressing support for the party center's decision, but nobody really knows what kind of mistakes Peng Zhen, Liu Ren et al. actually have committed."[56]

Work Teams

Liu Shaoqi, too, was bewildered, not to mention irritated. In private conversation in mid-June with a fellow Hunanese and old "white area" cadre with whom he had worked closely in the 1930s,[57] Liu voiced muted criticism of the force of the purges and the role of the PLA in particular. The PLA, Liu said, "is not protecting the healthy progress of the movement, not protecting the old cadres." Instead, "it is standing by with folded arms, waiting for leaders everywhere to collapse before moving in to tidy up."[58] After the Cultural Revolution, Liu's children claimed that when they asked him in early June why he didn't move to restore order, he had responded: "I have no experience of running a movement in this fashion under socialism; nor have I ever in the past come across our party using this form of rectification. We're going to have to wait a while and see."[59] Deng Xiaoping was equally unhappy. His wife's comment that Nie Yuanzi was "a bad person," one of their daughters recalled many years later, "was reflecting what my father thought. He was very much against this sudden assault."[60]

Liu Shaoqi's extraordinary admission of puzzlement and Deng's negative reactions illustrated the extent to which the Cultural Revolution was being orchestrated by Mao and his trusties behind the backs of the men who were nominally running the country during the Chairman's absence from the capital. Indeed, Liu and Deng were never quite sure where in the country Mao was, and Liu sent a secretary to the CC's General Office to find out if he was in Hangzhou.[61] But since they were nothing if not conscientious, they had to keep taking decisions while Mao was out of town, and with the campuses erupting, they could not afford to investigate too long.

CCP standard operating procedure when problems arose was to send in a work team. Consisting of trusted cadres drawn from uninvolved units, the numbers depending on the size of the target institution, its remit would be to stabilize the situation, establish the reasons for the problems, deliver a judgment, and distribute punishments and rewards. In places where "the leadership core has already become rotten," leadership was to be assumed by "competent work teams" organized and sent in by superior organs.[62] The powers vested in these ad hoc work teams were almost unlimited: working regulations drafted for them by the CCP center stated that they could "detain, isolate for self-examination, take into custody, sentence to [labor under] surveillance or imprisonment" persons found guilty of "criminal acts." One of the very few restrictions imposed was that the work teams had to consult with and receive permission from the central authorities before taking action against cadres at or above the rank of county governor or equivalent.[63]

Most recently, in the Socialist Education Movement work teams had been dispatched in huge numbers—20,000 to one rural Beijing county alone—and some were still busy executing the "four cleanups" when the Cultural Revolution began.[64] Many, if not most, of the people at the center of the Cultural Revolutionary drama had themselves been on work teams for shorter or longer periods since 1963: Liu Shaoqi's wife, Wang Guangmei, in a production brigade in the Hebei countryside, not far from the seaside resort of Beidaihe; Chen Boda in a rural brigade south of the city of Tianjin; Wang Dongxing and Mao's doctor, Li Zhisui, in rural Jiangxi; Guan Feng and Qi Benyu together in a brigade in rural Tongxian, east of Beijing. In the current upheaval, Li Xuefeng's North China Region had begun in the second week of May to send work teams to the Beijing Party Committee and its subordinate organs in effect to take over.[65]

On May 29, Liu, Zhou, and Deng Xiaoping decided to send in a temporary work team under Chen Boda to take over at the *People's Daily*, perhaps assuming that the head of the new CCRG was *au fait* with Mao's thinking and so better able to respond appropriately in a rapidly changing situation. Zhou Enlai immediately phoned Mao requesting and getting his permission.[66] On May 30, Liu, Zhou, and Deng followed up with a letter to the Chairman; Mao confirmed his permission that day, and Chen took over on May 31, his first major duty being the publicizing of the Beida big-character poster.[67] In a parallel move, the Central Committee Secretariat sent a work team to take over at the Propaganda Department on June 6. Lieutenant General Xiao Wangdong, who had been brought into the Ministry of Culture a year earlier as a deputy minister to help cleanse the Augean stables there, got Lin Biao's permission to bring in a work team of 300 officers.[68]

The most urgent question, however, was whether to send work teams into Beida and other Beijing colleges and middle (high) schools, where, as Liu's children reported to him, the students were in an uproar, confusion reigned, and schoolwork had ceased.[69] If Liu and his colleagues did not act swiftly, they were in danger of being unable to recover control and restore order.

When Zhou had phoned Mao on May 29 about the *People's Daily* work team, he had also requested permission for a Beida work team, which he, Liu, and Deng also considered necessary, and again he had obtained Mao's agreement.[70] On June 3, an expanded PSC meeting under Liu's chairmanship agreed that the new Beijing Party Committee should send in work teams to various municipal colleges and schools in order to lead the Cultural Revolution there. Chen Boda opposed the decision, but fell silent when Deng Xiaoping pointed out that he himself was currently heading a work team at the *People's Daily*. Work teams going to colleges were made up of cadres from departments of the CC and the State Council; those destined for middle schools were recruited from the Central Committee of the Communist Youth League.[71] On the same day the Beijing party announced the dismissal of Song Shuo, Lu Ping, and Peng Peiyun and the dispatch of a work team to Beida to guide the Cultural Revolution and assume the party leadership.[72]

Almost overwhelmed by the pace of events,[73] Liu Shaoqi decided to go with Zhou, Deng, Tao Zhu, and Chen Boda on June 9 to report to Mao in Hangzhou, where they stayed until June 12. Discussing the Cultural Revolution, Liu asked the Chairman: "How should we handle the schools? In some there have been power-seizures; in some they criticize the academic authorities and thereafter transform the teaching system, solving the issues of exams, teaching materials, and so on."[74] However, Mao refused to be pinned down. He said nothing to suggest that he opposed work teams per se, but commented: "Sending work teams in too early wouldn't be good; there would be no preparation. It would be better to let them raise Cain for a little, mix it up [with each other], and then send in work teams when conditions are clearer."[75] Since Mao had already approved the decision to send a work team into Beida,[76] and since Chen Boda again made the sending of work teams an issue by airing his opposition in front of Mao but failed to gain the latter's support, perhaps Liu thought Mao was musing aloud rather than hinting his disapproval. But in the light of his own uncertainties, he would obviously have been well advised to try to get the Chairman's overt agreement, asking him if he had reconsidered his earlier agreement. Instead, Liu attempted to get Mao to return to the capital and take over the running of the Cultural Revolution, but the Chairman laughed and refused.[77] Liu Shaoqi and his colleagues perforce returned empty-handed to Beijing, where the PSC met continually in expanded session under his chairmanship from June 14 to June 28.[78]

4

The Fifty Days

D uring the early weeks of June 1966, work teams totaling 7,239 cadres entered educational and cultural institutions in Beijing. Some of the teams were extraordinarily large relative to the size of the institutions they entered. The biggest of all and the one destined to become the most notorious was the work team of more than 500 men and women that entered Tsinghua University on June 9. Drawn from the party committee of the State Council's Industry and Communications Office, it was headed by Ye Lin, a deputy chairman of the State Economic Commission, who recollected thirty years later that he was totally unprepared for the job.[1] One of its members was a midlevel cadre (rank 14) from the CC's General Office, Liu Shaoqi's wife Wang Guangmei. Her confrontation with a twenty-year-old student in the Chemical Engineering Department named Kuai Dafu was eventually to become part of Red Guard lore and to be immortalized in novels and on the stage, even in the West.[2]

In the provinces, party committees also began sending out work teams soon after getting the lead from Beijing on June 3. In Shanghai, work teams entered forty universities and colleges and more than 160 middle schools. Work teams in Beijing to a large extent consisted of former PLA officers and men who since 1964 had been occupying nominally civilian posts in the government bureaucracy's so-called political departments. The latter had been set up on PLA lines after Mao had ordered everyone to take the PLA as a model. Provincial work teams were also drawn from the PLA, but consisted of serving officers and men from the provincial military district (MD). In Hangzhou, for instance, at the request of the provincial party committee, the Zhejiang MD contributed more than 200 cadres to the first work teams entering universities, the premises of the *Zhejiang Daily*, the provincial broadcasting station, and other cultural institutions.[3] In Hubei, the Cultural Revolution was seen by the party leadership under one of Mao's most trusted first secretaries, Wang Renzhong, as a new version of the 1957 Anti-Rightist Campaign, with the usual bourgeois suspects as the prime targets. The purges of the Beijing municipal party and of the Beida leadership were regarded as unusual and isolated incidents; any signs of anti-party activity at Hubei educational institutions were quickly suppressed by work teams.[4]

Big-Character Posters

Wherever they arrived, the work teams found academic institutions already festooned with big-character posters. In Beijing, Tsinghua University topped the list, with 65,000 posters appearing on campus in June. In the elite middle school attached to Peking University, "many thousand" posters appeared between June 2 and 15.[5] No premium was put on superficial uniformity: a poster might consist of no more than a few sentences, or it might be a massive treatise of 10,000 characters, even carrying appendices.[6] In the post and telecommunications sector in Beijing (which included the university known as the Beijing Institute of Posts and Telecommunications and various specialized vocational schools), one of the few for which contemporary calculations of this kind are available, each person wrote on average 7.3 big-character posters between June 4 and June 30, 1966.[7] In Shanghai, the first weekend in June witnessed an unprecedented "high tide" in big-character posters and a "free airing of views." According to the initial calculations of the municipal party authorities, no less than 2.7 million people had "thrown themselves into the movement" within days.[8] In the propaganda sector in Shanghai, some 88,000 big-character posters had appeared by June 18, attacking by name 1,390 persons. In the industrial, financial, scientific, and legal sectors, the number of big-character posters was slightly less; in the educational sector, as was to be expected, it was even higher.[9]

What were the posters about? Who was attacking whom? And why? The full implications of Mao's words that the stress of the Cultural Revolution was to be "on the inside and at the top" may not yet have fully sunk in. The work teams encouraged criticism of teachers, who were held responsible for "bourgeois" or "revisionist" curricula and pedagogy, usually on the flimsiest of grounds. On university campuses, students and junior staff took the lead in the "free airing of views," turning their pens against university leaders and senior professors, and just about anyone else whom they regarded as a potential member of the "counterrevolutionary black gang," a label used extensively by the party press in June and July, only to be quietly discarded after August for supposedly "failing to indicate the nature" of the person(s) thus labeled.[10]

In a whirl of conflicting emotions, students cudgeled their brains as to how to find fault with classroom teachers, with whom in many cases they had bonded. They did not want to humiliate them too drastically, but equally they wished to avoid criticism from their peers for being only indifferently revolutionary. They were also conscious that if, as so often before, there was a sudden change of direction in the movement, they could well become the targets of vengeful teachers, who had considerable power over their future educational or vocational prospects.[11] Their direct involvement in the Cultural Revolution having only just begun, they often lacked information of a more damaging nature about the "black gang" and had to be content with putting the maximum negative spin on whatever controversial fact or rumor they managed to get hold of.

At Peking University, a group of physics students put up a big-character poster charging university president Lu Ping with being a reactionary, utterly terrified of young people mastering Mao Zedong Thought. Why else, they asked, had his university leadership "by citing as their excuse the need to keep dormitories neat and tidy . . . forbidden the pasting up of quotations from Chairman Mao and slogans indoors"?[12] Students belonging to a branch of the CYL in the Chinese Language and Literature Department that only a month earlier had been granted the honorary title of a "Four Good Youth League Branch" on the forty-seventh anniversary of the May 4 Movement now put up a big-character poster in which they insisted that the designation be removed, because it had been granted by a university leadership that was "revisionist to the core" and therefore implied, falsely, so the students claimed, that the branch, too, was nothing if not a model of revisionism.[13] Tsinghua University, the alma mater of 1957 Nobel Prize laureates Chen Ning Yang and Tsung-Dao Lee (both "traitors," according to one on-campus poster, because "they have since become U.S. citizens"),[14] saw the appearance of a poster by a woman in the Department of Mechanics who denounced the university president and concurrent minister of higher education for the countless ways in which he allegedly "promoted peaceful evolution among female students":

Any female student who feels a bit queasy (Note: Some don't suffer from major illnesses at all), if she finds breakfast a bit too coarse, will receive a special provision of milk and eggs. Regardless of her financial circumstances, she gets 1.5 yuan [about one dollar] extra for food . . . If she's on the factory floor [doing an assignment], if she has her period, she only has to work a maximum of four hours/day and no night shift. If she has to operate a lathe or welding equipment, she gets an extra two or three days off. She doesn't have to do any heavy labor at all, not even bend her back washing vegetables! Is this labor? It's bringing offerings to the Buddha! Nurturing revisionism![15]

While such charges of gender-based pampering may have failed to rouse the revolutionary ire of many, the same was not true of alleged class-based discrimination, if anything a burning topic in elite institutions such as China's finest universities. The ten wounded Korean War veterans from peasant stock who had entered Peking University on a special quota in 1960 and whose discrimination case against "Lu Ping's black gang" was the subject of an angry big-character poster on June 10 stood a much better chance of winning an appreciative audience.[16]

Far more potentially damaging to faculty targets than the accusations made by the first waves of pen- and brush-wielding students were the posters emanating from colleagues and staff. Needless to say, those with access to confidential records or boasting high-level inner-party contacts were often able to blacken someone's reputation very effectively. If so-and-so had ever been involved in something that had left a mark in his dossier, now was the time to bring it up, not merely actions, but words, too. In their big-character poster "The wings of a crow will not keep the sun out!" the staff of one research institute denounced numerous remarks made over the years by the party general branch secretary in the Department of Biology. Among those they cited as proof of his inability to distinguish right from wrong was one that was later held up as the hallmark of Deng Xiaoping's sins, but one which this lowly party secretary had allegedly made in the wake of the Great Leap Forward, on February 14, 1961, a year earlier than Deng: "It doesn't matter if a cat is black or is white; so long as it catches the mouse it's a good cat."[17]

Obviously, if a suspected "black gang element" had been caught making what in retrospect turned out to be a highly inappropriate remark or observation, it was bad enough and likely to be added to whatever other proof there might be of his or her "criminal guilt." But being caught making what in retrospect turned out to be *too* "correct" a remark or observation was sometimes not much better. One poster-writer alleged, for example, that as early as the first week of April, the minister of higher education had told a colleague that Peng Zhen's February Outline was "anti–Mao Zedong Thought, and an all-out revisionist program." In June, this was *not* cited in the minister's favor as proof of his impressive powers of perception—it was, after all, precisely how the February Outline was to be characterized in the May 16 Notification—but, on the contrary, as circumstantial evidence of his having been leaked an early draft of the Notification by Peng Zhen. By implication, he was very close to Peng and, so the poster-writer declared, clearly "an important member of his anti-party clique."[18]

But it was not only about those with inside knowledge that a potential target had to worry; it was anyone with whom one had ever been in contact. Chauffeurs, for example, could do much damage. They might not only cite snippets of conversations they had overheard to cast doubt on the revolutionary credentials of selected passengers; at times, the simple fact of a journey on such-and-such a date to the offices or residence of so-and-so sufficed to suggest by implication that something "sinister" had been in progress. On June 17, a driver in the Ministry of Higher Education put up a big-character poster in which he said that whereas before mid-April his minister had never asked to be driven to the Beijing Party Committee, he had since been a frequent visitor, sometimes late in the evening. Clearly, the driver maintained, this change in behavior suggested that he had been involved in whatever nefarious activities Peng Zhen had been engaged in at the time.[19] A week earlier, a different driver working for Deng Tuo had made an almost identical allegation in his big-character poster, insisting that the official's recent journey in his car to Peng Zhen's residence cried out for an "investigation."[20]

Initially attempts were made to keep certain subjects off the big-character poster battlefield. On May 28, an ad hoc office set up by the Beijing municipal party authorities to monitor the progress of the movement declared "illicit sexual liaisons" and "moral depravity" off-limits.[21] But only a few days later this decision was challenged in a poster by a group of eighteen cadres with extensive experience in the rural Socialist Education Movement whose real-world experience told them that

the important techniques used by the bourgeoisie to bring about peaceful evolution include morally depraved lifestyles and sexual entrapment. These are used to strike at the weak-willed for the sake of usurping political power . . . This is a big issue of right and wrong. And yet the Study Office, for fear of seeing the masses reveal the decadent life of the black gang, has issued an order that states: "Big-character posters should not have as their subject illicit sexual relations and moral depravity." What is the point of hastily issuing pointers like these—to tell the masses not to do this, and not to do that? What is it you're really trying to achieve?[22]

In the end, hardly a subject remained taboo. Nie Yuanzi, for instance, was subject to no end of innuendo and allegations about the facts that she had remarried several times and that her latest husband was twenty-three years older than she. In the Ministry of Higher Education, poster-writing cadres in the Foreign Affairs Office denounced their boss for his "bourgeois lifestyle," alleging that during a visit to Morocco he had "played mah-jongg" and while in Paris he had "let a car drive him around the nightclub district."[23] A leading cadre in the CC's Propaganda Department was attacked by a man whose entry into the CCP he had once sponsored, the attacker now asserting that the senior cadre was "a piece of shit who screwed my wife, for which I've hated him ever since."[24] Sometimes the accusations brought too much shame for the target to bear: in June, when his staff accused him of sexual misconduct, the thirty-six-year-old head of propaganda in the Beijing CYL consumed a handful of sleeping pills, attempted to electrocute himself, and ended up semiparalyzed. He then became the target of what the record describes as an even harsher "high tide of exposure and denunciation by the masses." In August, his second attempt at suicide succeeded.[25]

Resisting the Work Teams

Attempts to impose control and supervision extended to more than the contents of big-character posters. On June 3, the PSC meeting chaired by Liu Shaoqi that decided on dispatching work teams to venues besides the *People's Daily* and Peking University endorsed an eight-point guideline put forward by Li Xuefeng that would soon be honored only in the breach:

1. Big-character posters should be put up only inside schools.
2. Meetings should not hinder work or studies.
3. There should be no street demonstrations.
4. Foreign students should not participate in the movement.
5. Targets should not be struggled against in their homes.
6. Attention had to be paid to security concerns.
7. People should not be hit or roughed up.
8. Active leadership was necessary to ensure that the struggle stayed on the right track.[26]

To enforce these rules would have been problematic under any circumstances, but the inherent difficulties of the task were compounded by the haste with which many work teams were dispatched, their poor preparation and briefing, and their sheer incompetence. Quite a few teams had to be recalled and replaced by others after just a few days. This was an unprecedented situation; nothing similar had happened during the Socialist Education Movement. Between June 20 and 23, work teams at thirty-nine universities in Beijing were hounded off campus by radical students and teachers who saw themselves as eminently more qualified than the teams' members and wanted to "run" the movement themselves, without "outside help."[27] The municipal, State Council, and CYL authorities responded by designating those who opposed the work teams as "rightist students," "bogus leftists/true rightists," and even "counterrevolutionaries."

In Beijing and elsewhere, a majority of teachers and students seem to have welcomed the work teams at first. Kuai Dafu recalled that on the evening of June 9, upon hearing of the arrival of Ye Lin's work team, he and his Tsinghua classmates were "elated and excited, rose and applauded endlessly, some even jumping up and down for joy, and shouted at the top of their lungs 'Long live the CCP!' and 'Long live Chairman Mao!'"[28]

But the exhilaration of some of the more radical students was soon replaced by suspicion when, as they perceived it, the work teams turned out to be just as hostile toward the "revolutionary left" as the original party committees. On June 21, Kuai Dafu scribbled at the bottom of a big-character poster: "We must all ask ourselves, revolutionary leftists, whether the power now in the hands of the work team represents us. If it does, then we should support it; but if it doesn't, then we should seize power once again."[29]

Statements by senior party figures from this period suggest clearly that the real mandate given the work teams was to deal with outspoken teachers and students like Kuai in the way the "bourgeois rightists" had been dealt with nine years earlier. At some universities the work teams even screened documentary newsreels from the Anti-Rightist Campaign in 1957 to hint at the analogy.[30] Vice Premier Bo Yibo, an alternate member of the Politburo who chaired the State Council's Industry and Communications Office Party Committee, told his work-team leaders on June 13: "The monsters and freaks have already come out of hiding. All department party committees should target their spearheads with accuracy. Don't meddle with the [monsters and freaks] while we're letting them have a go. Give them free rein." Once the work teams had the necessary evidence, they would pounce on the outspoken teachers and students. Again, in the words of Bo Yibo, "You trick the snakes into leaving their pit, and then you wipe them all out at the same time."[31] He was another who didn't get it.

In some cases, high-level policy like this was communicated to work teams by back channels, namely through the children of Politburo members. In June 1966 most Politburo members, with the exception of the childless Zhou Enlai, had offspring in one or more Beijing colleges or schools. Lin Biao's son Lin Liguo, who would later play a pivotal role in the most dramatic episode of the Cultural Revolution, was studying at Beida. One of Liu Shaoqi's daughters was at Tsinghua and another was enrolled at the girls' middle school attached to Beijing Normal University. One of Deng Xiaoping's children was enrolled at Beida, another at the Central Fine Arts Institute, and a third at the girls' middle school attached to Beijing Normal University. Liu Shaoqi personally guided the work team at the middle school attached to Beijing Normal University through his daughter Pingping, who became a work-team member on June 17. In her work diary, Pingping recorded page upon page of her father's remarks. One day he spoke to her about the "bourgeois" teachers and staff in China's middle schools: "They are simply insincere. They neither kill people nor practice arson, but just keep spreading poison. Hence you cannot arrest them and may not execute them. This is a big nuisance."[32] Despite the purge of Peng Zhen and other senior colleagues a month earlier, even a leader as experienced as Liu had apparently fallen into the trap of thinking that the main targets of the Cultural Revolution were the usual suspects, the intellectual bourgeoisie, with perhaps a few party intellectuals thrown in for good measure.

Like Liu's remarks, the words and deeds of activist teachers and students reflected contempt and even hatred. At Beida on the morning of June 18, a seminal incident broke the taboo on physical violence. While the members of the work team were tied up in a meeting, students from about six different departments got together to "struggle" Lu Ping and about forty other "monsters and freaks." Nie Yuanzi's supporters produced the following eyewitness account of the incident:

> That morning, students from all over campus were mobilized to form one boundless ocean of people's war. The black gang was swamped like rats, accompanied by shouts of "Beat them!" Dozens of heinously criminal black gang elements suffered the punishment they deserved from the revolutionary teachers and students. The battle of annihilation was like a tempest; those who yielded to it survived, while those who resisted perished. The privileges of the bastards who ruled Beida for decades came to an end like fallen flowers carried away by the flowing water, and the dignity and prestige of the black gang were swept into the dust. A red terror spread across campus as the black gang trembled

with fear and shook with fright, and the revolutionary teachers and students were filled with joy like never before![33]

According to one observer, a professor whose husband was among those humiliated, the students used wastebaskets instead of dunces' hats, "glued posters onto the backs of their victims, and sometimes even threw ink in their faces to show the degree of contempt in which these former holders of academic power were now viewed. No evidence, proof, or discussion of guilt was necessary."[34]

The Beida students and teachers were mimicking the "revolutionary" behavior of the poor peasants whom Mao had praised in his 1927 essay, "Report on an Investigation of the Peasant Movement in Hunan." In it Mao described how the peasants when rising up against their landlord exploiters would "at the slightest provocation . . . make arrests, crown the arrested with tall paper hats, and parade them through the village." Some people called this behavior "going too far" or "going beyond the proper limits in righting a wrong"; however, Mao had asserted that "such talk may seem plausible, but in fact it is wrong."[35] Leftist students and teachers found further theoretical support for their actions in the writings of Chen Boda, who, in a 1951 retrospective essay on the Hunan report, had referred to Mao's argument that in order to "right a wrong" one simply had to "go beyond the proper limits" as "an important objective law of revolution, and an objective dialectic of the revolutionary struggle of the masses." In the autumn of 1966, Red Guards reprinted this passage from Chen's essay extensively in their mimeographed publications.

But in June the Beida work team was not prepared to tolerate such violent behavior directed against cadres like themselves. Responding to the "chaotic" nature of the proceedings, they broke up the struggle meeting around noon and reported critically on it to the PSC. The team made a point of downplaying whatever possible political significance the "struggle" may have had and charged that by any normal standard, it had more than anything else been a case of hooliganism:

> What the essence of the incident consisted of becomes evident once we look at some of the people who dominated the chaotic violence . . . While struggling a female cadre, the sixth-year student Xia XX [a CCP member] in the Department of Wireless Communications ripped her trousers, fondled her breasts and genital area [*yinbu*]. In the crowd, he also touched the private parts [*xiashen*] of two female students. (His immediate expulsion from the party has since been announced.)[36]

On June 20 Liu endorsed the work team's action as "correct and timely" and had its report reprinted as a highly classified central circular issued as a guide for party committees all over China facing similar situations.[37]

Even so, on the Peking University campus a significant number of students refused to endorse the work team's characterization of the incident. A second-year student in the Department of Economics put up a big-character poster in mid-July in which she accused the work team of "serious rightist tendencies" and, speaking on behalf of an unknown number of fellow students, let it be known that "we were participants on 'June 18,' and it was with class hatred directed against the black gang that we shouted: 'Well struggled! Struggle is good! Let's have some more!'"[38] Three of her fellow students in the same department insisted that the whole incident had in fact been a "conscious act of revolution on the part of the masses" and that "it's like the Chairman says: those who were beaten up merely got what they deserved. To obsess about the violence to the point of censuring the revolutionary masses who, burning with bitter class hatred, beat these black gang elements, would be a very serious mistake indeed."[39]

Crucially important in understanding the failure of the official negative verdict on the "June 18 incident" to win universal acceptance among the students was the inexplicable behavior of Tao Zhu, who visited the Peking University campus on July 1 to deliver a public lecture celebrating the founding of the CCP forty-five years earlier. In his lecture, he remarked that on campus, "aside from a small number of bad elements resorting to violence on June 18, the movement has unfolded well."[40] But Tao, breaking ranks with his senior party colleagues, also said *off the record* that what had happened on June 18 had been "a terrific thing."[41] This remark gave no small measure of encouragement to those who felt that the work team had "suppressed" them, and that in actuality they had been in the right to "struggle" the "black gang." Tao's indiscipline reflected the fact that by the end of June the CCP leadership was becoming more and more divided over the issue of the work teams. Liu was clear that the party had to remain in control. In instructions given to the CYL on July 13 about the Cultural Revolution in middle schools, he emphasized reviving and strengthening party and CYL branches. But he seems to have been uncertain about the necessary duration of the movement. On July 11 he said that it would last until the end of the year in higher middle schools; two days later, he said that it would be over in August or September in lower middle schools and in September or October in higher middle schools.[42]

Meanwhile both Chen Boda and Kang Sheng were issuing signals to the effect that the work teams just might be in trouble almost regardless of what they did. They pointedly refused to give any words of reassurance to the leaders of one work team that they had called to their offices on July 15. When the question of support came up, Chen Boda said that it was wrong of the team to accuse the students who opposed it of opposing the CCP center. "Who are the masters of this movement? Is it the broad masses or the work team? . . . At some point, they may recall you, tell you to piss off [*gundan*]! The power to do so is theirs, not yours."[43] Later in the discussion, Kang Sheng added that if the "masses" resented it, the work team ought to withdraw.[44]

The search for a solution to the problems encountered by the work teams dominated the agenda of a "report-back meeting" convened in the name of the PSC in the second week of July. On this occasion Liu Shaoqi argued that the work teams "need to be given some education; they don't understand policy, nor do they study policy. The work teams that are no good should be subjected to overhaul, consolidation, and sorting out." A draft policy document discussed at the meeting stated that so far only a quarter of the work teams that had entered Beijing's 312 middle schools had succeeded in "exercising strong leadership, mobilizing the masses rather fully, gaining a basic understanding of the situation, and embarking upon the first struggles."[45] Liu's stance was that whatever steps were needed should be taken quickly to improve the performance of the teams. His wife, as a member of the work team that had entered Tsinghua University a month earlier, later admitted that "not for a moment had I considered the possibility of letting the Great Proletarian Cultural Revolution unfold in the schools without any work teams at all."[46]

Deng Xiaoping meanwhile seemed already to be thinking one step ahead. What is not known is whether he conceived of the work teams' activities as just another phase in a protracted Cultural Revolution or whether he assumed, by analogy with the Socialist Education Movement, that the work teams *were* the Cultural Revolution, and that once they had performed their duties, the Cultural Revolution might be regarded as having been completed. In any case, Deng proposed to the "report-back meeting" that "first the students should be organized and the power-holders weeded out; then, after that, the work teams, big and small, can be withdrawn."[47]

Liu and Deng were also worried about the spread of leftist agitation from campuses to workplaces. On June 30 they wrote to Mao explaining that the Five-Year Plan was far behind target, the production and quality of major commodities were down, and industrial accidents were increasing. Under the circumstances, they suggested that in industry, transportation, construction, commerce, and hospitals the Cultural Revolution should be combined with the ongoing SEM, on which, though they did not say this, the party kept a firm grip. On July 2 Mao replied, agreeing to their proposal.[48]

The PSC member formally in charge of the economy was Zhou Enlai in his concurrent role as premier, but in the second half of June he was on an official visit to China's European Communist allies. His reaction to Nie Yuanzi's poster indicates that Zhou initially supported sending work teams to schools and universities, but the PSC circular on the June 18 Beida incident which set the tone for work-team activity nationally had been formulated in his absence. By the time he arrived back in Beijing, CCRG officials evidently had sufficient insight into Mao's thinking to know that the Chairman would use the work-team issue against Liu, Deng, and others, but would want to keep the premier at his side. In the words of Wang Li:

> The premier returned from his visit to Romania and Albania on July 1 . . . I suggested to Kang Sheng that he tell the premier of the seriousness of the domestic situation as quickly as possible—that this was not an ordinary movement, that Liu and Deng and [Foreign Minister] Chen Yi had all become entangled in it, and that the premier must not under any circumstances become entangled in it too. At that point, I was working on the "Sixteen Points" [which would become the charter for the Cultural Revolution in August] in Chen Boda's office, and I remember running to where Kang was to get hold of him. Kang traveled in the same car as the premier back from the airport, and spent the entire ride telling him what had happened and warning him not to become entangled . . . [Kang said] Liu and Deng might not be able to survive . . . and he told the premier not to have anything to do with the work teams, but to take charge of the movement. [He added] that Chen Boda was not managing and that Jiang Qing was no good either.[49]

Zhou was canny enough not to take Kang up on his suggestion to take charge, and managed to stay away from the PSC meetings, beginning on July 11 when he traveled to Wuhan and Shanghai to meet with Mao and to act as host for the visiting prince of Nepal. Zhou met and spoke at length with Mao on July 11 and 12. Mao had shown him a copy of the letter he had written to Jiang Qing on July 8, in which he spoke of his plans for the Cultural Revolution and his desire to create "great disorder under heaven" and expressed concerns about parts of Lin Biao's speech to the expanded Politburo session on May 18. Flying back to

Beijing on July 14, Zhou made a detour to Dalian, where he briefed Lin Biao on his talks with Mao and Lin agreed to modify the official transcript of his speech in the light of Mao's comments after Lin returned to Beijing.[50]

How Mao Knew

In the latter stages of the Cultural Revolution, Mao's supporters advanced the argument that the Chairman had not been able to stay on top of what was happening in Beijing in the spring and summer of 1966 because the information he would have needed to do so did not get through to him. The truth is that Mao remained well informed throughout and was well aware of what had been happening in his absence, though he later implied otherwise.

During Mao's absence from Beijing, the CC General Office had a specially assigned aircraft make daily runs between wherever he happened to be and the capital, ferrying documents and papers that needed his signature back and forth. Even when Mao was some distance away from the nearest airport, this link was scrupulously maintained with local cooperation. So, for example, the official in charge of Mao's security while he visited his home town of Shaoshan in late June 1966 later recalled that "every day a special plane would fly in from Beijing with documents to Changsha airport, from where a car would transport them to Shaoshan for Mao Zedong to read."[51] It was well known in the highest circles that few things were as likely to arouse Mao's ire as a sign that information was being withheld from him. In the spring of 1965, Luo Ruiqing had remarked in conversation with Lin Biao, "I know that what Chairman Mao and you hate most of all is when you're not being kept informed." Lin Biao's response had been to agree.[52]

The secret intelligence reports Mao received dealt primarily with domestic events. By the time the Cultural Revolution began, China was covered by a vast secret network of "eyes and ears" *(ermu)*—the very term used to refer to the emperor's spies by the great Han dynasty historian Sima Qian. On this point, Mao's PRC was no different from its imperial and more immediate predecessors. The Qing emperor Yong Zheng (1722–1736), for example, was said to have been "informed of all the activities in which the provincial authorities engaged. In probably every part of the Chinese Empire there were secret agents privately sent out by him. In many cases, therefore, even people's private lives, and trivial matters concerning family members and their relatives, could not be kept from his notice."[53] And in Republican China, U.S. Army intelligence sources at one time in the 1940s estimated that Chiang Kai-shek's "spymaster" Dai Li had working for him "180,000 plainclothes agents—of whom 40,000 worked full time."[54]

Mao's "eyes and ears," some of them from what publicly counted as a very "bad" class background (seen as an asset when dealing with the enemies of socialism), were active among all social strata and operated covertly inside ordinary civilian workplaces such as factories and schools as well as in state organs.[55] Unfortunately, almost nothing is known about what role they may have played in Mao's perception of events or his relationships with colleagues. A more public sector providing the leadership with strategic intelligence included hundreds, possibly thousands, of well-placed journalists who, in addition to writing for the general public, wrote classified "reference" materials for a hierarchy of audiences ranging from ordinary cadres up to the handful of leaders who made up the PSC.

The Xinhua News Agency's oddly titled *Internal Reference Final Proofs (Neibu cankao qingyang)* was the most important channel through which the agency's own nationwide network of journalists provided the CCP leadership with current information on domestic affairs. Its readership encompassed only the full and alternate members of the Politburo and the members of the Central Committee Secretariat, though separate copies were made available to the CC's Propaganda and International Liaison departments and the Ministry of Foreign Affairs. A typical print run would thus have consisted of about thirty copies. The *Final Proofs*, supplementing the regular *Internal Reference*, also had a restricted but significantly larger readership: in 1960 the latter had reached an estimated 40,000 cadres nationwide, and the audience had only increased since then.[56] A senior cadre who suddenly found his access to *Internal Reference* curtailed knew he had problems. Out of the loop meant out in the cold.[57]

In the summer of 1966, the Xinhua News Agency began publishing a regular supplement to *Internal Reference* called *Cultural Revolution Trends*. By November 1966 it was appearing, like *Internal Reference,* twice daily. In addition to *Cultural Revolution Trends*, Mao liked to be given access to locally produced information, especially when he was traveling. The office of the Shanghai Municipal Party Committee Cultural Revolution Group, created on June 2 and headed by Zhang Chunqiao, put out two classified publications of the kind that Mao enjoyed reading: *Great Cultural Revolution Trends* and the *Great Cultural Revolution Bulletin. Trends* was distributed "instantly" on average five to six times a day to members of the municipal party secretariat only. The *Bulletin* appeared regularly once a day and was distributed to a wider audience that included the CCP center in Beijing. That there was a crucial difference in content between the publication intended solely for high-level local consumption and the one of which copies were shared with the central authorities is evident from what the publishers revealed in early 1967. When, at one point in the summer of 1966, journalists had been dispatched from the CCP center to Shanghai to gather information about the situation in the city, the office staff was ordered by the then municipal party leadership to lock up *Trends*, let them see only the *Bulletin*, which the center received regularly, and not provide them with any additional information concerning "the actual situation."[58]

But while Mao was an avid reader of this wide variety of intelligence reports, ultimately he may not have taken it with full seriousness. He once told a gathering of provincial leaders that a policymaker who did not have any intelligence at all might in fact be superior to one who put his faith completely in the products given him by his intelligence providers.[59] Well before he launched the Cultural Revolution, Mao had decided that he was, to some extent, being intentionally manipulated by the agencies supplying him with information. Accordingly, one of the first steps he took in the spring of 1966 was to set up a new, ad hoc intelligence collection unit serving, in essence, only his personal "proletarian headquarters."

When the CCRG was set up, its mandate was not divulged. The fact that it included many of the same scholars who had been part of the ad hoc Central Document Drafting Group indicated that it would continue to be involved in producing policy documents. But from the outset it was also to serve as the Chairman's very personal provider of alternative information. During his continued absence from Beijing in the summer of 1966, Mao had Mu Xin and Qi Benyu take turns sitting in on meetings convened by Liu Shaoqi in Beijing to discuss the Cultural Revolution. After the meetings, the two provided him with their own confidential summaries of what transpired at the meetings, summaries that would serve as correctives or complements to the official minutes that Mao also received. Many years later Mu Xin wrote that at the time he had failed to understand why this was necessary; but it did serve to sow seeds of doubt in his mind about the unity of the party's most senior leaders.[60]

In addition to providing Mao with alternative reports of what was happening inside Zhongnanhai, the CCRG in the summer of 1966 had a handful of investigative reporters working for it.[61] In the summer of 1966, their findings were distributed in issues of the CCRG *Cultural Revolution Bulletin*. It was in issue 13 of this *Bulletin* (the name was generic) that Mao had come across the text of Nie

Yuanzi's big-character poster. By early August 1966, news of the *Bulletin's* existence must have reached a fair number of senior cadres, because on August 12 the
CCRG informed Mao Zedong that "each of the provinces wants one copy of
[our] *Bulletin* to be sent to it."[62] There is reason to believe that Mao agreed to the
request, since it was around this time that one provincial leader, Shanghai's first
party secretary, Chen Pixian, described the CCRG *Bulletin* as "all one-sided."[63]

The CCRG became increasingly important as an information source for
Mao and his closest colleagues. Their insatiable desire for up-to-date political
intelligence prompted the creation of a separate so-called CCRG Journalists'
Station, in existence from September 1966 to May 1969. Commenting on its size
and operations, the wife of a deputy editor of *Red Flag* once observed that "the
Central Cultural Revolution Group sent close to a thousand people to every corner of the country in order to stay on top of developments." The station and its
"journalists," who roved the country under cover of temporary affiliations with
Red Flag or the *Liberation Army Daily*, had as their job "to collect intelligence."
On August 25, 1966, the station began putting out the *Rapid Reports (Kuaibao);*
distributed at irregular intervals, sometimes averaging one an hour, *Rapid Reports* was to become *the* foremost source of classified political intelligence upon
which numerous crucial decisions affecting the course of the Cultural Revolution would be based. The time lag between the occurrence of an event and its being reported in the *Rapid Reports* was typically less than twenty-four hours. The
distribution list included Mao, Lin, Zhou, the members of the CCRG, and just
a handful of other senior leaders. The first issue reported how young "revolutionary" students had ransacked the offices of China's "democratic" political parties
the day before; the following day, issue 19 reported that those same political parties had decided to "suspend activities" temporarily.[64]

Mao Returns to Beijing

The problem in the summer of 1966 was not that Mao was unaware of what was
going on. The problem was that he was keeping his colleagues in the dark about
what he was trying to achieve. Amidst the increasing confusion caused by the
Cultural Revolution, the seventy-two-year-old Chairman suddenly gave a triumphant demonstration of his continuing vigor: on July 16 he joined the 5,000
participants in Wuhan's eleventh annual cross-Yangtze swimming competition.
The Hubei provincial first secretary, Wang Renzhong, and six guards from the
Hubei First Independent Division were in the water with him to ensure his

safety.[65] While swimming and drifting with the strong river current for an hour and five minutes, covering a distance of ten miles in the process, Mao told a woman in the water next to him that "the Yangtze is deep and its current is swift. This can help you train your body and strengthen your will-power."[66] After seeing Mao emerge from the water, a Japanese woman present ridiculed those who had questioned the state of his health.[67] Two days later, Mao returned to Beijing.

Citing security concerns as his excuse, Mao did not go to Zhongnanhai, but took up temporary residence in the Diaoyutai compound on the western edge of the city.[68] Created in 1959 to house foreign dignitaries—Khrushchev and the Korean leader Kim Il Sung among them—attending the PRC's tenth anniversary, Diaoyutai comprised fifteen Western-style villas in what had once been part of an imperial park.[69] It was soon to become synonymous with the rapidly expanding CCRG, whose offices it housed during the next three years. As soon as he learned of the Chairman's return—he was given no advance warning—Liu hurried over to his residence to bring him up to date, only to be told by a secretary that Mao was resting and that Liu would be notified when it was convenient to report to him. It was an act of extraordinarily contemptuous discourtesy to his most senior colleague, for that first day back Mao had in fact preferred to get briefed by Kang Sheng and Chen Boda, who presented him with material on the Cultural Revolution at Beida, Tsinghua, Beijing Normal University, and China People's University. Not until the next day did he allow Liu Shaoqi to brief him, telling Liu that he was rather unhappy with the Cultural Revolution so far and ordering him to convene a series of expanded PSC meetings immediately to discuss the movement.[70]

By July 19, selected ministries in Beijing had already begun implementing Liu's call for work-team "overhaul and consolidation."[71] The agenda now switched to whether, and under what conditions, the teams could be withdrawn. Deng Xiaoping declared himself ready to accept a partial withdrawal of some work teams, saying, "We have no experience with this kind of a movement, and neither do they. Let the bad work teams pull out first, while the good ones remain to carry out the work of the party committees."[72] Liu later explained his own position on the eve of Mao's return: "I was still of the opinion, as I had been in the past, that the method [of employing work teams] was quite a flexible one. I did not make up my mind to withdraw [the work teams altogether], but wanted to wait and see . . . The Chairman would soon be back, and I expected to be able to ask him for instructions and a decision once he had returned."[73] Zhou

Enlai was present at the first PSC meeting and would have briefed Mao on what transpired at it during his meeting with the Chairman on July 20.[74]

Emboldened perhaps by discussions with Mao, on July 19 Chen Boda again suggested withdrawing the work teams, but the proposal was turned down by a majority led by Liu and Deng; Zhou Enlai's position is not clear.[75] On July 20 a decision was taken to establish an editorial committee for Mao's works headed by Liu, presumably with a view to reissuing them as a guide to the Cultural Revolution. On July 22 the meeting agreed on keeping strict control over Cultural Revolution activities in high-level academic institutions. As late as the afternoon of July 23, Liu was reaffirming to the increasingly stormy meeting his conviction that work teams were essential and that the great majority had worked well.[76] He was backed by Deng, Bo Yibo, and, from the PLA, Ye Jianying and Liu Zhijian. But there was a hint that Zhou Enlai was trimming his position. On the evening of July 23, Zhou conferred with Liu and Deng on the work-team problem. At four in the morning on July 24 he wrote to them as follows:

> I've been considering over and over again what we talked about last evening, and I've also looked at some documents; different opinions come principally from one's estimate of the situation and perception of the problems . . . In Beijing, there were common and necessary elements in sending in work teams, but the conditions produced by each work team in the unit to which it went also had their special features, and this requires on-the-spot investigation and concrete analysis . . . This morning I'm going to the Foreign Languages Academy to read big-character posters to increase my perceptual knowledge a bit.[77]

Zhou was prevaricating. He may have detected differences between Mao's ideas and Liu's and realized their full import. Chen Boda and Jiang Qing had visited the Beida campus on the nights of July 22 and 23 and doubtless communicated the rising tension there to Mao. Wang Li and Guan Feng made a secret visit to Tsinghua University, where, on Mao's orders, they had interviewed the "rebellious" and soon-to-be-notorious student Kuai Dafu (still detained and locked up in his dormitory by the work team) to learn about his ordeal and confrontation with the work team.[78] Yet when Mao finally summoned Liu Shaoqi to report on July 24, the latter, according to his secretary, was totally unprepared for Mao's condemnation. In the light of unceasing opposition to work teams from someone as close to the Chairman as Chen Boda, it is hard to see why.[79]

In a series of meetings with groups of party leaders on July 24, 25, and 26,[80]

Mao roundly condemned the "fifty days," the period when the work teams were in control of campuses. Mu Xin, who was present at the first meeting, held in Mao's temporary residence in the Diaoyutai compound, recalls that Mao was "waiting for us in the center of a large room on the ground floor, dressed in his worn old white pajamas."[81] Once all his colleagues were present, Mao began talking about the movement in general and the work-team issue in particular:

> I felt very sad after returning to Beijing, when I noticed how frigid the atmosphere is. Some schools have closed their gates, and one gets the feeling that the student movement is being suppressed. Who suppresses student movements? Only the northern warlords did! . . . Covering up big-character posters is something that cannot be permitted. It's an error in orientation that must be rectified right away. All these restrictions must be smashed to pieces . . . We must not restrict the masses. When Beida saw the students rising up, they introduced restrictions, which they gave the well-sounding name "putting things on the right course," whereas in fact what they were doing was putting things on the wrong course. Some students label the students counterrevolutionaries. Those who suppress the student movement will come to no good end![82]

At the meetings on July 24, Mao revealed his decision that the work teams had to be withdrawn. "Nobody stood up to him and opposed it," according to Tao Zhu's biographer.[83] Mao explained: "We should not use work teams and should not issue directives and give orders . . . Let the teachers and students themselves continue by themselves; that's the only good way to do it. None of us are any good, not even I. This is not just a matter of Beida; it concerns the entire nation. If we go on the way we started, then it's not going to lead anywhere."[84]

On July 28 the Beijing Party Committee dutifully announced its decision to withdraw all work teams from the city's colleges and middle schools. Leadership of the movement was to be left in the hands of "Cultural Revolution mass organizations," the members of which were to be elected by the "revolutionary teachers and students" themselves.[85] But not all members of work teams were withdrawn. At Beida, for example, in response to a request made to Kang Sheng and Jiang Qing by Nie Yuanzi, PLA navy officers remained behind in a new capacity as campus security guards.[86]

The Beijing Party Committee's decision, which had been drafted by the CCRG and finalized by Mao, was read out by its first secretary Li Xuefeng to a mass rally of some 10,000 college and middle school teachers and students in the Great Hall of the People on July 29.[87] The rally was addressed by Deng

Xiaoping, Zhou Enlai, and Liu Shaoqi (in that order). Deng said that the decision to withdraw the work teams had been "very necessary" and had been "based on the teachings of Mao Zedong Thought that the popular masses are the creators of the world, and that only by relying on and uniting with more than 95 percent of the masses . . . can we prevent revisionism." Both Deng and Zhou explained what had happened over the past two months as "old revolutionaries encountering new problems." "All in all," Zhou said, "this is a new thing, a new movement, and we were not familiar with it, especially those of us who are so old . . . We are going to come to you and learn from you." In a remarkable passage at the very beginning of his speech, Liu Shaoqi echoed this theme, as he had done with his children in June: "Now as for *how* to carry out a Great Proletarian Cultural Revolution, you're none too clear about it, and don't know too well, so you ask us how to do it. I tell you honestly, I don't know either. We're mainly going to be relying on you to make this revolution."[88]

Liu went on to emphasize the need to "protect the minority." One should not immediately curse, beat up, and arrest people who, like one Tsinghua student, wrote slogans such as "Support the party center; oppose Chairman Mao." They should be protected and permitted to write a few more slogans and make a few more reactionary statements. "Their actions will not affect the overall situation," Liu insisted. "Later, when we have sufficient documentation, then we can draw our conclusions . . . Then we can subject them to the dictatorship of the proletariat, deprive them of their freedom, and let them shoot their mouths off."[89]

During the rally, unbeknownst to Liu and his colleagues, the Chairman was listening to the whole proceedings from behind a curtain. According to his doctor, who was listening with him, when Mao heard the excuse that old revolutionaries were facing new problems, he snorted and said: "What old revolutionaries? Old counterrevolutionaries is more like it." At the end of the rally, Mao suddenly came onstage to be greeted by stormy applause and shouts of "Long Live Chairman Mao!" As he walked to and fro across the stage waving slowly, it became evident that he was ignoring Liu and Deng, distancing himself from them.[90]

Tapes of the rally were played on campuses all over Beijing. The country copied the capital, and work teams were withdrawn everywhere.[91] Early opponents of the teams became heroes, now called rebels or the minority faction, while the supporters of the teams were condemned as conservatives or the majority faction.[92]

The fifty days were over.

85

5

Mao's New Successor

Having evicted Liu Shaoqi from control of the Cultural Revolution, Mao now acted to reorganize the top leadership of the CCP to ensure that it would be more responsive and loyal to his unfolding plans. On July 24, the day he delivered his negative verdict on work teams, Mao ordered the CC to be convened for its Eleventh Plenum, its first in four years. To set the scene, the *People's Daily* on July 26 revealed Mao's triumphal swim in the Yangtze, underlining that the Chairman was fighting fit and ready to resume command. The following day, Liu Shaoqi's name was mentioned positively for the last time in China's most widely read paper, the internal publication *Reference News*.[1]

The plenum opened on August 1, after a preparatory work conference held from July 27 to July 31. Of the 173 CC members and alternates elected at the two sessions of the Eighth Congress in 1956 and 1958, only 141 attended the session, a sharp reduction from the norm and an indication that many leaders found excuses to stay away from what promised to be a stormy session.[2] For Liu, who could not stay away, it was a bitter moment. When the order to withdraw the work teams went out on July 28, he was at home with his family; five months later, one of Liu's daughters, a student at Tsinghua University, recalled that in her whole life she had never seen her father so upset as on that night. Both she and her stepmother wept bitterly.[3] Also present at the plenum were an additional 47 people, including senior party officials and, more importantly, members of the CCRG and two "revolutionary teachers and students" (Nie Yuanzi and a junior colleague and fellow poster-writer from Beida), visible harbingers of the shape of things to come.[4]

The plenum was originally scheduled to last five days, and the agenda as laid out by General Secretary Deng Xiaoping in the opening speech on August 1 was to consist of a report on central activities and decisions since the Tenth Plenum;

passage of a "Decision of the CCP CC on the Great Proletarian Cultural Revolution," as it was now to be called;[5] ratification of the decisions of the enlarged Politburo conference in May, at which Peng Zhen, Lu Dingyi, Luo Ruiqing, and Yang Shangkun had been purged; and passage of a plenum communiqué.[6]

Preparations for the plenum had been rushed; Liu Shaoqi's opening-day report on the policies of the center during the previous four years was not properly scripted; the decision on the Cultural Revolution was not ready.[7] But these turned out to be minor issues as compared to the tone of the conference set by Mao on the opening day. The Chairman aggressively interrupted Liu Shaoqi while he was delivering his report. When Liu took responsibility for sending in the work teams, Mao asserted that 90 percent of the teams had made mistakes of line, had stood on the side of the bourgeoisie, and opposed proletarian revolution. Implicitly he was indicating Liu's complicity in these fundamental errors.

To Rebel Is Justified

In an equally ominous move, Mao circulated to the plenum that day a copy of a letter he had just written to the very first Red Guard *(hongweibing)* organization, set up on May 29 by students at the elite middle school attached to Tsinghua University. A CC member who had been close to Mao for decades as his ghost-writer and secretary argued that the fact that Mao "looked for backing among the students shows that he had no backing [inside the party]."[8] The secretary missed the point. Mao was hardly likely to look for a constituency in an organization he was about to trash.

On July 28 the Tsinghua Red Guards had sent Mao two big-character posters titled "Long live the proletarian revolutionary spirit of rebellion!" Nos. 1 and 2, along with a covering letter requesting a reply. He promptly obliged, giving the nascent Red Guard movement a blank check, underwritten with all the political capital of his office and cult: "You say it is right to rebel against reactionaries; I enthusiastically support you." Less credibly, Mao pledged the support of his colleagues: "Here I want to say that I myself as well as my revolutionary comrades-in-arms all take the same attitude. No matter where they are, in Beijing or anywhere else in China, I will give enthusiastic support to all who take an attitude similar to yours in the Cultural Revolution movement." In one of those characteristically moderating passages with which he liked to pepper his speeches and writings, presumably to avert blame when things got out of hand, Mao went on to emphasize the need for uniting with as many as possible and the importance of offering a way out even for those committing serious errors. But the tocsin was "to rebel is justified [*zaofan you li*]," a phrase that echoed throughout the country and served as the justification for murder and mayhem over the next few years.[9]

Whether they liked it or not, Mao's colleagues now had to interact with the Red Guard movement. On August 3 Wang Renzhong invited the Tsinghua middle school correspondents to the Diaoyutai guest house complex to see the Chairman's letter. Their joy was boundless. Sometime around midnight on August 4, Zhou Enlai told a mass "mobilization rally" on the Tsinghua University campus at which the head of the departing work team had just made a public self-criticism and been made to listen to one "rebellious" Red Guard after another denouncing him: "Just now, the three young comrades from the middle school attached to Tsinghua were right when they spoke of how, when necessary, revisionist leadership has to be opposed and the revolutionary masses granted the right to rebel . . . With their big-character posters, they led a rebellion, responding to Chairman Mao's appeal. On this point, frankly, I should learn from you. I salute you."[10]

Liu Shaoqi, too, doggedly attempted to climb onto the revolutionary bandwagon. At midnight on August 1 he informed the Beijing first secretary, Li Xuefeng, that he wanted to investigate the situation at one of the capital's academic institutions where the work team had been withdrawn. The following evening, after some last-minute arrangements, he turned up at the Beijing College of Construction Engineering, escorted by a number of cadres, including Li Xuefeng and a CCRG stalwart, Qi Benyu, who carefully noted what he said. For three evenings, August 2, 3, and 4, Liu tried to discover what the work team had done wrong and to make sense of the struggle at the college between the "Revolution Corps" and the "August 1 Corps," which presaged the internecine warfare among Red Guard groups over the next two years. On the final evening, now addressing the members of the college's work team in Zhongnanhai, Liu was clearly distraught and knew his days were numbered. Adopting the rhetorical device of "If I were one of you, I would . . . ," he said:

> People rebel against me, but for fear of "great democracy" we don't let them. I've made mistakes: you may expose them. You may expel me from the party, you may remove me from office, and approve of him, give him the right guidance, in which case he will not rebel. Therefore, draw fire against yourself: *It is right to bombard the headquarters!* If you're a good person and [it turns out that]

to rebel against you was wrong, you're still a good person. If you don't permit them to rebel, they will get rid of you for sure. The work team did not permit people to rebel![11]

But on August 5, after another broadside from Mao, Liu telephoned Li Xuefeng and said he would not be going to the college anymore because "it seems that I am not qualified to lead the Cultural Revolution."[12] Meanwhile Qi Benyu probably provided Mao with a summary of Liu's address the night before, for it cannot have been a coincidence that the key phrase in it was one that Mao would promptly throw right back at Liu.

Mao Bombards the Headquarters

Mao's original plan had been to conclude the plenum on August 5. But he had been increasingly angered by the very lukewarm support from CC members in their speeches on August 2 and 3 for the withdrawal of the work teams. Many clearly if not explicitly took Liu Shaoqi's position.[13] So the Chairman suddenly changed the agenda, calling an unscheduled enlarged meeting of the PSC on the afternoon of August 4. At the meeting, he read the riot act to his colleagues and even referred without naming names to some of his PSC colleagues as "monsters and freaks":

> This so-called mass line, this so-called faith in the masses, this so-called Marxism-Leninism, it is all fake and has been for years . . . What we have here is suppression and terror, and this terror originates with the [party] center . . . Judging from the present suppression of the great Cultural Revolutionary activities of the students, I do not believe there is any real democracy or real Marxism. What we have here is standing on the side of the bourgeoisie to oppose the Great Proletarian Cultural Revolution. Because the center not only has not supported the movement of the young students, but in fact has suppressed the student movement, I am of the view that something has to be done.[14]

With Mao in the chair, Chen Boda delivered an address in the name of the CCRG that was no less aggressive:

> Quite a few comrades among us have become officials who always find accepting other people's opinions very difficult. Their own words cannot be infringed upon. (MAO ZEDONG: [What they say is] sacred and inviolable. They have become used to acting like high officials and overbearing bureaucrats.) This really

is a problem, one I have come across in many different settings. When he says something, it counts; when other people say something, it just doesn't! If this [problem] is not resolved, we shall see revisionism emerge.[15]

When Liu Shaoqi again expressed his willingness to take responsibility for what had happened, Mao said sarcastically, "You exercised dictatorship [here] in Beijing. Well done!"[16]

Mao proposed that his remarks be distributed to the delegates attending the plenum and discussed in small groups. The plenum was formally extended by a week. From August 4 to 6 the delegates met to discuss Mao's criticism, but again no warm support for the Chairman's views was expressed. On August 5 Mao condemned the circular endorsed by Liu, which had supported the actions taken by the Beida work team in suppressing the June 18 incident, and ordered it to be formally withdrawn. On the same day, in a written comment on the *People's Daily* article that had accompanied the publication of Nie Yuanzi's poster, he tried to pressure his colleagues by asserting that "erroneous leadership that harms the revolution should not be unconditionally accepted, but should be firmly resisted."[17] In a third move, on August 5, Mao scribbled "Bombard the headquarters—my big-character poster" in praise of Nie Yuanzi's poster on a two-month-old copy of the *Beijing Daily*. His secretary copied it for him onto a blank sheet of paper, Mao gave it its provocative heading, and two days later he had it distributed to the plenum. Recalling earlier disputes with which the conferees would have been familiar, it left no doubt that the Chairman had broken with Liu Shaoqi. It read in full:

> The first Marxist-Leninist big-character poster in the country and the *People's Daily* commentator article on it are indeed superbly written! Comrades, please read them once more. [They were appended.] But in the last fifty days or so, some leading comrades from the central down to the local levels have acted in a diametrically opposite way. Proceeding from the reactionary stand of the bourgeoisie, they have enforced a bourgeois dictatorship and struck down the noisy and spectacular Great Proletarian Cultural Revolution movement. They have stood facts on their head, juggled black and white, encircled and suppressed revolutionaries, stifled opinions differing from their own, imposed a white terror, and felt very pleased with themselves. They have puffed up the arrogance of the bourgeoisie and deflated the morale of the proletariat. How vicious they are! Viewed in connection with the 1962 right deviation and the erroneous tendency of 1964, which was left in form but right in essence, shouldn't this [behavior] prompt one to deep thought?[18]

Although it would be another six weeks before this text was officially distributed to party members all over China, and another year before it was published in the *People's Daily*, it leaked almost instantaneously.[19] Mao's plan should now have been plain for his followers to see. The combination of "To rebel is justified" and "Bombard the headquarters" meant that the Chairman was not just up in arms about the alleged misbehavior of the work teams, but that he intended to use it as justification for a top-level purge of the CCP.

In case there was any doubt, Kang Sheng, Jiang Qing, Zhang Chunqiao, and their leftist colleagues elaborated on the significance of Mao's words in the small group sessions and denounced Liu's "bourgeois headquarters." One member of Mao's claque, Minister of Public Security Xie Fuzhi, even attacked Deng Xiaoping; allegedly Jiang Qing had told him that Liu was no longer a threat but Deng was.[20] On August 5, after talking to Mao, Zhou telephoned Liu to suggest that he should not show his face in public or receive foreign guests in his capacity as head of state.[21] Yet though none dared to speak for the defense, enthusiasm was still muted. So far-reaching and profound were the political implications of Mao's "big-character poster" that some CC members refused to accept them. "After reading the Chairman's poster," Qi Benyu lamented in April 1967, "they still didn't understand its purpose or who he was talking about. Some still don't, which just shows that understanding a major struggle is not an easy thing to do."[22]

On August 6, Mao summoned reinforcements. He ordered Lin Biao, resting in Dalian during the first week of the plenum, to fly to Beijing. Lin had been absent from Beijing throughout the summer and managed to stay out of the conflict over the work teams and how the Cultural Revolution was to be run. Upon arrival, he was asked by Mao to denounce Liu Shaoqi. Maintaining that his frail health had prevented him from staying on top of what Liu had been doing these past years, Lin asked Mao and Zhou Enlai to provide him with an informed assistant who could help him draft a denunciation that would be on target. The assistant dispatched by Mao and Zhou was the same major general who had provided Lin with crucial damning information about Luo Ruiqing in 1965.[23] With instructions from both Mao and Zhou on what issues to raise, he drafted speaking notes for Lin that comprised twenty-three indictments, covering everything from serious "right opportunist errors" in policy during the late 1940s to impertinent remarks made in private during the years since.[24]

On August 8, at a meeting with members of the CCRG, Lin expressed total support for Mao's vision of the Cultural Revolution, urging them to "turn the world upside down, be noisy and boisterous, blow tempests and make big waves, cause major disturbances and lots of trouble to the point where for the next six months not only the bourgeoisie but even the proletariat will be unable to sleep." His rousing remarks, together with his May 18 speech to the Politburo meeting at which the purging of top leaders had started, were distributed to the conferees.[25]

The Sixteen Points

Yet Mao's blueprint for the movement, the "Decision of the CCP CC concerning the Great Proletarian Cultural Revolution," also known as the Sixteen Points, was a deceptively more moderate document than the fire-eating speeches of the Chairman and Lin Biao might have led conferees to anticipate. The text adopted by the plenum on August 8 was the thirty-first draft produced by the CCRG, which had been working on the document since at least June. Mao's comment on it, addressed to Chen Boda, had been: "Excellent revisions; please print and distribute."[26] It was broadcast on national radio the night of August 8 and published in the *People's Daily* the next day. Unlike the May 16 Notification and the other key documents of the Cultural Revolution so far, it was to be public intellectual property from the start. It even went on sale in record shops, as part of a set of four 33-rpm vinyl discs that included a studio recording of a *People's Daily* editorial titled "Study the Sixteen Points, Become Acquainted with the Sixteen Points, and Put the Sixteen Points to Use," as well as live recordings of the speeches by Lin Biao and Zhou Enlai.

The Sixteen Points started lyrically with an uplifting definition of the Cultural Revolution as "a great revolution that touches people to their very souls," but it soon shifted to struggle:

> Although the bourgeoisie has been overthrown, it is still trying to use the old ideas, culture, customs and habits of the exploiting classes to corrupt the masses, capture their minds and endeavor to stage a come-back. The proletariat must . . . change the mental outlook of the whole of society. At present, our objective is to struggle against and overthrow those persons in authority who are taking the capitalist road, to criticize and repudiate the reactionary bourgeois academic "authorities" and the ideology of the bourgeoisie and all other exploiting classes and to transform education, literature and art and all other parts of the superstructure not in correspondence with the socialist economic

base, so as to facilitate the consolidation and development of the socialist system.[27]

That description of the movement's aims, with its attack on what came to be known as the "four olds," suggested that the Cultural Revolution would continue much as before, involving only the cultural and educational spheres and denunciations of the "usual suspects" of bourgeois background. Indeed, early Red Guard activities were based on that assumption, and many Red Guard groups memorized that passage.[28] But later in the Decision came sentences that indicated and authorized a different objective: "The main target of the present movement is those within the Party *who are in authority* and are taking the capitalist road."[29]

As for methods, the decision gave carte blanche to student radicals to go on the rampage without let or hindrance:

> In the great proletarian cultural revolution, the only method is for the masses to liberate themselves, and any method of doing things in their stead must not be used . . . Don't be afraid of disturbances. Chairman Mao has often told us that revolution cannot be so very refined, so gentle, so temperate, kind, courteous, restrained and magnanimous. Let the masses educate themselves in this great revolutionary movement and learn to distinguish between right and wrong and between correct and incorrect ways of doing things.[30]

At first there were no exceptions, save for the one spelled out in the last but one of the Sixteen Points, that within China's armed forces the Cultural Revolution would be carried out in accordance with separate instructions issued by the MAC and General Political Department.[31] Then, on September 7, *Zhongfa* [1966] 459 was issued, listing the regions and counties along China's borders where "the method of having the masses directly 'dismiss officials from office' is *not* to be employed." From Shenzhen in the south to Erlian in the north, from Jilong on the border with Nepal to Yanji on the border with North Korea, in all such strategically important localities a premium was to be put on security rather than on "revolutionary disorder."[32] The exceptions proved impossible to maintain.

There was one notable omission from the Sixteen Points: any mention or endorsement of the Red Guards. In September, Zhou Enlai reassured Red Guards that they had been included in the "other" of point 9's mention of "Cultural Revolutionary groups, committees, and other organizational forms created by the masses."[33] The Sixteen Points characterized all these entities as "something new and of great historic importance."

A New Leadership

On the afternoon of August 12, the final day of the plenum, Lin Biao presided over a session added late to the original agenda, the formal election by secret ballot of a new eleven-member PSC. Only the seventy-four full members of the CC were entitled to vote, and all of them cast their ballots for Mao, Lin Biao, Deng Xiaoping, and Kang Sheng. Zhou Enlai, Chen Boda, and Tao Zhu received all but one vote each, perhaps modestly not voting for themselves. The chief planner, Li Fuchun, received seventy votes; Zhu De, Mao's military alter ego during the revolutionary wars, received sixty-eight; Liu Shaoqi, sixty-five; Chen Yun, whose political discretion had kept him out of circulation for four years, fifty-eight.[34] Li Xiannian, whose name was not on the ballot, received one vote.[35] The CC did not formally dismiss any of the CCP's five vice chairmen, but the party media no longer used this title when referring to Liu, Zhou, Zhu, or Chen Yun. In the most stunning leadership change at the plenum, Lin Biao had become the CCP's only vice chairman, taking over from Liu the role of heir apparent.

Yet the results of the voting for the PSC were not to Mao's liking, for they did not tally with the rank order he had already decided upon in consultation with Lin Biao, Zhou Enlai,[36] and Jiang Qing. In the event, Mao's preferred order trumped that voted by the CC: Mao, Lin Biao, Zhou Enlai, Tao Zhu, Chen Boda, Deng Xiaoping, Kang Sheng, Liu Shaoqi, Zhu De, Li Fuchun, Chen Yun. Mao chose to disregard the fact that Deng had received a unanimous vote[37]—Jiang Qing criticized Tao Zhu, Chen Boda, and Kang Sheng for having voted for Deng—and personally promoted Tao to fourth place, allegedly to balance Deng's power.[38]

It is not clear why Mao should have worried any longer about Deng's power. Supposedly the CC Secretariat was to continue to function after the plenum. In fact it never met again, and Deng's title of general secretary thus fell into abeyance. After replacing Peng Zhen as the body's "permanent secretary," Tao Zhu tried in vain to keep some semblance of its authority, but in so doing clashed with Mao, who was now referring to the Secretariat as a "strategic mistake."[39] In fact, Deng's empire, the departmental structure that operated under the orders of the CC Secretariat, had been in the process of dismemberment ever since the

May Politburo session. Inside the Zhongnanhai leadership compound, the leaderships of the "five big departments" had been subjected to a "cleansing" of unprecedented ferocity.

Given that the Propaganda Department had been branded an "underworld kingdom" at the May meeting, it would have been strange indeed if it had not become the scene of a purge in the summer of 1966. The appointment of Tao Zhu to replace Lu Dingyi as department head was followed on June 6 by the CC Secretariat's formal suspension of three of the department's deputy directors as well as the department secretary general. The 234 "lesser kings of the underworld" (that is, ordinary cadres) working within the department were shaken up by a reduction in its overall size and radical changes to its makeup, most notably the merger of a number of its key offices and sections into one big Office for the Propagation of Mao Zedong Thought.[40] By the end of July, nine of the Central Propaganda Department's eleven deputy directors had been formally ousted, the only two survivors being CCRG chief Chen Boda and the sixty-six-year-old Zhang Jichun, a veteran of the peasant movement in Hunan and Long March participant with seemingly impeccable revolutionary credentials. Zhang's fate was in the end no less tragic than that of a majority of his colleagues: on September 8, 1966, his wife (a Red Army veteran and revolutionary in her own right) died of what in all probability was a heart attack, though suicide was at first not ruled out; in the spring of 1967, his children were accused of being "active counterrevolutionaries," and he himself came under fire for alleged "counterrevolution"; an aging, lonely, and broken man, he died on September 12, 1968, from injuries sustained in a fall from an overcrowded trolley.[41] On June 1, 1967, the CCRG announced the abolition of the Central Propaganda Department and the assumption of most of its functions by a much slimmed-down CCRG "propaganda group."[42]

The CC Organization Department fared even worse than the Propaganda Department, with its director, An Ziwen, and all eight of his deputies being officially suspended from their posts on August 19, 1966. The suspension, announced at a mass meeting attended by the entire department staff, was a response to Mao's recent blunt assessment: "The CC Organization Department is not in our hands."[43] Obviously, so crucial a department had to be "in our hands," and during the weeks that followed, the vast majority of the 210 cadres working in the department were subjected to a major investigation.[44] Deputy Director Zhao Han committed suicide on December 14, 1966; some of his colleagues (most notably An Ziwen and the highest-ranking deputy director, Li Chuli) werc to endure brutal and systematic torture for failing to cooperate with their "investigators" over the years to come. Credit for providing the Politburo with sufficient dirt on An Ziwen to justify his ouster went to Nie Yuanzi: Jiang Qing eventually referred to her exposure of the "An Ziwen traitor clique" as one of Nie's "great contributions" to the Cultural Revolution.[45] In 1994, Nie still insisted that her denunciation of An, which she had passed on in great secrecy to Kang Sheng via Kang's wife in May 1966, had been essentially correct. An Ziwen had, she recalled, maintained a highly suspect affair with a woman with KMT connections and to bring this to the attention of Kang had been little more than her duty as a CCP member. In her post–Cultural Revolution memoir, Nie claimed that Kang Sheng had later told her that the woman was a British agent with a radio transmitter.[46] In May 1967, the CCP center entrusted the running of the Organization Department to the PLA.[47]

In the winter of 1966–67, Zhou Enlai justified *ex post facto* the onslaught on the two oldest and best-known of the CC's five big departments as "entirely correct and necessary": "Our own Organization Department ended up in the hands of An Ziwen, and ideological work ended up in the hands of Lu Dingyi. That's the source—the class source—of the inability of so many of our high-level cadres to be as dynamic as the young people have been in the Great Cultural Revolution."[48] But Zhou hesitated to speak in similarly negative terms of the department that he himself had supervised on behalf of the PSC for several years: the CC United Front Work Department, a highly secretive organization that oversaw the delicate relationship between the CCP and the country's "democratic personages," small "democratic parties," "patriotic" capitalists, religious figures, overseas Chinese, and non-party intellectuals. At the beginning of the Cultural Revolution, its director and most of its eight deputy directors were criticized for "errors" of one kind or another, but thanks to whatever protection Zhou was able to accord them, and doubtless because the people for whom they were responsible were not Mao's targets, they survived longer than most. Some ended up serving on the ad hoc bodies that—under Zhou Enlai's personal supervision—examined the wrongdoings of major "revisionists"; others ended up becoming the targets of those very same bodies. The latter included deputy directors Fang Fang and Zhang Jingwu, both of whom died behind bars in the autumn of 1971.[49] The United Front Work Department remained in a state of near-total chaos throughout 1967 and much of 1968 and did not resume anything even remotely resembling normal operations until July 1968, when two PLA officers were put in charge of running it.[50]

The International Liaison Department handled the CCP's overt and covert contacts with Communist parties in other countries. It was one of two CC departments that Deng Xiaoping supervised for the PSC.[51] Its leadership survived the summer of 1966 relatively unscathed, although Xu Li, the senior deputy director responsible for the training inside China of foreign Communist cadres, was attacked for "revisionism" and suspended from his post, together with a number of his subordinates in the winter of 1966–67. Director Wang Jiaxiang (who had been under a cloud since 1962 and whose health was poor), however, was singled out for a carefully premeditated attack in a big-character poster by one of his six deputies, CCRG member Wang Li. On June 9, 1966, Wang Li claimed under the provocative title "What kind of a struggle is this?" that to resist the kind of leadership that Wang Jiaxiang represented was to resist "a revisionist seizure of party power and capitalist restoration."[52] As the summer months wore on, most of the approximately 700 cadres employed in the department appear to have concluded that to challenge Wang Li's line of reasoning was pointless, especially since it had the explicit backing of Kang Sheng. On June 7 the CCP center had already announced in *Zhongfa* [1966] 292 that the third-ranking deputy director and concurrent party secretary of the All-China Federation of Trade Unions, Liu Ningyi, had been appointed acting director in Wang Jiaxiang's stead.[53] Together with deputy directors Zhao Yimin, Wu Xiuquan, and Liao Chengzhi, Liu Ningyi was soon regarded by Wang Li—and, far more important, by Kang Sheng and Deng Xiaoping—as representing a correct line for dealing with other Communist parties.[54]

The last of the "five big departments" of the CC was the Central Investigation Department, which was also supervised for the PSC by Deng Xiaoping. So secret was the work carried out by the department that even in classified internal communications it was more often than not referred to simply as the "Organs in the Western Garden," a fanciful name derived from its location in the former imperial garden in the vicinity of the Summer Palace.[55] Its name and current structure stemmed from a major shakeup of the CCP's intelligence community in 1955. The Central Investigation Department managed a number of tasks deemed crucial to the regime, including counterintelligence, the collection of political intelligence, ensuring the safety of senior officials traveling abroad, and supervising visits to China by foreign dignitaries and delegations. When the Cultural Revolution began, its director, Kong Yuan, and several of his deputies came under fire for alleged "revisionist" wrongdoings.[56] It is clear, however, that although in theory the Cultural Revolution was meant to "shake up" the entire party and state apparat, powerful arguments could be and indeed were made in favor of insulating this department from some of the worst chaos. Kang Sheng, who began overseeing its operations in Deng Xiaoping's stead shortly after the Eleventh Plenum, is said to have preferred to see it simply "keep to the conventional way of doing things."[57] On December 23, 1966, Kong Yuan's wife, an intelligence officer herself and a member of Zhou Enlai's personal staff since 1940, committed suicide; not long thereafter, rumors began to circulate in Beijing that the department director himself had attempted suicide as well, but failed. Kong Yuan was by now like so many other senior "revisionists" being denounced and humiliated at one mass rally after another, including one in early February 1967 at the Beijing No. 4 Middle School, where his son Kong Dan—an early Red Guard leader—was a student.[58] In March of that same year, with Mao Zedong's endorsement, Zhou Enlai ordered the imposition of direct military control over the department.[59] By the end of 1969, it had been merged with and become part of the PLA General Staff's Directorate of Intelligence.[60] Meanwhile Kong Yuan and all but one of his deputies were either behind bars or performing manual labor somewhere in China's remote hinterland. The sole survivor was Deputy Director Luo Qingchang; a biographical directory produced by KMT intelligence eventually noted that the Cultural Revolution had left him "unaffected [because of] his close relationship with Zhou Enlai."[61]

As the old leadership and its bureaucratic infrastructure were dismantled, a new leader took the stage and a new bureaucratic infrastructure burgeoned. At a work conference the day after the closing of the plenum, Lin Biao made some personal observations on the tasks now facing him: "I have recently been rather downhearted because my ability is not commensurate with the task and position I have been given. I anticipate that I shall be committing mistakes." Although Mao knew what he wanted, it was not always possible for other people "to understand what the Chairman has in mind." "We must firmly implement the Chairman's instructions, whether we understand them or not," he suggested. "We must believe in the Chairman's innate genius, in his wisdom, and in his intelligence, always ask him for instructions and then act accordingly, never interfering in big matters or bothering him with trifles."[62] Clearly Lin Biao hoped by adopting an attitude of total subservience to avoid Liu Shaoqi's fatal errors in the hot seat that he now occupied, even if he, too, failed to work toward the Chairman. Mao endorsed Lin's speech and ordered it distributed to every party member.[63] Even after he had been elevated to No. 2, Lin concerned himself first and foremost with military matters. The nomenclatura positions of his entire staff remained unchanged within the MAC bureaucracy and were not shifted to the CC General Office controlled by Wang Dongxing.[64]

In political matters, Lin delegated the running of the center's day-to-day affairs to Zhou Enlai. Two weeks after the Eleventh Plenum, Zhou began regularly chairing what for want of a better name was called the "Central Caucus" *(zhongyang pengtou huiyi),* a body for which there were no provisions in the party constitution. Insofar as its participants, agenda, and decision-making role in the winter of 1966 were concerned, it was in all but name identical with an enlarged session of the PSC minus Mao and Lin. Already on the eve of the CC plenum, Zhou had at Mao's request taken over the task of overseeing the drafting of key documents and their approval pending final ratification by Mao. Years later, Wang Li recalled that "in reality, at this point the premier was running day-to-day affairs."[65]

Despite the fact that on paper he was China's highest-ranking vice premier, Lin Biao did not involve himself in how the State Council was run. Zhou on the other hand took a keen interest, and as the Cultural Revolution progressed he remained intimately involved in all major decisions involving the PLA. According to the son of one of Lin Biao's generals, "my father remembered clearly the things that happened in the 'Cultural Revolution,' and he told me that the MAC Administrative Group [of which he had been a leading member] processed altogether over 1,300 documents, not a single one of which was not known to Chairman Mao, and not a single one of which was not personally handled by Premier Zhou."[66] But an even more significant new role that Zhou assumed from now on was that of overseeing the work of the CCRG.

The Central Cultural Revolution Group

News of the CCRG's existence and the names of its leading members were first revealed to an inner-party audience in the highly classified *Zhongfa* [1966] 281 on May 28, after its creation in the wake of the enlarged Politburo session that month.[67] Its name was first mentioned in public in July 1966, in the unusual context of a banquet celebrating the "triumphant closing" of an emergency meeting of Afro-Asian writers in Beijing. Upon Mao Zedong's return to Beijing, its members had visited one university after another as the Chairman's personal emissaries, gathering information and spreading the Cultural Revolution gospel. In the process, Jiang Qing made a point of telling audiences everywhere that "Chairman Mao has asked us to send you his regards; he takes a keen interest in your revolutionary cause!"[68]

The CCRG as an organization became the campaign headquarters for the

Cultural Revolution.[69] Beginning as a group of ten party intellectuals and the wife of the CCP Chairman charged with drafting policy documents for the PSC, by 1967 it grew into a bureaucracy employing hundreds, possibly thousands. Replacing the CC Secretariat, it became more powerful than the latter had ever been. On paper at least, it was formally the equal of the State Council and the MAC. On the eve of its dissolution in 1969, both Lin Biao and Zhou Enlai praised it for having "firmly carried out Chairman Mao's proletarian revolutionary line."[70]

Its humble beginnings before Mao and Jiang Qing returned to Beijing in July had been one villa in the Diaoyutai compound and a single secretary on loan from the CC's International Liaison Department. By the time the Eleventh Plenum was over, it occupied seven villas, with Chen Boda taking up residence in No. 15, Kang Sheng in No. 8, and Jiang Qing in No. 11. The offices of the CCRG were in villa No. 16, while No. 17 housed recreation facilities, including a projection room where Jiang Qing would watch foreign films. (Her favorites supposedly included Hollywood classics like *Gone With the Wind*.) The CCRG Journalists' Station, mentioned in the previous chapter, came to be located on premises neighboring the Diaoyutai compound.[71]

Like the campaign it was intended to help Mao run, the CCRG was in a state of constant flux. Ravaged by internal conflicts, by January 1967 more than half of the seventeen people listed as members, vice directors, adviser, and director in *Zhongfa* [1966] 281 had either been purged or otherwise rendered powerless and shunted aside. Not surprisingly, the official line was initially that the CCRG was a superbly united team that "worked together with one heart" with no other aim than to "raise even higher the great red flag of Mao Zedong Thought." Once the internal purges had proved beyond doubt that this was not true, a new line was formulated according to which those still in the CCRG had waged a constant struggle against those who no longer were, all of whom—once purged—had shown themselves to be people who "wave a red flag to oppose the red flag." All the available testimony indicates that the CCRG never became the well-oiled and smoothly operating Cultural Revolution machine that Mao presumably wanted. After the Chairman's death, Jiang Qing reminisced: "It was impossible to convene the CCRG: as soon as Kang *lao* and Chen Boda saw each other, they would begin arguing. Chen Boda would not even obey the premier, though he would do as I told him. So the premier got to work on Kang *lao* while I dealt with Chen Boda, and finally we were able to convene a meeting. Later we would have the same problem again."[72] Mu Xin eventually described it as "the most anarchic, the most disorderly" institution he had ever worked for, one in which "with each passing day, the contradictions between its members became ever more acute and their internal conflicts and struggles grew increasingly intricate."[73] In January 1967, Mao complained about the CCRG's relationship to himself. All its members presented their own versions of events, he said: Kang Sheng told his story, Chen Boda told his, and Jiang Qing told hers. As an institution, it submitted no reports.[74]

Despite the fact that Chen Boda was the titular director of the CCRG and Jiang Qing from September 1966 onward its quasi-permanent deputy director, neither chaired the group's regular meetings. These meetings, the "CCRG Caucus"—not to be confused with the "Central Caucus," mentioned earlier—were chaired by Zhou Enlai, who also set the agenda.[75] Such was the extent of the premier's power over the CCRG that he was himself, when he deemed it prudent, in a position to intervene directly in local disputes of a factional nature *in the name of* the CCRG.[76] Information about the formal relationship between Zhou and the CCRG that has been coming to light only in recent years does not invalidate the frequent claim that the Cultural Revolution involved a fundamental clash of interests between the group (an institution described by some authors as one with "little stake in the political status quo")[77] and Zhou Enlai's "establishment." But it does hint at how complex the setting was in which that clash played itself out. At a time when she would have had no reason to make up such a claim, the wife of Lin Jie, a senior staff member on loan from *Red Flag* who regularly attended the "CCRG Caucus," testified that Jiang Qing more often than not deferred to Zhou even on those occasions when the staff might have preferred her not to. Lin Jie had once explained to her, she said, that "comrade Jiang Qing is not certain about some things and always tells us to do what the premier says, which makes things difficult."[78]

This then was the ramshackle organization with which Mao Zedong hoped to create a brave new world. Having dismissed Liu Shaoqi from his role as heir apparent[79] and achieved through internal intrigue and deception the beginnings of a new leadership lineup—there were many purges still to come—it was time for Mao to embark on *his* Cultural Revolution and to press on with what he had criticized the old leadership for not doing: unleashing the masses. The cadres of the CCRG would be his shock troops.

6

The Red Guards

By the end of the Eleventh Plenum, the "masses" had already risen. A "red terror" spread rapidly through the campuses of colleges and middle schools of the capital. That violence was the product of the Red Guard movement.[1] Mao's endorsement of students' right to rebel had removed such restraints on violence as the work teams had selectively imposed. Various of his remarks indicate that Mao craved a measure of catalytic terror to jump-start the Cultural Revolution. He had no scruples about the taking of human life. In a conversation with trusties later in the Cultural Revolution, the Chairman went so far as to suggest that the sign of a true revolutionary was precisely his intense desire to kill: "This man Hitler was even more ferocious. The more ferocious the better, don't you think? The more people you kill, the more revolutionary you are."[2] Perhaps he was vicariously reliving his glory days of mobilizing peasants in Hunan and Jiangxi. Whatever the motivation, in the autumn of 1966 the violence ranged from the destruction of private and public property, through expulsion of urban undesirables, all the way to murder. Although the human toll of some subsequent phases of the movement was greater, it was the in-your-face nature of the "red terror" of August–September 1966 that stuck in popular memory.

"Beijing is too civilized!" Mao declared at a post-plenum work conference of central leaders. "I would say there is not a great deal of disorder . . . and that the number of hooligans is very small. Now is not the time to interfere."[3] Prompting Mao's comments most notably was an "Urgent Appeal!" issued on August 6 by Red Guards in the three elite middle schools attached to Tsinghua University, Peking University, and the Beijing Aeronautical Institute. The appeal spoke of "hooligans" masquerading as Red Guards going on a rampage, destroying state property, and beating people up at random, and it called on all "genuine, revolutionary" Red Guards to take action to bring to an end the "disorder" into which the capital was descending.[4] Mao called the need for such an appeal into question.

On August 5—the day he wrote "Bombard the headquarters"—Mao also revoked *Zhongfa* [1966] 312, which had endorsed the Peking University work team's breakup of the June 18 "incident." The members of the CCRG leaked Mao's personal opinion: in his view, what had taken place was "not a counterrevolutionary incident, but a revolutionary incident."[5] On August 13 an ambivalent Beijing Party Committee staged an event almost certainly intended to strike a blow at the "hooligans" mentioned in the Red Guard "Urgent Appeal" and in the process to mollify any sympathizers they may have had among the general populace. At a mass rally in the Beijing Workers' Stadium—the biggest facility of its kind in the city, completed in 1959 to celebrate the PRC's tenth anniversary—a crowd of some 70,000 young men and women saw about a dozen young "hooligans" being paraded out and denounced. But as the rally climaxed, the situation got out of hand, and they were beaten up. Wang Renzhong, present as the deputy director of the CCRG charged with monitoring the progress of the Cultural Revolution in Beijing, was unable or unwilling to interfere. That Saturday night, a "red terror" spread through the capital. Putting their recollections on paper a few months later, university students opposed to the violence spoke of the rally as having "an extremely bad impact."[6]

That an explosive mix of repressed anger and violence was brewing under the surface, waiting to explode at the first crack in the veneer of socialist order, was something the CC leadership had long been aware of but rarely discussed. In January 1965, Peng Zhen had broken the taboo, telling some of his colleagues in a speech on the progress of the Socialist Education Movement: "Indiscriminate struggle takes place in the schools, including those attended by your own sons and daughters." Citing the example of one Beijing middle school student who had done no more than write a silly poem, Peng said that his classmates had promptly accused him of "opposing Chairman Mao." "They beat him until he confessed. Then they accused him of wanting to kill Chairman Mao. He said he would never have dared to. So they accused him of dishonesty and beat him up again. Finally he confessed to having wanted to [kill Mao]. When someone tried to intervene, that person was beaten up as well. I am not making this up: the sons of some of you comrades sitting here today tried to intervene and were beaten up."[7] After Peng's fall, Zhou Enlai termed his speech "very bad."[8] Mao's reaction is not known, but he harnessed the volcanic energy that it revealed to his own grand design for the Cultural Revolution.

Curiously, Mao and Kang Sheng had misjudged where they could recruit the most fervent supporters for the Cultural Revolution, for, as Peng's story showed, it was in the middle and even elementary schools that the most terrible crimes took place, not at Beida or other colleges.[9] The most unquestioning and fervent supporters of the Cultural Revolution emerged from among China's 13 million middle school students. If mobilizing them meant putting up with a bit of disorder, mob violence, and a few "excesses," then so be it!

As mentioned in the last chapter, it was at the elite middle school attached to Tsinghua University that the Red Guard movement was born as early as May 29, when students there took it upon themselves to organize in order to defend the Chairman and his Thought, and to struggle against revisionism. According to one participant at the founding meeting, held by seven students in Yuanming Park after the evening study session, the choice of the movement's title emerged after only a brief discussion:

> "Listen, fellows. I think we should ask those who hold the same position as us at school to sign our posters in a common name." I put forward the suggestion...
>
> Someone suggested using the same pen name that the student Zhang Chengzhi had once used—the "Red Guard."
>
> "The Red Guard—how about it? It's great! The Red Guard of Chairman Mao and the Party Central Committee!"
>
> "The powerful guard of the red regime, or the honorable guard of the red country. Wonderful! So be it—the Red Guard!"
>
> The next day, a great number of wall posters written by "the Red Guard" covered the middle school attached to Tsinghua University, located in the western suburbs of Beijing.
>
> On June 2 and 3, students from middle schools in the Haidian and West City districts learned of the news and rushed to our school, supporting us with their own posters. At the end of almost every poster, the name "Red Guard" was signed in different ways.[10]

One of the posters put up on June 2 prophetically proclaimed what would become the hallmark of the movement: "Beat to a pulp any and all persons who go against Mao Zedong Thought—no matter who they are, what banner they fly, or how exalted their positions may be."[11]

A reason for the early activism in the elite or "key" middle schools was probably the composition and cohesion of their student bodies. These schools were not "elite" simply in educational terms: significant numbers of their students were either children or grandchildren of party and government leaders immensely superior in status to their teachers. From their parents they had heard stirring stories of revolution; now was their chance to emulate them, using their knowledge of inner-party affairs gained from reading secret documents delivered to their homes. And while elite universities had a geographically diverse student body chosen on merit from the intellectually most gifted from all over China, many of whom would have initially been strangers to one another, pupils at elite middle schools formed a far more cohesive group, having been drawn from relatively small catchment areas in the capital, with many having studied together in elementary school.

Revolutionizing Education

In early June, when the work teams fanned out across the capital, college and middle school students were encouraged to set up Cultural Revolution committees for their campuses and Cultural Revolution small groups for each class. Similar developments took place across the country, and provincial party leaders aped the capital by effecting the dismissals of university administrators and party secretaries.[12] After the CCP center's decision on June 13 to temporarily suspend all classes and have students devote themselves full-time to the Cultural Revolution, studies halted, and students read and discussed published polemics and Mao's comments on the educational system.[13] Inspired by Mao's "Letter to Comrade Lin Biao" of May 7, 1966, in which he had said that "there must be a revolution in education, as the phenomenon of bourgeois intellectuals ruling our schools can no longer be tolerated," some students initially wanted merely to turn their schools into military-Communist institutions like the CCP's Resistance University in Yan'an. According to the recollection of one of the most prominent early Red Guard leaders from the elite middle school attached to Peking University, "At the time, we were happy about the situation in China as a whole . . . [but] felt that China's entire educational system was definitely no good."[14] The work teams encouraged criticism of teachers, who were held responsible for "bourgeois" or "revisionist" curricula and pedagogy, usually on the flimsiest of bases. Big-character posters soon covered school walls. According to a student at an elite girls' school,

> The revolution kept on like this for several weeks, then the pace began to slacken. Whatever could be written had been written, and the number of new

105

posters put up each day decreased. The working group decided to let us out to see what other schools and universities were doing. We went to nearby schools to read their posters, then to Qinghua and Beijing universities, where the revolution had originated. I spent whole days in universities reading big-character posters . . . In late July I thought the time to wrap up the Cultural Revolution had come.[15]

But the Cultural Revolution was only just beginning.

Elite Red Guards, such as the children of ministers and generals, already had an inkling that the Cultural Revolution was not just about education. When they read the text of the Politburo's classified May 16 Notification (to which teachers did not have access, but which the students saw at home), they interpreted it as a call to arms to join an even bigger undertaking. One remembered: "We did not doubt at all what was said in the 'Circular' . . . We thought that for sure there was a Khrushchev next to Chairman Mao. If we did not rise up and fight this revisionism, our country would change its color."[16] At the end of June, in the first of four big-character posters titled "Long live the proletarian revolutionary spirit of rebellion!" the Tsinghua middle school Red Guards had declared: "We intend to strike down not only the reactionaries in our middle school, but also the reactionaries throughout the entire world . . . We are going to create a big proletarian commotion in the heavenly palace and zap forth a new proletarian world."[17]

These grandiose ambitions suddenly seemed more realistic when in early August Mao gave the Tsinghua middle school Red Guards his "ardent support," and the *People's Daily* quoted the Chairman as having told them to "concern yourselves with affairs of state, and carry the Great Proletarian Cultural Revolution through to the end." Now the Red Guard movement took off. Soon Beijing students were proselytizing around the country, as well as on their own campuses.[18]

The Red Guard Rallies

Attracted by what was happening in Beijing and availing themselves of the opportunity provided by the now extended summer vacation, out-of-town students had descended on Beijing in ever larger numbers since June. At this point it was not yet official policy to welcome out-of-town students. On August 12, in an internal memorandum that was the basis for an oral report to Mao, the CCRG minuted: "The provinces and municipalities should be urged not to mobilize large numbers of people to travel to Beijing. The people who have already come to Beijing should be urged by the provinces and municipalities to return home and make revolution. There are already 7,000 people from outside Beijing living on the Tsinghua University campus, and food and accommodation have already become a problem." But Mao disagreed, telling the CCRG that one of the reasons the Soviet Union had "discarded Leninism" was that "too few people ever saw Lenin in person." Mao insisted that "large numbers of China's younger generation—the more the better—should be given the opportunity to see the older generation of revolutionary leaders in person," namely, himself.[19] In the Little Red Book, *Quotations from Chairman Mao,* which would become the bible of the Red Guards, appeared the words: "The world is yours, as well as ours, but in the last analysis, it is yours. You young people, full of vigor and vitality, are in the bloom of life, like the sun at eight or nine in the morning. Our hope is placed on you . . . The world belongs to you. China's future belongs to you."[20] There was a touch of megalomania in his attitude; he once recalled: "Our people are very disciplined, which has impressed me a lot. Once I was on an inspection tour of Tianjin, surrounded by tens of thousands, and all I had to do was wave my hand and they dispersed."[21] Accordingly, on August 16 Chen Boda started publicly urging students to come to, rather than stay away from, the national capital.[22] This invitation was the prelude to eight massive Nuremberg-style rallies, "reviews" of "revolutionary teachers and students" by the Chairman, most of them held in Tiananmen Square, between mid-August and late November.

According to one participant in the first rally, on August 18, the decision to hold it was made only the day before. Starting at one in the morning on August 18, a million students and teachers were led into Tiananmen Square. At five, significantly wearing an army uniform, Mao came down from the rostrum atop Tiananmen itself, from which the leaders traditionally reviewed National Day parades, and mingled with the crowds, shaking hands. At eight, some students were issued silk Red Guard armbands and taken to meet Mao and his colleagues, including Jiang Qing, emerging from obscurity to helicopter into the twenty-fifth place in the official ranking. Close up, the leaders were less impressive than they were to the teenagers down below, hysterically chanting: "Long Live Chairman Mao! [*Mao zhuxi wan sui!*]" The Chairman "looked older than I had imagined and more than half his hair was white. His face showed marks of old age and did not glow either, as it was supposed to. His movements were sluggish. He was a senile old man . . . Lin Biao . . . was a small, thin, weak man, his face as white as paper."²³ Despite his appearance, Lin Biao signaled his new role by making a seventeen-minute speech to the assembly, calling on his young audience to energetically destroy all the "old ideas, old culture, old customs, and old habits of the exploiting classes."²⁴

At some point during the more than six-hour-long rally, Mao turned to Lin Biao and observed: "The scale of this movement is very large. It really has managed to get the masses mobilized. Insofar as the ideological revolutionization of the people of the entire country is concerned, it carries immense significance."²⁵

The high point of the day was when Song Binbin, one of the students chosen to meet the leaders, was allowed to put a Red Guard armband on Mao's arm, thus obtaining his imprimatur on the movement and signaling its legitimacy nationwide.²⁶ When Mao learned that her given name was "suave," he said that she ought rather to "be martial." Reading this exchange, some elite Red Guards wondered if Mao meant that they had been too refined in their activities until then.²⁷ The exchange certainly reinforced his earlier signals. In celebration, the drab and seemingly generic name of the Middle School for Girls Attached to Beijing Normal University was changed to the "Red 'Be Martial' School."

Understandably, some of the older CCP leaders found the rallies exhausting. While their colleagues holding a copycat rally in Shanghai on August 19 took advantage of heavy rainfall and darkness to let body doubles wave at the passing crowds part of the time, this was not something that Mao and his colleagues could do.²⁸ After the second rally, on August 31, at which Jiang Qing acted the part of master of ceremonies, Mao began to show the first signs of fatigue. Confined to his bed and running a slight fever, the seventy-two-year-old Chairman wrote to Lin Biao on September 13 to prepare him for the possibility that *he* might have to be the most senior participant at the next rally, slated for the following day or the day thereafter.²⁹ Surprisingly, according to Mao's doctor, the seemingly frail and sickly Lin, who normally led a mole-like existence in his home, was rejuvenated by the rallies: "The sun shines brightest in Beijing during the fall, and the wind atop Tiananmen is strong, but Lin Biao apparently no longer feared sun or drafts. He accompanied Mao each time, smiling and waving to the crowds below."³⁰ In the end, Mao regained enough strength in time to be present. As the leaders moved about the rostrum during the four-hour rally on September 15, at which Kang Sheng took over the master of ceremonies role from Jiang Qing, they were followed by Xinhua News Agency photographers whose job it was to record the proceedings for posterity. On this day, they slipped up. In the wake of the rally, the CC Propaganda Department failed to find a photograph showing Deng Xiaoping standing next to Kang. In the end, a cut-and-paste job was distributed nationwide, showing the head of Deng grafted onto the body of Chen Yi.[31]

As this episode demonstrates, media coverage of these events was tightly controlled. After the rally on October 1, National Day—at which 1.5 million people were present, including what the papers described as "friends from some seventy countries from five continents"—the square became the scene of an ugly incident that was kept out of the news, lest it be picked by the "imperialists, revisionists, and reactionaries of the world" to "tarnish the glorious image" of Mao's leadership and the Cultural Revolution. Once the official parade was over, Mao insisted on going for a motorized greeting session in the company of some of his "closest comrades-in-arms." Total chaos promptly ensued, in the words of Wang Li, as "the masses surged forward to shake Chairman Mao's hand and the cars were unable to move any farther." Beijing Garrison commander Fu Chongbi, whose men shared responsibility for the leadership's safety, had three ribs broken as he desperately sought to clear the way for the motorcade. About ten people were trampled to death, and nearly a hundred were injured.[32] Yet Mao was insouciant. Safely back behind the walls of the Forbidden City, he told the CCRG: "We're going to carry the Great Cultural Revolution through to the end: if it comes down to it, we'll all go down together!"[33]

For most of the rank and file in the square at any of the eight rallies, it was simply a day to remember. By November, when the last rallies were held, more than 200,000 people were coming on overcrowded trains to Beijing each day; on peak days the number reached 290,000, according to Zhou Enlai, who was in charge of logistics.[34] Even after the last rally, an additional 50,000 arrived hoping to see Mao, and an additional 60,000 wishing to submit petitions about the progress of the Cultural Revolution back home. At one point, there were no less than 3 million temporary visitors in Beijing, in addition to its permanent population of 7.7 million.[35]

Arriving at Beijing's main railway station or Yongdingmen Station, provincial Red Guards took buses or trekked to one of a few dozen Red Guard Reception Stations, where staff in turn directed them to one of over 4,000 reception points scattered across the city.[36] Military personnel from the Beijing Military Region were in charge of assigning them accommodation, either on one of the 59 college or 300 middle school campuses, or in factories or private homes. In their new quarters, other junior officers drilled them so that they would be ready to participate in the next rally. The cost of the operation was high, 15 yuan being allocated for one month's food for each Red Guard—there were meal coupons for breakfast (rice, water, pickles, and steamed buns) and lunch (two steamed buns and a dish of cabbage and pork)—though free accommodation was supposed to last only a week.[37] Additional costs were incurred when some Red Guards were trampled on in the hustle and bustle of the rallies and ended up in Beijing's hospitals. Zhou later told the PSC that they remained "in excellent spirits and are very happy,"[38] unlike Beijing's citizens, who resented the upheaval and inconvenience the Red Guards caused.[39]

By the last rally, on November 26, Mao had manifested himself to some 12 million Red Guards from all over China.[40] For them, it was an experience like no other. In a letter to colleagues from a Shanghai Red Guard, a twenty-six-year-old middle school teacher wrote on the evening of the rally on September 15, after he had seen Mao in person: "I have decided to count today as my birthday. On this day, I began a new life!!!"[41] Sadly, this idealist's new life was a short one. He committed suicide on October 2 after being savagely beaten and brutalized by some of his students, who accused him of having gone to Beijing solely for the purpose of establishing "counterrevolutionary contacts."[42] Had he known of this none-too-rare casualty of the Cultural Revolution, Mao would have had no sympathy: "People who try to commit suicide—don't attempt to save them! . . . China is such a populous nation, it is not as if we cannot do without a few people."[43]

Revolutionary Tourism

Mao did not just wish to have as many Red Guards as possible come to see him with their own eyes. He also backed the idea of their crisscrossing the country and "igniting the fires of revolution." "We must support the great exchange of revolutionary experience by the masses!"[44] By early September, all relevant authorities had been informed by the State Council that Red Guards engaged in such exchanges were to enjoy free travel, board, and accommodation. A remarkable autumn and winter of revolutionary travel and tourism was about to begin, as young people—some of whom may have read a bowdlerized Chinese translation of Jack Kerouac's *On the Road*, which had appeared four years earlier—set off on the journey of a lifetime.[45]

Popular destinations included the sacred historical sites of the Communist revolution: Mao Zedong's hometown, Shaoshan; and the provincial capital of Hunan, where he had gone to school; the wild and rugged Jinggang Mountains in Jiangxi province, where the Red Army had set up some of the first revolutionary base areas; the town of Zunyi in Guizhou province, where during the Long March, according to official histories, "Comrade Mao Zedong had once and for all established his leading position inside the party"; and the caves of Yan'an, the moral center of the revolution after 1937.[46] In addition, there were China's great cities, such as Shanghai, where the CCP had been founded in 1921. By the end of 1966, 1.6 million Red Guards from all over China had passed through the southern metropolis of Canton, ostensibly to visit the KMT Peasant Movement Training Institute, where Mao had lectured forty years earlier.[47] The truly adventurous traveled to really exotic destinations: official post–Cultural Revolutionary histories note that approximately 1,000 Red Guards from China proper (Sichuan and Beijing) managed to get to Tibet to "exchange revolutionary experiences." By mid-November 1966, in part because the winter made further travel into the region all but impossible, in part because of a hastily drawn-up policy of dissuading Han students from traveling into ethnic minority areas, their numbers grew no further.[48]

In the words of Zhou Enlai, speaking in the Beijing Workers' Gymnasium to an eager and enthusiastic Red Guard crowd about to head south, the "great exchange of revolutionary experiences" was an "excellent thing."[49] In conversation with Mao, on a more sober note, Zhou had let it slip that a lot of things needed to be prepared. Unperturbed, Mao responded: "What is there to prepare? Are you saying they might not find anything to eat where they're going?"[50] In Shanghai, which had been visited by 374,800 "revolutionary teachers and students" by the second week of October, the mayor fretted about the impact that revolutionary tourism was having on industrial production.[51] "It's no use saying the Central Committee doesn't know what's going on," he told his colleagues. "They know all right. The question is, do they see it in the same real terms as the people at the grass roots?" An Australian language teacher living in Shanghai at the time commented: "This statement attributed to Mayor Cao has the ring of truth around it. Once again we get the picture not of an evil man conspiring against the students or the Mao group but of a sincere administrator, genuinely concerned about the impact of the Cultural Revolution on Shanghai's industry and earnestly trying to make the CC see reason."[52]

Many Red Guards imagined themselves to be reliving the Long March, realizing the revolutionary myths on which they had been reared in school textbooks, in movies, and, if they were from an elite background, in the stories their parents had told them. Thirty years later, the daughter of two cadres in the Central Investigation Department, not quite sixteen and in middle school at the time, reminisced:

> We were not tourists. Our trip was not for fun and comfort. We were soldiers going out to war against an old world. In fact many of us thought at the time that this trip would be a turning point in our lives, the beginning of our careers as "professional revolutionary experts." *From now on, we no longer need envy our parents for their heroic deeds in revolutionary wars and feel sorry because we were born too late. Like the forerunners we admired, now we are going to places where forces of darkness still reign and dangers lurk. We will enlighten and organize the masses, dig out hidden enemies, shed our blood, and sacrifice our lives for the final victory of the Cultural Revolution.*[53]

The contemporary diaries of those who traveled reveal how hectic and exciting it all must have been. No longer did they compose elaborate entries the length and content of which had reflected a stifling boredom; now the handwriting deteriorated as they hurriedly jotted down bare-bones notes of what, when, and where on the basis of which the diarist perhaps hoped he or she would someday be able to reconstruct the fuller picture. On November 2, the Nanjing student whose thoughts on encountering a beggar are translated in Chapter 3 above wrote in his diary:

> Arrived in Tianjin at 1:10 A.M. on October 29, 1966. Stayed in the municipal People's No. 1 Middle School [formerly the Chengyouzhuang No. 2 Middle School], second building, classroom No. 6. Bought a Chairman Mao commemorative badge, visited the Red Flag and People's department stores, and walked along the Hai River. Today we're at the Tianjin Municipal Party Committee, reading big-character posters.[54]

Unlike the young travelers, parents and grandparents left behind were in two minds about the exercise. So much could obviously go wrong. In public, adults may have been prepared to agree that all such activity was for the good of the revolution, but in private they felt an understandable anxiety, and sometimes with good reason. Years later, a retired PLA officer in Shanghai recalled:

> An old comrade-in-arms of mine, in Beijing, had a son in middle school who when the great exchange of revolutionary experiences began took his little twelve-year-old sister along and set off from Beijing via Shijiazhuang, Taiyuan, Xi'an, Ürümqi, Zhengzhou, Wuhan, Guangzhou, and Changsha (where he

lost his little sister; he searched everywhere but was unable to find her), to Shanghai; then on to Qingdao, Dalian, and Tianjin, before returning to Beijing. What kind of "exchange of experiences" was that? Roaming all over the place . . .[55]

The most lethal consequence of the nationwide "great exchange of revolutionary experiences" has gone mostly unnoted. Before the autumn of 1966, outbreaks of epidemic cerebral-spinal meningitis had been rare in China, and highly localized, in large part because of a low degree of popular mobility. The sudden movement under extremely cramped and unsanitary conditions—"I pretty much spent the entire journey from Urümqi crammed into the toilet together with a group of other girls," a young woman from Shanghai recalled years later[56]—of millions of people from every corner of the country put an end to this situation and paved the way for a massive epidemic. By the end of 1967, 3.04 million cases of cerebral-spinal meningitis and more than 160,000 fatalities had been recorded. An official source notes that "worst affected were youths and children, a substantial number of whom were 'Red Guard' participants in the 'great exchange of revolutionary experiences.'"[57]

Eliminating the "Four Olds"

The prime task laid down in the CC's decision on the Cultural Revolution was the elimination of the "old ideas, culture, customs, and habits of the exploiting classes," an aim that was reaffirmed in Lin Biao's speech, approved in advance by Mao, to the August 18 rally, when the new heir apparent exhorted Red Guards to "energetically destroy" the "four olds."

During the summer months, only scant attention had been paid to this injunction, most likely because few people really knew what it was meant to entail in concrete terms. It did, however, become popular enough as a general idea to permit someone like the mayor of Shanghai to advocate the "destruction of the four olds, and fostering of the four news" without having to explain further what he meant.[58] On August 18, Zhou Enlai had shared with municipal cadres busy drawing up the plans for the rally on National Day his own idea of a destruction of "old habits": "This year," he told them, "we shall break with convention and have the parade march from west to east!"[59]

When the Red Guard movement took off, "destroying the four olds" became one of the first "glorious tasks" assigned this iconoclastic shock force by

Mao's heir apparent and the CCRG. At the second rally, Lin Biao showered praise on those Red Guards who during the past two weeks had "taken to the streets to sweep away the 'four olds.'" Zhou Enlai concurred fully, calling on his audience to join him in a "salute" to the heroism shown by "little Red Guard generals who destroy the 'four olds' and foster the 'four news.'"[60]

From the crudely written handbills, stenciled broadsheets, posters, and other ephemera that have survived, one gleans something of the eclectic nature of the movement. On August 24, Red Guards in Beijing's No. 66 Middle School presented the municipal party committee, Bureau of Public Security, and Bureau of Labor with a crude "Diplomatic Note" in which they called on urban neighborhood committees across Beijing to force undesirable "elements" to labor under "mass supervision," called for the imposition of a twenty-five-year age minimum on smoking and drinking, and demanded the immediate closure of all privately managed hospitals, restaurants, and barber shops.[61] An order *(mingling)* from the same time signed by "Mao Zedong-ism Red Guards" in Beijing's No. 6 Middle School demanded that all "members of the exploiting classes" henceforth "collect their own feces and deposit them in the night-soil collector carts themselves." The "revolutionary masses" were called upon to "supervise" the process of collection and deposit.[62] In mid-September, Red Guards in the Beijing School of Industry addressed an "Appeal to Fellow Students across Beijing" and told those who wanted revolution to "step forward" and those who weren't revolutionary to "piss off!" More than anything else, the authors of the appeal directed their ire at young people whose daily routine consisted simply of "three meals and a shit" and who instead of making revolution abused the relative freedom that the Cultural Revolution granted them by "knitting string bags and sweaters" or "preparing for the upcoming winter cold."[63] On August 2, Red Guards in Beijing's No. 29 Middle School distributed a broadsheet that denounced the foul and vulgar language in use in many parts of Beijing and called on "revolutionary comrades everywhere" to join in an effort to eradicate such language. "Slang that is intolerable to the ear and extremely shameless" was an "opium of the working people" and therefore "incompatible" with Beijing's reputation as "the home of the party center and Chairman Mao and the birthplace of the world revolution."[64]

Perhaps the most harmless aspect of the movement was the changing of names—streets, shops, schools, theaters, restaurants, hospitals, newspapers, journals, even the Red Guards' own given names, indeed anything that had a name in the first place. Personal names were changed from ones with "feudal" overtones to ones more fitting for a self-designated "revolutionary successor," names like "Protect Biao" or "Defend Qing."

In Beijing, Zhou Enlai allowed the name of the road on which the Soviet embassy was located to be officially changed from Yangwei Street to Anti-Revisionism Street, as requested by the Red Guards. But he warned the latter against attacking the embassy or pasting big-character posters on its walls, and sent extra garrison troops there to enforce his orders during the renaming ceremony.[65] Foreign journalists who had been specially invited estimated that the ceremony was attended by close to 100,000 Red Guards.[66] In Changsha, in response to a "demand by the masses," the name of the Zhongshan Library (named after Sun Yat-sen, the leader of the 1911 revolution) was changed back to Hunan Library, as it had been known in the winter of 1912–13, when Mao Zedong had spent some time there.[67]

Without exception, national- and provincial-level party papers promptly praised name changes like these as yet another proof that the Red Guards were "doing the right thing, doing the good thing!" The *People's Daily* editorial on August 23 called the changes "Excellent!" *Red Flag* rejected critics of the Red Guards who called them "both fanatic and childish."[68] Red Guards in neighboring Guangdong province even renamed Hong Kong. On September 16, *Reference News* carried a translation of an Associated Press telegram from Hong Kong which under the Xinhua headline "Red Guards Achieve Propaganda Victory" announced that, according to a spokesman for the colonial administration, "letters mailed from Red China to [Hong Kong but addressed to] 'Expel-the-Imperialists-City' *would* be delivered by the local postal authorities."[69]

For those who lacked such revolutionary creativity, Red Guards compiled lists of answers to the question once put by V. I. Lenin: "What is to be done?" A list of "one hundred proposals" for "destroying the old and fostering the new" put out by Red Guards in Beijing's "Maoism School" (which until only recently had been the Beijing No. 26 Middle School) included the following: "(No. 87): No manufactured goods in shops may be called by their Western names. Meaningful Chinese names must be used" and "(No. 95): Those who have [personal] names with feudal overtones will voluntarily go to police stations to change their names."[70] Now and then, chaos was the predictable outcome of uncoordinated name changes involving two or more competing groups of Red Guards.

Later, once the high tide of name-changing had passed, Zhou Enlai admitted that both he himself and Mao Zedong had found it a bit excessive at times. "You wanted to change the name of Tiananmen Square," he told Red Guards on

December 1, 1966, "but into what? Into 'The East Is Red'? . . . I asked the Chairman, and he didn't agree to changing it [to 'The East Is Red']. In fact he didn't want to change it at all . . . As for names, as long as they're not too feudal or too backward, then they're all right."[71]

The problem was that feudalism and backwardness lay in the eye of the beholder, and since Red Guards could not consult the premier in every instance, it was always safer for them to go along with changes than to oppose them. When a big-character poster was put up at a Beijing middle school proposing changes in dress and appearance, "Some Red Guards acted immediately. They stood on streets and stopped passersby to cut their narrow-legged pants and destroy their sharp-toed or high-heeled shoes. Girls' long braids were deemed feudal remnants and cut by force. Before Liberation women in China were not allowed to cut their hair short; now the Red Guards didn't allow them to wear it long."[72] An American member of the CCP, who witnessed such activities in Beijing's major shopping district, Wangfujing, observed: "It was comic opera. But tragedy flowed in its wake."[73]

7

Red Terror

The tragic side of the movement to "smash the four olds" began in the summer of 1966 with the searching of homes and the confiscation or destruction of property belonging to families of "bad" class background; in urban areas, this meant the bourgeoisie and petite bourgeoisie, in whose ranks many teachers and all former businessmen were classified.[1] In August and September, the homes of 33,695 families in Beijing were looted by Red Guards or people claiming to be Red Guards.[2] In Shanghai, 84,222 homes of "bourgeois" families were looted between August 23 and September 8; 1,231 were the homes of intellectuals or teachers.[3] In Beijing, Red Guards in slightly more than one month confiscated 103,000 liang (about 5.7 tons) of gold, 345,200 liang of silver, 55,459,900 yuan in cash, and 613,600 antique or jade pieces.[4] In Shanghai, in addition to large quantities of gold and jewelry, the Red Guards netted a great deal of cash: 3.34 million in U.S. dollars, 3.3 million yuan in other foreign currency, 2.4 million pre-Communist silver dollars, and 370 million yuan in cash and bonds.[5] In an official document circulated for reference at the central party work conference in October 1966, the confiscation by Red Guards all over China of a total of 1,188,000 liang (about 65 tons) of gold was praised as the "confiscation of the ill-gotten wealth of the exploiting classes."[6] After the Cultural Revolution, Shanghai set up a "Bureau for Sorting Looted Goods" to carry out an official policy of returning such items to their owners, but much of value had probably disappeared.[7] One Red Guard leader claimed at the time that Zhou Enlai accepted the idea of Red Guards' using confiscated money and goods "to cover the expenses they incurred" in the course of carrying out the Cultural Revolution.[8]

In cities across China, those who thought themselves fortunate not to have been targeted looked on in shock and bewilderment. A lab technician working in what in a bygone era had been Shanghai's Oriental Dispensary wrote in his diary on August 26, 1966:

Take ransacking people's homes: first they targeted capitalists and landlords, but soon they entered cadres' homes and the homes of persons attacked in the movement as well. At this point it is still getting worse, with similar things occurring in factories and enterprises. The name of the game is "destroy the four olds," but there are those who fish in troubled waters and seize the opportunity to attack others. Beware of pickpockets and scoundrels who seize the opportunity to molest and humiliate women! Some remove people's trousers and clothes in the street, cut their hair, and take their shoes. Forcing people to hand over all their books and magazines—bastards!

No doubt expressing what countless millions of other Chinese were feeling, he confided: "I can't explain what the actual task of the Red Guards is supposed to be. I don't know, and that's it."[9]

Nor were the Red Guards respecters of status if the person concerned was clearly bourgeois. On the night of August 29, Beida Red Guards broke into and trashed the house of Zhang Shizhao, an octogenarian onetime journalist, educator, and official, who had earned Mao's lasting gratitude more than forty-five years earlier for arranging financial assistance for the nascent CCP; indeed, Zhang had been one of a very exclusive group invited by Mao to celebrate his seventieth birthday in 1963. Zhang thus felt able to complain directly to the Chairman, and at Mao's prompting, Zhou Enlai was able to issue an order protecting the residences of a number of senior non-Communists, notably deputy state chairperson, Song Qingling, transferring some of them to PLA Hospital No. 301 for better protection.[10]

Destroying National Treasures

In addition to confiscating and destroying private property and humiliating its owners or worse, Red Guards attacked public property. Xie Fuzhi later revealed to the Tsinghua middle school students, including some of the original "Red Guards," that "Chairman Mao often asks us why middle school students are such a destructive force, why they destroy public property. We cannot come up with an answer either."[11] By the end of the Cultural Revolution, 4,922 of the 6,843 officially designated "places of cultural or historical interest" in Beijing had been destroyed, by far the greatest number of them in August–September 1966.[12] The Forbidden City (Palace Museum) escaped only because Zhou Enlai got wind of a planned Red Guard attack. On August 18 he had the gates closed and ordered the Beijing Garrison to send troops to protect it; on August 28, he told representatives from a student umbrella organization, the Capital's Universities and Colleges Red Guards' Headquarters (HQ) (later known as No. 1 HQ), led by the daughter of Wang Dongxing, that the Forbidden City, the Great Hall of the People, the broadcasting station, newspaper offices, and airfields were absolutely off-limits. But when Zhou tried to follow up by issuing a nationwide directive down to county and regimental levels, listing a wide variety of protected establishments, Mao vetoed the document. In early September, Zhou tried again, drafting a ten-point memorandum laying down rules restricting Red Guard behavior, and then trying it out on a mixed group of old cadres such as Tao Zhu, Li Fuchun, and Chen Yi and Cultural Revolutionaries such as Kang Sheng, Jiang Qing, and Zhang Chunqiao. The old cadres supported him, the Cultural Revolutionaries did not, and so he dropped the idea. A month later, Zhou had to head off a move by a middle school Red Guard group to rename Beijing "East Is Red City" and to replace the stone lions and pillars in front of Tiananmen with bronze statues of Mao and some heroic figures from Chinese history. In mid-November he added the Diaoyutai compound, the ministries of defense, public security, and foreign affairs, and the State Planning Commission to the list of places to be particularly well guarded.[13]

Perhaps the most remarkable act of destruction of a priceless cultural relic centered on the Confucius Temple in Qufu county, Shandong province, some ten hours by train from Beijing. In November 1966, around 200 teachers and students from Beijing Normal University led by one Tan Houlan, a young cadre on leave from her ordinary job, enrolled at the university as a student to raise her formal educational credentials, descended on Qufu and announced their intention to "thoroughly demolish the Confucius Family Shop." Before leaving Beijing, Tan and her comrades had been in touch with the CCRG. When he heard of their plans, Chen Boda himself had decreed that it was all right to dig up and level the grave of Confucius, but he cautioned against setting the Confucius Temple and its contents on fire. Chen did not object to burning the memorial tablets, but at the same time he allegedly "did not advocate smashing the Han dynasty steles."[14] During their four-week stay in Qufu, teachers and students from Beijing joined forces with members of the local population and with like-minded students from the Qufu Teachers' Institute. Together they managed to destroy 6,618 registered cultural artifacts, including 929 paintings, more than 2,700 books, 1,000 stone steles, and 2,000 graves.[15] They organized local mass rallies at which Confucius was duly denounced, among other things for his edu-cational philosophy. At one rally, a local "activist in the study of Mao Zedong's Works" declared:

> To be "nurtured" on the thoughts of Confucius never did anyone any good and only produced cowardly bastards who exploit, oppress, cruelly injure, and bully other people. What those in favor of "educating" people with the thoughts of Confucius want is to foster landlords, rich peasants, counterrevolutionaries, bad elements, rightists, monsters and freaks, foster counterrevolutionary revisionist elements, and hire men and buy horses for a capitalist restoration on behalf of the capitalists. Our response is to say no a thousand times over, to say no ten thousand times over![16]

When Tan Houlan and her group returned to Beijing, they had to confront ru-mors that their destruction had not been efficient and thorough enough and that they had "just made a lot of noise, not mobilized the masses enough." Defending them in front of a critic, a member of the CCRG staff announced: "What do you mean 'just made a lot of noise'? That was already no mean feat!"[17]

In one of the more bizarre acts of destruction outside the capital, on August 27 Red Guards from three Shandong middle schools destroyed the grave of the nineteenth-century cultural hero Wu Xun. An illiterate beggar who used what-ever money he garnered to found schools, Wu Xun was attacked by party ideol-ogues in the early 1950s as a "propagator of feudal culture" who had failed to challenge the imperial system.[18] The Red Guards exhumed Wu Xun's corpse, walked with it to a nearby public square, held a mass sentencing rally, and finally broke it into pieces and burned it. On Hainan Island, the grave of Hai Rui, the righteous Ming official who had been "dismissed from office," was also de-stroyed.

The destruction of at least some public property was far more organized and officially sanctioned than is acknowledged today, involving the complicity of the local state and the direct responsibility of central leaders, including Zhou Enlai.[19] In Foshan, Guangdong province, for example, the municipal government issued the following decree:

> Because of the launching of the Great Cultural Revolution, in order to adapt to the called-for destruction of the "four olds," a decision has been made to annul the decision promulgated in 1962 that designated as key protected cultural relics certain urban sites, for example, the Hall of Scriptures Right Monastery, Em-

peror Guan's Shrine-on-the-Water, the Southern Springs Right Shrine, and the Ancestral Temple of the Prince's Daughter's Husband. From this day on, these sites no longer enjoy protection as municipal key cultural relics, and the cultural contracts entered into between them and the municipal Cultural Bureau are rendered null and void.[20]

One group of Red Guards was even accompanied by a state film crew that recorded for posterity their destruction of Buddhist statues and incense burners in a monastery in Beijing's Western Hills.

Public libraries also suffered considerably from the destructive activities of Red Guards in the autumn of 1966.[21] Yet the loss of books during that relatively brief flurry of activity was small compared with that caused by the state's cutback in funding and almost total neglect of libraries after 1966. By the end of the Cultural Revolution, one-third of China's 1,100 libraries at or above the county level had been closed, and more than 7 million library books had been lost, stolen, or destroyed in the provinces of Liaoning, Jilin, Henan, Jiangxi, and Guizhou alone.[22]

The CCRG used the media to spur on the Red Guards. On August 27, *Reference News* used Mao's words "To be opposed by one's enemies is a good thing—Not a bad thing!" as its headline for a front-page report to the effect that "the U.S. imperialists use every ounce of their energy to attack our Great Cultural Revolution." The next day, its "daily Mao-quote," in a box on the top left-hand corner of page 1, read: "Everything our enemies oppose, we shall support; everything our enemies support, we shall oppose." A second report quoted the American press as saying that the CCP's new "thug rule" was nothing new, but something already tried and tested by Adolf Hitler. Off and on during the weeks and months that followed, *Reference News* would cite Chiang Kai-shek, Ch'en Li-fu, *Pravda,* and the Vatican as comparing the Red Guards to "wild beasts" and "rampaging hordes of destructive brutes."

When rumors began to circulate that the destruction had perhaps been excessive, *Reference News* promptly began printing translations from foreign sources of a different kind. In September, a telegram from an East German source was published under the heading *"Neues Deutschland journalist based in Beijing admits: China gives proper protection to historical relic."* By November, earlier reports in which the news agencies of the "imperialists and revisionists" lamented the wanton destructive actions of the Red Guards were replaced by accounts from recent French and Japanese visitors to China, the headlines of which asserted that "China's ancient works of art are being well preserved" and "Red Guards protect cultural artifacts."

Repatriation or Humiliation

Private citizens of "bad" class background who merely had their property confiscated, stolen, or destroyed were lucky. Some urban residents were thrown out of their homes altogether and forcibly repatriated to the villages whence their ancestors had come. According to a Beijing Red Guard handbill, such steps were taken "in order to make our capital purer and redder, and give our great seventeenth National Day a clean welcome."

In Beijing and elsewhere, the repatriation process involved tacit cooperation between Red Guards and the authorities.[23] In the capital, the program was enforced by the "West City Pickets," an elite Red Guard organization that enjoyed material support and political backing from the State Council General Secretariat and the municipal authorities, doubtless because its members included the children and grandchildren of cadres at key institutions.[24] The Pickets were funded through the State Council's Department of Administrative Affairs, the bureau that provided government funding to China's "democratic parties" and official "mass organizations."[25] Office space, two government trucks, two jeeps, and one motorcycle were put at their free disposal, in addition to large numbers of bicycles and bullhorns.[26]

One of the leaders of the West City Pickets was a son of Foreign Minister Chen Yi. In January 1967, a rumor circulated among students in Beijing that he had been sentenced to death for "excesses" he had supposedly committed during his tenure as Pickets leader, and that he had been reprieved because he was underage.[27] At the party center, his father was among those who endorsed the policy of repatriation, albeit reluctantly, telling Red Guards on August 30: "It is very good to repatriate the 'five black categories,' but the Red Guards should make contact with local police stations, and not cause the deaths of the people they repatriate . . . Some say I'm speaking up on behalf of the 'five black categories,' but that's not what I mean."[28]

Under enormous pressure to support the repatriation process regardless of the circumstances, party members did their best, but did not always succeed. A lesser cadre with the municipal Higher People's Court had to witness her ailing mother's forced expulsion from Beijing; later news arrived of her suicide en route to the ancestral home in Hebei, where the family had been landlords before 1949.

Although she lodged no complaint or protest, the daughter spoke with some sadness about the suicide to a colleague whose mother was also short-listed for repatriation. This act was enough to make the party branch to which she belonged charge her with "failing to draw a clear line of demarcation" between herself and her "wicked landlord mother." Doubting the wisdom of the party's policies was tantamount to taking a "seriously erroneous political stand."[29]

At lower levels, repatriation was more actively supported by party activists, police, and residential committees with access to lists of who was a "landlord element, rich peasant element, reactionary, hooligan, or rightist." In many cases, repatriation became a convenient way for crowded urban residents belonging to one of the "five red categories"—workers, poor peasants, soldiers, revolutionary cadres, martyrs' relatives—to secure additional housing space for themselves and their next of kin. Between August 18 and September 15, some 77,000 residents of Beijing, 1.7 percent of the city's population, were ejected from the capital. Of the total, some 30,000 were merely the spouses or children of "monsters and freaks."[30] In China as a whole, some 397,000 urban "monsters and freaks" were forced to return to their ancestral villages during the same period.[31]

For the top-level "revisionists," a different fate was in store: regular humiliation in front of tens of thousands of screaming Red Guards. These spectacles, often incited by the CCRG and addressed by its leaders, were political theater designed to rouse the youngsters to even greater fury against Mao's supposed enemies. Documentaries shot by state film crews show tens of thousands of people packed into a sports stadium, shouting slogans, their clenched fists in the air, and humiliated revisionists with signs hanging round their necks ("counterrevolutionary revisionist So-and-so") being forced down on their knees, roughed up, and abused physically and verbally. Between April 23 and October 27, 1967, Minister of Public Security Xie Fuzhi alone approved the convening of more than 100 large municipal-level mass rallies all over Beijing at which deposed senior members of the central and Beijing municipal government and party organizations were struggled. The leaders included Peng Zhen (on fifty-three occasions), Peng Dehuai, and others.[32] Thousands of lesser rallies, organized by a city district, a factory, or perhaps jointly by a group of universities, were convened in Beijing alone. Starting in the winter of 1966–67, the whole pattern was repeated all over China.

On December 12, 1966, Beijing's acting mayor, Wu De, gave the keynote speech at the first of this long series of rallies, organized jointly by a number of campus-based Red Guard groups. On this day, the latter had managed to cram

120,000 of their members and supporters into the preferred venue, the Beijing Workers' Stadium (designed to hold two-thirds that number). Wu De, a long-time party official who had been transferred to Beijing from the Northeast, denounced his former superiors and peers as the "scum of the party, the scum of the people, who colluded in a scheme to usurp the power of the party, the power of the army, and the power of the government." While the crowd shouted slogans, he continued: "Our fight against them is a life-and-death struggle! Today, you have dragged them out and exposed them to the light of day, and this is an excellent thing and a great victory for Mao Zedong Thought!"[33] On this occasion the most important of the more than a dozen party "scum" dragged out and "struggled" were the former leaders of the Beijing apparat, including Peng Zhen, Liu Ren, Wan Li, Zheng Tianxiang, and Wu Han.[34]

On April 10, 1967, Kuai Dafu's Jinggangshan organization at Tsinghua University, with the full cooperation of the central authorities and logistical support from the Beijing PLA Garrison, organized a huge on-campus rally attended by an estimated 300,000 curious onlookers at which the wife of Liu Shaoqi, Wang Guangmei, and more than 300 other so-called revisionists and capitalist roaders were publicly humiliated.[35]

Red Guard Circuses

The most gruesome aspects of the movement to smash the "four olds" and expose "monsters and freaks" were the torture and killing of innocent people and the suicides that were the final options of many who had suffered intolerable physical and mental abuse. There were many instances of humiliation and torture, and some of deaths, in Beijing and the provinces, during the "fifty days," especially when the work teams encouraged rather than restrained students.[36] In elementary schools alone in Beijing's six suburban districts, altogether 994 persons had been beaten and "struggled" between June 1 and June 25, 1966.[37] But it was only after Mao announced that "to rebel is justified" that the red terror really began. In August and September, altogether 1,772 people were murdered in Beijing.[38] In Shanghai in September there were 704 suicides and 534 deaths related to the Cultural Revolution.[39] In Wuhan during this period there were 32 murders and 62 successful attempts at suicide.[40]

Crucial in making possible the widespread mob violence of the autumn of 1966 was Central Document Zhongfa [1966] 410; Mao ratified it and it was issued on August 22. Consisting of a report to Mao and the party center from the

Ministry of Public Security titled "Mobilizing the Police to Suppress the Student Movement Is Strictly Prohibited," it ruled that

> not under any pretext is it permitted to mobilize the police to interfere with or suppress the student movement . . . the police, we reaffirm, must stay out of the schools . . . and not arrest anyone in the course of the movement, unless that person is a counterrevolutionary of whom it can be proved that he has murdered, practiced arson, poisoned people, engaged in sabotage, or stolen state secrets and so forth, in which case he should be dealt with according to the law.[41]

At a meeting of police officers in Beijing, Minister Xie Fuzhi tried to explain in practical terms how the police were meant to proceed from now on:

> I've just come back from a meeting at the center and want to say a few words: We must protect and support the Red Guards . . . Recently the number of people killed has gone up, so let us try to talk the Red Guards out of it and persuade them to act in accordance with the Sixteen Points. First support, then persuasion. The Red Guards are obedient, so talk to them and try to make friends with them. Don't give them orders. Don't say it is wrong of them to beat up bad persons: if in anger they beat someone to death, then so be it. If we say it's wrong, then we'll be supporting bad persons. After all, bad persons are bad, so if they're beaten to death it is no big deal.[42]

In one Beijing suburb, police officers were told that the gist of Xie's remarks was that "we must not be restrained by regulations stipulated in the past, by the state, or by the public security organs." According to Xie, "the people's police should be on the side of the Red Guards, establish contact with them, become friends with them, and provide them with information about what the five kinds of elements are doing."[43]

The police contacted the Red Guards and relayed Xie's remarks. The Red Guards realized what he meant and acted accordingly.[44] After the rally arranged by the authorities in the Beijing Workers' Stadium on August 13, at which 70,000 watched the dozen or so "hooligans" being beaten up, and once Mao on August 18 had told his young guest on the rostrum that she really ought to "be martial," Red Guards began organizing their own "mass meetings to denounce and struggle the black gang." The first was held in Sun Yat-sen Park, just off Tiananmen Square; there the Red Guards denounced, humiliated, and physically abused thirteen city education officials (including the director of the municipal Education Bureau, who suffered a broken rib). Thereafter the situation deteriorated rapidly as previous restraints on violent behavior were lifted. In Beijing's western district alone, in the course of little more than two weeks, the violence left close to one hundred teachers, school officials, and educational cadres dead. The number of those injured was, according to one investigation, simply "too large to be calculated."[45]

In every one of eighty-five elite colleges, middle schools, and elementary schools throughout China investigated by a Chinese scholar after the Cultural Revolution, teachers were tortured by students. At twelve of them, a teacher was beaten to death; at one school, two teachers were murdered. Of the thirteen institutions at which killings of teachers occurred, eleven were middle schools and two were elementary schools. Of the eleven middle schools, four were girls' schools.[46]

The more fortunate teachers, though they may not have thought so at the time, were those assigned to humiliating tasks such as cleaning latrines. A working-class public latrine attendant—nicknamed the "Shit Samaritan" because of his kindnesses—later reminisced about them:

> Many professors and scholars were labeled counterrevolutionaries, and yes, they were assigned to clean toilets. For people like me who did this for a living, we suddenly found ourselves with nothing to do. I wanted to work, but the students in Mao's Red Guard wouldn't allow it . . . Since I was used to doing hard labor every day, I got really bored. Sometimes in the mornings and evenings I would sneak out to the toilet to coach the professors on their technique . . . when you forced professors to clean toilets they considered it a huge loss of status. On the surface they acted as obedient as dogs. But many of them couldn't take it and hanged themselves with their belts inside the toilet stalls.[47]

The Red Guards did not limit themselves to teachers. At Beijing No. 6 Middle School, located across the road from Zhongnanhai, where senior leaders lived, the Red Guards turned the music classroom into a jail. On the wall they wrote: "Long live the red terror," and from time to time they repainted the characters of the slogan with the blood of their victims, according to some, with chickens' blood, according to others. In that jail, they beat to death a student, a janitor, and a local resident. A fourth victim was a vice dean who died a few weeks after being released from three months' incarceration there.[48]

While most ordinary students found the experience of watching someone being beaten to death in front of their very eyes terrifying to say the least, some hard-core Red Guards (like the following martyr's daughter) positively reveled in the opportunity to take out "class revenge" on their hapless targets. Li XX, a twenty-two-year-old student in the East Asian Languages Department at Peking University, wrote the following in a big-character poster put up on the premises of the municipal party committee on September 2, 1966:

> The class enemies are extremely sinister and ruthless, and I really hate the reactionaries to death! It was class hatred that made me denounce Li Jianping at the mass rally on August 27 and [class hatred] that drove the masses to such popular fury. They beat her—a counterrevolutionary element sheltered by the old municipal party committee for so many years—to death with their clubs. It was an immensely satisfying event, to avenge the revolutionary people, to avenge the dead martyrs. Next I am going to settle scores with those bastards who shelter traitors, butchers, and counterrevolutionaries.[49]

A younger woman who at the time was a student in an elite middle school in Beijing, a school attended almost exclusively by the children of the staff of the CCP center's "five big departments," wrote many years later about her traumatic involvement in the beating to death of somebody who might have been a "class enemy": "We must have inquired into his family background and family status . . . [But] The only thing I remember clearly is the pair of white cotton shorts he had on that night." The event occurred in Guangzhou, where a group of Beijing Red Guards had been given wrong directions by a man they convinced themselves was probably a rapist:

> As the interrogation went on, the man confessed that he had committed all the crimes we could think of. The words that dropped out of his mouth turned into facts in our minds. And these "facts" fueled our hatred toward him. He was no longer a suspect. He had become a criminal, a real class enemy. We started to beat him.
> The next thing he did was a real shock to all of us. In a shower of fists, kicks, curses, and trashes, he suddenly straightened up and pulled his white cotton shorts down. He had no underwear on. So there was his thing, his penis. Large and black. It stuck out from a clump of black hair. To me it seemed erect, nodding its head at all of us.
> I couldn't help staring at it. I was dumbfounded. I was embarrassed. I was furious. My hands were cold, and my cheeks were on fire. For a few seconds, none of us moved. We were petrified.[50]

Had the Red Guard contingent been all-female, this might have been the end of the story. They were after all mere teenagers, while their "class enemy," in the memory of the woman telling the story, was "a big, stout man in his thirties."[51] But waiting in the wings were the male Red Guards:

> All the female Red Guards ran out of the classroom. We stayed in the corridor. The male Red Guards charged forward. On their way they picked up long bamboo sticks to hit him.
> We all hated him! I could not tell who hated him more. The female Red Guards hated him because he had insulted all of us. The male Red Guards hated him too, because he was a scum of their sex. By exposing himself, he had exposed all of them. They were stripped. They were shamed. This time they beat him hard. No mercy on him. He did not deserve it. He was a bad egg!
> The sticks fell like rain. In a few minutes, the man dropped to the ground. The sticks stood in midair. Then someone pulled his shorts back up. After that we streamed back into the classroom. We looked. He did not move. He did not breathe. This man was dead![52]

Not only was criminal responsibility for murders such as this one not pursued by the authorities at the time; even after the Cultural Revolution, the CCP's policy was essentially one of proscription and of not inquiring further into the circumstances. "Students and Red Guards who when the 'Great Cultural Revolution' began were under eighteen years of age," an official manual from the 1980s states, "who later realized and admitted their errors, and whose current behavior is good, are not to have it held against them that they participated in mass beatings with a fatal outcome."[53]

Even at this early stage, the violence was by no means limited to urban China or to schools. In the greater Beijing area, the worst killings occurred in Daxing county, on the southern outskirts of the capital, and in Changping county, north of the city. On August 26, the Daxing Bureau of Public Security released the contents of Xie Fuzhi's speech to the municipal public security conference. People in Daxing interpreted the spirit of what was coming down from above as the qualified sanctioning of popular violence against selected targets, the "five black elements." At the time, it was rumored that not only would commune, county, and Beijing city officials not interfere with acts of violence against such elements, but "even Premier Zhou supports it." In Daxinzhuang People's Commune (one of thirteen communes in the county where killings took place), the catalytic event was a meeting of brigade cadres called by the commune leadership on August 31, at which the commune head and secretary of the commune CYL committee relayed the latest "spirit" from on high, which they claimed to have picked up at a nearby labor reform camp. Almost certainly incorporating key elements of Xie Fuzhi's speech to the municipal public security conference, merged with their own attempts at actualization of what that speech might entail locally, they called for the immediate wholesale extermination of "landlord and rich peasant elements" and all their kin in Daxinzhuang. Extermination was a matter of urgency, they explained, in order to preempt a massacre by "class enemies" of poor and lower-middle peasants; it was alleged that in Macun brigade, located some eighteen miles away, and only vaguely known to most of the cadres present that day, the "class enemy" had already begun to attack. Over the next few days, what began as the beating of selected "landlord elements, rich peasant elements, reactionary elements, and bad elements" with "bad attitudes" quickly escalated into the systematic extermination of "four kinds of elements," the fifth element, rightists, being nonexistent in Daxing.[54]

Who actually carried out most of the brutal butchery of the innocent that ensued that night is still only imperfectly known. Red Guards from urban Beijing were apparently not involved, though tales of their exploits were already serving as "inspiration" to local youths. The killers are known to have included local militiamen and activists such as the chairman of the Poor and Lower-Middle Peasants' Association in one brigade, who killed sixteen persons; their corpses were thrown into a dry well and eventually covered over when the stench had become unbearable. In one brigade, the dead, and in some cases the not yet dead, were simply buried in whatever conveniently located ditch could serve as a mass grave. A Chinese investigative journalist was told in 2000 that in one brigade, a little girl and her grandmother had been buried alive. "Granny, I'm getting sand in my eyes!" had been the girl's final words, to which the old woman had responded, "Soon you won't feel it any more." Survivors explained to him that, in their opinion, the killings were partially the outcome of the harsh policy of the preceding years, the "four cleanups" in particular. The death toll reached 325, spread out over thirteen communes and forty-eight brigades in Daxing county. The oldest victim was eighty years of age, the youngest thirty-eight days. Some twenty-two households were completely wiped out.

Not all brigade cadres present at the fateful meeting in Daxinzhuang on August 31 were prepared to carry out the "extermination order." Three of them, who had only just returned from Peking University, where they had read big-character posters about the Cultural Revolution, decided among themselves that the order was so extraordinary that it would have to be confirmed somehow before they would be prepared to consider implementing it. When the meeting was over they rushed off to central Beijing, where after a long delay the staff of the Municipal CCP Committee Reception Office met with them and told them that it contravened central policy. Returning in a hurry to Daxinzhuang with this news, they were able to prevent an even greater massacre, though the immediate reaction on September 1 from those who in the meantime had done their best to carry it out was extremely hostile.[55]

On September 2, the central authorities issued *Zhongfa* [1966] 445 in a first attempt to bring the "red terror" under control. This document, containing a report drawn up at Zhou Enlai's suggestion by the Ministry of Public Security's CCP Group, was meant among other things to "clarify" the relationship between Red Guards and the police. It cautioned Red Guards against "entering public security organs and beating up local police," as doing so was "not in the interest of protecting the Great Cultural Revolution." Addressing itself to the police, it went on to explain that

the revolutionary enthusiasm with which the revolutionary masses demand to be allowed to enter prisons, detention facilities, and labor camps to struggle and punish criminals is understandable, but in order to avoid criminals' availing themselves of the opportunity to escape or to riot, we welcome the masses to provide us with materials, and permit the staff of the dictatorship to punish the criminals [in their stead].[56]

As winter set in, the "red terror" gradually subsided. Four months after the Daxing killings, on January 1, 1967, Wang Li told a gathering of cadres from the State Council Secretariat and the CC's General Office that "we went to Daxing to investigate . . . and the situation there is excellent." Wang reminded his audience that "a struggle of this magnitude cannot always proceed smoothly."[57] In June 1968, Minister Xie Fuzhi inquired at a meeting with officials from the rural counties surrounding Beijing about whether the murders in Daxing county had been properly dealt with, to which someone in his audience replied that the matter had "already been taken care of."[58] What this statement meant is uncertain, but a Red Guard who had been incarcerated for having opposed the brutal "class" violence waged at the time recalled many years later that the main accusation against the perpetrators had concerned not their original murders, but the "slowness" with which they had reacted to the order from above to desist from further murder.[59]

Between them, Mao and Xie Fuzhi, working toward the Chairman, had sanctioned a reign of terror. The youth of China had been brought up in a culture of violence that class struggle represented. Whereas party violence had normally been carefully controlled and calibrated, now the rules had been suspended. Freed from parental and societal constraints, youths, both girls and boys, had been unleashed to perpetrate assault, battery, and murder upon their fellow citizens to the extent their barely formed consciences permitted. The result was the juvenile state of nature, nationwide, foreshadowed in microcosm by Nobel Prize–winner William Golding in *Lord of the Flies*.

8

Confusion Nationwide

ao was convinced that experiments like the Cultural Revolution had to be bold, even reckless, if they were to stand a chance of success. Speaking allegorically on his favorite subject of swimming, and flaunting some classical erudition in the process, he had once made this point by invoking the words of the philosopher Zhuang Zi: "If water is not piled up deep enough, it won't have the strength to bear up a big boat."[1] The deeper the water, Mao explained, the better; swimming close to the shore for fear of drowning was simply not an option.[2] Having hundreds of thousands of teenagers destroy the "four olds" in an orgy of violence and destruction was one experiment; tacitly supporting slightly more mature university students in a head-on conflict with the local state was another.

While the first wave of mostly teenage Red Guards fanned out across China in search of opportunities to exercise their new powers of "revolutionary destruction" and to "exchange revolutionary experiences," members of an older generation of students on the nation's university campuses turned their energies elsewhere. Concerned with what would happen to them upon graduation, when jobs would be assigned at least partially on the basis of their political performance and not merely according to scholarly excellence, they were eager to see whatever blots might have ended up on their records during the summer officially expunged. Having been labeled anything from "rightists" and "fake leftists" to "anti-party elements" and "troublemakers" for having resisted the local authorities (that is, the work teams) during the summer of 1966, their own rehabilitation was a number-one priority. Instead of seeking to "zap forth a new proletarian world" like their younger brothers and sisters, they joined forces behind rather more concrete goals. For example, the founders of the "East Is Red Commune" organization on the campus of the Beijing Geological Institute charged the ministry party committee that had dispatched the work team to their campus with "defamation," insisting that through its actions it had "injured the reputation" of countless innocent individuals. The highest-ranking party officials in the ministry, they insisted, had to issue written apologies for their personal complicity in the continuing "political harassment and suppression" of commune members. Finally, they demanded the release of all documents pertaining to the "calumny and persecution" to which their members had been subjected. Threats of hunger strikes, violent brawls, and four chaotic sit-ins on the grounds of the Ministry of Geology finally achieved their objective. The "Red Flag" organization from neighboring Beijing Aeronautical Institute, whose members were making similar demands, had to sustain a vocal and highly visible round-the-clock demonstration outside the National Defense Science Commission for almost a month before they emerged "victorious," in part thanks to a personal intervention on their behalf by Chen Boda.

Local officials viewed these university-based organizations of the so-called revolutionary masses with ill-concealed suspicion, hostility, and resentment. Probably typical was the view of one senior cadre in the Shanghai public security sector, who observed that only "careerists, the dissatisfied, and those who wanted to be in the limelight" joined them, and that their raison d'être was threefold: boasting and bragging, late-night meals, and "exchange of revolutionary experiences."[3] But Mao took a very different view; in particular, he seemed to regard the organizations as the likely breeding ground for his own revolutionary successors.

During the summer of 1966, Liu Shaoqi and Deng Xiaoping had used the unorthodox means of relying on their own children not merely to find out what was happening at some of Beijing's key schools, but also occasionally to influence what was happening. Now it was Mao's turn to use the same ploy. In mid-August he sent his twenty-six-year-old daughter by Jiang Qing, Li Na, to make contact with the Beijing Geological Institute students who had just formed the East Is Red Commune. Armed with an identity card, Li Na (who had graduated from Peking University's History Department in 1965) first presented herself as Xiao Li from the CC General Office and stated that she had come to gather information on the progress of the political movement on campus. By the time she came around again a few days later, the leaders of the commune had discovered who she really was. She now told them openly that her father had asked her specifically to find out more about what had motivated and driven the "revolutionary teachers and students" who had clashed in open confrontation with the work teams and by extension the local party apparatus during the initial phase of the

Cultural Revolution. Fully aware of the unique power this private back channel to the CCP Chairman gave them, the leaders of the East Is Red Commune (only one of whom was a CCP member, most being CYL members) were able, over the months that followed, to communicate their ideas and political aspirations directly to Mao and—more important—to gain occasional insights into what Mao was thinking. On other university campuses in Beijing, similar covert one-on-one links were established between the leaders of selected organizations and lesser members of the Politburo and CCRG.

In September, twenty-four of the campus Red Guard groups formed an umbrella organization, soon to become known as the "Capital 3rd HQ," claiming a membership of nearly 5,000. They defiantly styled themselves the "minority faction" in admission of their status at the start of the movement, but also no doubt recalling Mao's pronouncements from the time of the Great Leap Forward about how it was always the privilege of a minority to grasp the truth ahead of others. The Capital 3rd HQ was "commanded" by one Zhu Chengzhao, a co-founder of the Beijing Geological Institute East Is Red Commune, with whom Li Na was at this point in regular contact. When Zhou Enlai addressed the members of the Capital 3rd HQ for the first time, at a mass rally on September 26, he told them: "You really bring together—and your views represent—the people who have been suppressed. That's why in your case 'to rebel *is* justified.' *(Stormy applause).*"[4] With high-level endorsements coming from all the right quarters, the power and influence of the Capital 3rd HQ grew rapidly. Significantly, its leaders made a point of deemphasizing the family background and class origins of rank-and-file recruits. On this point, they echoed the views of Lin Biao, who argued in October that "among those who belong to the five red categories there are those who aren't red, just as among those who belong to the five black categories there are those who aren't black. We must not let class origins determine everything. It is better still to distinguish between left, center, and right."[5]

One of the least known but most significant occasions on which the Capital 3rd HQ interacted with the central leadership was when they helped organize—"in accordance with Mao Zedong Thought," according to Wang Li[6]—four days of "hearings" about the progress of the Cultural Revolution. Wang Renzhong called the hearings in his capacity as deputy director of the CCRG, and Zhu Chengzhao helped him identify and invite around twenty representatives of university-based organizations belonging to the "minority faction." From September 17 to September 20, in front of a panel chaired by Zhang Chunqiao, Red Guard leaders such as Kuai Dafu, Tan Houlan, and others not only gave impassioned accounts of their "sufferings" since the start of the movement, but also offered opinions on what needed to be done next to put it on a "healthier" course. The detailed minutes of the hearings were never made public or even distributed to a wider audience, but they were presented to Mao and allegedly fed into his assessment of the situation. Later some of the key participants were to claim that they had proposed that the central leadership communicate high-level disagreements over the progress of the movement to the general public, and not just to a privileged, select minority. Unless information was shared more widely, there could be no talk of the Cultural Revolution's ever becoming a genuine "mass movement."

By October 1, six weeks had passed since the end of the Eleventh Plenum, yet Mao had yet to come up with a unifying name for the sum total of errors that had characterized the "fifty days" and for which he held Liu Shaoqi and Deng Xiaoping responsible. In the wake of the hearings, a number of alternative formulations had been tinkered with, but Mao was still unable to commit himself. His indecision was now holding up the publication of the next issue of *Red Flag*, which was meant to introduce a unifying name or label in a key editorial. In his National Day speech in Tiananmen Square, Lin Biao had referred to a "bourgeoisie opposing revolution-line," but as Zhang Chunqiao pointed out to Mao that evening, it was grammatically flawed and far from ideal. At the very last moment, Mao decided to go with "bourgeois reactionary line," and once it had appeared in print in the thirteenth issue of *Red Flag* (distributed seventy-two hours behind schedule) on October 3, it became one of the most famous "technical terms" of the entire Cultural Revolution.[7] The CCP center then circulated *Zhongfa* [1966] 515, which in an "Urgent Instruction" drawn up at Lin Biao's insistence called for the immediate, full, and public rehabilitation of all the countless students and others who had been victimized while the "bourgeois reactionary line" had held sway. (Mao's comment on the "Urgent Instruction" was "Very good, very important.")[8] At a mass rally organized by the Capital 3rd HQ in the Beijing Workers' Stadium on October 6, Zhou Enlai and the CCRG announced to 100,000 ecstatic "revolutionary teachers and students" from all over China: "This is to announce the rehabilitation of all those revolutionary comrades who [since May 16, 1966] have suffered, at the hands of leaderships at various levels or work teams, such things as repression, attacks, struggle, even suppression."[9]

The Central Work Conference

In October the topic of the "bourgeois reactionary line" and its lingering influence dominated a major central work conference of central party and government officials and senior regional and provincial party leaders from all over China. Intended at first to last for only three days, then for a week,[10] in the end, in a reflection of the complexity of the subject, the conference lasted for almost three weeks, from October 9 to October 28. The conference was meant to resolve what was seen as a widespread "problem of understanding": officials everywhere either had never understood what the Cultural Revolution was about in the first place, or else had only a very partial or skewed understanding of Mao's aims.

Mao at first did not attend, though he was kept up-to-date on what participants were saying. Most of the time, he allegedly was disappointed. Although no explicit opposition to the Cultural Revolution was being voiced, support was at best muted and certainly not informed. On October 25 he described the statements made during the initial stage of the conference as "not really that normal." Presumably it was this impression which prompted Mao to extend it. "Only during the latter stage of the conference, after the comrades from the center had spoken and traded experiences, did things proceed a bit more smoothly," he explained.[11] In the absence of clear pointers from Mao or someone empowered to speak in his stead, it was obvious that participants had no idea what accorded with or violated Mao's grand design. Working toward the Chairman was hard for everyone.

Marking the conclusion of the first stage of the conference, on October 16 Chen Boda distributed to the delegates the text of a report titled "Two Lines in the Great Proletarian Cultural Revolution." On the same day he also read the text at a plenary session in the Great Hall of the People, but the printed text had been distributed beforehand at the suggestion of the Chairman, who may have feared that many in the audience would not be able to understand Chen's heavy Fujian accent. Revised repeatedly by Mao both before and after its delivery, the report amounted to an official assessment of the progress of the Cultural Revolution since Mao's return to Beijing on July 18.[12] It contained at least some of the pointers the participants had been waiting for.

The first, comparatively short, section of Chen's report described the situation as "excellent." The second section, on the "continuing two-line struggle," set out to explain why the Cultural Revolution was still encountering widespread resistance. One reason was the "lingering impact" of the bourgeois reactionary line. Chen made special reference to the increasingly ambiguous role of the sons and daughters of high-level officials; he described how some of them, as Red Guards, claimed to be the obvious successors of the revolution by birthright. Such a claim, he stated, was in total violation of Mao Zedong Thought. Some of these youngsters were even "about to embark on a revisionist road." In the third section of his report, Chen addressed himself directly to the many ordinary officials across China who made up what he called the "fearful" faction. They were utterly wrong, he said, to believe that the Cultural Revolution appeared to be mostly about "the masses acting recklessly" and "opportunists joining up with careerists, thugs, brutal savages, and the like to assume the role of Cultural Revolution 'activists.'" Claims of this kind were almost identical with those being made in the foreign press; hence they were obviously wrong and unacceptable. In the fourth and final section, Chen again addressed the Red Guards directly and impressed upon them the importance of "adhering to Chairman Mao's class line and uniting the majority."[13]

When Chen criticized the work teams, the irony would not have been lost on his audience that he himself had headed one of the first work teams of the Cultural Revolution. Indeed, while acting as the spokesman of Mao's "proletarian headquarters" in the Great Hall of the People, Chen was himself coming under fire in the offices of the *People's Daily*, where his team had held sway during the "fifty days." Some newspaper staffers were now claiming that Chen himself had in fact been a most faithful executor of the dreaded "bourgeois reactionary line." Chen's defenders, like the senior commentator Wang Ruoshui, argued that, on the contrary, he had managed to work his way around the "restrictions imposed by comrade Deng Xiaoping" and had "resolutely implemented and defended a proletarian revolutionary line represented by Chairman Mao."[14] By November, Chen Boda's critics were on the defensive, trying vainly to rebut charges of seemingly being "left" but in actuality being on the "right."[15]

On October 23, after conference participants had had a week to digest Chen's report, the two party leaders held responsible for the "bourgeois reactionary line" finally delivered their self-criticisms to a plenary session. Liu admitted to, and criticized himself for, having committed two distinct sets of "errors." The first were those of the summer, when he had been in day-to-day charge of the center in Mao's absence. These he was prepared to characterize as "serious errors in line" and as "right-opportunistic in nature." Citing verbatim a formulation used by Mao in "Bombard the headquarters," Liu conceded having "adopted the reactionary stand of the bourgeoisie, enforced a bourgeois dictatorship, and struck down the surging Great Cultural Revolution movement of the proletariat." The second set of errors were those "errors in principle and errors in line" that he had committed on various occasions in the past. Among these, the most serious, he admitted, were the two alluded to by Mao in "Bombard the headquarters," namely the "right deviation" of 1962 and the "seemingly 'left' but actually rightist erroneous tendency" of 1964. Nowhere in his self-criticism did Liu refer to himself as a "revisionist."[16]

Deng's self-criticism was significantly more personal in tone than Liu's. It dwelt at length on the ideas, habits, behavior patterns, and personality traits that supposedly inclined him to commit "errors": "I can definitely say that if I had been more modest at the time and listened more to the views of others and, in particular, constantly reported to and asked for instructions from the Chairman, I would certainly have received his instructions and help, which would have helped me correct my mistakes in time." Deng also spoke on a much more upbeat note than Liu about the Cultural Revolution, describing it as something that would "prevent China from ever changing color and [help China] avert the danger of revisionism and capitalist restoration." He ended by giving Lin Biao his strongest personal endorsement as Mao's new "assistant and successor" and announced that from now on he intended to emulate Lin where it mattered the most: "The one and only dependable way in which someone who has committed errors like myself can correct those errors and [once more] manage to do something useful for the party and for the people is by learning in earnest from comrade Lin Biao—by learning his way of holding high the red banner of Mao Zedong Thought and his way of creatively studying and applying the works of Chairman Mao." Like Liu, Deng refused to refer to himself as a "revisionist." But in what amounted to a highly significant distinction, he was—unlike Liu—prepared to speak of what he had done together with Liu in the summer as actually representing a "bourgeois reactionary erroneous line."[17] This was something that Liu refused to do: in two further self-criticisms, one in April and the other in July 1967, Liu still did not use Mao's all-important label, and seemed to imply that he was really unable to fathom what it referred to.[18] Neither Liu nor Deng, of course, ever admitted to having knowingly and intentionally opposed the "proletarian correct line represented by Chairman Mao."

The work conference was still in session when the party's propaganda machinery swung into action. Unmistakable signals were sent out showing just who was politically on the way out and who was on the way up. The day after Liu and Deng had made their self-criticisms, the Central Propaganda Department issued a nationwide alert, ordering the immediate suspension of the distribution and further sales of Liu's *How to Be a Good Communist.*[19] Mao called for Chen Boda's report to be "printed up in booklet form and distributed in quantities large enough to ensure that every party branch, every Red Guard contingent, has at least two copies."[20] On October 26, the day after Lin Biao—the only one of the CCP's five vice chairmen to whom the media still referred to by that title— had addressed a plenary session, the headline on the front page of the Xinhua News Agency's internal publication *Reference News* (with a readership perhaps in the tens of millions)[21] read: "Lin Biao is a plain, staunch, and modest person"; under it was a translation of a short laudatory biographical sketch of Lin by Edgar Snow published earlier in the month in a Japanese weekly and ending with the observation "Lin Biao's ascent to power shows that militant communism has the upper hand on bureaucratic communism."[22]

In closed communications with Liu and Deng before they delivered their self-criticisms, Mao had made some mildly positive comments on the texts. But when the official transcripts were finally distributed nationwide on November 9, Mao's remarks were not included. The official preamble that accompanied the transcripts read very differently: "At the central work conference, very many comrades criticized their self-criticisms and maintained that they were highly superficial. The aim of the bourgeois reactionary line they advanced in the Great Proletarian Cultural Revolution was to oppose the proletarian revolutionary line of the party center headed by Chairman Mao. In their self-criticisms, both evaded this substantial issue."[23]

If it was any consolation to Liu, Deng, and cadres guilty by association with them, Mao admitted in his final address to the conference that changes had been taking place at a remarkably fast pace, and some mistakes had been committed simply because people were unprepared and had not known what to expect. He assured his audience: "Who wants to topple you? I don't want to topple you, and I think the Red Guards don't necessarily want to topple you,"[24] and expressed the hope that "after this seventeen-day conference things will be a bit better."[25] The record does not give his audience's reaction, but could anyone have dared to trust him? Apprehension and a sense of impending doom would have been a more likely reaction, especially after Zhou Enlai's closing address: the premier prepared the audience for the likelihood of Red Guards' abducting them the moment they returned to their home bases. In the weeks that followed, Zhou expected everyone to "pass the test." The Cultural Revolution had only just begun, he said, and it might last "anywhere from five to ten years." There was still plenty of time to "accumulate experience." But for now, the most important thing was simply to "gradually understand the rules of the movement, gradually figure out its rules, and to discover—in the midst of chaos—the way ahead."[26]

In the immediate aftermath of the central work conference, once the implications of the fall of Liu Shaoqi began to sink in, the reopening of political cases in which the alleged crime had consisted of little more than criticism of Liu got under way. One case that would gain particular notoriety in 1967 was that of a man from Hunan who had been committed to a mental institution for criticizing Liu's *How to Be a Good Communist*. A senior official in the Ministry of Public Security was the first to call for a reversal of his case, but it was not until the CCRG realized its full propaganda potential that a discharge was finally arranged. In the spring of 1967, a play based on the story of—as Wang Li called him—*The Madman of the New Age* was performed in Tianjin and briefly touted as "the ninth model opera." An American Communist, moved to tears as he saw it, told the artists: "This is not a play that you are performing, it is a struggle! It reflects the Great Cultural Revolution the way it really is!" Unfortunately, once it became widely known that the original "madman" had not only criticized Liu Shaoqi's writings but some of Mao's as well, everyone who had been actively involved got into trouble.[27]

The Cultural Revolution Spreads to Farm and Factory

While the central work conference may have settled temporarily the issue of blame for the conduct of the Cultural Revolution during June and July, it did not deal with an issue that became increasingly serious during the autumn months: the disruption of the economy. As framed by Deng Xiaoping at the time, the "crucial question" was "whether or not we employ the method of extensive democracy and the method of mobilizing the masses to resolve certain long-standing, big, and difficult problems in our factories and mines."[28] The authorities used the media to try to convey the message to the population at large that China's economy as a whole was doing fine, despite what might appear to be the case in their own area. A steady stream of carefully edited reports from foreign news sources appeared in translation in *Reference News* under headings such as "China's Cultural Revolution Leads to Increased Productivity in Industry and Agriculture" *(Toyo keizai)*, "Advances in Production Thanks to Great Cultural Revolution" *(Neues Deutschland)*, and "Associated Press Forced to Concede Chinese Economy Made Strides in 1966."[29]

Was it desirable to have China's workers and peasants participate in the Cultural Revolution in the same way as students and urban intellectuals? In *People's Daily* editorials, the central party authorities had so far reiterated the initial policy from the summer of discouraging workers from participating in the Cultural Revolution, and of asking them instead to "remain at their production posts, and not leave their factories to engage in exchange of revolutionary experiences."[30] Zhou Enlai, who by the end of the year would have held over 160 meetings with representatives of the "masses," used almost every public occasion to call desperately for the insulation of the economy from the Cultural Revolution.[31] However, in their even more numerous face-to-face encounters with Red Guards and workers' representatives, the members of the CCRG downplayed the need to respect such stipulations. Jiang Qing justified this anomaly by stating categorically about China's factories that "wherever they're revolutionary, production is always doing fine." Lin Biao told those who maintained the opposite, and there were many, that "in principle, the Cultural Revolution should promote production, and in fact this has already been proven to be the case."[32] Foreign observers expressed guarded skepticism. One ambassador reported home from Beijing in the first week of January: "Industrial production, we are being told, has consistently surpassed the plan targets, which have never been made public, and is said in 1966 to have been a full 20 percent more than in 1965. Whether this—if it is correct—is due to an increased spiritual vigor brought about by intensive reading of Mao's writings or simply major investments made in the late 1950s must remain undecided."[33]

As on so many other occasions in the Cultural Revolution, the issue was decided not around a negotiating table in Beijing, but by rapidly unfolding events on the ground, in this case in Shanghai. On November 6, at a meeting in the Shanghai Liaison Station of the Capital 3rd HQ, worker "rebels" from seventeen factories across the city had formed what they called the Shanghai Workers' Revolutionary Rebels General Headquarters (WGHQ), with a thirty-two-year-old security guard by the name of Wang Hongwen as its "commander." The Shanghai Party Committee refused to recognize the new organization, thereby prompting close to 2,500 of its "members" to commandeer a train to go to Beijing to gain the center's support. When Zhou Enlai ordered the train stopped so that the problem could be solved locally, the WGHQ stalwarts found themselves stranded in the Shanghai suburb of Anting, where, in protest, they sat down on the rails and blocked traffic on the crucial Shanghai-Nanjing trunk line. There they remained for thirty-one hours, causing a transportation crisis,

141

until Zhang Chunqiao, dispatched by the PSC from Beijing, persuaded them to return to Shanghai for negotiations.[34] Zhang Chunqiao resolved the crisis by simply countermanding the municipal party committee's unanimous decision and giving way to all the WGHQ demands, including recognition and the assignment of all blame for their recent actions to the Shanghai party leadership. Zhang's betrayal infuriated the party committee as well as Tao Zhu, Zhang's superior as adviser to the CCRG, who called it "erroneous" and typical of someone "with no experience in handling mass movements." But in this crisis, Zhang had shrewdly and correctly calculated on getting ex post facto support from the CCP Chairman. On November 14, Mao called a meeting of the PSC at which he lectured from the PRC Constitution about the rights of citizens to organize, and went on to comment: "It's all right to act first and submit a memorial to the throne later. After all, first there are facts, then there are concepts." Tao Zhu was forced to make a self-criticism. Explaining his actions to workers in Shanghai, a jubilant Zhang took Mao's line, saying that in extending recognition to the WGHQ he had done no more than abide by the PRC Constitution: "As long as it's not a counterrevolutionary [organization], it's legal."[35]

But would this become national policy, or was Shanghai somehow special? This was not yet clear. The argument was joined at a series of meetings in November, convened to coincide with a national planning conference, and bringing together representatives from the State Planning Commission, the regional bureaus of the center, the industrial ministries, and China's major industrial cities, as well as members of the CCRG. The agenda was to "discuss matters in urgent need of resolution involving the movement and [industrial] production at present," and as it turned out such matters quickly overshadowed everything else, economic planning included.[36] The main bone of contention was a policy document being drafted by the CCRG that flatly rejected the notion of any conflict between production and revolution.

The meetings were stormy. When Zhou Enlai dropped in on one session he found ministers and vice ministers for railways, the metallurgical industry, water conservancy, and electric power in an uproar, and, he later recalled, "By the time I left, they were all on their feet." Most regional representatives were fiercely opposed to the creation of workers' organizations: a delegate from China's heavily industrialized Northeast insisted that if workers "are permitted to set up all kinds of organizations, there will be even more problems [than there already are]. Either they will begin fighting, or they will stop production." When the delicate subject of whether networking between workers and students was to be permitted came up, one minister asked: "The question is, are the students going to the factories to learn from the workers, or are they going there to lead the workers in making revolution? This is the essential question, the crucial question." Some participants demanded that a provision be drawn up, stating explicitly that "students and workers must not be permitted to join forces in rebellion."[37]

When the views of the ministers, planning officials, and regional representatives were presented to Mao on November 22, he rejected them as unacceptable. The members of the CCRG were immediately emboldened. Turning their ire primarily against Gu Mu, chairman of the State Capital Construction Commission, they hurled forth accusations that were nothing if not serious: Jiang Qing turned highly emotional and accused Gu Mu of having "absolutely no class feeling. Burdening the workers with rocks weighing hundreds of pounds—that revisionist stuff you're up to is counterrevolutionary through and through!" Kang Sheng dressed up his no less severe criticisms in concepts borrowed from Karl Marx's *Critique of the Gotha Program,* Lenin's *State and Revolution,* and Mao's hopelessly utopian musings at the height of the GLF: "Wages are still paid to each according to his work, and remnants of bourgeois right still exist . . . in our factories, where they are capable of generating capitalism. If the factories aren't handled well, we'll see revisionism emerge in them as well . . . From this point of view, the Great Cultural Revolution is even more important in the factories than in the schools."[38]

Unable to withstand this concerted onslaught and realizing that the views they had so far enunciated did not enjoy Mao's support, Gu's original backers also changed their stand and began making one startlingly frank admission after the other about past and present failures. Tao Zhu admitted the presence of problems in China's industrial sector that, he said, "did not just develop over the past few months, but have been accumulating for ten, twenty years."[39] Li Fuchun asked ministers and party secretaries present: "Now that the masses have stood up, has any one of us here won their support or become one of their leaders? Not a single one of us."[40]

The final document was a compromise, ratified at a session of the Politburo chaired by Lin Biao in the first week of December. With Mao's approval, it was issued on December 9 as *Zhongfa* [1966] 603 and became known as the "Ten Points on Industry." It affirmed the right of workers to join in the Cultural Revolution by setting up their own "revolutionary organizations," but added that the staff of these organizations was expected to continue to take part in production. In their spare time and locally, members of workers' organizations were granted the right to engage in "revolutionary" factory-to-factory networking.[41] On December 15, the Politburo ratified a similar document spelling out how the Cultural Revolution was to be carried out in China's vast countryside. Issued with Mao's approval as *Zhongfa* [1966] 612, it became known as the "Ten Points on Rural Villages" and reversed the policy in force until then of handling the Cultural Revolution in the countryside along the lines of the Socialist Education Movement. It gave the go-ahead to set up Red Guard organizations "the core membership of which is to consist of poor and lower-middle peasant youths" and stated that from now on, as in China's cities, the Cultural Revolution in rural villages was to involve "great contending and great blooming, big-character posters, debates on a grand scale, and big democracy." Networking between members of different brigades or communes was permissible so long as it did not interfere with agricultural production.[42]

Despite such qualifications, the twin decisions to open up farms and factories to the Cultural Revolution amounted to opening a Pandora's box. In principle, virtually anyone among China's hundreds of millions now had the right, indeed the obligation, to make revolution. Modern Chinese history showed that if unleashed students linked up with them, it would be an explosive mix. After all, that was how the Chinese Communists began their revolutionary saga, mobilizing peasants and workers. No wonder Mao's colleagues were fearful; Mao of course saw only the revolutionary potential.

The Iron Fist of the CCRG

If Mao had imagined that the leaders of the Capital 3rd HQ would end up becoming something akin to an extension of his own will, he was in for an early surprise. The Red Guards saw themselves as "natural-born rebels," even though they were told by Zhou Enlai that there was no such thing. Much as they were ready to serve as the "iron fist of the CCRG," their sense of discipline left much to be desired, and when, as happened with some regularity, they took the initiative themselves, they did not always act along lines that coincided with what Mao had in mind. From the outset, the relationship was characterized by friction.

The university-based organizations were if anything even more eager to leave their mark on the Cultural Revolution than the middle school Red Guards. On November 9, the "Red Rebel Regiment" at Nankai University in Tianjin wrote to Zhou Enlai to inform him that, in the process of digging deep into their

144

1. Mao having a Red Guard armband pinned on by Song Binbin at the first Red Guard rally on August 18, 1966, to show his support and encourage the movement to spread nationwide.

2, 3. Jiang Qing, Mao's fourth wife, in a publicity still (right) during her film acting days in Shanghai during the 1930s, and (above) during the Cultural Revolution.

4. Mao Zedong (left), with Marshal Ye Jianying to his left, and Xie Fuzhi to his right. Wang Dongxing, head of Mao's bodyguards, is sitting in the front seat next to the driver.

5. Mao (below) and his new heir apparent, Marshal Lin Biao, both wearing Red Guard armbands on the reviewing platform high on the Gate of Heavenly Peace (Tiananmen) at a rally.

6. Liu Shaoqi (above), emulating Mao and wearing military collar flashes, shaking hands with his future nemesis, Jiang Qing.

7. Kang Sheng (right), a security specialist and Mao's most trusted enforcer of radical policies.

8. Xie Fuzhi (left), minister of public security and a loyal ally of the Cultural Revolution Group until his death in 1972.

9. Marshal Chen Yi (below), foreign minister, and one of the most outspoken opponents of the mayhem of the Cultural Revolution.

10. Premier Zhou Enlai (above) photographed on Tiananmen with three leaders of the Cultural Revolution Group, Jiang Qing and her two Shanghai collaborators, Zhang Chunqiao (left) and Yao Wenyuan (right), who fired the first salvo of the Cultural Revolution.

11. Four junior activists (right) of the Cultural Revolution Group, (from the left) Qi Benyu, Wang Li, Guan Feng, and Mu Xin.

12. Wu Han (top left), historian and vice mayor of Beijing, whose play *Hai Rui Dismissed from Office* was denounced at the outset of the Cultural Revolution.

13. Deng Tuo (top right), a senior propaganda official of the Beijing party who was attacked along with Wu Han early on, committed suicide in May 1966 as the Cultural Revolution got rolling.

14. Lu Dingyi (bottom left), head of propaganda, who was one of the first four senior officials to be purged in spring 1966.

15. Yang Shangkun (bottom right), another of the first four leaders to be purged in spring 1966; long after the Cultural Revolution, in 1988, he became head of state.

16. Red Guards with pens as weapons.

17. Young Red Guards (above) marching with spears.

18. Red Guards (below) putting up posters.

19 (with inset, 20). Red Guard (above) loyalty dance.

21. A work team leader (below) in Heilongjiang province being accused of following the capitalist line and opposing the mass movement.

22 (below). Former defense minister Peng Dehuai and former Politburo member Zhang Wentian under fire. Peng Zhen (inset, 23), ex-Beijing party leader and first major victim of the Cultural Revolution, at a Red Guard denunciation meeting.

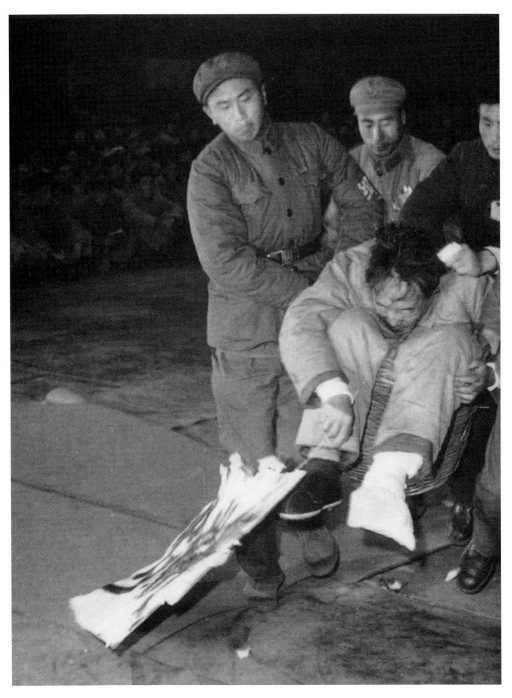

24. Former PLA chief of staff Luo Ruiqing being taken to a denunciation meeting in a basket after breaking his leg in a failed suicide attempt.

25. The governor of Heilongjiang province, Li Fanwu (top), having his head shaved because for political reasons he had allegedly cultivated a hair style that resembled Mao's.

26. The governor's wife (below), her face inked, being paraded in front of the crowd.

27. Huang Xinting, the commander of the Chengdu Military Region in southwest China, under attack.

28. Religion was a particular focus of Red Guard assault, as this picture of nuns being denounced shows.

29. Buddhist monks under attack.

30. Buddhist statues being destroyed by Red Guards in Anhui province.

31. A Buddhist statue festooned with posters in Beijing.

university's former party past, they had made the remarkable discovery that Liu Shaoqi and a number of senior CCP leaders were in fact "renegades." "There are hundreds of them, possibly a thousand," they insisted, "and they make up a vast bloc of renegades"—a "firmly rooted, vast, and very dangerous network." In the letter, the Red Rebel Regiment went on to propose that the party center immediately launch an inquiry into the matter and that they themselves be allowed to assist in the inquiry and in "completely eradicating this bunch of renegades."[43] On this occasion, the center at first hesitated to accept the services of the Red Guards; but later the Red Guards from Tianjin—in particular from Tianjin University as well as from Nankai University—were repeatedly brought in to help with just such inquiries.

How the center interacted with supposedly independent and "unofficial" investigations launched by the "revolutionary masses" remains largely shrouded in mystery. But what is known is that there were contacts: the CCRG was not averse to having members of organizations like those belonging to the Capital 3rd HQ perform certain delicate duties for it, in particular ones in which at some stage it might want to be able to deny complicity. And as the letter above suggests, gullible university students yearning to prove their revolutionary worth were often only too happy to express their devotion to the Cultural Revolutionary cause by agreeing to be gofers for the center.

In one extensively documented case involving a group of students from two universities and a research institute in Beijing, the case boiled down to whether Liu Shaoqi had betrayed the CCP organization in Tianjin in 1928. The students had launched their original somewhat amateurish and underfunded investigation into the matter after the issue had come up in conversation with a few old CCP cadres who themselves had worked closely with but clashed with Liu Shaoqi in the 1930s. In the spring of 1967, the students found themselves approached by the CC General Office and told that the center was prepared to help them with their investigation, on the condition that they agree to certain basic ground rules, of which the most important was not to divulge central involvement: "As you carry out your work, you must not say you've been sent by the CC General Office; simply say you're acting in the name of a mass organization. If you encounter problems, give us a call." A second, equally important rule was that on no condition were the students to "inquire into matters you're not supposed to know anything about."[44]

In the end, of course, it was this second rule that was to get the students into trouble. Although they did what they could to produce the kind of results they hoped would satisfy their CC General Office contacts, and even went so far as to subject a retired old worker to some very "hostile interrogation" in order to have him come up with the "right" answers, the students found nothing and were in the end told to cut short their work and forget about the whole affair.[45] In the interregnum, unfortunately for them, they had among themselves begun to suspect that none other than Zhou Enlai might have played a very suspect role in what had transpired in Tianjin back in 1928. When this possibility leaked to the authorities, not only were they not thanked for what they had done on Liu Shaoqi; on the contrary, they were all accused of having used their investigation as a pretext for digging up dirt on "comrade Enlai." In the end, instead of finding themselves rewarded with positions of some responsibility or at least a bright future upon graduation for their contributions to the Cultural Revolution, they found themselves assigned to miserable jobs in distant corners of China and stigmatized as suspected members of the "May 16 Conspiracy" (discussed in a later chapter).[46]

In October, central leaders such as Zhou Enlai and Tao Zhu still repeatedly urged Red Guards not to attack Liu Shaoqi and Deng Xiaoping by name in public, but to little or no avail. Justifying their actions by quoting Mao's famous 1957 dictum, "'He who is not afraid of death by a thousand cuts dares to unhorse the emperor'—this is the dauntless spirit needed in our struggle to build socialism and communism," Red Guards at Peking University were among the first to openly attack Liu Shaoqi by name, in a big-character poster on October 21 titled simply "Liu Shaoqi is China's Khrushchev!"[47] "Rebels" in party and government offices were not to be outdone. Within twenty-four hours of Liu's and Deng's self-criticisms at the central work conference on October 23, the entire hundred or so staff of a section in the Central Organization Department signed off on the first big-character poster to attack the CCP general secretary by name. "Deng Xiaoping is also China's Khrushchev!"—the name of the poster was clearly meant to associate it with the one at Peking University—and accused Deng of being responsible for the deletion of references to Mao Zedong Thought in the constitution of the Eighth Party Congress, of opposing the organized study of Mao's works among CCP cadres, and of promoting individual farming in the wake of the disaster of the Great Leap. It also for the first time revealed to the world at large that Deng in 1962 had made the highly un-Maoist claim that "the color of the cat does not matter, as long as it catches mice."[48] Tao Zhu, whose PSC portfolio at this point included both higher education and organizational affairs, pleaded with the poster-writers, saying: "It's wrong of you to make comrades Liu Shaoqi and Deng Xiaoping your primary targets."⁴⁹ But it was all in vain. One of Deng's daughters who made the rounds of schools and offices together with her sisters on their bicycles later recalled that "the vicious tone of the posters, their effort to paint Papa in the worst possible light, made my hair stand on end."⁵⁰

On January 1, 1967, the Cultural Revolution penetrated into Zhongnanhai. That morning, a handful of "rebels" employed in the leadership telephone exchange, calling themselves the "67.1.1 Combat Team," entered the courtyard where Liu Shaoqi lived and "decorated" it with huge slogans proclaiming "Opponents of Mao Zedong Thought will come to a no-good end!" and "Down with China's Khrushchev Liu Shaoqi!" One of the characters making up Liu's name *(qi)* was intentionally distorted and tilted on its side so as to resemble the character meaning "dog." Two days later, another group, consisting of some two dozen clerical staff calling themselves the "Red Flag Regiment," suddenly appeared at dinnertime and ordered Liu and his wife out into the courtyard to accept the "denunciation" of the "revolutionary masses."⁵¹ By mid-January the rebels (whose activities were carefully masterminded from behind the scenes by Qi Benyu) had put Marshal Zhu De, the eighty-year-old father of the PLA and Mao's first major comrade-in-arms, as well as Deng Xiaoping and Tao Zhu and their families through similar ordeals. On the evening of January 12, no less than 200 clerical staff "rebels," including the wives of Kang Sheng and Qi Benyu, appeared in the Liu Shaoqi courtyard, accompanied by a film crew, to launch a second round of "denunciations."⁵² The next day, Mao allowed Liu one final audience, but when Liu asked Mao for permission to resign and to withdraw to the countryside to live as an ordinary peasant "in order to make an early conclusion of the Great Cultural Revolution possible, and save the country some suffering," Mao turned him down.⁵³ Saving the country from upheaval was not what Mao had in mind.

Despite these humiliations—and, in Liu's case, denunciation by children of an earlier marriage⁵⁴—by virtue of the fact that they were members of the PSC, Liu and Deng never had to endure the fate that virtually all other top-level "revisionists" were to share with increasing frequency from now on: public humiliation in front of tens of thousands of screaming representatives of the "revolutionary masses." In sports stadiums and gymnasiums festooned with banners reading "Down with anyone who opposes Chairman Mao's revolutionary line!" and "Open fire on the bourgeois reactionary line!," on makeshift stages erected in the middle of soccer fields and public squares, a kind of political theater was played all across China to rouse the population to even greater fury against the supposed enemies of Chairman Mao.

The leadership of the Capital 3rd HQ in particular prided itself on the organizational skill and discipline with which it ran some of the biggest and most spectacular of these rallies in cooperation with the relevant authorities. Older cadres not at the receiving end of the "righteous indignation" of the "little revolutionary generals" gave them high marks on almost every count. A senior intelligence official who worked as Kang Sheng's personal emissary in Tianjin at the time told a group of friends visiting him in the spring of 1967: "They are really capable, those young kids, all in their early twenties . . . I told them to get a mass rally going and to drag out Li Xuefeng, and right away—within no more than an hour or two!—they had organized a rally of some 400,000 to 500,000 people. Discipline was excellent."[55] A slight exaggeration, no doubt, but a telling one.

On the eve of the GLF, Mao had complained that Beijing had never produced anything other than "bureaucracy."[56] Maybe the situation was different in other parts of China, but as if to prove him right a quasi-permanent "struggle administration" came into being, occupying if not actually employing hundreds. Premises on the second floor of the Ministry of Geology, for example, were provided free of charge to the Capital 3rd HQ to serve as the home of its "Reception Station of the Preparatory Office for Struggling the Peng Zhen–Luo Ruiqing–Lu Dingyi–Yang Shangkun Counterrevolutionary Clique." While the Preparatory Office sought permission from the CCRG to "struggle" various targets, called on the municipal party authorities to provide a suitable venue, and had the Beijing Garrison make sure that the target actually showed up, if necessary by forcibly escorting him or her under armed guard, the Reception Station handled contacts with the public. It printed advertisements well in advance of each major rally, indicating where people wishing to address it should submit their written "denunciations and exposure materials" for screening, when and at which one of four locations tickets could be obtained ("by groups in possession of a letter of introduction"), and what telephone numbers to use to obtain more information. Security may not have qualified as tight, but it was definitely not possible to just walk in off the street to see the "class enemy" get what he deserved. A newsletter produced by and for one of the member organizations of the Capital 3rd HQ revealed that a group of Swedish students visiting Beijing had attempted one evening to "crash" a rally at which a seventy-four-year-old deputy head of the

Chinese Academy of Sciences Philosophy and Social Sciences Department was being struggled.[57] They were turned away.

The mood at some of the bigger rallies was caught on film by crews from the Central News Reel Studios. A fifteen-minute documentary made by the Preparatory Office of a rally organized on a frigid winter day shows the disgraced mayor of Beijing and his most senior colleagues in the municipal government on their knees in a packed Beijing Workers' Stadium. Still, these events sometimes had their comical moments. Many years later, one of the "lesser kings of the underworld" from the Central Propaganda Department recalled what happened at one rally where he himself was to be struggled. At the time, the rally organizers were sufficiently confident that Yu Guangyuan would not run away that they let him live at home in between events and make his own way to the venue when called upon:

> On one occasion, the struggle rally was to take place in the Muxudi district of Beijing, on the campus of the Beijing Institute of Politics and Law. When I arrived that day, they asked me for a ticket at the gate. I told them I knew nothing about a ticket and said that I had not been told I would be needing one. The guard at the gate told me categorically "No ticket, no entry!" . . . I responded: "Other people may not be able to enter without a ticket, but I'm someone you're going to have to let in anyway." His response was: "No way!" His refusal to let me in drew a lot of attention, and by now there was an audience of onlookers wondering why he insisted on not letting me in while I insisted on being let in . . . Finally he got angry and said: "How can you be so unreasonable! It's as if, if we don't let you in, the rally will not get off the ground!" "Exactly! Without me, no rally!" I said, very self-confidently. Though he heard me say this, he still could not figure out what I was driving at. So I finally asked him: "What sort of rally is this that you're having today?" "A struggle rally," he answered. "And whom are you struggling?" I continued. "Yu Guangyuan." I said: "I am Yu Guangyuan. Do you think there will be a rally without me?"[58]

At this point Yu entered without a ticket, to be struggled in the notorious "jet-plane" position.

In November and December the political situation became increasingly chaotic in the absence of explicit and authoritative directives as to which senior leaders other than Liu and Deng could safely be attacked as representatives of the "bourgeois reactionary line" and/or the "enemy." Self-styled rebels in Beijing began attacking just about every power-holder there was, save for Mao himself.

While the Cultural Revolution was still seen in positive terms, this particular wave of attacks from below was labeled the "evil wind" of November and December, by virtue of the fact that it hit at even such bona fide "leftists" as Lin Biao and Jiang Qing. Recent Chinese histories attempt to impose a nonexistent coherent "anti-leftist" pattern on the attacks by overlooking the fact that the author of a fierce denunciation of Jiang Qing might at the same time be lauding Lin Biao to the skies, and the other way around. One group of university students based in the Beijing Forestry Institute put up a big-character poster calling on their fellow revolutionaries to "kick aside" the institution of the CCRG ("a stumbling block before the feet of Chairman Mao") and to "make revolution" by themselves; in the poster, they also declared such action to be entirely in line with firmly supporting Mao "and his deputy commander, Vice Chairman Lin."[59] Two students from a middle school attached to Beijing Agricultural University attacked Lin Biao in a big-character poster, maintaining that in view of his very limited grasp of Marxism-Leninism, the CCP under his leadership ran the risk of turning into a fascist party; in their poster, the two students on the other hand praised Zhou Enlai, Tao Zhu, and Chen Boda for having few if any of Lin's faults.[60] One Red Guard group on the Tsinghua University campus distributed a handbill in which they attacked Chen Boda and Jiang Qing for failing to abide by the basic tenets of Mao Zedong Thought.[61] Another Red Guard group that claimed to have members in seventeen universities in Beijing publicly called for the ouster of Guan Feng and Qi Benyu and insisted that Qi in particular was criminally responsible for "instigating the masses to fight the masses."[62] Scores of big-character posters attacked Liu and Deng. Caricatures of them and a multitude of their supporters and allies were printed and distributed.

Sometimes the handful of foreign journalists in China picked up news of such events. The Soviets in particular were good at doing this, and Red Guards became incensed when they heard that a "revisionist radio station" had broadcast the text of a "counterrevolutionary big-character poster" from the Beijing Foreign Languages Institute titled "What is Zhou Enlai up to?" In protest, Red Guards pasted up a traditional Chinese couplet at the entrance of the Soviet journalists' (TASS?) offices in Beijing: on one side, "*Pravda* does not tell the truth"; on the other, "*Isvestia* fabricates news"; and across the top, "Nothing but a load of crap!"[63]

The most virulent attacks on the CCRG in particular emanated from the "early" Red Guards, whose power and influence had been waning steadily since their glory days in August–September. Perhaps this decline was only to be expected. Of the people who predicted early on that the Red Guards would turn against the very leaders who had nurtured them, few were as perceptive as Chiang Kai-shek's erstwhile right-hand man, Ch'en Li-fu, founder of the National Cultural Reconstruction Association and promoter of the KMT's New Life Movement. In November 1966 Ch'en observed: "The Communist bandits are using 'Red Guard' youth organizations on the mainland to make rebellion and wreak havoc. This course of action is the most stupid of all: those who cheat and exploit the young will one day inevitably be spurned by them."[64] By the end of the year, some disillusioned later "rebels" who had no more begun to gain insights into what Mao's proletarian revolutionary HQ was all about before they set about questioning it also produced less angry but in some ways more sophisticated critiques. These now largely forgotten (as historically inconvenient) critics included Zhu Chengzhao himself, whose views as developed and enunciated in January 1967 were regarded by officialdom as "so reactionary that there is nothing to compare with them among all the students in China."[65] Zhu maintained that the entire nationwide exchange of revolutionary experiences, namely Mao's free travel scheme, had been "premature." He insisted that the CCRG was arresting too many Red Guards and that a number of the middle school students who had been members of the West City Pickets and similar "royalist" organizations were in fact genuine "leftists." In fact what the CCRG was doing, he said, was nothing short of "harassing the masses."[66] Once Zhu's views had become widely known, his career as a Red Guard leader was effectively over. Behind the scenes, however, he continued to enjoy the tacit support and admiration of many of his original followers.

Ordinary people and others not privy to the discussions inside Zhongnanhai were left to speculate as best they could about what might happen next. Sweden's ambassador to China assumed that the worst was just about over. For a while, he noted in a letter to his minister, the embassy had been guarded by nine police officers, but now "things have returned to normal, with just a single guard on duty."

On following pages: A caricature of a "hundred clowns." The trio at top left are Liu Shaoqi, Khrushchev, and Lyndon Johnson. In the row underneath: Liu, Deng Xiaoping, Marshal Peng Dehuai, Peng Zhen, Luo Ruiqing, Lu Dingyi; the second row includes Yang Shangkun, Marshal He Long, Wang Guangmei (Mme Liu Shaoqi), Bo Yibo, An Ziwen, and Tao Zhu. The two rows at bottom right, under the heading "Imperialists and all reactionaries are paper tigers," have a catholic selection, including Dulles, Eisenhower, and Johnson; Khrushchev, Brezhnev, Kosygin, and Sholokhov (!); Harold Wilson; Tito; Tsedenbal (Mongolia); Indira Gandhi; Chiang Kai-shek; Sukarno and General Nasution; General Ne Win; Miyamoto Kenji (Japan; Communist Party general secretary).

帝国主义者和国内反动派决不甘心于他们的失败，他们还要作最后的挣扎。在全国平定以后，他们也还会以各种方式从事破坏和捣乱，他们将每日每时企图在中国复辟。这是必然的，毫无疑义的，我们务必不要松懈自己的警惕性。

毛泽东

北京市革命委员会红画军总部合印

百丑图

帝国主义和一切反
动派都是纸老虎。

Begging to disagree with a recent editorial in the *New York Times* claiming that "a limited civil war has begun in China," the ambassador insisted that "as far as can be ascertained from Beijing, this claim would seem to be premature." But, he ended his letter, "the more one sees of Chinese society . . . the less inclined one is to speculate needlessly about the future."[67] This final observation was indeed the right one to make, as it turned out. Civil war was under way and already becoming unstoppable.

9

Shanghai's "January Storm"

Mao and Jiang Qing celebrated his seventy-third birthday, on December 26, 1966, by inviting six of their CCRG trusties—Chen Boda, Zhang Chunqiao, Yao Wenyuan, Wang Li, Guan Feng, and Qi Benyu—to dinner in Zhongnanhai at what was known to the cognoscenti as Mao's swimming-pool house. Zhou Enlai and Tao Zhu, who had been striving to control the chaos unleashed by Mao and the CCRG over the previous seven months, did not make the "A" list; more surprisingly, neither did Lin Biao or Kang Sheng. In this congenial group, Mao felt able to speak freely, giving a toast "To the unfolding of nationwide all-round civil war!"[1] The New Year editorial published jointly in the *People's Daily* and *Red Flag*, drafted by Guan Feng and finalized by Mao, echoed that toast in more circumspect language, predicting that 1967 would be "a year of nationwide all-round class struggle," in which "the proletariat will join the revolutionary masses in a general offensive on the handful of persons in power taking the capitalist road and society's monsters and freaks."[2] The prediction was accurate, and Mao almost got his wish.

The CCRG Moves Center Stage

Crucial to the process of promoting "all-round civil war" was the seizure of power by radical elements. At the center, this was facilitated by the Chairman's fiat. From early in 1967, any document emanating from Mao himself went to a very short list: Lin Biao, Zhou Enlai, and "the comrades on the CCRG." Within the CCRG, the documents went to Chen Boda, Kang Sheng, Jiang Qing, Wang Li, Guan Feng, and Qi Benyu, and to Zhang Chunqiao and Yao Wenyuan when they were in Beijing. PSC members Tao Zhu, Deng Xiaoping, Liu Shaoqi, and Chen Yun were excluded.[3]

Mao's creation of the Central Caucus after the Eleventh Plenum had increased the power of the radicals and prefigured these arrangements, dramatically expanding the ability of Mao's radical supporters to influence the entire spectrum of national affairs. The radicals' new powers were further increased by the disappearance of the Central Committee Secretariat, from which, before the Cultural Revolution, Deng Xiaoping had effectively run China on behalf of the PSC. Tao Zhu had replaced Peng Zhen as the body's "permanent secretary" and tried to maintain its authority. But Tao was purged early in 1967, and at some point in February Mao simply noted: "Now the CCRG has replaced the Secretariat." Already the CCRG had been added as a co-signatory to Central Documents, coming after the center (unspecified, but effectively Mao), the State Council, and the MAC. For six months, from the Twelfth Plenum in October 1968 until its dissolution after the CCP's Ninth Congress in April 1969, the CCRG would formally outrank even the State Council and the MAC on official documents.

The reach of the radicals was also extended by the gradual disappearance of the CCP's six regional bureaus, five of them in the winter of 1966–67 and the sixth in August 1967.[4] The regional first secretaries had been powerful figures—two of them had been appointed members of the Politburo—but as their institution faded away, the radicals were able to deal directly with the provinces without their interference. Lower-level organizations were eventually advised to address formal communications concerning the Cultural Revolution to "the center and the CCRG."[5] Zhou Enlai, in conversation with Red Guards, explained the division of labor among four key institutions that thenceforth constituted the central authorities by comparing the CCRG to Mao's "general staff," the MAC to his "high command," and the State Council to his "executive organ."[6]

The radicals and their adherents were now able to set about transforming the existing institutions at both the central and provincial levels.

The Shredding of the Central Government

While Mao had an interest in preserving the institutional integrity of the PLA at this stage of the Cultural Revolution, the Eleventh Plenum and its aftermath had already revealed that he had no such qualms with regard to the party machine. And however strenuously Zhou Enlai felt able to intervene on behalf of individual leaders, the premier was probably less concerned about the party apparatus as such. Since the GLF in 1958, he and the State Council had played second fiddle to the CC Secretariat in the overall running of the country.[7] With the disgrace of Liu Shaoqi, Deng Xiaoping, and Peng Zhen and the collapse of the Secretariat, under normal circumstances the State Council might have recovered the key national role it had played during the first FYP, 1953–1957. But circumstances were not normal, and now the time had come to deal with the government hierarchy, since no limitations had been put on the scope of the movement. Revitalization of all bureaucracy through upheaval and power-seizures was what the Cultural Revolution was about.

Mao's ideal government was a small one. In July 1966, complaining bitterly about the massive size of the State Council, he said that some ministries should be greatly reduced in size and turned into bureaus or offices with only a handful of staff.[8] Mao's romantic ideas may have resonated with the guerrilla ideal of the slim CCRG organization, but they were hard to reconcile with the realities faced by Premier Zhou Enlai. The CCRG was able to operate without its own cars, but only by borrowing transport (as it did after December 1966) from the Zhongnanhai car pool, and somebody had to maintain that kind of facility.[9] Normally, that somebody was a bureaucrat who reported to Zhou. Though Mao could never have made an accusation of laziness against Zhou stick—it was common knowledge elevated to the level of myth that Zhou worked around the clock[10]—the same was not true of the premier's ministers, and the Chairman could not abide "lazy" bureaucrats. "Laziness is one of the sources of revisionism," he had asserted in 1964.[11]

In that year, the last for which reliable statistics are available, the number of potential senior "revisionists" within the bureaucracy—ministers, vice ministers, and equivalent—had been just under 400. In late 1966 these men ran a central government bureaucracy under the State Council of some seventy-eight ministries, commissions, committees, staff offices, central bureaus, and equivalent organs. A large ministry might consist of between twenty and thirty departments and have a staff of anywhere from 500 to 2,000. The ministerial-level Department of Administrative Affairs was the largest, employing more than 2,500 people, but it had been without a functioning leadership since June 1966.[12] Some small committees and central bureaus consisted of only a handful of offices and fewer than 50 staffers.[13]

On January 8, 1967, Mao declared open season on this vast apparatus of government, declaring: "You don't necessarily need ministries to make revolution."[14] The effects of the simultaneous reform of the government and compulsory purge of senior staff on the different parts of the State Council varied greatly. Key organs of the military/industrial complex were the least touched; the worst hit were the supposed hotbeds of revisionism: culture, education, and public health. In theory, a distinction was to be made between organs where power-seizures were essential and those where they were not. But maintaining this distinction in practice was not possible, as Mao admitted to his closest colleagues. According to Zhou, Mao told the MAC:

> About seizing power: in the papers it says "seize power from persons in power taking the capitalist road and from stubborn elements persisting in the bourgeois reactionary line." But when the circumstances are not like that, can one still seize power? Now it appears as if such fine distinctions just cannot be made, so the thing to do is to seize power first and then deal with the rest later. Forget about metaphysics or you will have your hands tied. Once power is in your hands, the question of from what kind of person in power you have seized it can be determined at a later stage in the movement. Once you have seized power, report to the State Council to secure approval.[15]

In order to secure approval from the State Council, effectively from Zhou himself, the premier insisted that the rebels who took over had to establish "three-in-one" combinations of "revolutionary leading cadres, revolutionary mid-level cadres, and representatives of the revolutionary masses" who together would elect a revolutionary committee to supervise the Cultural Revolution and professional work throughout the ministry. However, existing party groups in the ministries could not be overthrown and would presumably continue to run affairs.[16] That was the road map; but it was rarely followed.

Even where rebels expressed their readiness in principle to follow this road map, Zhou might still end up giving them the red light. In the Ministry of Finance, which was headed by Vice Premier and concurrent Politburo member Li Xiannian, the rebels demanded that a vice minister, Du Xiangguang, be put in charge as the senior "revolutionary leading cadre" in the three-in-one combination. At a meeting with ministry rebels from two in the morning until dawn on February 17, Zhou flatly refused to accept such an arrangement. He began by asking Du politely to leave; when he refused, the situation deteriorated rapidly:

> Please leave! (*Crowd:* When the premier asks you to leave, you have to leave! Leave!) I've never seen anyone behave the way you do! (*Crowd:* Get out!) This is unacceptable, there's no talk about it! (*Crowd:* Get out!) Right! You won't even accept an order from the party center? (*Crowd:* Piss off!) Listen up, all of you! This is why we end up having chaos! (*Crowd:* Leave!) Leave! Leave! You're not going to obey the supreme instructions, are you!? (*The premier leaves his seat and steps up to the front. Crowd:* The premier's order must be obeyed!) I am con-

vening this meeting at the order of the Chairman, and this is how you behave!?
Red Guards, execute my order! (*Crowd:* Leave! Piss off! *Red Guards step forward to drag off Du Xiangguang.*) Liberation Army soldiers, arrest the man!
(*Crowd:* Arrest him! Take him away!) Wrecking our Great Proletarian Cultural
Revolution like this! I give him an order, and he won't obey! *(Prolonged applause.)* Thank you for supporting the decision of the party center. (*Li
Xiannian:* I also want to thank the comrades for your support.) His intention
was to seize supreme financial power from the party center! Some of you have
been hoodwinked; now is the time to wake up! (*Crowd:* Long live the dictatorship of the proletariat! A long, long life to Chairman Mao!! Wake up, hoodwinked comrades! Down with the royalists!)[17]

With Mao's backing, Zhou promoted the idea that a power-seizure was a
political and not a professional act; in other words, if Red Guards took over an
institution, they should not interfere with the routine performance of its designated duties.[18]

Power-seizures were followed by factional fighting between rival rebel groups.
The ministries could not function. Production suffered. Quite a few seasoned
administrators were unable to fathom the meaning of what was happening. One
Nanjing cadre in the banking sector gave voice to the question on the minds of
many when he asked: "Why does the movement have to proceed in this fashion?
If what the Chairman resents is that there are too many cadres, why not simply
tell those eligible for retirement to retire? Why go about it in this way?"[19] "Re-
medial" measures were considered and implemented, in a few cases amounting
to nothing less than the abolition of a ministry. In May 1967 the Ministry of Culture was abolished and its powers transferred to the Arts and Literature Group
under the CCRG, headed by Jiang Qing. Its fate had been sealed by the paralysis
induced by factional struggle; the victorious faction had expressed its revolutionary preference in a song—in E flat, *mezzoforte*, 2/4 time—titled "Smash the
Ministry of Culture, overthrow Xiao Wangdong!"[20]

In central government institutions, the dismissal from office "by popular demand" of every minister who was not also a vice premier was officially endorsed.[21] But dismissals did not lead automatically to the empowerment of internal "rebels" who had carried them out. Instead, the vice ministers and bureau directors who had seized the hour to accelerate their own promotions by rebelling
were at best given power to "supervise professional matters."

By May 1967, Zhou Enlai was forced to get Mao's permission to send the
PLA into the ministries, a last resort he had hoped to avoid. In the State
Planning Commission, the Ministry of Foreign Affairs, the Ministry of Com-

merce, the Ministry of Foreign Trade, and the People's Bank of China, PLA officers exercised joint leadership with a preexisting body of civilian "revolutionary" cadres and "masses." But in some cases, including the Ministry of Finance, the Ministry of Communications, the Ministry of Posts and Telecommunications, and the Ministry of Railways, military control commissions were established made up entirely of PLA officers. The PLA also took over complete control of defense-related industries, including machine-building, nuclear weapons, aircraft, electronics, conventional weapons, shipbuilding, and missiles. In the end, not a single ministry remained entirely civilian.[22]

When asked by a delegation from Anhui province to specify what "military control" meant, Kang Sheng replied bluntly: "Military control is autocratic rule. You obey me in everything. You put out a public notice in which you announce that you obey me."[23] Obedience meant also accepting near total reorganization and drastic reductions in numbers of subunits and staff. Beginning in 1968, between 70 and 90 percent of the original employees in most ministries would be "sent down" to "May 7 Cadre Schools," named in honor of the date in 1966 on which Mao wrote to Lin Biao stating that the PLA was a great school in which politics, military affairs, and culture were combined with agricultural and industrial production. "All the ones who aren't obedient," in the words of Wang Hongwen, "we send 'em there."[24] Often located in isolated rural areas in distant provinces and sometimes situated in converted labor camps, the schools were supposed to "reeducate" the rusticated cadres. Here they spent an average of two to three years doing manual labor and "getting closer to the poor and lower-middle peasants and in the process strengthening their intellectual and emotional ties to the laboring people." The schools, the *People's Daily* declared, were an integral part of the "revolutionization of government organs."[25]

The militarization of the Chinese government was surely the opposite of what Mao wanted. One of his fundamental precepts since the 1930s had been that "political power grows out of the barrel of a gun. Our principle is that the Party commands the gun; the gun shall never be allowed to command the Party."[26] Yet as the government crumbled, the PLA took over from the original party groups that ran the ministries. Not only did this development reverse the desired Maoist order of things; it also led to the corruption of the military. Looking back from the vantage point of the 1990s, one of Mao's radical followers, jaundiced but accurate, commented: "Large numbers of people in the military won promotions and made fortunes (of course, nothing as serious as what we witness today), gained access to housing and cars for their own use, and got

Beijing residence permits for their dependents. This all damaged the reputation of the PLA and destroyed its nature."[27] The pattern in the center was replicated in the provinces, where Zhou Enlai had even less control over the situation. At the beginning of October, he had anticipated that the Red Guard movement could be wound down early in the new year,[28] but two months later he was bowing to the inevitable:

> At the work conference in October, I said that the movement is in the ascendant, and the Chairman said we cannot put on the brakes now . . . By now it's just as chief Lin [Biao] put it, that the movement is deepening and broadening and turning into a force impossible to ward off. How could one ward it off? Comrade [Chen] Boda calls it a mighty revolutionary torrent that you can neither stop nor ward off.[29]

In the winter of 1966–67, that torrent engulfed Shanghai.

Beijing Red Guards Foment Rebellion

At the beginning of January 1967, Mao predicted that the major locations in the evolving nationwide class struggle would be the industrialized parts of China: Beijing, Shanghai, Tianjin, and the large cities of the Northeast.[30] Not that Mao had a strategy. Indeed, to have had a strategy for the mass movement and its "general offensive" would have contradicted the basic premise of the Cultural Revolution: the masses had to liberate themselves. As Mao was quoted in the *People's Daily* on February 19, 1967, "You only learn to swim by swimming"; equally one could learn to make revolution only by making revolution.[31] And for making revolution, Shanghai showed "great promise" because—and here Mao's impression was shaped by what he had been reading in the CCRG Journalists' Station's *Rapid Reports*—"revolutionary students, revolutionary workers, and revolutionary cadres have all stood up."[32]

The original spark was provided by Beijing Red Guards, who arrived in Shanghai in three waves and large numbers starting in late August 1966, and the violence in the city in September soon demonstrated that the new local Red Guard organizations were apt pupils.[33] But Shanghai would differ significantly from all other parts of the country as the one place where the "revolutionary workers" would swiftly displace the "revolutionary students" as the standard-bearers of the Cultural Revolution.[34] Ironically, it had been Liu Shaoqi and Deng

161

Xiaoping who got Mao's agreement as early as June for the suggestion to expand the Cultural Revolution from intellectuals to proletarians by experimenting in Shanghai factories. The first workers' big-character poster was put up on June 12 at No. 17 Cotton Mill by Wang Hongwen, who later emerged as head of the WGHQ. The poster campaign against power-holders in Shanghai factories soon escalated. Production was affected. Anxious to restore order and protect themselves, managers gave in to worker demands, leading to accusations of "economism."

Shanghai Workers Take Over

Although the formation of the WGHQ had been sparked by Beijing Red Guards at the Shanghai Liaison Station of the Capital 3rd HQ, the WGHQ had taken over as the leaders of the "rebel" forces in Shanghai as a result of the *Liberation Daily* incident in late 1966. Inspired by Nie Yuanzi, who as an unofficial emissary of the CCRG visiting Shanghai told them that the center was in fact secretly in favor of officials' being "dismissed . . . by the masses" rather than through traditional top-down procedures, Red Guards had occupied the offices of this official organ of the Shanghai party on November 30 and closed down the paper.[35] But when they came under siege by far superior numbers of citizens mobilized by the city authorities, they appealed to the WGHQ for help. Wang Hongwen came to the rescue, but his quid pro quo was the establishment of a united organization with the WGHQ as the dominant partner and himself in overall command. This was the moment when Red Guard power began to fade in Shanghai and workers took over the Cultural Revolution there.[36]

Such incidents constituted severe body blows for the Shanghai Party Committee, but though down, it was not out. As the *Liberation Daily* episode demonstrated, the party was still able to mobilize large numbers of citizens in its defense. Whereas the Shanghai Party Committee's nemesis, the WGHQ, had attracted a high proportion of disadvantaged temporary and contract workers, the city's regular workers, who had by and large benefited under its leadership, supported the political status quo. They formed themselves into the Scarlet Guards with a claimed membership of 800,000 in opposition to the WGHQ.[37]

Mao had not explicitly sanctioned violence as a means of resolving conflicts among "the proletariat and the revolutionary masses" themselves, but at the start of the Cultural Revolution he was widely quoted as arguing that "it's a mistake when good people beat up on good people, though it may clear up some misunderstandings, as they might otherwise not have got to know each other in the first place."[38] The links of the Scarlet Guards to the members of the Shanghai Party Committee—which was, in Zhang Chunqiao's view, "taking the capitalist road"—made it possible to justify a physical assault on them. When informed by telephone on December 28 that the Scarlet Guards not only had ransacked his home (which they had not) but also were planning to cut off water, electricity, and communications throughout Shanghai (which indeed they were), Zhang ordered the WGHQ to prepare for action. Meanwhile Shanghai's mayor, Cao Diqiu, had begun peaceful negotiations with both sides in an attempt to lower tension in the city. Cao's moves did not seem to interest Zhang, who told his wife in Shanghai over the telephone: "The peach of Shanghai is ripe now, and we must not let Cao Diqiu pick it."[39]

Before dawn on December 30, some 100,000 members of the WGHQ attacked about 20,000 Scarlet Guards stationed around the Shanghai party secretariat on Kangping Road. After four hours of bloody fighting, the Scarlet Guards capitulated.[40] Post–Cultural Revolution official historians would pinpoint the "Kangping Road incident" as signifying the "beginning of nationwide violence."[41]

At 1:00 A.M. on January 1, in order to prevent the situation from getting further out of hand, the commander of the Shanghai Garrison, Liao Zhengguo, ordered all members of the Shanghai workers' militia to temporarily hand in small arms, rifles, hand grenades, light and heavy machine guns, and light artillery and ammunition within three days, ostensibly for "inspection and repair of weaponry."[42] Starting on the same date, the garrison command also searched and disarmed persons entering Shanghai by train or boat.

Shanghai's "January Storm"

Two hours after the garrison commander's order, at a little past three in the morning on January 1, Zhou Enlai telephoned the Shanghai first party secretary, Chen Pixian, and ordered him to get back to work.[43] Chen, who was recovering from nose and pharynx cancer surgery, had put his deputy, Mayor Cao Diqiu, in the front line. Zhou told Chen that Shanghai could on no account be allowed to descend into chaos. In particular, something needed to be done instantly to disperse the close to 20,000 Scarlet Guards in Kunshan county, Jiangsu province, a few miles outside Shanghai, on their way to Beijing to petition the central authorities. Holding up no less than twenty-six passenger trains and thirty-eight freight trains, they were totally disrupting traffic along the crucial north-south trunk line that connected China's great industrial metropolis with the capital. The premier called on Chen to take immediate measures "in consultation with the organizations of the masses" to resolve Shanghai's current crisis.[44]

In response to Zhou's call, Chen immediately called in the leaders of Shanghai's major mass organizations for an urgent meeting, which got underway at about five in the morning on New Year's Day.[45] Wang Hongwen represented the WGHQ, and Zhang Chunqiao's aide Xu Jingxian represented the Shanghai Party Committee Agencies Revolutionary Rebel Liaison Post, the very group that Mao had had in mind when in the course of his birthday dinner he had commented positively on "revolutionary rebels rising up in party and state organs as well."[46] The meeting issued an order to the Kunshan petitioners to withdraw (which they eventually did, and traffic returned to normal by January 3) and also drafted an open letter calling upon the people of Shanghai to "grasp revolution, promote production, and thoroughly smash the new attack by the bourgeois reactionary line." The text of the handbill, the greater part of which was written by a liaising music academy student from the Capital 3rd HQ and some local workers, was submitted for comments to the leaders of several mass organizations on January 4. After revisions, the leaders of twelve mass organizations (a deputy signing on behalf of Wang Hongwen, who had flown to Beijing on January 2) signed their names to it and passed it back to Chen, who ratified it and ordered the *Wenhui Daily* (where a power-seizure was in full swing that day) to print 200,000 copies and have them distributed and pasted up throughout the city. On January 5 the *Wenhui Daily* published the text on its front page under the headline "Letter to the people of Shanghai."[47]

On January 4, Zhang Chunqiao and Yao Wenyuan arrived in Shanghai on a PLA air force plane in their dual capacity as representatives of the CCRG and senior local cadres. Zhang later told a meeting of Red Guard leaders that "the municipal party committee hoped we would return to Shanghai to act as their shield against incoming arrows, but we turned them down."[48] They came with enhanced authority, having been made members of the Central Caucus two days earlier. And, as one of their old Shanghai colleagues who had not seen them for a few months noticed, "they showed up wearing army overcoats, even though at the time neither of them held a position within the military. Once Mao Zedong started wearing a uniform at his reviews of the Red Guards, the members of the CCRG all showed up in uniforms too, PLA-chic they would live to regret."[49] Thus emboldened, they precipitated rebellions at the *Wenhui Daily*, *Liberation*

Daily, and the Shanghai radio and television stations, encouraging the media to demand the restoration of order and to blame the disruption of the past weeks on the Scarlet Guards. Simultaneously Zhang called upon the WGHQ and other rebels to organize a "Down with the Shanghai Party Committee mass rally."[50]

On January 6, 100,000 people gathered in Shanghai's People's Square to witness cadres, workers, and student representatives publicly denounce Chen Pixian, Cao Diqiu, and other members of the municipal party committee.[51] Though concurrently first political commissar of the Shanghai Garrison, Chen Pixian was expressly forbidden by the rally organizers to attend in full military uniform; PLA-chic was not for revisionists.[52] The mass rally issued three orders, the texts of which had been approved beforehand by Zhang and Yao Wenyuan. Order No. 1 declared: "Beginning on January 6, 1967, the revolutionary rebels and revolutionary masses of Shanghai no longer recognize the counterrevolutionary revisionist element Cao Diqiu as member of the municipal party secretariat and mayor of Shanghai." In Order No. 2, Chen Pixian was ordered to give a thorough account of how he had opposed the Cultural Revolution in Shanghai so far. Order No. 3 declared that the mass rally was in favor of "thoroughly reorganizing the municipal party committee."[53]

That evening Yao sent a message to the party center in Beijing: "The rally was successful, and very orderly. The municipal committee has in effect collapsed completely. The revolutionary situation is excellent."[54] The rally made political history: a powerful party committee had been overthrown by a mass rally, albeit guided by an emissary from the center. Of fifty-six members and alternate members of the committee, forty-five were thrown out, of whom four died as a result of their subsequent treatment. The mayor and his seven deputies were purged.[55] The rally also made media history: it was the first ever "struggle rally" to be shown live on television.[56] Over the next few days, Zhang and Yao moved swiftly to restore order and create a new type of regime in Shanghai.

On January 9 the *Wenhui Daily* and the *Liberation Daily* published a joint "Urgent Notice" from the WGHQ and thirty-one other "rebel" organizations, spelling out concrete measures to fight economic chaos in Shanghai.[57] After reading it, Mao told the members of the CCRG that both the policies and the actions of the Shanghai rebels were correct, and that "all over China, the party, government, armed forces, and people [should] learn from the experience of Shanghai, and take concrete action."[58]

With this aim in mind, Zhou Enlai presided over the drafting of a telegram in the name of the CCP center, the State Council, and the MAC congratulating the Shanghai rebels. The telegram was significant, not just because it was the first ever such public communication from the party center directly to a "revolutionary mass organization," but also because by personally adding—at the very last moment, without consulting Zhou—the name of the CCRG to the signatories, this was the occasion on which Mao publicly gave Chen Boda, Jiang Qing, and their colleagues a bureaucratic stature equivalent to the established institutions of the party-state.[59]

The text of the telegram was read out on Central Radio in the predawn hours of January 12. Two stunned workers with the WGHQ, in charge of their factory's radio recording and retransmission equipment that morning, were slightly at a loss about what to do next but decided not to waste even a second and to wake everyone up by retransmitting there and then on their factory's public address system: "Attention please! Attention please! Here is the WGHQ Factory 822 Joint Regiment 'To Rebel Is Justified' Broadcasting Station: we start our program early today . . . with a message of congratulations to our Shanghai rebels!"[60]

On January 16 Mao formally approved the seizure of power from the Shanghai Party Committee and municipal people's government.[61] Soon the first calls to make Zhang first party secretary and mayor of Shanghai and Yao his deputy began to appear in the form of graffiti and huge slogans on city streets.[62]

But Mao had something different in mind, and not simply the substitution of a few crucially placed individuals. From now on, all power previously divided between party and government would be centralized in one new organization. But what was it to be called? On January 19, a meeting of a number of university-based Red Guard organizations, called at the request of Zhang and Yao and chaired by Wang Hongwen, opted after much discussion to propose to Zhang and Yao that the new organization be called the "Shanghai Commune" and that its creation be formally celebrated on January 27; the day of the month was chosen to match that of the creation of the Paris Commune, on March 27, 1871.[63] On February 5 it finally came into being, at a mass rally in People's Square in central Shanghai, under the name Shanghai People's Commune and under the leadership of a "temporary committee" headed by Zhang Chunqiao and Yao Wenyuan. In its General Order No. 1, the "temporary committee" announced that it was "assuming all the powers of, and pronouncing the death sentence on, the old Shanghai municipal party committee and government."[64]

In the wake of the events at the municipal level, power at lower levels was also seized in one organization after another. Firsthand accounts by the leading cadres affected tell of considerable fear, confusion, and a sense of insecurity as to what constituted the politically appropriate course of action in a constantly changing environment. In his privately published memoirs, a retired PLA officer who a year before the start of the Cultural Revolution had been appointed deputy party secretary of a major land and sea transport bureau in Shanghai (number of employees: 120,000) tried to recapture the event:

> The day before the power-seizure took place, I had called a meeting of the party secretaries and political department directors at which we decided to allow each individual to deal with the situation as he/she saw fit, as long as power was not ceded to bad people. Of course the latter was a meaningless qualification, since what could one do if bad people demanded to be given power? When we arrived at work the next day, the leading cadres in our unit and I were ordered by the rebels not to leave. I was told to wait in building No. 4, where a few minutes later I heard the whistle blow, and everyone began to assemble. As the balconies and stairwells filled up, we ended up at the foot of the stairs, between buildings Nos. 3 and 4. At the time, there were two factions in the organs belonging to our bureau: one was the Rebel Brigade, with close to 300 members, the other the "East Is Red Regiment," with slightly more than sixty members. On this day, the Rebel Brigade was in charge: one of their bosses read a "Power-Seizure Public Announcement," and then he called on the bureau leadership to declare where it stood. Five of us were present . . . At first we glanced at each other in silence; then all the others started looking at me. Everything had happened so suddenly, and none of them quite knew the best course of action. I had had a vague inkling that something like this would happen; they all expected me, the deputy party secretary, to declare where I stood. So I looked at the crowd of people present, all of them cadres from our own organs—none came from outside organizations—and expressed my agreement. The other leading cadres then also, one after the other, expressed their agreement. When we were asked to hand over our official seals there and then, we also agreed. This completed the seizure and transfer of power.[65]

Well, not quite. A week or so after the above event, the same bureau leadership, having only just ceded power "downward" to the Rebel Brigade, was ordered to report in person to a new superordinate WGHQ-affiliated "Joint Command Post," which had recently seized power from the original Shanghai shipping authorities. When it was now told to cede power "upward," its spokesman announced: "We've already had our power seized from us by our staff. If it's what you want, you go talk to them about it."[66]

For reasons that are not totally clear, despite having more than once held up the Paris Commune as the model of revolutionary organization and dubbed the giant collectives of the GLF "people's communes," Mao was in two minds about this title. At some point in mid-January, he had Wang Li telephone Zhang and Yao in Shanghai to inform them that he himself had begun contemplating the setting up of a "Beijing Commune" and that, after drawing up a first list of names of those who were to be in charge of it, he was looking forward to their creation of a "Shanghai Commune" along similar lines.[67] What Mao neglected to do was to let Zhang and Yao know that after thinking some more about it, he ended up abandoning the idea. Not until the two men returned to the capital on February 12 did Mao update them on his own thinking in the matter:

> With the establishment of a people's commune, a series of problems arises and I wonder whether you have thought about them. If the whole of China sets up people's communes, should the People's Republic of China change its name to "People's Commune of China"? Would others recognize us? Maybe the Soviet Union would not recognize us whereas Britain and France would. And what would we do about our ambassadors in various countries? There is another series of problems which you may not have considered. Many places have now applied to the Centre to establish communes. A document has been issued by the Centre saying that no place apart from Shanghai may set up people's communes. [I think] that Shanghai ought to make a change and transform itself into a revolutionary committee or a city committee or a city people's committee ... The [Shanghai] people's commune is too weak when it comes to suppressing counter-revolution. People have come and complained to me that when the Bureau of Public Security arrests people, they go in the front door and out the back.[68]

Nomenclature, diplomatic recognition, and ambassadors seem absurd quibbles coming from someone who would normally deride such concerns. Probably the Chairman's real worry was contained in his last point, a fear that a "commune" would be too lax an organization to keep control of power. As the *People's Daily* had put it on January 22 in one of many editorials on the Shanghai experience, this one finalized by Mao himself:

> Of all the important things, the possession of power is the most important. Such being the case, the revolutionary masses, with a deep hatred for the class enemy, make up their minds to unite, form a great alliance, and seize power! Seize power!! Seize power!!! All the party power, political power, and financial

power usurped by the counterrevolutionary revisionists and those diehards who persistently cling to the bourgeois reactionary line must be recaptured.

So Zhang and Yao went back to the drawing board. On February 23, they announced that the name of the supreme "organ of power" in Shanghai would henceforth bear the official name "Revolutionary Committee of Shanghai Municipality" rather than "Temporary Committee of the Shanghai People's Commune."[69] Zhang became the chairman of the renamed body, Yao its first deputy chairman.[70] Wang Hongwen emerged as their principal deputy while they were busy with national affairs in Beijing. It was the start of his own extraordinary rise to national power.

10

Seizing Power

Provincial Red Guards had returned home from Beijing inspired by the Chairman and the great rallies and encouraged by their colleagues in the capital. Mao's injunction that they "learn from the experience of Shanghai and take concrete action" showed provincial radicals, who wanted nothing more than to "remain closely in step with" the CCP Chairman, what had to be done. "Seize power! Seize power! Seize power!" as Red Guards editorialized in one of their many tabloids. Action was the order of the day: students in particular were out in full force, taking over offices and official seals and issuing manifestos left, right, and center. Few were as hesitant as the heads of one CC department, who actually wrote a letter to Kang Sheng asking him for *permission* to "seize power."[1]

The Shanghai power-seizure may have been immensely encouraging, but the special circumstances of Shanghai could not be duplicated. Nowhere else was there a native son like Zhang Chunqiao who could return to lead the power-seizure with the authority of the Chairman and the CCRG and the support of the military; and in few other provinces did the Red Guards face the challenge of being supplanted by workers as leaders of the great rebellion. In the immediate aftermath of Shanghai's January Storm, most provincial power-seizures failed, and the center recognized only five others—Heilongjiang, Shandong, Guizhou, Shanxi, and Beijing—in the first half of 1967. Three other revolutionary committees were formed in the second half of 1967, but the other twenty not until 1968, a testimony to the bitter factional fighting provoked by attempted power-seizures and the refusal of the center to recognize power-seizures that it did not consider genuine transfers of power from "capitalist roaders" to "proletarian revolutionary rebels."[2]

In conversation with a delegation of visiting Albanian officers, Mao seemed to imply that the problems with creating new revolutionary bodies had to do with the makeup and organization of the new centers of power: "[My] original intent was to select some successors from among the intellectuals, but now, from the looks of it, it was not an ideal selection. The way we went about it in the case of the Beijing Revolutionary Committee was not necessarily appropriate. There has to be a reorganization."[3] Mao's audience on this occasion would have been pleased to know that the "reorganization" often ended up as an increase in the relative number of military officers like themselves.

The First Revolutionary Committees

To Heilongjiang belonged a double distinction. It was the first province to set up a revolutionary committee—on January 31, 1967—and it was the first of only three provinces in which the party first secretary was skillful and lucky enough to metamorphose into the chair of the committee. Pan Fusheng became famous throughout the country, and obtained Mao's backing,[4] for enthusiastically embracing the successive stages of the movement, meeting the masses, making self-criticisms, distancing himself from most colleagues, but ensuring that the provincial military commander was with him. As a result, when the provincial revolutionary committee was formed, the head of a mass organization emerged on top, and Pan and General Wang Jiadao were listed as advisers. But when the center finally put its imprimatur on the new institution in March, Pan and Wang were chair and deputy chair, and the original leader had to be content with standing committee membership. The *People's Daily* hailed the founding editorially on February 1 as a "new dawn in the Northeast" and singled out for praise the three-way combination of revolutionary masses, local military, and revolutionary former leading cadres as an ideal grouping for the seizure of power.[5]

The party first secretary of Shanxi province, Wei Heng, was politically less nimble than Heilongjiang's Pan, and found himself outsmarted by a colleague, party secretary Liu Geping, who enjoyed the personal support of Mao and Kang Sheng in particular.[6] Liu, who was a Muslim, boasted a unique claim to fame in that he had addressed the founding of the PRC in Tiananmen Square on October 1, 1949, as the official CCP representative of China's ethnic minorities. With the backing of key members of the Shanxi MD, Liu put himself at the head of the Shanxi General Command of Revolutionary Rebels, which took control of the provincial government on January 12. The power-seizure was celebrated by a

People's Daily editorial on January 25, and the new revolutionary committee was certified by the central government on March 18. Wei Heng was imprisoned and committed suicide on January 29. He was the third provincial-level first secretary to choose this escape route from struggle sessions; Wan Xiaotang in Tianjin had committed suicide at the age of fifty in September 1966; when half a million people turned up at a memorial ceremony, Mao criticized it as a demonstration of force against the party, "using the dead to oppress the living." Yan Hongyan, the Yunnan first secretary, committed suicide in Kunming on January 7, 1967, blaming Chen Boda and the CCRG for his action;[7] a week later Zhou Enlai told a delegation from Yunnan that "we sent a forensic expert from Beijing who confirmed that it was suicide: Yan Hongyan is a shameless renegade."[8]

The Beijing Municipal Party Committee and government were unique in having already witnessed a power-seizure at the start of the Cultural Revolution. But this fact did not prevent a new one from taking place, now that Shanghai had shown the way. In the words of Xie Fuzhi, the takeover of Peng Zhen's party apparatus in May 1966 had already been "a seizure of power under Chairman Mao's guidance."[9] But nothing could deter those who on the afternoon of January 18 launched another. First three rebel organizations led by middle school teachers announced that they had "taken over" the party committee and were setting up a general headquarters on the fifth floor of its main building. An hour later, thirty other rebel organizations made up of university students and workers announced that *they* had seized power and set up a takeover committee on one of the floors below. As confusion reigned and the first rebel organizations became de facto hostages to the second, a third rebel coalition, which had been secretly networking inside the party committee offices all along, set about to mediate and work out a more orderly power-seizure. In the early hours of January 19, Zhou Enlai issued a tentative seal of approval when he was told of the "victorious" power-seizure in the midst of an address in the Great Hall of the People; he immediately informed his audience that he wished to "congratulate the rebels from more than thirty different work units who, last night, entered the premises of the municipal party committee and seized power."[10]

But it was to take an additional three months of preparatory groundwork before the Beijing Revolutionary Committee was formally inaugurated, on April 20. After all, Mao's intention had been to achieve far more than merely the replacement of one set of cadres by another. The high point of that day was the symbolic act of smashing the old signboards that read "Beijing Municipal Party

Committee" and "Beijing Municipal People's Government." "A mere formality," according to Wu De (who retained his No. 2 position in the hierarchy), taken care of by eager "rebels," but one that was repeated over and over again across the country.[11]

Restoring Order

As winter gave way to spring in 1967, Zhou gained Mao's support for a number of measures designed to limit the confusion and damage to the nation's polity and economy. "Revolutionary students and teachers" were told to stop marching hundreds of miles to revolutionary shrines, where lack of accommodations and minimal facilities had led to outbreaks of infectious diseases, and go home. Provincials camped out in Beijing were told that their free lunches were coming to an end.[12] Ministries and industries connected with national security were declared off-limits for the exchange of revolutionary experience.[13] Primary school teachers and pupils were recalled to classes, followed shortly by middle school teachers and students and, a little later still, college teachers and students.[14] The resumption of revolutionary exchanges was cancelled, though the reiteration of this ruling indicated that it was not obeyed.[15] Red Guards were forbidden to punish party members, confiscated property had to be returned, and attempts to form national Red Guard organizations were quashed.[16]

Urban youths, who had been rusticated in earlier campaigns and had seized the opportunities afforded by the Cultural Revolution to exchange experiences in order to return home, were ordered to report back to the border regions and mountainous areas into which they had earlier been decanted.[17] Industrial and construction workers who had been transferred along with their plants from coastal provinces to build the Third Front deep inland were told to return to the Third Front industrial bases.[18] Temporary and contract workers, whose circumstances had been blamed on Liu Shaoqi and whose grievances made them ready allies of those who sought to upset the status quo at the outset of the Cultural Revolution, were told that there could be no immediate changes in their positions.[19] The eight-hour workday was declared inviolable; the Cultural Revolution should be a spare-time activity for miners and industrial workers.[20] All workers were presumably inspired by the rise of a workers' movement in Shanghai under the aegis of Zhang Chunqiao. Peasants—some of whom had taken the opportunity provided by the Cultural Revolution to complain vigorously of the

173

urban bias in the development process[21]—were exhorted to "work to seize victory in the spring cultivation," and power-seizures in production brigades and teams were declared undesirable.[22]

Vice Premier Li Fuchun, whose portfolio included overseeing the third Five-Year Plan, 1966–1970, put an optimistic gloss on the state of the economy, despite looming problems, to a meeting of military officers convened by Zhou Enlai and Ye Jianying from February 26 to March 25. During 1966, Li claimed, agricultural production had increased by 7 percent and industrial output by 22 percent.[23] But during the first two months of 1967, output figures for three key commodities—steel, coal, and oil—were less than during the equivalent period of 1966, and plan targets were not being met as a result of the "destructive counterrevolutionary economist practices of a tiny handful of party persons in power taking the capitalist road" and workers spending "a little too much time away from their production posts." But Li took encouragement from a rise in March over February in the daily outputs of his benchmark products. The annual plan for 1967 had been distributed to centrally managed enterprises; whether its targets were known to or being implemented by enterprises in the various localities was a different matter. In his talk, Li listed the major targets for 1967 and called on provincial leaders in his audience to stress plan implementation. Post–Cultural Revolution official statistics reveal how damaging to Li's hopes was the "all-round civil war" that so exhilarated Mao: industrial production, slated to increase by 16 percent, dropped by 14.9 percent; agricultural production, scheduled to rise by 6 percent, managed only 1.5 percent.[24] By June, Li Fuchun was forced to face facts, declaring that "armed struggles" had had a "very bad impact," especially on coal output and the railways. Military control of coal fields and key harbors was requested.[25]

Of particular importance to the officers in Li's audience was the impact of the Cultural Revolution on the Third Front. This program might have guaranteed very expensive protection from American bombers, but it did not ensure protection from Red Guards. There were "serious instances of work stoppages that warrant extreme concern," Li said. For him the only answer seemed to be military control of industry, agriculture, and commerce at the local level, as it had been imposed at the center.[26]

In addition to national security establishments, the organs of the CC, the ministries of public security, finance, and foreign affairs, the planning, economic, national construction, and scientific commissions, banks, and the national media were declared off-limits to Red Guards and rebels, and outsiders were ordered to leave.[27] The protection of confidential documents was strengthened, and the protection of state property was ordered.[28]

The Role of the PLA

The PLA was being assigned a double role. On the one hand, it had to maintain security and some semblance of law and order. Simultaneously it played a crucial role in the success of the early power-seizures: the key was the participation of the PLA, not the party, not the Red Guards, not even the "rebel worker" organizations. Even in the particularly advantageous conditions of Shanghai, Zhang Chunqiao himself said that the role of the CCRG should not be exaggerated, adding that what decided the issue was that "the head of the Shanghai Garrison issued a firm order, stating that anyone trying to smash the sign [reading "Government Offices of the People's Commune of Shanghai"] would automatically be labeled a counterrevolutionary and arrested."[29] Where the provincial military districts supported the same alternative leaders and popular organizations as the party center, the power-seizures succeeded, and the "civil war" that Mao had predicted was brief. Where they did not, the power-seizures failed. In either case, the PLA's behavior became the most powerful factor in shaping the further course of the Cultural Revolution.

By the end of the third week of January 1967, intelligence to this effect was arriving on Mao's desk by the hour, not merely from the CCRG but also through PLA channels. On January 21, one report containing an urgent message from the city of Hefei (routed in accordance with all the proper bureaucratic procedures via the Anhui MD, the Nanjing MR, the MAC, and finally Lin Biao) told the CCP Chairman that liaising Red Guards from the Capital 3rd HQ in Hefei were about to organize a mass rally at which they would denounce the provincial first party secretary and in effect proclaim a "seizure of power." Unless the Anhui MD sent a contingent of soldiers to back them up, so the Red Guards argued, the PLA would not be supporting the Cultural Revolution.[30] After reading the report, Mao sent a short handwritten note to Lin Biao in which he told his closest comrade-in-arms that "the military should be dispatched to provide support to the broad masses of the left."[31] Two days later, Mao's order became official policy when the CCP center issued *Zhongfa* [1967] 27, which stated: "When genuine proletarian Leftists ask the army for help, the army should send troops to actively support them."[32]

But this power carried penalties. The PLA could not act simply as a *deus ex machina.* It was inevitably sucked into the maelstrom, with profound political and institutional consequences. As early as October 5, 1966, Lin Biao had opened floodgates within the PLA by conceding to students at military academies and schools the same rights enjoyed by the Red Guards.[33] By January, frantic calls were coming from the regions about attacks by military Red Guards on senior officers. The commander of the Nanjing MR, a onetime Buddhist who had studied martial arts in the legendary Shaolin Monastery as a teenager before joining the Red Army in 1927, was drinking heavily and threatened to open fire if anyone tried to seize him. The commander of the Fuzhou MR, a highly decorated former deputy commander of the Chinese People's Volunteers in Korea, warned that if the situation were not brought under control, he would go off to the mountains and become a guerrilla leader.[34]

Lin Biao could not afford to have his power base eroded as Liu's and Deng's had been. On January 23, the participants in an expanded session of the MAC that had met on January 19–20 submitted a collective appeal ("request for instructions") to Lin and Mao for measures to be designed to restore order in the military. The following day, attesting to the urgency with which he viewed the matter, one of the MAC vice chairmen, Marshal Xu Xiangqian, went in person to Lin's home to plead the case that something had to be done. Lin agreed. An informal meeting of the top brass was called, a draft order was drawn up—its wording borrowed in part from the MAC "request for instructions," in part devised by Lin and the marshals—and then shared with the CCRG, which fine-tuned the political rhetoric. On January 25, Lin submitted it together with a note to Mao requesting his ratification. Unlike the PLA, Mao was not in a hurry; he called for further changes and for input from Zhou Enlai. On January 28 the order finally went out, with a powerful endorsement from Mao: "These eight points as drawn up are very good; issue them accordingly."[35]

The order was ambiguously worded, but its general thrust was in the direction of imposing law and order. It explicitly forbade all attempts to "assault" key military installations, outlawed the "arbitrary ransacking of homes," and warned against attempting to resolve "contradictions among the people" with methods designed to deal with "the enemy."[36] Zhou Enlai later spoke of it as an order that "protected the army," and on this point he was undoubtedly correct.[37] So striking was the way in which the order amounted to restraining the "mass" aspects of the movement that the printers who received it from the MAC on the night of January 28 believed it was spurious and refused to print it until they were shown Mao's original handwritten endorsement.[38] Nor was Mao against the partial insulation of the PLA from the disruption among the civilian population; after all, the PLA was his institutional base too. According to Ye Jianying, Mao did not want all the military regions to carry out the Cultural Revolution simultaneously, wanted to keep the movement inside and outside the armed forces separated, and wanted to postpone the movement in military regions that bordered enemy territory.[39] Zhang Guohua, the first secretary and military region commander in Tibet, benefited from this last consideration.[40]

In its first paragraph the MAC order countermanded the previous policy of nonintervention and instructed commanders to suppress rightists and counter-revolutionary groups and elements.[41] The order did not and indeed could not explain how to determine which organizations were leftist and which not. But in the immediate aftermath of the order, provincial military commanders interpreted it as an attempt to limit the chaos being produced by the Cultural Revolution. They acted with extreme prejudice to maintain "law and order," sometimes with, sometimes without, the prior knowledge of the MAC.

The "Three Supports and the Two Militaries"

For the ambiguous role of the PLA to be effective, internal discipline had to be restored. This was the burden of a number of MAC orders issued in early 1967.[42] The PLA's role in relation to the rest of society was to restore stability, often acting as a sort of fire brigade,[43] while ensuring that Cultural Revolutionaries came out on top. This policy was finally crystallized in the slogan "The three supports and the two militaries," issued by the MAC on March 19, 1967. The military was ordered to support the left, the peasants, and the workers and to carry out military training and control.[44] What training meant in practice had already been indicated by a Central Document, *Zhongfa* [1967] 85, giving the example of how a PLA unit had turned around a junior middle school in the Tianjin area, partly it seems with drill and other military exercises, but most effectively probably simply by being on the premises and tolerating no nonsense.[45] Military control meant putting a ministry or a province or an area under military rule, leaving the commander to restore order. By the time the policy was rescinded in August 1972 and PLA personnel were returned to their units, some 2.8 million officers and men had been seconded to various duties under its aegis.[46] After the Cultural Revolution, PLA officers found to their dismay that they had to self-criticize for excesses committed under this policy.[47]

The center was not always able to pinpoint the appropriate PLA officer to control effectively. Liu Xianquan, who had been ordered on March 24 to set up the Qinghai military control commission, was transferred on April 13 to Inner Mongolia, where the PLA as well as the party had fallen apart.[48] The center also set up military control commissions in Anhui and Guangdong, but rehabilitated a radical mass organization in Anhui[49] and faulted the Chengdu MR for having been deceived by conservative mass organizations.[50] The Shandong MD faulted itself for a similar error, and Mao praised its attitude as "Very good! Correct. Exemplary. To be emulated!"[51] Although it continued to prove impossible for PLA commanders fully to restore order, it was even more problematic, as the example of Sichuan below illustrates, for them to identify a truly Maoist mass organization, or to agree with the CCRG which among hostile rival claimants to choose.

In Huhehot, the capital of the Inner Mongolian Autonomous Region, a PLA officer shot and killed an unarmed student from the regional teachers' college demonstrating outside the headquarters of the Inner Mongolia MR.[52] In Kaifeng, in Henan province, units of the PLA 1st Corps opened fire on civilian demonstrators.[53] In Sichuan, the headquarters of the Chengdu MR was subjected to a six-day, seven-night siege by members and supporters of two great radical mass organizations—the "Chengdu Workers Revolutionary Rebel Regiment" and the "Sichuan University August 26 Battle Regiment" acting in coalition. Once the PLA had received the go-ahead to do so from Beijing, it responded by arresting close to 100,000 "rebels" in a province-wide crackdown.[54] Instead of running Sichuan in the name of the "revolutionary left," the rebels found themselves languishing in jail, where, according to one sympathetic contemporary account,

> they suffered every conceivable hardship, being locked up twelve people to a cell, measuring 3 by 3 meters, sharing one piss pot and one pot in which to wash their rice bowls; it was so crowded that moving was almost impossible even when crouching. Some were locked up in underground cells without any sunlight and without being able to move at all. The food was worse than pig feed . . . The wardens told them: "Red Guards are newborn counter-revolutionaries, and there's no way you will ever be rehabilitated here—the only thing you can do is go to Taiwan or to the United States!"[55]

It was to be almost two months before substantial numbers began to be set free. On April 20, the commander of the Sichuan MD informed the CCRG that some 27,865 of those detained in the crackdown had been released so far. Mao's reaction to the news was that clearly too many people had been arrested in the first place, but "mistakes are hard to avoid, and as long as they are conscientiously rectified, it's OK."[56]

The farther removed from the real action they were, the easier it was for commanding officers to convince themselves that what they were doing was merely "removing obstacles blocking the path of the revolution" or dealing a blow against the "class enemy." Much as they might have wanted to, ordinary soldiers did not always have the same option. To many, the experience of being made to shoot to kill unarmed civilians shouting "Long Live the Communist Party!" was highly traumatic.[57] In the aftermath of a bloody confrontation on the premises of the *Qinghai Daily* in Xining, a surviving Red Guard was told by a PLA soldier guarding him in prison that quite a few soldiers had cried on the eve of the confrontation. "I cried too," the Red Guard replied, only to have it explained to him by the guard that "they cried for a different reason. They knew the shooting was just about to begin."[58] The outcome of the shooting on this occasion was, according to an official estimate, that "the masses suffered 169 dead and 178 wounded, while the armed forces suffered 4 dead and 26 wounded."[59]

Behind the observations made in Western histories about "chaos and anarchy, until the military intervened to restore order,"[60] lay massacres like that in Xining, the precise circumstances of which remain highly contentious to this day. In some cases, even the post–Cultural Revolutionary authorities, with their intense desire to have but a single concise and "correct" history of events appear in print, have not been able to see this aim realized. The end of the occupation of the *Qinghai Daily* just mentioned is but one example. One version of events in a Chinese history of the Cultural Revolution, published in the late 1980s by a historian affiliated with the PLA, has it that once they had succeeded in occupying the premises of the paper, the Red Guards proceeded to

> beat, smash, steal, loot, and grab and subject the newspaper staff to a white terror, even beating some of them to death. Some of the illegal occupants shouted counterrevolutionary slogans, and with rifles and ammunition they had stolen from elsewhere they issued violent threats to the PLA soldiers who came to persuade them to change their ways . . . Seeking to provoke trouble, the occupants of the newspaper premises then shot at the armed forces, forcing them to counterattack. In the fighting that ensued, some people were shot dead on the spot while the rest were made to vacate the newspaper premises.[61]

An entirely different version of events can be found in the official history of the CCP in Qinghai, published in the 1990s:

Enjoying the support of [the commander of the Qinghai MD] Liu Xianquan, some people opposed to the decision to impose military control [over the *Qinghai Daily*] threw the soldiers who attempted to exercise that military control over the wall and off the premises. This provoked righteous indignation among the officers and men of the armed forces and the masses. By February 23, the number of people inside and outside the newspaper premises was greater than ever. Under these exceptionally chaotic circumstances, one soldier's weapon went off by accident, wounding a number of his fellow soldiers. This was mistakenly interpreted as the "August 18" rebel occupants of the newspaper premises having begun to fire shots [at the PLA] and in turn led to the military opening fire. Although no order to shoot had been given by the commander in charge, once the shooting began no prompt effective measures were taken to suppress fire.[62]

The end of the butchery (the ratio of forty-two dead civilians for every dead soldier speaks volumes) was not the end of the ordeal for wounded occupants and innocent bystanders. Some hospitals simply refused medical treatment to those who frankly stated that they had been shot or wounded by the Liberation Army.[63] A central inquiry in Beijing in March 1967 was told of a girl who had been hit by three bullets and who, as she lay wounded, had been asked first of all who had fired them. "She was told: 'If you say it was the *August 18* [rebels], I will attend to your wounds and treat you, whereas if you say it was the Liberation Army, I'll have you sent to prison.'" Terrified, the girl responded truthfully that she had actually seen the soldiers who had fired at her. As a result, she was sent to prison rather than hospitalized.[64]

By the second half of March, Mao had concluded that the delicate balance between the forces of "rebellion" which he encouraged and the military which he backed was beginning to be upset. Reinforcing this belief were intelligence arriving from CCRG reporters in the provinces and the findings of centrally conducted inquiries. In Qinghai, Zhao Yongfu was made a scapegoat, accused of carrying out a "counterrevolutionary coup" against the Qinghai Military District commander, Liu Xianquan, and then engaging in "ruthless armed suppression" of revolutionary mass organizations. Zhao was placed in solitary confinement to await trial, but the PLA's position in the province was strengthened, for Qinghai was put under a military control commission headed by Liu.[65]

In Inner Mongolia, a wholesale purge of the military leadership was effectuated together with a change in the status of the region from an independent MR to a subordinate part of the neighboring Beijing MR. In the Sichuan case, the center handed down a judgment against the PLA of pursuing a mistaken line, a move that was greatly resented.[66] In Xinjiang, where party first secretary Wang Enmao was in the enviably strong position of being concurrently military region commander and political commissar in a frontier region bordering a hostile state, the Soviet Union, clashes that resulted in 31 dead and 107 wounded were interpreted quite differently by himself and the CCRG.[67] These conflicts between regional military commanders and the CCRG in Beijing exposed a crack in the façade of unity of the disparate Maoist coalition.

On April 1 Mao gave expression to his concerns about the PLA's behavior in the provinces by adding to the draft of a Central Document, *Zhongfa* [1967] 117, dealing with problems in Anhui province, the following observation:

> [Here in Beijing] quite a few students from elsewhere in China have forced their way into Zhongnanhai, students from military academies have forced their way into the Ministry of Defense, but the center and the MAC have not reprimanded them, much less made them admit to crimes, issue statements of repentance, or produce written self-criticisms. It's sufficient to explain the matter clearly to them and then encourage them to return home. The localities are taking much too serious a view of the assaults on military institutions.[68]

To drive home the point that Mao viewed this as a general phenomenon, with implications extending far beyond the situation in Anhui, the CC General Office on April 5 issued a follow-up document calling specifically for the "organized oral transmission" of *Zhongfa* [1967] 117 across all of China. Indeed, the CCRG had already for some time recognized that their supporters were in retreat in many places as a result of the permission given to the PLA to restore order. In February, university Red Guards from Beijing had conducted an investigation into how their comrades-in-rebellion in Wuhan were doing; on April 2, on the basis of their report, the *People's Daily* editorialized in support of the beleaguered leftists.[69]

At this point Lin Biao, perhaps spurred by the editorial—the title of which was "Adopt a Correct Attitude toward the Little Generals"—sought to burnish his leftist credentials after a visit by Huang Yongsheng, the commander of the Canton MR. According to his secretary, Lin had hitherto kept himself detached from the tumult up and down the country, but he now decided that the eight-point order of January 28 needed to be superseded, and he drew up a ten-point order on the spur of the moment.[70] This was the order, issued on April 6, that was enthusiastically endorsed by Mao. Whereas the eight points had favored the PLA maintenance of order, the new ten points redressed the balance in favor of the rebels. The PLA was explicitly ordered not to fire on members of mass organizations; not to carry out arbitrary arrests, particularly large-scale ones; not to declare mass organizations reactionary—labeling was now to become the prerogative of the center, and opposing the PLA would not be a criterion for determining where on the political spectrum a mass organization lay—and not to take revenge on rebels who had attacked the PLA in the past. Actions taken counter to the ten points in the past had to be rectified immediately.[71]

It was to be Jiang Qing who, in a widely disseminated speech finalized by her husband, came to spell out how the new MAC order was to be interpreted and related to the earlier one.[72] The purpose of the eight-point MAC order of January 28, Jiang Qing explained, had been one of "supporting the army." The ten-point order of April 6, on the other hand, aimed at reminding the military of the need to "cherish the people."[73] Not that the orders were in any way contradictory, she insisted. The "spirit" of the first document was in conformity with that of the second. Anyone who tried to cite one against the other was either a "bad person" or a comrade "committing a mistake."[74]

According to Wang Li, anti-PLA riots broke out everywhere in response to the new order. Mao tried to reconcile the contradiction by coining the slogan "Support the army and cherish the people": cited in the press, written on billboards, embossed on Mao badges, and even painted on the weapons of the PLA, this was Mao's attempt to get the PLA and rebels to let bygones be bygones. Zhou Enlai, Kang Sheng, and Wang Li each elaborated upon it in conversation with agitated rebels and PLA officers from Inner Mongolia on May 26. Zhou said: "If someone is already dead, then you should not go too far in your attempts to determine [who was responsible]"; Kang Sheng took the same line: "For now, you should refrain from attempting to decide who deserved to die and who died in vain"; while Wang Li commented bluntly that it was "inevitable that people will die in the course of a revolution."[75]

Clearly, the CCRG needed to restrain law-and-order commanders in the provinces or its supporters would be decimated. It was also trying to extend its influence within the PLA. Liu Zhijian, who had collaborated with Jiang Qing in February 1966 in the preparation of the Summary of the PLA Forum on Literature and Art, had been forced to resign on January 4, 1967, after self-criticizing for alleged "mistakes in line" since the beginning of the Cultural Revolution. He was replaced as deputy director of the PLA General Political Department by a very active CCRG member, Guan Feng.[76] The PLA CCRG had been completely reorganized on January 11, 1967, and put under the nominal leadership of Marshal Xu Xiangqian, but it was effectively dominated by its new "adviser," Jiang Qing, who installed Guan Feng as a deputy head.[77] The head of the PLA's General Political Department, Xiao Hua, was made Marshal Xu's principal deputy, but within eight days, he, too, came under fire from the CCRG and disappeared.[78]

Mao and Jiang Qing also extended their personal influence over the running of the *Liberation Army Daily* in unusual fashion when their daughter Li Na, who recently had taken a job with the paper as a journalist/apprentice, and seven of her colleagues "seized power" from its editor-in-chief, Hu Chi. As a reward for agreeing to keep outside "mass organizations" from interfering, Li Na's self-designated shock brigade was quickly recognized as the paper's official "mass supervisory group" by the MAC. Lin Biao told its members in a letter of congratulations: "I firmly support you! Do not fear 'chaos,' as only in the wake of chaos can there be order."[79]

Jiang Qing and Lin Biao had contracted a marriage of considerable convenience to both at the outset of the Cultural Revolution. But as power-seizures took place and the CCRG sought a foothold in the PLA, their interests and purposes would begin to divide. For the moment, however, they still had to confront a common enemy. The provincial power-seizures and their repercussions led to crises and tension between the old guard and the civilian radicals. In February 1967 those tensions exploded in a confrontation between the CCRG and some of the most senior members of the MAC and State Council in Zhongnanhai.

11

The Last Stand of the Old Guard

Mao seems never to have ordered the liquidation of a senior colleague during the Cultural Revolution. Unlike Stalin, he did not feel the need for the safeguard of a final solution. Instead, he was content to leave his onetime comrades-in-arms to the tender mercies of the CCRG or Red Guards. If doing so led to their humiliation, torture, injury, or even death, so be it; that was what making revolution was about. Hence his insouciance about the denunciations of Liu Shaoqi and other PSC members at their homes in Zhongnanhai. He may have counted on the *Schadenfreude* of millions of his countrymen at the fall of the high and the mighty.

Zhou remonstrated with Red Guards about their rough treatment of party veterans[1] and also made attempts to protect individual party leaders, both at the center and in the provinces—he had Marshal He Long spirited away to the Western Hills outside Beijing in a manner reminiscent of a thriller movie[2]—but as the Zhongnanhai raids made clear, his powers were limited. On January 16, 1967, photographs of the first victims of the Cultural Revolution—Peng Zhen, Lu Dingyi, Luo Ruiqing, and Yang Shangkun—showed them with placards around their necks, heads bowed, as they were publicly humiliated.[3] On January 22, Minister for the Coal Industry Zhang Linzhi died under interrogation.[4] Deputy Director of the Defense Industry Committee of the MAC and CC member Zhao Erlu died about the same time under similar circumstances.[5] Finally, Zhou and his State Council colleagues drew up a list of thirty senior government officials who should be allowed to move into Zhongnanhai for protection and rest—though that concept had already proved problematic—and a second list of regional leaders who should be brought to the relative safety of the capital. Mao agreed to the lists, but the directive could not be enforced in all cases, as some provincial leaders were already in captivity.[6]

Even vice premiers came under attack, affecting the work of the State

Council. On January 8, 1967, Zhou told Zhongnanhai rebels that the center would not permit them to drag out Vice Premiers Tan Zhenlin, Chen Yi, Li Fuchun, and Li Xiannian.[7] But on January 24, Marshal Chen Yi was forced to self-criticize at a mass rally organized by rebels in the foreign affairs sector.[8] Other vice premiers came under attack. In conversation with senior Ministry of Finance staff, Zhou admitted to feeling "very uncomfortable" and "upset" about what was happening. Putting dunces' caps on the heads of old cadres, he said, was "bourgeois, feudal. If you were in power, and the younger generation were to treat you that way, would you accept it?" he asked.[9]

The premier's tenuous ability to protect colleagues was vividly illustrated by the fall of Tao Zhu in January 1967, an event that in turn helped precipitate the last stand of the old guard. Known as the "February Countercurrent," this was, according to Lin Biao's later judgment, "the most serious anti-party incident to occur in the wake of the Eleventh Plenum."[10] Translated from metaphor into plain language, it was the calling into question of the wisdom of the entire Cultural Revolutionary undertaking by some of the nation's most senior government and military leaders at two chaotic meetings in Zhongnanhai in mid-February 1967.

The Tao Zhu Case

After Tao had been helicoptered from his post as first secretary of the Central-South Region into the top ranks of the central leadership, Zhou had relied considerably upon him during the latter half of 1966 to second his efforts to protect individuals and institutions, and to maintain China on an even keel.[11] CCRG leaders, aware that they could not take on Zhou Enlai, had focused their hostility on Tao Zhu, whom—despite the fact that he was formally a member of the CCRG in an "advisory" capacity identical with that of Kang Sheng—they never truly regarded as "one of us." There were many clashes, and Tao was subjected to numerous petty taunts and serious accusations, and sometimes provoked to anger.[12] On November 27, 1966, at Jiang Qing's request, Guan Feng sent her a report detailing seven crimes which Tao had committed since coming to the center, and which allegedly amounted to supporting the Liu-Deng line and opposing the Chairman's call to "bombard the headquarters." Jiang Qing forwarded the report to Mao.[13] The following day at a big meeting, Jiang Qing pointedly omitted Tao Zhu's name from a list of the Chairman's close comrades-in-arms.[14]

Mao's reaction to Guan Feng's report is unknown. Indeed, the Chairman's role in the fall of Tao Zhu is still obscure. He was said to have signed off on documents prepared by Tao that did not really satisfy him; Zhou Enlai's rule of thumb, as noted earlier, was that unless Mao wrote something like "Very good" on a document, one should assume that the Chairman might have some doubts about it.[15] One insider felt that, from Mao's point of view, Tao Zhu was taking his responsibilities as if the situation were normal, which was the last thing the Chairman wanted.[16] At the time, misperceptions of Mao's attitude, induced by his contradictory behavior, quite probably helped to precipitate the February Countercurrent.[17] One could "work toward the Chairman" from different perspectives.

The first serious attack on Tao Zhu in a major forum occurred on December 6, when Wang Li and other members of the CCRG accused him at an expanded Politburo conference, chaired by Lin Biao, of using the shibboleth of production to suppress revolution.[18] But the issue that came to haunt Tao Zhu was his attempt to protect his former Central-South Region deputy, Wang Renzhong, who had also fallen foul of the CCRG despite having been made one of its vice heads at Mao's personal instigation. Tao Zhu made successive representations to Mao that Wang, who had long been a favorite of the Chairman's, should be allowed to leave his post and go to Canton to rest. Finally Mao responded, saying that Wang's future should be decided by the Politburo and the CCRG jointly.[19]

On December 26, when the CCRG toasted upheavals while celebrating Mao's birthday with the Chairman, Tao Zhu seems not to have been discussed.[20] On December 27–28, Zhou Enlai convened the meeting mandated by Mao to settle Wang Renzhong's fate.[21] Instead the CCRG leadership suddenly renewed the assault on Tao Zhu, along the lines of Guan Feng's charge sheet. To Tao's evident dismay, none of his Politburo colleagues saw fit to defend him; only Li Fuchun put in the lame suggestion that Tao should be transferred back to the Central-South Region.[22]

It was from this point on that Mao's behavior became confusing. On December 29, at a PSC meeting summoned by the Chairman, he criticized Jiang Qing for not having got permission from the center, presumably himself, before attacking Tao.[23] Mao praised Tao's work since coming to Beijing. After the meeting, in an hour's private chat with Tao Zhu, Mao described Jiang Qing as narrow-minded and intolerant and counseled Tao not to take offense at anything she said. He also advised Tao to change his own provincial workstyle, not to shoot his mouth off without thinking first, to become more modest and prudent. The two men then discussed the need for Tao Zhu to make a two-to-three-month provincial tour to inspect the progress of the Cultural Revolution, and the Chairman gave him a list of provincial leaders who could be criticized, but not burned to a crisp. Tao Zhu returned home elated, telling his wife that the Chairman had protected him and that his problems were not so serious after all. She later remembered that moment as the "last radiance of the setting sun"—a momentary recovery of consciousness just before death.[24]

So it proved. Late the following evening, a group of Central-South Red Guards blackmailed Tao Zhu into meeting them by threatening a hunger strike. Their avowed aim was to seize Wang Renzhong, but apparently they deliberately provoked Tao into angry responses to what he considered their impertinent attitude toward a national leader. When guards rushed in to protect Tao in the increasingly ugly situation, the Red Guards accused Tao of suppressing the masses with armed force.[25] Chen Boda and Jiang Qing followed up this confrontation with what turned out to be the coup de grâce on January 4. They denounced Tao Zhu to the Central-South Red Guards, describing him as "China's biggest protector of the imperial clique" for his efforts to safeguard Wang Renzhong.[26] Immediately "Down with Tao Zhu" posters sprang up everywhere.[27] A striking aspect of these accusations is that in addition to criticizing the party's fourth-ranking leader, the CCRG leaders seemed to feel that there was no problem in targeting Wang Renzhong, despite his past relationship to Mao.[28]

Later the same day, in response to a question from Mao, presumably prompted by CCRG allegations, Zhou Enlai denied that Tao Zhu was guilty of suppressing the masses who were seeking to drag out Wang Renzhong. The premier acknowledged that Tao might have an attitude problem, presumably a reference to the robust manner in which he had dealt with the Red Guards. However, Mao's demeanor was sufficiently ambiguous to cause the premier to call Tao in the early hours of January 5 and warn him not to leave his home for the next several days; and indeed by January 8, Zhongnanhai rebels were demanding the right to seize him along with Liu Shaoqi and Deng Xiaoping.[29]

On January 8, too, Mao commented (apparently in a message to a Red Guard rally) that the issue of Tao Zhu was "very serious." Tao was "very dishonest," but it had taken the masses to solve the problem. Mao blamed his transfer to the center upon Deng Xiaoping's recommendation, as if he personally had little knowledge of Tao. He wished the meeting good luck in its efforts to drag out Tao Zhu.[30] On the same day, Mao appointed Wang Li to succeed Tao Zhu as head of a central propaganda group to replace the CC's Propaganda Department,[31] and when Wang made his first speech to journalists on January 9, attacking Tao Zhu was his major concern.[32] Qi Benyu followed this up on January 12 with a speech to rebels in the CC's General Office attacking Deng and Tao.[33] By about January 20, Tao stopped getting official papers; thereafter his red telephone was removed and the electricity voltage to his house reduced.[34]

Just when the triumph of the CCRG over Tao Zhu seemed complete, Mao seemingly changed his position again. At first he only expressed irritation at the *modus operandi* of the CCRG. At a meeting with Chen Boda, Ye Jianying, Jiang Qing, and Wang Li on the night of February 3, Mao commented on the formal status of the CCRG as a party institution that had de facto replaced the CC Secretariat, but criticized its lack of "democratic centralism." Mao was apparently concerned less with the internal operations of the CCRG than with its relationship to himself. He received reports only irregularly. No formal decision had ever been taken about the manner and frequency of CCRG reports to the PSC. At present, Mao observed, all its members presented their own versions of events independently: Kang Sheng told his story, Chen Boda told his, and Jiang Qing told hers. The CCRG as an institution submitted no reports.[35]

Mao's irritation is understandable. Mao loved upheaval *(luan),* but he appreciated the services of a well-oiled and obedient bureaucracy. Unfortunately for him, the CCRG was not a tight-knit body responding instantly to its leader, like the CC Secretariat under Deng Xiaoping. Despite the CCRG's swelling bureaucratic tail, its leadership remained a congeries of *lumpen* radicals, recruited by Mao on the basis of their loyalty to him, and its foot soldiers consisted of "other ranks" recruited by CCRG leaders on similar grounds, all for the purpose of stirring the country up rather than running it smoothly. The timid Chen Boda never exercised authority over the impetuous and imperious Jiang Qing, while Kang Sheng kept his counsel until he was clear how he could best work toward the Chairman. Zhang Chunqiao was still too preoccupied with Shanghai to play the commanding role that he would later assume. No wonder Mao was irritated.

But this indication of the Chairman's dissatisfaction with the CCRG as a bureaucratic machine would not by itself have provided sufficient encouragement for the party old guard to have moved against it. For that, an indication that Mao shared their displeasure at some of the activities of the CCRG would be necessary. This occurred a week later, on February 10, when the Chairman summoned Lin Biao, Zhou, Chen Boda, Kang Sheng, Li Fuchun, Ye Jianying, Jiang Qing, and Wang Li to a meeting and attacked Chen Boda and Jiang Qing. According to Wang Li, Mao lost his temper after having read for the first time— highly unlikely, according to some[36]—a transcript of the attacks by Chen Boda and Jiang Qing on Tao Zhu on January 4. Mao accused Chen Boda of having been way out of line in "calling for the overthrow" of Tao Zhu. No one member of the PSC had the right to "strike down" another member just like that. "You and I have got along [fine] for so many years; this is not about you as a person." But that reassurance was undercut by Mao's allegation that "in the past, as far as relations between [Liu] Shaoqi and myself have been concerned, you've always been an opportunist." And in words reminiscent of his criticism of Deng Xiaoping at the outset of the Cultural Revolution, Mao claimed that "as many years as I've known you, you've never sought me out unless the matter involved you personally." Chen wanted to make a self-criticism then and there, but Mao told him not to. After the meeting Chen became suicidal and had to be dissuaded from drastic action by Zhou Enlai.[37]

Mao then turned on Jiang Qing: "You're someone who has grandiose aims but puny abilities, great ambition but little talent. You look down on everyone else." The other members of the CCRG, Mao added, had done nothing improper: "[Toppling Tao Zhu] was organized by just you two, nobody else!" Mao even seemed to criticize Lin Biao, albeit indirectly. Turning to Lin, he said: "See, it's still just like it was before! I don't get reports. Things are being kept secret from me. The sole exception is the premier. Whenever there's something important going on, he always reports to me." Concluding the meeting, Mao said that the CCRG should hold a meeting to criticize Chen Boda and Jiang Qing. But, he added, "the problem with Chen and Jiang" was on no account to be debated elsewhere. They were to be criticized only by the other members of the CCRG, and to that end Zhang Chunqiao and Yao Wenyuan were to be recalled immediately from Shanghai.[38]

One Chinese biographer of Tao Zhu has argued that Mao never wanted him to fall; he needed someone of his ability to aid Zhou.[39] The Chairman's complaints about lack of reporting from the CCRG suggest that Tao fell because Mao was not aware of what was going on. His denunciation of Chen Boda and Jiang Qing supposedly showed how angry he was when he did find out, but he did not reverse the decision for fear it would undermine the CCRG. This interpretation does not withstand scrutiny in the overall context of CCRG activities, the long gestation of the Tao Zhu affair, and Mao's behavior patterns.

CCRG leaders, even the thrusting Jiang Qing, were always aware of the source of their power. If Mao told them not to attack Zhou Enlai, they obeyed. It is highly unlikely that they would have carried on a two-month campaign against Tao Zhu without a strong sense of the Chairman's tacit approval. If Mao wished to protect Tao Zhu at the end of December, why did the CCRG persist? Or rather, why did Mao not tell them privately that he would not tolerate any more attacks on Tao Zhu? Why did he not give Zhou an unambiguous indication on the night of January 4–5 that Tao should be protected? Under other circumstances, when an aide whom Mao considered important was maltreated by Red Guards, the Chairman immediately rushed to his house to check up personally on his safety.[40] Though Tao lived quite close to Mao in Zhongnanhai, the Chairman did not see fit to rush round to reassure him on January 5. Instead, he tried to slough off the blame for bringing Tao to Beijing in the first place. The evidence suggests that Mao was well enough aware of the campaign against Tao to have saved him. The fact that he did not choose to do so indicates tacit support for the CCRG campaign, coupled with a desire to avoid blame for bringing down another so worthy a comrade on flimsy grounds. Mao sought to maintain deniability.[41]

Mao may have had an additional reason for castigating Jiang Qing. She was his loyal follower, his student as she called herself after his death, but as the CCRG became the engine of the Cultural Revolution, this strong-willed woman was becoming an increasingly self-confident and prominent political figure. With his patriarchal attitude toward women, the Chairman was warning her not to overstep her proper role. She was, after all, only his wife.[42]

Jiang Qing got the message. The subsequent retreat of the CCRG in the face of Mao's apparent anger bolstered his deniability. Later in the spring, the CCRG on various occasions attempted to downplay the role of Jiang and Chen in particular in the fall of Tao Zhu. At the pre-première screening of a major retrospective exhibit on the Cultural Revolution in Beijing, one of the CCRG's very first instructions to the organizers was that they redesign the exhibit that dealt with the events on and around January 4. A quotation from Chen Boda had to be removed, Qi Benyu insisted, and visitors "should be made to see that it was the revolutionary masses that dragged out Tao Zhu." "It was the masses that dragged him out; we [merely] gave them our support," Chen himself explained, backed up by Jiang Qing and Zhang Chunqiao.[43]

One additional explanation for Tao Zhu's rapid rise and fall suggests itself in the light of the care with which Mao had planned the earlier downfall of his other senior colleagues in 1965–66. By bringing Tao to the center, Mao separated a dynamic leader with high-level connections in the capital from his power base, a region that had traditionally been a haven for opponents of the national government.[44] Coincidence? Perhaps, but a fortunate one.

The February Countercurrent

Whatever Mao's motives in the Tao Zhu affair, there can be little doubt that his dressing-down of Chen Boda and Jiang Qing gave considerable encouragement to the survivors among the old guard; Mao himself certainly believed so.[45] Perhaps the Chairman, well aware of high-level opposition to the Cultural Revolution, intended to smoke out its most antagonistic opponents. It is certainly strange that even though he avowedly wanted to keep Chen's and Jiang's transgressions secret, at the end of this very same enlarged PSC meeting, on February 10, Mao ordered that an additional number of people in the future be called to such meetings, among them Chen Yi, Tan Zhenlin, Xu Xiangqian, Li Xiannian, and Xie Fuzhi.[46]

At any rate, whether he was meant to or not, Li Fuchun promptly shared the contents of Mao's criticisms at a hastily summoned meeting at his house with other members of the Politburo, including Vice Premiers Tan Zhenlin, Marshal Chen Yi, and Li Xiannian.[47] The result was a frontal attack upon the CCRG by the old guard in defiance of Mao's order that the faults of Chen Boda and Jiang Qing were to be discussed only within the CCRG. The conflict, later christened the "February Countercurrent" by Zhang Chunqiao,[48] took place at two meetings of the Central Caucus chaired by Zhou Enlai on February 11 and February 16.

Motivating the old guard, Chinese historians agree, were three issues, discernible through the cut and thrust of the debate: (1) Was the leadership of the party simply to be dispensed with, as in Shanghai? (2) Was every senior leader to be toppled? (3) Was the PLA to be destabilized?[49] Speaking to a *People's Daily* journalist more than a decade later, the seventy-six-year-old Tan Zhenlin recalled: "Those were all issues of a fundamental nature, ones that had cropped up in the course of this so-called 'Great Revolution' movement. To put it bluntly: Who were its ultimate targets? Who were to be relied upon to carry it out? Big issues, that is what they were!"[50]

The meeting on February 11 was supposed to discuss "grasping revolution and promoting production,"[51] but it quickly developed into a verbal brawl between the CCRG, seated on one side of the table, and the assembled marshals and vice premiers, seated opposite them. The CCRG was poorly represented, with only Chen Boda, Kang Sheng, and Wang Li participating.[52] Marshal Ye Jianying, who as secretary general of the MAC supervised the PLA on a day-to-day basis, accused Chen Boda (and by extension the CCRG, which he headed) of making "a mess of the party, a mess of the government, and a mess of the factories and the countryside," and "still you're not satisfied. You insist on making a mess of the army as well! What are you up to, going on like this?" Ye was backed up by Marshal Xu Xiangqian, who also attacked Chen: "The army is a pillar of the dictatorship of the proletariat, but the way you're making a mess of it, it's as if you didn't want this pillar. Are you suggesting that none of us are worth saving? What do you want? For people like Kuai Dafu [the Tsinghua Red Guard leader] to lead the army?" Kang Sheng intervened to defend Chen Boda, saying: "The army doesn't belong to you, Xu Xiangqian," but Ye returned to the attack:

> This power-seizure in Shanghai and changing its name to the Shanghai Commune—this is a big matter that affects the state system, but it wasn't discussed by the Politburo. What do you think you were doing changing the name without authorization? . . . We [i.e., the old guard] don't read books or newspapers, and we don't understand the principles of the Paris Commune. Please explain what its principles are. Can the revolution do without the party's leadership? Does one not need an army?[53]

Chen Boda abased himself, telling Marshal Ye that after his remarks, he was "covered in embarrassment." As the quarrel continued, Zhou Enlai terminated the meeting on the grounds that they had departed from the agenda. As they dispersed, Marshal Chen Yi whispered to Marshal Ye: "My duke [jian gong], you are truly courageous!"[54]

But how courageous? Did Marshal Ye have an inkling of Mao's thinking? For it was on the following day, February 12, that Zhang Chunqiao and Yao Wenyuan, returning from Shanghai at Mao's command, were whisked off from the airport to Mao's residence to be told by the Chairman to change the name "Shanghai Commune." Or was Mao trying to appease the marshals with an unimportant concession on nomenclature? At any rate, it was a clear setback for the freewheeling CCRG radicals. Two days later, their troubles were compounded by internal frictions when the CCRG met to conduct the criticism of Chen Boda and Jiang Qing that Mao had ordered.[55] How much the old guard knew about these developments is uncertain, but when Zhou summoned a second meeting of the Central Caucus on February 16 in a fresh attempt to discuss "grasping revolution and promoting production," the marshals and vice premiers were spoiling for a fight. Zhou did not even have time to announce the opening of the meeting before the recriminations began.[56]

Vice Premier Tan Zhenlin, Mao's chief agricultural aide during the GLF, immediately challenged Zhang Chunqiao to protect Chen Pixian, the ousted Shanghai leader, whom Tan had known when he had worked in the East China Region in the early 1950s. When Zhang said that this would have to be discussed with the masses, Tan exploded: "What masses? Always the masses, the masses. There's still the leadership of the party! [You] don't want the leadership of the party, but keep talking from morning till late about the masses liberating themselves, educating themselves, and making revolution by themselves. What is this stuff? It's metaphysics."[57]

After Zhang had explained that the party organization was in tatters in Shanghai and that every cadre above the rank of section chief was, for now, powerless, Tan continued, even more agitated:

> Your aim is to purge the old cadres. You're knocking them down one by one, until there's not a single one left . . . The "five black categories": some [of you] speak up on their behalf. But what about the children of high-level cadres: how come none [of you] speak up on their behalf? The children of high-level cadres are all being persecuted, every one of them. When you see a high-level cadre's son, you grab him. If this isn't the reactionary blood lineage theory, then what is it? It's to employ the reactionary blood lineage theory to fight the reactionary blood lineage theory. Isn't this metaphysics? . . . Today's rebels: aren't they all children of landlords, rich peasants, or capitalists? Who is this Kuai Dafu person? A counterrevolutionary, that's what he is! . . . Of all the struggles in the history of the party, this is by far the cruelest.[58]

Particularly striking was Tan Zhenlin's bitterness toward Jiang Qing, absent again because of illness. She had called him a counterrevolutionary to his face, he said. When her ally, Xie Fuzhi, the minister of public security, protested that Jiang Qing and the CCRG were protecting Tan, Tan snorted: "I don't want her protection! I work for the party, I don't work for her!"[59]

At this point, Tan began gathering up his papers and putting on his jacket preparatory to leaving in disgust, announcing: "If I had known at the beginning that it would come to this, I would never have joined the revolution or joined the Communist Party. I wasn't meant to live to the age of sixty-five. I should never have followed Chairman Mao all those forty-one years."[60] Zhou Enlai refused to let Tan leave. Chen Yi told him: "Don't go! You must fight!"[61]

The confrontation lasted for three hours with more of the old guard, especially Chen Yi, joining in what turned into a tit-for-tat struggle. In the end, Mao came to regard no single outburst as more hostile and personally offensive than one made by Marshal Chen Yi:

> Once in power, these are the guys who practice revisionism. Actually, back in Yan'an, Liu Shaoqi, Deng Xiaoping, and Peng Zhen, as well as Bo Yibo, Liu Lantao, and An Ziwen, were the most energetic supporters of Mao Zedong Thought! They never opposed Chairman Mao. [In fact] they had never even met Chairman Mao! We were the ones who had opposed Chairman Mao and who were criticized as a result. Wasn't the premier criticized? Didn't history prove who opposed Chairman Mao!? The future will prove it again. Didn't Stalin hand over to Khrushchev, who ended up a revisionist?[62]

At this point, Zhou interrupted Chen Yi, saying: "That's the very reason we're conducting a Great Cultural Revolution to expose Liu and Deng!"[63]

Significantly, Zhou Enlai did not support his comrades-in-arms from the State Council and the PLA, some of whom he had been associated with for forty years, and with whose views on the three basic issues he was in total agreement.[64] Criticism of his less than robust stance has even circulated in China,[65] despite the normally unalloyed respect with which Zhou is publicly portrayed. One can only speculate about the impact on Mao had the premier, on whom he so greatly relied, taken this rare opportunity of old-guard unity to side with the marshals and vice premiers and present to the Chairman a set of suggestions for dissipating the terror and chaos of the Cultural Revolution. Zhou Enlai did not take the risk of finding out.

Mao's Reactions

At seven o'clock Zhou Enlai announced that time was up and the discussion would have to "continue some other day."[66] As they were leaving, Zhang Chunqiao called Wang Li and Yao Wenyuan aside. After comparing notes to ensure that they were in agreement about what had been said, the three men, with Zhang taking the lead, set off to villa No. 11 in Diaoyutai to report to Jiang Qing. Her immediate reaction, not surprisingly, was that Mao would have to be told immediately. Between ten o'clock and midnight that same evening, Mao received the three (Jiang thought it best not to accompany them) in the Beijing Room of the Great Hall of the People, where they told him what had transpired. Wang Li later recalled that at first Mao seemed not to take it very seriously, and even laughed; it was when he heard about Chen Yi's remarks that his expression suddenly changed.[67]

As they had hoped, the CCRG trio was able to preempt rival accounts—Zhou Enlai seems to have been uncharacteristically slow off the mark on this crucial occasion—and present the events in a manner calculated to arouse the Chairman to anger against the old guard. As in 1959 at the time of the Lushan Conference during the Great Leap Forward, Mao was in the process of rectifying the excesses caused by a tumultuous mass movement that he himself had launched, and at such a time he took criticism of the campaign itself as a personal challenge.[68] In any case, the marshals and vice premiers had failed to appreciate that the Chairman might criticize the CCRG's mistakes, but he would reject any root-and-branch assault on its activities as a disavowal of the Cultural Revolution itself.[69] In a last desperate effort, Tan Zhenlin appealed to Lin Biao against the CCRG, but the latter merely forwarded Tan's letter to Mao with the observation that the vice premier's thinking had become totally confused and sunk to an all-time low.[70]

Possibly in order to avert the danger that the shared anger of the old guard might turn against himself, early in the evening of February 18 Mao signed off with a positive comment ("I agree with your viewpoint") on a *Red Flag* editorial draft submitted to him by Zhou Enlai titled "Cadres Must Be Treated Correctly." The editorial spoke critically of those who were under the mistaken impression that cadres with power were all no good and therefore had to be "struck down." After being leaked by Zhou to, among others, Chen Yi, it was reprinted in the *People's Daily*—a full week in advance of its appearance in *Red Flag*.[71] The real Mao, however, was furious, boiling over with anger. In the early hours of February 19, he summoned Zhou Enlai, Ye Qun (representing Lin Biao), Kang Sheng (representing the CCRG), Li Fuchun, Ye Jianying, Li Xiannian, and Xie Fuzhi to what was in effect a meeting of the Politburo.[72] Mao now vigorously counterattacked:

> The CCRG has been implementing the line adopted by the Eleventh Plenum. Its errors amount to 1, 2, maybe 3 percent, while it's been correct up to 97 percent. If someone opposes the CCRG, I will resolutely oppose him! You attempt to negate the Great Cultural Revolution, but you shall not succeed! Comrade Ye Qun, you tell Lin Biao that he's not safe either. Some people are trying to grab his power, and he should be prepared. If this Great Cultural Revolution fails, he and I will withdraw from Beijing and go back to the Jinggang Mountains to fight a guerrilla war. You say that Jiang Qing and Chen Boda are no

good; well, let's make you, Chen Yi, the head of the CCRG, and arrest Chen Boda and Jiang Qing and have them executed! Let's send Kang Sheng into exile! I'll step down, too, and then you can ask Wang Ming [the Moscow-trained rival defeated by Mao in a struggle for leadership in the late 1930s and early 1940s] to return to be Chairman.[73]

Afterward Kang Sheng told Wang Li that "in all these years I've been with the Chairman, I've never seen him this angry!" At the meeting, which lasted until daybreak, Zhou Enlai attempted to make Mao calm down and, with this aim in mind, criticized himself for not having handled the whole affair well. At the end of the meeting, Mao ordered that Tan Zhenlin, Chen Yi, and Xu Xiangqian were to "request leave of absence to self-criticize." Mao asked Zhou to work on Chen Yi; Li and Xie were told to work on Tan Zhenlin; and Ye Jianying, Li Xiannian, and Xie Fuzhi were told to work on Xu Xiangqian.[74]

At seven successive criticism meetings of the members of the Politburo, chaired by Zhou Enlai between February 25 and March 18, intense pressure was applied not only by the members specifically assigned by Mao to "work" on Chen, Tan, and Xu but also by the members of the CCRG. In the words of Wang Li, "Everyone criticized the three, some comrades simply . . . to show where they stood."[75] Red Guard outrage was meanwhile conveniently manufactured and guided by leaked snippets of the accusations made at these meetings. Kang Sheng insisted that the clashes in Huairen Hall constituted by far the most serious anti-party incident to have occurred since the Eleventh Plenum; Jiang Qing described them as an attempt to "protect not old cadres but a handful of renegades and special agents"; Chen Boda claimed that they had amounted to an attempted "subversion of the dictatorship of the proletariat."[76]

At Zhou Enlai's suggestion, in order to provide those who had not been present in Huairen Hall for the meeting but who had to criticize the old guard, a set of quasi-official minutes were now drawn up on the basis of Zhang's, Yao's, and Wang Li's notes.[77] In the weeks and months that followed, Zhou Enlai did his best to protect his vice premiers, insisting that there was no real urgency about "dragging them out." After all, "Chairman Mao observed Liu Shaoqi for over twenty years; only then did he write his big-character poster [against Liu]."[78] As if to ensure that remarks like these would not be misread to imply that the central authorities were endorsing a reduction in tempo of the movement as a whole, the members of the CCRG—using a recent quotation from Mao which they did not explicitly attribute to him—at the same time began arguing in public that "signs of counterrevolutionary restoration are everywhere, beginning at the top, all the way to the bottom."[79] In a sign of ambivalence, they qualified this observation by warning against exaggerating the force of this "adverse current." "Don't go overboard in dealing with it," Qi Benyu told Beijing Red Guards. "There's nothing extraordinary about it," Wang Li explained to the *People's Daily* staff.[80]

The United Action Committee

Whether out of compassion or, more likely, caution, Mao was not prepared to destroy totally the leaders of the February Countercurrent. He had been careful to condemn by name only the most outspoken, thus averting the danger that the old guard would unite against himself. Then, on April 22, he ordered the release of members of the United Action Committee arrested three months earlier.[81] This Red Guard organization was formed exclusively of the sons and daughters of high-level officials who came together when they suddenly realized that the targets of the Cultural Revolution were not the usual suspects but their own parents. On January 16, Mao talked to Vice Premier Xie Fuzhi, who was also minister of public security, about the behavior of the committee in terms of "class struggle."[82] On the following day, Xie had denounced the committee as a "reactionary organization" led by "counterrevolutionaries" to a gathering of public security officers.[83] During the February Countercurrent confrontation, Vice Premier Li Xiannian had challenged Xie to explain how it was possible for "seventeen-, eighteen-year-old babies" to be "counterrevolutionaries." All over China, Li said, confessions were being extorted from them.

Li was perhaps being disingenuous. The members of the United Action Committee were not unsophisticated. In their "charter"—a curious and possibly in part spurious document attributed to them by other Red Guards in 1967—they had pledged allegiance to "Marxism-Leninism and pre-1960 Mao Zedong Thought" and demanded the "firm though thorough, total, and clean destruction of the left-opportunist line pursued by the two chairmen [*sic*] and some other members of the CCP Central Committee."[84] In the final week of January, some 139 known and suspected members of the United Action Committee had been arrested and locked up in Beijing No. 1 Prison. Their crimes, aside from putting up "reactionary slogans" like "Fry Jiang Qing in shallow oil!," "Down with Chen Boda!," "Long live Liu Shaoqi!," and "Oppose the arbitrary seizure of elderly revolutionaries" in public places, included hooliganism and six attempts to "assault" the Ministry of Public Security. Jiang Qing told Nie Yuanzi, Kuai Dafu, and other Red Guard leaders that the members of the United Action Committee were no different from "landlords, rich peasants, reactionaries, bad elements, and rightists." Still, she hoped that "most of them will come back on to the right road again."[85]

Now in April Mao had given them that chance, telling them to return to their schools and behave themselves. Quite a few people, including ordinary cadres working for central party and government units, expressed bewilderment at this leniency. It fell to Qi Benyu to explain that by giving the most degenerate members of the United Action Committee the opportunity to continue to "get drunk, go out in the evenings, and behave in an utterly decadent fashion," the continued public distaste for them would be assured. "To lock them up," Qi suggested, "is not the way to go about it . . . as society at large must be given a chance to know what the 'United Action Committee' was all about. Otherwise, if you say it was no good and should be opposed, some people will simply feel sympathy toward them."[86]

However, the real motivation for Mao's leniency was probably a fear that harming their children was a surefire way to goad his senior colleagues beyond endurance. On the evening of April 30, he followed up with a "unity meeting," to which he invited Zhou Enlai to his house, and along with him the principal old guard protagonists in the February Countercurrent: Marshals Chen Yi, Ye Jianying, Nie Rongzhen, and Xu Xiangqian; Vice Premiers Li Fuchun, Tan Zhenlin, and Li Xiannian; along with Yu Qiuli and Gu Mu, two leading economic officials who had been invited to the meetings in the vain expectation that the original agenda would be discussed. He gave them permission to watch the May Day fireworks from Tiananmen, knowing that when the list of attendees was published, it would be a sign that they had not yet been consigned to outer darkness, even if appearance suggested otherwise. According to a Westerner who was on the Tiananmen rostrum that day, Marshal Chen Yi "looked like a ghost. His body was frail and emaciated, his wrists like tiny sticks. This once hearty man seemed shrunken and gray."[87] Chen Yi's appearance could have been taken as a metaphor for the condition of the once formidable leadership of the CCP.

The Wuhan Incident

D uring the summer of 1967, China descended into a state of what Mao later described as "all-round civil war," at the start of which rival groups used cudgels and knives, but soon moved on to machine guns and artillery.[1] According to Mao, "Everywhere people were fighting, dividing into two factions; there were two factions in every factory, in every school, in every province, in every county; every ministry was like that, the Foreign Ministry was split into two factions . . . the Foreign Ministry was in chaos . . . In July and August 1967, nothing could be done; there was massive upheaval throughout the country."[2] As Lin Biao put it in mid-1967, "The 'Great Cultural Revolution' has turned into the great martializing revolution!"[3]

At his birthday party the previous December, the Chairman had welcomed the prospect of civil war. Now he, or rather Zhou Enlai, had to deal with actual threats of anarchy.[4] The most dangerous incident occurred in central China, and embodied the potential fracture of the radical alliance of the PLA and the CCRG.

Tensions in Central China

The triple city of Wuhan—comprising Wuchang, Hankou, and Hanyang, separated by the Yangtze and its tributary the Han River—is the capital of Hubei province, and the most important industrial city in central China.[5] The country's fifth most populous urban area, with about 2.5 million people in 1967, it is a strategically key transportation crossroads, a transit point for Yangtze River shipping between Shanghai and Chongqing and rail traffic between Beijing and Canton.

The city was also the headquarters of the Wuhan MR, which embraced Henan as well as Hubei provinces. The regional commander in 1967 was a three-star general, Chen Zaidao. According to Red Guard allegations, General Chen was known within the PLA as a lecher, and in 1963 the Standing Committee of the Wuhan MR Party Committee had convened a meeting specifically to deal with his "problematic lifestyle."[6] However, Chen, a native of Hubei, liked to boast that the fact that he was "illiterate and crude" made him a genuine representative of the working class.[7] Perhaps this self-perception conditioned his behavior during the Wuhan incident.

Wuhan had a revolutionary history, being the site of the first uprising of what became the 1911 Republican revolution, which overthrew China's 2,000-year-old imperial system. It had already earned a place in Cultural Revolution legend because of Mao's swim in the Yangtze there in July 1966. Mao's senior companion in the water that day, Hubei first secretary Wang Renzhong, had later moved to Beijing at the Chairman's behest to become a deputy head of the CCRG, and from that vantage point had managed to keep his provincial subordinates apprised of and protected from the treacherous currents of the Cultural Revolution.[8] But after Wang's dismissal from the CCRG in late October and Tao Zhu's at the beginning of 1967, local party officials were on their own.

In the autumn of 1966, there were two city-wide, highly factionalized Red Guard organizations: the original Red Guards, most of them from "good" class backgrounds; and the Mao Zedong Thought Red Guards (also known as the 2nd Headquarters), whose membership was drawn more widely. The latter proved more daring in confronting local authorities. Their aggressive activities also inspired workers to liaise with students and to organize autonomously. A "Workers' Headquarters" was established on November 9, to be followed by the emergence of other workers' groups, some radical, some "conservative."[9]

By January 1967, when there were reportedly fifty-four Red Guard groups of various persuasions in Wuhan[10]—though ideological orientation was less important than factional allegiance—morale had collapsed within both the provincial and municipal party organizations. Worker and student rebel groups negotiated the formation of a "Wuhan Revolutionary Rebel General Headquarters" to seize power, but the coalition split over issues of power and turf, with one accusing the other of "Trotskyism."[11] Gradually three major rebel organizations would emerge: the "Steel-Tempered 2nd Headquarters," the city's largest student organization; the 480,000-strong "Steel-Tempered Workers' General"; and the "Steel-Tempered September 13," composed mainly of workers from the Wuhan Iron and Steel Corporation and the Ministry of Metallurgy First Construction Corporation. They allied eventually as the "Wuhan Steel-Tempered Three."

As confusion mounted, Chen Zaidao's forces took control of banks, prisons, granaries, warehouses, and crucial sectors of the infrastructure, including the Hubei broadcasting station. Ostensibly the PLA was performing its designated role of "supporting the revolutionary masses of the left." The question as elsewhere in China was who was the left and who was the enemy to be suppressed, or, in more starkly Leninist terms, "Who? Whom?"

Chen and the political commissar of the Wuhan MR, Zhong Hanhua, spent much of February at an MAC conference in Beijing. Chen took particular note of advice from Mao and Zhou. Mao told PLA commanders to be reasonable and to retreat a little in the face of rebel actions, and if that did not work, then to take a stronger line and find out who were the bad elements behind the attack on the military. Zhou was concerned above all with production, telling Chen and Zhong: "Seasons don't wait for man; if one doesn't manage production well, there'll be nothing to eat."[12] The Wuhan generals took these comments as giving them carte blanche in their efforts to restore order, especially as even the CCRG warned the Wuhan rebels against attacking the PLA. As a result of massive arrests and constant pressure, Chen Zaidao managed to outlaw the Steel-Tempered Workers' General, arresting 2,000–3,000 of its leading activists, and to engineer the collapse of the main radical student organizations in the course of March.[13]

Chen also clamped down with impunity on signs of unrest within the armed forces, arguing that a seven-point set of regulations issued by the MAC on February 11 gave him the authority to outlaw and dissolve rebel organizations, whose activities threatened to interfere with the smooth operation of the regional command's political and logistical structure.[14] No less than five battalions, commanded by Chen's deputy Yang Xiushan, descended on the Higher Infantry School in Hankou at one in the morning on February 21 to dissolve and round up members of two rebel organizations there. Yang claimed that the action had the support of the MAC, because even the movement of one company needed its permission. An even larger armed contingent, three regiments, took control of the PLA Air Force Radar School, where more than 90 percent of the staff and students had formed a "Red Rebel Headquarters." Arrests were carried out in more than a dozen military units belonging to the Wuhan MR, including the Xinyang Infantry School and the PLA Air Force Unit 005 in Henan province.[15]

Conservative mass organizations, composed mainly of cadres and activists, got stronger. Remembering Zhou's injunction and utilizing Mao's slogan, Chen set up an "Office for Grasping Revolution and Promoting Production," effectively a new provincial government. Mao's idea was that all such new organizations should be "three-in-one" alliance of the PLA, rebels, and old cadres, but in Wuhan the rebels were dispensed with while old cadres assumed accustomed roles. By the end of March, Chen was able to declare, perhaps tongue-in-cheek: "We have successfully crushed a counterrevolutionary adverse current. At present the proletarian revolutionaries are forming a great alliance, the rightist groups are falling apart, and the power usurped by a handful of careerists is being seized back. The progress of the Cultural Revolution in Wuhan is very good."[16]

Meanwhile, back in Beijing new judgments were being issued. Many took the ten-point MAC order of April 6 as heralding an open season on the PLA. Chen Zaidao was flabbergasted by the 180-degree turn of the April 6 order, coming hard on the heels of "Adopt a Correct Attitude toward the Little Generals," and Wuhan was among the cities in which the two documents had almost immediate impact.[17] Student rebels set aside their factional disputes and returned, united, to the streets, denouncing Chen as a latter-day representative of the February Countercurrent, nicknaming him the "Tan Zhenlin of Wuhan." Military training teams were forced out of colleges. The main newspaper offices were occupied. Chen Zaidao and Zhong Hanhua, who had returned to Beijing in late March for another extended MAC conference, met the CCRG on April 19 at their own request so that they could present a more accurate account of events in Wuhan than that supplied to the CCRG by its local correspondents.

The meeting was a success for the generals, but their satisfaction was short-lived. The Wuhan MR was cleared of making mistakes of line, and the CCRG undertook to persuade Wuhan rebels not to attack the PLA. Unfortunately for Chen Zaidao, the unauthorized release of the news by conservatives in Wuhan turned Jiang Qing against him again. The CCRG withdrew from its commitments and impounded all copies of the minutes of the April 19 meeting. Of all the participants at the MAC conference, only Chen and Zhong were not invited to stay on for the May Day celebrations. The situation in Wuhan became even more confused and volatile. With no official confirmation of the Jiang Qing–Chen Zaidao agreement available, both conservatives and rebels were able to claim that the CCRG in Beijing was on their side.[18]

The Million Heroes

Both sides now organized multi-organization alliances. The conservatives brought fifty-three groups together under a liaison station in mid-May, and then more tightly under a headquarters on June 3. This overarching organization, christened the "Million Heroes" in view of the claimed size of its membership, 1.2 million, was drawn mainly from the party—85 percent of Wuhan party members were apparently enrolled in it—and from government, trade union, and youth league cadres and rank and file, along with older workers, militiamen, and activists. Some of the workers belonged to a Red People's Militia created by the Wuhan city People's Armed Department in January and as such constituted the fighting arm of the Million Heroes. The elite among the students supporting the Million Heroes concentrated their efforts on intelligence and propaganda work and were members of a "Special Action Committee" *(tedong)*, the Wuhan equivalent of Beijing's United Action Committee formed by the sons and daughters of high-level officials and PLA officers.

In his memoirs, Chen Zaidao denies having been involved in the formation of the Million Heroes, and claims that at the time he did not even know the names of its leaders or what they looked like.[19] This claim seems barely credible, given that the leader of the Million Heroes was Wang Kewen, a member of the Wuhan municipal party secretariat and vice mayor, and his deputy was the director of the Wuhan municipal party Organization Department, Xin Fu.[20] Chen is more credible when he maintains that large numbers of PLA officers and men quite "spontaneously" developed an affinity for the political stand taken by the Million Heroes.[21] On the basis of this, the MR—if not Chen himself, who was in Beijing for long spells—directly aided the formation and operation of the Million Heroes.[22]

For its part, the Million Heroes maintained that the Wuhan MR had pursued a generally correct orientation in its "support for the left" and had acted in accordance with the instructions of the center. To call for a purge of the regional PLA leadership was incorrect. The provincial and municipal party leaderships, furthermore, had also pursued an essentially correct line over the previous seventeen years, most party cadres were on the whole good comrades, and demands that they be struck down were illegitimate.[23] Effectively, the Million Heroes were denying the need for a Cultural Revolution, at least as far as Hubei was concerned.

The rebels did not manage to organize as tightly as their rivals or to eliminate all factional differences, but in early May two united headquarters reemerged, the Steel-Tempered Workers' General and the Steel-Tempered 2nd Headquarters. These groups even managed to gain support from some units of the PLA air force. During May the radicals staged sit-ins and a massive hunger strike and began to win concessions. The formal grounds of dispute between the rival headquarters were whether or not the Wuhan MR had genuinely supported the left. In reality, the conflict pitted those who saw themselves as having a big stake in the pre-1966 political and social order against those who did not.

By late May, the first death had occurred, and by early June major clashes took place regularly with more loss of life as the Million Heroes sought to "liberate" buildings and even whole areas of the city from rebel control. Lances and knives were weapons of choice—this despite the fact that on June 6, at Mao's suggestion, a general order, Zhongfa [1967] 178, had gone out advocating struggle with words, not weapons, and forbidding armed conflict and arbitrary arrests.[24] (Appeals like the general order were a measure of the depth of the crisis nationwide and the inability of the center to contain it. In the words of one PLA historian, the "general order" was nothing more than a "worthless piece of paper.")[25] On June 24—the very day on which the center issued a renewed appeal to those in positions of power "not to take to the streets and demonstrate, not to fight, not to arrest people, not to obstruct rail, road, and river traffic, not to construct roadblocks, not to steal weapons, and not to shoot"[26]—the Million Heroes delivered a coup de grâce by capturing the rebel workers' headquarters, killing twenty-five defenders in the process.

Although ideological fervor and factional ties may have motivated many combatants, some were simply mercenaries: teenagers were paid cash to kill, as the following account by a seventeen-year-old Wuhan middle school student testifies:

Yesterday morning, before I had time to eat, the "Million Heroes" had organized more than 10,000 people. The chief was someone named Li, from the Wuhan Cotton Mill. At a meeting in the Jianghan Public Park, he said: "Our main aim today is to kill everyone in the Wuhan tri-city area's 'Popular Paradise of Nothing but Looting-Smashing-Thieving Monsters and Freaks' and to close down the 'Popular Paradise Liaison Station.'" When I heard the news, I rushed with two neighbors to the Six Crossings Bridge. After we got there, I killed five kids with my star-knife. I saw the Hongwubing kill thirty-six members of the "September 13" at the time. After they killed them, they quickly got rid of the corpses. At the time, if you ran into someone who shouted "Down with the Heiwubing!" you killed them. There was this female comrade, she also killed a bunch of kids with a knife. I killed five—one got it in the waist, the second, third, and fifth ones in the back, and number four in the neck. They were all maybe eight, nine years old. Killing a young boy would get you 20 yuan. For killing a "Combat Team" member, you got 50 yuan. For killing an enemy of the Hongwubing, you got 50 yuan. For the people you had killed, you picked up the money from the chiefs of the Hongwubing [at the Wuhan Cotton Mill]. We got the weapons we used to kill people from the Hongwubing during drills in the Jianghan Public Park.[27]

We have Mao's own word that killing was a paying proposition also in other parts of the country. In his home province of Hunan, "in some places you get 3 yuan in cash each day, while in others you get 100 yuan for fighting one battle. In yet other places you get 100 yuan for killing someone. Even if they survive, you still get 100 yuan."[28] In some rural areas surrounding Beijing, cash was supplemented with grain and "work points" as inducements to peasants to join a mercenary militia formed to attack the local soldiery.[29]

In Wuhan, the extent of the victory of the Million Heroes in late June alerted the CCRG to the imminent elimination of their allies there. On June 26 the CCRG and the PLA Cultural Revolution Group (dominated, it will be remembered, by Jiang Qing) cabled Chen Zaidao urging him to stop the violence and announcing that representatives of both sides would soon be invited to Beijing so that the CCRG could make a full assessment of the situation. An uneasy calm descended upon the city as the rival organizations prepared their cases for the Beijing meeting.

According to the Wuhan MR, the Million Heroes had the support of the people and had resorted to force only in the face of provocation; the rebels, on the other hand, had attacked 342 soldiers and wounded 264, some severely. Rebel statistics listed 174 violent clashes between the end of April and the end of June, all blamed on the conservatives, involving 70,000 people, of whom 158 were killed and 1,060 were seriously wounded.[30] Another rebel account claimed that "more than 7,000" of them were killed or injured during May, and 744 rebels were killed and 8,900 wounded in fighting after June 4.[31] A post–Cultural Revolution PLA historian gave figures of 108 dead and 2,774 wounded between June 4 and 30.[32] Whatever the actual figures, unquestionably industrial output and productivity had dropped a great deal, resulting in shortages of many daily necessities.[33]

Mao Returns to Wuhan

At the beginning of July, Chen Zaidao telephoned Zhou Enlai to tell him that the mass organizations and the MR had selected their delegates and prepared their briefs and were ready to come to Beijing; Zhou told him to await instructions. On July 6, 7, and 9, Mao held a series of central meetings at which he proposed making a southern tour of inspection. Despite advice to the contrary from colleagues concerned for his safety, he intended including Wuhan on his itinerary, ostensibly for another swim in the Yangtze.[34] On the eve of his departure, the Chairman addressed a gathering of senior PLA officers and repeated what by now would have been a mantra only too familiar to many of them:

> Don't be afraid of people making trouble. The bigger the trouble gets, the longer it lasts, the better. Trouble again and again, on and on—something is bound to come out of it! Things will become clearer. It doesn't matter how bad the trouble gets, you must not be afraid. Fear will only bring out an even greater number of monsters! But you must not open fire either; opening fire is never any good. Major trouble across all of China is not going to happen. [But] pustules and bacteria, wherever they are, are bound to burst at some point.[35]

Mao would have been aware that Wuhan was a "pustule" ready for bursting. According to Lin Biao, the Chairman "reads all the reports and all the telegrams from below very carefully and has a very clear understanding of the situation at the lower levels. The papers put out by the Red Guards: he reads them all himself."[36] Thus he would have known of the serious clashes and that, as Zhou Enlai put it, "the situation is very complex and the antagonistic sentiment of the masses is very strong. These are very good chaotic phenomena."[37] On July 10, Zhou Enlai telephoned Chen Zaidao to tell him that the scheduled negotiations between the rival factions to resolve this very complex situation would take place in Wuhan, not Beijing, but apparently not informing him that Mao or he would be coming there very soon.

Zhou Enlai left Beijing for Wuhan on an air force plane at 2:30 A.M. on July 14, accompanied by Li Zuopeng, a deputy chief of staff and first political commissar of the PLA navy. The tense situation in Wuhan directly affected the way in which the crucial issue of the personal safety of the visiting central leaders was handled. Mao's presence seems to have been kept secret from all but Chen Zaidao and Zhong Hanhua, and they were informed only a few days after his arrival. Unlike in the summer of 1966, when he came for his famous swim, the Chairman's safety was no longer the responsibility of the 1st Hubei MD Independent Division (a.k.a. PLA Unit 8201). Formerly a People's Armed Police public security force composed of more than 15,000 officers and men stationed across the province but with two guard regiments in Wuhan, Unit 8201 had become deeply embroiled in local factional politics by supporting the Million Heroes and as such would have appeared less than 100 percent reliable in the eyes of the center. Instead, contingents from the PLA air force, whose chief of operations had come down from Beijing with Zhou, would have that duty. Initially, the commander of the air force in the Wuhan region, Major General Fu Chuanzuo, was to have been the officer responsible, but because of his links to Marshal He Long (currently under investigation for alleged involvement in the so-called abortive February coup in 1966), he, too, was pronounced unreliable. Zhou was therefore greeted by the local PLA air force deputy commander, Major General Liu Feng, a veteran of Deng Xiaoping's Second Field Army, who had been alerted by the commander of the PLA air force, Wu Faxian, simply to meet a special plane.

Zhou was whisked off to air force headquarters, where he sent for Chen Zaidao and Zhong Hanhua. Zhou spent the day in discussions with various military leaders. He also consulted with Xie Fuzhi, Wang Li, and Lieutenant General Yu Lijin, political commissar of the PLA air force, as well as some Beijing Red Guards who flew in at noon from Chongqing. Xie's group had been on the road for almost a month on Mao's instructions, attempting to quell factional fighting in Yunnan, Guizhou, and Sichuan. Zhou had summoned Xie, the minister of public security, not so much to ensure Mao's physical safety—that was in the hands of the PLA acting chief of staff, Yang Chengwu, under Zhou's supervision[38]—as to facilitate dealing with the Wuhan military; Xie was from Hubei province and knew local commanders from his time in the military.

In the evening Zhou joined Mao, who arrived on his private train via Zhengzhou, accompanied by Wang Dongxing, the director of the Central Bureau of Guards and head of the CC's General Office, and Yang Chengwu. Before Mao's arrival at the East Lake Guest House compound, Zhou had ensured that the factional allegiances of the staff there would not endanger the Chairman's safety.[39] With Mao safely installed, the premier's principal task was to bring peace to Wuhan. His job was made much more difficult by the behavior of Xie Fuzhi and Wang Li.

In his post–Cultural Revolution account of events, Wang Li accused Xie Fuzhi of having "bungled things" late on the evening that Mao arrived: "He had insisted on reading the wall posters on the streets, and those of us who had come with him from Chongqing went along. (We had neither a guide from the Wuhan MR nor Liu Feng, who had gone with the premier to welcome the Chairman.) We were spotted by the crowds. They immediately had bands playing and set off firecrackers to welcome us, and both factions hurriedly put up slogans."[40]

In fact, the Chongqing contingent had visited Hubei University, a rebel stronghold, and the news that a "beloved delegation sent by Chairman Mao" had come to solve the Wuhan problem was marked the following day by massive demonstrations by rebels. They paraded through areas controlled by their rivals shouting: "Disband the bandit gang of the Million Heroes." The local loudspeakers blared back: "Smash the black Workers' Headquarters and suppress counterrevolutionaries." Clashes followed, and the rebels were routed, with ten killed, thirty-seven seriously wounded, and eighty injured.[41]

Curiously, when Xie and Wang first informed Zhou about their midnight misadventure, he was unperturbed. Already questions were being asked about the reason for the lights' going on in the East Lake Guest House; Zhou thought that people would now assume that the reason was that the Xie-Wang central delegation was staying there, and so Mao's presence was less likely to be revealed. This conclusion and his premature departure on July 18 indicate that Zhou greatly underestimated the depth of anger among the "conservative" politico-military establishment at having become the principal target of the Cultural Revolution, and overestimated the power of the military commanders to control the tense situation in Wuhan.[42] It proved to be a serious blunder.

Zhou acted as if he needed only to convince the leaders of the Wuhan MR to accept that they had made mistakes and let them correct them. Chen Zaidao and his colleagues had clearly been given the impression that the Wuhan problem would be settled on the basis of the presentation of rival cases by the two sets of mass organizations and the MR itself. In fact, a verdict had already been agreed upon in Beijing, and reaffirmed by Mao in discussions with Zhou, Xie Fuzhi, and Wang Li in Wuhan. It consisted of four main points: (1) the Wuhan MR had committed an "error in general orientation" in the course of "supporting the left"; (2) a decision by the MR to outlaw and disband the Steel-Tempered Workers' General should be publicly rescinded; (3) the MR should publicly announce that the Wuhan Steel-Tempered Three, which it had hitherto labeled "monsters and freaks," were in fact "revolutionary"; (4) and the Million Heroes constituted a "conservative organization."[43]

On the afternoons of July 15–18, Zhou Enlai, accompanied by Xie and Wang Li, and intermittently by other central officials, chaired stormy meetings with some two dozen members of the Wuhan MR Party Committee, some of whom reported on their work. If Chen Zaidao was accused of not supporting the left, he claimed to have been implementing the "three supports and the two militaries"; if he claimed he had followed the (pro-PLA) eight-point order, he was accused of not implementing Lin Biao's (pro-rebel) ten-point order. The contradictions that Mao had sanctioned were exposed. At the end of the sessions, Zhou in effect rejected the Wuhan MR's explanations and told them what had to be done to reform their work. When it became clear that even he did not have the authority to convince Chen Zaidao and Zhong Hanhua to write confessions, Zhou took the generals to see Mao on the evening of July 18.

Whereas Zhou, as the representative of the center attempting to compel compliance, had been perforce cast in the uncharacteristic role of "bad cop," Mao was the "good cop," all affability. The Wuhan situation was not all that bad. Why should there be struggles between groups of workers? What did it really signify that the Wuhan MR had made mistakes of line? When the meeting broke up at about ten o'clock, Chen and Zhong, whether convinced or not that they had erred, knew that they had to write confessions. Satisfied that the Wuhan crisis had been dispelled, Zhou Enlai left for Beijing at eleven.

Despite the lateness of the hour, Xie Fuzhi took his contingent to one of the rebel headquarters at the Wuhan Institute of Hydroelectric Engineering to spread the good news of the imminent climb-down of the Wuhan MR. On previous days, Xie and Wang Li had visited another rebel headquarters and even that of the Million Heroes, where they had become involved in a bitter confrontation. Since people were ignorant of the presence in the city of Chairman Mao and Premier Zhou, Xie Fuzhi and Wang Li were everywhere seen as the center's main emissaries. Despite Xie's seniority, Wang Li had emerged in the public mind as the principal arbiter. On the night of July 18–19, as the news of the settlement was spread throughout the city by the jubilant rebels, the two men were toasted or excoriated for imposing it. On the morning of July 19, the rebels broadcast tape recordings of the two men's speeches throughout the city. Chen Zaidao later blamed those speeches for triggering the Wuhan incident.

On the same morning, Chen Zaidao and Zhong Hanhua presented their self-criticisms at the headquarters of the Wuhan MR to its party standing committee. In the afternoon they attended a larger meeting of over 300 officers of division-level and above, which was addressed by Xie Fuzhi and Wang Li. Xie called upon the Wuhan MR to "make a 180-degree turnabout," which was bad enough, but Wang Li irritated the audience even more. In what appears to have been a highly condescending speech, he referred to the senior officers present as "elementary school students" who had not understood what the Cultural Revolution was all about, and he proceeded to lecture them at interminable length about its nature and course. Nor could the generals have been pleased when Wang Li explained that "at present, the main contradiction [in the Cultural Revolution] centers on a handful of capitalist roaders within the party and armed forces."[44]

The Wuhan Incident

By the time Wang Li had finished speaking at eleven o'clock on the night of July 19, the front gate of the Wuhan MR headquarters was blocked by a group of angry soldiers who demanded that Wang explain to them what he had meant by his speech at the Institute of Hydroelectric Engineering; some called Chen Zaidao a "capitulationist" for writing a self-criticism. Wang was taken out by the back door and escorted to the East Lake Guest House compound. Around midnight the frustrated soldiers were reinforced by several dozen truckloads of supporters from among the Million Heroes. Wang Li was called from MR headquarters and asked to return to the headquarters to talk to the protesters, but he refused, dismissing the demonstration as of little importance. The events of July 20 soon proved how wrong he was.

Early that morning, Chen Zaidao, who had moved into the East Lake Guest House complex after Zhou's arrival, wandered over to Xie Fuzhi's living quarters to discuss how to handle the Wuhan situation. Hardly had he sat down when some 200 members of the Million Heroes, mainly former cadres, burst onto Xie's doorstep demanding to see Wang Li. Xie and Chen hurriedly moved the group outside so that they would not locate Wang, and conducted negotiations while sitting on the grass. In return for Xie's promise to come that afternoon to answer all their questions, they agreed to leave the compound immediately.

Wang Li, who according to Chen Zaidao's later account had been cowering in his room, now felt it safe to emerge and join Xie and Chen on the grass. Just at this point, several hundred officers and men rushed up and began beating the "capitulationist" Chen Zaidao with their fists, feet, and rifle butts. Xie was left unharmed. Wang Li fled back to his room. When Chen Zaidao's guards finally persuaded the troops to stop the beating, the latter rushed inside and dragged Wang off to the Wuhan MR headquarters.[45]

When Xie Fuzhi brought the news of the incident to Mao's residence, the

Chairman, whose presence nearby was unknown to the mutinous troops, demanded that Chen Zaidao find Wang Li immediately. With Chen *hors de combat,* Zhong Hanhua took on the task, aided by Deputy Commander Kong Qingde and Ye Ming, deputy political commissar of the Wuhan MR.

In the meanwhile Yang Chengwu had telephoned Zhou Enlai with the news, and the premier had ordered him to focus only on the Chairman's safety until he arrived there later in the day. Lin Biao sent a letter to Mao, endorsed by Jiang Qing, carried by the head of the PLA logistical arm, Qiu Huizuo, urging the Chairman to leave Wuhan for Shanghai immediately because they were afraid that Chen Zaidao was launching a coup. The leaders left in Beijing may well have had in mind not only the Wuhan incident of October 10, 1911, which led to the unraveling and finally the collapse of the Qing dynasty, but also the arrest of Chiang Kai-shek in Xi'an in 1936 by one of his generals. The Xi'an incident, despite Chiang's later unconditional release, had led to a major change in the Generalissimo's grand strategy. Since the CCRG and even Lin Biao owed their current eminence to the Chairman's whim, the possibility that he might be caught in a situation in which he felt compelled radically to alter his Cultural Revolution policies could not have been welcome.[46]

Mao was well aware that the danger from the wounded Chen Zaidao was minimal, and he groused at the idea of abandoning his swim. Far more galling probably was the indignity of it all: Mao, the revolutionary victor and party leader, accustomed to the adulation of China's millions, was being forced to flee hugger-mugger because, as a result of events that he had set in motion, his safety from a mob of soldiers and party cadres could not be guaranteed. Yet as a former guerrilla warrior Mao knew that discretion had to take precedence over pride, even if it meant his going by plane, which he hated to do. At two in the morning on July 21 he left for Shanghai, escorted by air force fighters. Nevertheless, he maintained a convincing façade of insouciance and, characteristically, later blamed his hasty departure on his subordinates: "The trouble is that Wang Li provoked them into fighting. And when Zhou Enlai came to mediate the dispute, the fighting scared him to death. He forced me to flee to Shanghai in a hurry." Zhou Enlai had added his voice to those urging Mao to leave Wuhan upon his arrival late in the afternoon of July 20. The premier's conviction of the urgency of such a move would have been increased by his having himself been forced to land at the Shanpo air force base, almost forty miles from the city, instead of at the city airport, where his own safety could not be guaranteed.[47] In-

211

deed, some of the conservative faction had been heard shouting: "No matter how senior Zhou Enlai may be or how exalted his position, we'll drag him off his horse all the same."[48]

Having dispatched the Chairman, the premier focused on the rescue of Wang Li. The luckless Wang had been taken to the Wuhan MR headquarters, where he had been beaten up, had his leg broken, and feared for his life. Xie Fuzhi had come to the compound but had been turned back with threats. Zhong Hanhua had been allowed in but was unsuccessful in his plea for Wang's release. However, during mealtime Kong Qingde and Ye Ming managed to transfer Wang Li to the 29th Army Division (a.k.a. PLA Unit 8199), a main-force unit stationed in the Wuhan MR. Chen Zaidao later alleged in colorful language that the 29th Division commander botched the rescue operation in order to make political capital as the man who really rescued Wang Li. He "scared the shit out of Wang Li" by telling him that the place was surrounded by the Million Heroes, transferred him to another hiding place, and his chief of staff refused to say where when questioned by the commander of the First Independent Division sent by Zhou. Eventually Wang Li was located by the Wuhan air force deputy commander, Liu Feng, who transferred him to air force headquarters. In the early hours of July 22, Wang Li and Xie Fuzhi were brought to the Shanpo air force base. They were seen off by Zhou Enlai, who then rushed to the city airport, where he told Kong Qingde and Ye Ming that he was transferring the command of the Wuhan MR to them, to operate out of the 29th Division Headquarters, since the MR compound was no longer safe.

At 4:55 P.M. on July 22, Xie Fuzhi and Wang Li made a "glorious return" to the capital, landing at Beijing airport to be greeted by Zhou Enlai—who had ordered Xie and Wang's plane to keep circling so that his own could land first—and Chen Boda, Kang Sheng, and Jiang Qing.[49] That evening Lin Biao chaired a meeting attended by Zhou and the CCRG to hear Xie Fuzhi's report. It was agreed to designate the "July 20 incident" a "counterrevolutionary revolt."[50] At 3:00 A.M. on July 23, Zhou Enlai sent the telegram he had drafted for the center to the Wuhan MR. It ordered Chen Zaidao, Zhong Hanhua, Fu Chuanzuo, Liu Feng, the commander and political commissar of the First Independent Division, and half a dozen other officers to come to the capital immediately for a meeting. Chen's immediate reaction, as he later recalled, was "Either I'm lucky, and it's not a disaster; or else if it is a disaster it cannot be avoided anyway." Early on the morning of July 24, Liu Feng's air force troops put the twelve officers on a plane for Beijing. "It was a starry moonlit night," Chen remembered. "The guards who escorted us carried rifles with fixed bayonets. As they marched, the bayonets glistened in the moonlight. That was the kind of 'treatment' to which Liu Feng was subjecting us. It was unbearable."[51]

The treatment that Chen and his colleagues received in Beijing was no better. While Zhou Enlai took steps to safeguard them from Beijing Red Guards, they were put under de facto house arrest in the PLA-run Capital West Hotel. On the afternoon of July 25, a mass rally of a million people was held in Tiananmen Square to celebrate the return of Xie Fuzhi and Wang Li. The entire party, PLA, and CCRG elite were in attendance, save only Mao himself, who was still in Shanghai. Lin Biao's decision to attend was significant, since it publicly aligned him with the CCRG against the PLA generals. It also demonstrated his determination not to tolerate insubordination; he complained that the Beijing, Wuhan, and Chengdu MRs never listened to him.[52]

On July 26, under Zhou Enlai's chairmanship, the PSC held what Chen Zaidao remembered as a "marathon" struggle meeting lasting six to seven hours at the Capital West Hotel with the officers from Wuhan. The participants included the senior Politburo, MAC, and CCRG officials in the capital. The principal prosecutors were Xie Fuzhi and Wu Faxian. If Chen Zaidao ever entertained hopes that he would be able to state his side of the case, he was immediately disabused. This was a kangaroo court, and its verdict had been endorsed by Mao the day before. Egged on in advance by Jiang Qing, Wu shouted at Chen Zaidao and even boxed his ears, at which point Chen Yi and Tan Zhenlin walked out. When Wu accused Xu Xiangqian of being behind the counterrevolutionary rebellion, the marshal rejected the accusation and left. During a recess, the orderlies also beat up the Wuhan contingent. Zhou Enlai rebuked Wu and the orderlies, but does not seem to have taken sufficient control of the proceedings to ensure the protection of "comrade" Chen Zaidao and his colleagues, which had been Mao's declared objective before his departure for Wuhan.[53] At one point Chen tried to appeal to Kang Sheng as another elderly person who might sympathize with the desire of the accused to be allowed to sit down, but Kang Sheng cut him off abruptly and warned him that he could not rely on his past contributions to the revolution or Mao's use of the term "comrade" to save him.[54]

On July 27 the MAC dismissed Chen Zaidao and Zhong Hanhua, replacing Chen with Lieutenant General Zeng Siyu, the deputy commander of the Shenyang MR, and Zhong with Liu Feng, who was promoted three grades to the post of political commissar of the Wuhan MR. The Wuhan municipal People's Armed Department was taken over by the 15th Airborne Corps; the First Hubei MD Independent Division was forcibly disarmed and transferred to labor camps outside the greater Wuhan area, where the rank and file were subjected to what was euphemistically called "political training and consolidation." The 15th Airborne assumed control of its headquarters and what had been its 1st, 2nd, 3rd, and 5th Regiments, while the 29th Army Division assumed control of its 4th and 6th Regiments. The Million Heroes organization collapsed. The rebels staged daily rallies to celebrate the "second liberation of Wuhan." The Wuhan incident was over, but the killing continued. In the months that followed, more than 184,000 alleged members and supporters of the Million Heroes in Hubei province were beaten up or killed; in Wuhan, 66,000 were wounded, over 600 killed.[55] In May 1968 the MAC and the CCRG were still demanding that Wuhan rebels stop looting weapons.[56]

"Arm the Left"

Although the Wuhan incident was the most spectacular uprising against the Cultural Revolution by members of the Chinese politico-military establishment, and potentially the most threatening had Chen Zaidao really thrown in his lot with the Million Heroes, "civil wars" occurred elsewhere throughout the summer. According to a Chinese historian, "in actual fact, violent clashes occurred in all of China's cities. There were virtually no exceptions."[57]

Contributing to the increasing violence among workers in particular in the summer of 1967 were inflammatory remarks made by members of the central leadership, most notably Jiang Qing. In conversation with Henan rebels the evening after the Wuhan incident, she remarked: "I remember, I think it was in Henan that a revolutionary organization came up with this kind of a slogan, one that goes 'Attack with reason, defend with force.' This slogan is correct!" The official transcript notes that Jiang Qing's words were met with immediate and "enthusiastic applause."[58] A few days later, after the word was out that "comrade Jiang Qing says 'to defend with force' is good," the shooting began in earnest in the already tense province of Henan, with all sides claiming they were merely "defending" themselves. Armed clashes at the Zhengzhou Cigarette Factory and the Kaifeng Chemical Fertilizer Plant in the last week of July produced thirty-seven dead, 290 wounded, and 300 "prisoners of war," of whom 2 were later buried alive.[59]

Post–Cultural Revolution Chinese historians put much blame on Jiang

Qing for the summer of strife, but fail to emphasize the incendiary role of Mao himself.[60] "Why can't we arm the workers and students?" he had asked Zhou Enlai, Xie Fuzhi, Wang Li, Chen Zaidao, and Zhong Hanhua on July 18. Preempting any serious discussion of the pros and cons of such action, Mao immediately went on to add: "I say we should arm them!"[61] On July 31 in Shanghai, Zhang Chunqiao presented Mao with a formal request for permission to set up a workers' armed self-defense force. The Chairman responded positively, passing on the request to Lin Biao, Zhou Enlai, and the CCRG for additional comments; by late August, the charter of what was described as a municipal contingent intended to "organize the left, arm the left" had been circulated by the Shanghai Revolutionary Committee.[62] In a letter to Jiang Qing on August 4, Mao calculated that 75 percent of the PLA officer corps supported the right and concluded that this fact made it imperative now to arm the left.[63] "Arms seizures are not a serious problem." The Chairman also called for a mass dictatorship, a move that led to power-seizures in public security organs and the courts, and the establishment of kangaroo courts as legal norms. Clearly, Mao's first reaction to the Wuhan incident was to strengthen the left, not to back down for fear of a PLA revolt. The letter was circulated by Jiang Qing at an enlarged PSC meeting, at which everyone copied it in order to implement it. Thereafter there were large-scale arms seizures in Guangdong province, and even prisoners in the Chinese gulag began seizing guns.[64]

Wang Li was assigned to oversee the "arming of the left" in Wuhan under Jiang Qing's aegis. In a letter to her on August 6, Wang supported the idea of transferring to the radicals arms confiscated from the Million Heroes.[65] Zhou Enlai perforce supported the new policy. On August 7 he told delegates from Hunan province that it was both "understandable and natural" that the "real left" should demand arms, and that to supply them with arms was simply to act in accordance with "an instruction issued by our supreme commander-in-chief."[66] Indeed that very same day Mao signed off on a Central Document commenting positively on the formation in Hunan of a "revolutionary armed force of mass character" under the leadership of the preparatory group for a provincial revolutionary committee.[67] Whatever private concerns he may have had, Lin Biao obediently told a closed meeting of central leaders and senior PLA officers two days later: "We must comply with Chairman Mao's instructions, arm the left and distribute arms to the leftist masses."[68] On August 10, Mao signed off on a Central Document calling on the Jiangxi Revolutionary Committee Preparatory Group to arm the revolutionary masses "in areas where conditions are ripe."[69]

On August 13, Kang Sheng cited the slogan "Arm the left," and three days later he and Guan Feng accused the PLA unit about to enter the Wuzhong region of the largely Muslim Ningxia Hui Autonomous Region to "support the left" of being "too soft" and "unprincipled" in its dealings with a local "conservative mass organization." The PLA should resolutely support the local "leftists" and "if necessary provide them with arms for self-defense."

At five in the morning on August 28, during the brief incapacity of Zhou Enlai due to severe angina, Kang Sheng approved a plan of action for Ningxia submitted by the Lanzhou MR: the increasingly serious conflict between two Muslim factions paralyzing Qingtongxia county was—once all other options had been exhausted—to be resolved by having the PLA open fire on civilians. Kang quickly blamed local "party power-holders taking the capitalist road" for the bloodbath that ensued but also expressed regret at the "casualties on both sides," dismissing as unfounded "rumor" a claim that the total number of dead had been "more than 400." Eventually, three weeks after the event, he was able to defend himself by saying that the resolution of the Qingtongxia "issue" had been endorsed by Mao and Lin Biao, but what remains unclear is when that endorsement was given, before or after the event. A post–Cultural Revolution official inquiry by the central authorities into Kang Sheng's involvement in the incident determined that the PLA shot dead 101 and wounded 133 members of "the masses." An official history produced in Ningxia describes the incident as one involving two opposing factions of the "masses" and has it that the PLA shot dead 104 and wounded 133 members of one of these factions.[70]

With continuous high-level encouragement it is no wonder that calls for calm and compromise fell on deaf ears nationwide. Throughout August, one restricted-circulation news bulletin appearing in Beijing contained on average twenty to thirty reports of armed clashes in the provinces each day.[71]

Other Regions, Other Incidents

In the relatively prosperous coastal province of Zhejiang, whose capital, Hangzhou, Mao often used as a refuge from the bureaucratic tedium of Beijing, the familiar split between two rival "headquarters" spilled over into the military, as in Wuhan. The air force and the centrally controlled 20th Corps supported the CCRG-backed "Revolutionary Rebel United Headquarters," while the Hangzhou Garrison forces, the militia, and the navy supported the "Red Storm Provisional Headquarters." During the summer of 1967, reports of clashes in towns and factories leaked out to foreign correspondents. A CC document in July reported peasants' being incited to attack cities and holding up rail and river traffic. In the second week of August, "rebels" armed themselves with weapons and 1.27 million rounds of ammunition, "liberated" from two PLA storage facilities.[72]

Major engagements took place in the coastal port city of Wenzhou. On August 13, in the course of an attack on the "Wenzhou United General Command of Revolutionary Rebels" (supported by the Wenzhou Military Subdistrict) hiding on Huagai Mountain after being held responsible for burning some 20,000 square meters of the city's central commercial district, two PLA units mistaking each other for the rebels and their local military allies opened fire on each other, killing seven people.

In September 1967, Mao tried during a brief visit to get the rival groups to unite, but his call went unheeded. It was notable that, unlike the Million Heroes in Wuhan, Red Storm did not collapse when the center's preference for the United Headquarters was revealed, and indeed factionalism and clashes persisted until the end of the Cultural Revolution. In 1975, 10,000 soldiers from other areas were sent into the factories of Hangzhou in an attempt at pacification.

Of China's major industrial centers, Chongqing was among the worst affected, mainly because a heavy concentration of arms factories was the source of an almost endless supply of lethal weapons to the combatants. According to a postmortem conducted by the party center in 1970, the fighting on one particular construction site, on one occasion alone, involved close to 10,000 combatants "employing virtually every kind of conventional weapon available" and "resulted in the death or wounding of close to 1,000 class brothers, and the destruction of vast amounts of state property."[73] The Chaotianmen harbor district on the Yangtze River was razed to the ground in a battle that saw the use of tanks, mobile artillery pieces, and anti-aircraft guns. Some 10,000 artillery shells were fired in Chongqing in August 1967, and more than 180,000 refugees from the fighting were counted in the provincial capital Chengdu alone.[74] Shipping along the upper reaches of the Yangtze River was interrupted for over six weeks.[75]

In Hunan province, production at the Lianyuan Steel Plant had to be suspended in July for six weeks because of factional fighting that led to six dead, sixty-eight wounded, and estimated financial losses of 190,000 yuan.[76] In the Daqing oilfields, workers looted the local printing plant and railway station.[77] In August the central authorities imposed military control over the Anshan Iron and Steel Plant, where production was in disarray. At Canton International Airport on August 10, fifty-four Japanese were caught in crossfire between opposing factions and were left stranded when their panic-stricken pilot decided to take off ahead of schedule rather than risk his aircraft in the firefight.[78] Letters to Zhongnanhai from desperate ordinary citizens told of how biochemical research facilities storing deadly infectious pathogenic bacteria, poisonous plant samples, radioactive substances, poison gas, toxicants, and other dangerous substances were coming under attack in the course of armed struggles. In some places, residents of leper colonies—which existed in Shandong, Anhui, and Jiangsu—had joined rebel organizations and allegedly demanded the right to participate in power-seizures.[79]

At the Shanghai Diesel Engine Plant, a battle between two popular factions (the victorious one led by Wang Hongwen) resulted in 18 dead and 983 wounded, with 121 suffering permanent injuries. Damage to equipment was estimated at 3.5 million yuan, and production was at a standstill for two months, during which the loss in profits amounted to an additional 1.75 million yuan. The medical costs of treating the wounded in 1967–69 were estimated at almost 120,000 yuan.[80]

Even under these chaotic conditions, bureaucracy still ruled: if one could provide proof of having been involved in armed struggle out of sheer ignorance, it was possible to have one's injuries counted as an ordinary illness for medical purposes; assuming one was employed, the applicable compensatory regulations were those governing sick leave. If one could prove that one had participated in armed struggle solely to prevent armed struggle and to propagate the party's long- and short-term policies, injuries could be classified as work-related. On the other hand, anyone who could be proved to have been to some extent responsible for armed struggle would receive no compensation for medical bills and would not receive any salary during recuperation and absence from work.[81]

But no good bureaucratic regulations go unexploited. Beginning in June, armed struggles in Jiangsu, Zhejiang, Anhui, Jiangxi, and Sichuan had become so serious that people began to flee to Shanghai, where, rumor had it, "there's food and there's somewhere to stay, and it doesn't cost anything; the exchange of revolutionary experiences is free." By mid-July, Shanghai authorities estimated the number of refugees at over 15,000, including some 3,000 each from Wuhan and Wuxi. About 6,000 were workers who came originally from Shanghai but had been sent to work inland. In July the municipal "reception stations" for dealing with citizens' inquiries and complaints received an average of 2,355 visits a day, the number rising sharply in the second half of the month as a result of concerns about "armed struggles." By the end of August, the number of complainants had risen to over 4,000 a day, some 30 percent of whom were non-Shanghai residents worried about events elsewhere. In August the pressure exerted on Shanghai hospitals by the sudden influx of outsiders needing emergency care had become so heavy that the local authorities issued a special Notification *(tongzhi).* This document clarified the conditions under which non-Shanghai residents would be given urgent medical attention but also implied that nobody was to be turned away simply because of inability to pay the bill. Hospitals or medical posts that were in severe need of cash were to seek temporary loans from the authorities to tide them over.[82]

Nor was Beijing immune from upheavals. The creation of a municipal revolutionary committee, chaired by Xie Fuzhi, on April 20 had done little to restore what ordinary people might have recognized as law and order. "Armed struggles"—stemming from factional splits often focused on personalities rather than rival political programs or class origins—were becoming almost a permanent feature of life in the capital, especially in some of the bigger factories and on school campuses. At Peking University, former comrades split with Nie Yuanzi because of her "increasingly heavy-handed and dictatorial style of leadership."[83] City-wide, the Red Guard organizations of the various campuses had coalesced into two rival alliances: the "Heaven" faction, so nicknamed because the Red Flag Group of the Beijing Aviation Institute was a prominent component, and which included the major Red Guard organizations from other prestigious universities such as Peking (Nie Yuanzi's Xin Beida Commune) and Tsinghua (Kuai Dafu's Jinggangshan of Tsinghua University); and the "Earth" faction, nicknamed after the East Is Red Group of the Beijing Geology Institute, which, along with the Jinggangshan Group of Beijing Normal University, dominated this more numerous faction, composed mainly however of less prestigious schools.[84] Official figures compiled in May stated that during the ten days from April 30 to May 9, no less than 133 "armed struggles" occurred, involving altogether somewhere between 60,000 and 70,000 people, of whom 1,400 were wounded. By the end of June it was officially estimated that thousands of "armed struggles" had occurred since the formation of the revolutionary committee. In three Beijing suburbs, the situation was described as "explosive."[85]

Yet the situation could have been even more explosive—not just around the capital, but in any densely populated area anywhere in the country—as events in the Jilin provincial capital of Changchun make terrifyingly clear. Here two "organizations of the revolutionary masses" based in geological research institutes spent the summer engaged in wild experiments in unconventional weapons design and development. To these organizations belongs the dubious distinction of having first designed and tested (though—as far as is known—never actually used against human targets) various primitive "dirty bombs." During a test performed under controlled conditions, the "Geological Institute Mao Zedong Thought Combat Regiment" in the city of Changchun successfully exploded two "radioactive self-defense bombs" *(fangshexing ziweidan)* at 1:15 A.M. and 12:35 P.M. on August 6, 1967. In a statement released subsequently, the group explicitly committed itself to a no-first-use policy. Less than a week later, at between 9:05 and 9:20 P.M. on August 11, and again under controlled conditions—this time in the eastern garrison sector of the Changchun railroad maintenance area—the "Changchun Commune" successfully exploded two similar devices that it characterized as "radioactive self-defense mines" *(fangshexing ziwei dilei)*.[86]

As a result of this nationwide fighting and industrial disruption, the responsible State Council group under Li Fuchun told the center in October 1967 that in the previous month the national daily average output of steel and pig iron had fallen to 12,000 tons, or about 26 percent of the Five-Year Plan objective. Only 50 percent of the national industrial targets for the third quarter of 1967 had been fulfilled. In desperation, the State Council decided to spend $40 million, originally earmarked for grain purchases on the international market, on the import of 100,000 tons of rolled steel, 300,000 tons of scrap steel, and raw materials for the chemical industry.[87]

13

The May 16 Conspiracy

O f the countless national and local political initiatives, movements within movements, and ad hoc campaigns launched in the Cultural Revolution decade, none was stranger than the investigation into the "Counterrevolutionary May 16 Conspiracy." According to a cadre with the CCP Discipline Inspection Commission, the investigation targeted 10 million people nationwide.[1] Wang Li (initially accused of being a mastermind of the "conspiracy") estimated in 1981 that it involved the persecution of 3 million people; in 1983 he revised this number upward, estimating that it led to the arrest of 3.5 million.[2] The consensus among the CCP's own historians in Beijing today is that the particular class enemy that the investigation sought to identify and purge had in fact been nonexistent.[3] There never was a conspiracy in the first place.

CCP historians trace the origins of the May 16 Conspiracy to the emergence in Beijing, in the summer of 1967, of a Red Guard organization called the "Capital Red Guard May 16 Regiment."[4] The Regiment consisted of no more than a few dozen university students from Beijing's Foreign Languages and Iron and Steel institutes who believed that the belated publication of the CCP's May 16, 1966, Notification in the *People's Daily* on May 17, 1967, had signaled the impending downfall of Zhou Enlai as yet another "big capitalist roader." In the early summer of 1967, these students clandestinely distributed handbills and put up big-character posters in Beijing with titles such as "Drag out the chief backstage boss of the February Black Wind—Zhou Enlai," "The crux about people like Zhou Enlai is their betrayal of the 'May 16' Notification," "Thoroughly wreck the bourgeois headquarters! Hold Zhou Enlai to account," and "Zhou Enlai has disgracefully betrayed Mao Zedongism!"[5] In August 1967, the CCRG branded the Regiment a clandestine, illegal organization. Chen Boda called it a "conspiratorial organization" that by targeting Zhou Enlai "is in reality targeting the center. It has to be struck down!"[6]

Once it had been "struck down" in a few days of coordinated raids and arrests, the May 16 Regiment ceased to interest the central authorities.[7] Instead, the focus of a snowballing investigation shifted to its alleged "backstage bosses" and a putative nationwide conspiracy of "counterrevolutionary May 16 elements." A Central Document, *Zhongfa* [1967] 306, issued on September 23, described what these "backstage bosses" and "elements" had in common: "[They] resort to conspiracies from the right or from the 'left'—or from both directions simultaneously; they set out to sabotage Chairman Mao's proletarian headquarters, sabotage the PLA, and sabotage the revolutionary committees, these newborn things."[8]

Soon detailed charts and maps began to circulate claiming to describe a sinister open-ended network with its tentacles reaching deep into virtually every sector of state and society. The acting PLA chief of staff, Yang Chengwu, was quoted as saying: "the 'May 16' is very big and is made up of some eight front armies, of which the one confronting the 'Proletarian Faction in the Three Branches of the Armed Forces' is one made up of not too many people. It has liaison offices for every sector, including agriculture and forestry, finance and trade, foreign trade, universities, the military, middle schools and polytechnics, and overseas Chinese affairs."[9] In 1968 Yang himself would be accused of being one of the "backstage bosses" of the "May 16."[10] But in the late summer of 1967, the targets were the junior members of the CCRG. The catalyst was the sack of the British mission in Beijing on August 23.

International Dimensions

Since the Cultural Revolution was premised on Mao's idea that Soviet "revisionism" was insufficiently revolutionary in its opposition to U.S. "imperialism," it is hardly surprising that the domestic upheaval spilled over into foreign relations. The renaming of the road on which the Soviet embassy in Beijing was situated as "Anti-Revisionism Street" was only the mildest example of the xenophobia that the Red Guards exhibited. Every Chinese ambassador but one and up to two-thirds of embassy staffs were summoned home to participate in the Cultural Revolution,[11] and Chinese abroad were involved in confrontations with local citizens and police, often as a result of their own provocative actions.

Chinese students in the Soviet Union clashed with Soviet police when they tried to lay wreaths at the Lenin mausoleum in Moscow's Red Square in January

1967. During February, in the tit-for-tat struggle that characterized Sino-Soviet relations at the time, Soviet "citizens" trashed part of the Chinese embassy in Moscow, and Red Guards laid siege to the Soviet embassy in Beijing; and after Chinese students in Paris clashed with police preventing them from demonstrating against the Soviet embassy, the French commercial counselor in Beijing and his wife were dragged from their car and shouted at for six hours. In June, the Chinese-speaking second and third secretaries of the Indian embassy were beaten by Red Guards at the Beijing airport as they tried to leave the country after being expelled. Red Guards even denounced the Korean Communist leader Kim Il Sung as a "fat revisionist." In Burma and Indonesia, Chinese were beaten up and killed, and in the latter case thousands of Chinese were repatriated. By the end of September 1967, China had been involved in quarrels of varying magnitude with over thirty countries.[12] The Reuters correspondent in Beijing, Anthony Grey, described the form these took in China:

From June 1966 to August [1967] eleven missions were subjected to the now-familiar demonstration pattern unique in a world in which political demonstrations are becoming increasingly rampant . . . Now, long after some of the demonstrations have finished the embassies stand with their walls covered with a mess of posters, some have broken windows and stained walls and the Soviet and Indonesian embassies were burned in parts. The thing that distinguishes Peking demonstrations from those elsewhere in the world is their sheer size and iron discipline. . .

First come the poster stickers and road painters. They arrive to deface the embassy compound walls and the road outside usually late at night before the main demonstrating day. Some sporadic groups march by shouting slogans against the appropriate "ism." The next day in the morning school-age Red Guards and students begin streaming by with portraits of Mao, slogan placards and coloured paper flags bearing the same slogans.

Canvas-walled toilets are set up by the roadsides near the embassy concerned . . . and often carts come along selling tea and buns. As the day wears on factory workers and peasants finished with their shifts begin moving into the picture.

All concerned march in neat ranks chanting slogans read off a piece of paper by cadres marching alongside the columns . . . Fists and paper flags are waved as each shouts. Effigies are burned before embassy gates. I have watched [the Soviet leaders] Brezhnev and Kosygin, [British prime minister] Harold Wilson, [Indian prime minister] Mrs. Gandhi, [Indonesian leader] General

Suharto, [Burmese president] General Ne Win and Mongolia's Tsedenbal go up in smoke and blazing straw in Peking in the last few months.

For a really angry protest the highly efficient organisers can get a million people marched past the gates of an embassy in three days.[13]

Grey never sent that dispatch because, just as he was completing it, he became a pawn in a struggle between Britain and China.

The Burning of the British Mission

China's relations with some countries had specific dimensions that made explosions during the Cultural Revolution more likely and more bitter:[14] ideological schism with the Soviet Union, the 1962 border war with India, the widespread slaughter of Chinese in Indonesia during the anti-Communist pogrom of 1965. In the case of Britain, the crux was the continuing existence of the crown colony of Hong Kong, unmistakably on Chinese soil. Part of the problem, there as elsewhere, was the desperate urge of Chinese nationals abroad at the outset of the Cultural Revolution to prove that, despite living relatively comfortable lives in bourgeois countries, they were every bit as red as their less fortunate compatriots back home.[15]

In Britain, this necessity took the absurd form of a pitched battle on August 29 between embassy officials and London police. Far more serious in its consequences was the attempt by Communists and leftists in Hong Kong to prove that they had not been corrupted by the fleshpots of the colony. Zhou Enlai disapproved of their activities but proved unable to halt them.[16] From May 1967 on, unions called strikes; terrorist bombings caused five deaths; Chinese militia made raids across the border, in one of which five Hong Kong policemen were killed. Simultaneously a diplomat, Ray Whitney, was sent down from Beijing to help Her Majesty's consul in Shanghai, Mr. Hewitt, evacuate the post. In a long dispatch to Donald Hopson, the chargé d'affaires in Beijing, Hewitt described the events of the previous weeks, ending with his departure with his wife and three children on May 24:

> Our route to the airport was circuitous but, since traffic lights invariably changed in our favour long before we reached them, was obviously prearranged. The first Airport crowd was the Army check post; they hammered on the vehicle and viciously tried to drag the driver out: after Mr. Whitney and I had dismounted, been abused and received yet another written protest, we were allowed to proceed. There were very big crowds round the Airport buildings

and lines of buses and lorries which had brought them. To our pleasant surprise, Mr. Ksiesopolski, the Polish Consul General, and Mr. Van Roosbroeck
[a Belgian banker] were also present and they stepped forward and took a baby
each; my wife and eldest daughter were taken through the crowds to the
plane—though they were abused and bruised they were spared the worst. Mr.
Whitney and I had to run the gauntlet to the aircraft, and even the plane steps
were thronged with demonstrators. We were jostled, shoulder charged, tripped
and struck with fists and flag sticks, my jacket was torn and my tie pulled into
so tight a knot that it had later to be forced open with a tea spoon. The noise
and the venom were considerable and we were both hampered by having to
carry a heavy crossed bag. When at last we made the plane the Stewardesses refused to give us anything to drink, and throughout the flight we were regaled
with loudspeaker homilies on the wickedness of the British authorities in
Hong Kong.[17]

On July 19, a Chinese journalist was sentenced to two years' imprisonment
by a Hong Kong court in connection with the rioting there, and in swift retalia-
tion Reuters correspondent Grey was put under house arrest. A month later, on
the anniversary of the first great Tiananmen rally, Red Guards invaded Grey's
house, beat him up, killed his cat, trashed the premises, and confined him to a
tiny room.[18] When the Hong Kong authorities closed down three Communist
newspapers for publishing false and seditious material and arrested some of
the staff, the Chinese made an official protest to the British chargé d'affaires,
Hopson, on August 20, demanding the lifting of the ban and the release of those
arrested within forty-eight hours. In a dispatch to British Foreign Secretary
George Brown, Hopson explained what happened when the ultimatum expired
on August 22:

As night fell the crowd outside increased rapidly in numbers (the official Chinese report put it as 10,000). They were quiet and orderly, sitting down and
packed tight in their ranks, while the preparations for the drama were made.
Searchlights and loudspeakers were beamed at our building, and a sort of pro-
scenium was rigged up over our gateway. There were speeches, recitations,
songs, and a rather festive atmosphere prevailed. We did not know that the
audience were later to take over the role of actors in the grand finale . . . We
dined together in the office hall off a dinner of tinned sausages and peas, claret
and biscuits and cheese, prepared by the ladies. After dinner I went to the first-
floor [American second floor] to play bridge, while those of the staff who were
not at work watched Peter Sellers in a film entitled not inappropriately, "The
Wrong Arm of the Law"! . . .

At 10:30 P.M. I had just bid "Three no-trumps," when I heard a roar from the crowd outside. I ran to the window, which looked over the main gateway, and saw that the masses had risen to their feet and were surging like an angry sea against the small cordon of soldiers, who linked arms three deep before the gates. It was an extraordinary sight which will remain imprinted on my memory . . . Card players, film-goers and all [twenty-three, including five women] moved at speed into the area on the ground floor leading to the secure zone. . .

Outside the crowd broke the glass of the windows, but the bars and plywood shutters held . . . the mob then started to burn straw at the windows. We threw water through the gaps, but the room began to fill with smoke . . . Smoke in the room was making breathing difficult, we could see the glare of many fires, and as it was now clear that the mob would soon be through the wall and there was a danger that we should be burned alive if we stayed, I gave orders for the emergency exit to be opened . . . The mob greeted us with howls of exultation and immediately set about us with everything they had. The time was then about 11:10 P.M., barely 40 minutes since the attack began.

From that moment we were split up, except the girls who all had one or two men with orders to stick by them. We were haled by our hair, half-strangled with our ties, kicked and beaten on the head with bamboo poles. I do not know how long this lasted but I found myself eventually more or less out on my feet, by what turned out to be the side gate of the compound, though I had little idea where I was at the time. . .

Most of the staff who had been at the Office had had similar experiences to my own. Some were paraded up and down, forced to their knees and photographed in humiliating postures. All were beaten and kicked, and the girls were not spared lewd attentions from the prying fingers of the mob. Most of those who were wearing wrist-watches had them removed, and shirts, trousers and knickers were torn. So much for the morals of the Red Guards . . . Most of the staff were eventually rescued by the army and plain-clothes police agents and put temporarily in police-boxes as I was. . .

The Office is a total loss, though the strong room was untouched. All official transport was destroyed except the heavy lorry, and one bus which we kept for emergencies in a garage in the international compound. My house was sacked and its contents including my clothes destroyed. The signed photograph of The Queen, which I had earlier placed in the security zone of the Office, survived though slightly singed.[19]

Despite this ordeal, Hopson recommended that there be no rupture of diplomatic relations, and London agreed to this stance. But on August 30, Foreign Secretary Brown wrote to Foreign Minister Marshal Chen Yi asking if he thought it might be a good idea "if while maintaining diplomatic relations, both sides withdrew their mission and personnel from each other's capital for the time being."[20] Chen Yi, now under regular attack by Red Guards, did not reply. The British began to consider whether they might be forced out of Hong Kong. As late as March 28, 1969, the British foreign secretary, now Michael Stewart, circulated to the Cabinet Ministerial Committee on Hong Kong an interdepartmental study by officials "on the basis that we could not rely on remaining in Hong Kong on present terms until the lease of the New Territories lapsed in 1997."[21] But as the mobilization phase of the Cultural Revolution wound down later that year, calmer approaches to the future of Hong Kong began to be heard among British diplomats.[22]

The Leftist Ascendancy

Coming so swiftly on top of the Wuhan incident, the sack of the British mission was a turning point.[23] Zhou Enlai was reportedly furious about the attack and self-criticized that, weakened by tiredness, he had sanctioned the ultimatum.[24] Yet the triumph of the leftists, if sweet, was short. China's Foreign Ministry had come briefly under the sway of the former chargé d'affaires in Jakarta, Yao Dengshan, who had returned home to a hero's welcome and the title of "red diplomat fighter" after being declared persona non grata by the Indonesian government in April.[25] On August 4, in conversation with Yao Dengshan, Guan Feng and Qi Benyu had been extremely critical of the Ministry of Foreign Affairs. Qi had, according to Yao, characterized the "leading ideology" within the ministry as one of "having no end of misgivings" and of constantly "being afraid of this and of that." Even when other countries were "cursing us," Qi is alleged to have said, the ministry still pathetically referred to "the friendly relations of our two countries." Guan Feng had—if Yao's record of the conversation is to be believed—been of the same opinion as Qi:

The leading ideology within the Ministry of Foreign Affairs is not Chairman Mao's guiding ideology of daring to wage a tit-for-tat struggle, but one of fear! What's there to be afraid of? Look: Day out and day in, the capitalist countries' press keeps on cursing us, but for over a decade our country's press has not even dared to reflect this, much less counterattack! Why is this? Because their ideology is one of fear. What is it that they are afraid of? They're afraid of it impacting on the friendly relations of our two countries.[26]

227

In an earlier conversation with Yao Dengshan and a group of "rebels" from the Ministry of Foreign Affairs on August 7, Wang Li had been no less critical and suggested that one ought to get rid of a whole row of stuffy Foreign Ministry "bureaucrats" and replace them with daring "twenty-somethings."[27] Wang Li certified that it was all right to attack Chen Yi by name, as Mao had personally endorsed doing so.[28] Perhaps more importantly, Wang Li provoked the "rebels" in the Foreign Ministry by suggesting that they had been insufficiently firm in their revolutionary activities against the ministry old guard:

> In January you seized power, but how much power did you seize? How large is your supervisory capacity? Can you supervise? The office of the Party committee has not moved? The revolution did not remove it? What kind of great revolution is this if it is alright to leave it in place? Why can you not remove it? . . . The personnel department also has to be supervised, the line of the cadres has to be the guarantee of the political line. To choose cadres will then mean one chooses revolutionaries, not conservatives. To avoid unreasonable choice of cadres, you have to use your supervisory power even more . . . In my view you have not seized power well . . . Why are you so civilized? This is a revolution . . . Why should rebels not be able to read documents? . . . Why can only those who oppose Mao read documents? This is a joke.[29]

Wang's words in particular were promptly turned into something of a green light to ignore resistance to a Red Guard takeover of China's foreign affairs sector. As Yao Dengshan told a mass rally organized by "rebels" in the Ministry of Foreign Trade on August 15: "Do [our critics] mean that we Red Guards cannot handle foreign affairs? We can! *(Applause, slogans shouted)* Comrades, my sense of what's important in the spirit of what comrade Wang Li has said is that we must be thorough in our revolution, that we must be resolute and revolutionary all the way through!"[30]

Wang Li's speech appears to have encouraged the renewal of radicalism in the Foreign Ministry just when the Hong Kong situation was reaching a crisis point, with predictable results, though Wang himself later attributed the attack on the British mission not to Red Guards but to hooligans.[31] At the time, Zhou Enlai, who called the attack a manifestation of "anarchism," attributed Foreign Ministry extremism principally to Yao Dengshan:

> They [the rebels] sent telegrams directly to foreign embassies. As a result they were sent back. Yao Teng-shan [Dengshan] went everywhere making reports

and creating trouble . . . The Central Committee put forward the slogan "Down with Liu [Shaoqi], Deng [Xiaoping], T'ao [Zhu]." He put forward the slogan "Down with Liu, Deng, Ch'en [Yi]." How can you as a cadre at the head-of-department level . . . put forward such a slogan? Who gave you permission?[32]

But the spearhead of the attack on the mission seems to have consisted of radicals from the Institute of Foreign Languages and other Red Guard units, and, unlike Wang Li, Yao Dengshan was rehabilitated after the Cultural Revolution.[33]

Whoever was responsible, two days after the sack of the British mission, at the height of that summer of civil wars, Zhou Enlai revealed the depths of his despair to a distinguished foreign visitor whom he knew well. On the evening of August 25, the premier received Shirley Graham, the widow of W. E. B. Du Bois, the eminent American black historian and scholar, and confided to her: "The whole Chinese Revolution may go down to defeat for a while. We may lose everything. But never mind. If we are defeated here, you in Africa will learn from our mistakes, and you will develop your own Mao Zedong, and you will learn to do it better. And so in the end, we shall succeed."[34] Yet Zhou was on the verge of one of his many dramatic comebacks. His instrument was the crackdown on the alleged May 16 Conspiracy.

The Fall of Wang Li

In the predawn hours of August 25, Zhou had outlined his assessment of the situation in Beijing in the wake of the destruction of the British mission—"a disaster in the making"—in an extended one-on-one conversation with Yang Chengwu, who had just flown in from Shanghai, where Mao was temporarily residing. Zhou told Yang: "So many incidents have occurred that unless we come up with a way of explaining them, who knows, something even more terrible will happen. Where will it all end, if this is allowed to go on?"[35] Zhou said he saw no alternative but to ask the Chairman to take a stand, to issue instructions, to decide. Yang flew back to Shanghai immediately to update Mao. The Chairman allegedly slept for only two or three hours that night, then had his nurse call Yang Chengwu to his side first thing in the morning. Mao told Yang that Wang Li, Guan Feng, and Qi Benyu "are wrecking the Great Cultural Revolution and are not good people. Tell nobody but the premier about this, and see to it that they are arrested. I am putting the premier in charge of dealing with this matter." Just before Yang departed, Mao modified his directive slightly, telling Yang to tell Zhou to spare Qi for now. By noon on August 26, Yang was back in Beijing and briefing Zhou.[36]

Zhou wasted no time. One of the first things he did was to order Yang to travel on to Beidaihe to brief Lin Biao.[37] Zhou dispelled Yang's anxiety about "telling nobody but the premier about this" by reminding him that Lin was the vice chairman of the CCP and "not to tell him about something this important would not be good. If the Chairman asks, just tell him it was my idea!"[38] The pressure on Zhou was enormous, to the point where at dawn on August 27 he suffered a severe attack of angina that put him out of action for the next thirty-six hours.[39]

By August 28 at the latest, Wang Li for one knew that something untoward was about to happen to him. From snippets of a conversation that he overheard between Jiang Qing and Kang Sheng, he knew that a crash investigation into his past had been launched in the utmost secrecy at Mao's direct orders and that the "findings" would "show" that he was a member of the KMT rather than the CCP, that he was a Soviet agent, and that his entire family, including his in-laws, were nothing but a "burrowful of black trash." It is safe to assume that a parallel investigation into Guan Feng's past was being conducted and that it ended up pointing in a similar direction. On August 30, Wang and Guan were confronted with the investigation "findings" at an eleven-hour-long marathon session of the Central Caucus chaired by Zhou Enlai (who also conveyed Mao's directives on the matter). As was the long-established norm for such occasions, it fell upon Wang's and Guan's immediate superiors to present the "findings." This meant that Kang Sheng ended up speaking at length about Wang's "errors," while Chen Boda discoursed on Guan's. As had furthermore become the custom since the beginning of the Cultural Revolution, Jiang Qing was free to comment at will on the "errors" of both men. The session of the Central Caucus—from which Lin Biao was absent in Beidaihe and his wife/liaison officer Ye Qun had absented herself because of "illness"—ended up ordering Wang and Guan to "write self-criticisms," and put them under house arrest in the Diaoyutai compound.[40]

Little is known of the substance—if any—of the initial accusations made against Wang and Guan (and later Qi). But one accusation concerned their supposed responsibility for the chaos in the Ministry of Foreign Affairs that had culminated in the burning of the British mission. Mao's eventual comment on a transcript of Wang Li's August 7 remarks was that they amounted to a "big, big, big poisonous weed!"[41]

The PLA Dimension

A second issue that concerned Mao was the slogan "Drag out a small handful in the military!" Mao had begun to have second thoughts in early August about the "tactical" appropriateness of this formulation, which had been used against PLA leaders off and on since the beginning of 1967. The slogan was central to a *Red Flag* editorial, published on the fortieth anniversary of the founding of the Red Army on August 1, which was drafted by Lin Jie, revised by Guan Feng, and approved and signed off on by Chen Boda—"Excellent!" was Chen's comment, according to Wang Li. The text of the editorial was not submitted to Zhou Enlai or Kang Sheng for their comments before publication, nor was it read in advance by Jiang Qing.[42] It seems unlikely that it was read by Mao or Lin Biao.

According to one contemporary account, Mao first expressed doubts about the formulation while watching the raw footage of a newsreel about a pitched battle in the Shanghai Diesel Factory in which the slogan "Drag out a small handful in the military!" appeared twice. After remarking that "to drag out a small handful in the military" was wrong, Mao called for the frames containing the slogan to be edited out. Hereafter, "in accordance with the Chairman's instructions, the central leaders present in Shanghai at the time saw to it that this instruction of the Chairman's was transmitted to Vice Chairman Lin, the premier, and comrade Boda in Beijing."[43]

By August 11, the news had been conveyed to the members of the central leadership in Beijing that Mao had pronounced the call for "a small handful in the military" to be "dragged out" to be "tactically inappropriate."[44] At a meeting that same night with the leaders of Beijing's major Red Guard organizations, Chen Boda explained that this slogan had to be understood in its proper context and not be abused.[45] Four days later, on the night of August 15–16, Zhou Enlai told some of the same university Red Guard leaders that there should be no further use of this particular slogan.[46] Over the next few days, at one meeting after another, the members of the central leadership issued the same caution. On the evening of August 29, Wang Li himself told a meeting of members of the CCRG staff: "Some people advocate seizing a small handful in the military, but [in doing so] they are miscalculating the situation. Problems within the military can be solved by the military itself. The PLA is under the leadership of Chairman Mao and the command of comrade Lin Biao, so there's no need to go and seize a small handful in the military."[47] But if Wang was trying to jump on the bandwagon, he found that he had landed on a tumbril instead.

The additional accusations directed at this point at Wang Li and Guan Feng were at best highly tenuous: the claim that Wang was a KGB agent rested on the fact that during one of his visits to Moscow, he had had a conversation with Yuri Andropov, who became the director of the KGB in 1967. At the time of the meeting, however, Andropov had been head of the CPSU CC department in charge of relations with ruling Communist parties, and a meeting between the two men had been totally appropriate. Wang and Guan were also accused of having opposed their colleagues in the CCRG, notably Chen Boda, Kang Sheng, and Jiang Qing.[48]

On September 4, Qi Benyu wrote a letter to Mao in which he distanced himself from Wang Li and Guan Feng. Qi accused Wang and Guan of "very grave errors," which had found expression in "rashness" with a leftist inclination. For example, Qi said, they had assessed the situation in China as a whole erroneously when claiming that certain events suggesting a reversal should be interpreted as signs of a "nationwide restoration of capitalism." They had failed to see the positive outcome of the "struggle of the revolutionary masses." Wang and Guan had also made a mistaken assessment of the PLA when they had used the media to call for the arrest of "a small handful in the military." Finally, Qi said, they had "cast doubt on everything" and "whenever they felt like it, undermined the leadership of Chairman Mao's HQ." Their errors were ultimately rooted in "individualism, inflated egos, too high an opinion of themselves, believing they are more revolutionary than the rest, and being unable to accept the dissenting opinions of others." Mao's written comment on Qi's letter (which contained the obligatory self-deprecating self-criticism) was that "one benefits from committing a few errors, since they give one plenty of food for thought, which in turn allows one to correct them."[49]

Finally, the CC's General Office informed all concerned parties that as of midnight on October 8, 1967, Wang Li and Guan Feng were officially no longer trusted Cultural Revolutionaries; hence no official communications of any kind were to be shared with or addressed to them.[50] On October 16, the Beijing Garrison took official custody of Wang Li and Guan Feng and put them under house arrest in a villa in the Western Hills outside Beijing.[51]

Mao's decisive action to bring the leftists to heel and appease the generals was not limited to the removal from power of Wang Li and Guan Feng. Count-less lesser officials with links to the two men and/or the "excessively leftist devia-tions" for which they were made scapegoats also fell from grace in quick succes-sion. The core "elements" of the "May 16" group made up a veritable who's who of Cultural Revolutionary radicalism in the sense that they were almost all people who had enjoyed rapid promotions and ever greater influence in the party's academic and intellectual/propaganda sectors since the spring of 1966. In Beijing, they included Mu Xin, member of the CCRG and editor-in-chief of the *Guangming Daily;* Lin Jie, a CCRG staff member and *Red Flag* deputy editor-in-chief; Zhou Jingfang, secretary general of the Beijing RC; and Zhao Yiya, editor-in-chief of the *Liberation Army Daily.* The three most prominent "leftists" in the Philosophy and Social Sciences Department of the Chinese Academy of Sciences, Pan Zinian, Lin Yushi, and Wu Chuanqi, were arrested and accused of being May 16 elements after hiding out for some time in the countryside in cen-tral China. The most notable exception to this dominance of "intellectuals" was the inclusion, in the supposed core membership, of Yao Dengshan, the bureau chief in the Ministry of Foreign Affairs who was made the scapegoat for the burning of the British mission in August 1967. At one point Zhou Enlai re-marked cryptically of Yao that he "did not sign a [membership] form, claiming there was no need for him to join. He is a 'May 16' [element]."[52]

The Case of Wang Naiying

Yet the one fact that more than any other was seen by many as proof of the ex-tremely "sinister" nature of the May 16 Conspiracy was the apparent ignorance of even some of its core members of its very existence. It took more than the usual amount of carefully administered "persuasion" by determined interrogators to make a suspect arrive at a "correct" understanding of the nature of his or her "crimes" in this respect. The final items in the massive case dossier of one fairly well-known "May 16 element"—Wang Naiying, the wife of Lin Jie—makes this abundantly clear.

When Wang Naiying realized that her husband was in deep trouble and there was little else she could do, she put up a big-character poster at the edito-rial offices of *Red Flag,* demanding clarification. *"If,"* she said, Lin Jie had indeed "opposed the party center, Chairman Mao, and the proletarian revolutionary line," she would "definitely make a resolute, clean break with him, and join all of you in actively denouncing and overthrowing him, struggle him until he stinks, and never, ever, let him turn a new leaf." But for now, she insisted on "immediate information about comrade Lin Jie! I want to see Lin Jie!"[53] On September 7 she was herself placed under house arrest and called on to denounce her husband.[54]

For more than three years after her arrest, Wang produced pages upon pages of accounts of her every activity, her every relevant remark, everything of the slightest possible interest to her interrogators. In December 1970 she was finally called upon to admit her guilt. Her first admission (in her own hand) is the most telling, ending as it does in the following way:

> I was a follower of the May 16 counterrevolutionary bosses Zhou Jingfang et al. and was involved in a string of criminal May 16 counterrevolutionary activities, but before August 1967, when the party center publicly exposed the counterrevolutionary May 16 conspiratorial clique, I did not know of the existence of the counterrevolutionary organization that was the May 16, nor did I know of the existence of its counterrevolutionary program, plans, and membership. Nor had I become a member of it. I am [therefore] unable to confess to being a core member of the counterrevolutionary May 16 conspiratorial clique.
>
> *Wang Naiying*
> *December 10, 1970*[55]

Needless to say, this confession of Wang's did not make the grade. Nothing is known about what transpired during the next twenty-four hours, but on the following day she produced a new confession (in her own hand), this one ending in the following way:

> . . . there are indeed huge numbers of exposure materials that show that I am a counterrevolutionary May 16 core member, and extensive investigation and research has shown these materials to be reliable.
>
> *Counterrevolutionary May 16 Core Member Wang Naiying*
> *December 11, 1970*[56]

Finally, after yet another twenty-four hours and probably as a kind of formality—since the narrow, specific label "Counterrevolutionary May 16 Core Member" was not one that had yet found its way into the relevant laws and statutes governing counterrevolution and its punishments—Wang wrote a third and final confession:

> I admit to being guilty of crimes and to being, myself, an active counterrevolutionary guilty of May 16 counterrevolutionary activities. I admit these things to

the party and to the broad revolutionary masses and ask them to punish me. I am determined to sincerely mend my ways, forsake evil and do good, thoroughly remold myself, and become a new person.

Active Counterrevolutionary Element Wang Naiying
December 12, 1970[57]

But at least Wang Naiying survived. Others were not so fortunate.

To sway those who were inclined to interpret the difficulty involved in making people like Wang Naiying admit to the existence of, and their own direct involvement in, the May 16 Conspiracy as suggesting that indeed there may possibly never have been a conspiracy in the first place, the CCP center used the persuasive power inherent in its authoritative *Zhongfa* stream of documents to issue declarations like the following: "Some people maintain that the counterrevolutionary 'May 16' clique simply does not exist. They are very much opposed to the investigation launched into the 'May 16' and even go so far as to argue that the verdict on it should be reversed. This is altogether wrong."[58]

Reactions among radicals to the arrests of the first "backstage bosses" replicated those of Wang Naiying to the arrest of her husband, ranging all the way from anger and desperation to total incomprehension. When a close associate of Wang Li and Guan Feng, a sometime ghostwriter for *Red Flag*, heard on September 3 that a man who had been on the editorial board of the *Liberation Army Daily* had been purged with them and that Mao and Jiang Qing's twenty-seven-year-old daughter Li Na had been appointed the new editor-in-chief, he exclaimed: "Has Chairman Mao become all muddle-headed?" Later he went on to say: "It's never going to work, to think that contradictions can be mitigated by sacrificing a few individuals. Let alone that they're still not able to specify what those people have done . . . Even the people being struggled don't themselves know what crimes they [are supposed to] have committed!" A party secretary in the Central Institute of the Nationalities reacted scatologically to the arrest of Guan Feng's associate Lin Jie: "The fucking bastards [*tamade hundan*]! Only a couple of days ago he was still a revolutionary leftist and now he's counterrevolutionary?! This is nothing but a political frame-up!"[59]

Protecting Zhou Enlai

If Mao had been convinced of the need for a "frame-up" of the radicals in the wake of the burning of the British mission and the demands for "dragging out" a handful in the PLA, he may have hoped to make the anti–May 16 movement acceptable by focusing it on the need to protect Premier Zhou Enlai, who, he had clearly decided, was vital to ensuring that the country continued to function in the midst of its "civil wars." On September 5, Jiang Qing claimed in an "important speech"—tape recordings of which were given nationwide distribution "for study" by the CC General Office in October—to a provincial delegation from Anhui that "the counterrevolutionary organization 'May 16' has an extremely 'leftist' appearance, and its opposition is directed squarely against the premier."[60] Soon a major purge had been launched, and soon the name of this obscure rebel group had become a generic label affixed by the party to anyone anywhere in China who, either directly or by implication, appeared to be "ultra-leftist" and/or "anti-Zhou."

In the institution to which Zhou had particular ties, the Foreign Ministry,

> the campaign to "uncover" members or sympathizers of the [May 16] group began in January 1969 and reached its height in 1970. In the spring of 1970, Ma Wenbo, the military representative directing the campaign to purify the class ranks in the Foreign Ministry, reported to Zhou Enlai that more than 1,000 May 16 elements were discovered among the roughly 2,000 staff members of the ministry. In many departments of the ministry, 50 to 70 percent of their personnel was accused of belonging to the clandestine counter-revolutionary group . . . For the conservatives, the campaign was an opportunity to settle accounts with their former adversaries where personal vendetta played a major role.[61]

The list of people accused of being "counterrevolutionary 'May 16' elements" was to grow at a steady rate throughout the Cultural Revolution; and according to official CCP histories published in the 1980s, it eventually included "millions of innocent cadres and members of the masses."[62] In February 1968, despite turning Chairman's evidence against his erstwhile comrades-in-arms, Qi Benyu was arrested. (His arrest at first kept secret, his friends and colleagues were left to wonder what had happened to him; a rumor quickly spread that he had been dispatched by the center to Shanghai to assist with preparations for the Ninth Party Congress.)[63] In March, after the dismissal and arrest (under obscure circumstances, to be discussed later) of acting PLA chief of staff Yang Chengwu, PLA air force political commissar Yu Lijin, and Beijing Garrison commander Fu Chongbi, it was decided that these men, too (together with the former director of the PLA General Political Department, Xiao Hua), had maintained links with the May 16 group. By the end of the year, the party center had created an ad hoc leading group, chaired by Chen Boda, specifically to monitor the investigation of alleged members and "backstage bosses" of the May 16 group.[64] What happened after 1968 in the investigation into the "Counterrevolutionary May 16 Conspiracy" continues to mystify even the best-informed Chinese historians. One of them writes: "What motivated it? What was its aim? This author does not at present have sufficient factual information on which to base an analysis and a judgment."[65] By 1970, the hunt for May 16 elements had become quite confusing even for those charged with carrying it out. After the Second Plenum of the Ninth CC in the late summer of 1970, Chen Boda (once ferreter-in-chief) was accused of being its "sinister backstage boss."

The Campaign outside the Capital

The intensity of the hunt for "May 16 elements" varied greatly across regions, and this variation is to some extent reflected in recently published official provincial histories. One such history of Jiangsu describes the hunt for "May 16 elements" in the province as the "most brutal" in a "chain of movements" occurring after 1968. It states that more than 130,000 "May 16 elements" were "ferreted out" in Jiangsu as a whole and that of these, more than 6,000 were so badly treated that they either died or suffered permanent injuries.[66] Similar histories of Henan, Tibet, and Liaoning on the other hand pay significantly less attention to the "conspiracy." Guangxi was probably typical of those parts of China where the label "May 16" came to be used indiscriminately to refer to just about anything and anybody targeted by the sitting leadership as part of "conspiracies from the right or from the 'left' or from both directions simultaneously." In 1970 and 1971 the regional leadership in Guangxi asserted that a whole string of seemingly unrelated events in 1967 and 1968 had actually been part of the May 16 Conspiracy. These events ranged from the occupation of the premises of the *Guangxi Daily*, the theft of military hardware destined for Vietnam, protests against the transfer out of the region of a certain PLA main force unit, even to public performances of a supposedly sinister play titled *Southern Frontier on Fire (Nanjiang liehuo)*, and to a reluctance to clamp down on "sinister meetings, sinister plays" in the local cultural sphere.[67]

In February 1971, the CCP center set up a new central "May 16" coordinating unit (reporting directly to Zhou Enlai) to monitor the now massive, nationwide investigation.[68] As it announced the makeup and mandate of the group—most of the day-to-day work of which was to be led by its vice head, Major General Li Zhen, chairman of the revolutionary committee of the Ministry of Public Security—the CCP center also released a number of pertinent new quotations from Lin Biao and Zhou Enlai defining unit "policy." Lin Biao was quoted as saying that the "military is a tool of dictatorship. We must dig deep for 'May 16' [elements] and not permit a single one to get away." One of a number of extended quotations by Zhou Enlai hinted at the presence of powerful, high-level opposition to the investigation: "We issued a Notification [on March 27, 1970] warning against excessively broadening the scope [of investigation] into the 'May 16' Conspiracy. They then grabbed on to this and argued that in fact the whole thing should be cancelled altogether . . . But this time around we're going to get to the bottom of this, no matter what."[69] The record does not indicate the identity of the mysterious "they" referred to by Zhou. The mystery deepened even further on October 22, 1973, when Major General Li Zhen was found dead in an underground heating duct on the premises of the Ministry of Public Security. At first it was assumed that he had been murdered, and a major investigation proceeding from that assumption was launched under the leadership of Wang Hongwen. The final conclusion of the investigation was that Li had committed suicide for fear of having his own "illicit links" to the head of the "conspiracy" exposed—a verdict that Wang, however, refused to the end to accept and ratify.[70]

The hunt for May 16 elements ended soon after Li Zhen's demise.[71] But while the rout of the ultra-leftists starting in August 1967 helped Zhou Enlai, it was of no benefit to the party leaders who had been toppled a year earlier. And although an expansion of the system of revolutionary committees achieved a measure of pacification, civil strife abated little.

14

The End of the Red Guards

The attack on the May 16 group in the fall of 1967 was part of an attempt to bring the "nationwide all-round civil war" to an end by purging some of its alleged instigators. In pursuit of this aim, in October 1967 Mao called on "all revolutionary organizations to forge great alliances."[1] These alliances were to form "revolutionary committees" to replace the old organs of state power. After a year of struggle and the purge of many "bad people," Mao was anxious to get on with establishing a new order by summoning the CCP's Ninth Congress.[2] The *People's Daily* inveighed against anarchism and factionalism.[3] Yet internecine violence continued, exacerbated by a nationwide campaign to "cleanse the class ranks," and Mao set a bad example for potential uniters by finally consigning Liu Shaoqi to outer darkness.

Revolutionary Committees

When the first revolutionary committees (RCs) were created, in early 1967, they were greeted with much anti-bureaucratic rhetoric and talk about copying the democratic mechanisms of the Paris Commune. In the end, the institutions of the new political order were less utopian. Still, there were significant changes from the past. The old provincial structure had been formally composed of three nominally separate bureaucracies: departments under the party committee, departments under the provincial government, and the legal apparatus of the people's court and procurator. These were now replaced by a single bureaucracy under the revolutionary committees, made up of what were referred to as "functional groups."

These new groups were meant to be leaner and meaner than the departments they replaced. In 1969 the Liaoning Revolutionary Committee employed only 580 people, compared with 6,694 employed by the old provincial party committee and government on the eve of the Cultural Revolution.[4] Large numbers of dismissed officials were relocated to "May 7 Cadre Schools." But even in that supposedly idealistic enterprise, bureaucracy inevitably had its place. According to one participant, "people sent to the country were provided with two boxes [for belongings] at no cost, but additional ones were charged. All this came from documents issued by the May Seventh Office, which the State Council had newly established."[5]

Despite the reduction in cadre numbers, revolutionary committees were still essentially a traditional CCP-style bureaucracy, upholding the old distinction between the "revolutionary masses" and the "party vanguard." Even though provincial party committees had not yet been reconstituted, small "party nuclei" were set up in the revolutionary committees, and party members still enjoyed special powers and privileges, especially as far as access to information was concerned.[6]

By the time of Mao's call for great alliances in October 1967, revolutionary committees had been set up in only seven of China's twenty-nine provinces, central municipalities, and autonomous regions.[7] "Mao Zedong Thought Study Classes" were organized nationwide, and groups were brought to Beijing from problem provinces in the hope that local factionalism could be dissipated by Mao study; with 86.4 million sets of Mao's selected works and 350 million copies of the Little Red Book published in 1967, there was no lack of reading material.[8]

With the additional efforts, another eleven revolutionary committees—each consisting of somewhere between 100 and 200 members, with standing committees of between 20 to 50—were formed by March 30, 1968, when the *People's Daily, Red Flag,* and *Liberation Army News* published one of their joint editorials, titled "Revolutionary Committees Are Good," and confidently declared that the "formation of revolutionary committees in large numbers of primary-level units shows that the Great Proletarian Cultural Revolution is proceeding extremely well."[9] But not until September was the CCP center able to ratify the formation of the last provincial-level revolutionary committee (in Xinjiang) and declare in yet another joint editorial that "the mountains and rivers of the entire nation are red" and "an all-round victory in the Great Proletarian Cultural Revolution has been won!"[10]

Depending on the balance of local political, military, and popular forces, the drawn-out transition process leading to the formation of a revolutionary committee was either peaceful or violent. In many cases, the process was slow because of the complicated negotiations involved. At seemingly endless meetings in Beijing, often lasting from early evening until dawn the following day, and presided over by a member of the CCRG or Zhou Enlai himself, the parties involved would try to reach a consensus on who was to be a member and who was to be kept out. To judge by the number of times Zhou Enlai had to intervene personally in their problems in 1968, the difficult provinces were Guangxi (by far), followed by neighboring Guangdong, Shaanxi, Liaoning, Jilin, Hunan, and Jiangsu.[11]

The aim was to achieve a "three-in-one" combination of representatives of the PLA, "revolutionary cadres," and the "revolutionary masses." Typically, there was much disagreement over such questions as whether a commander of the resident PLA unit really deserved to be a vice chairman in view of his less than stellar performance in "supporting the left"; whether a former provincial vice governor was a credible representative of the party's revolutionary cadres when he had regularly put "economics [rather than politics] in command" before 1966; and whether a youthful representative of such-and-such mass organization needed to be given a seat on the standing committee of the province's most powerful body when until recently he had been a mere factory worker.

Even after the RCs had been set up and formally approved, internal conflicts and disagreements often continued. A month after the creation of the Hebei RC, its leadership reported to the central authorities in a remarkably forthright document that not only was it becoming abundantly clear that "to remain within the set staffing limits will not be easy," but, more important, that the needs of the new organization clashed sharply with "old concepts and unhealthy old workstyles." Some people

> have barely had time to take up their new jobs before they eagerly start issuing commands and ordering people about—well before they themselves have carried out investigations, gone among the masses, or bothered to find things out. Unprepared and without having done any investigating or research, they convene this or that kind of a meeting and issue all kinds of documents. Signs are that even major issues are being dealt with in a rash fashion by isolated individuals.[12]

The reaction of the central authorities was to call on RCs everywhere facing similar problems to copy the radical countermeasures already adopted in Hebei, namely to clamp down with impunity on any challenges to the new authority. Nothing must be permitted to challenge the power of the new revolutionary organs.

Peaceful Transition: Tianjin

The port city of Tianjin, about seventy miles southeast of Beijing, had been the capital of the province of Hebei until the end of 1966. On January 2, 1967, its status was upgraded to that of a municipality under the central government, equal to a province, one of only three such entities in China at the time, the others being Beijing and Shanghai.[13] The formation of the municipal revolutionary committee in Tianjin proceeded slowly but without major incidents.

When the first wave of power-seizures inspired by Shanghai's January Storm hit the city, there was a brief interlude of chaos, after which the local PLA garrison assumed control. By March, political and military power was firmly in the hands of an ad hoc transitional authority led by Xie Xuegong, a former member of the secretariat of the CCP North China Region; and Zheng Sansheng, the commander of the Tianjin Garrison. Zhou Enlai stated confidently that there appeared to be no major problems in the city preventing the swift and early establishment of a revolutionary committee.[14] But the garrison commander urged caution, noting that changes were taking place so rapidly that some power might well end up in the hands of "conservative organizations" while some bona fide revolutionaries were sidelined. Appearing to have in mind the intense Paris Commune–inspired rhetoric about direct elections popular among the city's many "organizations of the revolutionary masses," he noted that "on the surface," the ongoing process of creating a RC "looks very democratic. In actuality, it is not democratic."[15] By the second week of April, Zhou and the rest of the central leadership had drawn the same conclusion. Zhou observed in front of the members of a delegation from Tianjin summoned to the capital that "mainly there's been insufficient consultation. To carry out elections will be impossible." Kang Sheng reemphasized the point: "You must not make a fetish out of elections. In certain conditions, elections are inferior to consultative democracy."[16]

Slamming on the brakes, the central authorities then turned what had begun as an inconclusive power-seizure in the streets into a drawn-out process of negotiations in the conference rooms of the Great Hall of the People in Beijing, closely monitored and supervised by members of the CCRG. Zhang Chunqiao, giving the city advice drawn from what had already happened in his own Shanghai constituency, spoke of the need for pragmatism: "Making revolution is not like embroidery. It's never the way you envisage it: today we do this, tomorrow we do that, everything according to plan, never any complications. Neither is it like writing an article, when, if you're not happy with your first draft, you can just tear it up and start again from scratch. Revolutions don't let you do things like that."[17] For the rest of the spring and summer of 1967, most of the functions of the former municipal government, now inoperative, were assumed by a "Command Post for Grasping Revolution and Promoting Production," controlled by the PLA but staffed by members of the old civilian bureaucracy. The weaker party by comparison, the local "organizations of the revolutionary masses" and their supporters grumbled in private about what they saw as the perversion of the ideals of the Cultural Revolution. Much of their ire and sarcasm was directed at the role of the local military;

> Quite a few leading [civilian] cadres are spouses of senior military officers, and "pillow talk" can sometimes be quite powerful! So of course when the military based in the city are ordered to "support the left," they end up supporting the leading party and government cadres, not the opposition . . . To order the [locally based] military to "support the left" is fundamentally wrong. It cannot shoulder the task of "supporting the left."[18]

From August on, negotiations intensified. The local PLA self-criticized for some of the "errors" it had committed, and in November 1967 a ninety-seven-member Tianjin Revolutionary Committee membership list was finally submitted to the CCP center. Mao's comment was "Very good! Act accordingly." Xie Xuegong, now first political commissar of the Tianjin Garrison, was made chairman. His three deputies were Zheng Sansheng, the commander of the garrison; another senior military officer; and the head of the municipal Public Security Bureau.[19] On December 7 the *People's Daily* devoted its entire front page to the "victorious birth" of the Tianjin Revolutionary Committee at a mass rally attended by more than 250,000 people.

The political transition in Tianjin from the "old" party committee and people's government to the "new" revolutionary committee had been as orderly as could be expected. There had been intermittent factional fighting in the city's factories and universities. Productivity in the city's industries dropped by 23.7 percent, but the city's infrastructure remained almost intact and functioning, not always the case in the formation of other provincial RCs. The CCP center gave the PLA special credit for Tianjin's transition.

Violent Transition: Guangxi

Not all revolutionary committees were born at the CCP center's negotiating table. In the case of the Guangxi Zhuang Autonomous Region, on the border with North Vietnam, the revolutionary committee was literally born on the battlefield.[20] The center was particularly concerned about events there, because of its proximity to the Vietnam War zone, but an interim government set up by Zhou Enlai in March 1967—formally designated the "Guangxi Revolutionary Preparatory Group" in November—never succeeded in establishing any authority comparable to Xie Xuegong's in Tianjin, despite being, or perhaps because, it was put under the leadership of the incumbent provincial first party secretary, Wei Guoqing, who doubled as first political commissar of the Canton MR.[21] In August 1967, Wei had been beaten bloody and semiconscious by a mob of some 200 Guangxi rebels who traveled all the way to Beijing and managed to penetrate the PLA-run Capital West Hotel, where the first secretary was temporarily residing.[22]

By early 1968, the battle lines were drawn between two large organizations of the "revolutionary masses": the "Guangxi April 22 Revolutionary Action Command," whose members opposed Wei Guoqing but enjoyed the support of a PLA main force unit responsible to Beijing, stationed in the region's capital, Nanning; and the "Guangxi United Command of Proletarian Revolutionaries," loyal to Wei Guoqing and supported by local PLA units obedient to him in his concurrent capacity as first commissar of the provincial MD.[23] While some leaders of these two mass organizations were ready to compromise, others were not. An official history of the Cultural Revolution in Guangxi published in 1990 notes that "each of the two set out to suppress and annihilate the other by force."[24] Thus the process of forming a revolutionary committee was stalemated.

The standoff was broken when the main force unit was transferred out of Guangxi in the spring of 1968 and "April 22" lost its PLA support. At noon on July 16, after weeks of careful preparation, Wei Guoqing's forces began bombarding the parts of Nanning controlled by "April 22," and soon the city was ablaze. The next day, regular PLA units and heavily armed members of the United Command moved against a self-designated "April 22 Field Army" located on the

Nanning river front. In the ensuing battle, 166 boats were sunk, 3,600 tons of cargo destroyed, and dozens of buildings razed to the ground. On July 31, seven companies from the Canton MR, the Guangxi MD (a part of the military region), and the Nanning Military Subdistrict joined the United Command in a second battle with "April 22" in downtown Nanning. This time, property worth some 60 million yuan was destroyed and more than 50,000 people left homeless. Close to 10,000 survivors and supporters of "April 22" were taken prisoner, of whom 2,324 were later executed. Official photographs show rows of captured "members of the masses" being executed in a city street awash with blood.[25]

Wei Guoqing declared victory on August 8. The composition of the 133-member Guangxi Revolutionary Committee, headed by Wei and twelve vice chairmen, was approved by the CCP center on August 20, 1968. A week later, the *People's Daily* congratulated the "revolutionary people and heroic PLA forces of Guangxi" on the occasion of the "victorious birth" of the committee.

Composition of the Revolutionary Committees

In November 1967, the PLA had been ordered to desist from holding debates and pasting up big-character posters and to focus on reimposing discipline on its officers; military academies were told to form "three-in-one" alliances.[26] In December the PLA formally assumed control of public security units, many of which it already ran.[27] If unity was to be achieved, the PLA had to play the major role. As events in both Tianjin and Guangxi, and earlier in Shanghai, illustrated, whether the formation of a revolutionary committee was peaceful or violent, the key actor in the drama was the PLA. As a consequence, PLA representatives dominated the revolutionary committees. Of more than 48,000 members of revolutionary committees at or above the county level, the great majority were PLA officers. Representatives of the "revolutionary cadres" and the "revolutionary masses," supposedly equal participants in the "three-in-one" power structures, were relatively few in number and lacking in power.

At the time, some CCP leaders did not want to acknowledge that real power was in the hands of soldiers. Chen Boda declared: "Some people call the revolutionary committees 'military governments.' That is a reactionary KMT slogan."[28] But twenty years later, a PLA historian of the Cultural Revolution openly acknowledged that most revolutionary committees had been "mutations of military rule"—military control committees by another name.[29] Of the twenty-nine provincial-level revolutionary committee chairmen, six were generals, five were lieutenant generals, and nine were major generals. The remaining nine, though primarily party cadres, all served concurrently as PLA political commissars. In Guangdong, Liaoning, Shanxi, Yunnan, and Hubei, PLA officers chaired between 81 percent and 98 percent of all revolutionary committees above the county level.[30]

A similar process of militarization would take place when, after a hiatus of four years, provincial party committees were recreated in the winter of 1970–71. Six generals, five lieutenant generals, and eleven major generals became first party secretaries. Not since the early 1950s, when military control commissions ruled most of the country outside Beijing,[31] had China's armed forces played such an important role in civilian politics. Not until after the fall of Lin Biao would Mao be able to start trying to recover power for civilians.

The Purge of Yang Chengwu

Nevertheless, all was not smooth sailing for the PLA. The purge of the May 16 group angered the radicals, leading them to launch a campaign against the "revival of old ways" in an effort to ensure that their gains in the first year of the Cultural Revolution were not eroded. Reflective of the seesaw nature of Cultural Revolution politics, while local PLA commanders were consolidating their power by assuming leadership roles in the revolutionary committees, the Beijing-based PLA leadership suffered a considerable blow in the backwash of the radical campaign: the purge of acting chief of staff Yang Chengwu and two senior colleagues, Yu Lijin, the air force political commissar, and Fu Chongbi, the garrison commander.

As in the case of the purge of Peng Zhen and his three senior colleagues at the outset of the Cultural Revolution, different justifications were adduced in each case, but the objective seemed to be simultaneously to seize control of vital positions from men considered either antagonistic or insufficiently reliable by Mao, Lin Biao, and Jiang Qing.[32] Yang Chengwu was replaced by a Lin trusty, Huang Yongsheng, the Canton MR commander; unlike Yang, he was immediately accorded full not acting status. Yu Lijin's departure left another Lin trusty, air force commander Wu Faxian, more strongly in control of that arm of the PLA. The new garrison commander was Wen Yucheng, an ultra Lin loyalist who seemed destined for speedy elevation to the Politburo, but who fell foul of his suspicious patron and was posted to Sichuan a year later.[33]

The End of the Red Guards

The reconstructed political system was in the end not so much what Mao might have called a "negation" of what had preceded it, as a modified version staffed by new people, principally PLA officers. The weakness of the party cadre constituency in this modified system, the supposed "three-in-one" power structure, was attributable to the disgrace of so many of the old guard in the early Cultural Revolution. In October 1967 Zhou Enlai had told the CC's MAC that with the party and government "paralyzed," the PLA had to manage party, government, and military affairs, although he hoped that the "three-in-one" combinations would soon take over.[34] More striking was the absence of significant numbers of "revolutionary successors," the younger generation upon whom Mao had hoped to rely for his new order, notably the Red Guards and the Rebels. But their absence was attributable in part to the behavior of the "little generals" themselves.

In October 1967, the CCP center finally ordered classes to be resumed immediately, suspension of classes having lasted almost a year and a half. But even where this happened the question of content arose. Beijing's No. 23 Middle School was held up as an example to be emulated. Its PLA leadership reported: "What we have first of all resumed are classes devoted to Mao Zedong Thought and to firmly establishing the absolute authority of Mao Zedong Thought on a grand scale. We have also resumed classes devoted to the Great Proletarian Cultural Revolution, as well as set aside a very limited amount of time to a resumption of classes devoted to general cultural knowledge (for example, Chinese, mathematics, foreign languages)."[35] Problems abounded. There had been a massive reduction in the number of good teachers. In January 1968, the PLA military control committee managing the city's educational sector informed the Beijing RC that since the beginning of the Cultural Revolution, the total teacher contingent in the city's elementary and middle schools had shrunk by more than 2,700 and that the "contradiction" centering on the quality of the remaining teachers was "extremely sharp"—a roundabout way of noting that it was largely the good and best teachers who had been lost. As an emergency measure, personnel without formal qualifications were drafted to replace the teachers lost.[36]

On top of everything else, a serious interest in a good education was attacked. Cited as typical examples of "erroneous thinking" were comments like the following: "Enough of Great Criticism; let's get back to class! If we do our assignments, there'll be enough for us to do." "The Great Cultural Revolution has lasted for over a year now, [during which] I haven't acquired any education or learning. How am I supposed to be able to graduate?"[37] "I won't criticize any-thing as long as you give me some new knowledge and teach me stuff that will help me solve practical problems, and that's it."[38]

Discipline was another major problem; it had deteriorated to levels unheard of before the Cultural Revolution. Xie Fuzhi, addressing middle school students in the capital he was expected to run, said on October 14 that it was time for Beijing's 500,000 students to get back to school, one reason being the deteriora-tion of discipline that resulted in youngsters' just hanging out in the streets creat-ing trouble.[39] A Central Document, *Zhongfa* [1967] 179, painted a bleak picture:

> the hours that the students and the elementary school students in particular ac-tually spend in class are far too few. Some students only have one or two hours of classes a day. They have no homework at all, and when classes are over there is nobody there to encourage them to study on their own. Most of them spend most of their time just playing . . . Some students form gangs . . . carry knives, clubs, leather belts or other weapons and hide in dark corners in public parks and elsewhere. When the opportunity arises, they lure others into fights. Some have been wounded and some—on occasions when things really got out of hand—have even been killed. This is a very big problem.[40]

While waiting for something to happen, idle youngsters had plenty of time to ponder what the future might hold in store. Those who chose not to indulge in a revolutionary variant of gang warfare, but spent much of their time reading and just staying out of trouble, may have found inspiration in a remark which Mao was supposed to have made during a stopover in Wuhan in September 1967 and which, though never cited in the official media, was widely disseminated at the time: "On the basis of my own experience, I would say that in every revolu-tion that has taken place in China throughout history, the people for which there has really been some hope have been those who have pondered the issues and not those who have sought the limelight. Those who make a lot of noise and hubbub right now will certainly be nothing but transient figures in history."[41]

Sometimes young people confided to their diaries what they read into this and similar Mao-quotes. On January 27, 1968, a girl somewhere in Jiangsu wrote:

> Last night our political instructor presented me with a quote [from Mao Zedong's *Selected Works*]: "We should always use our brains and think every-thing over carefully . . . In other words, much thinking yields wisdom. In order to get rid of the *practice of acting blindly, which is so common in our party*, we

must encourage our comrades to think, to learn the method of analysis, and to cultivate the habit of analysis." How can I make this quote help me understand and solve my own practical problems? . . . Maybe most of the time I really don't like to use my own brain. I rarely ponder and don't have much of a method for analyzing objects. I really haven't developed an analytical habit. I know this much about myself, and from now on I have to improve. If I really want this quote to help me, I have to dig to the ideological roots of the problem.[42]

But while some youngsters indulged in introspection, many did not. They preferred the more exciting task of making real revolution, which meant taking part in the ferocious warfare between rival Red Guard gangs. One former Red Guard later told his biographer about the aftermath of one battle in 1968, when thousands of defeated Red Guards mourned their slain comrades:

At the head of the procession were the tens of dead, their comrades holding their blood-soaked bodies aloft for everyone to see. The wounded followed, aided, too, by their fellow rebels, and young female revolutionaries were honored to carry the occasional severed bit of a body—an arm or leg or a hand— as proof of the viciousness of the fight. Behind the wounded were the defeated troops, defiant and high-spirited even in retreat. A few carried guns but their primary weapons of war were the razor-sharp sickles originally destined for Castro's sugar fields. They marched in perfect formation . . . alternately chanting time and yelling slogans of defiance and revenge. They were proud to have risked their lives and would be willing to risk death again. They believed they were dying for Chairman Mao.[43]

Even campuses were not free of violence. Ironically, in desperation, Mao agreed to use the device for which Liu Shaoqi and Deng Xiaoping had been excoriated two years earlier: work teams. Whether the intelligence he was receiving through his various channels (the CCRG Journalists' Station, the *Liberation Army Daily,* the Red Guard press, his own "eyes and ears") prepared him for what would happen next is uncertain. He may well have had no inkling of the disaster that would attend his new venture.

Some 30,000 employees of sixty Beijing factories were organized into "Capital Mao Zedong Thought Worker Propaganda Teams" and were sent onto campuses to propagate Mao's directive to stop fighting and form alliances. The team that arrived at Tsinghua University on July 27, 1968, was greeted with shots and stones on the orders of the fiery student leader Kuai Dafu. Five members of the team were killed; many were injured. Having successfully resisted the work team in 1966, and subjected Liu Shaoqi's wife, Wang Guangmei, to public humiliation in 1967, Kuai was not about to knuckle under to this new attempt to suppress the "revolutionary masses."

For Mao, it was the end of his illusion that if "revisionist" party leaders could be swept aside and he could speak directly to the people, they would unfailingly follow him. The hearts and minds of his revolutionary successors, untrammeled now by revisionist party leaders, were not automatically synchronized with his own as he had hoped. Nor could they any longer be controlled by Maoist directives. They could be disciplined only by strong-arm methods. Failure to order such steps raised the danger that workers' groups backed by the military would take matters into their own hands, as in Wuhan a year earlier. Mao could not afford that risk.

On the day after the Tsinghua débacle, July 28, the Chairman called a meeting in the Great Hall of the People to which he officially "summoned" the principal Red Guard leaders of the capital:[44] Nie Yuanzi (addressed by Mao by her nickname "Old Buddha" [lao foye], which she had somehow acquired in the course of the Cultural Revolution and which had originally constituted the respectful title by which the eunuchs of the Qing court had addressed the Empress Dowager) from Peking University; Tan Houlan (Mao jokingly bestowed upon her the title "empress" of the Red Guard movement) from Beijing Normal University; Han Aijing ("You are a descendant of Han Xin," Mao told the twenty-two-year-old Red Guard, putting him on par with the legendary general and strategist who had helped found the Han dynasty) of the Beijing Aeronautical Institute; Kuai Dafu; and Wang Dabin, the young chairman of the Beijing Geology Institute Revolutionary Committee and a favorite of Mao's ("Come closer! Sit over here!"). It was an extraordinary gathering, illustrative of the status achieved by campus rebel leaders in a mere two years. To receive them, Mao had at his side Lin Biao, Zhou Enlai, Chen Boda, Kang Sheng, Jiang Qing, Lin Biao's wife Ye Qun, Vice Premier Xie Fuzhi, his deputy on the Beijing Revolutionary Committee Wu De, and the new PLA chief of staff, Huang Yongsheng. But despite this red-carpet treatment, the rebels had been summoned to hear the death sentence on their movement.[45]

Kuai Dafu had apparently justified his resistance to the Worker Propaganda Team on the grounds that some "black hand" was attempting to suppress the campus revolutionaries. Mao told the Red Guard leaders with mock jocularity that he himself was the "black hand," adding in the course of a conversation that lasted a full five hours that "we're so bureaucratic, not having called you to a meeting before."[46] He pointed out that Kuai and the other leaders could each rely only on 200 or 300 hard-core supporters, whereas he could send in 30,000 workers, not to mention the number of troops under Lin Biao. Mao and Lin emphasized that Red Guard violence had alienated all sections of the population, including many students; Red Guards were not engaged in the legitimate activity of "struggle-criticism-transformation" but in armed warfare. Mao indicated that his preferred alternatives were military control or "struggle-criticism-quit"/ "struggle-criticism-disperse."[47] In fact he chose both: in many places PLA units moved onto campuses, but simultaneously members of the principal Red Guard units were dispersed "up to the mountains and down to the villages" *(shang shan, xia xiang).*[48]

The title "Red Guard" was to live on for another decade: in China's middle schools as the successor to the Communist Youth League, and in elementary schools—under the name "Little Red Guards"—as the successor to the Young Pioneers. Its formal relegation to the "scrap heap of history" took place on August 19, 1978.[49] But the glory days of the Red Guards were over soon after July 1968. Even their leaders would now be sent down to farm and factory to make revolution as true proletarians. According to the Notification regarding work assignments for university graduates in 1968, "In general, graduates must become ordinary peasants or ordinary workers. A majority must become ordinary peasants . . . graduates who are members of Revolutionary Committees or who are leading members of mass organizations should play exemplary roles and set examples for others to follow."[50] Middle school graduates across China were told that the central authorities expected them to "put politics in command, fight selfishness and repudiate revisionism, put the public interest first, submit to the needs of the state and go to the countryside and factories and mines, where the conditions are the hardest."[51]

During the next seven years, 12 million urban youth, about 10 percent of the urban population, were sent to the countryside; over the twelve-year period 1967–1979, the number of rusticated "educated youth" totaled 16,470,000.[52] Shanghai registered the highest percentage, 17.9 percent. Most were rusticated within their home province,[53] the luckiest ones to the richer rural counties adjoining large cities. But eight cities—Shanghai, Beijing, Tianjin, Hangzhou, Nanjing, Wuhan, Chengdu, and Chongqing—sent large numbers to such border provinces as Inner Mongolia,[54] Xinjiang, Yunnan, and Heilongjiang; in the case of Shanghai, only 40 percent of its one million rusticated youths were sent to the city's suburban counties.[55] It cannot be coincidental that some of the worst violence during 1966–1968 occurred in these cities.

Harsh as it was, there was nothing sudden or ad hoc about this policy of sending educated urban youths "up to the mountains and down to the villages." In actuality, it had been among the very first concrete measures ever discussed in the context of what a Cultural Revolution might entail. Already in May 1964, the CCP center had called "educated youths going down to or returning to the villages" an "important step in carrying out a cultural revolution in the countryside."[56] That same year, more than 320,000 educated youths had been sent to the countryside after graduation.[57] The elements new in 1968 were the greatly expanded scope of implementation, the inclusion of university graduates, and its metamorphosis into the norm rather than the exception during the years that followed. A much-sought-after alternative for those with good connections, especially if they had already experienced the tremendous hardships of rural life, was entry into the PLA.[58]

Tragically, the dispersal of the Red Guards did not put an end to violence, but instead proved to be the prelude to an even wider-ranging campaign of terror during which even more people were tortured, maimed, driven mad, killed, or committed suicide.[59] Among the suicides were Jiang Yongning, Rong Guotuan, and Fu Qifang, the table-tennis stars who had led China to international preeminence in that sport.[60]

15

Cleansing the Class Ranks

C leansing the class ranks" was the first major campaign carried out by the new revolutionary committees. As its name suggests, this was a purge designed to eliminate any and all real and imagined enemies of the unity that was professedly the basis of the political order the revolutionary committees were inaugurating. To borrow a metaphor used on a similar occasion in the past by one of Mao's most prominent ghostwriters, socialist society was once more about to "defecate": "Societies are like that, [like people] they also have to defecate, which is not a bad thing. Once this truth has been made clear to people, it will no longer appear strange to them. Of course, differences in essence as well as process distinguish defecation by socialist societies from defecation by capitalist or feudal societies."[1] Thus "cleansing the class ranks" was all about getting rid of those whom the CCP regarded as waste matter. The movement provided whoever happened to be in power with an opportunity to get rid of opponents. It began gradually in places like Shanghai in late 1967, and was in full swing in most parts of China by the summer of 1968.

Mao never spoke at length on the subject in 1967–68, and he left most of the work of running the movement and keeping it on track to Zhou Enlai and the CCRG. Jiang Qing's role was widely recognized as being that of Mao's personal purgative, and by comparison with Zhou's, her part was—in the eyes of one Beijing cadre—the "easy" one: "The premier is the one who has to wipe the backside afterward, and that's the difficult part."[2] From the outset Zhou kept his options as open as possible: the movement was about getting rid of "bad people" broadly defined. "The bad people you have to drag out aren't just capitalist roaders," Zhou told a delegation from Zhejiang province on February 15, "but bad people inside your own ranks as well . . . Some of them have come from across the ocean while others have come out of the sky and wormed their way into your ranks."[3] Two weeks later, he quoted Mao to the leadership of the Jilin RC:

"Chairman Mao teaches us: 'Under normal circumstances, it is easy to tell a good person from a bad person. But under special circumstances, when there are bad people behind the scenes, you may easily be deceived. You should drag them out yourselves, since doing so not only won't harm your own organization but will make it even better.'"[4]

In some provinces and major municipalities (for example, Beijing and Shanghai) the cleansing of the class ranks was launched after the setting up of revolutionary committees, while in some it paved the way for setting up such committees. Soon it became almost impossible to keep track of all the variant interpretations of how it was to be carried out in different parts of the country. One example is the "three checks" that were meant to constitute one of the starting points of the process of cleansing. Special reference lists had to be compiled to allow readers of policy documents to keep track of the fact that whereas Jiangxi defined them as (1) "checking the behind-the-scenes activities of capitalist roaders," (2) "checking up on renegades and special agents," and (3) "checking for destructive acts by unreformed landlords, rich peasants, reactionaries, bad people, and rightists," Anhui defined them as (1) "checking alertness to enemy presence," (2) "checking determination to fight the enemy," and (3) "checking attitudes toward Chairman Mao"; and Guangxi in turn defined them as (1) "checking one's standpoint," (2) "checking one's loyalty," and (3) "checking one's determination to fight." Tianjin, Hunan, and Henan all used their own, very different, definitions.[5]

In Shanghai, activists engaged by revolutionary committees to perform the cleansing were provided with handbooks whose contents confirmed that the agenda represented a continuity of, rather than a break with, past practices. Despite having been formulated in an era when the "sinister influence" of Luo Ruiqing and Peng Zhen had supposedly been very pronounced, criteria for telling "good" from "bad" dating from the 1950s remained valid. By extensively reprinting detailed information on KMT and "puppet" regime networks in the city before Liberation, the Shanghai authorities in effect suggested that the movement was about rounding up the "usual suspects."[6] Principal targets included groups that had been responsible for the previous violence. An editorial in the Shanghai newspaper *Wenhui bao* in December 1967 listed persons engaged in "factionalism" as those to be cleansed, explaining that "they create disputes within our revolutionary ranks."[7] But the movement was by no means directed only against people who failed to accept the notion of "great alliances."

The first in a series of policy circulars issued by the CCP center dealing specifically with the new movement was *Zhongfa* [1968] 74, which was distributed on May 25, 1968, with an unusually personal endorsement from Mao ("Comrade Wenyuan: . . . Of this kind of written documents that I have seen, this is the best one.").[8] It contained a report originally published in the Xinhua News Agency's classified *Cultural Revolution Trends,* which described the experience of the New China Printing Plant Military Control Committee (made up of officers and men from PLA Unit 8341, the "security detail" of the Politburo) in cleansing the class ranks. In a brief preamble, the center called upon revolutionary committees, preparatory committees, and military control committees everywhere to adapt the experience of the New China Printing Plant to local conditions, "give full play to the great might of the dictatorship of the masses, and in stages and under leadership do a good job of cleansing the class ranks."

The catalogue of successful cleansing techniques employed by the officers and men of PLA Unit 8341 included "anti-enemy struggle mass rallies," "in-depth pursuit small meetings," "at-the-heart assaults," leniency and rewards to those who confessed their crimes, and severity and punishments for those who did not. But the document noted that it was wrong to think as some did that once a confession had been extracted, the matter had been settled. Such an attitude represented excessive leniency when dealing with counterrevolutionaries. Acceptable leniency meant sentencing to life imprisonment those who ought to have been executed, and handing ordinary wrongdoers over to the masses for dictatorship rather than putting them behind bars.

Zhongfa [1968] 74 concluded by revealing that the next aim of the Military Control Committee of the New China Printing Plant was to continue to "dig even further for more deeply entrenched spy elements."[9] Later policy pronouncements by CCP leaders revealed that this particular aim was thwarted as a result of the large number of suicides among those subject to cleansing. In the Daqing oilfield in Liaoning, one of China's foremost model industrial establishments, there had been fifteen suicides between January and April 1968, and no less than thirty-six in May–June.[10] This phenomenon worried the CCP center, since "class enemies" who had committed suicide were obviously useless as sources of information on additional "more deeply entrenched" class enemies. Suspects had to be kept alive until everything of interest to the party had been extracted from them.

In a talk to members of the Beijing Revolutionary Committee in May, Minister of Public Security Xie Fuzhi suggested that the movement should be suspended for a week or so, and that an effort should be made to quell the "wind of suicide." Xie explained that "while it is inevitable that one or two bad persons should commit suicide in a big movement such as this, it affects the progress of our work adversely if the number becomes too large. Many things can then no longer be investigated."[11] In conversation with members of the Shanghai Revolutionary Committee, Kang Sheng called for improvement in the "art of struggle." While "it does not matter if a few people die," he said, their deaths might "have a bad political impact, since leads to important cases might be lost."[12]

If judged exclusively on the basis of policy pronouncements by central leaders, the movement to cleanse the class ranks would appear to have had a reasonably well-defined target. But that target becomes blurred and the process becomes uncertain when sought in accounts of the movement outside the national capital and Shanghai, a phenomenon observable in other dictatorships.[13] Local officials invariably broadened its scope and used it as an excuse to intensify the level of organized violence in general. "In some places it became a massive pogrom against people of exploiting class background; in some places a campaign of retribution and murder against factional rivals; and in still others a massive campaign of torture and murder to uncover wholly imaginary mass conspiracies that could involve tens of thousands." One likely explanation is that most power-holders were newly and insecurely installed in office and therefore felt an urgent need to extirpate factional rivals and to evade accusations of insufficient zeal. This was probably why the movement in Shanghai, where Zhang Chunqiao and his colleagues had been firmly entrenched for a year, was well controlled and, by prevailing standards, relatively moderate.[14]

In Jiangxi, the provincial revolutionary committee under Major General Cheng Shiqing "cleansed" with extreme prejudice. In dealing with serious offenders, targeted for terminal cleansing, massive doses of terror were used to "kill the chicken in order to scare the monkey." In one production brigade, according to an investigation carried out in 1980 by the Ministry of Public Security, a "class enemy" accused of being a secret KMT agent had one ear cut off in public at a "struggle session" and was then left to bleed to death in front of his terrified kinsmen. The contemporary rationale for this unusual form of execution was that it was a waste of state property to kill counterrevolutionaries with bullets, the CCP center having recently issued an "urgent" circular demanding that "all units practice frugality while making revolution, and resolutely cut down on expenses."[15] The movement spilled over into the economic sphere, where a provincial leadership eager to prove its revolutionary credentials launched an experiment that in some ways presaged the thinking if not the brutality of the Khmer Rouge a decade later. In order to "eradicate once and for all" any signs of "capitalism," the Jiangxi Revolutionary Committee shut down and dissolved all of the province's cooperative shops and retail outlets and revoked the licenses of all private petty traders. The petty traders (some 15,900 in number) and about one-third (18,800) of the employees of the dissolved collectively run shops were relocated to the countryside, where they were assigned jobs in the agricultural sector. A further estimated 19,200 old, weak, and infirm shop employees were told to simply go home, while slightly more than 15,000 mostly younger staff were assigned jobs in state-run industries.[16]

In Jilin province, in northeastern China, the cleansing of the class ranks led to the "death from unnatural causes" of 2,127 and permanent injury of 3,459 cadres. The number of ordinary people who became victims of the movement is not known, and the official source from which the figures above are taken merely states the obvious, that "among the broad masses the number of those who were either killed or permanently injured was even larger."[17] In neighboring Heilongjiang, the cleansing of the class ranks broadened an already ongoing movement to "dig deep for traitors" among party and government officials. In early 1968, the CCP center had praised the provincial revolutionary committee for the energy with which it hunted down "traitorous" followers of "Liu [Shaoqi], Deng [Xiaoping], Tao [Zhu], He [Long], Peng [Zhen], Luo [Ruiqing], Lu [Dingyi], Yang [Shangkun], An [Ziwen], and Xiao [Hua], and told revolutionary committees and the PLA elsewhere in China to 'learn from Heilongjiang.'"[18] Now the net was cast more widely to include "Japanese and puppet spies, American and Chiang Kai-shek spies, and Korean, Mongolian, and Soviet revisionist spies." Cleansing the class ranks in Heilongjiang, according to one official post–Cultural Revolution account, resulted in "very large numbers of deaths from un-natural causes, and tens of thousands of people being seriously maimed both physically and mentally."[19] An official history of a county on the Soviet border notes that the local authorities at the time (mainly PLA officers and men) applied "thirty-three different forms [*zhong*] and 290 variants [*yang*] of torture" to 539 suspects and that this resulted in the death of 76 and the maiming of 192.[20] In another Heilongjiang county, some 2,125 suspects were arrested, and of these "38 were persecuted to death, 2 were maimed, and 7 suffered permanent wounds from torture."[21]

In Inner Mongolia, there was a wide-ranging witch-hunt in 1968. It included the reinvigoration of an ongoing campaign against deposed regional strong-man Ulanfu's "anti-party clique" and the ferreting out of suspected members of a "New Inner Mongolian People's Party," an alleged "counterrevolution-ary" underground organization of ethnic separatists with clandestine links to Outer Mongolia and the Soviet Union. Also under attack that year were the sup-posed instigators of the "Inner Mongolia February adverse current" of the year before. Most of the people at the receiving end of these local permutations of the cleansing of the class ranks were of Mongolian descent. A post–Cultural Revo-lution Central Document, *Zhongfa* [1981] 28, noted that in Inner Mongolia

> the number of people that were put in prison, criticized, struggled, isolated, and investigated in direct connection with the three big unjust cases totaled 790,000. Of these, 22,900 died and 120,000 were maimed. While "ferreting out and eliminating" additional enemies, some 8,000 herdsmen living close to the border with Outer Mongolia were forcibly resettled farther inland, and this caused the deaths of an additional 1,000 people.

So fearsome was the violence in Inner Mongolia that as early as 1969 the CCP center criticized the leading members of the regional revolutionary committee for taking the movement to cleanse the class ranks too far, and for creating "seri-ous interethnic tensions." Both the committee chairman (a lieutenant general of Han descent) and first vice chairman (a major general of Mongolian descent) were removed from office, and control of the region was temporarily assumed by a martial-law task force led by the commander of the Beijing MR, Zheng Weishan.[22]

In eastern Hebei, more than 84,000 people, including numerous CCP cad-res, were persecuted on suspicion of being members of an underground KMT network: tortured during interrogation, 2,955 of them died, and 763 suffered per-manent disabilities.[23] In Yunnan, according to calculations made by the provin-cial RC's Cleansing the Class Ranks Office in August 1969, 448,000 people were targeted in the province as a whole. Of these, some 15,000 were "cleansed" as ele-ments of one kind or another, and a staggering 6,979 died—*all* of them by "death from enforced suicide."[24] In Beijing, the cleansing of the class ranks resulted in the deaths of 3,731 people between January 1968 and May 1969—more than 94 percent of the deaths again registered as "suicides."[25] In Zhejiang, an estimated 100,000 people were "arrested, detained, dragged out, and struggled" in the course of the movement and a total of 9,198 officially "hounded to death."[26]

Nowhere was the movement more brutal than in the wild frontier lands of southern and southwestern China. In Binyang county, Guangxi, 3,681 mostly village residents were summarily executed and thrown into mass graves in one ten-day period in the summer of 1968.[27] And as publicly acknowledged by senior party historians writing about these events in China today:

> In a few places, it even happened that "counterrevolutionaries" were beaten to death and in the most beastly fashion had their flesh and liver consumed [by their killers]. This singular retrogression to a distant age of primitive savagery in the midst of what called itself the most utmost [*sic*] revolutionary "Great Cultural Revolution" certainly provides plenty of food for thought.[28]

The most notorious cases of Cultural Revolutionary cannibalism occurred in Wuxuan county, Guangxi, where a Chinese investigator/journalist in the 1980s found a "disturbing picture of official compliance in the systematic killing and cannibalization of individuals in the name of political revolution and 'class struggle.'"[29] Less well known is the case of Qiaojia county in neighboring Yunnan, where

> at a so-called Poor and Lower-Middle Peasant Sentencing Rally on June 10, 1968, the farmer Zhou Mingtai was sentenced to death and promptly executed. One Yang XX then cut out Zhou's heart and made a public display of it, while one Peng XX cut open Zhou's skull and removed his brain as well as his tongue. After one Xu XX had cut off Zhou's penis and testicles, one Yan XX proceeded to boil and eat them.[30]

Some have suggested that the cannibalism can be explained by "traditions" of the "minorities" in the region, but at least one writer rejects such analysis as nothing more than "Han chauvinism."[31] Nor can it be argued that communism impelled them to it: in the equally politicized environment of the KMT's persecution of suspected "spies" and "enemy agents" in China before 1949, agents and torturers of spymaster Dai Li on occasion also consumed parts of their victims.[32]

Though it persisted in some areas as late as 1971, as a nationwide movement the cleansing of the class ranks generally wound down during the winter of 1968–69. By then, even Mao appears to have felt that perhaps it had gone too far. In *Zhongfa* [1968] 170, addressed to revolutionary and military control committees all over China, he noted: "Among those who have committed capitalist-roader errors, the arch-unrepentant ones are only a minority, while those who are capable of accepting education and of correcting their errors are a majority. Hence you should not automatically assume that all of those referred to as 'capitalist roaders' are bad persons."[33] Later, at the CCP's Ninth Congress in April 1969, Mao specifically criticized the handling of the movement at Peking University. Out of 10,000 students and staff, 900 apparently had been arrested by the PLA's 63rd Corps, whose officers and men had been sent to the campus "to provide support to the broad masses of the left." In Mao's opinion, "to arrest some 0.1 percent, 0.2 percent, or 0.3 percent is enough. The rest can be set free . . . If they rebel, we can simply arrest them again."[34]

In 1972–73, the Beijing Revolutionary Committee reopened the cases of hundreds of cadres who had been investigated and cleansed in the course of the movement, typically by being dismissed and sent to perform manual labor in the countryside. The surviving records of the cases of 131 of those cadres provide a reasonably accurate picture of what the "cleansing the class ranks" movement entailed in Beijing. Particularly striking are the many references to "historical problems" and "malicious slander of the three Red Banners." In vast numbers of cases, what led to the targeting of a particular individual was not some recent event, but simply a reinterpretation of the political significance of a past event. Still, recent "errors" were also involved, and they give a flavor of the times that no amount of statistics or official histories can match.

Consider the case of Heng Yingzhu, a lower-level (rank 18 of 24) cadre born in 1934 who had joined the CCP in 1952 and who, when the Cultural Revolution began, had been a deputy section chief in the clerical department of the Beijing Party Committee. She was found to have made "reactionary remarks amounting to grave errors," and at the end of the "cleansing of the class ranks" she was placed on probation within the CCP for two years. Among her forty-nine "reactionary remarks" (not including a number of positive remarks about Peng Zhen made after the beginning of the Cultural Revolution), the one she made about Mao and four about Jiang Qing are typical.[35]

At the end of 1966, Heng had "attacked Chairman Mao" by commenting on Mao's big-character poster "Bombard the headquarters": "The Chairman is really quite hard in his criticism of Liu Shaoqi when he says: 'They have puffed up the arrogance of the bourgeoisie and deflated the morale of the proletariat. How vicious they are!'" In September or October 1966, in an argument with her husband, Heng had remarked: "All comrade Jiang Qing has to do is call Ma so-and-so 'Wang Guangmei's henchman' and that's the end of Ma so-and-so as a cadre." In the winter of 1966, while commenting on a speech by members of the central party leadership, Heng had said: "When she speaks, comrade Jiang Qing is sometimes imprudent and not careful about what she says." That same winter,

Heng had remarked in front of her husband that "so-and-so opposes Chairman Mao, and so-and-so opposes Chairman Mao. Jiang Qing, you're [supposedly] the only one who doesn't oppose Chairman Mao." At the end of 1966 or beginning of 1967, while talking to her husband about Jiang Qing having been an actress, Heng had said comrade Jiang Qing "was in the movie *Old Bachelor Wang.*" And in early 1968, Heng had told her husband at home that "in the future everything has to be done in accordance with Mao Zedong Thought. When something accords [with Mao Zedong Thought], then it should be implemented, and when it doesn't, this should be pointed out, regardless of who is involved, be it the Central Cultural Revolution Group, or be it comrade Jiang Qing." All these remarks, according to the Beijing RC, counted as "vicious attacks" on Jiang Qing.[36]

A fundamentally different case involved the targeting of another member of the same group of Beijing cadres. Yang XX, born in 1927 of poor peasant stock, had joined the CCP in 1939. By 1966 he was deputy head of the Beijing Municipal Bureau of Civil Affairs and also the acting party secretary in the bureau. During the "cleansing the class ranks" movement, he was found to have a number of "problems" that resulted in his formal expulsion from the CCP as a "capitalist roader." Yang was accused, first, of never actually having joined the CCP as a twelve-year-old in 1939. Investigators were told by one person who had known him at the time: "I remember Yang XX was very young. He wasn't a party member!" Another person told investigators: "I can't remember his being a party member. He was very young at the time." On the basis of these recollections, Yang XX was labeled a "fake party member." Second, he was accused of having provided false information about his whereabouts and activities from 1942 to 1944. (He had been at home with his parents, recovering from illness, but later claimed to have been involved in a children's training camp run by the CCP.) Third, he had walked the capitalist road. Proof of this included what investigators regarded as an implicit attack on Mao Zedong in the form of a remark that "one should not follow blindly, but think independently!" Additional proof of his walking the capitalist road was an alleged affair with a female colleague from a PLA background.[37]

In the context of the "cleansing of the class ranks," Heng's and Yang's crimes were regarded as comparatively minor, as evident in the light punishment meted out to them. The fact that both lived in the relatively civilized environment of the national capital also played a role. There are no official estimates of the total number of people killed in all of China during the "cleanse the class ranks" movement, but information extracted from more than 1,500 county gazetteers published after the Cultural Revolution has been used in one very authoritative sociological analysis of the movement in rural China. This study estimates that around 36 million people were persecuted. "This is a staggering number," the study acknowledges, "but it is arrived at through fairly conservative assumptions about the completeness and accuracy of the sources . . . our best estimate for the numbers killed is between 750,000 and 1.5 million, with roughly equal numbers permanently injured."[38] The toll in the cities, where close to 18 percent of the population of China lived at the time, has not yet been reported. But once the numbers are in, it, too, will undoubtedly be staggering.

The Mao Cult

The "cleansing of the class ranks" was, according to the official classification, a movement meant to resolve "contradictions between the enemy and us." A second, kinder gentler movement, aimed at resolving "contradictions among the people," was promoted at roughly the same time by the PLA under the name of the "three loyalties and four boundless loves": "loyalty to Chairman Mao, Mao Zedong Thought, and Chairman Mao's proletarian revolutionary line; boundless love for Chairman Mao, the Communist Party, Mao Zedong Thought, and Chairman Mao's proletarian revolutionary line."[39] What had begun at the time of the founding of the PRC as a more or less widely felt genuine popular reverence for Mao as the "great leader" of the Chinese people had by 1968 been replaced by a state-sponsored cult complete with carefully orchestrated rituals, the transformation of even the most banal utterances by Mao into holy writ, and coercive mechanisms for dealing with acts of deviance and heresy. The essential ideological justification for this cult had been formulated by Mao himself in the wake of Khrushchev's denunciation of Stalin in 1956, when Mao had gone on record as saying: "The question is not whether or not there should be a cult of the individual, but rather whether or not the individual concerned represents the truth. If he does, then he should be worshipped."[40] Ten years later, the hard practical justification for the cult had to do with political control, pure and simple.

The movement was characterized by a focus on ritual and ritualized speech, the latter involving the creation of no small number of neologisms. Some of the best-known rituals of the "loyalty-fication of the entire day" were the joint products of an inventive mass base and a powerful central propaganda machinery.[41] A case in point was what in abbreviated form became known as "asking for instructions in the morning and reporting back in the evening," first practiced by the roughly 2,000 mostly female workers in the Beijing General Knitting Mill. A contingent of officers and men from PLA Unit 8341 serving on the mill's military control committee wrote about it to the Chairman in November 1967. As they described it, the ritual consisted of four separate acts: (1) at the start of the working day, one turned to Chairman Mao's portrait and "asked for instructions" in order to be able to "see and think clearly and gain a sense of direction"; (2) while at work, one studied Mao's words on the factory wall "quotation board" in order to derive from them "a mighty increase in working enthusiasm"; (3) when changing shifts, one exchanged Mao-quotes with fellow workers as a way of "showing concern and offering help"; and (4) at the end of the working day, one turned once more to Chairman Mao's portrait and by way of "reporting back to him" reviewed critically one's work and one's thoughts during the day. Mao's reaction to the long report from the Beijing General Knitting Mill, of which the description of this ritual was only a minor part, was to write on it: "I've read this, and it is very good. Thank you, comrades!" The report was immediately distributed nationwide for what the CCP center called "implementation accordingly in the light of actual conditions."[42] By early 1968, more or less elaborate variations of the ritual were practiced by millions upon millions of people all across China. The future Nobel laureate Gao Xingjian described the process thus:

> At six o'clock in the morning, the bugle call got people up, and they had twenty minutes to brush their teeth and have a wash. They then stood before the portrait of the Great Leader on the wall to seek "morning instructions," sang songs from Mao's *Sayings* and, holding high the little red book, shouted out "long live" three times before going to the dining room to drink gruel. Assembly followed, and Mao's *Selected Works* were recited for half an hour before people shouldered their hoes and pickaxes to work on the land.[43]

One of the practitioners may have spoken for many when she wrote later: "I found the ritual pointless, humiliating and monotonous, but of course I couldn't say so."[44]

Throughout the "three loyalties and four boundless loves" movement, revolutionary committees published booklets containing commandments and precepts on how a true revolutionary should speak. Typically, "in everything we say, we must refer to class. In everything we say, we must refer to the [socialist] road. In everything we say, we must refer to the [revolutionary] line, and firmly denounce revisionism . . . [Otherwise] we shall not count as having shown our loyalty to the great leader Chairman Mao."[45] There was even a "loyalty dance," with the movements of which everyone had to be familiar. At the Shenyang city train station, passengers were for a brief period required to perform the loyalty dance before being permitted to board their train.[46]

Ever larger Mao badges were perhaps the most visible aspect of the movement. Whereas at the beginning of the Cultural Revolution only a privileged few (that is, those of good class background) had been permitted to wear them, by 1968 the badges were on virtually everyone's chest. The biggest could be up to ten inches in diameter, and some were battery-powered devices that shone in the dark. In March 1969, Zhou Enlai told a national planning conference that some 2.2 billion aluminum Mao badges had so far been produced by factories that received their raw material through the Ministry of Allocation of Materials. This figure did not include badges made of other materials, nor did it include aluminum badges produced by the PLA or by units using aluminum originally allocated for other purposes. In Hangzhou, Mao badges and other "loyalty objects" were offered for sale in the municipal Worker-Peasant-Soldier Treasure Request Shop. In Shaanxi, where 30 million badges were produced in 1968, the revolutionary committee in one weapons factory handed them out (together with a cigarette) to people under investigation as a reward for "making a clean breast of everything they know."[47]

Many other well-known rituals that became part of the cult of Mao emanated from the PLA, where practices such as the "daily reading of Mao's works with problems in mind" dated back to well before the beginning of the Cultural Revolution.[48] But probably the most extreme attempt at ritualized regimentation in the name of a "correct worship" of Mao was civilian and emanated from Shijiazhuang, the provincial capital of Hebei.[49] In the spring of 1968, delegations came to Shijiazhuang from throughout China to learn how to "Mao Zedong Thought-ify everything in a day" and to express their "three loyalties and four boundless loves." A delegation from Nanjing described the city as a place where the "glittering, shining, magnificently radiant character 'loyalty' [zhong]" decorated every wall, every street, every public and private space. According to their report, they heard the people of Shijiazhuang speak the "language of loyalty" and saw them perform the "acts of loyalty" one would expect from "persons of loyalty." As they got up in the morning, the first words to pass the lips of the citizens of Shijiazhuang were "Long live Chairman Mao!," the first song they sang was "The East Is Red," and their first act of the day was the study of Mao's works.

Some aspects of the cult as developed to perfection in Shijiazhuang have long since been forgotten, including, probably, some of the more elaborate theoretical arguments created to explain its particularities. Some aspects of the cult have found their way into collections of jokes about the Cultural Revolution, including the one that concerned the "Mao Zedong Thought-ification" of the language used in commercial transactions. As it was explained to the delegates from Nanjing, this particular way of showing loyalty was but one part of an elaborate set of rituals that began the moment shops opened for business, or even before:

> The shops open their doors some fifteen minutes before the start of the business day, and the staff embark upon "three loyalties" activities together with the customers . . . Together, staff and customers salute Chairman Mao, sing "The East Is Red," respectfully wish Chairman Mao a long long life and Vice Chairman Lin excellent health, and jointly study the *Supreme Instructions* [three old passages, four new ones] and [Lin Biao's] "Preface to the New Edition" of the Quotations from Chairman Mao.[50]

Once sales staff and customers got down to business, they began every dialogue with a Mao-quote. The delegation from Nanjing took down some examples, shown in the table below. At the end of the day, sales staff would perform variants of the "reporting back in the evening" ritual created in Beijing:

> Either by oneself, standing, facing Chairman Mao's portrait, examining and reporting on the day's events. Or, sitting down [as a group], employing quotes from Chairman Mao to comment positively on other people's strong points as a way of encouraging them. Finally, a record is kept in the "Fight Self, Repudiate Revisionism" Struggle Notebook (also known as the "Three Loyalties" Activities Notebook). Finally, one would sing quotations from Chairman Mao set to music, before calling it a day.[51]

There were of course people who found getting used to these rituals very difficult. As the delegation from Nanjing was told:

> At first, a small number of people did not sufficiently appreciate the profound meaning of this movement. They remained far from conscientious and effective in their attitude toward it and suffered from various ideological impediments.

Typical uses of Mao-quotes, by social category

Customer category	When sales clerk says . . .	customer responds by saying . . .
Workers	Vigorously grasp revolution,	energetically promote production.
	Within the working class,	there is no fundamental conflict of interests.
Soldiers	One should support the army,	and cherish the people.
	The army and the people	united like one.
	When the army organizes study classes,	soldiers should participate.
	The entire country should learn from the Liberation Army,	the masses are the true heroes.
	Carry forward the revolutionary tradition,	strive to achieve yet greater honors.
	Grasp revolution and promote production,	promote work and war preparedness.
Peasants	Grasp revolution,	promote production.
	Grasp grain and cotton production firmly,	strive for even greater bumper crops.
	Self-reliance,	ample food and clothing.
Students	Study well,	make progress every day.
	Read Chairman Mao's books,	heed what Chairman Mao says.
	Education needs a revolution,	the period of schooling must be shortened.
	Keep in step with Chairman Mao,	never cease to make revolution.
Cadres	One must not rest on one's laurels,	but make new contributions.
	Fight self, repudiate revisionism,	overcome selfishness, foster a public spirit.
	Keep in step with Chairman Mao,	never cease to make revolution.
	Study the *Three Constantly Read Articles* conscientiously,	thoroughly change one's world view.
	Serve the people,	entirely, thoroughly.
Elderly people and housewives	Let us wish Chairman Mao a long life!	Long live Chairman Mao! Long live, long live!
	Be industrious and thrifty in managing a household,	build the country through thrift and hard work.
	Let us respectfully wish Chairman Mao eternal life without end!	Eternal life without end! Eternal life without end!

In the beginning, they found it difficult to get used to propagating Mao Zedong Thought and were embarrassed and fearful. As soon as they began to speak, their faces turned all red, and they became all flustered. Some worried about how it all might affect their work, while others were afraid of not being up to it and of making mistakes. Some people who had been influenced by anarchism were unwilling to propagate [Mao Zedong Thought].[52]

Fear and intimidation played a crucial role in sustaining the Mao cult well through the spring of 1969 (when the central authorities made the first serious attempts to dismantle it). Lifted out of its original context, a remark like "from their attitude toward the 'three loyalties' one can tell the real revolutionaries from the bogus revolutionaries" appears to carry little real meaning. But in Shijiazhuang at the time, and in countless other parts of China in 1968, it was far from a theoretical observation. It was an implicit threat, hinting at what might happen to those whose language, acts, or personalities were less than sufficiently "loyal." On October 7, 1968, a middle school teacher in Fucheng county, Hebei, was sentenced "in accordance with the law" to nine years in prison for having, among other crimes, written in his private diary that a certain Mao-quote gave him "boundless energy," then changed that to "very much energy."[53] On October 15, 1968, a typesetter with the *Handan Daily* was sentenced to twenty years in prison as an "active counterrevolutionary" for mistakenly(?) typesetting a sentence wishing Mao Zedong "eternal life without end" *(wanshou wujiang)* as one wishing him "no long life without end" *(wushou wujiang)*.[54] There is no way of knowing whether the punishments meted out in these two cases were typical for China as a whole; examples of less severe punishments for similar offenses are also on record. When a cadre with the Beijing procuracy remarked in April 1968 that all this prostrating in front of Mao's portrait reminded him of his elementary school days in Japanese-occupied Manchuria, when students at the beginning of classes each morning had to salute the portraits of the puppet emperor Pu Yi and the emperor of Japan, his words were recorded in his dossier as a "malicious attack on our great leader Chairman Mao." But the punishment meted out to him was no more severe than a demotion and a few years of labor in rural areas on the outskirts of Beijing.[55]

The "three loyalties and four boundless loves" movement was officially called off by the CCP center in June 1969, but in China's rural areas it continued until well after the death of Lin Biao in 1971. Mao Zedong, in conversation with Edgar Snow in December 1970, claimed to have deplored the "excesses" of the movement, but to have understood why people had gone along with it: "If you did not take part," he noted, "you would be accused of being anti-Mao!"[56]

Economic Impact

Whatever they secretly felt about the cult of Mao, most Chinese doubtless took part just for the sake of a quiet life and to avoid drawing the authorities' attention to themselves. But the main concern of the average Chinese during these years of upheaval was as much physical survival as political survival, most importantly getting enough to eat at a time when the civil wars of 1967 and the terror campaign of 1968 inevitably had a disastrous effect on the economy.

The value of industrial and agricultural production declined by 9.6 percent in 1967. Since much of the upheaval had been urban, industry was worse hit, declining by 13.8 percent in value, compared with only 1.6 percent for agriculture. Whereas steel output declined by almost one-third, to 10.3 million tons, coal, the country's principal fuel, to which Zhou Enlai had paid particular attention, declined by 18 percent, to 206 million tons, and oil dropped 670,000 tons, to 13.88 million tons. Grain production rose by a little under 2 percent, to 217 million tons, and cotton output by a little under 1 percent, to 2,354,000 tons. But construction declined by one-third, imports by 12 percent, and the state was in deficit to the tune of 2.25 billion yuan.[57]

As part of his strenuous efforts to keep rail freight moving despite the swamping of the rail network by Red Guards traveling free and the fighting that periodically engulfed important hubs, Zhou received railway officials and workers more than 100 times during 1967, and he is given principal credit for hammering out three-way alliances in the railway system's eighteen bureaus, fifty-two sub-bureaus, and even some of the main train stations.[58] Even so, rail freight declined almost 25 percent, from 549,510,000 tons in 1966 to 420,950,000 tons in 1968, before recovering; during the same period, the Red Guards helped to increase the passenger load by over 20 percent.[59]

Industrial decline continued steadily in 1968, and the disruption of transport and distribution had an increasing impact on agriculture. As a result of persistent fighting and anarchy in the rural areas of Shaanxi, for example, by June 1968 the provincial revolutionary committee was forced to ration kerosene, matches, cigarettes, and soap. Roadblocks were common in parts of the province as banditry proliferated. Fighting in urban areas made workers afraid to work the night shift; day-shift workers came late and left early. Arrangements for the third FYP (notionally 1966–1970) were totally disrupted, and production proceeded without guidance. Assets that were not needed for military purposes were frozen down to the county level. By the spring of 1968, all this upheaval had affected state procurement of grain. The local PLA command estimated that grain reserves would soon be down to half the 1967 amount, the lowest they had been since the famine of the early 1960s.[60] In China overall, grain production declined by 4 percent, to 209 million tons, though cotton output was maintained at the 1967 level.[61]

In 1968, the regions worst hit were not the same as in 1967. Industry in eastern China did comparatively well, and the value of production in state-owned enterprises in Shanghai, Shandong, Anhui, Jiangsu, and Jiangxi was up moderately. Central-south and southwest China did extremely badly, however. The output value of industry in the central-south provinces of Henan, Hubei, and Hunan combined declined by 25 billion yuan. In southwest China, output value was down by more than 41 percent; in Yunnan, the output value of state-owned industries dropped by almost two-thirds.[62]

For China overall, 1968 was another disastrous year for industry, with output value falling by 5 percent. Coal output registered a welcome increase of almost 7 percent, but production was still well below the pre–Cultural Revolution level. Steel production dropped another 12 percent, to just over 9 million tons; the value of basic construction fell by almost 20 percent.[63]

On the eve of 1968, local authorities reminded Chinese citizens that the Cultural Revolutionary ideals of propagating new ideas, culture, customs, and habits were still very much alive and that traditions like calling on others to wish them a happy and prosperous new year, sending out New Year cards, and organizing New Year parties were still frowned upon.[64] In the first week of January 1968, the central authorities affirmed in a Notification distributed nationwide that "on no conditions" would such traditional practices be permitted during the upcoming traditional Chinese New Year (the Spring Festival) either.[65]

Once into the new year, the negative impact of the Cultural Revolution on the economy would have become increasingly evident. Each new call on the "revolutionary masses" to "practice frugality while making revolution" seemed to confirm that, contrary to what upbeat editorials in the *People's Daily* were saying, China was not in good shape. An urgent circular from the central authorities in February froze bank assets of most state companies and ordered all expenditures other than salaries to be reduced by 30 to 40 percent in 1968. Travel beyond provincial borders was to be curtailed. Unauthorized borrowing and lending of funds was strictly forbidden, as were other forms of "back-door" illicit economic activities.[66] Private bank accounts of suspected "capitalist roaders" and other "bad" persons were to be frozen if there was reason to believe that they were used to fund "illegal activities and counterrevolution."[67]

If people grumbled in private, they ran the risk of being exposed. After hearing about the freezing of bank accounts of alleged "capitalist roaders," a clerk with the old Beijing Municipal CCP Committee told her friends in the spring of 1968: "Nowadays you can't complain about anything. As soon as you do, you become an enemy . . . Whatever it says in Chairman Mao's books, that's the only thing you can say, with no variations whatsoever. Don't say anything other than that: if you do and they give you a label, it's bound to be 'counterrevolutionary.'" The clerk was informed upon by her friends and ended up being placed on probation within the CCP for two years for "serious errors in the form of reactionary statements."[68]

Rationing had been a permanent aspect of urban life in China since 1953, and in 1968 approximately 100 common products (the exact number varied among provinces and from year to year), including cooking oil and rice, were obtainable only by those in possession of the proper coupons or ration books.[69] In June 1968, the central authorities announced a further reduction (over 1967) in the amount of cotton cloth that ordinary citizens were able to purchase each year. Supplementary rations previously made available to certain categories of urban residents (including a "supplementary cotton ration for children residing in cities open to foreign visitors") were abolished across the board. The official announcement of the reductions was prefaced by quotations from Mao Zedong (from the previous autumn) in which the Chairman declared that "the situation in the Great Proletarian Cultural Revolution nationwide is not merely good, but excellent. The situation as a whole is better than on any previous occasion" and "in another couple of months' time, the situation as a whole will have become even better."[70]

But the "situation as a whole" was by no means uniformly "excellent" in all of urban China, as the example of Jiangxi, noted above, demonstrates. To the extent that CCP cadres concerned themselves with the issue of gaining and maintaining popular support for the "revolution," they were on the whole more concerned with the general sentiment among China's peasantry—the 82 percent of the total population that lived in rural townships and villages—than with the residents of the country's urban centers. The reasons for this were rooted in a particular understanding of what had shaped China's history, which assumed that the only serious domestic threat to CCP rule (revisionist or otherwise) was a peasant rebellion. As the chief prosecutor of Beijing municipality put it in 1962 (in what at the height of the Cultural Revolution was to be described as an oblique attack on Mao Zedong himself), "The reason why China's past emperors fell from power was always because they offended the peasantry."[71]

By the beginning of 1968, the single issue uniting peasants and the CCP remained what it had been since time immemorial: assuring a supply of food to what was now a nation of 650 million people.[72] In this respect, at least, life in the countryside in 1968 was not necessarily worse than it had been in recent years. By 1966, grain output had finally recovered to 214 million tons, a level higher than it had been in 1957, on the eve of the Great Leap Forward. With the exception of significant but not disastrous setbacks in 1968 and 1969, it continued to rise throughout the Cultural Revolution, reaching 286 million tons in 1976. This increased production failed to benefit the cities because of the disruption of the economy, transportation, the local state bureaucracy, and a decline in grain imports from Canada and Australia, from 6.43 million tons in 1966, to 4.59 million tons in 1968, to 3.78 million tons in 1969. The extent of the shortfall can be gauged by comparison with the 8.12 million tons imported in each of two relatively stable years, 1973 and 1974.[73] None of this had much of a negative impact in the still largely subsistence rural economy. In fact, quite the contrary.

To be left alone was what many peasants secretly wished for, and when the state's tax collectors failed to show up on time or in force because they were involved in struggles, the peasants were content. In parts of rural China, an unintended by-product of a dysfunctional state bureaucracy was hailed as a great, newborn thing. In Shehong county, Sichuan, peasants were told that "Cultural Revolution means no more grain deliveries to the state!" In a dozen or so counties in Henan, government finance bureaus were so badly affected by factional fighting that regular personnel simply were unable to attend to their tax collection duties. In Dongsheng county, Inner Mongolia, the official chop of the Bureau of Finance disappeared in the midst of a factional conflict; as a result, the bureau was unable to issue the proper agricultural tax collection receipts and had to temporarily suspend tax collection altogether. In Dayong county, Hunan, armed struggles were so intense that agricultural tax collection throughout the county was delayed by weeks in November 1967. Widespread armed struggles in the entire southeastern part of Shanxi in November 1967 delayed the collection of more than 100 million jin (50 million kilograms) of taxes in grain for weeks. In the two subprovincial regions of Suzhou and Zhenjiang, in Jiangsu, agricultural taxes equal to 200 million jin of grain were simply never collected. The situation was similar in the subprovincial regions of Enshi and Xiangyang, in Hubei, where agricultural taxes equal to 60 million jin remained uncollected.[74]

In some parts of China, the years 1967–1969 saw a resurgence of household-based farming, which the peasants preferred. In Yibin prefecture, Sichuan, some 8,355 of 49,349 production teams were by 1969 redistributing fields to individual households *(fentian daohu)*, contracting production out to individual households *(baochan daohu)*, and/or what contemporary sources described generally as allowing the "seizure of the collective economy" by private interests.[75]

In the face of this nationwide economic disruption, Mao fiddled. Meeting in late 1968, the CC focused not on the economy, but on the final resolution of the case of Liu Shaoqi.

16

Dispatching Liu Shaoqi

Mao's intention had all along been to time the CCP's Ninth Congress to coincide with the successful conclusion of the "first" Cultural Revolution.[1] But before beginning the construction of his brave new world, Mao evidently decided it was necessary to prepare the ground by completing the destruction of the old order. This principally meant finally disposing of Liu Shaoqi, the satanic figure of Cultural Revolution demonology. The dénouement was accomplished at the CC's Twelfth Plenum, which met in Beijing from October 13 to 31, 1968, a little over two years after the dramatic Eleventh Plenum at which Liu had first been toppled from his place as heir apparent.

The Twelfth Plenum was chaired by Mao and was one of the most remarkable gatherings in the party's forty-seven-year history. At the Eleventh Plenum, Mao had had to bully his colleagues, whose lack of enthusiasm for his measures was evident. By the time of the Twelfth Plenum, those colleagues who had survived were too cowed to drag their feet or offer lukewarm support. Almost three-quarters of the full and alternate CC members formally qualified to attend had come under suspicion of being "traitors" or "counterrevolutionaries." Of the eighty-seven living full members, only forty were invited to attend. Of the ninety-six alternate members appointed at the two sessions of the CCP's Eighth Congress in 1956 and 1958, only nineteen were at the plenum. Ten alternates (including four generals, one lieutenant general, and four political commissars) were appointed to full membership on the opening day to replace the ten who had died since the Eighth Congress, two by their own hand during the Cultural Revolution. These promotions brought the number of full members present up to the 51 percent needed to make any plenum vote formally legal. In addition to the fifty-nine full and alternate CC members, seventy-four members of the CCRG, MAC administration, provincial revolutionary committees, military regions, and organs directly under the CC attended this "enlarged" plenum and were accorded voting rights. In short, the plenum was attended by more voting nonmembers than members of the CC.[2] Its agenda, presented by Zhou Enlai, consisted of four points: the upcoming CCP Ninth Congress; the draft of a new party constitution to be adopted at the congress; the international situation; and the investigation of leading CC members, most notably Liu Shaoqi.[3]

As the content and tenor of Mao's opening address made clear, however, the CC Chairman was not about to let a formal agenda impose any limitations on the deliberations or even the duration of the plenum. He began by announcing that the plenum would meet for "maybe a week, or seven to ten days," and he then revealed his own personal preference for a much more unstructured approach by asking: "Let's think, what questions should be raised?"[4] Proceeding with a speech almost entirely devoted to comments of a personal nature on the supposed revolutionary credentials of selected CC members, Mao set the stage for what was to become a plenum devoted to matters of people and problems rather than principles and policies.

It was clear that at this stage of the Cultural Revolution "cleansing" was the issue uppermost in Mao's mind. Excerpts from his opening speech convey the flavor:

> There is a comrade, Zhang Dingcheng [procurator general], who's not a spy suspect, nor a spy or counterrevolutionary; why hasn't he shown up for this meeting? . . . [Zhou Enlai: . . . His collusion with Gao Gang and Rao Shushi needs to be investigated.] Wang Renzhong [first secretary, Hubei] is a hidden traitor and KMT member. Tao Zhu also has historical problems. Wang Yanchun from Hunan [second secretary]—he's no good either. So far, we have not found any historical problems with Deng Xiaoping other than his desertion from the Seventh Army . . . From the looks of it, Jiang Hua [first secretary, Zhejiang] can no longer be protected. What do you say? [General Xu Shiyou replies: If the Chairman says he's not to be protected, then I won't protect him anymore!][5]

On preparations for the Ninth Congress, Mao suggested to the plenum: "You talk about it among yourselves first; then at the tail end we'll get to matters like that."[6]

In a four-hour-long keynote address on October 26, Lin Biao maintained that the February Countercurrent of 1967 had been the "most serious anti-party incident . . . since the Eleventh Plenum" and had seriously disrupted Mao's "strategic plan" for the Cultural Revolution. It was absolutely imperative that the "current" as such be "criticized in earnest" in order to prevent the Cultural Revolution from "miscarrying."[7] As in the case of Chief of Staff Luo Ruiqing three years earlier, Lin was protecting his position at the head of the PLA, on this occasion by stigmatizing his peers among the marshals who had participated in the February Countercurrent.

The quality of the criticism "in earnest" called for by Lin has since the end of the Cultural Revolution been illustrated in Chinese histories by incomplete passages and sentences from speeches made at the plenum by members of the CCRG and Lin's own generals taken out of context. Chinese histories do not mention, much less quote, the keynote address Zhou Enlai made on the subject, but since Zhou outranked Chen Boda, Kang Sheng, and Jiang Qing, his speech was more significant. Zhou, unlike Lin Biao, had clearly taken his cue from the Chairman on opening day, since he too concentrated entirely on the personal rather than on principle, and his attacks on military leaders demonstrated the willingness of the premier to help shore up Lin Biao's position.

Zhou held Marshal Nie Rongzhen responsible for the death of Zhao Erlu, deputy director of the Defense Industry Committee of the MAC and CC member, and countless problems in the national defense sector, rattling off a litany of complaints against him as well as against Marshal Xu Xiangqian, not forgetting to include Xu's daughter, whom Zhou described as "very reactionary." Zhou blamed his ally Marshal Ye Jianying for any number of concrete incidents since the beginning of the Cultural Revolution. To prove that Ye "does not have an ounce of class sentiment for our Great Leader Chairman Mao," Zhou read out a poem that Ye had written upon hearing of Marshal Luo Ruiqing's attempted suicide in March 1966: "A jump and the general's body is ruined, his reputation destroyed; recollections of old friendship become a final parting." These lines showed, Zhou insisted, the kind of attachment Ye had to "a careerist who had plotted to usurp party power, military power, and government power." Zhou claimed that his loyal supporter at the Foreign Ministry, Marshal Chen Yi, had "always opposed Chairman Mao," while Marshal Zhu De really didn't know a thing about how to fight a war. For good measure, Premier Zhou attacked three vice premiers who had been his valued economics brains trust in the State Council: Li Fuchun had "all along not been faithful to Chairman Mao"; Li Xiannian had, back in the 1930s, "stood on Zhang Guotao's side"; while Chen Yun's economic thinking was all about "fostering a privileged stratum." Another vice premier, Deng Zihui, was someone with "Right inclination . . . spreading poison everywhere."[8]

Lin Biao's own denunciation of the February Countercurrent was a remarkable revision of history, holding former CCRG members Wang Li, Guan Feng, and Qi Benyu and Generals Yang Chengwu, Yu Lijin, and Fu Chongbi partially responsible for it. Whereas Zhou had merely noted in passing that these six individuals had "joined forces" with the vice premiers and MAC vice chairmen, Lin went on to explicate and to describe the "current" as one in which those responsible for it had

> assumed the roles of backstage bosses and instigated the masses to fight the masses. They proposed that, in state organs, all cadres above the department director level should be "baked [thrown out]," including cadres who held high the bright red flag of Mao Zedong Thought and gave prominence to proletarian politics. These actions of theirs resulted in the paralyzing of numerous state organs. The wind of arrests, the wind of dragging out high-level cadres in the military, the wind of attacking military organs, the instruction to carry out the "four greats" in companies as well, and so on—the members of the "February Adverse Current" are responsible for every one of these things. They made unfounded counatercharges and tried to put the blame on the CCRG. Now the facts are all too clear: it wasn't the CCRG, but them![9]

At the beginning of his speech, Lin had declared himself far from well-informed about current events and about the progress of the Cultural Revolution as a whole.[10] Kang Sheng commented on this disclaimer by insisting confidently that, "in actuality, he understands the actual situation even more and even more deeply than we do, and this modest attitude of his should be a lesson to us all."[11]

Although Mao wanted the leaders of the February Countercurrent criticized, he did not want them purged. As in February 1967, Mao chose to move carefully where PLA marshals were involved. In his closing address on October 31, he said: "They wanted to make their views heard. They're Politburo members, vice premiers, some of them vice chairmen of the MAC, so I'd say it's all right from the viewpoint of intra-party life. And also they were open about it." The Chairman insisted that the comrades responsible for the February Countercurrent should be made delegates to the Ninth CCP Congress. Mao knew that the guilty men included some of his most loyal and longest-serving supporters. By pardoning them, he ensured that he had old comrades to fall back on if his current colleagues failed him.[12]

Coup de Grâce

The most critical decision taken at the Twelfth Plenum was to expel Liu Shaoqi from the CCP and to dismiss him from all his posts "once and for all." The plenum communiqué referred to this decision as having been taken "unanimously," but in fact at least one CC member, labor union official Chen Shaomin, did not raise her hand in support, to the amazement of those who did.[13] The seventy-four-page indictment of Liu Shaoqi's alleged crimes had been prepared for the plenum by the Central Case Examination Group (CCEG, discussed below), which reportedly assigned 400,000 people to pore over 4 million files covering the period since the Sino-Japanese War. Yet the indictment dealt almost exclusively with events that had taken place before the founding of the PRC and contained no documentation of any event more recent than 1929.[14] All the "crimes" were dismissed as baseless when Liu was posthumously rehabilitated after the Cultural Revolution.

The CCEG report detailed how Liu had "betrayed" the revolution on three occasions in the 1920s. It formally labeled him a "traitor, renegade, and scab." In dealing with the thirty-nine years since then, it referred only to the existence of "extensive, concrete, and profound" documentation that was to be the subject of a forthcoming separate report. No such report was ever issued. In his comments on the findings of the CCEG Lin Biao is alleged to have described Liu as an "exceptionally big bastard" and maintained that "Liu is the ultimate, most highly venomous [*wudu juquan*] renegade, and there's a mountain of iron evidence proving that he's guilty and deserves to be accused of the most heinous of crimes."[15] The son of a PLA general who at one point had been a member of the CCEG maintains that Zhou Enlai's comment had been "This one can be executed [*ciren kesha*]," but no independent corroboration of this claim has come to light.[16] What Mao thought of the report is not known, but in any case Liu was not executed.

When he was informed of the decision of the Twelfth Plenum to expel him from the CCP, the hospitalized Liu "immediately broke out in a sweat, became short of breath, began to vomit. His blood pressure and body temperature shot up." From this moment until his death in 1969, he never spoke again, and refused to answer all questions.[17] He was allowed to waste away in a cruel, drawn-out process. Already afflicted with diabetes, he was unable to get out of bed to go to the toilet, became covered in bed sores, and had to be fed though nasal feeding tubes. On October 17, 1969, during a war scare, he was evacuated from Beijing along with other leaders. Liu was flown to Kaifeng, where he remained anonymous to his guards. Doctors were refused the drugs they requested for him. He died of pneumonia on November 12.[18] Whether Mao ordered Liu's health to be neglected is unknown, but, as his protection of Deng Xiaoping would show, a word from him could have ensured that his erstwhile comrade-in-arms at least suffered with dignity. Liu's wife, Wang Guangmei, whom he did not see after the summer of 1967, had also been investigated, and was imprisoned for twelve years.

The New Party Constitution

The plenum ratified the draft of a new party constitution that had been prepared in Shanghai, at Mao's insistence, under the supervision of the CCRG to replace the existing one, which the media claimed had been "brimming with the sinister revisionist wares of China's Khrushchev."[19] The draft (to be formally adopted at the upcoming Ninth Party Congress) had gone through numerous revisions in the course of an unprecedented, year-long process of opinion-solicitation and "discussion, among the broad members of the party and the masses," including input from 126 provincial revolutionary committees and PLA units.[20] Zhang Chunqiao, who had been at the center of this process, at one point allowed himself to make the following personal observation: "I was a delegate to the Eighth Congress, and we did not receive the party constitution until it was time to meet, raise our hands in approval, and adopt it. This time around, it's been different."[21]

The most remarkable feature was a reference in the constitution's preamble to Lin Biao as Mao's designated successor. Appropriately, the process initiated at the Eleventh Plenum by which Lin replaced Liu Shaoqi as party No. 2 was to be codified now that Liu had been expelled from the party. At the very end of his long speech to the plenum on October 26, Lin announced that personally he would have preferred to see the reference dropped:

> I have a reservation to make, and it has to do with my name's being written into the party constitution. I feel very uneasy about this, very uneasy. My view is that a party constitution is a major thing and that it is not suitable, that it is unsuitable, to write my name into it. I have raised this matter with the center in the past, but not managed to have it resolved. While I maintain my reservation, I submit to the organization. But my reservation stands.[22]

In his speech to the plenum, Kang Sheng explained that "Comrade Lin Biao, who is very modest, wanted us to delete this passage, but in our opinion it must be retained." Jiang Qing insisted that "the passage stays, or we will not approve [the new constitution]."[23] With Mao and the rest of the center insisting on retaining it, the passage not surprisingly appeared, unchanged, in the version adopted at the Ninth Congress.

In another constitutional issue, the Twelfth Plenum saw the formal elevation of the CCRG to the pinnacle of its formal power. Since the beginning of 1967, the State Council, MAC, and CCRG had been listed in official communications in that order. At the plenum, a new ranking order was established: CCRG, State Council, MAC.[24] The symbolic significance of this change was close to zero in the military sector, from which the CCRG was all but excluded. In the civilian sector, on the other hand, it finally spelled out what everybody had known for a long time anyway, that the responsibility of the CCRG for what was happening in the Cultural Revolution was far greater than that of the MAC. It seems not improbable that this division of responsibility (and possible future blame) suited military leaders, including Lin Biao, just fine. In his speech at the plenum, Lin had the following to say about the CCRG: "Finally, I would like to say . . . that for all of the past two years, it's mainly been a matter of Chairman Mao's leadership and mainly the practical implementation by the CCRG. In particular the role played by comrade Jiang Qing, the premier, comrade [Chen] Boda, comrade Kang Sheng, and the other comrades on the CCRG. As far as I am concerned, to be frank, I haven't done very much."[25]

Other Verdicts

In striking contrast to his unforgiving consignment of Liu to the dustbin of history and to an ignominious and anonymous death, Mao was curiously lenient in other cases. In his concluding speech on the final day of the plenum, Mao made a point of protecting Deng Xiaoping:

> You all wanted to expel Deng Xiaoping [from the CCP], but I have some reservations . . . He won't rebel. What characterizes him is that he's too far removed from the masses. These thoughts of mine may be a bit conservative and not to your liking—the fact that I am saying a few nice words about him. Anyway, he waved a goose-feather fan: the real decision-makers were other people.[26]

The plenum dismissed Deng Xiaoping—characterized for two years as "the other biggest party-person in power taking the capitalist road"—from "all posts both inside and outside the party," but did not expel him from the CCP. A 15,000-character-long report outlining Deng's key wrongdoings was circulated at the plenum but never made public.[27] Eventually, a 26,500-character-long written self-criticism submitted by Deng to the people handling his "case" on the eve of the plenum was leaked to a wider audience. In it, Deng admitted to a long list of mistakes and "crimes" committed against the revolution since the 1920s. "I have utterly failed to live up to the trust and hope bestowed upon me by the party and Chairman Mao for so long," he said. "It is with deep regret that I look back upon my past. In the years that I have left, I wish to repent, make a fresh start, become a new man, and strive hard to transform my bourgeois world view with the help of Mao Zedong Thought." Deng told the CC to "feel free to dispose of me in any way you please," and promised "never ever to reverse the verdict you pass on me. I have absolutely no wish to remain an arch-unrepentant capitalist roader."[28] Unlike Liu Shaoqi, Deng displayed "repentance" and denounced himself, presumably believing it was preferable to lose face than to forfeit any hope of a future. At the end of 1969, Deng was exiled to a tractor repair shop in rural Jiangxi until Mao recalled him in 1973.

In his concluding speech, Mao again made a string of comments on people, including some of his Politburo colleagues ("Chen Yi says he's not qualified to attend the Ninth Party Congress, but I say he is!"), past party leaders ("Don't conclude from the fact that it produced Chen Duxiu [the CCP's first general secretary in the 1920s] that there were no good people on the Central Committee!"), senior academics ("Jian Bozan [historian] and Feng Youlan [philosopher] spread poison . . . but we should feed them"), worker delegates ("This man's name is Wang Hongwen: Stand up so they can see you! . . . Too bad there aren't more young comrades attending this meeting"), and ethnic minority delegates ("Do you speak the Han language? Are you a real Tibetan or a fake Tibetan?").[29]

Mao's defense of Deng should be compared to his comments on Marshal He Long at the very end of his speech, added almost as an afterthought:

> We used to say as far as He Long was concerned that he should (a) be denounced and (b) be protected. The reason was, he represented the Second Front Army. Now it seems we can no longer protect him, because of the things he did that we did not know about. Judging from the revelations made by Cheng Jun, Xu Guangda, Liao Hansheng, and others, he's been destroying this

army of ours. Behind our backs, it turns out he tried to usurp military power and oppose the party, but then he ran out of time. There's He Long, Liu Zhen, Wang Shangrong, Xu Guangda—these guys. Still, let's not get off the topic, but leave it at that. Meeting over.[30]

The claim "it seems we can no longer protect him" was Mao's perverse way of announcing that Marshal He Long, unlike Deng Xiaoping, was slated for terminal cleansing from the revolutionary ranks. In January 1969, the "He Long Case Group" under the CCEG embarked upon a program of intentional mismedication in an effort to speed up the deterioration of He's already frail health. He finally died in the PLA-run Hospital 301 in Beijing on June 9, 1969.[31]

The communiqué of the Twelfth Plenum, published in the *People's Daily* on November 2, 1968, referred to the meeting as having been "united to an unprecedented degree," and as the "mobilization for total victory in the Great Proletarian Cultural Revolution." In his closing address, Mao said that "the meeting wasn't too bad; in fact it went quite well."[32]

The Central Case Examination Group

One reason why the plenum went well from Mao's viewpoint was the dirt dug up on his colleagues, particularly Liu Shaoqi, by the CCEG—a far more shadowy organization than the CCRG though created simultaneously in 1966. At the plenum, Lin Biao singled it out for special praise, and made a point of mentioning Jiang Qing and Zhou Enlai:

> Our Special Case Group has been very efficient—comrade Jiang Qing in particular has maintained a tight leadership and grasp of its cases—and has produced conclusive evidence in the form of human testimony and material and circumstantial evidence about what to us were unheard-of and utterly shocking things. It came as a sudden realization to us. Otherwise, with no facts, one is always slightly confused and not that clear . . . Now these guys have been exposed. As far as the issue of these cases is concerned, of course, in addition to the comrades on the CCRG, we have had the premier take part and exercise leadership. Thanks to the hard effort made by all these comrades, by the entire Special Case Group, we're now able to see the images of these monsters and freaks in the demon-detecting mirror with their masks ripped off.[33]

Unlike the CCRG, whose actions and pronouncements were prominently displayed in the media, this second institution created at the Politburo meeting in May 1966 was secret, its name never appearing in the press. Yet during its thir-teen-year existence, the CCEG had powers far exceeding not only those once exercised by the party's Discipline Inspection Commission and Organization Department, but even those of the central public security and procuratorial or-gans and the courts. This group made the decisions to "ferret out," persecute, ar-rest, imprison, and torture "revisionist" CC members and many lesser political enemies. Its privileged employees were the Cultural Revolution equivalent of Lenin's Cheka and Hitler's Gestapo. Whereas the CCRG at least nominally dealt in "culture," the CCEG dealt exclusively in violence. If the CCRG was the alpha of the Cultural Revolution, the organization that sparked much of the up-heaval, the CCEG was its omega, the organ charged with making the final de-termination of the cases that CCRG activism had produced.[34]

The CCEG grew out of the Special Case Examination Committee set up by the Politburo on May 24, 1966, to "examine" the cases of Peng Zhen, Luo Ruiqing, Lu Dingyi, and Yang Shangkun.[35] Like the CCRG, the CCEG was di-rectly responsible to the PSC, which ultimately meant Mao Zedong.[36] Before the CC's Eleventh Plenum in August 1966 and again for nine months in 1975, the PSC member formally supervising the work of the CCEG was Deng Xiao-ping, but for the greater part of the Cultural Revolution that role was played by Zhou Enlai. The group's members included virtually the entire CCRG, with Kang Sheng—the gray eminence of the Cultural Revolution, often described as its evil genius[37]—and Jiang Qing assuming particularly active roles in its opera-tion. Other members at the time of the CC's Twelfth Plenum included Xie Fuzhi, the minister of public security; Wang Dongxing, who would be head of the CCEG at the time of its dissolution in the winter of 1978–79; and Lin Biao's wife, Ye Qun.[38]

Although it was created as an ad hoc body, the CCEG soon became a per-manent institution similar to any other CC department or State Council minis-try, but substantially more powerful. It employed a permanent staff of thousands, including at one point 789 PLA officers. Of these officers, 126 were heads or dep-uty heads of some of the CCEG's many case groups. On the eve of the Twelfth Plenum, a staggering eighty-eight members and alternate members of the Cen-tral Committee were having their "cases" checked by the CCEG on grounds of suspected "treachery," "spying," and/or "collusion with the enemy."[39]

Ironically, in view of the fact that Liu Shaoqi presided over the Politburo meeting that founded the CCEG, the biggest case group of all turned out to be the one charged with investigating him. It began life as the Wang Guangmei

Case Group, set up on December 18, 1966, to investigate his wife. While holding a reception for Red Guards at one of Beijing's airports in late March 1967, Mao gave Kang Sheng the go-ahead to turn the group's focus more directly on Liu himself.[40] By early summer that year, the group had begun outsourcing some investigations into Liu's "sinister past" to small groups of university-age Red Guards in Beijing and Tianjin. Only too eager to prove their revolutionary credentials in this way, the Red Guards rarely hesitated to act as Mao's willing inquisitors.[41]

By the fall of 1967, the number of cases being investigated by the CCEG had grown so large that the workload was too big for the existing organization. The Luo Ruiqing Case Group under the PLA air force commander, Lieutenant General Wu Faxian, for example, had already branched out into at least three subcase groups, dealing with cases that were only incidentally connected to Luo.[42] At the orders of Mao and Zhou Enlai, the CCEG bureaucracy was subdivided into two separate offices. The First Office, linked to the CC's General Office under Wang Dongxing, continued to handle most of the cases from the initial phase of the Cultural Revolution, including those of Peng Zhen, An Ziwen, Liu Ren, and Zhou Yang, deputy director of the Central Propaganda Department and member of Peng Zhen's original Group of Five. The Second Office, which was linked to the MAC and of which Yang Chengwu was made concurrent head, took over a dozen or so cases involving senior PLA officers, including that of Marshal He Long.[43] After Yang Chengwu was purged in March 1968, he was replaced as chief of staff and head of the Second Office by General Huang Yongsheng.

In 1968 a Third Office was created, headed by Xie Fuzhi and linked through him to the Ministry of Public Security. The initial task of the Third Office was the investigation of the May 16 Conspiracy, but later it handled many other cases as well. Of these, the most notorious were probably the "Chinese (Marxist-Leninist) Communist Party Case," in which a researcher from the Institute of Economics of the Chinese Academy of Sciences admitted under torture the existence of a secret "shadow" CCP led by Zhu De with links to the KMT, the CPSU, and the Mongolian Communist Party;[44] and the case of the alleged murder (suicide, according to the forensic evidence) of Su Mei, Kang Sheng's sister-in-law and mistress, which led to the persecution of ninety-nine individuals, of whom nine ended up in prison, twenty-three were put under house arrest, three went mad, and two perished at the hands of their interrogators.[45]

Serving the needs of the CCEG became a priority of many party, government, and military institutions. A special Central Enemy and Puppet Archives Examination and Investigation Small Group, created in October 1967 with permanent branches in eighteen cities outside Beijing, provided information on the political past of suspects. In August 1968, when Xie Fuzhi ordered a thorough search of the entire archive of the Ministry of Public Security, the PLA lent him more than 700 men, who spent eighteen months finishing the job.[46]

At one point, the Politburo appears to have planned to dissolve the CCEG, like the CCRG, at the Ninth Party Congress;[47] but by 1969, the CCEG had become too useful to be easily dispensed with. In 1970, it would be charged with the "examination" of the Chen Boda Case, and a year later the Lin Biao Case. The CCEG would finally be abolished after the Cultural Revolution, by decision of the Third Plenum of the Eleventh CC in December 1978. Ironically, its last task was preparing the post-Mao leadership's case against the "Gang of Four."

17

The Congress of Victors

Mao intended the CCP's Ninth Congress to be the watershed, between old and new, bad and good, pollution and purity, revisionism and revolution. It was to be the forum at which victory was to be declared, and indeed, the first public communiqué issued in its name announced that it was being held "at a time when the Great Proletarian Cultural Revolution personally initiated and led by Chairman Mao has won great victory."[1]

But it did not work out that way. The congress in April 1969 has since become a transitional rather than a terminating event in histories of the Cultural Revolution. The final stages of the movement in which, according to the *People's Daily*, the "proletariat and the revolutionary people of the world who are fighting imperialism, modern revisionism, and all reaction [find] tremendous inspiration, bright prospects, and greater confidence in victory" were yet to be completed in parts of the country, and had not even begun in others.[2] Mao admitted as much in one of his speeches at the congress, insisting that "this Great Cultural Revolution . . . has been quite thorough, judging from the looks of it. [But] the job of the Great Cultural Revolution is not yet finished. We still have to continue to grasp it in a meticulous, down-to-earth, and conscientious way."[3] Whether because his timetable had been untenable from the start, or because Mao really did not have too clear an idea about what to do in a post–Cultural Revolutionary world, and hence preferred—consciously or not—to postpone its arrival indefinitely, his reluctance to give up made any form of real closure impossible for now.

Nobody was able to speak confidently in the spring of 1969 about what would happen next. A month after the end of the congress, the two great political theorists on the PSC, Chen Boda and Kang Sheng, tried to explain to a gathering of Zhongnanhai staff how to interpret the spirit of the Ninth Congress and Mao Zedong's most recent pronouncements about the future. Whatever Chen

Boda said is unlikely to have been what he himself believed: it was barely three months since his opinion—"to develop production, to do a good job of production, and to raise labor productivity" ought to be given priority once the congress was over—had been severely criticized as fallacious at a meeting in Mao's presence.[4] Kang Sheng—whose remarks, unlike Chen's, were printed and distributed to a wider audience—did manage to elaborate at some length on the finer points of the Cultural Revolutionary timetable, but he ended up having little substantial to say about the future other than that even after a "great" victory, "the main point is that we must not lower our guard and become careless or relax our vigilance. We must never forget class struggle!"[5]

To the extent that the Ninth Congress marked anything at all, it was neither the victory nor the end of the Cultural Revolution. It was but the beginning of an ending so painfully drawn out, so tortuously slow, that it would last more than twice as long as the event it supposedly brought to a close. And what until recently has been obscured by a paucity of documentation is the immense human cost of that ending, all too often treated by past chroniclers as merely a "restoration of order," followed by years when not much seemed to be happening in China other than the rise and fall of a tiny handful of members of the political elite.[6] A greater number of ordinary citizens died while revolutionary committees across the country "finished the job" that Mao had mentioned at the Ninth Congress than at the hands of rampaging Red Guards in 1966–67 or in armed combat between "mass organizations" competing for power in 1967–68.

Preparations

The CCP's Ninth Congress had taken at least eighteen months to organize. In fact, Mao had told the CC as early as August 1966 that "we should probably hold [the congress] some time next year," but that was not to be. Discussion of the congress started in earnest in October 1967, when *Zhongfa* [1967] 322 was issued by the party center. Mao had earlier entrusted Zhang Chunqiao and Yao Wenyuan with researching the subject in Shanghai, and the document included Yao's suggestions to the Chairman. Delegates could be chosen as a result simply of discussions: "What matters is not the form, but the content; not the name, but the substance," people were allegedly saying. Yao quoted Shanghai Red Guards as hoping that a sizable contingent of Red Guards would not only be allowed to be present at the congress, but would also be admitted beforehand to the party, obviously in order to qualify as proper delegates.[7] By late November 1967, the subject of the congress had been discussed nationwide. There was said to be nearly universal grassroots unanimity on the proposition that Liu Shaoqi, Deng Xiaoping, Peng Zhen, Tao Zhu, and all the other major leaders who had fallen in the past year and a half should not be delegates. "One hundred percent of the grass roots will not accept those people as delegates," *Zhongfa* [1967] 358 claimed, quoting "countless comrades" as saying: "With them, it's not a matter of electing them or not electing them to be delegates, but a matter of discussing how to dispose of them and of expelling them from the party."[8]

Talking about the prospective congress to members of the CCRG on November 5, 1967, Mao made some bold comparisons: "A human being has arteries and veins through which the heart makes the blood circulate, and he breathes with his lungs, exhaling carbon dioxide and inhaling fresh oxygen, that is, getting rid of the stale and taking in the fresh. A proletarian party must also get rid of the stale and take in the fresh, for only thus can it be full of vitality."[9] Turning to the realities of the Cultural Revolution, Mao said: "We've had over a year of fighting and come up with quite a few bad people, now let's have a [political] party—a party full of people who are full of vigor and vitality."[10] Activist elements from among workers, poor peasants, and Red Guards should be recruited; organizational life should be restored, but not in the old style. Mao invited the MAC to prepare a document criticizing Deng Xiaoping, but expressed his continuing desire to differentiate Deng from Liu.[11] In *Zhongfa* [1967] 358, a prime goal of the Ninth Congress was revealed to be the elevation of the status of Lin Biao. In December, *Zhongfa* [1967] 391 asked localities to emulate the Shanghai Revolutionary Committee's formula for mass discussion of revising the party constitution.[12] As we have seen, there was a year of bloody carnage before Lin's heightened status and the draft of a new party constitution were agreed to at the Twelfth Plenum in the autumn of 1968.

Yet another five months elapsed and a 128-person preparatory conference was held under Zhou Enlai's chairmanship before the 1,512 delegates to the Ninth Congress met from April 1 to April 24, 1969. Notionally, they represented 22 million party members, notionally partly because the delegates were chosen by discussion rather than by formal election, partly because some were not party members, partly because under the onslaughts of the Red Guards the party itself had become notional, with little institutional life below the top.[13] The oldest delegate at the congress was the eighty-three-year-old Dong Biwu, who, like Mao, had been present at the founding of the CCP at the First National Congress in Shanghai forty-eight years earlier; the youngest delegate was a nineteen-year-old Red Guard who had entered the party only the year before.[14] Altogether 422 delegates (28 percent of the total number) represented the armed forces.[15]

The congress met under conditions of secrecy unprecedented even by the standards of the world Communist movement. Contrary to the practice established at the Eighth Congress in 1956, the Ninth Congress was not announced in advance, and the first the party and the country knew of it was when a communiqué was issued on the opening day. To maintain security, no foreign guests were invited, reporters were not allowed to gather material freely, and the delegates were kept incommunicado.[16] Provincial delegations were flown in on specially chartered air force planes after dark. "When we got off the plane in Beijing," delegates from Shandong later recalled, "we were told to say that we were in town to attend a study class . . . We had to promise to abide by the 'five nos': not to go out, not to receive any guests, not to make any phone calls, not to write any letters, and not to talk to anyone else about the preparations for the congress."[17] After the turmoil of the previous three years, perhaps Mao felt uncertain about what sort of delegates would turn up and how the congress would go.

The congress was eight years overdue. According to the CCP constitution passed at the Eighth Congress, congresses were to be held every five years. Kang Sheng's explanation of the delay to a group of foreign Communists was that it would not have been a good idea to hold a congress in 1961 or in 1966, since at that time "the traitor Liu Shaoqi" had not yet been exposed. "Better to delay a congress, than to hold it in the company of traitors; what matters is the thinking that guides a congress, not whether it is early or late, or strictly in accord with the party constitution."[18] Even Kang Sheng was not prescient enough to realize that, despite the delay, the Ninth Congress was nevertheless held in the presence of traitors, and that after only eighteen months their identities would be successively unveiled.

For the moment, however, Mao was quoted in a contemporary, Stalinist-style transcript of his opening address as hoping that "the present congress will be a congress of unity and a congress of victory *(Enthusiastic applause)* and that, after its conclusion, still greater victories will be won throughout the country *(Prolonged enthusiastic applause and shouts of Long live Chairman Mao! Long live! Long long live! Eternal life to Chairman Mao!)*." For Mao, or the "Chairman of the National Revolutionary Committee," as Yao Wenyuan referred to him, this was the conclusion of the Cultural Revolution, the end of destruction and the start of construction, and delegates echoed those sentiments in the days that followed. Wang Hongwen, once leader of the Shanghai WGHQ and later third secretary of the Shanghai CCP Committee (under Zhang Chunqiao and Yao Wenyuan), promised on behalf of the working class to "resolutely surpass" the targets for the national economy once the congress was over. Chen Yonggui, leader of the Dazhai model brigade eventually and deputy secretary of the Shanxi CCP Committee, said that "we poor and lower-middle peasants will hold even higher the great red banner of Mao Zedong Thought, and . . . make preparations for war and natural disasters, and do everything for the people." Premier Zhou Enlai expressed his "firm belief" that Mao's call for post-congress unity and still greater victories "will surely be realized."[19]

Lin Biao's Report

The brief congress agenda consisted of a political report from the outgoing Eighth CC, to be delivered by Lin Biao; passage of the revised party constitution; and the election of a new CC. Initially Chen Boda had been designated to oversee the drafting of Lin's report, but as he said many years later, "I did not want to work together with Zhang and Yao. And since my name was at the top of the list of draftees, I decided to go ahead by myself instead."[20] However, Chen's text (titled "Strive to Build Our Country into a Powerful Socialist State") was rejected by Mao less than a month before the opening of the congress, in part because of its content, in part because of Chen's exclusion of Zhang and Yao from the drafting process.[21] Zhang Chunqiao argued that Chen's text paid too much attention to the role of "productive forces," and Mao may well have agreed, though he called for some of Chen's views to be retained as Zhang and Yao, supervised by Kang Sheng, hurriedly produced a new draft.[22] This was in turn criticized by Chen as reminiscent of the German revisionist Eduard Bernstein, full of the importance of "movement" but lacking any sense of "direction"—a feature that may have been attractive to Mao.[23] Although the Chairman had relied on Chen's ideological expertise for thirty years, he preferred the Zhang-Yao text, which he revised several times.[24]

Lin Biao made no contribution whatever to the preparation of the report, and indeed did not read it over even once (despite being asked repeatedly by Mao to do so)[25] before delivering it on the opening day of the congress.[26] As an experienced soldier, the marshal possibly did not feel it worthwhile to battle over mere verbiage that had no relevance to the political power structure; he was certainly too canny to interfere in Mao's sphere of ideology. Lin once characterized his own relationship with Mao Zedong Thought in the following way: "The center is the sun, and just as the nine big planets revolve around the sun, so all our work revolves around the sun. Chairman Mao is the sun. Mao Zedong Thought is the sun."[27]

"Lin's" eight-part report was heavily devoted to presenting a Maoist version of the thirteen years since the Eighth Congress in terms of the putative struggle against revisionism, both internationally against the Soviet Union and domestically against Liu Shaoqi. Liu was repeatedly criticized by name, especially for his "revisionist line on party building," but the errors of other members of his "bourgeois headquarters" (for example, Deng Xiaoping) were not mentioned. A week before the congress, Mao had himself told the members of the CCRG that "the only names to be mentioned in the report are those of myself and Liu Shaoqi."[28] The movement to "cleanse the class ranks" had to be brought to a successful conclusion, and, in what was almost certainly a passage retained from Chen Boda's discarded text, the party was told to "bring the revolutionary initiative of the people of all nationalities into full play, firmly grasp revolution, energetically promote production, and fulfill and overfulfill the targets for developing the national economy." For although victory in the Cultural Revolution had been won, the report said, quoting Mao, "we cannot speak of a final victory. Not even for decades."[29] There was, in short, to be no relaxation of vigilance, and struggle figured importantly as an inescapable and central element of the socialist stage of history that China had reached.

Yet for now the theme was unity. In consonance with Mao's opening address, Lin asserted that the outgoing CC was convinced that, after the congress, the Chinese people would "unite even more closely under the leadership of our great leader Chairman Mao and win still greater victories in the struggle against our common enemy and in the cause of building our powerful socialist motherland."[30] A week after the congress, Lin reiterated this point in conversation with a delegation from Sichuan, adding: "If you want revolution, you must unite, since without unity there can be no revolution. No unity is the same as no revolution, which is the same as aiding the enemy."[31]

Lin's report was approved by a show of hands at a plenary session on April 14, and no objections were raised when Mao asked whether delegates minded if further changes were made to the text before publication.[32] Zhou Enlai praised Lin's report in a special statement, prepared in close consultation with Mao:[33]

> [It] expounds brilliantly Chairman Mao's theory of continuing the revolution under the dictatorship of the proletariat. It proves and explains how this great

290

theory of Chairman Mao's amounts to a general and creative development of the Marxist-Leninist theory of uninterrupted revolution, and how it has been proven absolutely necessary by the concrete practice of China's socialist revolution and the international communist movement.[34]

Zhou's statement dealt less with Lin's report than with Lin Biao the person and his contributions to the Chinese revolution over the previous forty years. In a remarkable passage, seemingly aimed against Marshal Zhu De, Zhou referred to Lin as a "glorious representative [of those] who after the defeat of the Nanchang uprising [in 1927] led a group of insurrectionary forces to Jinggangshan to accept the leadership of Chairman Mao."[35] Zhou seemed to be trying to convince the congress that Lin, not Zhu, had been the cofounder of the Red Army with Mao, a revision of history that the Chairman endorsed shortly after the congress.[36] Zhou concluded his paean to the "deputy supreme commander of our proletarian headquarters" thus: "We do not only feel boundless joy because we have as our great leader the greatest Marxist-Leninist of our era, Chairman Mao, but also great joy because we have Vice Chairman Lin as Chairman Mao's universally recognized successor."[37] Zhou was making it abundantly clear to his congress audience that he accepted his own, formally subordinate, position within the party leadership and had no intention of challenging Lin Biao.[38]

The New Party Constitution

There were only insignificant differences between the new party constitution approved by the congress on April 14 and the draft agreed to at the Twelfth Plenum. The most remarkable passage in the constitution was the reference in the preamble to Lin Biao as Mao's designated successor. Despite the reservations he had already expressed at the Twelfth Plenum, with Mao and the rest of the central "organization" insisting on retaining it, the passage remained unchanged. Lin's role as Mao's heir—a provision unique in any Communist constitution—was formally agreed to at the congress after the now-customary expressions of support for Lin by the rest of the party leadership. At one point Jiang Qing explained that "writing Vice Chairman Lin's name into the constitution will reduce the likelihood that others will covet the position [of Mao's successor]," thus inadvertently hinting at what she thought she might be losing by the provision.[39] Reading in the party press about what had transpired at the congress, Deng

Xiaoping, still under house arrest in Zhongnanhai, wrote a letter to Mao, Lin, and the party center on May, 3, 1969, "in support of the resolutions passed by the Congress."[40] After the Cultural Revolution, free to speak his mind, Deng Xiaoping would describe the practice of a leader's personally choosing his successor as "feudal."[41]

The constitution's most striking feature was its brevity, being only a quarter of the length of the one it replaced. It contained fewer specific provisions concerning the rights and obligations of party members than previous constitutions. Kang Sheng, who had supervised the drafting work since the end of 1967, noted in a specially prepared statement that the constitution was "to the point, not burdened with trivial detail, well structured, very logical, concise in its language, easily remembered, and easily understood . . . I hear that many workers and peasants are able to recite it from memory."[42]

The constitution reaffirmed the leftist positions of the Cultural Revolution and laid down that "Marxism-Leninism Mao Zedong Thought is the theoretical basis guiding the party's thinking." This formulation represented a departure from the 1956 constitution, which mentioned only Marxism-Leninism, and a return to the 1945 Yan'an party constitution.[43] In recent years, CCP historians have been at pains to assert that the dropping of Mao Zedong Thought from the constitution at the Eighth Congress had been at the Chairman's suggestion, or at any rate with his consent, and it is certainly possible that in 1956 Mao might have been prepared to adopt a lower profile during the Soviet-led attack on Stalin's "cult of personality" in the world Communist movement. But the restoration of Mao's thought to the constitution during the Cultural Revolution suggests that the Chairman had not liked its excision earlier, and had resented those who had supported that decision.

A New Leadership

On the last day of the congress, April 24, a plenary session chaired by Lin Biao "elected" a new CC consisting of 170 full members and 109 alternates. Zhou Enlai had suggested that the CC should be limited to 115 full members and 95 alternates in line with the general slimming down of the bureaucracy characteristic of the Cultural Revolution, but Mao opted for a larger body, doubtless realizing that the movement had thrown up a lot of new activists who would expect preferment.[44] The Presidium Secretariat, run by Zhou, issued guidance for choosing CC members: a list of the names of candidates (identical in number with the projected new size of the body) was issued to each delegate, and "election" consisted in crossing out the names of candidates whose revolutionary credentials one was less than 100 percent prepared to endorse. Names of candidates were divided into four categories: members of the CCRG Caucus and outgoing CC, other "revolutionary leading cadres," PLA officers, and grassroots representatives. If a candidate managed to avoid having his or her name crossed out by more than half of the delegates, election was guaranteed. At a trial run of the election halfway through the congress, the number of candidates receiving the necessary number of endorsements to make it onto the CC fell short of the projected total, and in the end 5 members were added and 2 replaced by "democratic consultation."[45] In the middle of the election proper, chaos ensued when one delegate, after having placed his vote card in the ballot box, jumped onto the stage where Mao was sitting to shake the hand of the Chairman; within seconds, others attempted to follow his example, prompting the intervention of bodyguards (emerging from behind the curtains en masse) and the erection of a temporary human shield between the party leadership and the voting delegates.[46]

Of the 279-person body, only 53, or 19 percent, were carryovers from the previous CC. Among the new members were the wives of Mao, Lin Biao, Zhou, and Kang Sheng, who raised the proportion of women on the CC.[47] There was also a dramatic increase in the number of workers and peasants. But the most significant increase was in the number of PLA members, altogether 99, or more than 35 percent of the total.[48] The congress delegates who resented this development were told "to make some allowances, given the large number of older comrades in the PLA."[49] Yet there were still complaints from PLA delegates representing units in Hebei, Shanxi, Inner Mongolia, Beijing, and Tianjin, and Mao admitted that "some provinces are more fully represented, others less so . . . But most significantly, we're getting rid of Liu Shaoqi and his crowd. That's a major victory!" In an effort to console those who felt aggrieved that they had not made the cut, Mao remarked that not all of those elected were necessarily ideal choices, and that there were also "many good comrades" among those not elected—cold comfort in any political system.[50]

One odd but inevitable outcome of the election procedure was that candidates about whom little or nothing was known were less likely to have their names crossed out than those about whom something (possibly controversial) was known. In the end, only two candidates received the endorsement of all 1,510 voting delegates: one was Mao, and the other was Wang Baidan, a completely unknown thirty-four-year-old steelworker from Harbin whose name not a single one of the delegates had chosen to cross out.[51] Zhou Enlai received 1,509 votes and Lin Biao 1,508, both men choosing to cross out their own names on the ballot; Jiang Qing received 1,502 votes and subsequently launched a secret investigation to identify and punish those who had failed to endorse her.[52]

Those who failed to be nominated may have resented the slots accorded "older comrades." Knowing that probably nobody else would dare put their names forward, Mao selected a number of senior but unthreatening figures who had been in various degrees of disgrace even before the Cultural Revolution, men such as Zhang Wentian and Wang Jiaxiang, both of whom had played helpful roles at the start of Mao's rise to power in 1935. These senior figures also included what Mao himself referred to explicitly as his "opposition," ten members of the Eighth CC who became the subject of a carefully designed voter manipulation scheme that would give them a sufficient number of votes to make it onto the new CC, but not so many votes as to create an impression that their politics actually enjoyed widespread support. They included the father of the Red Army, Zhu De (809 votes); Chen Yun (815 votes); Deng Zihui (827 votes), who had been in charge of agriculture until he fell out with the Chairman over collectivization; and most of the key players in the February Countercurrent, including Marshals Chen Yi (867 votes), Ye Jianying (821 votes), Xu Xiangqian (808 votes), and Nie Rongzhen (838 votes), along with Vice Premiers Li Fuchun (886 votes) and Li Xiannian (922 votes).[53]

It appears that quite a few delegates doubted the wisdom of electing "old rightists" to the CC, but Mao overrode them. "What's wrong with having a few opponents in the party?" he asked. Turning to the first political commissar of the Chengdu Military Region, Lieutenant General Zhang Guohua, he added: "You must not assume that all those who oppose you are necessarily bad people."[54]

The dismal fate of the Red Guards and rebels after their glory days two years earlier was illustrated by their results in the elections to the CC and thereafter. In recognition of their roles in bringing down Li Jingquan, the powerful head of the Eighth CC's Southwest Region in the winter of 1966–67, the nationally famous husband and wife rebel pair Liu Jieting and Zhang Xiting from Sichuan were elected to the Central Committee, Liu (with 1,435 votes) to full membership and his wife (with 1,400 votes) to alternate membership.[55] Before the end of the year, however, their involvement in what they claimed was merely "resisting the revival of old ways," but which the PLA in southwest China insisted was tantamount to "resisting the center" got them thrown off the Sichuan RC, relieved of their positions on the CC, and within another year expelled from the CCP.[56] Nie Yuanzi of Peking University had by August 1968 become the target of what Mao at the congress called an excessively zealous hunt for class-alien elements.[57] Released from seven months of solitary confinement on the eve of the congress, she was elected a CC alternate (receiving 937 votes) not because, in her own words, she was "qualified," but as an "ornament" serving "a political need at the time"; in the wake of the congress, she first spent some time in a May 7 Cadre School in Jiangxi, and then laboring (cleaning toilets) and "repenting" on the Beida campus for a number of years.[58] Kuai Dafu never made it to the congress in the first place, much less onto the Central Committee; yet in one of his speeches, Mao mentioned his name, describing Kuai as someone whose "attitude" had benefited from having been "sent down."[59] In December 1968, Kuai had been assigned a job in a factory under the Ministry of Metallurgy, located in the Ningxia-Hui Autonomous Region on the western outskirts of the Great Wall, a traditional place of internal exile. In a private letter to Jiang Qing in the summer of 1969, he told her that as he gazed across a seemingly boundless expanse of "mountains upon mountains, rivers upon rivers," he realized what a "bosom friend" she had indeed been to him.[60]

The new Politburo, named, as was customary, at the First Plenum of the new CC immediately following the congress, was made up of twenty-one full and four alternate members, about the same size as the body it replaced. During discussions preceding the plenum, some CC members proposed that the Politburo be enlarged to about three dozen members, while others favored shrinking it to only a dozen members. Mao and a majority favored continuity on this issue.

The composition of the new Politburo reflected the factional divisions that had emerged under Mao during the Cultural Revolution. There were the survivors of the old guard who had been members of the outgoing Politburo: Zhou Enlai, Vice Premier Li Xiannian, and Ye Jianying, secretary general of the MAC, were the only ones who still wielded any real executive power; but Marshals Zhu De and Liu Bocheng and party elder Dong Biwu also belonged in this category. All but one had been members of the Politburo at least since the Eighth Congress in 1956, Ye having been co-opted at the Eleventh Plenum in 1966. Mao knew he could rely on the first three to run the country and the army loyally on his behalf, and on the second three as unquestioningly supportive votes if he ever needed them. Upon being reelected, Li Xiannian told the members of the CC: "I have committed many errors, and am not qualified to be a member of the Politburo," to which Mao responded: "Here is a comrade who's mended his ways. I am sure others who've committed errors will be able to as well."[61] Ye Jianying, aside from being an old associate of Zhou's, also commanded the gratitude of the Chairman, whose life he had saved during the Long March.[62] But most of the survivors who retained their seats on the Politburo were rarely summoned to the meetings where most of the decisions in the name of that body were made from then on. They were attended principally by members of the other factions, the CCRG, and the PLA. An emerging group, the beneficiaries of the Cultural Revolution, officials such as Wang Dongxing who had risen as their superiors had fallen, would not rise to power within the Politburo until after the CCP's Tenth Congress.

The Chairman was well aware that this new Politburo was a congeries of factions rather than the happy band of brothers that should have been the product of the Cultural Revolution. In one of his comments on unity at the congress, Mao asserted: "For the sake of victory, more people need to be united. It does not matter which mountaintop or which province they're from, or whether they're from the south or the north . . . Our contradictions are contradictions among the people, so why the tension? Always this faction, that faction"—a richly disingenuous comment from the man who more than anyone else had promoted the factionalization of the CCP over the previous three years.[63]

Party Institutions

The institutions enshrined in the new constitution conformed to the realities of intra-party life in the late 1960s: the CC Secretariat and the partywide network of control commissions, which had not functioned since late 1966, were abolished. Mao was taking steps to prevent the rebirth of a powerful central party machine that might constrain him in the way he alleged Liu, Deng, and their lieutenants had done before the Cultural Revolution.

The constitution also did not mention the CCRG, and Mao seems to have vacillated about what to do with it. In March, when discussing the Ninth Congress documents, he had told some of the CCRG members that since the Cultural Revolution was over, there was no need for the CCRG, which had been running it; the PSC would take its place.[64] Yet in the immediate aftermath of the congress, Mao may have reconsidered this decision. On May 29, 1969, in conversation with Zhou Enlai, he approved in principle a plan according to which the CCRG together with the CC's General Office, its Organization Department, and its International Liaison Department (the latter two organizations were at the time led by senior PLA officers) would be retained as organs of the party leadership, while its Propaganda Department, Investigation Department, Discipline Inspection Commission, and so forth would be "transferred down" to a lower level in the bureaucratic structure or merged with related PLA or State Council organs. On July 3, Mao reaffirmed his commitment to this plan "in principle."[65]

Nevertheless, the CCRG began winding down operations as the summer wore on. It continued to issue a slowly shrinking number of documents in its own name and to remain an addressee of documents sent to the central authorities concerning matters of a vaguely cultural nature, such as a provincial census, an archaeological discovery, or a patriotic health campaign. On September 12, 1969, it finally suspended operations altogether, and the powers hitherto vested in it were transferred to the newly elected Politburo.[66] Having rid the party of traitors and revisionists, Mao could try to restore it to normalcy, winding up the guerrilla organization he had spawned to attack it. But the purged party leaders were not to benefit, for behind the scenes the CCEG entered a period of significant expansion. On October 12, 1969, the Politburo formally approved the creation of yet another new ad hoc body directly under the CCEG to examine the "cases" of the seven senior PLA officers and CCRG members who had fallen from grace: Yang Chengwu, Yu Lijin, Fu Chongbi, Xiao Hua, Wang Li, Guan Feng, and Qi Benyu.[67] Insofar as the CCEG constituted the biggest inquisition in the history of the CCP after 1949, the Cultural Revolution was by no means over for Mao's onetime colleagues.

The remaining leaders of the CCRG who had not hitherto been Politburo members, Jiang Qing, Zhang Chunqiao, and Yao Wenyuan, now benefited in theory from an older and surer legitimacy than could have been derived from an ad hoc body; supposedly they should have had no need for an independent power base if they were going to be able to operate from the party's highest organ. But in practice, the new arrangements represented a setback for the CCRG leaders. True, they now occupied the seats of the high and the mighty whom they had done so much to help overthrow. But their new legitimacy trapped them within a power structure that they did not control, committed to a constructive agenda for which most of them, like Mao himself, had little aptitude or taste.

In the two years before the Ninth Congress, the forum of elite decision-making in the absence of Mao was usually a CCRG caucus, chaired by Zhou Enlai. After the Ninth Congress, the regular forum of formal elite consultation became the Politburo, or rather the Politburo's "everyday work meetings," the meetings from which most of the old guard were excluded.[68] On a few rare, if important, occasions, Mao or Lin took the chair, but the vast majority of the 142 Politburo meetings known to have been held from the Ninth Congress through the end of 1972, an average of about 40 a year, were chaired by Zhou.[69]

Many sessions dealt with aspects of China's rapidly developing ties with the West, notably with the United States and Japan, subjects unfamiliar to the CCRG leaders, but indicating trends surely worrisome to self-anointed guardians of the revolutionary flame. Sessions dealing with provincial problems no longer aimed at takeovers by leftist factions, but rather the extinction of factionalism and the creation of stable leadership groups. Moreover, officials working for the Politburo, unlike those under the CCRG, would be more likely to look to Zhou for instructions than, say, Chen Boda or Jiang Qing. Quite a few of the original shock troops of the CCRG had by now been dispersed to the countryside, to May 7 Cadre Schools or even to labor camps. For ex-leaders of the CCRG, this was hardly a brave new world, simply the old world redux, albeit reduced in size. Only Shanghai still represented what might have been. Under these difficult new circumstances, the alliance forged in the crucible of the Cultural Revolution began to crumble.

Division in the Revolutionary Ranks

The Politburo's "everyday work meetings" brought together the civilian and military Maoists. The civilians included the CCRG stalwarts Chen Boda, Kang Sheng, Zhang Chunqiao, Jiang Qing, and Yao Wenyuan, and their firm ally Vice Premier Xie Fuzhi, concurrently minister of public security, chairman of the Beijing RC, a member of the MAC management group, and head of the Third Office of the CCEG.[70] Xie had been made an alternate member of the Politburo at the Eleventh Plenum and was promoted to full membership at the Ninth Congress.

Chen Boda was the senior member of the civilian faction, moving up from the fifth- to the fourth-ranking position on the PSC as a result of the purge of Tao Zhu. But in real terms, Chen's position was by now not very powerful; when he retained his PSC position after his fiasco with the congress political report, Zhou Enlai even told him: "I did not expect your name to be on the list!"[71] Kang Sheng also retained his PSC position and seemed to have the ear of the Chairman, but beginning in late 1970 he gradually withdrew from active politics because of illness. Thus Jiang Qing emerged as the leader of the civilian Maoists, whose main power base was Shanghai, but who were also influential in Beijing, at least until the death of Xie Fuzhi in March 1972.

Whereas the civilian Maoists were ultimately dependent on the Chairman for their authority, the PLA Maoists were a tight-knit faction of five, loyal in the first instance to Lin Biao, and presumably expecting their fortunes to continue to rise with his. The faction coordinator was its least distinguished member, Lin Biao's wife, Ye Qun, a member of the MAC administration, but whose most influential formal position was that of director of her husband's private office. Second to her was the head of the MAC administration and PLA chief of staff, General Huang Yongsheng. Huang had taken part in the Autumn Harvest Uprising led by Mao in 1927 and had joined the Red Army and the CCP that same year. In 1969 his concurrent civilian posts included head of the Second Office of the CCEG and, until June, chairman of the Guangdong Revolutionary Committee. Curiously, at the Ninth Congress Mao claimed not to have got to know Huang until he moved to Beijing in 1968.[72] The three remaining members of Lin's faction were lieutenant generals (or equivalent) and deputy chiefs of staff, all of whom, like Huang, had been close to Lin since the 1930s: air force commander Wu Faxian; Li Zuopeng, the first political commissar of the navy; and Qiu Huizuo, director of the PLA General Logistics Department. (Two other generals, Chen Xilian and Xu Shiyou, who had been brought into the Politburo at the Ninth Congress, owed their preferment not to links with Lin Biao—they had none—but to the importance of their status as regional commanders.)

These civilian and military wings of the Cultural Revolution alliance had coexisted loosely since 1966, but they now began to solidify into cliques with diverging interests. The military wing, strongly entrenched at the center and in the provinces, could be satisfied with the status quo, and wait for their leader to inherit power. The civilian wing, on the other hand, had lost influence through much of the country, and had to fear exclusion from power when the military were no longer held in check by Mao.

Outwardly, cordial relations were maintained between the two wings, one centered on Maojiawan, the residence of Lin Biao and Ye Qun, the other centered on the Diaoyutai Guest House complex, the headquarters of Jiang Qing, Zhang Chunqiao, and Yao Wenyuan. Ye Qun tried to do favors for Jiang Qing, presenting her now and then with gifts that ranged from an imported ionizer meant to help her with her insomnia to watermelons coming "from Lin Biao personally." Jiang Qing in turn made almost daily inquiries over the telephone about Lin Biao's health and engaged in polite chitchat. At the same time, her paranoia left her constantly on guard: in January 1969 she had told her staff that she suspected her residence in villa No. 11 was being bugged, and she ordered a move lock, stock, and barrel to villa No. 10. Her personal secretary later insisted that Jiang had suspected Ye Qun of doing the bugging.[73] At the combined post–Cultural Revolutionary trial of the "Lin Biao–Jiang Qing counterrevolutionary clique," Jiang Qing expressed great indignation that the two "wings" were being thus lumped together: "It's wrong," she insisted, maintaining that "Lin Biao had one clique, which included Chen Boda. I myself, Kang *lao*, Zhang, Yao, and Wang were another one . . . Lin Biao was the head of theirs, but I wasn't the head of ours; Chairman Mao was."[74]

Chen Boda, hitherto Jiang Qing's nominal boss, a bookish man with a virtually incomprehensible Fujian accent, had always seemed an unlikely, uncharismatic leader for the CCRG, even though he had ghostwritten or edited some of Mao's most revolutionary works. His failure with the report to the Ninth Congress suggested that even his grip on theory, or at least on the current cast of Mao's mind, was slipping. Chen became unhappy with Jiang Qing, feeling thrust aside in favor of Kang Sheng.[75] In the second half of 1969, deprived of his CCRG power base and increasingly alienated from his former colleagues, he apparently took the fateful decision to hitch his wagon to the rising star Lin Biao and, like Lin's principal generals, was increasingly seen at Maojiawan (a fact that they all tried to keep concealed from the Diaoyutai clique).[76] One day Mao would die, and Lin was designated to succeed him; Chen could legitimately have harbored the ambition of being the indispensable man, principal theorist to the leader of China, whoever he might be.

It must have seemed a good idea at the time, given that PLA officers emerged at the Ninth Congress as the major constituency within the upper ranks of the CCP, having earlier taken the leading positions in an overwhelming majority of provincial revolutionary committees. By the end of the lengthy and bitterly contested post-congress process of forming provincial party committees in August 1971, the PLA would supply twenty-two of the twenty-nine first secretaries and the absolute majority of cadres running provincial party bodies.[77] The radical constituency, on the other hand, had been eviscerated, while surviving old cadres were still in shock and had to walk warily.

Whatever Lin Biao's personal ambitions, objectively the prospect was that if he became party Chairman, the army would effectively command the party rather than vice versa as Mao had always insisted.[78] Lin's long years of apparent illness meant that he had no constituency outside the PLA, and he would almost certainly have had to rely upon his clique of senior generals in the center and PLA first secretaries in the provinces; a vigorous campaign to send the PLA back to its barracks, such as Mao and later Deng Xiaoping initiated, would have been against his interests. Such a reversal of the Chairman's principles on the party-army relationship would need to be justified by ideological legerdemain, and Chen Boda may have seen himself as just the man to provide it.

But Chen's transfer of allegiance to Lin proved to be a colossal mistake. Within eighteen months, Chen would be purged. Less than a year later, Lin himself would be dead and disgraced as a traitor.

The "One Strike, Three Anti" Campaign

Even while the Ninth Congress was in session and delegates were making their pledges to "unite to win still greater victories," the situation outside Beijing remained highly volatile. Despite the "cleansing of the class ranks," talk of a "restoration of order" remained premature; anarchy was still prevalent in many parts of China, including parts of the industrial heartland, where armed struggles between long officially disbanded "organizations of the revolutionary masses" continued to flare up. In the coal fields of Henan, Shandong, Shanxi, Inner Mongolia, Yunnan, Guizhou, and Sichuan, production was down for reasons that Zhou Enlai suspected had far more to do with "factionalism" than with anything else. In the transport sector, more than 2,000 railway carriages were said to have been damaged in "accidents," a claim that Zhou found utterly inexplicable and refused to believe. In one of the biggest steel plants in all of northern China, in Baotou, Inner Mongolia, the local leadership blamed a total halt in production for almost two weeks on railway stoppages, but Zhou's alternative sources of information suggested that "serious anarchy within the plant itself" was to blame.[79] A Chinese historian later summed up the situation, saying that neither the political nor the economic conditions in China in 1969 were such that a return to "normal" productivity was possible. With the sole exception of crude oil, no item in the plan for the national economy in 1969 met the assigned target.[80]

By the end of 1969, it must have appeared evident to the central leadership that radical measures were again necessary to improve the situation. And so, just in time for the Spring Festival holiday in February 1970, it launched yet another brutal movement, which quickly became known as the "One Strike, Three Anti" *(yi da san fan)* campaign. The "strike" referred to a nationwide crackdown on "counterrevolutionary destructive activities" ordered in *Zhongfa* [1970] 3, drawn up under Zhou Enlai's supervision and issued with Mao's express approval ("Act accordingly!") on January 31.[81] *Zhongfa* [1970] 3 called on local leaderships all over China to

> resolutely put down those active counterrevolutionary elements who collude with the enemy and betray the nation, conspire to revolt, gather military intelligence, steal state secrets, commit murder and physical assault, commit arson and poison people, counterattack to settle old scores, viciously slander the party and the socialist system, plunder state property, and disrupt the social order . . . Resolutely execute those counterrevolutionary elements who are swollen with arrogance after having committed countless heinous crimes and against whom popular indignation is so great that nothing save execution will serve to calm it.[82]

The targets of the "Three Anti" were specified in *Zhongfa* [1970] 5 and 6, issued on February 5. The first target was labeled "graft and embezzlement," but was defined in such a way as to include all forms of unauthorized economic activities. For instance, it explicitly banned "exchange of goods for goods in the name of 'cooperation.'" The second target was "profiteering."[83] The third target, discussed in detail in *Zhongfa* [1970] 6, was "extravagance and waste." Examples of what was regarded as such and explicitly banned included "erecting, expanding, or rebuilding office buildings, large halls, and guest houses . . . Using public funds to purchase sofas, carpets, spring beds, electric refrigerators, and other similar high-grade consumer goods . . . Using public funds to give dinners or send gifts, watch plays or movies." To come to terms with the "Three Anti" targets, the CCP center called for a nationwide all-out "high tide of large-scale denunciations, exposures, condemnations, and sorting out" and—"with the power of a thunderbolt and the speed of lightning"—the "mobilization of the masses in struggle."[84]

Needless to say, what local authorities came to regard as appropriate targets of the "Three Anti" did not always conform to the vaguely formulated intentions of the CCP center. Still, the go-ahead had been given for what was to become one of the most severe crackdowns on anything and everything regarded at the local level as vaguely "counterrevolutionary" in intent or nature. Whether or not they had contributed to the anarchy that Zhou Enlai had wanted to overcome was beside the point. In Yinchuan, the capital of the Muslim Autonomous Region of Ningxia, a dozen or so "sent-down" university graduates who called themselves the "Communist Self-Study University" were arrested at the beginning of 1970 and accused of having engaged in "counterrevolutionary" activities while merely pretending to be studying Marxism-Leninism. Three of them were sentenced to death and executed on August 29, 1970: one of them for having, among other things, desecrated a copy of the *Quotations from Chairman Mao* by writing "Crap!" in the margin of Lin Biao's preface.[85] In Hunan, in a May 7 Cadre School run by the State Science and Technology Commission, an outspoken cadre named Yu Ruomu was branded an "active counterrevolutionary element," put in solitary confinement, subjected to public abuse at "struggle rallies," expelled from the CCP, and dismissed from all her posts for having availed herself of the opportunity provided by the "Three Anti" to put up two highly inflammatory big-character posters, the first titled "The lid has to come off to expose extravagance, waste, and spending without restraint—Jiang Qing is the biggest exploiter and parasite in the party," the second, "The lid covering up extravagance and waste has to come off—is Jiang Qing a Marxist-Leninist or a revisionist element?" Had Yu's husband not been Chen Yun, she would almost certainly have met an even worse fate.[86]

Still, it would probably be a mistake to assume that almost all or even necessarily a majority of the people who became the targets of the "One Strike, Three Anti" were inquisitive young students with critical minds or politically outspoken cadres. In the Zhabei district of Shanghai, a mere 6 percent of the total number of cases dealt with in the campaign concerned "political problems"; the absolute majority involved financial matters.[87] The targets also included numerous ordinary criminals or offenders, as the record from many "mass sentencing rallies" shows.[88] And the contemporary record of what ordinary people understood the "One Strike, Three Anti" campaign to be about suggests that it was precisely the hope of reestablishing some familiar sense of "law and order" and of just possibly giving "good people" a chance to once again get the upper hand over "bad people" that made it attractive. Struggling to express themselves in the politically appropriate way, the elderly residents of one residential area in central Beijing had this to say about the campaign in the early autumn of 1970:

> The "One Strike, Three Anti" has to be done. A lot of foreign guests visit China, our Chairman Mao is the leader of the peoples of the world, the situation in China is excellent, but there are still bad people. Protection has to be done well, we cannot let bad people create trouble [*daoluan*] . . . The "One Strike, Three Anti" is Chairman Mao's instruction, and we have to go deep and comb carefully. When I think back to the Great Cultural Revolution, back

then, to the number of people who were just creating trouble, I think, factional battles just show that there are class enemies creating trouble, treating good people like enemies . . . Good people are not afraid of bad people. The bad people, the people who instigate trouble, have to be identified. We trust in the party, trust in the masses. The party supports us: what are we afraid of?[89]

In 1982, even someone as deeply involved in the post-Mao negation of every-thing the Cultural Revolution stood for as Mao's onetime secretary, Hu Qiaomu, was prepared to describe the "One Strike, Three Anti" campaign in positive terms, as one that actually had dealt a blow to some "real enemies" and not just what he called "phoney" ones.[90]

In China's cities, the crackdowns on "bad people" or "real enemies" became known as "red typhoons." In Shanghai, with Wang Hongwen in charge of run-ning the campaign, red typhoons blew on average every two months in the early 1970s. Held up as models for emulation nationwide, the Shanghai typhoons in-volved the massive mobilization, usually on the eve of major holidays or before visits by foreigners, of anything from a few tens of thousands to hundreds of thousands of militia, police, and activists in gigantic preemptive raids through-out one or more city districts, sometimes the entire city. "The targets of these crackdowns can only be enemies of the people or serious criminal offenders," a visiting delegation from Yunnan was told as it prepared to emulate the "progres-sive experiences" of Shanghai. A list of concrete cases offered to the delegation included, in addition to those of obvious murderers, thieves, rapists, and the like, those of "criminals who sabotage the policy of sending urban youths up to the mountains and down to the countryside."[91] It was, however, highly doubtful whether all who were classified as such really satisfied the criteria of "enemies of the people." With a variety of purely linguistic means, those who blew the red typhoons were capable of upgrading almost anything to a "serious crime." The label "underground," for example, was attached with impunity to any form of vaguely organized activity occurring in the vast gray zone that separated the ex-pressly state-encouraged from the decidedly illegal. It gave rise to designations such as "underground library," "underground concert," "underground studio," and "underground marriage partner introductory service." Anything that in-volved more than one or two people might be designated a "gang." Actual exam-ples from Shanghai include the "Topple-the-New-Regime Gang," "Gang of Gamblers," and "Gang of Hooligans and Ruffians."[92]

The dossiers compiled on the activities of some of these gangs make for fascinating reading and open a rare window on a seamier side of life at the height of the Cultural Revolution. Here the working class is no longer represented by labor heroes or by activists in the study of Mao Zedong Thought, and days and nights are certainly not spent debating how best to "grasp revolution, promote production." A flavor of a life in the Cultural Revolution miles removed from the propaganda filling the pages of *China Pictorial* and *China Reconstructs* comes across in the following extract from a confession by a member of the Nanjing Motorized Tricycle Repair and Assembly Plant's "Youth Choir," a gang led by a twenty-seven-year-old welder charged with counterrevolution in the "One Strike, Three Anti" campaign:

> When the men in our counterrevolutionary group—the "Youth Choir"—got together, either we talked about how to give the factory leadership a hard time or we simply talked about the most vulgar things . . . Liu XX used to spend all his spare time out by the entrance to the female workers' lavatory, and he would say things like: "We're paid less because we work in the rear of the plant, but each day we get to see a lot of women. Women who look like this; women who look like that; this place has really good *fengshui!*" . . . When he had night duty, he would sometimes ask me not to return home but to keep him company and sleep in the plant. In the morning he would wake up, pull away the quilt, point at his hard-on, and say: "What do you think? Think those women like my tool? None of you has one as big as mine!" I would say: "What's the point of having a big one? You'll just scare them off!" Sometimes when I wasn't paying attention he would crawl on top of me from behind. Each time, when I finally managed to shake him off, I would swear at him: "You horny bastard!" Now and then he would say things like: "Awgh! Life is really boring nowadays. What I want is for a woman to come around every morning for me to poke. I heard that in the past, in Shanghai, you could pay someone to supply you with women to look at and enjoy. They would strike all kinds of poses. Now that's all gone."[93]

The members of the Youth Choir were alleged to have committed a whole range of "counterrevolutionary" offenses, including listening to "enemy" (that is, Nationalist) radio broadcasts and, by talking about what they had heard, "singing the praises of the Soviet revisionists and the U.S. imperialists." So, for example, they had claimed that "the fighting at Damansky Island just goes on and on; the Soviet revisionists could launch a missile from Mongolia that would hit Nanjing in twenty-three minutes" and "Our radar is no good: it doesn't detect the incoming U.S. imperialist and Soviet revisionist aircraft."[94] Nothing is known about their ultimate fate, but in the tense political climate prevailing at the time the members of the Youth Choir may well have been treated with extreme prejudice for their hooliganism and for making remarks like these.

In cases in which the crackdown on graft, embezzlement, profiteering, extravagance, and waste involved the recovery of monies and other valuables, central regulations not surprisingly stipulated that they be handed over to the state or the collective. In distant areas of rural China, these regulations were not always adhered to, or so it would seem from a carefully worded Notification issued by the Guizhou RC some nine months into the "One Strike, Three Anti" campaign. The final passage read: "In rural communes and brigades, excess wealth found to have been concealed by landlord and rich peasant elements (including property that ought to be confiscated from landlords who previously escaped being classified as such) should be used for common accumulation and development of the economy and should no longer be distributed to the poor and lower-middle peasants."[95]

In urban Beijing, the "One Strike, Three Anti" campaign lasted until the end of 1970, when the municipal revolutionary committee reported the "ferreting out" of some 5,757 "renegades, special agents, counterrevolutionaries, and other bad elements" from among the legal and illegal permanent and temporary residents of the city; the solution of some 3,138 "counterrevolutionary and fairly major criminal cases"; and the identification of more than 6,200 cases of alleged graft, embezzlement, or profiteering.[96] In most other parts of China, including Shanghai, the campaign lasted significantly longer, with reports on its "successful conclusion" not reaching the central authorities until 1972 or 1973. In January 1972, the Heilongjiang Revolutionary Committee ascribed the exposure "on the provincial finance and trade front" of 3,173 "political cases" and 37,462 "economic cases" to the successful implementation of the "One Strike, Three Anti" campaign.[97] That same month, the authorities in Guangzhou municipality announced that the campaign had made it possible to crack 2,168 "major cases" and to identify 147 "counterrevolutionary cliques."[98] In Baoding municipality, Hebei province, the campaign lasted until December 1972, high points of intensity occurring during seven consecutive public sentencing rallies at which 17 people were executed and another 1,325 given punishments ranging in severity from imprisonment to the unspecific "resolution of a contradiction between the enemy and us as if it were a contradiction among the people."[99] In Shanghai, too, the campaign began to wind down at the end of 1972. In the ten rural counties surrounding the city, 64,000 people were "dragged out and struggled." Among these were 520 "other-than-normal deaths."[100]

There are no known estimates of the human toll of the "One Strike, Three Anti" as a whole. The only figure made available by the CCP concerns the first ten months of the campaign: the number of people said to have been arrested as "counterrevolutionaries" and the like by the end of November 1970 exceeded 284,800.[101] But although the campaign lasted far longer in many parts of China, by November 1970 Mao was busy with a more important and by now very familiar task: ferreting out "counterrevolutionaries" within the top ranks of the party.

18

War Scares

To the rank-and-file delegates to the Ninth Congress, Lin Biao must have seemed the ideal choice as a successor.[1] Most important, he had been handpicked by Mao, and who better to stand beside the Chairman than one of the CCP's greatest generals at a time when China was surrounded by hostile superpowers? Indeed, the congress met at a time when war with the Soviet Union seemed a real possibility.

The previous year, Soviet-style revisionism, the cardinal sin that the Cultural Revolution was designed to extirpate in China, took an alarming new turn. In the summer of 1968, the Soviet Union invaded its satellite Czechoslovakia in order to eliminate *its* revisionism, the "communism with a human face" introduced by First Secretary Alexander Dubček and his colleagues. The overthrow of the Dubček regime had subsequently been justified by the "Brezhnev doctrine," which held that Moscow had a right to dispose of any government that betrayed Communist principles. While Beijing in the throes of Cultural Revolution was hardly sympathetic to the "Prague spring," the implications of the Brezhnev doctrine were deeply unsettling for a Chinese regime that Moscow manifestly detested. The Chinese dubbed the Soviet actions and doctrine "social imperialism."[2] As Zhou Enlai later put it to a Vietcong delegation, "This has created a precedent that allows a socialist country to intervene in another socialist country's affairs."[3]

Simultaneously, conventional "imperialism" was a potential threat on China's southern border. Mao had launched the Cultural Revolution on the assumption that the Vietnam War would not spill over into China at a time of internal upheaval.[4] Even so, in the mid-1960s he had ordered the transfer of vital industries to the far interior, the so-called Third Front,[5] a massively expensive dislocation of the economy—over 200 billion yuan according to a later Chinese estimate[6]—and at a CC work conference in the autumn of 1965, national defense, including further development of the Third Front, was laid down as the first priority of the third FYP (1966–1970).[7] The Cultural Revolution soon exacerbated the economic upheaval caused by the Third Front. It also distracted the political and military leaderships from economic and defense issues. Fortunately for them, the process of forming provincial revolutionary committees was completed in September 1968, and while the *People's Daily's* proclamation of this as a great victory did not mark the end of upheavals, the relatively greater stability enabled Mao and his colleagues to ponder the threatening international environment.

Their initial response was primarily rhetorical, but a major clash on Zhenbao/ Damansky Island, on the Ussuri River boundary with the Soviet Union, in March 1969, injected urgency into their planning. As compared with the first half of the 1960s, the number of Sino-Soviet border clashes had increased 150 percent from late 1964 through March 1969. But the Zhenbao Island incident was very different in nature from earlier clashes, being the occasion for a massive escalation in the Soviet use of firepower. According to a former CIA director, American satellite photographs revealed that "the Chinese side of the [Ussuri] river was so pockmarked by Soviet artillery that it looked like a 'moonscape.'"[8] Whoever initiated the incident, the Chinese came off considerably the worse.

The Ussuri River Incident

Hitherto available contemporary Chinese accounts of the clashes in March 1969 were all of the sort intended for widespread public and foreign consumption. These accounts asserted that Soviet forces "recently . . . made successive armed intrusions into our territory Zhenbao Island" and that, "driven beyond the limits of forbearance," Chinese frontier guards "fought back in self-defense, dealing the aggressors well-deserved blows and triumphantly safeguarding our sacred territory."[9] Soviet sources, on the other hand, always insisted that the fighting began with a Chinese ambush. In the 1990s, Chinese historians of the Cold War began to make subtle changes in the way they described the incidents, admitting implicitly that there was a problem with the original Chinese version. By 2001, something akin to a consensus had begun to emerge among Russian and Chinese scholars, that the fighting on the Ussuri in March 1969 had in fact been instigated by the Chinese.[10]

That the version of events released by the Chinese for public consumption in 1969 was part of a major (and quite successful) disinformation strategy is borne out by a previously unavailable firsthand account from a PLA officer delivered to a restricted high-level audience in the wake of the Ninth Party Congress in April 1969.[11] In this account, the speaker used language more or less identical with that employed by Chinese historians today but scrupulously avoided in Chinese propaganda at the time: he described the event on March 2, 1969, as a Chinese ambush (*maifu*). He began by describing the run-up, in which the Soviets had been caught "clandestinely moving the border markers in our direction." The Chinese side had promptly informed the Soviets that if they moved the border posts "ten meters in our direction," they would be told to dig them up again, move them back "thirty meters," and position them well inside the border on the Soviet side. On March 2, an armed Soviet contingent sixty-one strong had been ambushed and "totally annihilated" after entering Chinese territory. Two severely wounded Soviet soldiers who survived the ambush were later "jolted to death" (*diansi*) by infuriated Chinese militiamen who, one infers from the context, were meant to carry them away from the scene of the fighting to receive medical treatment.[12] According to a contemporary secret Soviet report,

> During the provocation, the Chinese military committed incredibly brutal and cruel acts against the wounded Soviet border guards. Based on the on-site inspection and the expert knowledge of the medical commission which examined the bodies of the dead Soviet border guards, it can be stated that the wounded were shot by the Chinese from close range [and/or] stabbed with bayonets and knives. The faces of some of the casualties were distorted beyond recognition; others had their uniforms and boots taken off by the Chinese.[13]

On March 15, in what the Chinese account describes as a "retaliatory attack" (*baofu*) by the Soviet Union, the Soviet side again entered Chinese territory with a battalion. Initial PLA plans to lure the enemy deeper were prematurely upset when an inexperienced young PLA conscript lying in ambush lost his nerve: "He asked repeatedly for permission to fire, which his commanding officer would not give him. He then recited [Mao's words] 'Erroneous leadership must not be obeyed' and opened fire of his own accord."[14] As a result, so the account had it, the battle that ensued resulted in casualties on both sides and no clear victory for either the Soviets or the Chinese. On March 17, a third and final battle took place, a battle that the speaker acknowledged "we have never reported publicly."[15] In this final "even bigger retaliatory attack," the Soviet side deployed a new kind of battle tank previously unknown to the Chinese and two battalions in armored personnel carriers under the command of a lieutenant colonel. It was presumably the PLA's experience in this third clash that led Zhou shortly thereafter to state that it was "very important" to have more anti-tank weapons, as well as anti-aircraft guns.

However, the speaker may have been carried away in calculating the size of the Soviet force, which seems too large in proportion to the size of the island—only about a square kilometer. According to a later Chinese account, on March 17 the Russians deployed only three tanks and 100 infantry; it was probably the "fierce" artillery barrage under whose shelter the Soviet forces advanced that caused the most grief to the Chinese forces.[16] The Chinese estimated the total number of Soviet casualties (no Chinese casualty figures are provided) in the three clashes as "in the hundreds." According to Zhou Enlai, the Soviets lost 36 dead in the first clash and 203 in the second, but he did not mention the third, nor did he give Chinese casualties. According to a recent Russian account, 58 Soviet soldiers were killed on March 2 and March 15.[17] The Chinese claimed to have taken "more than 60 prisoners of war."[18]

If the Chinese side indeed instigated the fighting, to what end? And precisely at what level in the chain of command was it instigated? According to one authoritative Chinese account, in response to an incident on Qiliqin Island in January 1968 the MAC instructed the Shenyang MR to prepare to retaliate strongly on any future occasion. But though Shenyang drew up plans, and stationed some crack troops near Qiliqin Island, the border quieted down, apparently because the Soviets were too busy in Eastern Europe, handling the overthrow of the Dubček government in Czechoslovakia.

Serious incidents on Zhenbao Island on December 28, 1968, and January 23, 1969, led the Heilongjiang Military District (part of the Shenyang MR), responsive to the year-old order from the MAC, to propose giving the Soviets a strong lesson if they came again with military force. The Heilongjiang MD's proposal was agreed to by the Shenyang MR, and then transmitted to Beijing. After further serious incidents on the island in February, General Headquarters and the Foreign Ministry agreed to the Heilongjiang plan on February 19, and, after it was endorsed by the MAC, and at some point probably by Mao himself,[19] Shenyang MR prepared for battle. Three reconnaissance companies, numbering about 200–330 men, were selected from each of three armies and given special training. These were the troops who were involved in the clashes on March 2 and March 15. The latter battle was in fact directed from Beijing, where the MR commander, General Chen Xilian, had gone to participate in the preparations for the Ninth Congress. General Headquarters set up a special room in the

PLA run Capital West Hotel and installed a direct telephone line so that Chen could communicate directly with the front line. Vice Foreign Minister Qiao Guanhua was charged with monitoring the international dimensions, and was in touch with Zhou Enlai.

On March 15, the Soviets brought several dozen vehicles and about a dozen tanks onto the tiny island. There were no Chinese troops stationed on Zhenbao Island at this point, but Chinese artillery had been carefully placed, and, after Chen Xilian got Zhou Enlai's permission, it laid down a tremendous barrage for half an hour, knocking out all the Soviet vehicles. The Soviets did not send in reinforcements but retaliated with artillery fire. On March 17, the Soviets apparently initiated the third battle. If the Chinese had hoped that their first two ambushes would teach Moscow a lesson, Beijing now learned that such border clashes could escalate in a devastating manner. This episode should have prompted Mao to start rethinking how best to preserve China's security.

For now, the clashes gave the Chairman and his colleagues the opportunity to use patriotic fervor to mobilize the people. Speaking in the final week of March 1969 at a high-level meeting called to set the agenda for the Ninth Party Congress, Zhou Enlai made a direct connection between the fighting on the Ussuri River and the domestic troubles facing the central leadership in the Cultural Revolution:

> Chairman Mao says: "Faced with a formidable foe, we had better get mobilized." The enemy's provocations allow us to mobilize the people. Even though people hold this viewpoint or that viewpoint in the Great Cultural Revolution, or have split into different factions, or in some cases haven't managed to unite yet (and there are still bad people around), under these circumstances one has to prepare for the worst . . . and when the worst is exposed, it serves the dictatorship of the proletariat even better.[20]

As leaked by Zhou, Mao's comment on the need to "get mobilized" dated from a briefing on the fighting on March 15, 1969. On that occasion, of course, the context had not been the Cultural Revolution but a purely military one.[21]

The disinformation campaign launched after the first ambush began with a joint *People's Daily* and *Liberation Army Daily* editorial, finalized and ratified for publication by Zhou Enlai on March 4, titled "Down with the New Czars!"[22] It is clear that the civilian and military leadership in Beijing played the "external threat" card domestically for all it was worth over the weeks and months that followed, not just in the media aimed at the "broad revolutionary masses," but also in closed communications aimed at exerting pressure on provincial revolutionary committees and PLA units across the country. Two cases in point were Inner Mongolia and Guizhou, where strongly worded orders from the central authorities demanding an end to factional infighting and a "rectification" of disruptive local policies were given an added dimension of urgency by calls for "unity in the face of the common enemy."[23]

As the border clashes continued, with a very serious one occurring in Xinjiang on August 13, the Chinese learned of rumors emerging from Eastern Europe that Moscow was consulting its allies about a possible "surgical strike" against Chinese nuclear weapons sites. Since the views of the Soviet satellites were hardly likely to determine Soviet behavior, it is more likely that the rumors were put about by Moscow as part of its war of nerves against Beijing, and in an effort to elicit Western attitudes. Washington was in fact sounded out by Moscow.[24] Earlier, the new Nixon administration had hinted to the Soviets that it would maintain benevolent neutrality in a Sino-Soviet clash in return for Soviet help in restraining North Vietnam. But by mid-1969, Nixon and Kissinger had concluded that the Soviets would not or could not influence the North Vietnamese leadership, and in a 180-degree turnaround Washington now indicated to Moscow that it would regard an attack on China as a threat to peace.[25]

However, a September 1969 visit to Hanoi by Soviet premier Alexei Kosygin for the memorial service of Ho Chi Minh provided the opportunity for a top-level Sino-Soviet meeting to discuss the border in an effort to defuse the immediate danger of another major clash. According to Chinese sources, the meeting was suggested by a member of Kosygin's entourage and agreed to by Mao on condition that it take place at the Beijing airport and be presented as an unofficial stopover. By the time the Chinese reply reached Hanoi, Kosygin was already in the air headed for Moscow, but he turned his plane back and met Zhou at the airport on September 11. Border talks were agreed to.[26] But the prospect of talks did not dispel the strong perception of threat to the country's northern borders that the Chinese leadership had felt for much of 1969.[27]

In March 1969, Mao twice warned of the need to prepare for war in case the Soviet Union attacked. The political report to the Ninth Congress in April discussed the same danger in more general terms. On August 27, learning of the rumors circulating in Eastern Europe about a Soviet surgical strike, the Chinese established a People's Air Defense Small Group under Zhou to organize the dispersal of the urban population and the resiting of factories, and to encourage workers and urban residents, relying on their own efforts, to build shelters— Shanghai became a "huge construction site, with clouds of dust in the air and piles of dirt along every road"[28]—and stockpile grain and other wartime necessities. The following day military units and citizens in Xinjiang were put on high alert.[29]

On September 16 the CCP Politburo met to discuss the implications of the Zhou-Kosygin meeting and concluded that the Russians were laying down a smoke screen. The following day, Mao signaled his concern by adding an item to the formal injunctions that would be issued in honor of the PRC's forthcoming twentieth anniversary: "The peoples of the whole world should unite to oppose any aggressive war launched by imperialism or social imperialism, and especially oppose aggressive war using nuclear weapons."[30] The Politburo met again on September 18 and 22 to continue discussing the possibility of war. Kosygin's visit was compared to the Japanese ambassadorial negotiations with the United States on the eve of Pearl Harbor, that is, designed to lull suspicion. Taken as indicative of Soviet intentions were a number of straws in the wind: Kosygin had failed to guarantee that the Soviet Union would not launch a nuclear attack on China; he had been met at the Moscow airport only by low-ranking officials, an indication that the Soviet leadership did not approve of his peace gesture to Beijing; officials of the Soviet foreign and defense ministries were issuing threatening statements. Mao, who seems to have been chairing the meetings, subscribed to these views, and the Politburo agreed on a series of emergency measures preparing for war. Zhou notified the Foreign Ministry and other relevant units to draft plans for the dispersal of secret files and archives, and to mobilize their personnel. On September 22, he summoned an all-PLA emergency strategic work conference and told the meeting: "The international situation is tense. We must be prepared to fight a war. Preparing for war is the new strategic plan. We must really make sure that preparedness averts danger."[31]

From September 25 to September 27, the MAC held a war-fighting conference, attended by the commanders, political commissars, and other senior officers from the military regions, as well as General Headquarters staff, to consider strengthening combat readiness in the north, northeast, and northwest. In a closing speech, Lin Biao instructed the conference on its central duty: "Examine everything, investigate everything from the viewpoint of waging war."[32] On September 27, Mao received military commanders.[33] The central PLA leaders in the Politburo loyal to Lin Biao and running the MAC—Chief of Staff Huang Yongsheng, air force commander Wu Faxian, navy commissar Li

Zuopeng, logistics chief Qiu Huizuo, and Lin's wife, Ye Qun—agreed with the Chairman's ominous assessment, which had the additional benefit of providing a justification for the newly prominent role of PLA officers at the apex of the political system.

The B Team Reports

Yet an alternative, less gloomy assessment by senior military figures was available to the Chairman. On February 19, 1969, Mao had appointed four marshals who doubled as vice premiers—Chen Yi, Xu Xiangqian, Nie Rongzhen, and Ye Jianying—to meet as a group to do research on international relations. Whose idea it was to set up this team of men who had been in semidisgrace since the February Countercurrent in 1967 was unspecified, but Zhou implied it was Mao's.[34] At first glance, it might seem like a way of second-guessing the premier and the Ministry of Foreign Affairs, but in fact Zhou was the beneficiary. These were comrades with whom he had worked closely over the years, a team of marshals who outranked the generals of Lin Biao's clique, and who had been told by Mao not to be hidebound in their thinking.

At first the four marshals seem not to have taken their duties very seriously; perhaps they regarded it as make-work for has-beens, since they were well aware that foreign policy decisions were made by Mao and executed by Zhou. When Zhou received their first report in early June, the premier admonished them not to regard their assignment lightly and to think hard about foreign and defense policy, since he did not have time to do so. According to Zhou, Mao believed that the objective situation was changing rapidly and that China's leaders' subjective understanding had to keep up with it. Zhou delegated two senior Foreign Ministry officials to help Chen Yi and his colleagues and made sure they got relevant documentation.[35] Thus the premier had control of the materials and advice given to the four marshals, and he instructed Chen Yi that all reports should go to him before being passed on to the Chairman.

Spurred on by Zhou's strictures, from early June to mid-September the marshals met sixteen times for a total of almost fifty hours. They sent Zhou a second report on July 11 and a final one on September 17. The group focused on two questions: Which was the main enemy, the United States or the Soviet Union? Was war indeed likely? The Chen Yi team reached far more sanguine conclusions than currently prevailed in the Politburo, downplaying the danger of attack from either the Soviet Union or the United States. Both countries mouthed anti-Chinese rhetoric, but neither wanted to attack; Europe remained the main focus of Soviet-American rivalry. Despite the Zhenbao Island incident, the Soviet Union feared the political and diplomatic consequences of aggression against China. The marshals emphasized the importance of delaying any possibility of hostilities while China improved its economic, military, political, and diplomatic position.[36] In a personal, "unconventional" comment made orally to Zhou after the second report, Chen Yi suggested that since ten years of Warsaw talks had produced nothing, perhaps it was necessary for the United States and China to meet at the ministerial level or even higher, an indication that he considered the Americans a lesser threat. Here was an early hint of how China might escape from the circle of superpower hostility.

Defense Measures

For the moment, however, Mao ignored this analysis, and pessimism prevailed. In June 1969, just as the Chen Yi group was beginning its deliberations, Chief of Staff Huang Yongsheng and his colleagues held two conferences to consider the threat from the north, and Mao ignored the group's final report when the Politburo met in mid-September; indeed, Politburo members may not have known about the Chen Yi group's deliberations. Defense spending escalated, up by 34 percent from the 1968 figure, followed by increases of 15 percent in 1970 and 16 percent in 1971, greatly distorting the economy.[37]

Overestimates of the external threat were paralleled by overoptimism about domestic economic possibilities, with Mao again fantasizing about massive increases in industrial and agricultural production. The significant increases in output that did occur were achieved at the expense of economic balance; one Chinese historian has characterized 1970–71 as two years of blind advance, the term also used to describe the Great Leap Forward. As Mao's strategic answer to external aggression, the Third Front in the western provinces benefited from a second high tide of investment, absorbing over 55 percent of the total in 1970, while in a new wrinkle in strategic thinking, a planning conference in early 1970 split the country into ten cooperative zones and ordered each to establish independent war industries, a move that led to GLF-type decentralization, duplication, and confusion.[38]

In the meanwhile, anarchy still prevailed in some provinces—notably Shanxi, Henan, Jiangsu, and Hubei; the calls for unity at the Ninth Congress had failed to halt internecine struggles, often with weapons. In Shanxi, for example, adopting the slogan "Seize political power by military means!," rebel organizations disrupted rail lines, attacked trains, seized banks and warehouses, built their own strongholds, forced workers to strike, and incited peasants to attack cities. To suppress this kind of behavior so that provinces could focus on defense preparations, the center issued a proclamation—*Zhongfa* [1969] 41—on July 23 that proved only partially effective, followed by *Zhongfa* [1969] 55 on August 28—after the Sino-Soviet clash in Xinjiang on August 13—commanding rival factions and leftist guerrilla groups to stop fighting immediately.[39]

As a result, in the last quarter of 1969 the provinces began to follow up on Zhou Enlai's instructions, exhorting their citizens to be ready for war, set up command posts, construct air-raid shelters, organize militias, and evacuate colleges and middle schools from the cities.[40]

Lin Biao's First Order

In this crisis atmosphere, Lin Biao, who for much of the Cultural Revolution had sequestered himself in his residence, inspected defenses in and around the capital. After a visit to a Beijing airfield on September 30, he ordered the immediate dispersal of aircraft at bases in the Beijing area, the placing of obstructions on runways, and the provision of weapons to remaining personnel in case of paratroop attacks. At this time the leadership feared that the Soviets would take advantage of China's October 1 National Day celebrations to launch a surprise attack as they had done against Czechoslovakia. Shortly after that danger point was passed, Lin flew to inspect other bases in Shanxi and Hebei. He ordered Chief of Staff Huang Yongsheng to go to Zhangjiakou district, northwest of Beijing in Hebei province, to check on defense preparations on what could have been an invasion route. The MAC executive group moved its headquarters to the western side of the city. Zhou Enlai ordered the compilation and distribution of documentation on Pearl Harbor and the German blitzkrieg attacks on Poland and the Soviet Union in World War II.[41]

This time Mao feared a Soviet surprise attack at the start of the border talks in Beijing on October 20, when the Chinese guard was down.[42] According to authoritative Chinese histories, the Chairman's assessment spurred Lin Biao to take emergency measures.[43] According to other authoritative Chinese accounts, Lin Biao chaired a Politburo meeting in mid-October at Mao's behest, which, unsurprisingly, unanimously endorsed the Chairman's suspicions and seconded his desire to evacuate the Chinese leadership from the capital. It is unthinkable that the Politburo would have taken such a decision without the Chairman's imprimatur.[44] The Chairman personally decided where each person should be sent;[45] he himself went to Wuhan on October 14.[46] While Mao's old colleagues may have appreciated his continuing concern for their safety, they surely resented the often contemptuous treatment they received from provincial authorities, which was a product of their humiliation at the Chairman's hands earlier in the Cultural Revolution.[47]

These details are critical for understanding why Lin Biao, who flew to Suzhou on October 16 as part of the evacuation, put together an emergency six-point directive on October 17, titled "On Strengthening Defenses and Guarding against an Enemy Surprise Attack."[48] The directive, surely the prerogative of the man who was formally charged with day-to-day control of the MAC, required that the "armed forces be put on red alert, production of weaponry [especially anti-tank weapons] be speeded up, and commanders get into combat positions," and a close watch be kept on the Sino-Soviet border.[49] On the evening of October 18, Chief of Staff Huang Yongsheng issued the directive to the eleven military regions, the PLA navy and air force, and the Beijing Garrison, under the heading "Vice Chairman Lin's First Verbal Order."[50] Mao hit the roof.

To explain Mao's anger at Lin's initiative, many later Chinese commentators have claimed that Lin acted behind the backs of Mao and the CC.[51] Wang Dongxing, who, as head of the CC's General Office, was the main formal channel to the Chairman, states that Lin Biao tried to run the document by Mao, sending it via the premier for the latter's prior approval. Zhou refused to comment, simply forwarding the order to Wang, who took it to Mao on October 19. Mao read it, exclaimed, "Burn it!," and proceeded to do so; Wang intervened to plead that he needed some documentation to report from and managed to save the accompanying letter. When Zhou learned from Wang of Mao's displeasure, he again withheld comment, but warned Lin of Mao's reaction.[52]

Wang's own interpretation of the episode was that Lin was probing to see how far he could go in taking over Mao's leadership role, and that Mao—though the Chairman never spoke ill of his vice chairman in front of Wang—resented this *lèse majesté*.[53] Although this analysis fits with the official view of Lin Biao as a traitorous plotter against the Chairman, it is totally out of keeping with Lin Biao's behavior during the Cultural Revolution up to that point. Whatever his private views, Lin's iron rule of thumb as reported by his secretary was always to agree with the Chairman and never to act or vouchsafe an opinion until he knew what the Chairman thought.

Could Huang Yongsheng have jumped the gun, issuing the order before Lin had had a chance to do what he always did: gain Mao's clearance? Apart from the unlikelihood that the chief of staff would have made so elementary an error, Lin Biao's secretary states that the text was sent to Mao two hours before it was sent to Huang and was not countermanded. It seems more likely that Lin understood, on the basis of earlier Politburo discussions, that he had been authorized, perhaps even ordered, by Mao to alert the PLA to the possibility of a Soviet blitzkrieg attack. To judge by his secretary's account, Lin perhaps imagined himself back in his wartime role, when he was accustomed, self-confidently, to give his orders and assume that Mao would endorse them later, but when it was suggested that he should clear the order with Mao first, he readily agreed.[54]

On the assumption that the Chairman did see Lin's directive in advance, it was surely its manner rather than its matter that enraged him. He could hardly have been angered by its content, which was simply the logical consequence of his own analysis. But he may well have seen the form in which it was issued, especially the title given it by Huang Yongsheng, as usurping his supreme authority. Wang Dongxing may have been wrong about Lin Biao's motives, but correct about how the Chairman interpreted them. The issuance of a "first" order by the vice chairman could suggest that a whole stream of orders would follow—and in fact three did follow on the same day[55]—and that Lin would take over Mao's role as commander-in-chief. Although the first order was rescinded once Mao's reaction was known, it had, however briefly, galvanized the whole PLA: ninety-five divisions, some 940,000 troops, 4,100 aircraft, and 600 naval vessels plus large numbers of tanks and artillery were dispersed; vastly increased numbers of rail cars were used for transporting men and matériel.[56] Whatever the intention, it was a massive demonstration to the Chairman how easily control over the ultimate basis of his power could shift to his heir.

There is at least one other possible explanation for Mao's anger. Perhaps the Chairman floated the Pearl Harbor scenario after the border clashes for political reasons, just to keep the country mobilized as the Cultural Revolution died down, and to rally everyone behind the supreme leader of the revolution and the Korean War. Shipping VIPs out of Beijing to safety was a low-key way of underlining the message, with the additional benefit of removing possibly inconvenient colleagues from the politics of the capital. But by taking Mao seriously, Lin Biao turned costless political mobilization into high-profile military mobilization with the danger that the specter of a Soviet attack might actually become a reality. Mao would have been hoist with his own petard.[57]

Whatever the reason for Mao's wrath, had the Chairman not worried hitherto about the militarization of the Chinese polity, this episode translated the institutional reality into potential personal danger. Even a leader less paranoid than Mao could legitimately have been worried.[58]

The Opening to America

There is no clear evidence as to exactly when Mao began to espouse the more sanguine viewpoint about the international scene adopted by the four marshals. The timing suggests that although the Soviet threat was obviously the crucial background to Mao's rethinking, Lin Biao's "first order" was the trigger. Mao did nothing until after the putative moment of maximum danger to China—the arrival and departure of the Soviet delegation after abortive negotiations[59]—had passed. But Lin's order demonstrated to him that, if preparing for war remained the principal preoccupation of the Chinese state, then inevitably the PLA and its leaders would dominate the political stage. Defense requirements would dominate politics, distort the budget, and disrupt social life, and indeed continued to do so through 1970.[60] Only by lifting the perception of dire and immediate threat, which Mao himself had done most to foster, could the PLA gradually be eased back into a more customary supporting role.

Fortunately for Mao, signs had been accumulating of the desire of the new Nixon administration to adopt a radically new posture toward China.[61] Nixon's "Guam doctrine" of July 25, 1969, indicated the president's aim of avoiding future commitments to help out with internal security problems in Asia of the type that had drawn the United States into its massive deployment of troops in Vietnam. Implicitly, Nixon was indicating his desire to withdraw from that quagmire. Such a shift would remove the potential American threat from the south and would confirm the Soviet threat from the north as the main danger to Chinese security. If the Soviet threat could be neutralized by an opening to the United States, then the role of the PLA could be diminished. Domestic pressures and international opportunities made the time ripe for Mao to play the "American card" (and for Nixon to play the "China card") against the Soviet Union.

On January 1, 1970, the official Chinese press greeted the New Year with somewhat lessened emphasis on defense, but the first important indication of a reappraisal by the Chairman came after the Americans had made significant concessions in the January ambassadorial meeting in Warsaw. On that occasion, the Americans also offered to send a senior emissary to Beijing. At the February

Warsaw meeting, the Chinese welcomed the idea of a senior emissary. But for much of 1970, Sino-American relations were in the doldrums, largely because in May the United States sent troops into Cambodia, an action that Mao had to denounce.

In October 1970, Nixon asked Pakistani president Yahya Khan to tell the Chinese that the Americans were prepared to send a high-level emissary to Beijing. In early December a reply came from Zhou Enlai saying that the emissary would be welcome.[62] Later in the month, Mao sent a further signal to Washington. A picture that had been taken of him and the American journalist Edgar Snow watching the National Day parade on October 1 was published in the *People's Daily* on Mao's birthday, December 26, 1970, but its significance seems to have been lost on the China watchers in Washington, possibly because the Nixon White House distrusted Snow.[63] In April 1971, Mao made a further gesture, allowing the American table-tennis team that had been competing in the world championships in Japan to come to China to play friendly matches, and while the world wondered how far "Ping-Pong diplomacy" could go, behind the scenes Zhou told relevant officials that the U.S. team's visit had initiated a new era in China's foreign relations.[64] In May Mao told a foreign guest that the world was moving in the direction of revolution rather than global war, and over the weeks that followed, Chinese propaganda gave the war danger diminishing prominence.[65] Behind the scenes, in great secrecy, with the Pakistani government continuing to act as intermediary, the Chinese and the Americans continued their negotiations to bring about the major geopolitical reconfiguration that the Nixon visit to Beijing in February 1972 would represent.[66]

The Sino-American breakthrough was an extraordinary event in the context of the Cultural Revolution. It had been the Soviet search for détente with the United States that had led Mao to accuse Moscow of abandoning Lenin's foreign policy of implacable hostility to imperialism in favor of appeasement. He had attributed that revisionism to the Soviet leadership's desire to restore capitalism, and the Cultural Revolution had been launched to prevent similar backsliding in China. Now Beijing was itself seeking détente with the United States, making nonsense of all its ideological hyperbole of the previous five years.

Internally, the Chinese justified their *volte-face* by reference to Mao's writings during the Sino-Japanese War, when he had argued the need to make common cause with imperialist America and Britain against the greater danger of imperialist Japan. But that was an argument from expediency, just like the Soviet argument that its détente with the United States was necessitated by the danger of mutual nuclear annihilation. In the Sino-Soviet dispute, the Chinese had rejected Moscow's justifications as cowardly or a smoke screen, and had depicted themselves as occupying the high ground of ideological principle. Now they, too, were being expedient, and if not cowardly, certainly circumspect.

Yet by the time Henry Kissinger came to Beijing in July 1971 to negotiate the Nixon visit, how expedient did the Chinese need to be? True, the Soviets had sent six new divisions armed with battlefield nuclear weapons to the border,[67] but the Sino-Soviet border had been defused, and would remain quiescent provided the Chinese offered no provocation. A Soviet "surgical strike" was by now unlikely, if not inconceivable. If the four marshals had been right to be sanguine in 1969, the situation was even more favorable in 1971. The Americans were disengaging from Vietnam, even if at times, as in the case of the Cambodian invasion, their maxim may have seemed to the Chinese to be *sauter pour mieux reculer.* For Beijing, it was far safer in the early 1970s than it had been in the late 1960s to maintain ideological purity and wish a pox on the houses of both superpowers. But Mao chose otherwise.

Can one conclude that the Chairman's anger at the Soviet Union was provoked less by its "revisionism" than by its leaders' refusal to elevate China's international aims into prime goals of Soviet foreign policy; that once he saw an opportunity to break out from the hole-in-the-corner ambassadorial talks in Warsaw and engage America as an equal, as the Soviet Union had so long done, he chose national interest over ideological rectitude? And if so, did Lin Biao demur? It is one of the many question marks still hanging over Lin's demise.

Five months after Lin's death in an air crash in Mongolia in September 1971, Mao told Nixon: "In our country also there is a reactionary group which is opposed to our contact with you. The result was they got on an airplane and fled abroad."[68] Yet Lin Biao had not taken any great interest in foreign affairs during the Cultural Revolution,[69] and on all documents relating to the U.S.-PRC opening that he was sent, he simply wrote: "I completely agree with the Chairman's instructions."[70] To judge by Zhou Enlai and the four marshals, the opening to America was welcome to the old guard, whom Mao was trying to cultivate in the aftermath of Lin's defection and death, and the suggestion that his late heir apparent was against it—relevant portions of Mao's discussion with Nixon would be circulated among the elite—could have been calculated to show how fortunate it was that Mao had rebuffed Lin.

On the other hand, inviting Nixon to China *was* turning the world upside down—or, as Nixon put it at his final banquet in China, "This was the week that changed the world"[71]—and in private to his family, Lin Biao did indicate that he thought the policy was disastrous.[72] Lin Biao may have felt that China could continue to go it alone, and if not, then the Communist Soviet Union rather than the imperialist United States was more obviously the superpower to make peace with, especially since, whatever Moscow's intentions, its troop strength along the border had to be counted a threat. But if those were his thoughts, he kept them from his family, and he certainly did not voice any such views to Mao or other colleagues. Indeed, Mao learned of Lin's skepticism about the opening to America only after Lin's death, from his daughter's testimony.[73] So Mao's suggestion that this was the reason for Lin's defection seems simply self-serving. The issue was not policy but power; but it came to a head, oddly, in a debate over an institution without power.

19

The Defection and Death of Lin Biao

D espite his formal elevation at the Ninth Congress to the role of successor, Lin Biao had reason to be concerned about his position. Under the
old, two-front succession system devised by the Chairman, Liu Shaoqi
and other senior colleagues took charge when Mao was out of town or could not
be bothered. The creation of the post of honorary chairman in the new constitution adopted at the CCP's Eighth Congress had been an implicit undertaking
that one day Mao would retire permanently to the Second Front, handing over
the reins of party leadership to Liu. Mao seemed to take a major step in that direction in 1959 when he vacated the state chairmanship in Liu's favor, and from
that time on, every National Day, the *People's Daily* printed the pictures of the
two chairmen side by side and equal in size. Mao had also identified Liu as his
successor in conversation with Britain's Field Marshal Lord Montgomery, and
that personal commitment had circulated throughout the party leadership. In
the end, none of this saved Liu from disgrace at Mao's hand, but for a decade
there had been in place an apparently working succession process suggesting that
Mao would hand over power in his lifetime.

Under the constitution adopted at the CCP's Ninth Congress, however,
there was no hint of a succession process. The provision for an honorary chairmanship was dropped, possibly as a result of the experiment in handing over
power to Liu, and this change carried the implication that Mao intended to die
in office. Nor was it clear from the deliberations and decisions of the congress
whether there might be an interim step, such as occupying the position of head
of state, which could be taken to confirm Lin Biao's formal role as heir apparent.
Lin could have acted as if the two-front system were still in place by chairing Politburo meetings regularly in Mao's absence, but perhaps the fate of Liu Shaoqi
as well as his health problems decided him to leave that chore in the safer hands
of Zhou Enlai.[1] Lin, indeed, could have been forgiven for wondering if the

Chairman's decision to install him as his heir was simply to establish a system that could allow for a Maoist zealot to be inveigled into the top job in due course. Why else would the Chairman suggest to Lin, much to the latter's discomfiture, that he, too, should name an heir and propose the name of Zhang Chunqiao?[2] Even though Mao apparently made no attempt to push his suggestion, it was at the very least an indication that he regarded his wife and her henchmen as his true ideological heirs.

The ambiguities of the succession finally came to a head over the issue of who, if anyone, should succeed Liu Shaoqi as chairman of the PRC.

The Head-of-State Issue

On March, 8, 1970, Wang Dongxing journeyed from Wuhan to Beijing to relay Mao's opinions to the Politburo on rebuilding the institutions of the Chinese state. During the upheaval of the previous four years, the ranks of the vice premiers and government ministers had been seriously thinned, though a skeleton State Council had continued to try to carry out essential functions under Premier Zhou's leadership. The National People's Congress had not been summoned, and after Liu Shaoqi's disgrace his duties in the office of head of state were performed by the elder statesman Dong Biwu, chosen on the eve of the Cultural Revolution as one of Liu's two deputy state chairpersons.[3]

On the surface, then, Mao's interest in convening the Fourth NPC, whose agenda would include agreement upon a revised state constitution abolishing the office of head of state—a radical step on which he had not consulted his senior colleagues[4]—seemed a logical step in his efforts to move toward reconstruction after the destruction wrought by the Cultural Revolution.[5] Nor was Mao's rejection of the state chairmanship surprising. The Soviet Union under Lenin and Stalin had done without a powerful head of state, so clearly the office was not an essential part of a revolutionary state.[6] Besides, Mao had already held that office and had disliked the formalities incumbent upon it, and he had no need for the trappings of power.

Yet it seems curious that Mao interested himself in the state structure at a time when the far more gravely damaged institutions of the far more important CCP still awaited rebuilding. At this point, despite the fact that the Ninth Congress had been held a year earlier, and despite the publicizing of grassroots models of party building, so few county committees had been established[7] that a decision had been taken to start from the top, with provincial committees.[8] Even so, the first provincial committee, in Mao's native Hunan, was not formed until December 1970. Under those circumstances, Mao's attention to state institutions in which he had hitherto shown little interest prompts at least a question about his motives.

In the light of later events, it is legitimate to wonder if Mao hoped that the abolition of the office of head of state might be an issue with which he could trap Lin Biao, on the assumption that Lin might believe that, as heir apparent, he ought to occupy that post just as Liu had done. This possibility gains credence from the revelation in the memoirs of Wu Faxian that Wang Dongxing read Mao's own words to the Politburo: "I, Mao Zedong, do not want to be Chairman. If [the Politburo] decides to maintain such a position, it is Lin Biao who should hold the position." According to Wu's account, Wang invited Lin Biao's senior military colleagues to dinner and repeated the Chairman's preference for Lin to be state chairman if that office were recreated. Allegedly, Lin's wife, Ye Qun, was eager for him to have it, perhaps so that she could become first lady, and activated his supporters in furtherance of this aim.[9] However, there is no proof either of Ye Qun's ambitions or that Lin wanted the post, and reportedly he vigorously rejected the idea later in the year.[10]

Although party historians have been encouraged to condemn the concept of and the need for the Cultural Revolution, none has ever dared claim that in order to bring it about, the Chairman was prepared ruthlessly to resort to plotting the downfall of his former close comrades-in-arms. The master strategist gone astray in his old age is an acceptable image; the gang leader masterminding dirty tricks is not. The impact on the party's legitimacy would be too great.[11] Yet if Mao plotted successfully to remove his first heir apparent, there is no prima facie reason why he should not have set about plotting to remove his second one, as part of an effort to undo PLA dominance within the reconstructed CCP. After the Cultural Revolution, the head-of-state issue was deemed proof of Lin Biao's plot to "capture supreme power."[12] Could Mao have been setting him up for such an accusation? The facts may never be known; motivations are still obscure. But why else would Mao have claimed, when he was still building his case against Lin Biao and *before* Lin's flight and death, that "a certain person was very anxious to become state chairman, to split the Party, and to seize power"?[13]

Mao was in Wuhan when he made his proposal. He ordered Wang Dongxing to return to Beijing to inform Zhou Enlai. The same day, March 8, 1970, Zhou presided over a Politburo meeting at which Mao's proposal was predictably endorsed, and three groups were organized to manage the logistics and prepare the necessary reports. On April 11, however, Lin Biao in Suzhou had his secretary phone Mao's secretary—the Chairman was by now in Changsha—and suggest that the post of head of state should be retained and that Mao should fill it. Later in the day, Lin's secretary phoned the Politburo office and elaborated on Lin's message to Mao. For Mao not to be head of state would be contrary to the psychology of the people. There was no need for a deputy head of state and anyway he, Lin, would not be appropriate for it. Again, Zhou immediately summoned the Politburo, whose members (including some of Jiang Qing's followers), with the text of the phone conversation before them, endorsed Lin Biao's proposal. When his secretary had reported Lin's proposal to Mao, the Chairman had merely laughed and sent his best wishes to Lin; but when the Politburo's endorsement reached him, he wrote on it: "I cannot do this job again; this suggestion is inappropriate."[14]

It has been persuasively suggested that Lin's proposal, its acceptance by the Politburo, and later moves to get Mao to accept the post of head of state could have been motivated in large part by ignorance of the Chairman's real desires—his response to Lin Biao's telephoned suggestion certainly did not indicate antagonism—and a feeling that he would not be displeased if his lieutenants kept trying to honor him.[15] If so, it would be another example of "working toward the Chairman," the attempt by uncertain subordinates to flatter their leader by going beyond what the latter may have really wanted. Their problem was complicated by the absence from Beijing of both Mao and Lin, which underlined yet again the extraordinary way in which the country was run from afar during much of the Cultural Revolution: the Chairman sends a message to Beijing to indicate his wishes, and the Politburo carries them out; the vice chairman makes a counterproposal, also from afar, and it, too, is adopted. Even had the two principals been in the same room with their colleagues, it is unthinkable that Lin would have confronted Mao and asked him to come clean about his intentions so that they could fulfil them, but somebody as subtle as Zhou Enlai or as canny as Kang Sheng might at least have learned something from the discussion or just the body language.

Moreover, Mao's opposition to reviving the post of head of state was again put in doubt when the office of Wang Dongxing, the Politburo member in closest regular contact with the Chairman, circulated two draft constitutions, one with and one without the state chairmanship.[16] Along with Wang's earlier quotation of Mao to the Politburo, this move lent credence to the idea that the Chairman was less interested in abolishing the office than in not occupying it himself. Indeed, in late July, Mao reportedly had his secretary phone Lin Biao's office with the following message: "As to the state chairman, I will not hold the position, and neither will you. Let Old Dong [Biwu] be the state chairman and, at the same time, put several younger people in the position of vice chairman."[17] This, too, could have been a provocation: Would Lin continue to decline the office when faced with a threat that younger men might take it and perhaps challenge his position?

And yet, whatever their ultimate objective, anybody who advocated retaining the state chairmanship had to insist that Mao should take the post, even as he kept refusing it. Thus, whether "working toward the Chairman" in Lin Biao's case, or perhaps out of family ambition on her own initiative in Ye Qun's case, both pursued the issue, pressing the military members of the constitution drafting committee, Generals Wu Faxian and Li Zuopeng, to insist on a state chairmanship. The constitution drafting committee divided on factional lines, with the generals and Chen Boda in favor of the office, and Kang Sheng and Zhang Chunqiao against. Both factions were trying to work toward the Chairman. The impasse was left for the Politburo to resolve.[18]

Confrontation at Lushan

By the time the CC met in the southern mountain resort of Lushan for its Second Plenum in late August, it must have been clear to the Chairman, whatever his original motives, that Lin Biao was as determined as Mao himself to refuse to be head of state. As it turned out, it was a different though related issue that sparked confrontation at Lushan: how to honor Mao in the new constitution. On August 13, on the eve of the Lushan meeting, the constitutional committee again split on factional lines, this time over whether the constitution should include the statement that Mao had developed Marxism-Leninism "with genius, creatively, and comprehensively." As all members of the committee knew, this was Lin Biao's encomium in his preface to the second edition of the Little Red Book.[19] Zhang Chunqiao, knowing that the Chairman had vetoed these three adverbs' being written into the party constitution a year earlier, suggested that they not be used; but Wu Faxian, who saw this suggestion as an attack on Lin Biao, accused Zhang of taking advantage of Mao's modesty to attack his thought. Both men may have been trying to work toward the Chairman, but Lin Biao's supporters were exuberant, believing they had found an issue on which to cripple the rump of the CCRG.[20]

On the afternoon of August 22, Mao summoned to his office the other members of the PSC—Lin Biao, Zhou Enlai, Chen Boda, and Kang Sheng, with Wang Dongxing to take notes—to discuss the arrangements for the upcoming plenum, the agenda of which was to include three main items: the revision of the constitution, the economic plan, and the strategic plan. For once, Mao's four PSC colleagues united to work seemingly against but certainly toward the Chairman, each in turn urging the revival of the post of head of state and Mao as its occupant. Well aware of Mao's boredom with protocol, Zhou suggested that the formal foreign relations duties of the office could be delegated to others. Kang Sheng bemoaned the burden that Mao's reluctance had placed upon the constitution drafting committee, which knew that the whole country wanted him to do the job; while Chen Boda, with Lin Biao concurring, emphasized how encouraged the people would be if he took it on. Mao said that if they all wanted to recreate the office, they could, but he would not assume it. Leninist discipline dictated that Mao accede to the demands of the majority of the PSC and what would doubtless have been unanimous votes in the Politburo and the CC. But the imperial Chairman was above party discipline. Later in the day, Zhou explained matters to the constitution drafting committee.[21] The head-of-state issue was dead.

Or was it? When the PSC reconvened briefly before the first plenary session the following afternoon, Lin unexpectedly announced that he would like to say a few words, and with Mao's agreement the agenda was set aside for him to speak first. Mao later claimed that Lin had not consulted with him or shown him what he was going to say;[22] the weight of evidence, however, suggests that Mao lied as part of his effort to discredit Lin, and that Lin did alert him about what he would say. Lin explained, with Zhou's backing, that he wanted to speak about the constitution because of the quarrel between Wu Faxian and Zhang Chunqiao on the genius issue, that Zhang had wanted to eliminate the reference to Mao's contribution. The Chairman gave permission to Lin to address the issue, stating that it must be Jiang Qing who was behind Zhang and that anyway Lin should not accuse Zhang by name.[23]

Why did Mao give permission, and in this provocative manner? He believed that his criticism of CCRG leaders had resulted in the February Countercurrent in 1967.[24] Did he hope now to provoke a similar reaction, which he could then use as grounds for an assault on Lin and his colleagues? Mao's behavior at Lushan also recalls his treatment of Peng Zhen in 1966 when he approved the latter's February Outline, but shortly thereafter roundly denounced it. This time it would take him only forty-eight hours to react angrily.

Lin Biao's unscripted speech eulogized Mao and his thought in characteristic stylc. In deference to the Chairman's repeated refusal to return to the office of head of state *(guojia zhuxi)*, Lin used a less formal term *(guojia zhi yuanshou)* to convey the idea of Mao as maximum leader. As he had done in the past, he asserted that without Mao and his thought, the CCP would not have achieved its victories—because of them, the subjective world could transform the objective world—and that the important thing about the new constitution was that it embodied Mao's role. More important, he implicitly defended his use of the three adverbs—although unlike Zhou Enlai at the Ninth Congress he chose not to use them[25]—arguing that because the world had changed since the times of Marx and Lenin there were ideas in Mao's works that could not have been in the classics of communism. "The talents, learning, and experience of Chairman Mao himself have created new things."[26] To adapt and reverse a favorite Cultural Revolution condemnation of crafty behavior—waving the red flag to knock down the red flag—Lin Biao avoided raising the three adverbs in order to raise the three adverbs. His supporters followed up.

At an enlarged Politburo meeting that evening, Wu Faxian suggested to general agreement that the agenda (the constitution, the economic plan, and war preparations) should be set aside to allow the conferees to hear Lin's speech again. Zhou agreed to this and also, after getting Mao's consent, to a suggestion that Lin's speech should be printed and circulated. The following morning, after sitting twice through the tape recording of Lin's one-hour speech, the participants discussed it in their regional groups for the rest of the day. Years later, Nie Yuanzi's recollection was that "everybody listened attentively . . . nobody sensed anything [out of the ordinary]."[27]

Ye Qun had warned Lin Biao's supporters not to raise the question of having a head of state, but rather to focus on the genius issue as the one on which Zhang Chunqiao was most vulnerable. Scattered among different groups and armed with a set of quotations justifying the notion of genius culled from the Marxist classics by Chen Boda, Lin's generals did just that. Although Zhang's name was not mentioned, once people began to realize that he was in fact the target there was widespread denunciation of anyone who would presume to doubt Mao's genius. Doubtless for many Zhang personified the mayhem of the Cultural Revolution, and they eagerly exploited the opportunity to attack him, albeit anonymously. One account indicates that in Zhang's own East China Group, there were calls for him to be sentenced to reform through labor;[28] even Zhang's Shanghai lieutenant Wang Hongwen supported the concept of genius. In the Northeast Group, Zhou Enlai supported Lin Biao's speech.[29]

But it was the speeches in the North China Group, summarized in a bulletin, that encouraged Zhang's opponents at the plenum and soon spurred Mao to action. Chen Boda and Wang Dongxing indicated that there were plotters within the CCP who still wanted to deny Mao's genius. These were "representatives of the Liu Shaoqi line in the absence of Liu Shaoqi" and the "running dogs of the imperialists, the revisionists, and the counterrevolutionaries" who should be thrown out of the party. Their speeches garnered wide support in the group and engendered enthusiastic demands for Mao and Lin to be chairman and vice chairman of state under the new constitution.[30] Wang Dongxing reported that such was the hope of the CC's General Office and PLA Unit 8341.[31] He also knew, though he could not reveal, that it was also the wish of the PSC. But since he had heard Mao summarily reject the PSC's plea, why did he revive the suggestion? Did he hope that Lin Biao would assume the post in lieu of Mao despite his equally strenuous disavowal of interest in the job? Chinese sources indicate that Wang was in regular contact with Lin's group through Ye Qun, and like Chen Boda, he could have been investing in his future. Even so, no CCP leader would consciously defy the Chairman. During the Cultural Revolution that was a sure way to have no future.

And why did Wang Dongxing, as close to Mao as any Politburo member, jump on the anti-Zhang bandwagon, and allow his audience to infer that he spoke for the Chairman? Supporting the concept of Mao's genius, even advocating that he should resume the office of head of state, could simply have been another example of working toward the Chairman. But did Wang believe that participating in a concerted attack on Zhang was also working toward the Chairman? Was he spurred on by Mao's implicitly critical remarks about Zhang and Jiang Qing when the Chairman signed off on Lin Biao's opening speech?[32]

In his memoirs, Wang states that when Mao quizzed him about the head-of-state issue, he explained that in the enthusiasm of the moment after hearing Chen Boda's speech, he had lost his head.[33] One wonders why Mao would retain so unreliable an official in the key positions he occupied so close to himself. The Chairman would excoriate Chen Boda. Why not Wang? It raises the possibility that, unbeknownst to him, Wang had done just what the Chairman hoped he would do: help to stir up emotions against the rump of the CCRG, giving Mao the justification for moving against the military faction loyal to Lin Biao.

Chinese sources, in which allegations of deviousness on Mao's part are politically sensitive, say only that Jiang Qing took Zhang Chunqiao and Yao Wenyuan to see Mao on the morning of August 25 and that their complaints of calls to drag "people" out led him to call an expanded Politburo meeting that afternoon and launch a counterattack, which he directed mainly against the weakest link in the Lin Biao camp, Chen Boda. It has been argued that Mao saw the implicit attacks on Zhang Chunqiao as effectively an onslaught on the Cultural Revolution itself, the February Countercurrent revisited, and that he would have been confirmed in this suspicion by the strong support of Marshal Chen Yi for the anti-Zhang tide. Hence the vigor of a response that the issues of head of state and genius would have been unlikely to engender; and certainly Kang Sheng quickly drew the parallel between the two events.[34]

But in fact there was a fundamental difference between the two events, which Mao surely perceived. In 1967, Chen Yi and his colleagues were indeed opposing the Cultural Revolution itself because of the chaos it was causing. But in 1970, there was no reason for Lin Biao, Chen Boda, or any of Lin's PLA followers to oppose the Cultural Revolution as such, since they were among its principal beneficiaries. Moreover, the PLA ran most of the country, the Red Guards were dispersed, the CCRG was no more, and Jiang Qing and Zhang Chunqiao's capacity to stir up trouble was greatly limited. Where there was upheaval—the campaign to "cleanse the class ranks," for instance—the PLA was usually in charge, not the radicals. Lin Biao may have thought to gain credit with his constituency by bringing retribution down upon a man who had been a thorn in the side of the PLA a few years earlier; Chen Boda might have wanted revenge for humiliation at Zhang Chunqiao's hands. But whatever Chen Yi may have thought or Kang Sheng claimed, Lushan 1970 was not a renewed onslaught against the Cultural Revolution, but a factional struggle among its beneficiaries with primacy at Mao's court as the aim.

This explanation leaves unanswered the question of Mao's role in helping to stir up this factional struggle. Mao's criticisms of the CCRG in 1967 almost certainly sparked the February Countercurrent, enabling him to smoke out the most vocal opponents of the Cultural Revolution and to justify criticizing and sidelining them. In August 1970, his implicitly critical remarks to Lin Biao about Jiang Qing and Zhang Chunqiao similarly emboldened the opponents of the CCRG rump, as Mao could have anticipated. The net result of the episode was that Mao was enabled to launch an attack on Lin Biao's faction and thus to begin to undermine the role of the military at the apex of the CCP.

Throwing Stones . . .

As so often, Mao described his action in colorful terms. He was "throwing stones, mixing in sand, and digging up the cornerstone." "Throwing stones" meant attacking the members of Lin's clique, though not Lin himself. Indeed, in an effort to lull Lin Biao into a sense of false security, as was his habitual tactic, Mao told him that he would be handing over power to him in two years.[35] But Mao wanted his supporters to self-criticize. Zhou Enlai passed on that message to Wu Faxian, Li Zuopeng, and Qiu Huizuo at Lushan. The missile launched at Chen Boda was more like a massive rock; the Chairman gave Chen his comeuppance for deserting his trusted CCRG for Lin Biao.[36] With characteristic ingratitude, Mao denounced as a false Marxist the theoretical guru who had helped him in the "sinification" of Marxism and certainly had ghostwritten some of his works.[37] In view of their thirty-odd years of ideological collaboration, if Chen was a false Marxist, what did that make Mao?[38] And if he had become a special agent of the KMT as early as 1931 and subsequently a follower of Mao's main rival from the late 1930s, Wang Ming, as Mao now alleged, why had the omniscient Chairman not spotted this before?[39] No CCP leader was bold enough to ask. Instead, at a North China conference attended by Politburo members and military leaders from December 22 to January 26, 1970–71, Chen Boda was further denounced as "a traitor, a spy, and a careerist."[40] But Lin Biao's generals—especially Huang Yongsheng, who had not been at Lushan when Chen Boda was spearheading the assault on Zhang Chunqiao—had little feeling of guilt and, despite prodding from Zhou Enlai, made only pro forma confessions, which angered Mao. Indeed, as late as July, the Chairman appeared more interested in the activities of Lin's supporters than in the secret visit of Henry Kissinger.[41]

"Mixing in sand" meant adulterating the composition of the MAC administration, adding a civilian—a Politburo alternate, Ji Dengkui—and a general whom Mao could trust—Li Desheng[42]—to keep an eye on Huang Yongsheng and Wu Faxian. "Digging up the cornerstone" meant reorganizing the Beijing Military Region. As at the beginning of the Cultural Revolution, Mao wanted to ensure that troops around the capital were loyal to him and to nobody else. The region's commander and the second political commissar were suspended from their posts and ordered to write self-criticisms.[43]

Lin's Abortive Coup?

The official Chinese version of elite politics in 1971 is that Lin Biao conspired against Mao in a plot called "571," *wuqiyi*, which in Chinese could sound like "armed uprising." Lin's agent in this enterprise was his son, Lin Liguo, a PLA officer who, despite his youth, had attained considerable power in the air force because of the favoritism of Wu Faxian. Lin understood that his father's position was threatened, and strong measures had to be taken to protect it. He recruited like-minded fellow officers into what they called a "joint fleet." From the documents later distributed by the CC to party officials, it is clear that the plotters had taken to heart Mao's call to "dare to think, dare to speak, dare to act," but shared a view of the Chairman greatly at odds with the official picture:

> Today he uses this force to attack that force; tomorrow he uses that force to attack this force. Today he uses sweet words and honeyed talk to those whom he entices, and tomorrow he puts them to death for some fabricated crimes. Those who are his guests today will be his prisoners tomorrow.
>
> Looking back at the history of the past few decades, [do you see] any one whom he had supported initially who has not finally been handed a political death sentence?
>
> Is there a single political force which has been able to work with him from beginning to end? His former secretaries have either committed suicide or been arrested. His few close comrades-in-arms or trusted aides have also been sent to prison by him. . .
>
> He is a paranoid and sadist. His philosophy of liquidating people is either don't do it, or do it thoroughly. Every time he liquidates someone, he will put them to death before he desists; once he hurts you, he will hurt you all the way; and he puts the blame for all bad things on others.[44]

It seems likely that Lin Liguo would have framed this condemnation of Mao on the basis of what he had learned from his father. The conspirators evidently saw no need to emulate their elders in "working toward the Chairman," and one wonders if their analysis of the Chairman struck a responsive chord among the many party officials to whom their opinions were later circulated.

The "joint fleet" at first discussed how best to arrest Zhang Chunqiao and Yao Wenyuan. The idea of assassinating Mao, codenamed "B52" after the big American bomber, allegedly arose when the Chairman was touring seven southern provinces from mid-August to mid-September, making provocative anti-Lin remarks in thirteen speeches to civilian and military cadres. Mao alleged that he had been seeking out Lin Biao, but Lin had avoided him. This was a lie *(sahuang)*, according to Chinese party historians. In fact Lin had tried to see Mao several times, but, as in the case of Luo Ruiqing in 1965, Mao was not prepared to meet Lin. As a result, Lin chose to live outside the capital, in Suzhou and Beidaihe, and his son tried to take action.[45]

The methods canvassed among the plotters included attacking his special train with flamethrowers, 40-millimeter rocket guns, or 100-millimeter anti-aircraft guns, dynamiting a bridge that the train had to cross, bombing the train from the air, or simply face-to-face assassination with a pistol.[46]

Either the conspirators were insufficiently determined or strikingly incompetent, or Mao, ever the wary guerrilla warrior, and perhaps forewarned,[47] outsmarted them, moving his special train swiftly back to Beijing—only stopping briefly in Shanghai to ensure the loyalty of the Nanjing MR commander, Xu Shiyou[48]—before they could implement their plans.[49] At any rate, no assassination attempt was made, and on September 12, hearing that Mao had returned to the capital, Lin Liguo ordered his followers in effect to kidnap Lin's four generals and fly them to Canton the next day with the objective of setting up a rival party headquarters there under Lin Biao. That evening Lin Liguo himself flew to Beidaihe, where his parents were holidaying, to fly them also to Canton.

The events of the next few hours reportedly were highly dramatic, involving an unsuccessful attempt by Lin Biao's daughter, Doudou, to prevent the rest of the family from fleeing; a midnight dash by her father, mother, and brother to the nearby airport; and an equally unsuccessful effort by Zhou Enlai to prevent any planes from taking off from there. Zhou had earlier offered to fly to Beidaihe to prevent their flight, but Mao had vetoed the suggestion.[50] But instead of flying to Canton, the Lin family trio ended up flying to the Soviet Union. As the plane approached Mongolian airspace, Zhou asked Mao if he should order it to be shot down. The Chairman replied with a characteristic verbal shrug of the shoulders: "Rain has to fall, girls have to marry, these things are immutable; let them go."[51] In the event, the plane crashed in Mongolia, perhaps short of fuel, and Lin Biao, Ye Qun, and Lin Liguo were killed.[52]

Precisely because of the dramatic nature of the events of September 12–13, the veracity of the official Chinese sources and the accounts of Chinese historians has long been subject to question in Western publications.[53] For historians of the Cultural Revolution, however, one fact seems indisputable: from the Lushan plenum on, Mao put Lin Biao and his allies under continuous and escalating pressure. During Mao's southern tour, which immediately preceded the "September 13 incident," the Chairman made it clear that the man he really blamed for the events at Lushan was Lin Biao and that the affair was a "line struggle," which meant that it was as serious as the struggle with Liu Shaoqi.[54] Whether Lin Biao participated in Lin Liguo's alleged plot against Mao or passively awaited his fate remains unknown. There can also be legitimate doubt as to whether Lin Biao, who had taken a sleeping pill and gone to bed on the night of September 12, was fully conscious of what was going on when his wife and son rushed him into a car and off to the airport. But there could have been no doubt in Lin Biao's mind that his bright political future as heir apparent was over. Why was Mao after him?

One explanation rejected above, offered at the time by Kang Sheng and endorsed by some Western scholars, is that Mao saw the attack on Zhang Chunqiao as an attack on the Cultural Revolution and thus as an attack on himself. But there was little justification for him to believe that. Moreover, there are too many questions concerning Mao's handling of the head-of-state issue before the Lushan plenum, his prevarication about Lin Biao's plenum speech taking him by surprise, and the unexpected behavior of the Chairman's trusty Wang Dongxing at the North China Group meeting.

The more likely explanation, consistent with the political guerrilla tactics used by Mao against Peng Zhen, Liu Shaoqi, Deng Xiaoping, and others, is that the Chairman tried to entice Lin Biao to let his name go forward to take Mao's place as head of state; his acquiescence could have been used later to denounce him as a careerist who coveted the office of head of state, as was alleged in the indictment of Lin after his death.[55] This ploy foundered on the rock of Lin's immovable opposition to accepting the post. At the Lushan plenum, Mao encouraged Lin with his hints about Zhang Chunqiao and Jiang Qing to see where this tactic would lead. Conceivably, he encouraged Wang Dongxing to support Lin Biao's speech on the genius issue—another point in the indictment of Lin—to pour fuel on the flames. This time it took less than fifty hours rather than fifty days for Mao to spring his trap and start his attack on Lin Biao and his military faction.

Whatever explanation emerges when the CC archives are finally opened, Mao's use of the Lin Biao affair to begin a drive to eradicate PLA dominance of the CCP is not in doubt. As became clear at their trial in 1980–81, Lin's four generals had no knowledge of any plot against the Chairman or of the proposal to form a rival headquarters in Canton. But their immediate arrests as Lin's co-conspirators eradicated the influence of the central military authorities in the Politburo; the PLA faction disappeared. Later in the Cultural Revolution, Mao would use Deng Xiaoping to reduce PLA power in the civilian party in the provinces. For the moment the Chairman could be reassured that he had averted any danger of a military coup and that the specter of Bonapartism had been exorcised. But Mao's victory over Lin Biao was won at great cost: the discrediting of the Cultural Revolution.

32. Denunciation of capitalist-roaders in Wuhan; children were brought to witness evil being uncovered by armed Red Guards.

33. Yao Dengshan (middle), the diplomat allegedly responsible for the destruction of the British mission, in an earlier moment of triumph with Zhou Enlai, Jiang Qing, Mao Zedong, and Lin Biao.

34. Liu Shaoqi and his wife, Wang Guangmei, in a happy moment during their official visit to Indonesia.

35. Liu Shaoqi on his lonely deathbed in Kaifeng.

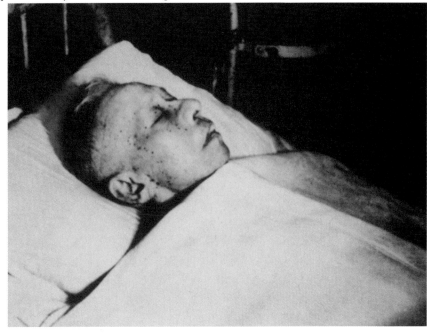

36. Wang Guangmei forced by Tsinghua University Red Guards to wear a traditional *qipao* over her trousers and a necklace of pingpong balls symbolizing the pearls she wore in Indonesia.

37. Kuai Dafu, the Tsinghua University student leader responsible for humiliating Wang Guangmei.

38. A Mao Zedong Thought Propaganda Team spreads the word as Mao attempts
to quiet the campuses.

39. Educated youth—Red Guards—join peasants attempting to till the frozen ground in Heilongjiang province.

40. Lin Biao and his son Lin Liguo (center).

41. Lin Biao's wife, Ye Qun (top right), who ran his private office.

42. The wreckage of the plane in which Lin Biao and his wife and
son were trying to flee to the Soviet Union.

43. The campaign to criticize Lin Biao and Confucius continued for several years after Lin's death.

44. President Nixon and his wife arrive in Beijing to be greeted by Premier Zhou.

45. The young Shanghai worker Wang Hongwen (left), chosen by Mao as heir apparent after the death of Lin Biao.

46. Mao greets a rehabilitated Deng Xiaoping (below) in 1974 prior to entrusting him with running the country as Zhou lies dying.

47. A year before his death, an ailing Zhou Enlai leaves hospital to address the National Peoples Congress on the four modernizations.

48. Mourners throng the Martyrs Memorial in Tiananmen Square to place wreaths and read the memorial writings to Zhou Enlai in the days leading up to the Qingming festival on April 4, 1976.

49. A visibly ailing Mao in his last appearance with a foreign visitor, Pakistani Premier Bhutto, on May 27, 1976.

50, 51. In photographs published of the obsequies following Mao's death (top and middle), gaps in the ranks of the leadership underline the fact that since then the Gang of Four had been arrested.

52. The temporary lineup of the leadership (bottom) at the CCP's Eleventh Congress in the year following Mao's death: Hua Guofeng, Marshal Ye Jianying, Deng Xiaoping, Li Xiannian, and Wang Dongxing.

53. The formal picture of the trial of the leading Cultural Revolutionaries, with ten of them seated between the court and the carefully chosen audience.

54. Zhang Chunqiao (above), who did not speak during the trial.

55. Jiang Qing (below), arguing with the court during her trial.

56. Victims of Cultural Revolution violence appeared in Beijing and elsewhere to claim compensation.

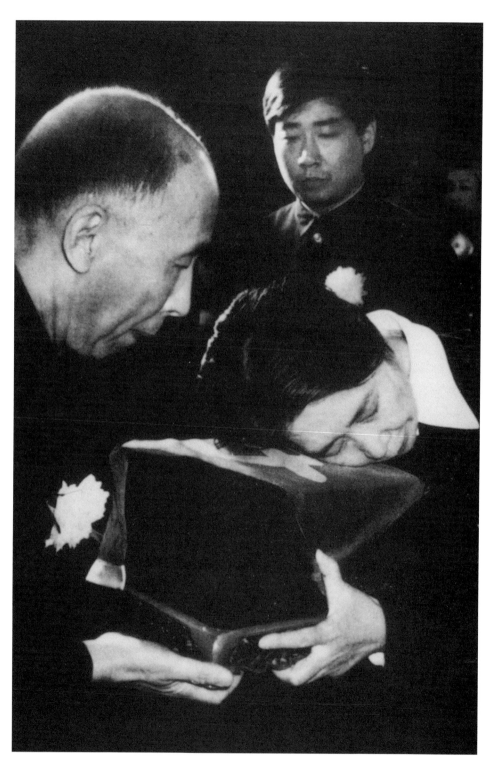

57. Liu Shaoqi's widow, Wang Guangmei, receives his ashes in May 1980, eleven years after he died.

Mao Becalmed

No immediate publicity was given to the events of September 13 as the leadership decided how to handle this political disaster, the "major turning point" that "objectively proclaimed the theoretical and practical defeat of the 'Great Cultural Revolution,'" according to Mao's official biography.[1] A top-secret Notification on September 18, *Zhongfa* [1971] 57, began the briefing of senior party officials. The dismissal of Lin's four generals on September 24 was a signal to the upper ranks of the PLA. Disgraced members of the old guard, including Marshal Chen Yi and other participants in the February Countercurrent, were briefed at a meeting that started on September 26.[2]

Lin's fellow marshals quickly fell into line and denounced their former comrade-in-arms. Their criticisms were long on history and outrage but, given the circumstances, predictably short on observations that might just qualify as Marxist or "theoretical" in nature. Yet they were important for Mao in shoring up his military constituency. General Luo Ruiqing's attempted suicide in 1966 provided a justification for hitherto-unconvinced top brass to denounce their erstwhile colleague as betraying the party. So in 1971, Lin Biao's flight to the Soviet Union salved the consciences of China's marshals as they turned on this national traitor.

Zhu De looked back at the decades he had known Lin and concluded that "there is nothing accidental about his stepping onto the anti-party counterrevolutionary road." Liu Bocheng recalled that "Lin Biao told you one thing to your face and then said something completely different behind your back; in all the decades I knew him, he never spoke the truth." Chen Yi's characterization of Lin was similar to Liu's in that he too mentioned Lin's "sinister conduct, double-dealing, cultivation of sworn followers, and persistent scheming," but Chen allowed himself to add: "I don't want to deny that Lin Biao previously did some useful things, under the leadership of the Chairman and the party center." Nie

Rongzhen admitted that he never for a moment expected Lin to be "so sinister, so full of hate toward Chairman Mao that he would actually plot to assassinate Chairman Mao and then betray his country, seek refuge with the revisionists, and turn into a shameless traitor and collaborator."[3]

Lin's absence could not be concealed for long. Even without any open admission of the crisis, the abrupt cancellation of the customary October 1 National Day celebrations in Tiananmen Square, when Mao and his current comrades-in-arms watched and were seen by a massive parade, signaled to the nation at large that something big was up.[4]

Over the next several months denunciations of Lin were distributed to ever-widening circles of the population; in the province of Jiangsu (population 54 million) alone, 1,577,000 individually numbered "top secret" copies were printed of *Zhongfa* [1972] 24, a ninety-two-page document treating the alleged crimes of Lin Biao and his generals.[5] With that kind of distribution, soon everybody knew, even foreigners, although until Lin was publicly denounced at the CCP's Tenth Congress in August 1973, he was referred to in the official Chinese press only as a political "swindler of the Liu Shaoqi kind."[6]

As knowledge of it spread, the Lin Biao affair had a profoundly negative impact on perceptions of the Cultural Revolution among all Chinese who had any pretensions to political literacy. For many who had accepted, if reluctantly or in astonishment, the early purges of the upper ranks of the CCP and the elevation of Lin Biao as being necessary for the reasons given by Mao and his CCRG lieutenants, the death and denunciation of the marshal were a profound shock. How could a man who had been at Mao's side for four decades, who had been the Chairman's best pupil and personally chosen heir apparent, have tried to assassinate his patron? More important, how could the all-wise Mao, who had detected revisionism among so many old comrades, have been unable to spot Lin Biao as being worse than all of them? The "September 13 incident" lifted the scales from the eyes of many Chinese. A devoted onetime party member wrote later about its impact on her and her husband:

> The revelations were shattering for me . . . So many of us had dedicated our lives to the future of our country, but what use were our efforts when the society was being directed by people like Lin Liguo? Both Lao Tang and I were disillusioned, aware that something was fundamentally wrong with the system in which we had believed so devotedly. I guessed that we were not the only

ones whose faith in the Party wavered, but no one could communicate his misgivings.[7]

For many, the Cultural Revolution was transformed from a crusade for ideological rectitude that would give birth to an egalitarian and collectivist society into a power struggle.[8] This perception, too, was misguided; had the Cultural Revolution been simply a power struggle, Mao could have ended it in early 1967. But this popular revulsion would help to make it possible in the immediate aftermath of September 13 to moderate the Cultural Revolution, and in due course to negate it completely.

The Lin Biao incident was a profound shock for Mao, too. He may have hoped to ease Lin Biao into retirement or disgrace, presumably on the grounds of ambition and duplicity elaborated by him on his southern tour. There would still have been unfavorable repercussions, but not nearly as damaging as what actually occurred. Doubtless as a result of the political setback he had suffered, Mao's "physical decline after the Lin Biao affair was dramatic":

> he became depressed. He took to his bed and lay there all day, saying and doing little. When he did get up, he seemed to have aged. His shoulders stooped, and he moved slowly. He walked with a shuffle. He could not sleep. His blood pressure . . . shot up . . . His lower legs and feet swelled, especially at the ankles. He developed a chronic cold and cough and began spitting up heavy amounts of phlegm. His lungs were badly congested.[9]

Wooing the Old Guard

Despite his physical condition, Mao understood that he had to recover from the political blow he had suffered. As a citation in a massive index of Mao quotes, published a year earlier, put it: "We must constantly revise our plans according to how our actual work progresses."[10] Mao chose reconciliation with "capitalist roaders" and "revisionists" whom he had discarded earlier in the Cultural Revolution. The policy was justified by another Mao-quote cited in a *People's Daily* editorial: "We should remain convinced that more than 95 percent of our cadres are good and fairly good, and that a majority of those who have committed errors are able to change."[11]

The briefing of the old guard on September 26 was a start. More dramatically, on January 10, 1972, Mao suddenly, and uncharacteristically, decided to

leave his bed to attend the memorial ceremony for Chen Yi, who had died of co-
lon cancer four days earlier.[12] "He did not even bother to dress. Hastily, he
slipped on a silk robe and leather slippers and insisted that we leave immediately,
ignoring our warnings about the bitter cold and gusty wind. We managed to
cover him with a coat and hat . . . and he walked stoically to his car." Hearing of
Mao's decision, Zhou Enlai immediately raised the status of the ceremony by inviting the exiled Prince Sihanouk of Cambodia and his wife, as well as senior
Chinese leaders.[13]

At the memorial hall, Mao told the marshal's widow: "Chen Yi was a good
comrade." He appeared to be crying, but his doctor judged that he was "putting
on a good show, blinking his eyes and making an effort to wail." In conversation
with Sihanouk, Mao exonerated Chen Yi and the February Countercurrent; the
marshal and the other veteran leaders were trying to oppose Lin Biao, Chen
Boda, Wang Li, and other subsequently disgraced leftists.[14] Mao also told Chen
Yi's family that the problem of Deng Xiaoping, currently in exile in Jiangxi, was
a "contradiction among the people," and Zhou told them to spread this verdict
around.[15] It was these conversations that gave Zhou Enlai the signal and the permit to revise policies, revive past practices, and rehabilitate earlier victims of the
Cultural Revolution.

For some it would be too late: Liu Shaoqi, Tao Zhu, and Marshal He Long
had died in disgrace in 1969; and the unexpected deaths of other CC members
around this time led Zhou to order medical checkups, and hospital treatment if
necessary, for all cadres at or above the vice-minister level, regardless of their
current political status.[16] But for those still living there was now a possibility of a
return to privilege if not necessarily to power, even at levels far below the CC,
because, for the first time in a long while, there was a credible scapegoat on the
very left of the political spectrum on whom those who were eager for change
could pin any number of "problems" seemingly in need of rectification. Zhou
Enlai worked hard to ensure that just such a rectification was launched, from top
to bottom.

Rehabilitation of Junior Officials

At intermediate and lower levels, the political fallout from the Lin Biao affair affected the criteria used to judge the cases of some of the early victims of the Cultural Revolution. In Beijing, a special tribunal was set up to reexamine the verdicts on numerous municipal cadres from Peng Zhen's city government and

party apparatus who had been laboring in factories and rural brigades in Beijing's suburbs since around the time of the Ninth Party Congress. Their rehabilitation—in part necessitated by an acute shortage of competent staff, identified as early as 1970—was now significantly facilitated by the identification of Lin Biao as an "ultra-leftist" on whom any number of errors could be blamed.

One widely accepted political practice of the Cultural Revolution was that comments on formulations, slogans, policies, and so forth directly associated with a specific senior leader were judged correct or incorrect depending on the standing of that leader, rather than on any intrinsic quality of the comments. The fall of Lin Biao and his transformation from a comrade-in-arms to an enemy of the people enabled the Beijing tribunal swiftly to dismiss the numerous "errors" that had consisted of no more than a critical remark about Lin. For example, it concluded that although a deputy director of the Beijing Municipal Planning Commission had indeed argued against the policy of "not under any circumstances dispensing with the daily study of Chairman Mao's works," it was no longer appropriate to make a big case out of this, since "those had been the traitor Lin's slogans."[17]

Alleged attacks on Mao's person or political comments previously judged to have been "malicious" in intent were also reassessed and in many cases found to have been far less serious than originally claimed. In April 1969, an entry had been made in the dossier of a senior official in the Beijing party Organization Department, alleging that he had "Slandered Chairman Mao's precious red book *Quotations from Chairman Mao*." Approached by a colleague suggesting that they go swimming, the official had agreed, responding: "I always carry my swimming trunks and *Quotations from Chairman Mao* with me, just in case I should need them." The tribunal downgraded the accusation of "slander" to one of "flippancy."[18]

In some rare cases, the tribunal went so far as to admit that it was unable to determine what a cadre's original "error" had actually been. A deputy director of the Beijing Municipal Bureau of Commerce had been accused of "opposing the study of Chairman Mao's works"; his original accusers had cited an alleged remark of his to the effect that when studying Mao's works "one must not pursue formalism, and not stress quantity but quality instead." The tribunal's conclusion was: "In our reexamination, we have not been able to identify in what way this remark amounted to opposition to the study of Chairman Mao's works."[19] By as early as March 1972, 90 percent of the altogether 6,627 department-level Beijing cadres who had been sent down to the countryside, dismissed, and so forth in

1969 had been "liberated."[20] Some central government officials became cockily confident that soon everything would be back to normal.[21] Similar processes were at work elsewhere in the country. Even though they did not all get meaningful jobs back for a year or two, they were nonetheless put back on the government payroll.[22]

The Wretched of the Earth

Changes for the better came more slowly, if at all, to the high-level "counterrevolutionary revisionists" and other political prisoners languishing in maximum-security prisons like the notorious Qincheng, in Changping county, an hour's drive from central Beijing, controlled by the PLA since 1967. Here is how Wang Li described the situation in Qincheng after his eventual release in 1982:

> Conditions in Qincheng prison were utterly inhuman, and more fascist than fascism! Especially during the first five years [1968–1972] when we were not even once allowed out of our cells to get some exercise and were given nothing whatsoever to read, not even the *Quotations from Chairman Mao*. Why, even in Zhazidong prison [operated by the KMT during the Sino-Japanese War] one was allowed to read the [KMT organ] *Central Daily News* . . . Especially inhuman was the practice of covering the windows so you could not tell if it was day or night, keeping the loudspeakers blasting out noise for 24 hours, not letting you see a doctor, force-feeding you a kind of drug that induced hallucinations, and finally announcing over the loudspeaker that today you would be executed and then calling off the execution at the very last moment.[23]

Mu Xin, who entered Qincheng around the same time as Wang Li, has confirmed the use of a variety of drugs in a harrowing account of the seven years and four months he spent there. The prison medical staff clearly regarded inmates as little more than human guinea pigs, and "there were certain doctors," Mu alleges, "who either consciously and of their own free will or because they were being forced to . . . not only did not set out to cure the sick but, on the contrary, 'vaccinated' the healthy with diseases and made the sick perish prematurely."[24] Between 1967 and 1971, more than sixty Qincheng inmates are alleged to have gone insane. During the same period, an additional thirty-four were either "tormented to death" and/or committed suicide.[25]

One of the Qincheng inmates who survived this ordeal and lived to write about it for a foreign audience was Sidney Rittenberg. An American resident of

China since the mid-1940s, fluent in Chinese and a member of the CCP, he had been an early supporter of the Cultural Revolution and made quite a name for himself as a speaker at Red Guard rallies, at which he was billed as a "staunch internationalist antirevisionist fighter."[26] Rittenberg had ended up in Qincheng on February 21, 1968, on the very day that Jiang Qing had announced in front of a Tianjin delegation that he was a "foreign special agent" suspected of being involved in the May 16 Conspiracy. Rittenberg recalls:

> My interrogations had stopped after Lin Biao's death. I should have been relieved at the end of that type of pressure, but I wasn't. They were my only chance at human contacts, my only assurance that my keepers had not forgotten me. Now I was completely alone. How was I to live like this, perhaps for the rest of my life? The walls were grey. The floor was grey. The door was a dull reddish color. Sitting on the low-slung bed, staring at the wall, I felt the room full of aloneness. It was not just the absence of other human life, but the presence of aloneness that seemed to fill the room, to shimmer between me and the wall, to weigh down the otherwise empty air until it seemed to press in and threaten to suffocate me.
>
> Alone alone alone alone alone. The walls beat my solitude into my head through aching eyes every hour of the day and night—great spots and bands of color floating and pulsating before my eyes, silence making my ears ring.[27]

In December 1972, Mao Zedong suddenly took an interest in conditions in Qincheng. In reaction to a personal letter from the wife of a vice minister who had been wasting away in Qincheng since 1968, he asked Zhou Enlai: "Who has prescribed these fascist methods of interrogation?" Adding that "they should be done away with, all of them," Mao ordered Zhou to launch an investigation, something the premier did immediately.[28] As it happened, the PLA ended up being given most of the blame for the "fascism" that had outraged Mao, and on January 8, 1973, control over Qincheng reverted to the Ministry of Public Security. Official sources all note a marked improvement thereafter in "the living conditions of persons being interrogated," but the extent of that improvement should not be exaggerated.[29] In 1975, just before his release from Qincheng, Mu Xin still had to suffer treatment that was, if anything, hard to distinguish from "fascist":

> They put drugs in my food and drink, tormenting my brain. Some drugs made me hallucinate, others induced a feeling of terror. Still others created an irrepressible urge to talk. And then there was one drug which totally inverted the

nature of everything I recalled. Day after day, when it was time to go to sleep, the drug would take effect and from then on every person or thing coming to mind would appear politically suspect. Come morning, the effect of the drug would have worn off and my mental faculties and my memory returned to normal.

Their intention, in tormenting me like this, was evidently to force forth some kind of confession that would then serve as an excuse for obstructing my release.[30]

By early 1975 Zhou Enlai and the CCEG would receive instructions from Mao to the effect that the examination of the cases of the major victims of the Cultural Revolution was to be concluded as soon as possible, and that "people are to be let out." In February and March that year, a series of meetings of senior CCEG members was held, to lay down guidelines for the speedy conclusion of the "cases" of, and the passing of an official verdict on, a number of Qincheng inmates.[31] On March 6, 1975, CCEG members Wang Dongxing, Ji Dengkui, Hua Guofeng, and Wu De presented Zhou with a draft report addressed to the center in which they noted among other things that "basic clarity" had been reached in a majority of the cases of the altogether 670 cadres being investigated by the First and Third Offices of the CCEG and its special "May 16" Case Group.[32] "An absolute majority of them," the report proposed, could be released. In the end, not an absolute majority, but somewhat more than 300 were released in the late spring and summer of 1975.[33]

There would be an irony about the discrimination with which amnesties were granted to prisoners across the entire political spectrum in that penultimate year of the Cultural Revolution. The only blanket amnesty granted was to the 293 remaining KMT, Manchurian, and Xinjiang "puppet regime" war criminals still behind bars. They were all given full citizens' rights and jobs upon release, and even allowed to travel to Taiwan if they wished to do so.[34]

On the other hand, there was no amnesty for members of the first group of victims of the Cultural Revolution, those CCP cadres whose crimes had put them on the revisionist end of the political spectrum, only a conditional release on a case-by-case basis into internal exile to some remote part of the rural hinterland with a variety of restrictions imposed. For example, the former party first secretary of the Northwest China Region, Liu Lantao, was released from Qincheng in May 1975, but forcibly resettled in Anhui province without the right to contact his family.

Worse still, the prospect of many more years in prison and a very slim likelihood of any pardon was the fate of those CCP members who were—and in many cases prided themselves on being—on its extreme "leftist" end (for example, the May 16 "conspirators" and the leading survivors of the Lin Biao clique).[35]

The Role of Zhou Enlai

In China to this day, Premier Zhou is given enormous credit for ameliorating the impact of the Cultural Revolution, both on individuals and on the country. But during the long-drawn-out process of rehabilitation after the Lin Biao incident, it was clearly Mao who took the initiatives and Zhou who implemented them. In the small number of CCEG cases for which such details are available, it was Mao who took the final decision. There is no evidence that Zhou played any major autonomous role in this realm. According to one leading member of the May 16 group who had to wait until 1982 for his release from Qincheng Prison:

> Today's historians have become partial and fail to respect history [when dealing with this question]. Mao Zedong is given all the blame for striking people down, while Premier Zhou is given all the credit for protecting people. This does not accord with the facts. As far as I know, all the decisions to protect people were taken by Mao Zedong and executed by Zhou Enlai. Had Mao Zedong not taken the decision, Zhou Enlai would not only not have dared, but not have been able to act either, since he was not in a position to decide what was to be done about important cadres. One cannot separate Mao Zedong and Zhou Enlai—make one into a bad guy, the other into a good guy; make one into a muddle-headed person, the other into someone with a clear mind; and say that one is wrong while the other is right.[36]

Yet in the immediate aftermath of the Lin Biao incident, according to one Western commentator, "1972 belonged to Zhou Enlai rather than to Jiang Qing's radicals."[37] The fundamental reason for this was the leeway provided to him by the condemnation of Lin Biao as a leftist.

The CCP leadership's first serious assessment of the post–"September 13" situation took place at a five-week-long "Criticize Lin and Rectify Work-Style Report-Back" conference in Beijing in May–June 1972, attended by 312 senior cadres from all over China. Zhou Enlai set the agenda and delivered most of the keynote speeches, albeit in daily consultation with Mao, who chose not to attend. At the first plenary session of the conference, Zhou announced that "after Liu Shaoqi, it was [Lin] who took the lead in opposing the Chairman."[38] At the conference, non-Politburo members were told for the first time of the existence of the letter from Mao to Jiang Qing, dated July 8, 1966, which showed, according to Jiang Qing, that Mao had early on realized that Lin Biao was up to no good, that "he didn't discuss Marxism-Leninism, classes, party leadership, or the broad masses; he only discussed the individual and palace coups, and he [Mao] saw that ideologically and theoretically he [Lin] was not a Marxist-Leninist." The original letter had been torn up and destroyed at the time, but now an edited version, reconstructed from a copy, was circulated.[39] Thirty years later, Xu Jingxian remembered that the editorial changes to the copy were no more than one or two at most, and very minor, such as altering the reference to Chiang Kai-shek as having in 1949 "fled [*tao*] to an island in the ocean," to read "buggered off [*gun*] to some islands in the ocean."[40]

The conference passed the verdict that "at every stage in the history of China's revolution, at every crucial stage in the two-line struggle within the party, Lin Biao always stood on the side of the erroneous line, opposed Chairman Mao's revolutionary line, resisted Chairman Mao's strategic policies, and more than once plotted to usurp Chairman Mao's leadership."[41]

There were no official minutes of the conference, but participants were expected to transmit the "spirit" of what had transpired to their respective constituencies and a wider audience. A transcript of what a Sichuanese audience was told indicates that the conference labeled virtually all of Lin's most recent "crimes," save that of fleeing to the Soviet Union, "extreme 'leftist'":

> In the Great Proletarian Cultural Revolution, Lin Biao emerged as an extreme "leftist" and put forward a number of reactionary ideas . . . Some years ago, the emergence of anarchism and birth of an extreme "leftist" trend of thought that prevented many good cadres from being liberated—these were the evil consequences of Lin Biao's pernicious influence . . . Together with Chen Boda and Huang [Yongsheng], Wu [Faxian], Ye [Qun], Li [Zuopeng], and Qiu [Huizuo], Lin Biao wantonly preached the counterrevolutionary thesis of "doubting everything," stirred up an extreme "leftist" trend of thought, spread slanderous rumors about certain leading comrades at the center, and furthermore covertly compiled sinister files on leading comrades at the center in a conspiratorial effort to bombard the proletarian headquarters.[42]

The radicals perceived the danger of this ideological framework to themselves. After all, Jiang Qing had first come to prominence in 1966 as an arbiter of cultural policy under the aegis of Lin Biao. Fortunately for Jiang Qing, she,

Zhang Chunqiao, and Yao Wenyuan were in effect running the new Central Propaganda Group created after the 1970 Lushan plenum—making it into a CCRG redux, according to some Chinese historians—and they were able to use this organizational base to advantage.[43] Accusations of Lin's being a rightist emerged: "Extensive documentation shows that the bandit Lin was a Soviet revisionist special agent boss who remained deeply hidden for a long time."[44] Zhang Chunqiao used Lin's treachery to try to refocus the argument: "What Lin Biao did was betray the country and defect to the enemy: this will be obvious to the people of the entire country right away. There's nothing worth criticizing here. In the future, the real danger is still that of Liu Shaoqi's revisionist line and of a leisurely, peaceful transition. Consequently, the emphasis should still be on criticizing Liu and not Lin."[45] But for most of 1972, Mao remained passive on the left-right issue, and Zhou was able to seize this opportunity to cool the temperature of the Cultural Revolution, most notably in foreign affairs.

International Relations

The most conspicuous and lasting changes in 1972 were in China's international relations, though they had their origins in decisions taken by Mao earlier. The announcement on July 15, 1971, that Nixon would visit China in February 1972 had transformed Beijing's global standing. From the Chinese perspective, the leader of the most powerful nation in the world was coming to Beijing like a foreign tributary to the emperor's court in imperial times. Other nations got the message. On October 25, 1971, the PRC was voted into the China seat on the United Nations Security Council with U.S. support. The U.S. State Department had lobbied for dual representation in the General Assembly, but with Kissinger again in Beijing to arrange the details of the Nixon visit precisely when the votes were being tallied, it was hardly surprising that the efforts of UN Ambassador George Bush failed to keep the Republic of China, soon to be known almost everywhere as just Taiwan, in the UN.[46]

The announcement of July 15, 1971, also had an impact in major foreign capitals. In London, the government of Prime Minister Edward Heath, which had been negotiating an upgrading of existing diplomatic ties to ambassadorial status, was furious: lack of any advance notice had undercut its own bargaining position. The Chinese government knew it had no need to make concessions. But at least Zhou Enlai had told his subordinates that the British should be informed that the attack on their mission in the summer of 1967 had not been sanctioned by the party or government.[47] Equally, Premier Kakuei Tanaka had to sacrifice Japan's very close ties with Taiwan before signing a normalization communiqué with Zhou Enlai in Beijing on September 25, 1972.[48]

These various breakthroughs, particularly the one with the United States, ended the isolation into which China had plunged as a result of the Cultural Revolution. For the first time, relations with the leaders of the "imperialist camp" had been blessed by Mao himself. Jiang Qing, whom Nixon described as "unpleasantly abrasive and aggressive," escorted the president to see one of her revolutionary operas, *The Red Detachment of Women,* and asked him: "Why did you not come to China before now?"[49] What she may have subconsciously meant was "Why did you come to China now?" For the opening to the capitalist West had to be discomfiting to radicals, who had hitherto had the luxury of pursuing their policies in a hermetically sealed nation. Moreover, it inevitably raised the profile of Zhou Enlai, the master diplomat and the radicals' main concern, as a torrent of visitors poured into China. Jiang Qing's consolation was that the newly established U.S. Liaison Office in Beijing provided her with movies; her first request was for a film about political assassination, *The Day of the Jackal.*[50] She also attempted to raise her profile abroad by giving long interviews to an American scholar, but sadly for her the biography appeared only after she had been overthrown.[51]

The Thaw

Zhou's achievements in 1972 should not be exaggerated. The political temperature still hovered close to freezing and was nowhere within the range within which it had fluctuated before the Cultural Revolution. Take publishing. The gradual resumption of the regular publication of books and journals with other than purely political content had begun in the wake of a national conference on publishing in the summer of 1971. At the time, Mao had even given the go-ahead for a massive project to reprint China's dynastic histories, and by 1972 the first volumes had begun to appear. But with junior cadres in the propaganda sector still very much concerned with not committing "errors" and worrying about where the line would ultimately be drawn between the permissible and "spreading feudal, capitalist, and revisionist poison," the actual sale of these and other books did not always proceed smoothly.

In February 1972, an irritated Zhou Enlai asked why only foreigners and no Chinese were allowed to buy the copies of China's classic novels *Dream of the Red*

Chamber, Romance of the Three Kingdoms, Journey to the West, and *Water Margin* on display in the largest bookstore in central Beijing. If the store had copies to sell, it ought to sell them to Chinese as well as to foreign readers, he argued. If it did not have copies to sell, it ought not to display the books in the first place, since all it did was "give the enemy an excuse to spread rumors!" Zhou's personal intervention appears to have made a difference, since only two months later the first 200,000 copies of a reprint of the classic novels went on sale to readers of all categories across China.[52]

In special bookshops off-limits to foreigners and most ordinary Chinese, but open to senior cadres and other privileged individuals, the first new translations of foreign works in years began to appear on the shelves. In January–February 1972, Richard Nixon's *Six Crises* and selections from his other writings were published. Later in the year, in connection with the establishment of full diplomatic relations, a number of histories of foreign countries appeared in translation.[53] By December 1972, the first new translations of foreign fiction had appeared, three Soviet novels. In 1973 a new "internal" journal, *Translated Selections,* devoted entirely to the critical introduction of foreign literature, art, philosophy, and social science and reflecting the views of the radicals, began to be distributed from Shanghai.

On university campuses, highly heterodox writings were once more made available to students starved for a more varied ideological fare than Mao Zedong Thought. At Fudan University in Shanghai, the Institute for Research into the Economies of Capitalist Countries not only published fairly uncontroversial reference books like *United States Government Organs* and *The Post-War Economy of West Germany,* but also put out translations of the most recent writings of Western Trotskyites. Intended to be denounced for their "reactionary ideological content," these writings may just possibly have struck a chord in the hearts of former Red Guards when they spoke of how a "fresh generation of revolutionary youth has come upon the world scene and is playing an ever more important part in its politics."[54]

In conversation with journalists from the Xinhua News Agency, whose investigative journalism was expected to uncover "unhealthy tendencies" among the younger reading public and report on it to the authorities, educators soon complained about the immense popularity of "obscene" books. Most were hardly obscene by Western standards, including as they did Dumas's *Count of Monte Cristo* and J. D. Salinger's *Catcher in the Rye.* In Shanghai, the black market price for a tattered copy of the former could be as high as 50 yuan, the equivalent of two months' wages for a young factory worker. The price on the Shanghai black market of anything containing images of nudes was, so the Xinhua journalists were told, "very high." "Obscene" books were alleged to be taking over "the cultural front" not just in large and medium-sized cities but in rural townships and villages as well. In many cases, their source was said to be Hong Kong, but in Beijing the authorities also pointed the finger at the foreign residents of the diplomatic quarter and major hotels.[55] Western-language novels and magazines, presumably more obscene still, remained under lock and key in university libraries.[56]

But young minds could not be shackled. The demise of Lin Biao and the opening to the United States sparked unprecedented soul-searching among countless young people in the cities as well as among those who had been sent "up to the mountains and down to the rural villages" to remold themselves with physical labor. In some cases, the ferment assumed artistic forms. The first sprouts of what eventually was to become a whole new school of genuine "underground" art and literature began to germinate. In Beijing, an ex–Red Guard by the name of Xu Haoyuan organized an informal literary "salon" among her elite friends, which met in the homes of their various families.[57] Budding singers, painters, and poets, as well as their groupies, exchanged forbidden books, sang banned songs, and dreamed impossible dreams. Invisible to foreign observers, and under conditions of extreme adversity and danger, the level of intellectual ferment in China was in fact rising, if ever so slowly.[58] As one foreign political scientist was subsequently able to illustrate, "acts of dissidence had been on the rise already before the start of the *Pi-Lin pi-Kong* (Criticize Lin [Biao], Criticize Confucius) campaign in mid-1973, and after 1973 signs of what in Eastern Europe was at this time being called a "second society" were visible.[59] The catalytic event had been the Lin Biao "affair."

As in the past, the CCP could mobilize the full resources of the dictatorship of the proletariat to disseminate propaganda about "orioles singing and swallows darting," the symbolic sign of the "excellent situation at home and abroad." The lone dissident, on the other hand, faced almost impossible difficulties in making his or her views heard by more than a tiny handful, not to mention almost certain detection, arrest, and punishment of unprecedented harshness. Those who actually dared to voice their opposition and dissent in public did not exhibit particularly profound powers of analysis or articulation, just bravery bordering on the suicidal.

In the spring of 1973, a forty-one-year-old engineer at the Chengdu Institute of Telecommunications, a CCP member of twenty years' standing named Tu Deyong, mailed copies of his "Ten Indictments against the Great Cultural Revolution" to a number of universities and revolutionary committees in different parts of China. Arrested in 1975, he explained his action to the police, saying that "after Lin Biao had detonated and blown himself up, I clearly realized that these evil creatures who made their fortune in the Great Cultural Revolution . . . are all jackals from the same lair and archcriminals and chief culprits intent on creating chaos everywhere."[60] Tu's "Ten Indictments" included the following:

★ The Great Cultural Revolution has subjected more than 90 percent of cadres and more than 60 percent of the masses to mindless attacks of every possible kind, political persecution, sometimes even physical ruin. It has seriously affected the eagerness with which cadres and the masses build socialism as well as the loyalty they feel toward the party. . .

★ The Great Cultural Revolution has had an extremely destructive impact on industrial production, with production stagnating, financial resources drying up, the state treasury being emptied, and people's standard of living declining. . .

★ The Great Cultural Revolution has led to an unprecedented (since Liberation) degeneration in social morals and has guided young people onto a road of criminality. . .[61]

On May 23, 1976, Tu was sentenced to life in prison for what was described as tantamount to "active counterrevolution." At one point during his interrogation he noted that "if someone like me, who has never been particularly sensitive in political matters and who has really deep feelings for the party and Chairman Mao, is now having thoughts like these, one can easily imagine how other people look upon the Great Cultural Revolution."[62]

One of the "other people" who Tu imagined had to be out there was a twenty-six-year-old worker in an optical instruments factory in Changchun, the capital of Jilin province, called Shi Yunfeng. In late October 1974, Shi sent multiple copies of what according to CCP Vice Chairman Wang Hongwen was an "extremely reactionary" pseudonymous handbill to fourteen different local government organs in Changchun. In the handbill, Shi subjected the Cultural Revolution to a damning denunciation, insisting among other things that "after" the Cultural Revolution, "society became increasingly chaotic as attempts were made everywhere to turn back the clock, and unhealthy tendencies became even more pronounced as the standard of living declined and the supply of goods failed to meet popular demand." China's universities, which in theory were now to have become institutions of higher learning for "workers" like himself, had in actuality been turned into "enter-through-the-back-door universities," he said. He accused Jiang Qing personally of having deprived China's 800 million citizens of their "national culture, traditional culture." But Shi's most damning accusation was reserved for the CCP Chairman, Mao's way of running the party and his "ultra-leftist" line:

> The leader of the party is an ordinary party member too. Oppose "blind faith in the individual"! Oppose "worship of the individual"! The Communist Party should not have a "party Emperor"! . . . To have a [Cultural Revolution] movement every seven or eight years is a line that spells the end of the party and the end of the country . . . Advance along the line set by the center at the "Eighth National Congress"! . . . The purge of comrade Liu Shaoqi was a conspiracy carried out by careerists who had risen to power illegally on a tide of ultra-leftism! It will stand forever in history as a flagrant injustice![63]

As if such "personal effrontery" was not enough, Shi had the audacity to propose that "comrades Zhou Enlai and Deng Xiaoping organize a temporary Central Committee and set up a special case group to examine the errors of the Great Cultural Revolution."[64]

Shi Yunfeng's handbills were taken very seriously indeed, not just in Jilin but also by the central authorities in Beijing. A high-powered team of investigators from the Ministry of Public Security quickly joined more than 6,600 specially assigned members of local security personnel in what became the biggest manhunt in the history of the province. The assumption of the investigators was that they were looking for a disgruntled cadre in a leading party or government body. Their surprise was said to have been great when they discovered that a "mere worker" had formulated all those "reactionary" statements by himself. After two years of interrogation and denunciation, Shi would be executed as an "active counterrevolutionary" on December 19, 1976—after the end of the Cultural Revolution—drugged and with his lips sewn together with surgical thread so he would not confuse his executioners by shouting revolutionary slogans (for example, "Long live Chairman Mao!") at them.[65]

By far the most famous and politically most sophisticated dissident critique of the Cultural Revolution to appear in China in the post–Lin Biao period was the 20,000-word-long big-character poster titled "On socialist democracy and the legal system," pasted up on a busy downtown street in Guangzhou in November 1974. Its authors, three former Red Guard "rebels" writing under the collective pseudonym Li-Yi-Zhe, subjected what they for tactical reasons called the "Lin Biao system," but which every reader easily recognized as China here and now, to a forceful critique. Unlike Tu in Chengdu and Shi in Changchun, they succeeded in finding a wide sympathetic audience, even among moderate officials in the Guangdong party and government apparatus. After a carefully worded assessment of the positive aspects of the Cultural Revolution, they went on to argue:

> However, the Great Proletarian Cultural Revolution has not completed its task because it has not enabled the popular masses to grasp tightly the weapon of the broad people's democratic dictatorship. In the summer of 1968, the rule of law under socialism "suddenly did not operate," and what operated in its stead was "political power is the power to suppress." Across the length and breadth of the land, everywhere there were arrests, everywhere there was suppression and imprisonment of the innocent. Where had socialist legality gone? It was said that it was no longer of any use because it pertained to the old constitution and the new People's Congress was still pending. It was a time of sheer lawlessness! This was a rehearsal for socialist-fascism in our country, and Lin Biao was the rehearsal's chief director.[66]

Though things had seemingly got better in recent years (and Li-Yi-Zhe made particularly positive references to the situation that had prevailed in 1972), countless problems remained. Addressing themselves to the upcoming session of the National People's Congress, which would be the first meeting of that assembly since before the Cultural Revolution, the authors maintained:

> But in many cases, among many of the genuine revolutionaries who launched a fight against the Lin Biao system, the executed remain executed, and the imprisoned are still in jail. The dismissed officials are still dismissed . . . People are not fools! . . . They demand democracy, demand socialist legality, and revolutionary and personal rights that protect the popular masses.[67]

At the time, these were highly provocative views. Timed to coincide with the National People's Congress in Beijing in mid-January 1975, the Guangzhou Revolutionary Committee at the orders of the central authorities launched a city-wide campaign to denounce those who held these views.[68] Although Li-Yi-Zhe were incarcerated for their dissidence, they were also able at what were

353

nominally "denunciation rallies" (but in actuality resembled public lectures) to enunciate their views further in front of wide and often secretly quite receptive audiences.[69]

Left Is Right

Whether by the mid-1970s an increasingly frail Mao still received, read, and digested information about this kind of popular dissidence is not known. Rumor has it that he did at one point read the Li-Yi-Zhe poster, or a summary thereof, and, waving a copy of it in the air, asked the key members of the Politburo if they thought they could write a credible refutation.[70] (None of them did, but the Guangdong Revolutionary Committee at least tried, describing the poster as an attempt to "gather together all the monsters and freaks and instigate the masses in a vain attempt to create chaos and reenact the Hungarian uprising on China's soil.")[71]

But it seems that in or around 1972, Mao had begun to rely even less on regular information channels than in the past. More and more, he restricted himself to reading not the Xinhua News Agency's current information reports and the like, but simply letters, sent to him from people he knew, from their children, or from the occasional ordinary citizen, and typically preselected, edited, abstracted, and typed up for him by the CC's General Office in its daily *Selected Essential Letters* and twice-daily *Summaries of Incoming Letters*. Zhou Enlai, Jiang Qing, and their colleagues, on the other hand, continued to read, react to, and more often than not attempt to manipulate the political agenda—and Mao Zedong—with the help of what they read in sources such as the Xinhua News Agency's *Internal Reference Final Proofs*.

The crucial task for the radicals was to rid themselves of the incubus of the campaign against Lin Biao's leftism. Much of what happened in 1972 would not have been possible had it not been for Mao's failure to define openly the "essence" of Lin Biao's "line" in terms of left or right. For months, Zhou Enlai had used Mao's ambiguity to push for changes that were implicitly anti-leftist. By October, internal reference material produced for the benefit of newspaper editors in Beijing was full of lists of suitable "formulations" to be used in a "denunciation of ultra-'left' ideological trends."[72] But behind the scenes it became increasingly obvious by late autumn of 1972 that the correct positioning of Lin Biao along the political spectrum would have to be resolved, since two diametrically opposite views had already taken shape and were competing. Matters came to a head in late November–early December, when Zhou Enlai declared himself "inclined to agree" to a "thorough denunciation of the ultra-leftist trend of thought and anarchism stirred up by the Lin Biao anti-party clique" proposed in a classified document from the Ministry of Foreign Affairs, while Zhang Chunqiao openly questioned the wisdom of this move and Jiang Qing announced that "personally, I am of the opinion that we should denounce the traitor Lin's ultra-rightism while we simultaneously denounce him for being 'left in form but right in essence' in certain matters."[73]

On December 5, a *People's Daily* editor, Wang Ruoshui, wrote a letter to Mao in which he described himself as in favor of going public with Zhou's formulation "the right is bound to return, unless we thoroughly denounce the 'left.'"[74] Wang's letter became the catalyst that prompted Mao to intervene. On December 17, Zhou Enlai, Zhang Chunqiao, and Yao Wenyuan were informed by the CCP Chairman that the essence of Lin Biao's line had been "ultra-right" and not "ultra-left"! The extant record of what exactly Mao told them is incomplete and not fully coherent, but it has Mao listing Lin Biao's alleged "revisionism, splittism, schemes and intrigues, betrayal of the party and of the country" in support of his contention.[75]

Mao's new authoritative characterization did not instantly surface in the media and become consistently used.[76] In most contexts, the trend was still to avoid, whenever possible, explicit references to extremes on the "left" as well as the "right."[77] The 1973 New Year's editorial in the national party and PLA press spoke at some length about the need to grasp the "essence" of Lin Biao's "revisionist line" and to subject it to "in-depth denunciation," but neglected to dub it either "ultra-left" or "right." Over the months that followed, the CCP's propaganda apparatus seemed concerned to explain why "ultra-left" was an *in*appropriate description of Lin's line, rather than to show why "ultra-right" was the appropriate one.[78] Given how counterintuitive some of the relevant arguments sanctioned by the party center at the time must have seemed to editors, it is perhaps not surprising that the first half of 1973 was a time when "political typos" appeared in great number in the party press.[79] Further adding to the highly esoteric quality of much public political writing at the time were strictly enforced censorship rules that

★ Forbade direct references to Lin Biao and Chen Boda by name (prompting the use of cryptonyms like "swindlers of the Liu Shaoqi kind")

★ Warned against quasi-transparent combined references to Liu Shaoqi by name and Lin or Chen by cryptonym (it was, for instance, *not* permissible to say "swindlers of the Liu Shaoqi kind and Liu Shaoqi")

★ Sanctioned denunciations of "real socialism," but frowned upon public use of the expression

★ While insisting that "revisionism" was indeed "counterrevolutionary" after May 1972, no longer favored use of the expression "counterrevolutionary revisionism" because it might seem to imply that there existed an alternative "revisionism" that was *not* "counterrevolutionary"[80]

Mao's pronouncement concerning the supposed "essence" of Lin Biao's line could and would be interpreted as an indirect criticism of Zhou Enlai. And at around this time, Mao was in fact already taking steps to counterbalance him.

Succession

For Mao faced a more concrete and potentially more serious problem than the characterization of Lin Biao's errors: who was to succeed the late marshal as heir apparent. By the summer of 1972, the four surviving members of the PSC were in a bad way. In quick succession, three of them received open "invitations to see Karl Marx," the news of serious medical conditions that would cut their lives short. Mao's collapse during treatment of his lung infection in January 1972 was nearly fatal. Kang Sheng, already suffering from clinical depression, was found to have developed bladder cancer. And on May 18, 1972, Zhou Enlai's doctors told him that he, too, was suffering from bladder cancer. Disbelieving in the efficacy of medical treatment of cancer, Mao's first reaction was to refuse to let either have surgery. Only Chen Boda, languishing in Qincheng Prison, was spared similar news, although the summer brought news of the termination of his political life when a Central Document, *Zhongfa* [1972] 25, formally labeled him a "KMT anti-Communist element, Trotskyite, renegade, special agent, and revisionist, guilty of the most heinous crimes."[81]

So who would run China after Mao? The Cultural Revolution had always been about the rearing of revolutionary successors. As the CCP's ninth polemic against Soviet revisionism had put it in 1964: "Comrade Mao Tse-tung has pointed out that, in order to guarantee that our Party and country do not change their color, we not only must have a correct line and correct policies but must train and bring up millions of successors who will carry on the cause of proletarian revolution." Indeed, as the polemic made clear, "in the final analysis" it was the succession question rather than the question of line that would be decisive in deciding the fate of communism in China.[82] This was why Mao had begun to tackle the issue of his heir apparent even before he settled the question of Lin Biao's line. In September 1972, he moved Wang Hongwen from Shanghai to Beijing.

Since helping Zhang Chunqiao seize power in January 1967, and with Zhang and Yao Wenyuan at the center, Wang had become effectively the party and government leader of Shanghai. In April 1972, he was made political commissar of the PLA's Shanghai Garrison. On September 7, Wang was summoned to Beijing, where he reportedly had several talks with Mao and was told to read lots of books. At a central work conference in May 1973, Wang would be assigned, along with Ji Dengkui and Wu De, to participate in Politburo work.[83]

Wang had a number of points to recommend him to the Chairman. He was of peasant stock, he had served in the military, and he had become a worker. Indeed, had he succeeded Mao, he would have been the first worker to lead the party of the proletariat after a succession of intellectuals and peasants. Wang was also young, probably thirty-eight. In a sense, Wang was Mao's pledge to the Red Guards that he had not forgotten them. If they could use their reeducation in farm or factory to become more like Wang, their future, too, might be transformed as dramatically as his. Mao had taken a risky gamble. The role of heir apparent had been transferred from the "best pupil" to a revolutionary symbol. It was a gamble that Mao would lose.

21

Zhou under Pressure

Wang Hongwen did not have the star power of a Lin Biao, so he would have to understudy for the part of successor. For the moment, Zhou had to occupy the uncomfortable role of No. 2 to which Lin's demise had elevated him. But Zhou's health posed a severe problem for the Chairman. On the one hand, since Mao could not be sure that he would outlive Zhou, he had to find means to constrain the premier and protect the legacy of the Cultural Revolution. On the other hand, Zhou's illness caused uneasiness among the elite. If Zhou were to die before Mao, who would emerge as heir apparent? Wang Hongwen might seem like a comer to Mao, but to veterans of the Long March he was but a whippersnapper, "a puppy, / Barely weaned."[1] In his enfeebled condition Mao could not risk a backlash among the PLA generals. He had to find somebody who could restrain Zhou Enlai and simultaneously inspire trust among the old guard. So Mao took another, even riskier gamble. In the spring of 1973, he recalled Deng Xiaoping to the colors.

The Return of Deng Xiaoping

The No. 2 "capitalist roader" had spent the previous three and a half years in Jiangxi province. Like other senior cadres, he had been evacuated from Beijing in October 1969, when Mao feared a Soviet surprise attack. Deng was moved with his wife, Zhuo Lin, and stepmother to a small apartment on the grounds of an old infantry school on the outskirts of the provincial capital, Nanchang. Deng and Zhuo Lin worked mornings in a local factory that repaired agricultural machinery. Deng was found a job as a fitter, doing what he had done as a work-study student at the Renault factory in France forty years earlier. A young soldier was assigned to them to look after the heavier household chores. Their elder son, Pufang, crippled as a result of a jump from a dormitory window at Peking University to escape Red Guard persecution, was eventually permitted to join them. Their other children managed to visit occasionally. For over a year Deng and Zhuo Lin even received their full Beijing salaries, later sharply reduced to cover only living expenses.[2]

On November 8, 1971, two days after learning about Lin Biao's death at a factory meeting of party members, Deng Xiaoping wrote to Mao expressing support for his "brilliant leadership" in the handling of the Lin Biao affair, and requesting that he again be allowed to "do a little work for the party. Naturally, it would be some sort of technical job," by which he apparently meant investigation and research. He also asked for two of his children to be allowed to go to college. The latter request was granted in April 1972, making it clear that Mao had received his letter and that his rehabilitation was in process. In May, Zhou Enlai ordered the restoration of Deng's original salary, and in October his son Pufang would be transferred to a hospital in Beijing for treatment at Deng's request.

In the meanwhile, Deng was getting impatient. In early August 1972, he again wrote to Mao asking to be returned to duty so that he could "make up for the past to the best of my ability."[3] On August 14, in a cover note to Zhou Enlai attached to Deng's letter, Mao explained why he had always distinguished Deng from Liu Shaoqi: Deng had been the leader of the so-called Mao faction in the 1930s, he had never surrendered to the enemy, he had proved himself in battle, and he had done well after the revolution, notably in leading the CCP delegation in its struggle with the CPSU.[4] Mao had given his imprimatur on Deng's return.

On February 22, 1973, Deng and his family returned to the capital. On March 9, Mao approved Zhou Enlai's report that the Politburo had proposed that Deng be restored to his office of vice premier and that the party, nationally, be so informed. Simultaneously Zhou started a brief sick leave, telling the Politburo that Ye Jianying would take charge of Politburo and MAC work; Jiang Qing and Zhang Chunqiao would handle organization and propaganda; Li Xiannian would run the State Council; and Ji Dengkui, General Li Desheng, and Wang Dongxing would implement cadre policy. Zhou returned on March 24 with his condition supposedly stabilized, and on March 28, accompanied by Li Xiannian and Jiang Qing, he met Deng for the first time in seven years; Jiang Qing's presence telegraphed to Deng the power realities to which he was returning. On the following day, Zhou took Deng to see Mao, who instructed the premier that in his restored role as vice premier Deng should take care of foreign affairs, and that he should sit in on Politburo meetings when important policy issues were discussed. Thereafter Deng was in attendance whenever Mao received foreign visitors if Zhou was hospitalized.[5] It would be Deng whom Mao would send to the United Nations in 1974, much to the disgust of Jiang Qing and the radicals, to expound the Chairman's theories of international relations.[6] But for the moment the Chairman proceeded with deliberate speed, perhaps to reassure the radicals, perhaps to show Deng that he was on probation. At any rate, Deng would not be returned to the Politburo on the next suitable occasion, the party's Tenth Congress.

The Tenth Party Congress

The irony of having a party constitution in which Lin Biao was still inscribed as the Chairman's most loyal supporter, close comrade-in-arms, and successor could not have been lost on Mao himself. Though he was clearly not a politician who bothered about legalities—except when he could twist them to his advantage[7]—the constitution in its present form was an official and continuing reminder of his folly for 28 million party members. Every new recruit would diligently read it and wonder. Only a party congress could revise the constitution—under Mao every congress produced a new constitution to reflect his changing political priorities—so the Tenth Congress had to be convened unusually early.[8] On the same day that he laid down the ground rules for Deng's return to duty, March 29, 1973, Mao ordered Zhou to get the Politburo moving on preparations for the congress.[9] Ad hoc groups were promptly set up to supervise the selection of delegates, draft a political report on behalf of the outgoing CC, produce a report and formal resolution concerning the "crimes of the Lin Biao anti-party clique," and, of course, revise the party constitution.

The Tenth Congress, held in Beijing on August 24–28, 1973, was attended by 1,249 delegates—not all of whom were party members[10]—but because of his deteriorating health Mao was rarely in attendance. He was suffering from anoxia (a shortage of oxygen), and his doctors had to install oxygen tanks at key places in the Great Hall of the People to allow him to attend at all.[11] During the Ninth Congress, he had delivered a number of speeches, some of them far from brief. On this occasion, he made no speeches, and indeed failed to produce even a single coherent "quotable" remark for the party press. The only thing he is known for certain to have said, during his one brief appearance presiding over the opening plenary session, was "Ah! Correct!" when Zhou Enlai, delivering the political report, had just said that since the death of Lenin, "the era has not changed" and "the fundamental principles of Leninism are not outdated; they remain the theoretical basis guiding our thinking today."[12] Seemingly an arcane ideological point, Zhou's statement represented a repudiation of a formulation once enunciated by Lin Biao to the effect that this was a new era in which the Thought of Mao Zedong had replaced Leninism.[13] Of course Lin Biao's words then were no more his than was Zhou Enlai's report "his" report. Zhou told senior delegates: "It may have my name on it, but I did not write it. It was drafted by comrade Zhang Chunqiao in accordance with Chairman Mao's thoughts, and has been gone over by Chairman Mao."[14] But Zhang Chunqiao, too, disclaimed authorship, telling a Shanghai delegate that all he had done was to string together a number of Mao-quotes, not all of which he himself had fully understood.[15]

But Mao's interventions had strongly influenced preparatory work and determined the congress agenda. As on the eve of the Ninth Congress, Mao reiterated the need for unity within the party, adding this time that one had to "adhere to principles, while not ruling out the necessary flexibility." This time, too, he was insistent on the elevation of a new leader, Wang Hongwen. On hearing that Deng Xiaoping had proposed that some old comrades might be employed as advisers, Mao jumped at the idea, proposing the creation of an advisory commission with himself as chair, only to meet with the united opposition of his colleagues. Unlike at Lushan three years earlier, this time he obeyed the will of the majority.[16]

The job of the Tenth Congress was to reaffirm the line of the Ninth Congress, which had trumpeted the victory of the Cultural Revolution, while denouncing its main beneficiary, Lin Biao. So both Zhou and Wang Hongwen, who reported on the new party constitution, asserted that the experience of the past four years, and the defeat of the Lin Biao "anti-party clique" in particular, had proved the essential correctness of the line adopted by the Ninth Party Congress. They cautioned party members against merely following whatever "tendency" happened to be the strongest at any given moment. At some point in the future, a new Lin Biao was bound to appear, and "independently of man's will" a new line struggle would then unfold. The only way to win that struggle and to defeat new forms of "revisionism" was to act in accordance with what Mao had already identified as a basic "principle of Marxism-Leninism," to "dare to go against the tide," "fearing neither removal from his post, expulsion from the party, imprisonment, divorce nor guillotine," as Wang's report put it, echoing Maoist standards that the Chairman himself would never be called on to live up to.[17]

The revised party constitution went beyond excising Lin Biao, inserting a number of passages reflecting the concerns of the radicals who had drawn it up. Additions included criticizing revisionism, the need to train revolutionary successors, the inviolability of party leadership over other institutions, most importantly the PLA, and the impermissibility of suppressing criticism. While the Cultural Revolution had supposedly concluded with the Ninth Congress, Wang's report and the general program of the new constitution asserted that "revolutions like this will have to be carried out many times in the future." But Zhou Enlai quoted Mao as saying: "Probably another revolution will have to be carried out after several years." Did Zhou Enlai reject the new constitution's formulation in the report Zhang Chunqiao wrote for him?[18]

Zhang Chunqiao, who had supervised the revision of the constitution, and Yao Wenyuan, who wrote Wang Hongwen's report on it,[19] were not the least bit interested in accommodating last-minute suggestions made by delegates on its wording. A proposal by a Qinghai delegate that a reference indirectly according quasi-permanent status to Red Guards as an "organization of the masses" be deleted was rejected out of hand. Also rejected was a proposal by a delegate from a State Council ministry that the term "arch-unrepentant capitalist roader" be deleted on the grounds that such people simply did not exist in real life.[20]

On the final day of the congress, having unanimously endorsed a decision taken by the outgoing Politburo, to "expel Lin Biao and the principal members of his counter-revolutionary clique . . . from the Party forever and remove them from all of their posts inside and outside the Party,"[21] delegates elected a new CC, consisting of 195 full and 124 alternate members. Mao, too frail to attend, had Wang Hongwen put his ballot in the ballot box for him: one delegate later described it as a brilliant exercise in symbolic politics, since "it showed that Wang Hongwen enjoyed Chairman Mao's trust to the fullest and that Chairman Mao had personally picked Wang to be his successor."[22]

A Shanghai history reveals how the CC list was generated: on the evening of August 27, the day before the election was supposed to take place, the delegates met in regional groups. The Shanghai group was only now told that it had been asked to add eight new members to the CC in accordance with certain criteria (the need for candidates from preferred constituencies, such as workers and peasants) drawn up by the congress screening committee led by Zhang Chunqiao and Wang Hongwen. But the delegates from Shanghai were not given the option of picking or proposing their additional representatives; that was being done for them by the screening committee. The outcome was that five of the new CC members "representing" Shanghai were not even among the delegates attending the congress. Not surprisingly, many of the actual delegates grumbled about this result. Some of the new CC members were awakened in the middle of the night in Shanghai, told they had been elected to the CC, and put on a plane to Beijing. The process gave a new meaning to the concept of the "helicopter promotion."[23]

But the key aspect of the new CC was that the number of military cadres on the CC dropped by almost half, the majority of those who disappeared having some form of association with the disgraced Lin Biao. The restoration of civilian dominance of the CCP was well begun. Another important aspect was the continuing propitiation of the old guard. At least forty full members—including Deng, Chen Yun, Li Jingquan, Ulanfu, and such February Countercurrent stalwarts as Li Fuchun and Tan Zhenlin,[24] all former Politburo members—and twelve alternates of the new CC were rehabilitated cadres who had been removed from office during the early stages of the Cultural Revolution.

On August 30, the new CC held its First Plenum. Mao failed to attend, again for health reasons.[25] In his stead, Zhou Enlai chaired the proceedings, limited to the election of a new Politburo and the ratification of a proposal from the MAC for a radical increase in its membership, from an existing twenty-eight to an unprecedented sixty-three.[26] Just before the plenum, Zhou and Wang Hongwen had together written to Mao and Kang Sheng and pointed out certain problems relating to the Politburo election procedure, arguing that it was imperative that there be ample advance consultation and exchange of information; otherwise "there can be no talk of democracy. If there are more than two hundred [CC] members and none of them knows anything [in advance], it's tantamount to forcing a decision upon them." Mao's answer was presumably positive, since an extraordinary "preparatory meeting" was held on the day of the plenum, at which Zhou spoke about procedural and organizational matters.[27]

The reason for the joint démarche is unclear, but if it reflected an attempt by Zhou to revive procedures adopted at the pre–Cultural Revolution Eighth Congress and abandoned at the Ninth, it would have been of little comfort to rehabilitated members of the old guard. The PSC was significantly enlarged, from five to nine, of whom four—Mao, Wang Hongwen, Kang Sheng, and Zhang Chunqiao—could be categorized as radical supporters of the Cultural Revolution; another two, Zhu De (aged eighty-six) and Dong Biwu (aged eighty-seven), were grand old men with little clout whom Mao could count on for knee-jerk support; General Li Desheng was a beneficiary of the Cultural Revolution, having risen rapidly as a result of his sensitivity to radical demands. That left only Zhou and Ye Jianying actively representing the survivors among the old guard and standing for moderation at the apex of the CCP. Presumably, Mao felt that in the aftermath of the Lin Biao affair he could no longer justify a five-man PSC of whom four were radicals, but though the appointments of Zhu and Dong were concessions to the old guard, Mao would normally be assured of an easy majority, even supposing anyone dared to oppose him.

Equally dismaying to the old guard would have been the ranking of the PSC. From the CCP's Eighth Congress in 1956 to the outbreak of the Cultural Revolution, the practice had been to have multiple, ranked vice chairmen. After the Ninth Congress, Lin Biao was confirmed as the party's only vice chairman under Mao. The First Plenum of the Tenth Congress marked a return to the earlier practice. Zhou Enlai was inevitably the first vice chairman, but Wang Hongwen's extraordinary rise was confirmed by his ranking as the second. Under them came three more vice chairmen, Kang Sheng, Ye Jianying, and Li Desheng, the last having risen almost as meteorically as Wang Hongwen. The three remaining members of the PSC, Zhu De, Zhang Chunqiao, and Dong Biwu, were unranked.[28] That Zhang Chunqiao was unranked underlined the galling elevation of his former subordinate over him. For the old guard, however, the grim fact was that Mao had again chosen a radical as his ultimate successor, and the standing of the radical group had been greatly strengthened. The old guard could only hope that Zhou, with over half a century of revolutionary struggle behind him, would be able to control Wang Hongwen, whose experience was only just over half a decade.

The Politburo as a whole consisted of twenty-one full and four alternate members. Of the twelve full members outside the PSC, two were radicals (Jiang Qing and Yao Wenyuan); five had risen to high office during the Cultural Revolution and as its beneficiaries could be assumed normally to side with Mao and the radicals: Ji Dengkui, Wang Dongxing, Hua Guofeng, Wu De, and Chen Yonggui;[29] Marshal Liu Bocheng, aged eighty-one and ailing, was another old comrade who would normally support Mao; two regional commanders, Xu Shiyou and Chen Xilian, were also beneficiaries of the Cultural Revolution who had weathered the purge of their central military colleagues; and only Li Xiannian and Wei Guoqing, the victor in the bloody battles in Guangxi in mid-summer 1967,[30] could be counted as active survivors from the old guard.

From the Tenth Congress on, the CCP leadership could be divided into three groups: survivors, radicals, and beneficiaries. Since the beneficiaries were indebted to Mao, they were natural allies of the radicals. But the radicals were not satisfied with being in the majority. They wanted to get rid of their potential enemies, and so long as he lived Zhou represented a grave threat. The Tenth Congress, far from promoting the new unity that Mao had enjoined upon his followers, became the springboard for a new assault on the premier.

Cracks in the Façade

The seriousness of the premier's position was underlined at the congress by the differences between the reports of Zhou and Wang Hongwen on issues of foreign policy, normally the premier's preserve. Indeed, since Yao Wenyuan wrote Wang's report, these differences are explicable only if Zhou chose to modify the draft given him by Zhang Chunqiao. Zhou stressed the need to uphold proletarian internationalism and the party's consistent policies, whereas Wang mentioned only proletarian internationalism, implying that other policies such as the opening to the United States were not "consistent" and might be abandoned. Zhou expressed solidarity with the proletariat and the peoples of the whole world subject to imperialist aggression, but Wang vowed to stand together only with the proletariat and the "revolutionary people" of the world. When citing the danger of war, Zhou warned of the possibility of a surprise attack by Soviet "revisionist social imperialism," but Wang warned against surprise attacks from both "imperialism and social imperialism." Both men quoted Mao's statement that "the danger of a new war still exists," but Wang, unlike Zhou, omitted the optimistic rider that "revolution is the main trend in the world today," as if wanting to emphasize the continuing need for Cultural Revolutionary policies.

Since the main substance of the differences between the two reports, other than greater radicalism in Wang's, was implicitly attitudes and policy toward the United States, the way Zhou justified the policy was particularly striking. After the announcement of the Nixon visit, the startling change of policy toward the United States had been justified by references to a wartime article by Mao explaining that it was acceptable to ally with the imperialist powers, the United States and Britain, against Japan, because the latter was the greater danger. But in his report, Zhou relied instead on Lenin's justification of making peace with the Germans in the controversial Treaty of Brest-Litovsk in 1918.[31] Had Mao begun to sour on the opening to the United States? Was he offended by reading reports that Western newspapers described the policy as Zhou's?[32] Only Mao could have authorized so flagrant an attack on Zhou's characterizations of the international scene.

In November 1973, after another visit by Kissinger, which included an interview with the Chairman, Zhou's handling of relations with the United States came under fire. Mao, who had told Kissinger that he did not believe in a peaceful takeover of Taiwan, possibly thought that Zhou had overemphasized that possibility. At a Politburo meeting ordered by Mao and extending over several days, Jiang Qing and Yao Wenyuan described the criticism of Zhou as an eleventh line struggle. To Zhou's evident surprise and dismay, Deng Xiaoping participated in the meeting and also criticized him; according to Deng's daughter, he had no option, because Mao had "demanded that every participant criticize Zhou Enlai." Doubtless this was the reason why many officers in China's Foreign Ministry believed that Deng had been brought back specifically to check Zhou.[33] But the radicals were not content with a single meeting; they launched a campaign against the premier.

Criticizing Lin Biao and Confucius

The *Pi-Lin pi-Kong* (Criticize Lin, Criticize Confucius) campaign was launched in the summer of 1973, transformed into a campaign to "criticize Confucianism, appraise Legalism" in 1974, and remained a prominent vehicle for allegorical politics, Cultural Revolution style, until the very end. But the ultimate target of the campaign was Zhou Enlai.

At the height of the campaign to "smash the four olds" and the denunciation of Liu Shaoqi's "Confucianist" *How to Be a Good Communist* in 1966–67, China's patron sage had not figured prominently among that which was to be "smashed."[34] In the overall scheme of things, the destruction of the Confucius Temple in Qufu in the winter of 1966 had been but a minor episode of rendering inoperative "Liu Shaoqi's central command for the worship of Confucius and restoration of the ancients."[35] At the Twelfth Plenum of the Eighth CC in October 1968, Mao had mentioned Confucius in passing in the course of rendering judgments on some of the PRC's "big intellectuals," as he called them. After accusing senior bourgeois historians Jian Bozan and Feng Youlan at Peking University of "spreading poison," and then openly disagreeing with the CCP's own historians Fan Wenlan and Guo Moruo for their positive assessment of Confucius, Mao ended by saying: "This is all archaic. I am not encouraging you comrades to do research on this stuff."[36] Before 1973, Mao's concern with Confucius and Confucianism had on the whole been peripheral to his overriding strategic aim of dealing with enemies closer at hand, both in space and in time.

With Lin Biao, however, things may have been a little different. In 1973, research on Confucius suddenly acquired a novel political dimension when it was discovered, during an examination of the contents of Lin's residence in Beijing, that the disgraced CCP vice chairman had been in the possession of "material" (for example, calligraphy, books, and index cards containing scribbled notes and quotes) implying a secret fondness for some of the basic philosophical and ethical principles associated with Confucius. Mao Zedong, it was said at this time, had long known that Lin had neither understood nor believed in the "isms" of Karl Marx and V. I. Lenin. In July 1966, according to Jiang Qing, Mao had already seen that "Lin Biao was not a Marxist-Leninist."[37] The newly discovered material permitted the central authorities to spin the Lin case in such a way as to imply that what Lin had been "as far as his thinking and his theorizing was concerned" was a closet Confucian.[38]

At a work conference in May 1973, called to prepare for the Tenth Party Congress, those attending were told that Mao had recently observed that "Confucius has to be criticized."[39] The group charged with building the case against Lin promptly put the incriminating "material" prominently on display in Lin Biao's and Ye Qun's bedrooms, so as to suggest that it had all along been an important part of their private lives; then they invited a handful of "big intellectuals" to inspect and develop from it an ideological critique of Lin.[40] Professor Yang Rongguo from Zhongshan University in Guangzhou soon became the best known of these "big intellectuals." After his article (personally endorsed by Mao) "Confucius—A Thinker Who Stubbornly Upheld the Slave System" appeared in the *People's Daily* on July 7, 1973, he was inducted into the *Pi-Lin pi-Kong* campaign, and received invitations to lecture on the subject of Lin and Confucius to audiences all over China. Here is what he told an audience in Hubei three months later:

I visited Lin's sinister thief's den in Beijing. "Dissipated and unashamed" is how I would sum up my impression of it. It was full of espionage equipment for use in a fascist coup d'état. He had quotations from Confucius and Mencius hanging on his wall and wantonly advocated their *Dao* [way]. He also had copied down, one by one, extended passages of Confucius on filial piety. You could see how he intended to advocate the *Dao* of Confucius and Mencius in his fascist coup d'état and how, had he succeeded, he would have peddled their philosophy even more wantonly. So we have to understand the great and profound significance of denouncing Confucius.[41]

The ideological or philosophical connection between Lin Biao and Confucius was tenuous at best. As Yang Rongguo put it:

> Their idea of covering for each other originated with Confucius. The members of the Lin Biao anti-party clique covered for each other, doing a lot of bad stuff, and they got this from Confucius. It was a concretization of his thinking ... Lin Biao picked up his scheming and craftiness from Confucius ... and that was also where he picked up his double-dealer workstyle ... No sunlight enters Lin Biao's bedroom, it's all gloomy. Everything about him was Confucian, from his ideas to the way he lived.[42]

For obvious reasons, much of the *Pi-Lin pi-Kong* campaign came to center on texts and commentaries on texts. The most influential of the latter originated with CCP-led research and writing collectives based on some of China's foremost university campuses. In Beijing, a number of "worker-peasant-soldier students" who had entered Peking University and Tsinghua University in 1970 (and who tended to be proudly ignorant of Confucius and Confucian philosophy) were drafted into a "*Pi-Lin pi-Kong* Research Group," where they found themselves working alongside the same bourgeois professors whom Mao in 1968 had accused of "spreading poison" (for example, Feng Youlan), but whose classical erudition was now found to be indispensable. Eventually, Jiang Qing was to refer to the group and its successor, the "Great Criticism Group of Peking University and Tsinghua University," usually abbreviated to Liang Xiao (Two Schools), as her very own "team of theorists."[43]

The team's members were only too eager to please their powerful benefactress. After being invited to join her on an "inspection tour" of Tianjin, the ailing Feng Youlan presented Jiang Qing with the following poem: "Bringing unity once more to the shattered mountains and torn rivers, the poor and common people are made equals of the most powerful clans; [Wu] Zetian was bold enough to declare herself empress, and since time immemorial, such have been the women heroes of anti-Confucianism."[44]

One of Liang Xiao's first significant products was the compilation *Lin Biao and the* Dao *of Confucius and Mencius (Documentation I)*.[45] A slim volume of excerpts from a broad range of texts, it acquired an extraordinarily wide audience when, in January 1974, Mao Zedong agreed to a direct request from Wang Hongwen and Jiang Qing to have it circulated nationwide as the first Central Document of the new year "in order to help further deepen the present criticism of Lin and Confucius."⁴⁶ *Zhongfa* [1974] 1 employed the familiar Cultural Revolutionary means of selective contrastive quotations to support the claim that Lin Biao had attempted to "strike a pretentious pose, deceive and intimidate people, prepare counterrevolutionary public opinion, conspire wantonly, and furiously attack the proletariat."⁴⁷ Under the heading "Modeling Himself on Confucius 'to Subdue One's Self and Return to Propriety' and Vainly Attempting to Restore Capitalism," it reproduced the following quotations on its first page:

Lin Biao
Of all the myriad things,
herein alone lies greatness,
to subdue one's self and return to propriety.
Written for Comrade Ye Qun
Yurong [Lin Biao–ED.]
October 19, 1969
(Calligraphy scroll, Lin Biao's bedroom)

Confucius and Mencius
To subdue one's self and return to propriety is perfect virtue. If a man can for one day subdue himself and return to propriety, all under heaven will ascribe perfect virtue to him.
The Analects: "Yanyuan"⁴⁸

To help readers arrive at a politically correct understanding of what these passages "really" meant, the editors included a translation into modern Chinese of the archaic quotation from *The Analects* and a contextualizing exegetical note to the calligraphy sample from Lin Biao's bedroom. The note read in full:

Note: "To subdue one's self and return to propriety" was the reactionary guiding principle of Confucius' restoration of the slave system. Between October 1969 and January 1970, in less than three months, Lin Biao and Ye Qun wrote out the above passage [on] four [different occasions]. This fully revealed the urgency with which they pursued their wild ambition to subvert the dictatorship of the proletariat and how they regarded the restoration of capitalism as the biggest of all things.

The "reactionary guiding principle of restoration" mentioned here had in fact been a key element in Professor Yang Rongguo's pathbreaking article, which had attacked Confucius without linking him with Lin Biao. "Restoration" became one of the two major themes of the *Pi-Lin pi-Kong* campaign,[49] and ultimately an allegorical vehicle for an attack on Zhou Enlai.

Professor Yang had argued that a fundamental principle of Confucius had been to restore the disappearing slave-owning society and to suppress the new things emerging in feudal society. Confucius' political slogan had been "Revive states that have been extinguished, restore families whose line of succession has been broken, and call to office those who have retired to obscurity." Confucius had advocated "benevolence," but only toward the declining slave-owners; they should not be abandoned if they had done nothing seriously wrong, but should be united to prevent the slaves from staging rebellions. When a disobedient disciple had helped to carry out reforms, Confucius apparently denounced him as betraying the "code of the Duke of Zhou." With that reference to Zhou Enlai's historical namesake, one of the most respected Chinese statesmen of all time, Professor Yang hardly needed the quotation from Mao on the importance of historical analysis for guiding current movements to point out the contemporary moral, especially as in private among the elite, Zhou had sometimes been referred to as the Duke of Zhou (*Zhou gong*) as early as the 1950s.[50] Yang's article was a counterattack against Zhou's rehabilitation of people and policies in 1972. In a later Yang article linking Confucius with Lin Biao, the theme of restoring old families disappeared.[51]

Since Mao and the CCP center had not given the *Pi-Lin pi-Kong* campaign a more substantive target than "manifestations" of whatever reactionary ideology Lin Biao and Confucius may have espoused, it was only to be expected that opportunistic political actors everywhere and at all levels would try to claim for themselves the right to define, circumscribe, and control the concretization of those "manifestations." Everybody with the rhetorical means at his or her disposal promptly set about turning individual targets of choice into targets of the *Pi-Lin pi-Kong* campaign.

The agenda of the Liang Xiao team, for instance, was clearly to strike a fine balance between the minimum necessary criticism of Lin Biao and a more immediately relevant criticism of [other] so-called "present-day Confucians." In June 1974 Jiang Qing had complained to the members of the team that few articles mentioned the latter: "Are we to conclude that there are no present-day Confucians? If that is the case, why are we criticizing Confucius? Why are we having this big a campaign? . . . You must not assume that once we have social-ism we have no more Confucians; in fact our party has seen the emergence of no small number of Confucians."[52]

Unfortunately for those who like Jiang Qing wished to target the *Pi-Lin pi-Kong* more strongly at the "present-day Confucians," some of the techniques de-vised in cooperation with the CCEG made doing so difficult, for example, the practice of anchoring key accusations in "materials" found in Lin's home. The latter, after all, were limited in range and volume. While compiling *Lin Biao and the* Dao *of Confucius and Mencius (Documentation II),* which at Jiang Qing's re-quest was to be more openly allegorical than *Documentation I* and to target the "present-day Confucians," but which, possibly for this very reason, was never finalized even after having gone through nineteen typed-up drafts, the Liang Xiao team had no choice but to make the occasional false attribution.[53]

At one point, Jiang Qing and her team maintained that corrupt practices in the form of gaining admission to university and avoiding being sent "up to the mountains and down to the rural villages" by using private connections were ob-vious choices for inclusion among those things that ought to be condemned in the *Pi-Lin pi-Kong* campaign. "Then there's the issue of 'gaining admission through the back door,'" the head of the Liang Xiao team Chi Qun announced at the same rally at which Jiang Qing had demonstrated machismo by bragging about killing a local despot during land reform. He then went on to answer in the affirmative the rhetorical question: "Should the *Pi-Lin pi-Kong* be linked to it?"[54] But no sooner had Mao been informed of this particular linkage (which Jiang Qing and Yao Wenyuan appear to have endorsed) than he expressed his firm opposition. The matter of using connections to get ahead was an issue of major proportions that involved millions of people, Mao insisted. "Among those who have entered through the back door there are good people, too," he ex-plained, "just as there are bad people, too, among those who have come through the front door."[55] Those who were far from eager to see the practice of going through the "back door" become a target of the *Pi-Lin pi-Kong* included Zhang Chunqiao, whose daughter had used connections not only to join the PLA (rather than be sent down to the countryside) but also to enter university.[56]

As the weeks wore on, the central authorities found the progress of the cam-paign at the local level increasingly difficult to control. In many parts of China, it was quickly hijacked by forces whose concern was less with denouncing the reac-tionary commonalities that may or may not have linked Lin Biao to Confucius and Mencius than with enemies closer to home. In eastern China, CCP Vice

Chairman Major General Li Desheng (who had moved through the ranks at lightning speed since the beginning of the Cultural Revolution, when the 12th Corps he commanded had been stationed in Anhui) was targeted by those who not only disagreed with his policies, but who also believed he fitted the profile of the "present-day Confucians" and "Confucians inside the party."[57] On March 31, a last-minute telegram from the center was all that prevented the Anhui provincial trade union from denouncing Li in absentia at a mass rally in the provincial capital of Anhui. In Zhejiang, Hunan, Hubei, Xinjiang, and elsewhere, similar mass rallies targeting senior officials with a local connection of one kind or another were either held without explicit permission or aborted at the last moment as a result of a direct intervention by the man heading the center's seven-man ad hoc *Pi-Lin pi-Kong* monitoring group: Zhou Enlai. By mid-April, enough of a clear trend in how the campaign was being used and abused at the local level had taken shape for the central authorities to be able to issue the first of two rectifications.[58]

Beginning in June 1974, a new dimension was added to the campaign as articles appearing in *Red Flag*, the *Journal of Peking University*, and a new Shanghai-based journal, *Study and Criticism* in particular began to highlight the many supposedly progressive qualities of a historical alternative to Confucianism, the philosophical school of the Legalists. In the winter of 1973, Mao had informed the members of Liang Xiao that "all reactionary classes . . . venerate Confucianism and oppose Legalism, and oppose Qin Shi Huang."[59] The image of Lin Biao slowly faded into the background as more and more energy was focused on creating a historical discourse in which a clear red thread appeared to link the post–Cultural Revolutionary CCP to a number of "progressive" rulers of antiquity.

From now on, until the death of Mao Zedong and the definitive end of the Cultural Revolution in the autumn of 1976, a continuous stream of articles and books devoted to the "history of the Confucianist-Legalist Struggle" appeared in China. Some were doubtless meant to be, and could be read as, examples of historical scholarship, albeit of a very politicized kind. But all too many amounted first and foremost to allegorical commentaries on the present, with partisan commentaries on the sinister faults of particular latter-day "Confucianists," which were meant to be understood as attacks on leaders like Zhou Enlai, Deng Xiaoping, or Ye Jianying, and as shamelessly ahistorical praise of some reputed "Legalists," in reality nothing more than a cryptic affirmation of Jiang Qing's leadership credentials.

After the Tenth Congress, then, elite politics developed into an intense struggle between the radical rump and the survivors, with the succession to Mao as the prize. Veteran leaders who had been rehabilitated after the Lin Biao incident clearly cheered silently for Zhou Enlai. The beneficiaries, sandwiched uneasily between the two factions, doubtless hoped that obedience to Mao would excuse them from choosing sides or would at least inform them on which side they should be.

Meanwhile, Back on the Farm

The Aesopian language in which the confrontation was presented to the public was above the heads of the *laobaixing,* the "old hundred names," the common people. Only peasants with the Confucian surname, Kong, suffered, as in Dachuan in Gansu province.[60] But elsewhere, even if violence had by no means ended, these obscure debates were a welcome change from the days when anarchic Red Guard mobs had roiled town and country. Had the lives of ordinary Chinese changed for the better as a result of the supposed rollback of revisionism, feudalism, and Confucianism? All available data suggest not; rather, the Cultural Revolution had failed miserably to benefit those for whom it was supposedly launched. As one senior veteran, Chen Yun, put it dryly to the leadership of the People's Bank of China in 1973, "at this point, a considerable distance still separates us from that era that Lenin described as one when some public toilets will be made out of gold." Chen went on to conclude that China needed to do more research on how things were done in capitalist countries.[61]

Even with a return to an apparent normalcy, life was still tough in rural China. A nationwide survey of 27,433 rural production brigades in twenty-seven provinces and autonomous regions carried out under the overall supervision of the Ministry of Finance in 1974 painted a less-than-rosy picture of life in the Chinese countryside. The commune member's annual income in 1973 averaged 77.9 yuan in cash and 431 jin of grain, and had increased by an annual average of 1.7 yuan and 3.6 jin since 1965. A growing number of miscellaneous fees were being extracted from production brigades, amounting on average to somewhere between 4 and 10 yuan per year per commune member (equal to the extraction of an additional 50 to 100 percent of the state agricultural tax). A survey carried out in 217 people's communes in Jilin province in 1973 found that the fees were used to pay the salaries of local teachers and "barefoot doctors" (local paramedics), to supplement the earnings of brigade cadres, and to pay for militia training and miscellaneous infrastructural works. Although many of these uses benefited the rural population, the same cannot be said about the moneys extracted in the name of agricultural tax by county governments. According to the provincial authorities in Sichuan and Hunan, county governments were putting agricultural tax funds to illicit uses (for example, guest houses, football fields, opera stages) on a scale unheard of before the Cultural Revolution.[62]

Indigence led to migration. In theory, travel and movement, across provincial borders in particular, were firmly regulated with the help of such measures as domestic travel permits and locally issued rationing coupons with restricted validity. In reality, significant segments of the rural population, particularly in impoverished areas, remained largely unaffected by such regulations and migrated as they had always done from one part of the country to another under the most adverse circumstances in search of a better life. Between 1971 and July 1973, over one million "floating population" entered one of the traditional destinations, Heilongjiang province, though some "floated" out again. In January 1974, the Heilongjiang CCP Committee called on rural people's communes and production brigades in the province to "take the situation as a whole into consideration, adopt a spirit of responsibility toward the masses . . . and find ways of resolving the problems of production and livelihood" of the new arrivals. It also noted that since 1968, the province had succeeded in absorbing over 600,000 migrants, though nearly 300,000 remained "unabsorbed."[63]

Not all migration was voluntary. In April 1974, Hebei province reported to the State Council that since 1968, in a mere five counties in the province, some 300 young women from two areas of Sichuan had been "abducted and sold" to men in those five counties.[64] What was done about that case is unknown, but the problem was not limited to Sichuan and Hebei. In July 1974, the Heilongjiang Revolutionary Committee called on public security organs and courts across the province to intensify efforts to put a stop to the abduction of and trade in women as part of a general crackdown on forced marriages, sexual molestation, and violence toward women.[65] Women's rights became a prominent subtheme of the *Pi-Lin pi-Kong* campaign. Eventually, in February 1975, the CCP center prepared to revive the Women's Federation, dormant since the start of the Cultural Revolution.

Poverty in the countryside impinged on the towns. A prime concern of the central authorities was to prevent waves of unsightly beggars and petitioners from entering major cities, where they might disrupt law and order and, certainly in the cases of Beijing, Shanghai, and Guangzhou, give an unfavorable picture of China to the increasing numbers of Western visitors. After receiving a report from the Ministry of Public Security and the Zhongnanhai Central Guard Unit on June 13, 1972, Zhou demanded the speedy formulation and implementation of effective countermeasures.[66] In Hebei, the province surrounding the capital, the provincial party committee immediately sent a work team to Beijing to repatriate all petitioners who had got that far. Hebei also created four "Persuade and Prevent Points" at each of the four traditional entry points to Beijing, the cities of Tangshan, Zhangjiakou, Baoding, and Handan.[67]

This migration to the cities was hardly surprising. Urban living conditions were indeed better. Untold numbers of peasants would have been overjoyed to change their social status to that of an urban proletarian. But even for the proletariat, conditions had deteriorated. At work, the number of fatal industrial accidents had increased markedly. At the end of 1970, when it became possible to start collecting national statistics again, it emerged that fatal injuries in enterprises above the county level had increased 2.85 times from what they had been in 1965. The figures for the hodgepodge of small-scale subcounty rural enterprises, if they had been available, would almost certainly have been worse. Efforts by the central authorities to alleviate the situation foundered on their desire to keep the gravity of the figures secret.[68] As a result, in 1971 the number of fatal industrial accidents rose to 4.24 times what it had been in 1965, and in 1972 it was 4.31 times greater.[69] Half of the ventilation machinery in China's foundries was inoperable, according to official figures from the early 1970s; hence it was not surprising that the number of confirmed cases of silicosis in 1975 was double the figure for 1963.[70]

There was some progress in workers' conditions. Exactly a month before the "Lin Biao incident," the CCP center and State Council formally approved the first across-the-board wage increase in years for 28 percent of the nation's workers.[71] But there was pitifully little to spend the money on. At the end of 1971, the Chongqing Revolutionary Committee was forced to admit that "in recent years" more than 500 different kinds of light industrial products for daily use had essentially disappeared from the shops, mainly as a result of an enforced policy of "self-reliance," when in actuality no self-reliance was possible. In April 1972, the provincial labor bureau, in a denunciation of Lin Biao, compared the conditions of workers in capitalist countries—who lived "in hell"—to those of workers in socialist Sichuan—who lived "in heaven." The very same month, the Chongqing authorities began rationing liquor and pastries.[72] In Heilongjiang in July 1973, the revolutionary committee forbade all units or individuals in the province from operating distilleries and/or trading in alcoholic beverages without permission;

presumably bootlegging was rife because liquor was short.[73] In 1974, a classified State Council document produced by the Ministry of Commerce spoke of numerous instances of the "masses being instigated to make panic purchases." Items persistently in short supply or unavailable at this time mentioned in a history of Shaanxi province included "plain sugar, powdered milk, bicycles, sewing machines, soap, light bulbs, various items made of chemical fibers, porcelain, or glass, and wooden furniture."[74] The Ministry of Commerce later revealed that "because of a shortfall in industrial output, the market supply situation remained very tense throughout the entire year, with an estimated 1.8 billion yuan discrepancy between social purchasing power and market supply."[75]

Living conditions might have been improving, but slowly. In some respects they had got worse. In Harbin, the average city resident now had 2.28 square meters of residential space to live in, compared with 3.62 square meters at the time of the founding of the PRC. In Beijing, residents were better off in absolute terms, but here, too, life had become more crowded. City parks suffered from serious neglect and had in some places shrunk dramatically since the beginning of the Cultural Revolution. In Chongqing, 71 percent of the 81.73 hectares of "green" urban spaces that had disappeared by 1975 had been taken over illegally by urban families and residents desperate for additional living space.[76]

In Beijing, urban residents took matters into their own hands in what in some sense must count as the very first "Tiananmen Square incident": on October 31, 1972, thousands of ordinary residents of the capital descended on the square and dug up and carted off more than 20,000 decorative flowers that had been planted around the Monument to the People's Heroes. Zhou Enlai, infuriated that the municipal Public Security Bureau had been caught totally unprepared, read the riot act to the Ministry of Public Security and the Beijing authorities and invoked the same passage in "On Discerning Traitors" that Lin Biao had used in his May 18, 1966, speech: "When a halo of color surrounds the moon, there will be wind; and when the stone in which a pillar is set is damp, there will be rain." With so many "eyes and ears" out there in society, Zhou asked, why had nobody seen this coming? He concluded that effective measures must be put in place swiftly to prevent even more serious incidents. On December 22, an interim report from the Beijing authorities on the measures put in place so far was circulated nationwide in *Zhongfa* [1972] 45: there had been improvements in the way popular petitions were being dealt with, improvements in traffic management and firefighting capabilities, and changes relating to law and order, including better supervision of potential counterrevolutionaries in the national capital.[77]

The digging up of the Tiananmen Square flowers symbolized the disruption of socialist controls. The Beijing *laobaixing* had taken to heart Mao's adages, and had dared to think, dared to speak, and dared to dig. Zhou presumably understood the implications, but his fury at the lackadaisical policing was undoubtedly due in part to his begrudging the time spent moonlighting as a police inspector. He had far larger and more serious problems to cope with.

At the end of 1971, a concerned premier announced that China had recently achieved two simultaneous "breakthroughs," neither of them positive from a fiscal standpoint: the number of employees in state-owned enterprises had broken the 50 million mark, and state salaries now exceeded 30 billion yuan. Measures were needed, he insisted, to slow the further growth of these figures. Yet in 1972 the trend continued unabated: the number of employees in state-owned enterprises grew by 5.5 percent, to 56.1 million, and state salaries by more than 12 percent, to 34 billion yuan. In early 1973 Zhou Enlai announced yet another, even more worrying, development: "The amount of currency issued has also made a breakthrough. This is none too comfortable. Capitalism experiences economic crises, and even though we are fundamentally different from them, this is still not very comfortable."[78]

One uncomfortable example was Chongqing, possibly an extreme case but almost certainly not an isolated one: in the first half of 1972, a number of the city's industrial enterprises were so beset by difficulties that they had to increase their borrowing from the People's Bank of China by more than 6.7 times what the annual plan had anticipated for the entire year.[79] State Council officials such as Vice Premier Li Xiannian, whose portfolio included overseeing China's financial sector, were well aware of the extent and seriousness of this and similar national financial problems, but were unable to devise effective remedies. After reading a report about a profoundly mismanaged and consistently loss-making chemical plant in Harbin titled "Losing Money Is Unavoidable If a Factory Is Run in This Fashion," Li's only reactions were to feel "appalled" and to call on the provincial authorities to do something.[80] In October 1973, a devastating report about the Heilongjiang Production and Construction Corps informed Li that the corps had accumulated a deficit of 537 million yuan over the previous five years and that the size of the annual deficit was growing rapidly. Li's limp reaction was to say: "I don't think the people in the corps are content to let things continue in this way!" and, in a blinding glimpse of the obvious, added: "The problem is whether long- and short-term policies are correct or not; unless they are correct, it will not be possible to mobilize people's enthusiasm."[81] On the basis of his record as minister of finance before the Cultural Revolution, a fair number of intermediate-level finance officials in China had long regarded Li as "obedient, but incompetent," and in December 1974 Mao himself concurred by describing Li as "rather weak" by comparison with the "talented and capable" Zhang Chunqiao.[82]

A mortally sick premier beset with too many problems, big and small; an experienced and wimpy vice premier, incompetent or ineffective or both; a putative heir apparent without the skill, knowledge, or authority to step into the breach: under these circumstances, Mao decided that he had no option but to transfer the responsibility for running China to Deng Xiaoping.

22

Deng Xiaoping Takes Over

I f 1972 had been Zhou's year, 1975 was largely Deng's; or, as the radicals later referred to it, the year when "China's Imre Nagy, that arch-unrepentant capitalist roader Deng Xiaoping, attempted the all-round restoration of capitalism";[1] or, as it was redesignated after the radicals had been purged, the year that "witnessed an unprecedented awakening among people all over China, and the speeding up of the decline of the 'Gang of Four.'"[2] As in 1972, Mao was curiously unresponsive to the alarm of his radical allies. Like Zhou in 1972, Deng in 1975 took advantage of the Chairman's passivity to try to reverse the damage caused by the Cultural Revolution.

In choosing Deng, Mao was in part pursuing his aim of reducing the role of the PLA in civilian affairs. The "Lin Biao incident" had enabled Mao drastically to diminish the role of the military in the central party apparatus. However, PLA officers still ran most of the country outside Beijing. On December 12, 1973, in a series of meetings with a Politburo work conference and the MAC, Mao complained that the "Politburo did not deal with politics" and the "MAC did not deal with military affairs," a broad hint to the PLA to withdraw from politics. He supported what was reportedly Ye Jianying's proposal to order eight of the eleven military region commanders to exchange posts, thus removing them from areas where they were well entrenched and had long-standing ties to both civilian and military cadres. The sweetener was Mao's proposal that Deng Xiaoping should return to the Politburo and the MAC. Since these two démarches were simultaneous, Mao's tactic was plain. In order to persuade the regional commanders to leave their bailiwicks, he was implicitly promising them that, although Zhou Enlai was fading from the scene, they could be confident that his place would be taken by a member of the old guard, a Long March veteran with strong party and military credentials, rather than Wang Hongwen. The importance of this quid pro quo was underlined by Deng Xiaoping after the Cultural

Revolution when he hinted at his surprise that Mao's orders had been carried out within the time limit prescribed. After the anarchy he had inflicted upon the country, Mao could no longer count upon the automatic obedience of the PLA generals.[3]

In promoting Deng, Mao was also bowing to other forms of *force majeure*, Zhou Enlai's increasing feebleness and Wang Hongwen's clear ineffectiveness. Zhou Enlai's health had by now deteriorated to the point that the meetings of the State Council and Politburo he chaired could no longer be held in the Great Hall of the People or Zhongnanhai, but had to take place in the hospital. He took an active part in the preparations for the long-delayed Fourth NPC in January 1975, and even rose from his bed to make the principal report. It was an appropriate swan song. Zhou was permitted to reaffirm the need for the "four modernizations": agriculture, industry, defense, and science and technology. These goals had been proclaimed on the eve of the Cultural Revolution, but had been overwhelmed in the general upheaval.

Mao suggested that Zhou retire after the NPC, saying: "Your health is no good. After the Fourth National People's Congress you must relax and take treatment. Leave the State Council to Xiaoping."[4] On February 1, 1975, Zhou gathered the members of his cabinet by his bedside one last time to inform them that he was in effect withdrawing from active politics. "In future meetings of this sort [of the State Council]," he said, "comrade Xiaoping will preside." The next day, Zhou wrote to Mao and informed him of the new division of labor on the State Council. Deng, he said, would be "in charge of foreign affairs" and would be "running the State Council and sign off on major documents on behalf of the premier."[5] Mao raised no objections. It was, after all, his idea.

The other factor in the return of Deng Xiaoping was Mao's disappointment with Wang Hongwen.[6] On October 4, 1974, Mao had a staffer telephone Wang Hongwen, who was in day-to-day charge of CC work, to tell him that Deng should be appointed senior vice premier of the State Council. For the radicals the writing was on the wall. Moreover, Mao was not available in Beijing for the radicals to contact in crises as they had often done in the past. In mid-July, in search of better health, Mao went south and stayed there until mid-April 1975.[7]

After a stormy Politburo meeting on October 17, 1974, at which Deng and Jiang Qing clashed, the radicals deputed Wang Hongwen to fly to Changsha to see the Chairman, convalescing in his home province of Hunan. Wang warned Mao that the political atmosphere resembled that of the 1970 Lushan plenum, and accused Zhou of plotting with Deng and others despite his illness. But instead of sharing Wang's alarm, Mao told him to unite with Deng Xiaoping and warned him against Jiang Qing.[8] Mao was well aware that to associate with Jiang Qing and her Shanghai henchmen would be the political kiss of death for his young protégé, because he, too, would be tarnished with the radical upheavals of the late 1960s. But by now, the Chairman could see that, despite his high rank, Wang was Jiang Qing's catspaw, and unlikely to distance himself from her and his Shanghai patrons. Even if he did, he was unlikely to be able to carry the burden of running the country. At the end of December, in conversation with Zhou Enlai, and with Wang himself present, Mao remarked about Wang that "politically, he's not as astute as Deng Xiaoping." Deng, Mao insisted, was "politically and ideologically astute" and had "rare talent."[9]

So feeble was Mao by this time, and so unintelligible his speech, that this last remark did not come across; Mao was forced to try writing it down, although he got no more than halfway, when Zhou understood what he was about to say and filled in the rest.[10] But Mao was in sufficient command of his senses to propose that Deng now be made a CCP vice chairman, MAC vice chairman, and PLA chief of staff, the first civilian to be given the last post. It was a bitter blow to the radicals, and to allow them to maintain some credibility and influence, Zhang Chunqiao was appointed to take over the PLA's General Political Department and to be second-ranking vice premier.[11]

Even after the Fourth NPC, an increasingly frail Zhou Enlai continued to chair meetings of the Politburo and its Standing Committee, but in practice the day-to-day work of the party center was now also handled by Deng.[12] Deng, like Zhou before him, still did not have the power to issue *Zhongfa* documents on his own say-so. Such documents, and whatever policies and decisions were contained in them, had long needed the imprimatur of the party Chairman to become valid.[13] But with Mao still retaining that ultimate power of ratification, at some point around the beginning of June 1975 Mao Zedong and Zhou Enlai agreed between themselves that from then on Deng Xiaoping would chair the meetings of the party's highest decision-making body.[14] Thus during much of 1975, at Mao's orders, Deng Xiaoping had oversight of the Politburo, the State Council, and the MAC.

Getting China Moving

The reactions of the radicals to the rise of Deng were predictable. Wang Hongwen allegedly complained bitterly, mostly about the fact that he now clearly was no longer being groomed to take over from Mao: "What power do I have? The power of the party, the power of the government, the power of the military—I have none of it." "All that talk about wanting me to run things: they're the ones who made my life a living hell!" Wang also complained about Deng's being given access to Mao while he himself was not.[15]

Jiang Qing's complaints suggested that she was simply not able to cope with the steamroller methods with which Deng now ran things: presumably she had felt herself capable of manipulating the way in which Zhou handled decision-making, but Deng was an entirely new element. This is how she eventually described the way in which Deng operated in 1975:

> He doesn't give people time to think, doesn't circulate the documents [that are to be discussed/approved] ahead of time, so that by the time you receive them, you don't have time to read them. When you arrive at the meeting, there's a whole stack of them that you don't have time to read through, but he [nonetheless afterward] says "approved by the Politburo" and passes them on to the Chairman, forcing the Chairman's hand. Then he utilizes his encounters with the Chairman at meetings with foreign dignitaries and says "that's the Chairman's [opinion]" as a way of exerting pressure on the Politburo.[16]

Deng's method was to tackle problems promptly and head-on. Most formidable and urgent were those affecting the state of China's economy and armed forces. Symptomatic of how the Cultural Revolution had affected the performance of the economy (where roughly one-third of all enterprises were running a deficit) was the kind of thinking allegedly common among enterprise leaderships, that is, that being in the red was actually safer than making a profit, since it spared one the accusation of having "put profits in command."[17] On the State Council, Deng was aided by Li Xiannian, who by virtue of his seniority probably commanded greater authority within the government bureaucracy than any of the ten other vice premiers. His experience as minister of finance in the 1950s and 1960s should have been of great help to Deng. Mao, however jaundiced his opinion about Li Xiannian, had always been partial to having an older rather than a younger colleague overseeing the economy. Back in 1930, he had insisted, while commenting on what sort of person was likely to have the clearest grasp of socioeconomic circumstances, that "as far as age is concerned, old people are the best, because they have a wealth of experience and not only understand present circumstances, but know about their causes."[18] In dealing with the PLA, Deng worked in tandem with Ye Jianying, who by decision of the Politburo was put in charge of a reconstituted MAC Standing Committee on February 5. The MAC Standing Committee had ceased to meet soon after the "Yang [Chengwu]-Yu [Lijin]-Fu [Chongbi] incident" in March 1968, perhaps because Lin's generals felt that it inhibited their control of the PLA, and had been formally abolished as an institution by the Ninth CC. Its revival was one of many unmistakable signs of a return to pre–Cultural Revolution order within the PLA.

The long-term objective that Deng set out to work toward was the "four modernizations" that Zhou Enlai had spelled out in his recent NPC report. "The entire party and nation must strive for the attainment of this great objective. This constitutes the overall national interest," Deng maintained.[19] His immediate short-term goal was what he called "all-round readjustment," and his rallying call was a simple programmatic formulation consisting of three "directives" from Mao. First, there were Mao's words to the effect that it was necessary to study and arrive at a better understanding of the "theory of the dictatorship of the proletariat"—an idea that had apparently come to Mao while lying sleepless at the time of his eighty-first birthday on December 26, 1974[20]—in order to prevent the emergence of revisionism.[21] Then there was a remark that Mao had repeated a number of times, most recently while listening to Zhou Enlai informing him in Hangzhou about progress at the Second Plenum of the Tenth CC, which he himself was too unwell to attend: China needed "stability and unity."[22] Finally, Deng brandished Mao's instruction to Li Xiannian and Wang Dongxing in November 1974 that it was now imperative to "boost the economy."[23] According to Deng, these "three directives" should form "the key link in our work for the present period."[24] For public consumption, Deng maintained that all the quotes were equally important. In practice, he clearly gave priority to boosting the economy.

In late February 1975, the Politburo had called a national conference of party secretaries to tackle problems in the transport sector. Factional strife, labor unrest, and strikes were seriously disrupting the railways. Since this was the principal means of transport for industry, particularly for coal, China's prime fuel, the result was massive economic dislocation. In order to "boost the economy," Deng argued, one had to begin with the weakest link. "If the problems in railway transport are not solved, our production schedules will be disrupted, and the entire plan will be nullified."[25] On March 5, the Politburo took a formal decision, ratified by Mao and circulated as *Zhongfa* [1975] 9, to "improve railway work." The Ministry of Railways, just recreated after having been part of the Ministry of Communications since June 1970, was given extensive new powers. Railway officials were given until the end of March to get the trains rolling again. If they failed, Deng announced, their "misdeeds" would be treated as "crimes," and they would be punished accordingly. "Stop paying wages until he submits," Deng proposed; if someone's real "trade" was factionalism, then "why should we keep him on the payroll?"[26] Over the next couple of months, public security organs across China came down hard on so-called counterrevolutionaries and other criminals on the "railway front," subjecting more than 11,700 of them to public "denunciation and struggle," imposing formal sentences of varying severity on more than 3,000 "serious criminal offenders," and swiftly executing, amid a major propaganda blitz, eighty-five of the "criminals guilty of the most heinous crimes." In the words of an official source, these measures "basically put a stop to the evil wind of theft and looting of railway shipments, and allowed some degree of control over disturbances, including travel without tickets and clinging onto and traveling on the outside of trains."[27] By April, all but one of China's major trunk lines were operating normally again.[28] Deng Xiaoping had succeeded where Wang Hongwen had failed.

Deng turned next to industry, specifically to iron and steel and the aerospace sector. Here, too, he was not prepared to wait. "The experience gained in handling the problems in railway work will be useful to the other industrial units," he warned relevant officials.[29] By mid-May 1975, China's steel industry was lagging behind the plan target by 2.02 million tons, and Deng now called for immediate and rapid changes.[30] "The main cause of our sluggish iron and steel production is the leadership, which is weak, lazy, and lax."[31] In *Zhongfa* [1975] 13, issued on June 4, the Politburo ordered the reorganization of "leading bodies at all levels," beginning with the Ministry of Metallurgical Industry. Leading cadres should ask themselves: "Is your ideological-political line proper? Has a powerful leadership nucleus been set up? Has factionalism been overcome? Are the party's policies being conscientiously implemented? Has a resolute blow already been struck at the destructive activities of class enemies?" If the answer was no, then they should do something about it, and stop procrastinating.[32] At a national forum on the iron and steel industry, Deng told delegates to stop worrying about accusations of capitalist "restorationism" and to act with greater determination. In this way, they would come out on top in the end. By the end of the first six months of 1975, China's steel production was still lagging behind the national plan—output had so far been a mere 42.2 percent of the target for the whole year—but the daily output figure was up significantly.[33]

Deng's particular worry was the giant iron and steel complex in Anshan, built with Soviet assistance in the 1950s. Located in Liaoning province, where Mao Zedong's young nephew Mao Yuanxin had advanced at lightning speed to the position of political commissar of the Shenyang MR and vice chairman of the provincial RC during the Cultural Revolution, it was already 400,000 tons behind target by the end of April 1975 and underproducing by an average of 2,000 to 3,000 tons each day. Deng's preferred solution to the problem was a thorough restructuring of the complex and the creation of an Anshan Steel and Iron Corporation resembling that which had existed before the Cultural Revolution. Mao Yuanxin and his followers, however, spoke disparagingly about how "some old geezers at Anshan Steel are eager to set up a corporation and dream of once more becoming managers or vice managers and of satisfying their bureaucratic craving!" Not until Mao Yuanxin left Liaoning for Beijing in September 1975 to become his uncle's private liaison officer did Deng, in one of his last acts before falling out of favor again, override local opposition and get his way. On November 18, 1975, the CCP center called on the leadership of what was to be the all new Angang Steel Corporation to "conscientiously implement and carry out Chairman Mao's three important directives." To coincide with the establishment of the corporation there was a massive clampdown on "factionalism."[34]

The Seventh Ministry of Machine Building, responsible for missile and satellite development, was also riddled with problems. Disruptive factional infighting had been endemic since the very beginning of the Cultural Revolution. Years of stressing political "redness" at the expense of scientific expertise were said to have been indirectly responsible for a failed satellite launch in November 1974. Deng adopted the same measures he had used in the transport sector: a forcefully worded Politburo decision, a deadline for compliance, and a visit by a high-powered work team, this one led by General Zhang Aiping, director of the National Defense Science and Technology Commission. At the end of May, Deng told a meeting of the State Council:

> We told the Ministry of Railways, we would wait for only one month. Now we're telling the Seventh Ministry of Machine Building the same thing, that we'll wait only until June 30 . . . Come July, we're not going to be polite any more. We're not going to wait for anyone. I don't care if you're a tiger's arse or a lion's arse, I'm going to pat you anyway, fight you, and fight you resolutely.[35]

On June 30, the CCP center purged the ministry party committee by issuing *Zhongfa* [1975] 14. In a move that symbolized Deng's determination to put capable officials in key jobs whatever their political past, the most senior target of China's first Marxist-Leninist big-character poster in 1966, Peking University president Lu Ping, was made vice minister of the Seventh Ministry of Machine Building subsequent to a formal rehabilitation. Meanwhile, Lu's most senior attacker in 1966, Nie Yuanzi, languished in the political wilderness, a worker in an instrument factory on the Peking University campus.[36] Factionalism remained a problem well into the winter—on November 23, Mao himself complained to Deng about the "waging of factional battles" in the ministry[37]—but the impact had clearly been reduced or at least confined to nontechnical personnel and no longer impeded "vocational work." In the final months of 1975, four successful satellite launches were carried out in quick succession. With pride, the Chinese media now spoke of "three stars shining brightly from on high," and Western news sources concluded that the successful recovery of the fourth satellite indicated that Chinese scientists were "close to test firing an intercontinental missile."[38]

The formal decisions taken by Deng and the Politburo to make changes in the railway, iron and steel, and aerospace sectors became programmatic documents for how to proceed with readjustment elsewhere in the economy. In July, the State Council submitted a report to the Politburo on industrial production during the first six months of the year. It showed a constant increase in the production of crude oil, coal, electricity, chemical fertilizer, cement, and so forth since March. The plan for the first six months of the year had been fulfilled by 47.4 percent.[39] As Deng's "all-round readjustment" took effect, China's economy was beginning to recover.

Of course, readjustment was not so much a matter of fine-tuning economic priorities and practices as of taking decisive measures to deal with striking workers and procrastinating middle managers: banging heads. Here Deng was in his element. Before Mao had put him in charge, he had praised Deng in front of the Politburo, saying that "he scares some people, but he is quite competent."[40] In the summer of 1975, Deng showed these sides of his personality over and over again.

When readjustment in the province of Zhejiang was being obstructed by a radical workers' faction on the provincial RC, Deng sent a high-powered work team led by Wang Hongwen, Ji Dengkui, and the director of the CCP's Organization Department, Guo Yufeng, to the provincial capital to sort out the situation.[41] After three weeks of heavy pressure, the radicals caved in. A predawn raid on the headquarters of the workers' faction was followed by the arrest of Weng

Senhe, the factional leader known as "the Wang Hongwen of Zhejiang," who was caught red-handed in his residence frantically burning incriminating documents.[42] The provincial RC was thoroughly reorganized. The new leadership transferred in to replace the disgraced radicals included one Zhang Zishi, son of the third-ranking CCP vice chairman, Kang Sheng. Zhang was promoted from his post as secretary general of the party committee in his father's home province, Shandong, to become vice chairman of the Zhejiang RC and concurrently first secretary of the Hangzhou CCP Committee. PLA units were dispatched to key factories to forestall unrest.[43] Implicated party leaders were relieved of their duties, and the three members of the provincial RC seen as the most deeply tainted by "bourgeois factionalism" were exiled to the countryside to engage in manual labor and to be "reeducated by the poor and lower-middle peasants." In August and September, a massive campaign to denounce "factionalism" was carried out in the province.[44]

Deng made a more fearsome use of the PLA to resolve ethnic conflicts. The most flagrant case was the "Shadian incident" in the summer of 1975. Shadian was a Muslim hamlet, a rural production team with a total population close to 8,000, in southern Yunnan province, some fifty miles from the border with Vietnam. Serious ethnic conflicts had first erupted there in 1968, in the course of Cultural Revolutionary attacks on "backward" religious practices, and continued off and on through the early 1970s. By late 1974, after an abortive public protest by more than 800 Muslims from Shadian in the provincial capital, Kunming, demanding that the state honor the freedom of religion granted in the constitution—the delegation was accused of "creating a disturbance" and of "opposing the leadership of the party"—violence erupted between a locally organized "Muslim Militia Regiment" and the non-Muslim county administration's militia command. In early 1975, representatives of both sides in the conflict were called to Beijing, where a truce was negotiated, only to be broken immediately on the ground in Shadian when confusion arose about how the handing in of illegal arms was to be managed. Village-state relations deteriorated to the point that the villagers protested by refusing to pay grain tax to the state. On July 5, the CC issued *Zhongfa* [1975] 15, signed off on by Mao himself, which gave the PLA the go-ahead to enter Shadian to bring the situation under control if all other attempts to end the now increasingly tense standoff peacefully failed. With Deng in his capacity as PLA chief of staff giving the order—and at the direct request of the provincial authorities—the PLA was finally called in to settle the conflict. At dawn on July 29, Shadian and an additional half-dozen neighboring Muslim hamlets were surrounded. The PLA forces included a division from the 14th Corps, soldiers from the Mengzi military subdistrict, one artillery regiment, and people's militia. When the fighting ended twenty-one days later, Shadian had been razed and more than 1,600 villagers, including 300 children, elderly, and sick attempting to flee, had been killed.[45]

Rectifying the PLA

Although the PLA was a key tool in Deng's struggle to restore order throughout China, the military, too, had to undergo "rectification." Within weeks of the death of Lin Biao, in October 1971 Mao had announced that this process would begin at an expanded MAC conference in early 1972. Ye Jianying had already fixed a date for the conference to begin, prepared an agenda, and produced the first drafts of various conference resolutions. But perhaps Mao felt that the September 13 incident had left him politically too exposed to undertake a frontal assault on the PLA, that assembling the nation's generals might be counterproductive, for at the last moment he aborted the conference. "We should not be in a hurry," he told Ye: "At this point we should concern ourselves with the superstructure."[46] The meeting was changed into the month-long "Criticize Lin and Rectify Work-Style Report-Back" conference in the spring of 1972.

By 1975, with Deng in charge, it finally became possible to hold the long-anticipated expanded MAC conference. It became the lead item of the working agenda of the reconstituted MAC Standing Committee from its inaugural meeting in February until the conference opened on June 24. The conference, which lasted exactly three weeks, was attended by more than seventy senior PLA officers from all branches of China's armed forces.[47] Deng Xiaoping and Ye Jianying gave the keynote speeches and dominated the proceedings. In the wake of the conference, there was a nationwide reshuffle of senior officers, although at least one eagerly expected promotion failed to occur: on Army Day, August 1, 1975, the very first Xinhua News Agency dispatch from Shanghai describing the city's celebrations listed Wang Hongwen as a MAC vice chairman, but the error was corrected when the text reached Beijing.[48]

The conference assessed the danger of war within the next three to five years as small, but argued that ultimately the superpowers and China would become embroiled in some form of military confrontation. This was a significant reduction in threat assessment, especially compared with Mao's in autumn 1969. It permitted Deng and Ye Jianying to embark upon an ambitious program of cut-backs in personnel, and to stress the importance of "professionalism" and modern equipment in a way that had not been seen since before the Cultural Revolution.[49]

In a speech on July 14, Deng Xiaoping summed up the shortcomings of the PLA in five words, "bloating, laxity, conceit, extravagance, and inertia," all of which Deng saw as rooted in developments under Lin Biao and "especially in the later period under him."[50] "Bloating" was of course overstaffing. At the beginning of 1975, the PLA employed 1,526,000 cadres, or 467,000 cadres more than authorized. Overstaffing had always been widespread, but this was too much. One provincial military district boasted no less than fifty-eight district commanders, political commissars, chiefs of staff, and political and logistics department directors. The number of active PLA soldiers was also excessive, in view of the perceived lowered international tension. The MAC, itself "swollen" to an unprecedented degree, from sixteen members in May 1966 to sixty-three members in August 1973, proposed that the size of China's armed forces be reduced from 6.1 million to 4.5 million within three years. Both the PLA railroad corps and engineering corps had expanded their personnel since the beginning of the Cultural Revolution, mainly, one suspects, as a result of the massive manpower needs of the logistically complex Third Front relocation of entire factories from coastal China to remote and mountainous inland regions. They were ordered reduced, by over 60 percent. Least affected by cutbacks in personnel were the air force and the navy. Ye Jianying was, with Mao's consent, made head of an ad hoc group of six charged with reshuffling the leadership of crucial PLA bodies. The group completed its task in short order by the end of August, and a spate of dismissals, transfers, and new appointments was formally ratified by Mao. By the end of 1976, the total number of PLA officers and men had been reduced by 13.6 percent.[51]

By "laxity," Deng meant chiefly "factionalism and an inadequate sense of organizational discipline." He did not cite specific examples of military districts or army units that were affected, probably because the problem was widespread. Since the PLA's entry into the Cultural Revolution in 1967, far too many officers and men had in Deng's opinion become "embroiled in factional politics," and this involvement was having a serious impact on intra-army discipline. Deng's preferred solution was to relieve PLA officers of the civilian posts they had accumulated since the beginning of the Cultural Revolution, and when necessary to transfer them and their units to other provinces. Such reassignments were made in a number of provinces in 1975, including Deng's own strife-ridden home province of Sichuan.[52]

"Conceit," Deng admitted, had always been something of a problem within the PLA, but in recent years, things had gone from bad to worse, for in the course of the "three supports and two militaries," PLA officers had amassed more power than ever before. "Some members of the armed forces," Deng said, had become "arrogant" and "overbearing." When ordinary people complained about them and said: "Uncle Lei Feng isn't around any more," they were justified in doing so. "It would be dangerous to underestimate the gravity of these things or to lower [our] guard against them," Deng warned.[53]

Cases of intra-army "extravagance" were "increasing and have so far gone unchecked," Deng maintained. Some PLA units took things from civilian units at will, or bought them without paying the full price. Some officers "seek ease and comfort, higher salaries, more housing space, and indeed top conditions in every respect." The situation had to be changed. The sanitized partial transcript of Deng's speech distributed nationwide in the wake of the MAC conference had him abruptly concluding his call for a clampdown on extravagance by saying: "I am sure every comrade knows of examples in the army, so I need say no more on this point."[54] Given Deng's bluntness, his speech may well have originally included more than one powerful and telling example. As a concrete measure, shortly after the conference, the MAC for the first time, at least since the beginning of the Cultural Revolution, stipulated exactly how many cars, domestic staff, and secretaries a high-ranking PLA officer had a right to.

"Inertia," finally, meant an unwillingness to assume responsibilities. Some high-ranking officers no longer put any conscientious effort into their work, Deng maintained, nor did they lift a finger themselves, nor did they "use their own minds." Echoing Mao's observations on the same subject in August 1971, when the Chairman had complained that Lin Biao and Huang Yongsheng had become too dependent on their secretaries,[55] Deng now added a note of sarcasm: "They rely on their secretaries to do everything and even ask others to write a five-minute speech for them, and then they sometimes read it wrong." Mistakes were unavoidable, he admitted, and should be criticized. "But," he added, in a more conciliatory mode, "once they are corrected, that should be the end of it."[56]

In rectifying the PLA, Deng was doing precisely what Mao wanted: forcing the military out of civilian politics. Wang Hongwen could never have bent the PLA to his will in the same way. But Deng was taking a risk. In the event of

Mao's death, he would need the PLA generals on his side against the radicals. Yet he was prepared to risk their anger by depriving them of power and privileges as part of the process of restoring party control over the gun. Privately, the radicals would have welcomed his efforts in the military sphere. But not so in a field where they had held sway since the beginning of the Cultural Revolution: education.

Educational Readjustment

Mao's utopian ideas about changing completely "the phenomenon of our schools' being dominated by bourgeois intellectuals" had totally disrupted the pre–Cultural Revolutionary order.[57] Attempts at creating a redder, better alternative in its stead had made little headway, but Deng could assume that the radicals would strenuously resist any backsliding. Fortunately, Deng had staunch allies willing to go out on a limb for him. In education he was backed by Zhou Enlai's onetime aide and secretary general of the State Council, Zhou Rongxin. The Ministry of Education had been abolished in 1970, when some of its functions were assumed by a minuscule State Science and Education Group. The ministry staffers were "sent down" to a May 7 Cadre School in Anhui, some 625 miles from the capital, to have their "worldviews" transformed. When the ministry was finally recreated by the NPC in January 1975, Zhou Rongxin, who had fallen from grace in the winter of 1966 and only just reappeared, was appointed minister, though only after some complex negotiations and compromises among the members of the Politburo. Zhou Enlai, Li Xiannian, and Ji Dengkui got their way by ceding control over the Ministry of Culture and the National Physical Culture and Sports Commission to candidates put forward by Zhang Chunqiao.[58] Zhou Rongxin's appointment came as a major disappointment to Chi Qun, the chairman of the Tsinghua University Revolutionary Committee, who had coveted the ministerial position for some time and had been expecting to get it with the backing of the vice premier holding the education portfolio, Zhang Chunqiao.[59]

Beginning in May 1975, Zhou Rongxin set about shaking up the educational bureaucracy. In speech after speech, he pointed at, on the one hand, the huge distance that still separated China from the avowed goals of the four modernizations and, on the other hand, the fundamentally counterproductive policies being pursued and the inherent contradictions in them. For many years, the media, controlled by the radicals, had been denouncing what they called the notion of "studying to become an official." Zhou now asked if the assignment of a graduate from a poor peasant background to a job as a state-employed technician also counted as "becoming an official." In the media, workers who "returned to production" upon graduation were singled out for praise. Zhou asked why a worker after having gone to university for a few years apparently no longer qualified as someone who "returned to production" if he went on to become an engineer. In 1972, an attempt had been made to demand at least a minimum of educational qualifications from students vying to enter university, and not to take only their class backgrounds into account. In 1973, this attempt had backfired when denounced as a "reversal." Zhou insisted that something be done to remedy the situation that had existed since, with no clear criteria one way or the other in force. "In 1972," he said, "we issued a document saying that the interference exerted by Lin Biao's line should not be underestimated. In 1973, we issued a document saying that it should not be overestimated. The linking of the criticism of Lin to what goes on in the educational field is just one big mess."[60]

Like Deng overall, in the educational sector Zhou Rongxin was calling for a reassessment of the negative judgment passed on the "seventeen years," the period from 1949 to 1966. That judgment had been passed at a national conference on education in 1971 and spelled out by Zhang Chunqiao in the minutes of the conference (*Zhongfa* [1971] 44): Mao's "proletarian line in education" had on the whole not been implemented during the "seventeen years," and those who had received their education then had on the whole not altered their "bourgeois worldview."[61] Zhou Rongxin wanted to see this assessment overturned in a new policy document on education that could supersede the earlier "minutes."[62] Ultimately, he was to fail, with tragically fatal consequences for himself.

Controversies over "Empiricism" and Factionalism

Mao's contradictory behavior in the spring of 1975 involved backing Deng in practical politics, but continuing to support radicals like Zhang Chunqiao and Yao Wenyuan in the ideological realm. In the same conversation with Zhou Enlai and Wang Hongwen in December 1974 in which he had referred to Deng Xiaoping as someone with "rare talent," Mao also spoke of Zhang Chunqiao as "a man of ability."[63] Zhang's "ability," of course, was in a different domain altogether from Deng's "talent." The first of the trio of directives from Mao that, together, to Deng represented the "key link in our work for the present period" indirectly acknowledged this. In the Politburo's circular *Zhongfa* [1975] 5, "On

Studying Chairman Mao's Directives concerning Theory," issued on February 18, 1975, Mao was quoted as saying:

> Why did Lenin speak of exercising dictatorship over the bourgeoisie? Articles should be written. Tell Chunqiao and Wenyuan to find the many passages in Lenin's works addressing this question. Set them in large type, and give them to me. We should read them first, and then write articles. I want Chunqiao to write these kinds of articles. If this question is not clarified, revisionism will develop. The whole country must be made aware of this.[64]

To alert "the whole country" to the danger of revisionism, Mao and the Politburo launched a major movement to study the writings of Marx, Engels, and Lenin on the dictatorship of the proletariat. Zhang and Yao put together a collection of thirty-three relevant quotations from the Marxist classics and had them published in the *People's Daily* on February 22, 1975. Jiang Qing would later remark sarcastically: "Don't tell anyone I said this, but by comparison, when it comes to studying Marxism–Leninism–Mao Zedong Thought, the Politburo is the worst. Of the thirty-three quotations, they studied only three, and then they stopped. Sometimes it is just not possible to convene the Politburo, and when it does meet there's always a row."[65] Zhang and Yao also wrote two major treatises to set forth their own views and Mao's. Yao's was "On the Social Basis of the Lin Biao Anti-Party Clique," published in *Red Flag* on March 1, 1975; Zhang's was "On Exercising All-Round Dictatorship over the Bourgeoisie," published in *Red Flag* on April 1. Both articles stressed the overriding importance of class struggle and the proletarian dictatorship, spoke of the danger that commodity exchange might undermine the socialist planned economy, pointed at the worrying emergence of new bourgeois elements encouraged by material incentives, urgently called for pressing forward to higher stages of collective ownership and then to state ownership, and warned of the continuing danger of China's turning revisionist.

Revisionism was the target designated by Mao for the movement to study political theory, but Zhang and Yao managed by way of subtle shifts in formulations and rhetoric to retarget the movement at a subdeviation labeled "empiricism," and more importantly at Deng Xiaoping and his praxis of "all-round readjustment." Addressing a PLA audience in his new capacity as director of its General Political Department on the day Yao's article appeared in *Red Flag*, Zhang made the claim that "empiricism" should be a target of criticism by quoting Mao's preface to the book *Empiricism, or Marxism-Leninism*, first published in the aftermath of the Peng Dehuai affair in 1959 and most recently reprinted after the death and demise of Lin Biao. There Mao had maintained that "theoretically, we in the past criticized dogmatism but not empiricism. Now, the main danger is empiricism."[66] "The way I see it," Zhang explained, "the Chairman's words still remain valid today . . . Very many issues, unless you clarify them theoretically, will lead you to commit errors in policy, whereupon ideological errors in turn will become political errors, resulting in capitalism's spreading unchecked."[67] Jiang Qing concurred with Zhang and Yao at a meeting in the Great Hall of the People with workers from the Xinhua Printing Plant, insisting that "the main danger within the party at present is not dogmatism, but empiricism." After the meeting, well into the night and apparently after deciding that she might not have made her point forcefully enough and might be misinterpreted as too moderate, Jiang Qing had her secretary phone and explain to the Liang Xiao writing group that "the main danger at present is empiricism: it is the great enemy, the accomplice of revisionism, and the great enemy facing us that has to be struck down."[68]

The Chinese national media were at this stage firmly in the hands of Zhang Chunqiao and Yao Wenyuan. The Central Propaganda Department was no longer institutionally functional; most of its staff had been languishing in a May 7 Cadre School in Ningxia since 1970, and the supervision and control exercised by the central authorities over time became highly personalized. In Beijing and Shanghai, one newspaper article after another attacked "empiricists," who were "wrapped up in unprincipled practicalism, content to engage in myopic routinism, and who conduct everything according to their own particular experience, while refusing to listen to the views of others."[69] By implication, Deng Xiaoping, with his brusque, results-oriented style of running meetings, was just such a person.

In April 1975, perhaps worried by the way the movement to study theory was developing, Deng approached Mao during a reception for the visiting North Korean "great leader" Kim Il Sung to find out where he stood. Mao not only gave Deng his backing, but also said to Kim while pointing at Deng: "I don't want to talk about political affairs . . . You can talk with him about them. His name is Deng Xiaoping. He knows how to fight wars, and he knows how to fight revisionism. The Red Guards attacked him, but now there's no problem. He was forced out of office for several years, but today he's back. We need him."[70] Deng's argument as restated a few weeks later in conversation with members of the State Council was simple, and it hinged on the distinction in Chinese between the word for "empiricism" *(jingyanzhuyi)*—literally "experience-ism"—and plain "experience" *(jingyan)*. "We maintain," Deng said, "that empiricism is bad, but forget the two characters meaning 'ism.' Experience is precious, and must not be neglected."[71]

For once, in a matter of theoretical import, the Chairman came down on the side of Deng Xiaoping. When the Xinhua News Agency through Yao Wenyuan submitted a report to Mao proposing that the national media henceforth should "propagate in particular how cadres at all levels, through study [of the theory of the dictatorship of the proletariat] have understood and denounced the danger of empiricism, and consciously set about overcoming empiricism," Mao responded with a strongly worded comment directed above all, but not only, at Yao Wenyuan. First of all, Mao emphasized, the right way to state the problem was "to oppose revisionism, which means opposing both empiricism and dogmatism." Furthermore, Mao continued: "There are not many people in our party who really understand Marxism-Leninism. Some people think they do, while in actuality they don't really. They consider themselves always in the right, and keep lecturing other people at every opportunity which in itself is also a sign of not understanding Marxism-Leninism."[72] Most ominously for the radicals, Mao ended his comment by calling for the matter to be debated by the Politburo. Jiang Qing later insisted that the succession of meetings that ensued had been organized by Deng Xiaoping without Mao's consent, but this claim was clearly false. Later rumors emerging from China suggested that the meetings had been devoted entirely to criticizing the radicals. But Jiang Qing claimed that Deng Xiaoping and his supporters had distorted the truth about the proceedings, and that the meetings had criticized "both" sides to the conflict.[73]

But as of mid-1975, one thing could not have been in doubt, even for Jiang Qing: Deng was firmly in command.

23

The Gang of Four Emerges

Deng's position of strength in 1975 owed everything to Mao's blessing. The Chairman had not just rehabilitated him and given him important posts; Mao's criticism of the radicals convinced party officials that he backed the policies Deng pursued. In particular, when Mao began to label the radicals—Jiang Qing, Zhang Chunqiao, Yao Wenyuan, and Wang Hongwen—as a "Gang of Four," and made particularly biting remarks about his own wife, Deng and his colleagues could reasonably have concluded that the Chairman was finally waking up to the depredations committed in his name over the previous decade. Mao's new line would later prove a godsend to post-Mao historians. If the Chairman could not be exculpated for launching the Cultural Revolution, he could be excused from some of its horrors, just as Mao himself used Lin Biao as a convenient scapegoat to explain why marshals and generals had been treated badly.

For the outside observer, however, Mao's behavior remains a puzzle. If Mao really had been waking up to illegitimate acts by the Gang of Four, he could have had them purged with a snap of his fingers. But he would not, because the Gang of Four were his ideological praetorian guard. They, and perhaps only they, would propound and defend the ideals of the Cultural Revolution to the end. In that case, why did he undermine them to the benefit of Deng in 1975?

At the time of previous ideological breakthroughs—collectivization in 1955 and the commune movement in 1958—Mao had stressed the need for the achievement to be sanctified by improved living standards. The notional liberation of China from the tyranny of "revisionist" leaders during the Cultural Revolution needed to have had the same effect. Mao had looked to Zhou and was now looking to Deng to propel China toward prosperity. On those previous occasions, however, Mao had had to intervene forcefully to prevent backsliding from the ideological innovations. No longer physically capable of playing that role, Mao had to assign it to Zhang Chunqiao and Yao Wenyuan, particularly Zhang.

Jiang Qing and Wang Hongwen were less essential for that purpose, but Mao could not cast them off. After failing to detect the turpitude of his "best pupil," Mao could hardly admit to having made the same mistake with his wife. Equally, having chosen one disastrous successor in Lin Biao, Mao could not admit to another colossal error with Wang Hongwen. Besides, Jiang Qing, as his wife, and Wang with his high rank, did lend cachet to Zhang and Yao. So despite a series of attacks on Jiang Qing and the Gang of Four from July 1974 to September 1975,[1] the Chairman did not allow the matter to get out of hand. Nor did he allow it to rise to the top of the CC's agenda: "I'd say it's not a big issue, and we should not exaggerate it, but since it is an issue we should be frank about it. If it cannot be resolved in the first six months of the year, then let's resolve it in the remaining six months. If it cannot be resolved this year, then let's resolve it next year. If it cannot be resolved next year, then let's resolve it the year after."[2] A senior CCP ghostwriter who worked for Deng Xiaoping in 1975 said later that the only way to understand these words was that the CCP Chairman simply did not intend to "resolve" the "issue."[3] But there must have been times when the Gang of Four worried.

For instance, what proved to be the last Politburo meeting chaired by Mao, on May 3, 1975, was, ironically, devoted to a denunciation of the Gang of Four, "anti-empiricism," and the problem of factionalism. Mao maintained that "those who criticize others for being empiricists are themselves empiricists. They don't have much Marxism-Leninism. I'd say Jiang Qing is herself a tiny little empiricist."[4] At the same time, Mao, who had personally approved Zhang's and Yao's articles after having had them read out to him before publication, blamed himself for "making a mistake in not spotting . . . the part in [Zhang] Chunqiao's article where he talked about empiricism."[5] Bringing up the problem of factionalism, Mao told Jiang Qing et al. "not to behave like a gang of four," and reminded them that he had criticized them on this point a few times already, but all to no avail. "Why don't you unite with the over 200 members of the CC?" he asked. "Just a small number of people is no good, and never has been."[6]

Lending credence to Jiang Qing's claim that Mao also criticized other members of the Politburo for "factionalism" is the fact that Mao by this time was concerned with the emergence not merely of a "Shanghai gang" or a "Gang of Four," but with other cliques as well.[7] Official Chinese histories merely note that on

July 17, 1974, Mao had told Jiang Qing et al.: "You'd better pay attention: don't let yourselves become a small faction of four."[8] But the full record goes on with Jiang Qing saying cryptically that "now [Ji] Dengkui has moved in too," prompting Mao to continue by issuing the warning: "You be careful over there; don't become one of five!"[9] In March 1975, in conversation with some members of the Politburo, again according to the fuller record prepared at the time but never made public, Mao said: "you must not form any gangs, such as the Guangdong gang, the Hunan gang." An irritated Mao was hitting out left, right, and center at all kinds of factionalism, not just the Gang of Four.[10]

It is not clear what or whom Mao had in mind: Ye Jianying (born in Guangdong)? Hua Guofeng (a longtime Hunan official)? Or was he just rambling? This was after all an occasion when Mao was so blind with cataracts that he did not even recognize whom some of the voices around him belonged to, but had to ask his favorite woman assistant, Zhang Yufeng: "Uhuh. Who was that?" only to have her tell him: "Comrade Jiang Qing!" But Mao must have known that only eliminating factionalism and hammering out some kind of unity between Deng Xiaoping and Zhang Chunqiao offered any hope of China's becoming prosperous *and* remaining true to the ideals of the Cultural Revolution. And he underlined for the Gang Deng's special place in his memory by telling the May 3 meeting that Deng was the sole survivor of the "Mao faction" that had suffered on his behalf in the 1930s.[11]

At Mao's orders, the Politburo met again, now under Deng's chairmanship, on May 27 and June 3 to "help" Jiang Qing and her allies to mend the error of their ways. All subsequent official accounts of the meetings depict them as settings of "battle lines clearly drawn from the outset, with the two armies facing each other across the table."[12] Indeed, the keynote speakers on May 27, Deng, Ye Jianying, and Li Xiannian, subjected the Gang of Four to some very sharply worded "help." But again, the full record shows that Deng understood that Mao was worried about factionalism in general and wanted him and Zhang Chunqiao to work together to eliminate it:

> Not eradicating factionalism is out of the question. I always agreed with [Zhang] Chunqiao's interpretation that factionalism now is different from what it was before. We must be on our guard and not be blind to sectarianism or the emergence of a Gang of Four. It is not as if somebody had been provoking the issue. I am a believer in what the Chairman has said. It is not simply

the Gang of Four: We must all be on our guard. The Politburo is responsible for putting the fine traditions of the Chairman into effect.[13]

In his address to the meeting on June 3, Ye Jianying elaborated on factionalism and concurred with Deng that the situation was indeed different from "what it was before," a reference to the 1970 Lushan plenum and the "tenth two-line struggle" in the history of the CCP that had ended with the fall of Lin Biao and his cabal.[14] In short, neither Deng nor Ye made capital out of Mao's attacks on the Gang of Four. No wonder Mao's subsequent assessment of the meetings on May 27 and June 3 was "very good."[15] Maybe Deng and Ye could work with Zhang Chunqiao.

After the first Politburo meeting on factionalism, the one chaired by Mao, Zhou Enlai drew up a set of formal bureaucratic rules that might in theory, had they ever been adopted and implemented, have helped ameliorate the extremely unregulated politics that characterized the "issue" without actually necessitating the purge of the Gang of Four or any other faction. Nothing is known about what happened to the rules or whether they were even shared with anyone else.[16] But the Gang played the game according to the traditional procedures.

On June 28, Jiang Qing submitted a written self-criticism to the Politburo in which she admitted the "objective existence" of a "Gang of Four," and said that her own "factionalism" had indeed become so serious that it might yet threaten to "split the party center." She appreciated the criticisms and help she had been given at the recent meetings of the Politburo, she said, but still had problems seeing things the right way. The crucial passage in Zhang Chunqiao's written self-criticism read: "I will resolutely act in accordance with the Chairman's instruction not to form a Gang of Four, and do my utmost to promote unity. The least I can do is not to give the Chairman additional burden." Yao Wenyuan admitted in front of the members of the Politburo that it was "lopsided" to criticize only "empiricism" and not "dogmatism" as well. After being criticized by Mao in December 1974, Wang Hongwen had already written a 1,000-character-long self-criticism in which he admitted that "my errors are serious."[17] For the next three months, the members of the Gang of Four avoided each other's company to show that they no longer engaged in factionalism. Jiang Qing even managed a polite visit to the Deng Xiaoping household upon orders by her husband, but it did little to reduce tension. Deng later told his children that during the visit Jiang "blew her usual trumpet. Pretty low quality stuff."[18]

Although what had transpired at the Politburo meetings in the summer was meant to remain a closely guarded secret, news of the apparently declining fortunes of the Gang spread quickly within the upper echelons of the CCP and PLA. Wang Hongwen maintained that insidious "political rumors" had spread like wildfire after the enlarged MAC conference in July.[19] Jiang Qing claimed in September that "some people spread a rumor that the Chairman had criticized me for committing errors, but the Chairman hasn't criticized me. Some people on the Politburo just spend all their time spreading rumors." In March 1976, when the campaign against Deng was well under way, she was more explicit, insisting that all the "rumors" had emanated from him and his supporters, whom she described as the "biggest rumor mill of all."[20]

Deng's Think Tank and Policy-Making

In search of solutions to deep-seated, long-term economic problems, Deng launched further initiatives. One was setting up his own "think tank," the State Council Political Research Office, in the summer of 1975 to supervise the drafting of new policy documents, and to wrest control over political-ideological discourse from Zhang Chunqiao, Yao Wenyuan, and radical ghostwriter teams such as the Liang Xiao organization. The Research Office was headed by Hu Qiaomu, Mao's onetime political secretary and according to Deng Xiaoping "our party's number-one pen."[21] This think tank produced three major policy documents in the second half of 1975, but none of them were in the end ratified by Mao Zedong or distributed for implementation.[22] The first document, titled "Some Problems in Accelerating Industrial Development," stated that China's industry was doing badly because a handful of "bad people were sabotaging work under the banner of 'making rebellion and going against the tide,'" because management was "in chaos," and because of low productivity, low quality, expensive maintenance, high costs, and frequent breakdowns.[23] The second document, titled "Outline Report on the Work of the Academy of Sciences," pressed for better training, higher educational standards, more expert leadership, and more time spent on science (and, by implication, less on politics).[24] In finalizing this report, Hu Qiaomu and his colleagues solicited and received crucial input not only from Deng Xiaoping and Li Xiannian, but also from Hua Guofeng, who lamented the state of China's high-tech sector at a meeting called to discuss the report on September 26, 1975: "Out of every 1,000 semiconductors we produce, only one is up to standard. In Japan, a factory of 2,000 workers produces 7 million semiconductors in one month. With us it is entirely by chance that we make one that is up to standard. I don't know why, but so much is being wasted."[25]

The third and hardest-hitting policy document produced by the Research Office was titled "On the General Program of Work for the Whole Party and Nation."[26] As former members of the editorial committee for Mao's *Selected Works*, Hu Qiaomu and some of his fellow staffers buttressed their arguments by quoting Mao extensively. In effect, they cited the moderate Maoism of the 1940s and 1950s to criticize obliquely the radical Maoism of the 1960s and 1970s. To undermine the position that stressing economics was tantamount to revisionism, they cited Mao's 1942 book *Economic and Financial Problems,* in which he had said: "Talking of education or study separately from economic work is merely using superfluous and empty words. Talking of 'revolution' separately from economic work is like making revolution against the Finance Department and against yourselves. The enemy will not be in the least hurt by you."[27] In defense of their drive to "boost the economy" they cited Mao's words from 1945: "In the last analysis, the impact, good or bad, great or small, of the policy and the practice of any Chinese political party upon the people depends on whether and how much it helps to develop the productive forces, and on whether it fetters or liberates these forces."[28] In conclusion, they insisted that Mao's criterion of the productive forces was, and should be, "the only criterion that permitted one to distinguish real Marxism from sham Marxism, correct lines from erroneous ones, real revolutionary and socialist action from its phoney counterpart, and the true value of the work carried out by cadres." Yao Wenyuan commented that this formulation constituted a "perversion of Marxism-Leninism, and return to the theory of the productive forces."[29]

The finalized text of "On the General Program" was to have appeared in the inaugural issue of a new journal, sponsored by the Research Office and tentatively called *Ideological Battle Lines.* Though the publication of that journal had to be aborted as the campaign against Deng gathered steam,[30] "On the General Program" was published "for internal criticism" in August 1976, subsequent to discussion and approval by the Politburo, together with the two earlier documents produced under Deng's aegis. The publication of these texts—by then labeled the "three big poisonous weeds"—in the form of three little booklets and the distribution of 81,310,000 copies nationwide (in Chinese, Mongolian, Tibetan, Uighur, Kazakh, and Korean) constituted a major tactical error by the

Gang of Four, since most readers, just like Deng, found them quite "fragrant."[31] By making the content of the documents widely known, the radicals undermined their own position and buttressed that of their most formidable enemy.

"Criticize *Water Margin*, Denounce Song Jiang"

"The Chairman spent two months reading the 71-chapter edition of *Water Margin*, and then he made a whole bunch of comments." That is how Deng Xiaoping allegedly explained what the "Criticize *Water Margin*, denounce Song Jiang" campaign was all about, according to big-character posters appearing on Chinese university campuses in the winter of 1975–76. The poster-writers critical of Deng took this comment as revealing his disrespectful attitude toward Mao Zedong and his painful ignorance of Mao Zedong Thought. The campaign was really, they insisted, an integral part of the great Cultural Revolutionary effort "to heighten the capacity of the people to tell correct lines from erroneous lines, and to raise the level of their conscious opposition and resistance directed at revisionism."[32]

The novel *Water Margin*,[33] dating from the early sixteenth century, was one of the handful of classical titles reprinted in 1972 during the post–Lin Biao "thaw" in the cultural sphere. Jiang Qing had long been particularly fond of one of the main characters in the book, the leader of a peasant rebellion by the name of Song Jiang. When representatives of a Japanese TV company visited China in early 1973, intent on making a TV series based on the exploits of Song and his "heroes of the marshes," she had done everything she could to help them. In Jiang's opinion, as she explained it at the time, Song was "a remarkable historical figure, wise and resourceful, with a sense of justice, who robbed the rich and helped the poor, knew how to unite people, and as a result enjoyed the love and esteem of the masses."[34]

What Jiang Qing clearly never anticipated was that two and a half years later, her husband would suddenly make a number of statements concerning Song Jiang and *Water Margin* that were the very opposite of her own. The good thing about the book, according to Mao, was in fact that it taught "by negative example" what "capitulationists" were like. Song Jiang, who in the final chapter of the 71-chapter edition of the book accepts an imperial offer of amnesty, was, Mao opined, "no good as the leader of a team of rebellious peasants" because "he capitulated and practiced revisionism." With the appearance of an editorial in the *People's Daily* on September 4, 1975, this assessment by Mao, the contemporary relevance of which was if anything obscure, became the focus of a nation-wide campaign meant to complement the movement to study political theory. Detailed media analyses of the principal characters in the novel immediately gave rise to speculation among ordinary Chinese as to whether other senior con-temporary figures besides Lin Biao and Liu Shaoqi might in due course be iden-tified as "capitulationists"; but at first the thrust of the material was cautious. Western students, who had begun to arrive at China's universities in small but growing numbers by 1975, all of them eager to understand the finer points of the unfolding campaign, were baffled. How was the charge of "revisionism" leveled at the leader of a peasant uprising in the early twelfth century to be squared with the definition of revisionism in the most authoritative Cultural Revolutionary dictionaries as a deviation from Marxism proper, when Marxism as a coherent theoretical construct capable of "revision" had not emerged until a full seven and a half centuries later? Their teachers responded that Mao was using the term "re-visionism" very creatively and that, as a matter of fact, not only Song Jiang but Confucius too had "in essence" been revisionist!

Jiang Qing stressed the importance of understanding Mao's denunciation of Song Jiang in allegorical terms during a visit to Politburo member Chen Yonggui's model agricultural brigade Dazhai in Shanxi province in September.[35] Carefully not naming any specific targets, she said:

> It's not purely a matter of literary criticism, or purely a historical matter, but something of present-day practical significance, since, in our party, we've [so far] seen ten line errors and we're likely to see additional ones in the future. Having altered his appearance, the enemy will continue to hide inside our party . . . The foreigners call it a "Trojan Horse." Here in China we say (Lu Xun has said this and our Chairman has too) that the most frightening thing is to see one's fort being taken over from the inside. To make a long story short, the capitulationists and revisionists in our party are doing stuff that our open ene-mies are incapable of . . . You don't have to look far; just look at Lin Biao![36]

Zhou Enlai took this bizarre campaign very seriously and personally. Whether Mao really regarded him as "capitulationist" in his dealing with Henry Kissinger will probably never be known. But on September 20, as he was about to be wheeled into the operating theater for major cancer surgery that he might not survive, Zhou stated firmly and loudly for all to hear—Deng Xiaoping, Zhang Chunqiao, Li Xiannian, Wang Dongxing, Zhou's wife Deng Yingchao, and a handful of others—"I am loyal to the party, loyal to the people! I am not a capitulationist!"³⁷ Zhou survived the surgery, and Deng Yingchao asked Wang Dongxing to transmit his words to Mao Zedong.

The "Criticize *Water Margin,* denounce Song Jiang" campaign in late 1975 was one of the more relaxed campaigns of the Cultural Revolution: no struggle sessions, only a very limited dose of Marxism–Leninism–Mao Zedong Thought, and instead hundreds upon hundreds of pages from a popular classical novel that people were free to discuss at length during "political study sessions." But it was the stillness before the storm.

Reversal

On October 26, a senior provincial leader who had attended a recent Politburo work conference in Beijing told his subordinates that Deng Xiaoping's policies of "all-round readjustment" definitely had the backing of the party Chairman. In the course of "transmitting the spirit of speeches by leading comrades at the center," Jiangxi first party secretary Jiang Weiqing reported that

> [Deng Xiaoping] said Chairman Mao approves of making readjustments in all sectors . . . [Deng] said he'd reported to the Chairman about problems in the army, and more recently in agriculture, industry, commerce, culture, and education, and how they need to be solved one by one. The Chairman endorsed [Deng's views]. The Chairman said you go ahead and find ways of solving the problems . . . It was with the Chairman's approval that [Deng] raised, explicitly, the subject of party rectification.³⁸

Jiang Weiqing was unaware that literally as he spoke, the Chairman was having a change of heart. Within another week, he would in effect withdraw his approval and endorsement of Deng's policies. One reason was that he was being fed critical accounts of what was happening outside the walls of Zhongnanhai by his nephew Mao Yuanxin; another was an attempt, in which Deng was implicated, to discredit and purge the most radical elements on the Tsinghua University Party Committee. Mao eventually concluded that Deng was "one, dissatisfied with the Great Cultural Revolution and, two, out to settle accounts, settle accounts with the Great Cultural Revolution."³⁹

Mao Yuanxin had come to Zhongnanhai in September 1975 to act as a liaison officer between Mao and the Politburo. When asked, Mao Yuanxin fed his uncle's paranoia by giving him highly critical accounts of what was happening "out there" in society at large. "I don't worry," he said, "about things like earth-quakes, crop failure due to waterlogging, natural calamities, or shortcomings in our work. I remain confident on these points."[40] But in Liaoning, a "wind" of criticism had been blowing since the start of the year, targeted against the Cultural Revolution. A lot of people were asking pointed questions like these:

> One, how do we judge the Great Cultural Revolution? What about the balance between its essentials and nonessentials; should it be 30/70 or 70/30? Do we affirm it or reject it? Two, how do we judge the *pi-Lin pi-Kong* movement? . . . Three, is it still necessary to criticize the lines of Liu Shaoqi and Lin Biao? The line of Liu Shaoqi is no longer mentioned very often . . . To sum up, should we or should we not continue to criticize the lines of Liu Shaoqi and Lin Biao, and the revisionist lines pursued on the different fronts during the seventeen years [before 1966], as we have done so far in the course of the Great Cultural Revolution?[41]

The new "wind," Mao Yuanxin told his uncle, "appears even to be fiercer than the 1972 criticism of ultra-leftism"; that is, whoever was criticizing the Cultural Revolution now was doing so even more strongly than Zhou Enlai had done then. Mao Yuanxin had no doubt about where the "wind" was actually coming from: "I've been paying great attention to the speeches comrade Xiaoping makes, and I see a problem in that he rarely brings up the achievements of the Great Cultural Revolution, or criticizes Liu Shaoqi's revisionist line." Although Deng claimed to be taking all three of Mao's "three directives" as the "key link," Mao Yuanxin insisted, he really paid attention only to the one about "boosting the economy." "[I am] worried about the center," Mao Yuanxin told his uncle, "and fear there will be a reversal."[42]

While Gang of Four supporters like Mao Yuanxin were attempting to dis-credit Deng and his "all-round readjustment" to Mao, Deng's supporters did not remain idle. They wrote letters denouncing selected followers of the Gang of Four. One obvious target consisted of Peking and Tsinghua universities and their respective radical leaderships, not least because of their being the home bases of the Liang Xiao group, to which Jiang Qing in particular maintained such close ties. The radicals saw these letters as merely one part of a wider insidious campaign to discredit the Cultural Revolution. In November 1975, the chairman of the Peking University RC, Wang Lianlong, a former PLA officer with the 8341 Central Guard Unit, told a meeting of the university party's Standing Committee: "At no point since the founding of the People's Republic have there been more rumors in circulation in society than this year, especially since July–August. How widely these rumors are spread and how frightening their malicious content is! Here at Peking University, too, we have had anonymous letters making all kinds of false allegations!"[43]

In the late summer of 1975, an anonymous member of the "masses" (in all likelihood a member of the Peking University staff) wrote a letter to the MAC denouncing Guo Zonglin, a senior member of the Peking University leadership, for his alleged factionalism, nepotism, and promotion of personal followers to party membership on dubious grounds. The MAC appears to have taken the accusations seriously: its written comment on the letter called on Wang Lianlong to have Guo transferred back to the PLA and away from the university. But instead of obeying orders, the university leadership showed the original letter and the MAC comment to Guo, who exploded, denouncing both the author of the letter and whoever had written the MAC comment as "bastards." In further defiance of the MAC, the university leadership passed the letter on to the campus security unit and had it conduct a secret investigation in an attempt to identify the anonymous letter-writer on the basis of the handwriting, and to punish him.[44]

This letter criticizing the radicals on the Peking University campus had only a limited impact. But two letters denouncing Chi Qun, the most powerful party official on the Tsinghua University campus, had serious repercussions. This letter was signed by four senior members of the Tsinghua University party leadership, and it was sent not to the MAC, but to Mao Zedong himself. Well aware of the obstacles that would prevent their letter from reaching Mao if sent to him through "regular" channels, the dissident academics used their private connections to give it to a senior official in the Ministry of Education; he in turn handed it over to Hu Qiaomu, who passed it on to Deng Xiaoping, who gave it directly to Mao Zedong.[45]

In their first letter, dated August 13, the authors accused Chi of having failed to resist the corroding influence of an increasingly privileged lifestyle and of having become something of an imperial overlord:

These past years, all the good publicity [that Tsinghua University has enjoyed] has gone to Chi's head and had a very big effect on him, ideologically. He has become a big bureaucrat with ever wilder ambitions, imperious and despotic. His word is law, and the way he deals with people is high-handed . . . We have

on numerous occasions behind closed doors attempted to help him, but he refuses our help and clings obstinately to his course.[46]

The authors described themselves in both letters as "in the midst of implementing your three directives." In the second letter, dated October 13, they not only
continued to criticize Chi but also expressed serious reservations about his close
colleague Xie Jingyi: "These past two months, he has become even worse, despite our patient attempts to help him . . . We had hoped that Xie [Jingyi] would
engage Chi in a struggle, but she is increasingly partial to and sides with him.
After the Fourth National People's Congress, Chi grumbled [about not getting
a promotion], while Xie went down on her knees in front of him. We can't
stand it."[47]

Whereas the first letter is not known to have prompted any immediate reaction from Mao, the Chairman reacted very sharply and critically to the second.
There was no significant difference in the political content of the two letters,
but by criticizing Xie Jingyi, the authors—knowingly or not—were attacking a
young woman for whom Mao had great affection. Hence his reaction, put on paper on October 19: "Their motives are impure: they wish to topple Chi Qun and
little Xie, and in their letter, they are pointing the spearhead at me!" Deng
Xiaoping at first tried to keep Mao's comment secret, but when news of it leaked,
Jiang Qing managed to get her hands on a photocopy.[48]

In response to the "worries" raised by his nephew about Deng and the "three
directives," Mao clarified his own position, telling Mao Yuanxin: "Stability and
unity don't mean abandoning class struggle. *Class struggle* is the key link, and everything else hinges upon it. Stalin made a big mistake on this point."[49] Deng,
Mao maintained, was obviously having a relapse into his old pre–Cultural Revolutionary pragmatic behavior:

> [Deng] Xiaoping suggested taking the "three directives as the key link," with-
> out inquiring about the views of the Politburo or conferring with the State
> Council. He didn't report to me either, but just went ahead and put it like that.
> He's someone who doesn't grasp class struggle, and who never mentions this
> key link. It's still all "white cats and black cats," no matter if it's imperialism or
> Marxism.[50]

Mao insisted that the problem with Deng was a "contradiction among the people." He repeated his firm conviction, spelled out many times in the past, that

Deng was different from Liu Shaoqi and Lin Biao. While the latter two had been unwilling to "engage in self-criticism," Deng could when necessary be counted upon to criticize his own faults. What he needed was "help." According to Mao, "to criticize his faults is to help him. Just yielding to him is no good, and we are going to criticize him." "But," Mao added, "he must not be finished off with one blow." At the end of one of their conversations, Mao Zedong told his nephew to sit down together with Deng, Wang Dongxing, and Chen Xilian ("Tell them you're acting on my instructions," Mao explained) and to convey to them the gist of his own comments.[51]

On the evening of November 2, the thirty-six-year-old Mao Yuanxin confronted Deng Xiaoping (twice his age) with Mao's comments. Deng Xiaoping's daughter's account of the meeting (presumably retelling her father's) suggests that Deng was very much in control and bluntly refused to be "helped." Once Mao Yuanxin had spoken his part, he found that Deng Xiaoping was not prepared to "engage in self-criticism," but, rather, insisted on putting up a spirited defense of his own actions over the past months:

> You should give the matter some more thought . . . According to you, the Central Committee has been carrying out an entirely revisionist line, it has abandoned Chairman Mao's line in every respect. The Central Committee is headed by Chairman Mao. I don't think you can say it has been carrying out a revisionist line . . . What kind of work have we implemented in the past three months? That's something that can be discussed. The responsibility is mine. Has the national situation improved, or has it become worse? Comrade Yuanxin has his own opinion on that. The facts can show whether things are better or worse . . . Last night . . . I asked the Chairman what he thought of the orientation and policy of our work in this recent period. He said they were correct.[52]

Two days later, Mao Yuanxin told Mao of the confrontation with Deng. The CCP Chairman was clearly irritated by what he saw as Deng's refusal to give way. Had he himself not always maintained in front of others that one of Deng's positive traits was his readiness to engage in self-criticism when "in the wrong"? And yet now he seemed as dead set against backing down as had Lin Biao after the Lushan plenum in 1970. It was time to put Deng's loyalty to the test. The Chairman told Mao Yuanxin to prepare for a gathering of Politburo members to consider specifically what in their view ought to be the verdict on the Cultural

Revolution. Mao's aim was to have a meeting of the Politburo, *chaired by Deng*, arrive at a consensus in support of his own verdict that it had been 70 percent success, 30 percent failure. Mao also wished to see a formal resolution to that effect drafted and passed.

The Politburo duly met on November 20 to discuss and evaluate the Cultural Revolution. Deng had initially suggested to Mao that Wang Hongwen, who had recently returned to Beijing from Shanghai, ought to chair the meeting, but Mao had been adamant that it had to be Deng. Altogether seventeen people attended, including what Mao at one point referred to as "old comrades . . . the middle-aged, and the young." No full list has ever been made public, but the group almost certainly included Wang Dongxing, Chen Xilian, Li Xiannian, Hua Guofeng, Ji Dengkui, Zhang Chunqiao, and Mao Yuanxin.[53]

As for how to evaluate the Cultural Revolution, this was not really something that the Politburo was genuinely in a position to discuss, since Mao had already made up his mind that it was to be 70/30, with the positive outweighing the negative. The Politburo meeting was simply expected to affirm Mao's evaluation officially. In this way—so Deng's daughter would later argue, presumably mindful of the Leninist rules of intra-party discipline—most critics of the Cultural Revolution would be effectively silenced. Mao was also providing Deng Xiaoping with one last chance to alter his critical stance.

But Deng balked. Indeed, he refused to deal with the resolution at all, pleading ignorance of what had transpired at the highest levels of the party during much of the Cultural Revolution. "For me to supervise the drafting of such a resolution," he said, "is inappropriate." Quoting the reclusive poet Tao Yuanming (A.D. 376–427), Deng explained: "I come from the Peach Blossom Spring, where 'they had never heard of the Han, let alone the Wei and the Jin [dynasties].'"[54]

Repulsing the Right-Deviationist Wind

Simultaneously with the secret Politburo meeting, the radicals—for whom even Mao Zedong's "70 percent positive, 30 percent negative" verdict on the Cultural Revolution must have seemed unduly conservative—launched a public lobbying campaign from the northwest corner of the capital, where universities and academic institutions were concentrated. In the words of one senior radical, "we saw revisionism emerging at the center, and our aim was to break the blockade, crush the resistance, and denounce Deng."[55] On November 20, somewhere in exccss of 1,300 sheets' worth of big-character posters went up on the Tsinghua University campus, denouncing individuals who had the audacity to "negate the Great Cultural Revolution" and "attack the proletarian revolution in education." The posters were by no means spontaneous expressions of the "indignation of the revolutionary masses," but part of a carefully orchestrated campaign led by the university authorities and at first confined to a special "poster sector" of the campus. On November 22, in step two of the campaign, that sector was made open to the public. Over the next three months, more than 377,000 people from all over China visited Tsinghua to read and "study" the posters. As the days and weeks wore on, the university authorities set up the by now typical ad hoc institutions needed to run what became known as the "great farrago on the educational front," including a dedicated reception office and editorial groups that churned out a steady stream of inflammatory propaganda with such titles as "Whipping Up a Storm of Verdict Reversals" and "The Capitalist Roaders Are on the Move."[56]

The campaign was sanctioned by the Gang of Four, but response outside the immediate radical bastions of Tsinghua and Peking universities and Shanghai was muted. To conceal this fact and make it appear that the attacks were far more widespread than was the case, the preferred tactic was the clandestine distribution of documents that could not be traced, including unauthorized transcripts of and quotations from speeches by Deng Xiaoping, Zhou Rongxin, and other "revisionists." At Peking and Tsinghua, massive quantities of such "materials for criticism and denunciation" were compiled. In Shanghai, Fudan University became the key printing and distribution point for the nationwide dissemination of 760,000 items over the next nine months.[57] Shanghai RC member Xu Jingxian later testified: "When I passed them on to another university, I would say: 'Don't let on that these came from me, but pretend you copied them from somewhere else'; when I passed them on to a middle school, I would say: 'Deny you were given these by your superiors and say instead that you had them printed up yourselves.'"[58] The obvious purpose was to fabricate a vocal majority, but the majority remained silent—for now. When asked by one Shanghai official whether proceeding in this fashion was really appropriate, Zhang Chunqiao assured him that so long as nothing could be traced back to the municipal CCP committee, there was no problem.[59]

Meanwhile, on November 24 at Mao's orders, Deng Xiaoping convened a meeting that bore a previously unheard-of label: "Cautioning." Its purpose was described by a senior official:

I've been around for twenty-some years, and rarely have I heard of a cautioning meeting. What does it mean? From what I understand now, a cautioning meeting is to caution the capitalist roaders still on the move . . . Subject them to a bit of a drizzle, give them a prophylactic inoculation, have them sober up and not misjudge the situation altogether, and not overrate their own abilities to a point where they end up completely shameless.[60]

Deng Xiaoping simply announced that the purpose of the meeting was to help "some comrades" avoid "making any new errors."[61] The crucial points for "caution" were summed up in *Zhongfa* [1975] 23 on November 26, 1975, issued at first only to senior provincial leaders, but shared with a wider audience after December 10.[62] It exhorted its readers not to believe those who (like Deng Xiaoping and Zhou Rongxin) claimed to be concerned only with "the educational front": their true agenda was to settle scores with the Cultural Revolution as a whole.[63] In December 1975 and during the first weeks of 1976, the CCP Politburo met almost daily in a tense atmosphere to criticize Deng Xiaoping. Deng himself chaired the meetings, but according to his own subsequent account, this role involved little more than saying: "Let's begin!" at the start and "Meeting over!" at the end of each session. Most of the time he remained silent. On December 20, he delivered a purported "self-criticism," but the record suggests that he was only going through the motions and using this opportunity to show his contempt for the whole spectacle. Speaking without notes, his opening words seemed laced with sarcasm: "First I would like to thank the Chairman for his teachings, and to thank the comrades [present]—the younger comrades in particular—for the help that you have given me. It's only step by step that I myself have come to appreciate these errors of mine." Deng ended by attributing any errors he might have committed to a profound inability to appreciate what the Cultural Revolution was all about. So unacceptable was his "self-criticism" deemed—it solicited no response from Mao Zedong—that the Politburo made him give a "supplementary self-criticism" on January 3. Though reading from a prepared text, he simply repeated what he had said on the first occasion, but added "at the suggestion of . . . other people" an admission to the effect that he had not asked Mao for permission, or solicited the views of the rest of the Politburo, before advancing the slogan "Take the three directives as the key link." Mao was clearly not impressed: on January 14 he called on the Politburo to continue to "debate" Deng's self-criticisms. Turning down calls for face-to-face encounters from Jiang Qing as well as from Deng, Mao may have wanted to distance himself somewhat from what was happening. Yet he gave Jiang Qing a clear signal as to where he stood: he ended his brief note turning down her request for a meeting with the words "The situation as a whole is fine."[64]

Mao's interest was in maintaining the campaign's momentum. On December 14, 1975, he asked the CCP center to give it a powerful positive endorsement by distributing to party branches in schools all across China, together with a positively worded comment, a "Situation Report from Tsinghua University on the Great Debate on the Revolution in Education" (*Zhongfa* [1975] 26), in which the minister of education was sharply denounced.[65] He maintained the pressure by ordering wide distribution a week later of the minutes of a conversation between Zhang Chunqiao and an Albanian delegation (*Zhongfa* [1975] 27) in which Zhang was quoted as saying that in the educational sphere, during the seventeen years before the Cultural Revolution "the bourgeoisie exercised dictatorship over us." Zhang continued: "But some people maintain that those seventeen years were very good, that they were actually Marxist-Leninist while on the contrary, since the Cultural Revolution, the schools haven't been any good, quality has declined, classroom hours have been reduced, and university students don't even learn as much as high school students used to in the past."[66]

The Central Document containing the Foreign Ministry's transcript of Zhang's conversation was supposedly for limited, high-level distribution, but at least in Shanghai, Zhang's followers promptly leaked it widely to bolster their assault on Deng.[67] In his capacity as vice premier holding the education portfolio, however, Zhang's immediate target was the minister of education, Zhou Rongxin. Within days of the first big-character posters' appearing on the Tsinghua campus, Zhang had purged Zhou by putting a "temporary leading group" in charge of the ministry in his stead, a group led by a steel plant worker cum workers' militia commander from Shanghai. After months of countless "struggle meetings" and investigations into his "wicked past," the minister would die at the age of fifty-nine on April 12, 1976, "persecuted to death" in post–Cultural Revolution language.

But by then, Deng's year was long over, and Deng himself had been purged again.

24

The Tiananmen Incident of 1976

I n the last year of his life, Mao looked back and claimed two great achievements: conquering China and launching the Cultural Revolution.[1] The first could never be denied him. The second could. Mao's new campaign to avert a reversal of verdicts on the Cultural Revolution was his last chance to preserve that legacy. His rapidly declining health foreclosed any other.

In mid-1974, grumbling mightily, Mao had finally agreed to be examined by specialists: by ophthalmologists, because cataracts had made him blind, and by neurologists, because his speech had become virtually unintelligible. But he rejected the results and refused treatment. The fact that Zhou Enlai had to have repeated operations for his cancer confirmed Mao in the belief that doctors simply could not cure people. In late January 1975, a four-day medical examination of the CCP Chairman found that he "had cataracts, amyotrophic lateral sclerosis, coronary heart disease, pulmonary heart disease, an infection in the lower half of both lungs, three bullae in his left lung, bedsores on his left hip, and a shortage of oxygen in his blood (anoxia). He also had a slight fever and a severe cough."[2] In February 1975, Zhou left his hospital bed to chair a special meeting of the Politburo to hear the doctors' reports and discuss treatments for Mao.

The easy part was to deal with Mao's eyes. With the Politburo's agreement, the doctors experimented on forty elderly peasant men, too poor to afford the cataract operations they needed. Half of them underwent a less invasive traditional treatment; the other half underwent the more aggressive Western-style surgery. When Mao was handed a report on the experiment, he opted for the traditional method as safer, speedier, and less painful. A year after the original diagnosis, Mao's right eye was operated on, and soon he could read official documents with the help of glasses.

The difficult, indeed terminal, issue was that the neurologists had diagnosed Mao as having, not Parkinson's disease as at first thought, but Lou Gehrig's disease, amyotrophic lateral sclerosis (hereafter ALS). The motor nerve cells controlling Mao's "muscles of the throat, the pharynx, the tongue, the diaphragm and intercostal muscles [between the ribs, governing breathing], the right hand and the right leg" were deteriorating.[3] When a patient reached this stage, as Mao had, he was unlikely to live more than another two years, during which period he would require nasal feeding and a respirator just to prolong life. Rare enough in the West, the disease was virtually unheard of in China. Mao himself believed he had laryngitis, even though he now had to be fed a semiliquid diet, lying on his side, by his young female attendants. He had to abandon his beloved swims because he choked if he swallowed water.

Zhou Enlai and his Politburo colleagues had difficulty absorbing the fact that the cause and, more important, a cure for this disease were unknown.[4] They expressed confidence in the doctors, but agreed that Mao have the last word on his treatment. The PSC plus Jiang Qing took on an oversight role for Mao's case.[5]

An unexpected aspect of Lou Gehrig's disease is that the patient retains his mental faculties despite suffering debilitating physical symptoms. Indeed, Mao continued to receive distinguished foreign visitors until May 27, 1976.[6] Thus Mao can be assumed to have been aware of the ongoing political struggle, informed or misinformed by Mao Yuanxin and the few others who had access to him. By this time, the most important of the latter was Zhang Yufeng, the onetime railway dining car attendant to whom Mao had first taken a fancy in October 1962. In his present health crisis, Mao's instinct was to trust her medical nostrums over the considered judgment of China's best doctors, to the latter's frustration and alarm. But the political question mark is over the degree to which Ms. Zhang was able accurately to interpret the Chairman's grunts and scrawled characters. Since nobody else could even begin to, the Politburo had to rely on her, *faute de mieux.*[7] Mao was increasingly isolated in a "bunker" created by his physical ailments. His will was law, but his subordinates could not be sure what his will was. Working toward the Chairman had never been so difficult. The Chinese political system had reached an extraordinary pass.

The Death of Zhou Enlai

By the end of 1975, the contending factions of the Politburo—the survivors, the radicals, and the beneficiaries—knew that they had a limited time in which to establish an ascendancy that might survive Mao's death, no more than a year if the mid-1974 diagnosis was correct. But it was the death of Zhou Enlai that precipitated the first stage of the inevitable succession crisis.

On December 20, Zhou had his final meeting with a representative of a central CCP department. The topic was not the revolution in education or the criticism of Deng Xiaoping. The official who was called was in charge of counter-intelligence and "work vis-à-vis Taiwan," the head of the Central Investigation Department, Luo Qingchang, who had worked closely with Zhou at least since the 1940s. During their last conversation, Zhou drifted in and out of consciousness and ran a high fever, but he nonetheless inquired about old KMT friends and sent them a few parting words, like "Don't forget to serve the people!" Zhou had founded the CCP's intelligence services in the 1920s; it was not an inappropriate way to go.[8]

At dawn on January 9, a solemn radio broadcast on national radio announced that Zhou had "died of cancer at 0957 hours on January 8, 1976, in Beijing at the age of seventy-eight." The spontaneous reaction of one Chinese university student awakened by the news over the campus loudspeakers was "I bet the Chairman cried when they told him!"[9] In fact, Zhou's death had little impact on Mao or his inner circle of female attendants, guards, and doctors.[10]

China now went into a period of nationwide mourning. A foreign news agency reported from Beijing that the capital was "like a ghost town on 10 January, with almost no shopping save for silk embroideries carrying the likeness of the late premier." Deng Xiaoping, who had spent time with Zhou in France as a teenage worker-student, made what was to be his last public appearance for a year to deliver the eulogy at the memorial ceremony on January 15, paying tribute to a man who "fought all his life for the realization of the great ideal of communism." Zhou had been a major figure in Chinese politics for more than fifty years. He had been premier of the PRC for the quarter-century since its founding in 1949. Mourning arrangements, condolences, and assessments of the contributions of this towering figure to the Chinese revolution and to world affairs dominated the media for over a week, in unprecedented nationwide and worldwide expressions of respect for a Chinese leader.[11]

Yet the Cultural Revolution was not Zhou's finest hour. In an assessment made four years after his eulogy, Deng said that Zhou had been "in an extremely difficult position [during the Cultural Revolution], and he said and did many things that he would have wished not to." Deng excused him because by surviving he had been able to play a neutralizing role and so reduce losses and protect people.[12] The record of Zhou's effectiveness, however, is much more ambiguous;

Deng's assessment avoided the vital question: Would China have been better off if the premier had used his immense prestige and influence in the CCP and the PLA to rally his colleagues in an effort to stop the Cultural Revolution in its tracks early on?

But for the people, Zhou was a symbol of the moderation that they had been denied for a decade. Tens of thousands of Beijing citizens, many weeping, braved the bitter cold and took to the streets to say farewell when Zhou's body was transported from the hospital to be cremated in the Baobaoshan Cemetery, although no announcement of the route had been made.[13] Even in Qincheng Prison, the "entire prison had melted into a paroxysm of grief. The guards and prisoners alike were united. I could hear weeping in adjoining cells. I could hear weeping in the hallways. Everyone was crying. From far away I could hear a prisoner's voice, an elderly man, wailing. 'China has lost her last hope. What are we to do? What is to become of us?'"[14]

But for those who wept the premier's passing, there was still one last hope: Zhou's colleague Deng Xiaoping would carry on his work. He was the obvious successor. It was not to be.

Deng Sidelined

A few days after he had read his eulogy, Deng was relieved of his duties as the senior vice premier running the day-to-day work of the State Council in Zhou's stead. Exactly 365 days after his informal appointment to that job, the CCP issued its first Central Document of 1976, the first sentence of which read: "As proposed by our great leader Chairman Mao and unanimously agreed by the Central Politburo, comrade Hua Guofeng is appointed acting premier of the State Council."[15] When Mao Yuanxin conveyed the Chairman's message to the Politburo, Deng is said to have been the first to voice support.[16] But Zhang Chunqiao was outraged; as the highest-ranking vice premier after Deng, he had expected to receive this promotion himself. In private he put his bitterness on paper, insisting that Hua was "overestimating his own power" and predicting that "the faster he climbs, the harder he will fall."[17]

But even some of Zhang's closest supporters could sense why he had not been promoted. Xu Jingxian eventually recalled: "In my mind, I wanted Zhang Chunqiao to be made premier, but I sensed that he had made too many enemies, that his qualifications weren't sufficient, and that he wouldn't be able to strike a balance."[18] Ma Tianshui's feelings were similar: "My initial reaction to the announcement that comrade Hua Guofeng had been made acting premier was surprise, but later I also felt that it was appropriate and struck a balance."[19] Again according to Xu Jingxian: "Both Ma Tianshui and I were of the opinion that comrade Hua Guofeng had positioned himself somewhere in the middle and that consequently he would be acceptable to the left as well as to the right."[20] These two radicals had intuited Mao's strategy. Zhang Chunqiao was unacceptable to the survivors of the old guard and the PLA generals. An unrepentant Deng Xiaoping was unacceptable to the Chairman. A beneficiary had at least the chance of bridging the divide and, more importantly, standing by the principles of the Cultural Revolution that had brought him to power. Hua, in other words, was the perfect compromise. Why only acting premier? Having made mistakes with Lin Biao and Wang Hongwen, perhaps Mao was getting cautious in his old age.

As for Deng, from this moment on he went to Politburo meetings only if summoned. Otherwise, as his daughter later wrote, "he felt much better at home with his children and grandchildren than having to look at the mad faces of the 'Gang of Four.'"[21] (At the meetings to which he was summoned, when attacked by someone like Zhang Chunqiao, Deng claimed that his poor hearing prevented him from understanding much of what was being said, which in turn infuriated Zhang, who insisted that Deng was not the least bit deaf: "When Hua Guofeng way at the other end of the table in a low voice announces 'meeting adjourned,' he hears it immediately and, pushing back his chair, gets up to leave! He's merely pretending to be deaf!")[22] Also "staying at home" after Mao's decision not to promote Deng was Marshal Ye Jianying. "During comrade Ye Jianying's illness," the second half of *Zhongfa* [1976] 1 had read, "comrade Chen Xilian will, in his stead, be managing the day-to-day affairs of the MAC."[23] The question for some was whether Ye Jianying was ill or "ill." In conversation with a member of the Peking University leadership, CC member Xie Jingyi, a deputy secretary of Tsinghua University Party Committee, insisted that "Marshal Ye is not ill! It's because of the criticism of Deng Xiaoping; he has simply decided to stay at home."[24]

The day on which Mao signed off on *Zhongfa* [1976] 1 was Spring Festival—the Chinese lunar New Year. Unlike Deng and Ye, Mao spent it neither in the company of children and grandchildren nor feigning illness. Mao had no next of kin by his side, and his illness was real. In her memoirs, Zhang Yufeng wrote:

It was a cold winter night with a few dim stars in the sky. Chairman Mao's residence seemed to be shrouded in darkness. There were no visitors, no family members. Chairman Mao spent his last Spring Festival with those who served him. I had to feed him his New Year's eve dinner with a spoon, since he could not use his hands. To open his mouth and to gulp down his food also was increasingly difficult for him. I helped him from his bed to the sofa in the sitting room. For a long time, he put his head on the back of the sofa without uttering a word . . . Suddenly, from far away, we heard firecrackers. In a low and hoarse voice, Mao asked me to explode some firecrackers . . . A faint smile crept over his old and weary face when he heard the firecrackers in the courtyard.[25]

Zhang failed to mention that the firecrackers set off a major commotion: they had been banned in Zhongnanhai because they sounded too much like gunfire. Mao's residence suddenly swarmed with nervous guards. Mao's personal physician later reported that the incident had started a rumor that the Chairman had celebrated Zhou Enlai's death with firecrackers.[26]

In late February, senior provincial-level leaders from all over China were called to Beijing for a second "cautioning meeting," this one presided over by Hua Guofeng. Hua announced that this "is not a meeting at which concrete problems are to be resolved. Therefore, the earlier we can bring it to a close, the earlier you can return home and launch a struggle to beat back the right-deviationist wind to reverse correct verdicts." "Where there are problems of one kind or another, you should now execute a turn," Hua said. "After this meeting, if you still don't turn, then that's bad. This applies equally to subprovincial leaderships as well." On the condition that leaderships promptly "executed a turn," the center was prepared to draw a line and "assume responsibility for problems predating this cautioning meeting."[27]

The "turn" was of course meant to be to the left. Jiang Qing explained informally but at great length to a gathering of delegates: "First study the Chairman's important instructions, and then concentrate the spearhead of struggle on the person of Deng Xiaoping. Otherwise there's going to be chaos. It's time to sum up our experiences!"[28] The instructions in question, which were disseminated at the meeting, and subsequently, with Mao's agreement, nationwide "for study" in Zhongfa [1976] 4, had been recorded by Mao Yuanxin, presumably with the help of Zhang Yufeng, on several occasions since the autumn of 1975. They were the last coherent and extended dicta laid down by the Chairman, and they were explicit in their criticism of all that Deng had stood for over the previous year:

The thinking of some comrades, mainly old comrades, has never progressed beyond the stage of the bourgeois democratic revolution. They do not understand the socialist revolution. They resent it, and even oppose it. Toward the Great Cultural Revolution, their attitude is either one of dissatisfaction or of wanting to settle accounts. They want to settle accounts with the Great Cultural Revolution.

Mao was directly critical of Deng Xiaoping, as we saw in the previous chapter, and much of the following passage would be quoted extensively in big-character posters on university campuses during the spring and summer:

The problem with Xiaoping is still a contradiction among the people, and given proper guidance it need not become antagonistic, as happened with Liu Shaoqi and Lin Biao. There are still some differences between Deng on the one hand and Liu and Lin on the other. Deng is willing to engage in self-criticism . . . To criticize him is necessary, but he should not be finished off with one blow.[29]

The Gang of Four and their closest allies were determined that Mao's "important instructions" reach as wide as possible an audience and as quickly as possible, so they leaked them to selected cadres at Peking University and Tsinghua University even before Mao had agreed to their wider distribution nationwide. Members of the Liang Xiao team were told that this privileged early access to Mao's words equaled that normally granted only to members of the Politburo.[30]

Presumably the Gang of Four believed that the Chairman's instructions would have the same galvanizing effect on the "broad masses" as they had on their allies. If so, they deceived themselves. Despite his access to an almost unlimited fare of overt and covert, formal and informal domestic intelligence, Yao Wenyuan dismissed what resistance to the criticism of Deng Xiaoping he learned of as little more than a "frenzied counterrevolutionary countercurrent."[31] Jiang Qing was also seriously divorced from reality. At one point in the "cautioning meeting," she claimed that the "masses" were "happy, elated, and feel that [Deng] should have been dragged out a long time ago." She insisted that the documentation she received showed that the political "consciousness of the masses is very high, and they certainly are very sensible indeed."[32] But the documentation told Jiang Qing only what she wanted to hear. It did not prepare her for the increasingly vocal and open public resentment toward the dismissal of Deng and the Cultural Revolution in general.

The Consciousness of the Masses

The movement to "beat back the right-deviationist wind to reverse correct verdicts" encountered particularly strong resistance in Deng's home province of Sichuan. The political situation there was so volatile that the entire province had been closed to foreign visitors for years. On February 18, 1976, a thirty-one-year-old technician named Bai Zhiqing put up a big-character poster titled "I love my country" in the city center of Chongqing, praising Deng's "all-round readjustment" policies of 1975 and asking the pointed question: "Who is it, really, who has ruined the wealth of the nation and the prosperity of her people?"[33] On March 4 he put up a second poster, this time in the busiest part of the provincial capital, Chengdu, titled "May I ask whose 'ism' this is?—A critique of Zhang Chunqiao's 'Eradicate the Bourgeoisie's Ideology of Rights.'"[34] The next day a major street brawl erupted between a group of workers who attempted to tear the poster down, a crowd that wished to see it remain, and the local police. Arrested as a "counterrevolutionary," Bai became the focus of one mass rally after another across Sichuan in April and May, forced to stand in the airplane position under banners that read "Denounce Deng Xiaoping! Crack down on counterrevolution!"[35]

But it was not merely in places like Sichuan that the "masses" insisted on being less than what Jiang Qing had called "happy, elated." In eastern China, in the provinces around Shanghai that the Gang of Four tended to regard as their territory, popular resentment was also vocal. In Hangzhou, the provincial capital of Zhejiang, a twenty-three-year-old factory worker by the name of Li Junxu concocted something called "Premier Zhou's Last Will," and within days, copies of this pro-Deng anti–Jiang Qing "testament" were finding an eager underground readership all over eastern China. The Ministry of Public Security in Beijing called for swift action against this "counterrevolutionary fabrication" and the punishment of its author, but with limited results; the testament continued to spread far and wide.[36] In Anhui, a university student, a middle school student, and a worker calling themselves the "children of the party" went on late-night slogan-pasting sorties in the city of Wuhu, announcing "Chunqiao, Chunqiao, farting and rumor-mongering; slandering the premier, your crimes will not go unpunished!" and "Jiang Qing! Jiang Qing! Poisonous snake, devil woman! You cruelly injure the loyal, and bring calamity to the country and the people!"[37]

In March, the Jiangsu provincial capital of Nanjing became the scene of two incidents involving the radical Shanghai mouthpiece *Wenhui bao,* in which Yao Wenyuan's attack on Wu Han's play *Hai Rui Dismissed from Office* had kicked off the Cultural Revolution. Kang Sheng, who had died three months earlier, once expressed strong irritation with "people who read the newspapers as if they were deciphering code," and what happened on both occasions showed that the Nanjing readers of the *Wenhui bao* were just such people.[38] When they discovered on March 5 that Zhou Enlai's calligraphic inscription in praise of the great paragon of proletarian virtue Lei Feng was missing from a set of inscriptions reprinted in the paper that included Mao's and Zhu De's, they were incensed. Outraged students from Nanjing University wrote to the paper demanding an explanation for this intentional and "sinister" deletion, though not without local opposition.[39] Years later, the publishers claimed, unconvincingly, that the decision to leave out Zhou's calligraphy had been made purely for reasons of space—unconvincingly because if that had been the case, they should have dropped the inscription of the lower-ranking Zhu De.[40] Yao Wenyuan likened the entire affair to something "about as important as a fart."[41]

Three weeks later, on March 25, the *Wenhui bao* provoked readers even more when it included a cryptic but unmistakable attack on Zhou Enlai in an otherwise dull news item about the circumstances of Deng Xiaoping's return to power a few years earlier: "That capitalist roader inside the party [i.e., Zhou] helped the still unrepentant capitalist roader [i.e., Deng] onto the stage." In the final days of March, slogans like "Down with the big careerist, big conspirator Zhang Chunqiao!" and "Down with those who oppose Premier Zhou!" appeared on the streets of Nanjing. On the sides of trains bound for Beijing, large slogans were painted, proclaiming: "Somebody behind the scenes is responsible for the *Wenhui bao* of March 5 and March 25, and that somebody is at the center [in Beijing]!" and "Whoever pointed the *Wenhui bao*'s spearhead at Premier Zhou on March 5 and March 25 deserves to die 10,000 deaths!"[42]

On March 30, in conversation with a *People's Daily* editor, Wang Hongwen called the events in Nanjing "directed at the center."[43] On April 1, the increasingly nervous central authorities telephoned Nanjing, calling for immediate and effective measures to curb such serious "political incidents" and to find and punish the "behind-the-scenes plotters" responsible. Nothing of the sort happened. On the contrary, increasingly large numbers of people, estimated to total 600,000–700,000, took to the streets of Nanjing in protest marches.[44] But it was in Beijing that popular sorrow at the death of Zhou and anger at the sidelining of Deng coalesced into the biggest seemingly spontaneous political demonstration since the founding of the PRC.

The First Tiananmen Incident

At the very beginning of the Cultural Revolution, during the high tide of "eradicating the 'four olds,'" Red Guards otherwise adamant that traditional festivals with a "feudal flavor" should no longer be observed in socialist China had nevertheless been ready to retain the Qingming Festival. "We will continue to observe the 'Qingming' Festival by sweeping the graves of revolutionary martyrs—not by visiting the graves of our ancestors."[45] Unfortunately for the Gang of Four, the most prominent martyrs' "grave" was the Monument to the People's Heroes, right in the center of Tiananmen Square. It provided the residents of Beijing and visitors to the capital with a justifiable location to celebrate one of the greatest CCP heroes and to comment on the current political situation. Nor was remembering Zhou at this festival confined to Beijing,[46] but events in the capital became the focus of domestic and foreign attention. To this day, it is uncertain whether the movement was totally spontaneous or whether there was "backstage" encouragement at any point, as the radicals would suspect, "a serious class struggle at the back of the wreaths," as the head of the capital's Public Security Bureau would suggest. But the Gang of Four had only themselves to blame for what happened. Since January, they had used their control of propaganda to suppress mourning for Zhou in order to maintain focus on the struggle against Deng. At some point, popular emotions had to explode.

Cow Lane Primary School set the fuse. Its pupils laid the first wreath to Zhou at the monument on March 19. Four days later, a man from Anhui province laid another. Both were quickly removed by the police. But at dawn on March 25, a middle school left its wreath, and shortly thereafter some workers left theirs beside it; on March 30, the first group of soldiers left theirs. None were removed. The news spread. All over the capital, schools, colleges, factories, shops, troops, ministries mobilized. Delegations marched in single or double file, sometimes long distances, to Tiananmen Square, headed by somebody carrying the wreath. Often they wheeled bicycles, ringing their bells in a melancholy lament. Wreaths were soon piled high immediately around the monument, so groups brought easels as stands for their tributes: "The wreaths were elaborately wrought of homemade flowers of silk paper. White, the traditional mourning color of China, predominated, but red and yellow, the colors in the national flag, were also much used . . . From each wreath hung two broad ribbons of white silk on which were brushed in black ink words of homage to Zhou and the name of the unit that had made it."[47] In the middle of the wreath might be a picture of Zhou, a hammer and sickle, or a paean to the dead premier:

Qingming is not clear and bright:
Heaven weeps with unending rain.
The nation has mourned for eighty-six days
Till tears are dry and sobs are hushed. . .[48]

For you no monument is raised,
For you no plinth for statue laid.
Yet the monuments to you are legion,
Deeply rooted in the people's hearts. . .[49]

Arriving in the square, groups held a short ceremony, dedicating themselves to the ideals they attributed to Zhou. Then they joined the throngs reading the individual tributes. By April 1, the tributes crowded the square: Birnam Wood had come to Dunsinane.[50] Their ranks were not serried, but in their peaceful and massive profusion they demonstrated solidarity more impressively than the terracotta soldiers of Xi'an.

For the Gang of Four they demonstrated something more alarming: the people had mobilized for Zhou but equally against them. It was almost impossible to get close to the wreaths that featured condemnations of the Gang, so mobbed were they by eager readers. All four were attacked, but Jiang Qing had pride of place:

You must be mad
To want to be an empress!
Here's a mirror to look at yourself
And see what you really are.
You've got together a little gang
To stir up trouble all the time,
Hoodwinking the people, capering about.
But your days are numbered. . .[51]

On April 1, 1976, leaders of the Beijing city party met in expanded emergency session. Officials were cautioned that "sweeping graves during the Qingming Festival is an old tradition, an old habit" and were ordered to "mobilize the masses not to go to the Monument to the People's Heroes to deposit wreaths, since a tiny handful of people are spreading all kinds of rumors attacking leading comrades at the center, which is absolutely impermissible." The municipal public security apparatus was ordered to greatly intensify surveillance operations. On April 4, the municipal authorities estimated that close to 2 million people had been in the square that day.[52]

On the evening of Sunday, April 4—Qingming itself, according to the traditional calendar—Hua Guofeng called a meeting of the Politburo in the Great Hall of the People. Old guard survivors such as Deng, Ye Jianying, and Li Xiannian were absent.[53] The sole topic on the agenda was Tiananmen Square. Having visited the square in the early hours of April 3, Wang Hongwen could report on the flavor of the popular mood in the tributes he had managed to read by torchlight. Wu De, in his capacity as party first secretary and mayor of the capital, could be more precise: there were 2,073 memorials in the square, representing 1,400 units; but in the past two days alone, 927 units had brought in 1,200 tributes, an indication that the momentum was increasing. The good news for the Gang must have been that, as of April 2, there were only 48 memorials that slandered Mao or other leaders.[54] Wu said there had been no movement like this since the start of the Cultural Revolution. In fact there had been no spontaneous movement like this in the capital since the Communists took over in 1949. And if anti-Gang posters were relatively few, the juxtaposition of the wreaths with the picture of Mao over the Tianan Gate was a stark indication of a popular preference for Zhou's moderation over the Chairman's class struggle. Not until students erected a statue of the "Goddess of Democracy" in Tiananmen Square in 1989 would there again be so flagrant a juxtaposition, implicitly rejecting what Mao stood for.

On the night of April 4, 1976, the problem for the Politburo was what to do about all the wreaths, poems, manifestos. How to defuse the situation? In his minutes of the meeting, delivered to Mao Zedong at dawn the following day and meant to represent the substance of the Politburo's deliberations, Mao Yuanxin highlighted the following: Quite a few of the poems in the square were actually not commemorating Zhou Enlai but were thinly disguised "attempts to split and attack the center," some even going so far as to "directly attack Chairman Mao." On no occasion since 1949 had people congregated in Tiananmen Square to hear what amounted to "counterrevolutionary speeches, directly attacking Chairman Mao."[55] In a phrase that he knew would strike a chord with his uncle, Mao Yuanxin claimed that the dead were being used to exert pressure on the living; the prestige enjoyed by Zhou Enlai was being channeled into support for Deng Xiaoping.[56] Anyone who dared voice criticism of Deng in the square was accused of denouncing Zhou Enlai. That something on this scale was taking place at Qingming was clearly the result of planning and coordination by person or persons unknown. Pressing another Maoist button, Mao Yuanxin stated: "It is evident, this time, that there is an underground 'Petöfi Club' that is organizing this in a planned fashion. Therefore, just in case, certain necessary measures must be adopted."[57]

The most immediate of these measures, which Mao Zedong ratified *ex post facto,* was the cleansing of the square.[58] Between 1:00 and 2:00 A.M. on April 5, some 200 trucks from the Beijing Garrison and municipal transport corporation came and carted off everything. All but a few were taken to Babaoshan in western Beijing to be incinerated. Fifty-seven late-night visitors to the square, among them people copying down poems by flashlight, were interrogated, and seven of them were detained for further questioning. By dawn, the emptied square had been cordoned off, and access was being denied to the public.

When people began arriving to discover what had happened, their mood quickly turned from surprise to outrage and anger. Before long, the first scuffles between outraged citizens and policemen erupted. When a plainclothes officer headed for the Great Hall of the People on the west side of the square in the aftermath of one such scuffle, the crowds concluded that it was there that whoever was responsible was hiding. Foreigners who had been welcomed in the harmonious atmosphere of the previous few days were now summarily ejected and sometimes manhandled. "This is the business of the Chinese people; go away."[59]

A few hours into the morning, a crowd of some 10,000 had gathered outside the Great Hall shouting loudly for the return of the wreaths and their arrested "comrades-in-arms." In a vain effort to make the crowd disperse, the authorities dispatched two loudspeaker vans to the square, broadcasting a message that warned against sabotage by the class enemy and called on all "revolutionary comrades" to leave promptly. Nothing of the sort happened; instead, a handful of infuriated people immediately overturned one of the vans and smashed its loudspeaker; the occupants of the second van were allowed to drive away after their loudspeakers had begun instead to broadcast the simple message "Long live Premier Zhou!"[60]

By noon, the attention of the crowd had been drawn to a small building in the southeast corner of the square, where it was claimed (correctly) the forward "joint command post" of the public security personnel, the PLA, and the workers' militia was located. In the words of one Chinese historian, "The masses, singing 'The Internationale,' advanced in rows, arm in arm, upon the little gray house. Once there, they chose four representatives . . . [all of whom were later arrested] to put forth three demands."[61]

To no avail. The authorities refused to communicate with the protesters. At 1:00 P.M., a car parked outside the building was set on fire, and later in the afternoon two jeeps and a minibus delivering food to the militia suffered the same fate. Finally, at 5:00, rioters entered and looted the "command post" and proceeded to set it on fire also. The most senior and no doubt terrified occupants—including two alternate members of the Central Committee, two deputy commanders of the Beijing Garrison, and two deputy directors of the municipal Public Security Bureau—made a hurried escape through the back door.[62]

From behind the window curtains in the Great Hall of the People, members of the Politburo were indeed following developments that day, in person. Two weeks later, Zhang Chunqiao wrote to his son describing the scene:

On April 5, I went to the Great Hall of the People, from where it was like watching the Hungarian uprising unfold. I could see it all clearly through my binoculars. To his face, I cursed Deng Xiaoping, calling him [Imre] Nagy. He stuck to his odious attitude but had no choice but to nod his head in silence. Finally, I had been able to vent some of my anger as it became my good fortune to see this Nagy meet his disgusting end. (Don't start bragging about this, as I have not told anyone about it.) Who will prevail has been decided, and we are in the midst of expanding our victory.[63]

The director of the Beijing Public Security Bureau, Liu Chuanxin, later claimed that his police officers had underestimated the ferocity of the protesters and had been taken off guard and put on the defensive.[64] Beijing Garrison commander Wu Zhong admitted that his troops, too, had been unprepared and disorganized: when the first car was set ablaze, he said, "we should have mobilized, but our efforts to do so were ineffective."[65] It took the authorities until late afternoon to come up with strategy for dealing with the worsening situation.

At 6:25 P.M. on April 5, the voice of the chairman of the Beijing RC, concurrently first political commissar of the Beijing Garrison, Wu De, was suddenly heard crackling from the public address system in the square. In a brief speech, broadcast repeatedly over the next few hours, Wu called on the "revolutionary masses" to vacate the square immediately:

> Comrades! In the past few days . . . a tiny handful of bad elements with ulterior motives made use of the Qingming Festival to deliberately create a political incident, directing their spearhead at Chairman Mao and the party center in a vain attempt to change the general orientation of the struggle to criticize that unrepentant capitalist roader's revisionist line and beat back the right-deviationist wind to reverse correct verdicts. We must clearly see the reactionary nature of this political incident, expose the schemes and intrigues of the bad elements, heighten our revolutionary vigilance, and avoid being taken in . . . The revolutionary masses must leave the square at once and not be duped by them.[66]

Most people obeyed. Out of sight, the militia, police, and PLA troops were quietly assembling in readiness to expel those who did not.

At 9:30 P.M., the floodlights were turned on. More than 10,000 members of the People's Militia, 3,000 policemen, and five battalions from the Beijing Garrison, all armed with clubs, entered the square running. With the public address system now blaring out the PLA's "Three Main Rules of Discipline and Eight Points for Attention"—presumably to remind the forces that the "masses" were citizens who should be treated with restraint—the slightly more than 200 people still in the square who had not wanted or managed to escape, huddled around the Monument to the People's Heroes, were beaten up and dragged away by force. But brutal as the operation may have been, it seems that no one was killed or died from injuries sustained in the process.[67] Among those detained was the son of Yao Dengshan, the Ministry of Foreign Affairs "rebel" held responsible for the sacking of the British mission in August 1967; the father had been one of Zhou Enlai's bêtes noires, but the son was redressing the balance.[68] In the end, 59 of the people apprehended in the square that night were sentenced to jail terms of varying lengths.[69] All but 3 were cleared after the Cultural Revolution of the charges of "counterrevolution" made against them; the exceptions were apparently pickpockets and the like, charged with ordinary criminal offenses.[70]

At dawn on April 6, Mao Zedong was briefed by his nephew about what had happened in the square. "The enemy," Mao Yuanxin insisted, had really given himself away this time, by setting fire to a building and vehicles, beating people up, and engaging in "counterrevolutionary propaganda." His suppression by a joint contingent of militia, soldiers, and public security personnel had significantly "boosted the morale" of the revolutionary masses.[71] After a few hours of sleep, Mao delivered his first official pronouncement, at 11 A.M. It read, in full: "Boosted the morale is good! Good! Good!" On the following morning, April 7, Mao again called his nephew to his side.[72] Since their last encounter, Mao had learned more by reading issues of *Circumstances Gathered (Qingkuang huibian)*, a classified news report put out by the *People's Daily* and edited by Yao Wenyuan.[73] Nodding in agreement when his nephew credited Zhang Chunqiao with making a comparison between what had happened and the Hungarian uprising, and between Deng Xiaoping and Imre Nagy, Mao announced: "That's right. This time, one, [in] the capital; two, [in] Tiananmen [Square]; three, burning and beating. Enough is enough. The nature has changed." Making a gesture with his hand, Mao added, with Deng in mind: "Therefore, throw him out!" At the end of their conversation, Mao told his nephew that he wanted to see Hua Guofeng made premier and ordered both his decisions to be made public as quickly as possible.[74]

On April 7, at Mao's orders, a frantic effort began to put together an official version of events that could be published in the *People's Daily* the following day. With Yao Wenyuan as the chief censor still sitting in the Great Hall of the People, and the offices and printers of the *People's Daily* quite some distance away, page-proofs were shuttled back and forth by car. So intense was the increase in traffic that members of Beijing's tiny foreign community "noticed a flurry of limousines in the neighborhood of Tiananmen" without knowing what it was about.[75] Chinese outside the capital were in a worse situation. Unless they had been telephoned by friends or relatives in Beijing, or had access to foreign broadcasts via a shortwave radio, they had no means of knowing that there had even been an "incident" until three days later.[76]

When the official version of events appeared on April 8, it was headlined "Counterrevolutionary Political Incident at Tiananmen Square." But despite Yao Wenyuan's best efforts, so detailed an account inevitably revealed the popular nature of the demonstration. Yao had no way to explain how "a handful of class enemies," "a few bad elements, sporting crew cuts," a "bad element wearing spectacles" could have made so much trouble for so long had the revolutionary masses indeed "showed their utmost hatred for this counterrevolutionary incident."

Symptomatic of the anxiety felt by Yao and his colleagues in the Gang of Four were three mentions of attacks on Qin Shi Huangdi, the ruthless sovereign who founded the Chinese empire by conquest in 221 B.C., and to whom Mao was often—and liked to be—compared. A harmless aside by Lin Biao about Qin Shi Huangdi when talking with Mao years before the Cultural Revolution was used as evidence to blacken him after his defection and death. According to the official account of the Tiananmen incident, the handful of class enemies "brazenly clamoured that 'the era of Chin [Qin] Shi Huang is gone.'"[77] Clearly, Yao hoped that by suggesting that the enemies in the square were anti-Mao, he could generate more sympathy than by quoting anti-Gang remarks, none of which were mentioned. But the focus on the Qin emperor underlined the Gang's fear of a genuinely anti-Mao movement, because they were totally dependent on him for their positions.

That same day, April 8, the formal decisions taken by the Politburo in response to Mao's "throw him out" also appeared in print. Hua Guofeng became first vice chairman of the CC and premier, and as such clearly heir to Mao as well as to Zhou.[78] The decision on Deng said that his problem had become an "antagonistic contradiction" and that on "the proposal of our great leader Chairman Mao, the Politburo unanimously agrees to dismiss Deng Xiaoping from all posts both inside and outside the Party while allowing him to keep his Party membership so as to see how he will behave in the future."[79]

In radical strongholds like Tsinghua University, the official reaction was one of "resolute support for the two wise decisions." Behind the scenes, however, there was disappointment as well. Chi Qun grumbled, saying: "Deng Xiaoping may have been purged, but still I'm not able to attend even the meetings of the Politburo."[80]

Should Mao really be held responsible for decisions like these? Mao's doctor, Li Zhisui, later maintained that in February 1976 "The Chairman's mind was still clear."[81] As late as July, Li insisted, Mao was still "very alert. His mind was clear. He was blind in his left eye, but he saw well with the right one. Nothing of importance could be kept from him."[82] But in 1980 Mao's personal attendant, Zhang Yufeng, wrote as follows to the CCP center in a letter concerned specifically with the events on and around April 5, 1976:

> Every decision at the time was taken by way of a discussion in the Politburo, about which the Chairman would receive a report. The Chairman, too weak to inquire about the details, was in a position only to nod his head, thereby acknowledging that he had been informed. During this period, the center made a whole series of erroneous decisions: clearly, it is not appropriate to pin the responsibility for these decisions on a dying, bedridden man who already for some time had been unable to speak and to eat [unaided], and who was barely able to breathe![83]

Ms. Zhang almost certainly spent more time with Mao than did Dr. Li, but she was testifying at a time when Deng and his colleagues were preparing their assessment of Mao and the Cultural Revolution and wished to ensure that as much of the blame as possible was shifted to the Gang of Four. Dr. Li, by contrast, was writing outside China with no political pressures upon him, so it is likely that his assessment, in line with ALS cases elsewhere, is nearer the truth. Moreover, had the decision been left to the dominant radicals in the Politburo, there would have been no question of allowing Deng to retain his party membership. And if Mao was responsible for that decision, he must be credited with the others as well.

Even without the complete disgrace of Deng, Yao Wenyuan was so elated that late in the night of April 7, unable to go to sleep even after taking sleeping pills, he wrote in his diary: "The three basic lessons learned from crushing this counterrevolutionary coup d'état are to act in the interest of the proletariat, to smash all bourgeois democratic conventions and fetters (like convening a plenum and having an 'election,' or obtaining the approval of the 'National People's Congress,' etc.), and to take decisive organizational action to get rid of bad people."[84]

Some of Yao's colleagues were energized by an idea to have Deng seized by "the masses" on the grounds that he had masterminded the Tiananmen incident. Wang Dongxing was deputed to ask Deng if he had visited the square. In fact, Deng had forbidden his family to visit the square, and his one trip to the neighborhood was to get his hair cut at the Beijing Hotel. But Wang's real objective was to prevent an attack on Deng, and on April 7, with Mao's agreement, he secretly moved Deng and his wife, Zhuo Lin, to a villa in the old legation quarter; renovated for Zhou Enlai in the early 1970s, it had never been lived in by him once he was diagnosed with cancer.

Deng and Zhuo Lin spent a little over three months there, separated from their family again, under effective house arrest under the watchful eyes of the 8341 guards. From here, the day the "two decisions" appeared on the front page of the People's Daily, Deng wrote to Wang Dongxing and the CCP center, giving Hua Guofeng's appointment his backing and saying how much he appreciated having been allowed to retain his CCP membership.[85] Deng could afford to be ingratiating. He could guess that he would be protected from humiliation or worse. He was down, but he was not out.

25

The Last Days of Chairman Mao

L esser mortals were not as lucky as Deng. The events in the provinces in March and the "counterrevolutionary political incident" in Tiananmen Square provoked a nationwide crackdown. Between April 4 and May 21, the Ministry of Public Security issued five "Telephone Notifications" to its organs nationwide, urging them repeatedly to strike hard against persons who "fabricate or spread counterrevolutionary rumors," as well as anyone caught disseminating "the so-called Premier Zhou's last will."[1] The intensity of the ensuing crackdown varied greatly among localities. In Mao Yuanxin's home province of Liaoning, a two-week-long meeting of senior party and public security officials in the second half of April identified "counterrevolutionary rumormongers" as key targets of a more general crackdown on "counterrevolutionary activities." By September, some 685 suspects had been investigated and 213 detained for what was rarely more than an expression of guarded sympathy for Deng Xiaoping and muted criticism of Jiang Qing et al.[2] In the Hebei provincial capital of Shijiazhuang, every urban resident known to have visited Beijing in late March/early April was investigated, and among them some 280 (one in four) persons who turned out to have been in the square were made to surrender 154 photographs of "activities and reactionary poetry."[3]

Estimates of the severity of the post-Tiananmen crackdown in China as a whole vary tremendously. One almost certainly misleading claim by the Ministry of Public Security has it that "within forty days, some 1,662 persons had been detained and 390 arrested nationwide."[4] A detailed German study cites Hong Kong estimates to the effect that "millions . . . were drawn in nationwide" and Taiwan intelligence sources claiming that "close to 10,000 lost their lives, nationwide"; the study points out that if figures like these are to be believed, this would have been "one of the biggest mass persecutions in the history of the PRC."[5] A senior CCP historian made a soberer assessment in 1984: "How many were seized [*zhua*]? How many were interrogated? How many died? No [aggregate] statistics exist, only fragments . . . [On the basis of these figures] one arrives at an estimate of close to 10,000 formally arrested nationwide. In actuality, the number of those who did not end up in police offices but were isolated and investigated within their own units was far, far greater."[6] Regardless of where the truth lies, Yao Wenyuan concluded at the time that brute force was proving effective. On May 7 Yao impressed upon one of the senior ghostwriters working for the Shanghai RC that "violence" had been at the core of both the Cultural Revolution and the suppression of the Tiananmen incident. He concluded: "In struggles to come, it'll still be violence that does the trick."[7]

For those who escaped the threat of violence there was the boredom of ritual, a predictable string of propagandistic rallies all over China. On April 8, the Beijing municipal committee of the Communist Youth League held a first mass rally attended by some 13,000 young workers, students, and militia men and women who swore to "firmly support the two decisions of the party center smashing the counterrevolutionary countercurrent" and to "carry out the struggle to repulse the right-deviationist wind to reverse correct verdicts through to the end." The next day, more than 100,000 Beijing residents took to the streets in a citywide demonstration addressed by Wu De, who asserted that the "swift dismissal" of Deng Xiaoping had "dealt a heavy blow to the class enemies at home and abroad," and not only "truly brought elation to the hearts of the people" but also had shown that "the situation is indeed excellent."[8] A foreign resident noted:

> The older housewives were happy to have time off from their routine work. The sun was shining and it was a nice day to be outdoors. Some hobbled on tiny bound feet and others waddled and puffed as they moved in small groups toward the square. They came directly from their workshops, and were dressed in faded jackets and worn clothes. Each carried a pink paper flag condemning Teng [Deng]. Occasionally their leader interrupted the chatter and rallied them to shout, "Down with Teng Hsiao-ping [Deng Xiaoping]!" and then they continued talking. A young factory worker was having a wonderful time loudly beating a big red drum balanced precariously on the back of a three-wheel bike. As a joke the driver suddenly swerved to one side, and the drum almost toppled over. Everyone around him laughed, and the drummer joined in also.[9]

Throughout April, similar rallies and demonstrations of support for the two decisions were held all over China. In Shanghai, Roderick MacFarquhar and a parliamentary colleague followed throngs of people marching through the streets and ended up at a mass rally addressed by local party leaders in the main square, once the site of a racetrack. In Beijing on April 26, Hua Guofeng, the Gang of Four, as well as Chief of Staff Chen Xilian, Wu De, and other leaders received representatives of the Capital Workers' Militia, People's Police, and guards who had rendered "meritorious service" in the Tiananmen incident.[10]

Unsatisfied with just public rallies, the radicals attempted to craft a coherent "theory" surrounding what had happened in Tiananmen Square and why. In mid-April, the Propaganda Group of the Beijing Municipal Party Committee organized a week-long conference of "theory workers" from twenty-six units in the capital, including Peking University and Tsinghua University. Much of the debate came to center on the alleged emergence of a "bourgeoisie inside the Communist Party."[11] The Gang of Four had for some time been calling on writers and artists to devote themselves to this particular subject matter in the arts and in popular literature. As Zhang Chunqiao explained to Minister of Culture Yu Huiyong:

> There are still no works with depth that describe the struggle against the capitalist roaders inside the party in the era of the socialist revolution. We simply must pay attention to this. If we don't properly investigate what constitutes the distinctive characteristic of the struggle in the era of the socialist revolution, and the distinctive characteristic and essence of capitalist roaders inside the party, we will have great difficulty writing good works of quality devoted to this topic. Such works would not only be able to teach the people of today something, but also have an educational value for future generations.[12]

Yu Huiyong, in turn, passed on the message to a group of senior playwrights in the Beijing opera community:

> To write about the struggle against the capitalist roaders, that is the urgent task at present . . . With artillery shells in the form of outstanding achievements, we must strike back at the right-deviationist wind to reverse correct verdicts and at the revisionist line pursued by [Deng Xiaoping]. Didn't [comrade] Jiang Qing use to talk about firing artillery salvos? It's time now for a new salvo![13]

Hua Guofeng's Credentials

For China's new premier, the concerns were more practical than theoretical. Hua Guofeng was virtually unknown to the people of China, and even within the Politburo his authority was far more tenuous than his formal titles suggested. For the old guard survivors, he was a puny substitute for Deng Xiaoping; for the radicals, he simply was not one of them. Fortunately for Hua, he was soon able to grasp at some straws of credibility handed him by the Chairman. When Mao received New Zealand's Prime Minister Robert Muldoon on the evening of April 30, Hua was able to stay behind afterward and have a rare conversation with the Chairman. On this occasion, Mao, whose speech was increasingly incomprehensible even to Hua, scribbled on scraps of paper three sentences that were to play a crucial role in the post-Mao succession struggle. They read: "Take your time, don't be anxious," "Act according to past principles," and, most immediately relevant to Hua's purpose, "With you in charge, I'm at ease." After Mao's death, this phrase became Hua's talisman, and was used to suggest that Mao meant it for general application. But as Hua explained to Foreign Minister Qiao Guanhua when he (Hua) caught up with the Muldoon entourage later that evening, the context of the remarks was only the volatile situation in southwest China, where the campaign to criticize Deng Xiaoping continued to encounter strong resistance.[14] Appropriately, the very last instruction Mao handed down to Hua, when they met on June 25, was "Pay attention to domestic affairs."[15]

Doubtless conscious that Wang Hongwen's failure to handle domestic affairs had led the Chairman to discard him as heir apparent, Hua tried to follow Mao's stricture as best he could. On June 26, he intervened in Shanxi by issuing a sharply worded central document in an effort to quell a rapidly escalating factional/labor conflict that was threatening to disrupt railway transport in and around the city of Datong, situated in one of the country's major coal fields.[16] Hua also attempted, without success, to bring to an end the state of near civil war that had persisted for years in the Hebei industrial city of Baoding.[17] In a number of provinces, the situation was extremely volatile, including in Mao's own home province, where a riot outside the headquarters of the Hunan Party Committee left twenty people wounded.[18] Meanwhile the Ministry of Public Security—which Hua concurrently headed—called a two-week-long conference of public security chiefs from all over the country to discuss the domestic situation in general as well as "the machinations of the enemy at present."[19]

Countdown

Mao's final instruction to Hua had been given in between heart attacks. Few people outside the walls of Zhongnanhai knew anything about these grave threats to the Chairman's life. He suffered the first attack on May 11, during an argument with his constant attendant, Zhang Yufeng.[20] His condition then stabilized, but on June 15 the foreign press was told by a government spokesman that "Chairman Mao is well advanced in years and is still very busy with his work. The Central Committee of our Party has decided not to arrange for Chairman Mao to meet foreign distinguished visitors."[21] The same message was conveyed to the Chinese public in a Foreign Ministry "General Circular."[22] Then on June 26, the day after that last instruction to Hua, Mao suffered a second myocardial infarction, more severe than the first. This prompted the issuing of a Notification to senior party officials across the country to the effect that Mao Zedong was indeed seriously ill.[23] In June, planning began for the construction of his memorial hall.[24]

For superstitious members of the Chinese public and officialdom, doubtless a high proportion, there were other portents that the year 1976 was ending an era. Zhou was dead. On July 6, the leading revolutionary general, Marshal Zhu De, died at the age of eighty-nine. It had been Zhu's loyalty that enabled the Chairman to ensure early on that the military was subordinate to the party. Zhu's passing was symbolic. The generals were already contemplating their first coup against civilian leaders.

But for traditionalists, the most potent signal of a disjuncture in human affairs was the massive earthquake that shook north China on July 28. Measuring 7.8 on the Richter scale, the earthquake obliterated much of the Hebei coal-mining city of Tangshan, killing, according to official figures, more than 242,000 people and leaving more than 164,000 seriously injured.[25] In Beijing, about 125 miles away, strong shock waves caused much damage, forcing many residents of buildings deemed unsafe in the event of aftershocks out into the streets and into makeshift accommodations for weeks, in some cases well into the early winter. In Zhongnanhai, Mao was awakened by the earthquake and agreed to be wheeled on his hospital bed to a safer building.[26] In Deng Xiaoping's compound, frantic family members had to break down his bedroom door—always locked for safety—and lead their groggy parents outside; sedatives had enabled the elder Dengs to sleep through the shock.[27]

For Hua Guofeng, the earthquake was an ideal opportunity to display leadership. He headed a top-level investigation team and took overall charge of the rescue operations, signaling national self-confidence by refusing foreign aid.

For the Gang of Four, by contrast, the earthquake was a political disaster. They claimed that the rescue efforts were being used to suppress the campaign against Deng. Arguing that the nation had other great affairs with which to be concerned—"study, criticizing Deng, grasping revolution, promoting production"—Yao Wenyuan limited the publication of articles on the relief operation. Under his direction, the *People's Daily* printed an editorial warning that whenever there were natural disasters, opportunists tried to use the temporary difficulties as excuses to change the direction of the revolution and restore capitalism.[28]

Perhaps conscious of the bad image the Gang of Four was projecting, in late August Chi Qun and Yao Wenyuan attempted to use the *Beijing Daily* to publicize Jiang Qing's recent visits to the Xinhua Printing Plant, Peking University, and Tsinghua University—where most of the staff were living in makeshift tents—under the banner headline "CCP Politburo Member Comrade Jiang Qing, Representing Chairman Mao and the Party Center, Calls on the People of the Capital." This move seems to have been too much for Wu De to stomach. Years later he claimed that he had been reluctant to have the report and the headline appear in the official organ of the Beijing RC, which he chaired. He decided to solicit Hua Guofeng's opinion before releasing the page-proofs for publication. Not surprisingly, Hua was even more reluctant and simply told Wu to sit on the page-proofs for now and, should anyone inquire about them, claim that he had handed them on to Hua.[29] Mao still had a few weeks to live, but the battle to spin his legacy was in full swing.

Preparing for Anything

The events in Tiananmen Square in early April and Mao's imminent demise prompted concern with domestic affairs among Hua Guofeng and other Politburo members. The very day Mao suffered his second heart attack, General Chen Xilian—commander of the Beijing MR and, since February, in charge of the day-to-day running of the MAC in place of Ye Jianying—called on Wu De to draw up contingency plans to respond to "possible counterrevolutionary political incidents." Wu assigned the job of drawing up plans to a joint task force that included the director of the Beijing Public Security Bureau, Liu Chuanxin, and the leadership of the Beijing militia. The joint task force submitted its contingency plans for approval to Wu De and Chen Xilian on July 9.[30]

The plans, titled "Envisaging Responses to Possible Counterrevolutionary Political Incidents"—were three in number. Contingency plan 1 was designed to deal with incidents "smaller than" the events in Tiananmen Square on April 5 and involved drawing on some 30,000 Workers' Militia, 500 police officers, and eight companies from the Beijing Garrison. Plan 2 was designed for incidents "comparable to" those in Tiananmen Square and involved employing 50,000 militia, 1,500 police officers, and ten battalions from the Beijing Garrison. Finally, plan 3 was designed for serious incidents of "even greater" magnitude, and involved throwing 100,000 militia, 3,000 police officers, and twenty-four PLA battalions into the fight against "counterrevolution." As for deadly force, the general principle was to deal with unarmed rioters primarily with nonlethal weapons, including clubs, and to deal with armed rioters with superior firepower.[31]

Contingency plans similar to those in Beijing were being drawn up in Shanghai. From his central vantage point in Beijing, Wang Hongwen had daily phoned his subordinates Ma Tianshui and Wang Xiuzhen on the Shanghai RC while the events in Tiananmen Square were still unfolding, telling them to have the Workers' Militia "get out there" and "prevent incidents similar to that in Tiananmen Square from happening in Shanghai." At 3:00 A.M. on April 8, Wang had phoned Wang Xiuzhen and shared with her ("Don't go public with this") some of his own views on the none-too-efficient Workers' Militia in the capital. In some places in Beijing, he said, "They have the militia, but the militia have no cars; in others they have cars, but they don't have any militia. There's no coordination. On top of this, they have one-way streets in Beijing that cause additional delays."[32] Implicitly, Shanghai would have to do better than that. After a day of intense conferring about how to respond, Wang Xiuzhen and her colleagues hastily drew up three alternative contingency plans, codenamed "Counterattacks" 1, 2, and 3, involving public security units and the Workers' Militia, and designed to deal respectively with "localized" incidents, incidents "likely to expand," and "situations entering a serious state." Exactly how many men were meant to be called upon in each case, and what their armaments were meant to be, are not known. As a measure intended to beef up security in general, some 200 to 300 roving Workers' Militia groups began to patrol the Shanghai streets at night in April and continued to do so until October 1976.[33]

Whether similar contingency plans were being drawn up in other parts of China at this point remains unclear. But few if any delegations from other parts of China came to the capital to pick up "progressive experiences." Beijing had a "bean-curd militia," according to Wang Hongwen. He had been outraged to hear that some militia contingents had been unwilling to take part in the crackdown in Tiananmen Square on April 5.[34] With the propaganda sector firmly controlled by the Gang of Four, the national model for "riot control" was still what it had been for some time, Shanghai. In the summer of 1976, after the Tiananmen events, six delegations from municipalities in China's three northeastern provinces, the area under Mao Yuanxin's influence, as well as neighboring Jiangsu, paid visits to study the work of the Shanghai Workers' Militia.[35]

Wang Hongwen was doubtless reliving his glory days in the "January Storm," when he led the Workers' General Headquarters to victory over the Shanghai party machine. But he should have remembered that even Zhang Chunqiao had attributed the triumph to the backing of the local military commander. The danger to the Gang of Four once Mao's protection was withdrawn by death was not a popular uprising in the streets projected by the first two contingency plans; it was what to do in the event of really serious firepower, that is, the PLA's, being used against them. Beijing's militia might not have been up to much, but Wang should have noted that its third contingency plan envisaged calling in twenty-four PLA battalions. Ding Sheng, the commander of the Nanjing MR, in which Shanghai was situated, was making supportive speeches alongside the Gang's satraps in the city,[36] but would he rally his battalions to the radical cause in a crisis? Without that guarantee, there was an air of unreality in Wang's planning.

Members of the Gang were aware of their problem. Zhang Chunqiao knew how highly disliked he was by the PLA. On the evening of April 5, as he watched the clearing of Tiananmen Square from behind the curtains in the Great Hall of the People, his thought had been: "What if the armed forces were to turn their guns around, at us? Then what?"[37]

Zhang Chunqiao carried pitifully little weight even in the PLA's General Political Department, of which he was concurrently director and party first secretary. To judge from the available record, in the campaign to criticize Deng Xiaoping and identify and punish those who were responsible for "political rumors" in the spring and summer of 1976, Zhang did everything possible to make the department toe the radical line, even going so far as to threaten it with dissolution if it did not come around to his stand.[38] Yet Zhang's deputy Liang Biye—a lieutenant general and Long March veteran in charge of the day-to-day operations of the department—simply disregarded most of what Zhang said. An increasingly frustrated Zhang enlisted the support of Wang Hongwen (in his capacity as member of the MAC Standing Committee) to back him up and increase the pressure on Liang. The latter in turn simply got General Chen Xilian to back *him* up, making it possible for him to continue to resist and obstruct whatever wishes were voiced by Zhang. Many years after the end of the Cultural Revolution, Liang wrote with some pride in his memoirs of how "during the more than ten months that the 'criticize Deng, oppose rightism' movement lasted, the General Political Department did not issue a single 'criticize Deng, oppose rightism' document."[39]

Underlying the Gang's military problem was a major political miscalculation, a failure to give Mao's game plan at least a chance of working. Members of the Gang of Four scorned Hua Guofeng in the months after his promotion to heir apparent. Yet the Tiananmen events had demonstrated that they had good grounds to make common cause. When they did, they could prevail. Attacks on the Cultural Revolution endangered beneficiaries as well as radicals. Deng was a common nemesis. The PLA was a potential threat to both groups. Maybe the old guard would always have won, but by failing to reach out to Hua and his colleagues, the Gang of Four never gave Mao's concept a chance to succeed.

The Gang's tactics were as flawed as their strategy. Ten years as Mao's powerful courtiers generating the chaos of the Cultural Revolution from Beijing had infected them with hubris. They had wielded power from the capital under the admiring gaze of their political and intellectual lackeys. They had enjoyed privileges and a lifestyle that the Cultural Revolution had been supposed to eliminate. On the one hand, in their public attacks on "capitalist roaders" they would accuse people like Deng Xiaoping of desiring "bourgeois rights." On the other hand, in closed settings, they admitted that they themselves were no different. On March 2, 1976, Jiang Qing had told senior provincial cadres that the bourgeoisie was no longer the surviving old capitalists from pre-Communist days. Rather, it was the "persons in power inside the party walking the capitalist road, big officials, with us right here! . . . Someone like me, I don't have to even ask for things, people will provide me with them . . . I don't have to take the back door; others will have taken care of all of that for me."[40]

How, with Mao gone, Jiang Qing expected to survive in power for any length of time is a mystery. The Gang controlled neither the military nor the party organizational apparatus. The Gang had forgotten that their power in Beijing was merely a reflection of Mao's, not their own, authority. Shanghai, however, was their own genuine power base, and the lesson of Mao's revolutionary struggle from the 1920s to the 1940s was that when faced with a superior force, one should relocate to a safe base area. It would surely have been wise, as Mao's life ebbed away, for either Wang Hongwen or Zhang Chunqiao to have returned to Shanghai to ensure that China's major industrial city remained a hefty bargaining chip in any post-Mao division of the spoils. But they did not.

The Death of Mao Zedong

At ten minutes past midnight on September 9, 1976, the fluttering line on Mao's electrocardiogram turned flat. The mantra "Long live Chairman Mao! Long live Chairman Mao! Eternal life to Chairman Mao!" spoken many million times over by many millions for so many years had finally failed to work its magic.

Zhang Yufeng, Mao's closest personal companion in his final years, wailed: "The Chairman is gone . . . What will happen to me?"[41] Jiang Qing, Yao Wenyuan later recalled, broke down and clutched her husband's lifeless body, crying: "Doctors! Quickly! Save the Chairman! Why don't you save him?"[42] But Mao's doctors could do no more. "We have done all we can," Mao's personal physician had whispered hoarsely to Hua Guofeng shortly before midnight.[43] Hua now turned to Wang Dongxing, ordering him to call a meeting of the Politburo. Held in Mao's swimming pool residence, it was to be what Zhang Chunqiao called the "most depressing Politburo meeting ever, everybody grieving deeply, speakers breaking down in midsentence, crying."[44] It approved the text of a "Message to the Whole Country," announcing that Mao had "passed away . . . as a result of the worsening of his illness and despite all treatment, although meticulous medical care was given him in every way after he fell ill." The message called upon "the whole Party, the whole army and the people of all nationalities in the country to resolutely turn their grief into strength" and "carry on the cause left behind by Chairman Mao."[45] The "Message" was made public by the Xinhua News Agency in its Chinese and English services at 4:00 P.M. that same day.

"I felt no sorrow at his passing," Mao's personal physician claimed many years later.[46] Zhang Chunqiao told a close colleague: "These past few years I've been on the medical teams of the revered Kang, the premier, and the Chairman, and not a single one of them did we manage to save. In the future, I'm not going to be on anybody's medical team."[47] Some immediately began worrying about how Mao's passing would affect the political balance. A member of the Standing Committee of the NPC admitted the day after Mao died: "After I heard the news of Chairman Mao's passing I thought, now that the Chairman is gone, whom do we rely on? . . . I don't trust the center without the Chairman."[48]

Messages of condolence arrived in Zhongnanhai from near and far. The Liang Xiao team wrote to Jiang Qing: "In this incomparably sorrowful moment, we sincerely hope that you, our most respected comrade Jiang Qing, take good care of yourself for the sake of the revolution!"[49] One CCP member wrote and suggested that Jiang Qing be appointed party chairman in order to ensure that the late "Chairman Mao's CCP center" end up in the right "hands."⁵⁰ Jiang Qing herself claimed she was receiving messages from Tibet written by those who feared that with Mao now gone, the Dalai Lama might return and the CCP center might turn "revisionist." "Don't worry!" she responded: "Should the sky cave in, we'll cope!"⁵¹ The more than fifty foreign governments that flew flags at half mast included, surprisingly, those of West Germany, Canada, France, and New Zealand.⁵² "Quite remarkable!" was Jiang Qing's reaction to what she characterized as "the sorrow felt by the people of foreign countries."⁵³

The day Mao died, the Beijing Garrison commander, Wu Zhong, put into effect the emergency plan for dealing with "possible counterrevolutionary incidents" drawn up by Wu De in July. Efforts to read and monitor all mail moving in and out of the capital were stepped up.⁵⁴ Surveillance of what might be called "the usual suspects" was greatly intensified. In Shanghai the next day, more than 6 million rounds of live ammunition were distributed by the municipal Workers' Militia Command as the city was put on an immediate "war preparedness" alert that lasted until September 23, when the Shanghai RC agreed to have the number of men affected by the alert reduced by two-thirds.⁵⁵

Popular reaction to Mao's death was muted. "There were many who wept, but there was not the same stunned grief as there had been for Zhou," according to one foreign resident, confirmed by another: "Instead of throngs of people weeping on the streets as they had done after Chou [Zhou] En-lai's death, I saw only a few people displaying deep emotions." In Shanghai, a foreign teacher noted in her diary a rumor that the local leadership had been summoned to Beijing because people seemed less moved than in Beijing. She added: "And, in fact, here people do weep less and make fewer scenes. Which accounts for the repetition and the beefing up of ceremonies, and the invitations—not public, needless to say—to cry harder."⁵⁶ But among the tens of thousands of Chinese families who had suffered during the Cultural Revolution all around the country, doubtless there were only crocodile tears:

The news filled me with such euphoria that for an instant I was numb. My in-grained self-censorship immediately started working; I registered the fact that there was an orgy of weeping going on around me, and that I had to come up with some suitable performance. There seemed nowhere to hide my lack of correct emotion except the shoulder of the woman in front of me, one of the student officials, who was apparently heartbroken. I swiftly buried my head in her shoulder and heaved appropriately. As so often in China, a bit of ritual did the trick.[57]

Nor was there any concerted action of protest or revolt by the regime's "counterrevolutionary" enemies safely wasting away in Qincheng Prison. Wang Li recalled seventeen years later that "I began weeping the moment I heard the broadcaster announce the news of Mao Zedong's passing. Qincheng Prison was filled with the sound of people weeping. The Qincheng administration turned down my request for permission to wear a black armband."[58] How much Wang Li's memory was clouded by a need to attest his loyalty to the Chairman in his ultimately vain effort to seek rehabilitation is uncertain. But a foreign Maoist incarcerated in the same prison had a different recollection of the atmosphere:

> I couldn't understand my reaction. In my mind, Mao was the most important man in the world, wise, gifted, philosophically sound, strategically masterful . . . And yet, I could not produce a single tear when news came of Mao's death. Not one. "What will the prison personnel think?" I wondered . . . And yet I needn't have worried. The keepers, the security personnel, my fellow prisoners—I could neither hear nor see much emotion from any of them either.[59]

At 3:00 P.M. on September 18, the mourning climaxed in a mass memorial meeting in Tiananmen Square, chaired by Wang Hongwen and attended by one million people and broadcast live on television and radio throughout China. After a three-minute silence and solemn music played by a 500-man military band, Hua Guofeng delivered the eulogy, in which the most apposite quote from the Chairman for the days ahead was: "Political power grows out of the barrel of a gun."

Two days earlier, a joint editorial in the *People's Daily, Liberation Army Daily,* and *Red Flag* had proclaimed that Mao had "adjured us to 'Act according to the principles laid down.'" What these words of Mao's referred to was unclear. Supposedly whispered to Zhang Chunqiao only a few days earlier at their final meeting on September 5,[60] they were virtually identical in meaning with the proposal "Act according to past principles" that Mao had communicated to Hua Guofeng at their late-night meeting on April 30. Eventually Hua was to charge the Gang of Four with having "tampered with Chairman Mao's words" and with having made up the "false" adjuration about acting in accordance with "the principles laid down."[61] At this point, however, according to a source close to Zhang Chunqiao, the Gang of Four had managed to "sneak" the adjuration into an editorial that the other "comrades on the Politburo signed off on at a moment when they were simply too busy with the funerary arrangements for Chairman Mao [to notice]."[62]

As soon as they saw the September 16 editorial, the Liang Xiao team added somewhere close to the top of their September–October agenda the task of writing "ideological critiques" that would drive home the point that "to act according to the principles laid down is to act in accordance with Chairman Mao's proletarian revolutionary line and policies and, for that reason, to be invincible."[63] In Shanghai on September 17, in the first of many articles on this theme, the organ of the municipal RC announced more explicitly that "to act according to the principles laid down" meant carrying on with the "struggle against capitalist roaders" and further "intensifying the criticism of Deng [Xiaoping]."[64] Soon even a song by the name "Act According to the Principles Laid Down" could be heard on Chinese radio, competing for airtime with music of mourning like the recently released "Chairman Mao Lives Forever in Our Hearts."[65]

The Arrest of the Gang of Four

On September 11 and 12, a number of provincial party committees received phone calls from a secretary in the CC's General Office who ordered them henceforth to communicate directly with a new "duty office" directly under Wang Hongwen, and not with whomever they might have communicated regularly in the past, in all matters of importance that called for central involvement. In Hunan, Hua Guofeng's longtime colleague and second-ranking member of the provincial party committee, Zhang Pinghua, decided that this was a somewhat irregular order and called Hua in person to have it confirmed, only to be told that Hua had no knowledge of such an order. Hua's conclusion, once he had determined that Hunan was not an isolated case, was that the Gang of Four had begun to make the first moves toward seizing power.[66]

Prompted by such developments, Hua decided on September 11 to begin grappling with the Gang of Four issue right away. That day, he called on Li Xiannian, asking him to get in touch with Ye Jianying immediately to draw up a plan of action, since otherwise it just might be the "end of the party, the end of the country, and the end of all of us!" Ye needed no further explanation, for he had talked the matter over with Hua on two previous occasions. Also on September 11, Hua called on Wang Dongxing and secured his unequivocal backing for a resolution of the Gang of Four issue.[67]

At this point, Hua and his putative allies had not yet firmly decided what form the "resolution" was to assume, much less exactly when it was to take place. On an evening near the end of the month, Hua Guofeng, Li Xiannian, and Wu De again discussed the respective pros and cons of proceeding by way of a vote of dismissal at a meeting of the Politburo. Wu De, who was in favor of a vote, believed that "we will have a majority of comrades behind us."[68] But the three men were forced to admit that there was considerable uncertainty about how the full CC might vote if and when it would have to be called upon to ratify the dismissal. In the end, after agreeing among themselves that the Gang of Four had no support within the PLA and were in any case genuinely unpopular among the population at large, they decided that simply to seize them was probably safer.[69]

Meanwhile there was no shortage of issues great and small over which the Gang of Four, and Jiang Qing in particular, clashed with Hua Guofeng. When Mao Yuanxin wrote to Hua asking for permission to return to Liaoning now that he was no longer needed by his uncle's side as his "liaison officer," Hua sought Jiang Qing's opinion, and Jiang at first raised no objections. But when the matter came up for decision at a session of the Politburo on September 29, the Gang of Four all suddenly objected strenuously, Zhang Chunqiao in particular. Jiang herself now insisted that Mao Yuanxin simply had to remain in Beijing and that this was, in fact, a "family matter." Many years later Wu De recalled what happened next:

> Jiang Qing went so far as to say that . . . if other people did not want to be bothered, they did not have to listen. At the time, we didn't want to hear any more of her unreasonable nagging and were extremely fed up, so one by one most people left. I recall Wang Dongxing staying on . . . It became a marathon session that lasted until five the next morning. Hua Guofeng controlled his temper, listening patiently. Finally, he asked Jiang Qing: "Are you done?" and Jiang Qing said she was. Hua Guofeng immediately announced: "Meeting over! Mao Yuanxin will return to Liaoning all the same." Jiang Qing's unreasonable nagging no longer worked.[70]

When Jiang Qing insisted at the same Politburo session that she be given custody of her late husband's papers, Hua balked, and a formal decision was taken to have the CC General Office assume control of everything left behind by Mao. "Jiang Qing was extremely resentful about this," Wu De recalled, and again "ended up arguing and fighting at great length with comrade Hua Guofeng, both in direct confrontation and over the telephone."[71]

In extreme secrecy, Wang Dongxing began handpicking the fifty or so officers and men who would in due course be called upon to encompass the purge of the Gang, all of them from among his direct subordinates in the CC General Office and PLA Unit 8341. One group, by far the smaller one, led by Li Xin, Kang Sheng's former secretary, was charged with what Wu De later described as "preparing the relevant documents," drafting a decision to establish a memorial hall for Mao in Beijing to "perpetuate his memory" and a decision to publish the fifth volume of the *Selected Works of Mao Zedong* as soon as possible and "make preparations for the publication of" Mao's collected oeuvres.[72] Both decisions were to be made public immediately after the arrest of the Gang of Four with the aim of convincing the public that Hua Guofeng was Mao's legitimate heir.

The second, significantly larger group, led by Wang himself, was made up of the men and women who were to carry out the actual arrests. Knowledge of these tactical moves was strictly on a need-to-know basis; even Li Xiannian was not informed of such details as exactly how and when the coup would be carried out.[73] Ye Jianying, meanwhile, was acting to minimize the possibility of any sudden action by PLA units stationed in or around Beijing should confusion suddenly arise at the crucial juncture about what was happening and about who was moving against whom. The 6th Tank Division, for instance, stationed in Changping county, was regularly visited by Zhang Chunqiao's younger brother Zhang Qiuqiao: Could it be relied upon to obey the orders from the center? Hua Guofeng and Wu De eventually decided that in order to ensure that units belonging to the Beijing MR stayed out of what was going to happen, they would have to involve Wu Zhong, the commander of the Beijing Garrison, in their plans. Wu responded that if worse came to worst, a tank battalion under his command stationed on the flank of the 6th Tank Division could be relied upon.[74]

General Yang Chengwu, who was privy to some of what was going on, concluded from his last conversation with Jiang Qing before her arrest that "the 'Gang of Four' had no idea about the moves that were under way."[75] At one point, however, Hua Guofeng and Wang Dongxing almost began to suspect otherwise, when Jiang Qing suddenly announced that she wished to leave Beijing for an inspection tour of Shijiazhuang. If the CC General Office had raised objections, she might have been alerted to the fact that something unusual was happening. Hua and Wang decided to let her go so as not to arouse suspicion, and this turned out to be the right move, from their point of view. At a stop along the way, about halfway to Shijiazhuang, Jiang Qing got out and picked some wildflowers by the tracks, had a conversation with members of the train crew, then asked them to return to Beijing rather than go on. Wu De later maintained that, if anything, the aborted journey to Shijiazhuang had been "her way of probing the situation."[76]

Ye Jianying's original plan had been to move against the Gang on or shortly after October 10, on the assumption that some ten days after National Day would be needed to make all the preparations. But a seemingly threatening article by Liang Xiao in the *Guangming Daily* on October 4 and rumors that the Gang were telling their followers to expect "great news" by October 9, possibly even earlier, convinced Ye that his original timetable had to be shortened.[77] In highly secret consultation with Hua Guofeng, the decision was made to preempt whatever possible move the Gang might be contemplating and to have its members and their principal supporters seized on the night of October 6.[78]

Ye informed Wang Dongxing of Hua Guofeng's "instructions" that same morning, October 4. Wang agreed to take action, and later that day twice telephoned Hua's office requesting Hua to meet him at his (Wang's) home in Zhongnanhai. Hua seems to have had a hard time making what was indeed not an easy decision. He was going to authorize a coup against the only members of the leadership who were committed, like himself, to the fruits of the Cultural Revolution; if it was successful, he would have only other beneficiaries to support him against the survivors among the old guard. But finally he set off by car from his home on a street just west of Zhongnanhai, getting his driver to drive him around the city first to ensure he was not being followed, finally entering Zhongnanhai by the western gate and arriving at Wang's residence after 11:00 P.M.

Hua's first question to Wang Dongxing was: "How will you do it?" Wang then laid out his plan of action. The PSC would be called into session, and the Gang of Four would be arrested there. Wang later reported that the meeting lasted until 3:00 A.M. and that both men were in a "state of extreme nervous tension." Hua then took the precaution of not returning home that night, but slept in temporary accommodations in Zhongnanhai arranged for him by Wang, who also ensured that a platoon of particularly reliable guards would maintain his security. At 9:30 A.M., Wang visited Hua in his temporary quarters and told him whom he had selected to carry out their plan. After lunch and a brief rest, both men left Zhongnanhai in separate cars, with Hua taking the precaution of visiting Beijing Hospital to throw possible followers off the scent. Both men were heading to the Western Hills residence, to which Ye had moved for fear of being arrested by the Gang of Four at his home. They were met at the sentry post by

Ye's staff officer and taken to the marshal's house, where they put the finishing touches to their plans.

After further discussions among the three the next morning, they decided to activate their plan at 8:00 P.M. the following day. On the morning of October 6, Hua Guofeng signed a Notification calling a meeting of the PSC, as on so many occasions in the past, in Huairen Hall in Zhongnanhai; it was circulated by Wang Dongxing in the name of the CC General Office.[79] Yao Wenyuan, though not himself a member of the PSC, was asked to attend because of the agenda, which included making some final revisions to the contents of volume 5 of Mao Zedong's *Selected Works,* due to be published some time in the near future.[80]

Wang Hongwen was the first to arrive. "I'm here for a meeting! What are you doing?" he protested, violently resisting the guards who grabbed him as he entered. After Hua Guofeng had read out the decision to have him arrested for "crimes against the party and against socialism," Wang is said to have muttered to himself, "Didn't think it would happen this soon," as he was led away. Zhang Chunqiao arrived next, clutching his briefcase. "What's going on?" he said again and again as the guards grabbed him. Standing on shaky legs and wiping the fog off his glasses, he remained quiet while Hua read out the decision, and made no attempt to resist as he was led away. Yao Wenyuan, who was next, had apparently told his staff, "It's about time we had this meeting!" as he set off for Huairen Hall. When the guards grabbed him, he protested loudly, saying: "I have come to discuss volume 5 of Mao's *Selected Works!* How dare you!" Jiang Qing, meanwhile, was arrested in her Zhongnanhai residence by a group of guards led by the commander of Unit 8341, Zhang Yaoci. Asking "Why? Why?" again and again, she asked for and was given permission to visit the bathroom before being led off. As she came out she refused to hand over the keys to her private safe directly to the guards, and insisted on putting them in a sealed envelope on which she wrote: "To be opened personally by Premier Hua."[81]

With the Gang of Four disposed of, Ye Jianying and Hua Guofeng traveled to the Western Hills, where Ye informed the PLA high command and intelligence department that a coup d'état by the four had been successfully thwarted, and ordered them to keep a close watch on any international reactions. The two men then went to Building No. 9 to begin a meeting of the CCP Politburo to be chaired, so the two of them decided between themselves, by Hua Guofeng. The meeting lasted from 10:00 P.M. until dawn the next morning. Present in addition to Wang Dongxing were Li Xiannian, Chen Xilian, Su Zhenhua, Ji Dengkui, Wu De, Ni Zhifu, Chen Yonggui, and Wu Guixian. Those present were subsequently not permitted to return to their respective homes, but ordered to remain in the Western Hills for the time being. The next priority was informing Deng Xiaoping and other former leaders. On October 7, the process of briefing senior provincial cadres about what had transpired began.[82]

The most delicate problem was how to deal with how Shanghai might react to the news. At 3:00 A.M. on October 7, the CC General Office ordered Ma Tianshui, the highest-ranking party official in Shanghai, to come to Beijing, informing him that a special plane would pick him up later that day.[83] When told by Hua Guofeng about the arrest of the Gang of Four, Ma admitted a month later, it was "as if I'd suffered a staggering blow with a club. How come those who in my mind were the leftists had all been rounded up and isolated? . . . I didn't sleep at all that night . . . and even thought might this not be a palace coup? . . . Transfer me out of here, best of all to somewhere far away like Xinjiang or even Tibet."[84]

On October 8, an increasingly panicky Shanghai RC leadership, unable to get through to Beijing on the telephone and sensing that something highly unusual was going on, concluded that in all likelihood a military coup was under way in the capital. That afternoon, they ordered 31,000 of the city's Workers' Militia to assume a state of high alert; 2,500 militia were to await further orders. At around 10:00 A.M. the following day, news reached leading members of the Shanghai RC through contacts in the Ministries of Culture and Public Health that Hua Guofeng had been appointed Chairman of the Central Committee and MAC. Now desperate for firsthand information about the fates of Zhang Chunqiao, Yao Wenyuan, and Wang Hongwen, the Shanghai RC insisted that Beijing put them in touch with Ma Tianshui.[85] To the question from Shanghai about what the city's reaction should be to the news of Hua Guofeng's appointments, Ma now replied over the phone: "An enthusiastic attitude of firm support!" To the question whether he had seen Zhang, Yao, and Wang and how they were, Ma replied: "I've seen them, they're all quite well, though rather busy and unable to talk to me one on one."[86]

The reaction of the Shanghai RC, where Ma's lie was taken as gospel, was one of immense relief. That evening, the state of alert for the 11,000 Workers' Militia, the number that had actually had been put on alert, was called off, though the 2,500 told to await further orders were asked to remain on standby, just to be on the safe side. At the same time, the Shanghai RC promptly sent off a telegram to Beijing, congratulating Hua Guofeng on his appointment. As Xu Jingxian, a high-ranking RC member, testified in November 1976, it was "not that we really supported Chairman Hua Guofeng. We had misjudged the situation and concluded that the 'Gang of Four' supported him. Therefore, we supported him." On the morning of October 10, still unable to determine exactly what had happened in Beijing and why, the senior members of the Shanghai RC concluded from that day's ambiguously worded joint editorial in the *People's Daily, Liberation Army Daily*, and *Red Flag* that "somebody may have opposed comrade Hua Guofeng, but the 'Gang of Four' had stood by him and come out on the winning side." Xu Jingxian added: "We nonetheless suspected that something had happened at the center. We suspected the key leading comrade [Wang Dongxing] in the CC General Office."[87] In the end, deprived of leadership, the Shanghai revolt that Hua and Ye had feared never took place.

By October 12, what had happened in the capital was a secret no longer. That day the London *Daily Telegraph* reported an attempted coup in China and the arrest of the four radical leaders. On October 18, the Beijing authorities made it official by publishing their version of the events. In the capital, it was the height of the crab season. To celebrate the news, parties would order four crabs, three male and one female, and plenty of liquor. The *People's Daily* trumpeted: "A Great Historic Victory!" in an editorial. The Cultural Revolution was over.

Conclusion

During the Cultural Revolution, people were "rebelling," whereas before that people were "making revolution." However, after the end of the Cultural Revolution, people avoided talking about rebelling, or simply forgot that part of history. Everyone has become a victim of that great catastrophe known as the Cultural Revolution and has forgotten that before disaster fell upon their own heads, they, too, were to some extent the assailants. The history of the Cultural Revolution is thus being continually revised. It is best that you do not try to write a history, but only to look back upon your own experiences . . .

Furthermore, it is very likely that when people have forgotten about it, it will make a comeback, and people who have never gone crazy will go crazy, and people who have never been oppressed will oppress or be oppressed. This is because madness has existed since the birth of humanity, and it is simply a question of when it will flare up again.
—Gao Xingjian, *One Man's Bible* (pages 151, 195)

The Cultural Revolution ended as it began, with a coup against a gang of four. But the coups differed: in 1966, a political coup; in 1976, a military one. At the start of the Cultural Revolution, Mao was able to manipulate the party to ensure a procedurally correct condemnation of his enemies. By its end, the Chinese political system was so paralyzed by top-level factionalism that only the use of armed force could effect a change of leadership.

But Ye Jianying, Hua Guofeng, and Wang Dongxing could justify their action as likely to be widely, indeed wildly, popular, and in a confident break from precedent, they provided graphic evidence of their triumph. The November issue of *Renmin huabao (People's Pictorial)* published a photograph of the mass meeting in Tiananmen Square on September 18 in memory of Mao, at which the Gang of

Four had occupied prominent positions. The traditional Communist method of doctoring photographs that included "non-persons" was to insert other faces or to squeeze the survivors together. This time the victors chose to advertise the fate of the Gang of Four by simply airbrushing them out, leaving conspicuous gaps in the photograph.[1]

The Fall of Hua Guofeng

Once the Gang of Four had been arrested, Deng Xiaoping's rehabilitation was inevitable. Ironically, it was Mao's purge, recall, and second purge of Deng that made it so. Shorn of power at the start of the Cultural Revolution, Deng bore no blame for it. His later recall showed that the Chairman himself had considered Deng the only man capable of matching Zhou Enlai. Deng's subsequent disgrace told everyone that he had defied Mao and the Gang of Four, and valiantly tried to restore sanity to PRC policy-making.

For Hua Guofeng, Deng's return would be a bitter pill, and he resisted it as long as possible. Premier already, Hua was made chairman of the party and the MAC at a Politburo meeting the day after the purge of the Gang of Four. Theoretically, he now combined the institutional clout of Mao and Zhou, and his elevation could not have occurred without the strong support of Ye Jianying and Li Xiannian, the dominant survivors among party and military elders in the leadership. Indeed, Hua was emboldened to tell a conference of senior officials that in the new order they had to continue to criticize Deng, to oppose the "right opportunist wind to reverse the verdicts," and to adopt a correct attitude toward the Cultural Revolution.[2]

Hua sought to bolster his position by ensuring that Mao's shadow continued to loom large over the land. It was swiftly decided that a mausoleum for an embalmed Mao would be erected in Tiananmen Square, in defiance of a twenty-seven-year-old agreement between Mao and his colleagues not to emulate the Soviet pattern of honoring leaders by erecting tombs and naming cities and streets. Hua also took control of Mao's legacy by assuming the editorship of the remaining volumes of his *Selected Works,* which would cover the years of the PRC.[3]

Mao's commendation "With you in charge, I'm at ease"—the spurious proof of Hua's legitimacy—was now much quoted. An oil painting of Hua receiving this benediction from his predecessor was made into a poster and distributed in vast quantities. The new chairman reinforced that link to his predecessor by promoting a slogan devised by another beneficiary of Mao's patronage, Wang Dongxing: "Whatever policy Chairman Mao decided upon, we shall resolutely defend; whatever directives Chairman Mao issued, we shall steadfastly obey." But the "two whatevers," as this slogan came to be known, and Hua's ill-advised indication that it meant that there would have to be future cultural revolutions, undermined whatever support he may have had among party veterans, who were determined that China, and particularly the party and themselves, should never undergo such terrible times again. But considering that Hua seemingly possessed all the levers of power, how the veteran survivors brought Deng back and eased the beneficiaries out was a striking proof that officials counted for more than institutions in China, as Mao had demonstrated during the Cultural Revolution.

Reportedly, senior generals threatened that Hua's appointment by the Politburo would not be confirmed by the CC, as was formally necessary, if Deng were not returned to power. Yet as late as a work conference in March 1977, when Hua came under fire from the former PSC member Chen Yun and General Wang Zhen, the new chairman held fast to his position and refused to let his critics' speeches be published in the official record. But by the time Hua convened the CC's Third Plenum in July, he had to give way on Deng, apparently getting the latter's support for his leadership in return. Presumably Hua's patrons, Ye Jianying and Li Xiannian, had told him they could not hold the line against Deng in view of the strength of opinion among party veterans. The plenum approved the restoration of Deng to all his offices: CCP vice chairman and member of the PSC, vice premier, vice chairman of the MAC, and PLA chief of staff. It was surely no coincidence that the plenum also confirmed Hua in his positions.[4]

In the wake of this compromise, Hua summoned the CCP's Eleventh Congress in August, at which Deng emerged as the third-ranking leader, after Hua and Ye. Both Hua and Deng exercised some restraint in their speeches, with Deng referring to Hua as "our wise leader." But to reassert his legitimacy Hua delivered a long and effusive eulogy to his predecessor as chairman, and reaffirmed the necessity for and success of the Cultural Revolution, the correctness of the line of the Tenth Congress, at which he had entered the Politburo, and the need to persist in class struggle and the revolution under the proletarian dictatorship. Had Hua emphasized instead the other half of his dual legacy, the moderate image of his predecessor as premier, Zhou Enlai, he might conceivably have survived. But although he declared that the Cultural Revolution had concluded, he kept referring to it as the first of its kind, and what probably sealed his fate was his chilling Maoist prediction: "Political revolutions in the nature of the Cultural Revolution will take place many times in the future." Less than eighteen months later, at the Third Plenum of the Eleventh CC in December 1978, reinforced by the return of Chen Yun and others to leadership positions, Deng took over effective control of the party even though Hua still retained all his offices.[5]

In the interim, Deng and his supporters had mobilized elite opinion among the "silent majority" of older party members who had been humiliated and alienated by the Cultural Revolution. Theoreticians, encouraged by Hu Yaobang, head of the Central Party School, devised the slogan "Practice is the sole criterion of truth," which struck at the claim of the "whatever faction" that Mao's words provided guidance in all things.[6] Deng's legitimacy was strengthened when, following the dismissal of Beijing mayor Wu De, the Tiananmen incident of April 5, 1976, was formally reassessed by the city party as being "completely revolutionary." Simultaneously, grassroots backing for Deng began to appear in the form of posters put up on what became known as "Democracy Wall" in the center of the capital. Support was expressed for him as the true heir of Zhou Enlai.

After the Third Plenum, Hua's position became untenable. In January 1979, it was Deng, the "paramount leader," not Hua, the premier and party chairman, who went to the United States to mark the normalization of diplomatic relations between Washington and Beijing.[7] Early in 1980, Hua was forced to agree to the dismissal from the Politburo of the "small gang of four," his fellow beneficiaries in the "whatever faction": Wang Dongxing, Wu De, Ji Dengkui, and General Chen Xilian. He was now isolated. Thereafter he was successively deprived of his grand titles, ceding the premiership to Zhao Ziyang later in 1980 and, in 1981, the party chairmanship to Hu Yaobang and the MAC chairmanship to Deng Xiaoping. He was given the face-saving title of party vice chairman, but at the CCP's Twelfth Congress in 1982, even that was taken away, and he was left as a simple CC member. Mao's attempt to put in place a human guarantor of his legacy had failed.

Exhumation: Victims Return

The reform era was launched at the Third Plenum, but three items of business remained by which Deng would draw a line under the Cultural Revolution.

First, as agreed at the plenum, victims had to be rehabilitated, even if posthumously. Familiar faces returned to the Politburo and the CC. Older grandees were shunted into a new Central Advisory Commission, which Deng planned as a graceful way for them to fade into the sunset, but which occasionally would be a source of conservative opposition to his reforms. At lower levels, cadres came back, often to find that they would have to work alongside those who had denounced them. Some senior officials reportedly wanted to sweep out all such beneficiaries of the Cultural Revolution, but since about half of the party's 38 million members had joined during that decade, it would have involved a purge of extraordinary proportions. The CCP leadership wanted nothing that might resemble a rerun of the Cultural Revolution.

The trickiest but most important rehabilitation had to be Liu Shaoqi, Mao's primary target. His case was treated with kid gloves so as not to damage further the late Chairman's reputation. Even though the Central Discipline Inspection Commission cleared Liu of the crimes imputed to him at the Twelfth Plenum in 1968—describing that indictment as the "biggest frame-up the CCP has ever known in its history, which had been created out of thin air by fabricating materials, forging evidence, extorting confessions, withholding testimony"—its report generated heated discussion at the CC's Fifth Plenum, which finally and formally exonerated Liu in February 1980. The continuing delicacy of the issue may explain why his ashes in Zhengzhou were not returned to his widow, Wang Guangmei, until May 14, 1980. Three days later, Deng gave the tribute at Liu's memorial service in Beijing.[8]

Exorcism: The Trial of the Gang of Four

The second outstanding item was to bring the Gang of Four and the "Lin Biao clique" to trial. The party and the public needed to see the instigators of their suffering being duly punished. After hundreds of investigators had compiled evidence from masses of documents, the trial was held from late November 1980 to January 1981. The gravamen of the indictments was persecution of other Communist leaders and attempts to usurp power. The verdicts were never in doubt. This was a Nuremberg-type trial in which the victors assumed guilt in advance and the only question mark was over the sentences.[9]

To try to ensure dignified and satisfactory court proceedings, party officials pressured the defendants in advance of the trial to agree to confess. Ironically, the final negotiations with Jiang Qing were handled by one of that first gang of four,

Peng Zhen, now rehabilitated and back in the Politburo. Despite an agreement to behave herself in court, the feisty Jiang Qing soon lost patience, becoming defiant, trading accusations, giving as good as she got, maintaining vociferously that she had only done what Mao had ordered. When accused of being responsible for Liu Shaoqi's persecution to death, she retorted that the presiding judge himself and most other CC members at the time had competed with each other to denounce Liu.

Zhang Chunqiao, by contrast, refused to utter a word. Both he and Jiang Qing were given death sentences with a two-year suspension to encourage repentance. Jiang Qing may have believed that Deng would not dare to execute Mao's widow, especially as even at the height of the Cultural Revolution, no leaders had been executed. At any rate, neither she nor Zhang repented, but the sentences were commuted to life imprisonment in 1983.

Jiang Qing was confined in the notorious Qincheng Prison on the outskirts of Beijing, where some of her victims had spent many years, but she was treated far better than they. In the mid-1980s, she developed throat cancer and was transferred to the Public Security Hospital. From then on she alternated between prison and the hospital, but later seems to have been allowed to exchange prison for house arrest. In hospital again in spring 1991 with a recurrence of her cancer, she committed suicide by hanging herself.[10] Jiang Qing's passing was briefly noted by the official news agency. Zhang Chunqiao was released after serving twenty years and lived out his final years in freedom together with his wife, probably under the watchful eyes of the local public security authorities.[11] His death in 2005 was also briefly noted in the official Chinese media.

Fortunately for the judges, who were often exasperated by Jiang Qing, especially when she ignored their orders to "shut up," all the other defendants were much more cooperatively confessional than Zhang and Jiang Qing. Wang Hongwen was sentenced to life in prison, where he died in 1992, apparently of a liver complaint. The other member of the Gang of Four, Yao Wenyuan, received a twenty-year prison sentence dating from his arrest in 1976, and was duly let out in 1996. Forbidden to return to Shanghai, he was forced to spend his final years in his family's ancestral region, Chuji county, Zhejiang province. Chen Boda, imprisoned in late 1970 after the Lushan plenum, was given eighteen years; released in October 1988, he died the following year.

Family members of the Gang of Four reacted in the self-protective manner all too sadly common in political campaigns before the Cultural Revolution. Zhang Chunqiao's wife told investigators from the Shanghai Public Security

Bureau: "I heard some time ago that there would be a trial, so I was mentally prepared for it. I resolutely support it and have already drawn a demarcation line between myself and the 'Gang of Four.'" Yao Wenyuan's paternal grandmother told her neighbors: "I knew nothing about the bad things my grandson was up to. His father was not my own son anyway, and we never had that much contact. Never thought he would do so much bad. He himself is to blame." On hearing news of the trial on the radio, Wang Hongwen's daughter exclaimed angrily in the presence of her mother: "What right does China have to conduct this trial? They should be tried in an international court!"[12]

The trial of the alleged members of the "Lin Biao clique" was less riveting. The four former central military leaders—Chief of Staff Huang Yongsheng, air force head Wu Faxian, logistics head Qiu Huizuo, and chief naval commissar Li Zuopeng—drew sentences of either sixteen or seventeen years. But apart from working with Lin Biao, their main crimes emerged as persecution of other generals rather than being part of Lin's alleged plot to assassinate Mao.[13]

The generals, the Gang of Four, and those who were close to them got their deserts. But the majority of people who committed crimes during the Cultural Revolution did not.[14] Reportedly, some in the CCP's Organization Department wanted a drastic weeding out of guilty party cadres, but that would have involved a massive purge at a time when Deng wanted to emphasize harmony and turn the country away from political struggle. Besides, the only fault of many such cadres had been to hew to the party line emanating from Mao, and since the CCP relied on discipline, party leaders could assume that they would obey the new line equally faithfully. An attempt was made to ensure that former Red Guards attempting to enter or reenter universities had not been guilty of murder or assault, but how successfully this distinction was drawn is uncertain.

Explanation: The Resolution on CCP History

The rehabilitations responded to the party's need for justice and relegitimation; the trial may have satisfied its desire for vengeance, but Deng evidently felt that these were not enough. A third step had to be taken. He would not descend to the level of making a secret speech, but the public deserved some kind of explanation, even expiation, for the maelstrom of the Cultural Revolution, "responsible for the most severe setback and the heaviest losses suffered by the Party, the state and the people since the founding of the People's Republic." How could the CCP, which claimed the right to run the country and protect its people, have allowed this to happen? The answer was given in an official CC *Resolution on Party*

History during the PRC years—Deng's third measure—from which that description of the Cultural Revolution is taken.[15]

Issued on the CCP's sixtieth anniversary, July 1, 1981, the *Resolution* had its origins in discussions among 4,000 party officials and historians, thereafter being passed to a drafting group of forty, later reduced to twenty, with regular interventions and instructions by Deng. At some point, it was suggested that the Twelfth Plenum, at which Liu Shaoqi had been read out of the party, and the Ninth Congress, at which Lin Biao had been named heir apparent, should be declared illegitimate. Deng rejected this proposal strongly as being "tantamount to saying that the party ceased to exist for a period of time." "Some comrades have argued that the Party ceased to exist during the 'Cultural Revolution.' We can't say that. Though the Party's regular activities stopped for a period, it did in fact exist. If it didn't, how could we have smashed the Gang of Four without firing a single shot or shedding a single drop of blood?"[16]

The *Resolution* boldly stated that the Cultural Revolution was "initiated and led by Comrade Mao Zedong." It rejected as conforming "neither to Marxism-Leninism nor to Chinese reality" Mao's "theses" that representatives of the "bourgeoisie" and "counterrevolutionary revisionists" had sneaked into leading organs and could only be eradicated by mobilization of the masses. Mao had been "a leader laboring under a misapprehension"! Unlike Liu Shaoqi and others who fell during the Cultural Revolution, whose entire political careers had been subject to condemnation, Mao emerges from the *Resolution* as a tragic hero whose leftist error, "comprehensive in magnitude and protracted in duration," was that of "a great proletarian revolutionary." The legitimacy of the party still rested heavily on Mao's revolutionary achievements. Unlike the Soviets, the Chinese had no Lenin to fall back on; Mao was both Lenin and Stalin. As Deng put it, "discrediting Comrade Mao Zedong . . . would mean discrediting our Party and state."[17] So the *Resolution* tried to absolve Mao from the worst events of the Cultural Revolution:

> As for Lin Biao, Jiang Qing and others who were placed in important positions by Comrade Mao Zedong, *the matter is of an entirely different nature.* They rigged up two counter-revolutionary cliques in an attempt to seize supreme power and, taking advantage of Comrade Mao Zedong's errors, committed many crimes *behind his back,* bringing disaster to the country and the people.[18]

To ensure that this version of history remained sacrosanct, academic research on the Cultural Revolution was strongly discouraged, and university courses on it were eschewed. Deng's hope was that once the *Resolution* was published, "common views will be reached and, by and large, debate on the major historical questions will come to an end."[19]

But rather than just heaping the blame on a few individuals, Marxist party leaders felt obliged to offer two more analytical explanations of the Cultural Revolution. Both explanations had merit, but they seemed designed also to excuse themselves from not having prevented it. Because the CCP had come to power suddenly after long years characterized by class struggle, it was second nature for cadres to regard new problems as manifestations of class struggle and to fall back on familiar tough methods for dealing with them. "As a result, we substantially broadened the scope of class struggle . . . this led us to regard [this] error . . . as an act in defense of the purity of Marxism." The error was compounded by the Sino-Soviet dispute, which led the CCP into a struggle against domestic "revisionism" "so that normal differences among comrades inside the Party came to be regarded as manifestations of the revisionist line or of the struggle between the two lines."[20]

The second explanation returned to Mao. The Chairman's prestige grew, and his arrogance alongside it. He gradually acted more and more arbitrarily and increasingly put himself above the party's CC. "This state of affairs took place only gradually and the Central Committee of the Party should be held partly responsible." But even this guarded hint of the fear and pusillanimity that gripped Mao's colleagues, transfixed like rabbits in front of a cobra, was reasoned away, pleading the difficulty of eliminating "the evil ideological and political influence of centuries of feudal autocracy":

> And for various historical reasons, we failed to institutionalize and legalize inner-Party democracy and democracy in the political and social life of the country, or we drew up the relevant laws but they lacked due authority. This meant that conditions were present for the over-concentration of Party power in individuals and for the development of arbitrary individual rule and the personality cult in the Party. Thus, it was hard for the Party and state to prevent the initiation of the "cultural revolution" or check its development.[21]

True, the Chinese tradition was emperor worship; true, the CCP tradition was struggle. The fact remains that party leaders of considerable ability, experience, toughness, and prestige failed—all of them—to struggle against an "emperor" when he ran amok, as Mencian doctrine permitted.[22]

Watershed

So accounts were settled and a line was drawn under the Cultural Revolution. In the succeeding quarter-century, Mao's worst revisionist nightmare has been realized, with only himself to blame. Deng will get historians' credit for the capitalist-style modernization of China ("reform"—*gaige*) and its incorporation into the wider world ("opening up"—*kaifang*), but it was Mao's disastrous enactment of his utopian fantasies that freed Deng's mind from Communist orthodoxies. Mao's greatest post-1949 victory, the collectivization of agriculture, has been set aside. Only his major achievement, the 1949 revolution itself, is still in place, saved by Deng Xiaoping and the PLA in Tiananmen Square on June 4, 1989, when the CCP could no longer cope. Arguably only Deng had the determination and the prestige to order the suppression of the student democracy movement with deadly force, and thus his action on June 4 posthumously justified Mao's refusal to consign him to outer darkness during the Cultural Revolution.

Mao's 1949 revolution had been termed the "Liberation" by the party, but it fitted the Chinese people into a procrustean bed of Marxist-Leninist orthodoxy. In the wake of the Cultural Revolution, popular liberation finally did begin to flourish. The humiliation of party cadres high and low destroyed the authority of the CCP in the eyes of the Chinese people, who took to heart the Maoist message of daring to think, speak, and act. Today, all over China, people protest what they consider to be unjust treatment by corrupt officials. The Cultural Revolution was truly the watershed in the history of the People's Republic of China.

But the Cultural Revolution was also a watershed in Chinese modern history. For well over a century, since the Opium War of 1839–1842, the Chinese had struggled with how to modernize while preserving their integrity as a people and a culture. The slogan that gained currency in the mid-nineteenth century was "Chinese learning for the essence, Western learning for practical use." But early in the twentieth century, Chinese learning crumbled. Confucianism was abandoned as state ideology; the 2,000-year-old imperial Confucian state gave way to a republic; Confucianism as a social philosophy came under attack from intellectuals as inegalitarian and paternalistic. The nature of the Chinese "essence" became unclear.

In its place, the CCP offered Marxism-Leninism, a foreign "essence" as totalist in its reach as Confucianism, which promised and, under Mao, delivered success. But by the late 1950s, Mao had tired of aping foreigners. The GLF was his first attempt to find a distinctive Chinese road. By the mid-1960s, he could justify his distaste for the Soviet model with the specter of revisionism. The Cultural Revolution was declaredly Mao's attempt to vaccinate his people against the Soviet disease. But more importantly, it was his last best effort to define and perpetuate a distinct Chinese essence in the modern world. His was truly the last stand of Chinese conservatism.[23]

The chaos, killing, and, at the end, the stagnation of the Cultural Revolution—which together had cost China well over a year's worth of national income[24]—led Deng to abandon this vain search for a Chinese version of modernity that had preoccupied the nation's politicians and intellectuals for well over a century. China had to jump on the bandwagon of successful Western-style modernization that had proved so effective on Taiwan and elsewhere in East Asia. The Cultural Revolution became the economic and social watershed of modern Chinese history.

The change in Chinese economic thinking fostered by the reform program was striking. Down the centuries, Confucian mandarins, like their Communist cadre successors, had believed that government should dominate the economy, and had frowned on the profit motive as corrosive of personal morality and social harmony.[25] Officialdom insisted on monopoly control of key commodities; its philosophy was spelled out as early as the famous debates on salt and iron in the second century B.C.[26] Merchants were discriminated against, economically and socially. Commerce flourished under the Han and Tang dynasties, but "in spite of, not because of, governmental policies."[27] Though government monopolies were gradually abandoned in later dynasties, merchants grew wealthy and powerful only by a symbiotic, subordinate, and often corrupt relationship with the bureaucracy.[28]

In 1949, after the Communist revolution, the CCP quickly established a similar dominance over commerce and industry, first by political controls, then by total or partial takeovers via joint state-private enterprises. In the symbiotic relationships established, there was plenty of corruption, which the CCP tried to root out.[29] In the later critique of Soviet revisionism, as evidence of Khrushchev's alleged determination to restore capitalism were reports of illicit business activities culled from the Soviet press. At the outset of the Cultural Revolution, former capitalists were among the usual suspects targeted by the Red Guards.

In the reform era, under "market Leninism," there has been a sea change. No mandarin would have intoned "To get rich is glorious," even though the prosperity of the people was supposed to be his central concern. As significant was Deng's 1983 statement: "Some people in rural areas and cities should be allowed to get rich before others."[30] Capitalist incentives were in, as shown by the praise given to peasant households that earned 10,000 yuan a year. In two decades, that figure became totally out of date as some people got really rich before others: by 1993, a writer had been paid an advance of 1 million yuan (about $125,000) for a soft-porn novel;[31] by 2003, *Forbes* magazine was listing 100 Chinese private entrepreneurs with a personal wealth of over $100 million.[32] Old cadre attitudes persist, and uppity tycoons can run afoul of the law.[33] But profit is no longer a dirty word, and in 2004 private ownership was finally enshrined in the constitution. This is truly a historic cultural revolution.

Political Stasis

Though willing to adopt any policy to get China back on the road to wealth and power, the aim espoused by all patriots at the start of the twentieth century, Deng did not pay much heed to the goal of democracy espoused by the leading Chinese revolutionary of that time, Sun Yat-sen. Though the CCP claims to be the legitimate child of the May Fourth Movement of 1919, it has embraced only one of its two goals: "Mr. Science," not "Mr. Democracy." For Deng, with his memories of the Cultural Revolution, giving power to the people could easily degenerate into mob rule. As he asserted shortly before the Tiananmen events in 1989, "The key to our success in modernization, the reform and the opening up to the outside is stability . . . China cannot afford any disorder."[34]

The basis for stability was to be four cardinal principles: the socialist road, the dictatorship of the proletariat, the leadership of the CCP, and Marxism-Leninism and Mao Zedong Thought.[35] By the early twenty-first century, the one truly cardinal principle was the rule of the party, enforced as it saw fit and deemed possible. Yet the foundations of party rule had been undermined. There was no revolutionary giant to give purpose to the regime and impose unity and discipline upon the country. The Cultural Revolution and the reform era had destroyed respect for the ideology that had given the party legitimacy and glued the system together. Party members were for the most part careerists without a cause and, more dangerously for them, unrespected by their people. And stability as the CCP once defined it no longer existed: on July 5, 2005, the minister of public security told the Standing Committee of the Chinese People's Political Consultative Conference that there had been more than 74,000 mass protests in 2004, up from 10,000 a decade earlier, and involving some 3.76 million of China's 1.3 billion people. In 2005, the figure rose to 87,000.[36]

461

At some point, the exigencies of governing a vast, restive, and increasingly sophisticated population of 1.3 billion may make the party decide that political pluralism is an opportune way to diffuse responsibility and deflect criticism.[37]

If so, a favorite observation of Mao's—"Out of bad things can come good things"—may be applicable also to the Cultural Revolution: a terrible era, but out of which has emerged a saner, more prosperous, and perhaps one day a democratic China. Then, Chinese may be ready publicly to confront the horrors of what they did to one another during the Cultural Revolution and render a final verdict on the responsibility of the Chairman who unleashed them.

Glossary of Names and Identities

Offices are those held at the beginning of the Cultural Revolution, unless otherwise indicated. A rough guide to Chinese pronunciation: $q = ch$, $x = sh$. The sources consulted in preparation of the following biographical sketches include Sheng Ping, ed., *Zhongguo gongchandang renming da cidian* (Large Biographical Dictionary of the CCP) (Beijing: Zhongguo guoji guangbo chubanshe, 1991); *Zhongguo gongchandang lishi da cidian* (Large Encyclopedia of the History of the CCP) (Beijing: Zhonggong zhongyang dangxiao chubanshe, 1991); *Lijie Zhonggong zhongyang weiyuanhui renming cidian* (Biographical Dictionary of the Members of Successive CCP Central Committees) (Beijing: Zhonggong dangshi chubanshe, 1992); *Dubao shouce* (Newspaper Reader's Handbook) (n.p., 1969).

AN ZIWEN (1909–1980) Member of eighth CCP Central Committee and director of the Central Organization Department. Purged in Cultural Revolution as one of the "Sixty-one Renegades," a group of CCP cadres released from KMT prisons on the eve of the Sino-Japanese War.

BO YIBO (1908–2007) Alternate member of CCP Politburo, vice premier, and director of the State Economic Commission. Purged in Cultural Revolution as one of the "Sixty-one Renegades," a group of CCP cadres released from KMT prisons on the eve of the Sino-Japanese War. Returned to influence after Mao's death.

CAO DIQIU (1909–1976) A senior member of the Shanghai party and city mayor on the eve of the Cultural Revolution, he fell when Zhang Chunqiao engineered the collapse of the Shanghai leadership in 1967.

CAO YIOU (1903–1989) Wife of Kang Sheng, who was sent by her husband to Peking University campus in the spring of 1966 to stir up opposition to the school's leadership.

CHEN BODA (1904–1989) Alternate member of CCP Politburo, editor of *Red Flag*, and one of Mao Zedong's ghostwriters. Appointed director of the Central Cultural Revolution Group in May 1966. Promoted to Politburo Standing Committee at Eleventh Plenum. Member of Central Case Examination Group. Officially No. 4 in the party hierarchy after the Ninth Party Congress. Purged in 1970 and subsequently accused of being a follower of the disgraced Lin Biao. Imprisoned until 1988.

CHEN PIXIAN (1916–1995) Replaced Ke Qingshi as first secretary, Shanghai CCP, on Ke's death in April 1965. Lost his post as a result of the overthrow of the Shanghai party and government leadership engineered by Zhang Chunqiao in 1967, but returned to office as a vice chairman of the Shanghai Revolutionary Committee in 1975. Held a number of posts after the Cultural Revolution, including first secretary, Hubei province; member of the CC's secretariat; and member of the eleventh CC.

CHEN SHAOMIN (1902–1977) A member of the eighth Central Committee, she was the only one of fifty-nine full and alternate members present at the Twelfth Plenum who did not vote in favor of permanently expelling Liu Shaoqi from the party. Not reelected to the ninth Central Committee.

CHEN XILIAN (1915–1998) A general who commanded the PLA Artillery Corps from 1950 to 1959, the Shenyang Military Region from 1959 to 1973, and the Beijing Military Region from 1973 to 1980; vice premier in 1975. Member of Politburo, ninth–eleventh CCs. Lost his party and government posts in 1980 as part of the purge of the "little gang of four" or "whatever faction" (Chen Xilian, Ji Dengkui, Wang Dongxing, Wu De).

CHEN YI (1901–1972) Member of CCP Politburo, vice premier, and foreign minister. In the Cultural Revolution, Chen's career quickly took a turn for the worse, especially as a result of the February Countercurrent, but as a PLA marshal who enjoyed Mao's protection he managed to hold on to his Central Committee membership. Died of cancer.

CHEN YONGGUI (1914–1986) Party secretary of Dazhai brigade in Xiyang county, Shanxi, the role model that peasants were told to emulate in the movement "In Agriculture, Learn from Dazhai," launched on the eve of the Cultural Revolution. His career peaked in the mid-1970s, when he was a member of the CCP Politburo. Was allowed to retire in 1980.

CHEN YUN (1905–1995) A member of the Politburo from the 1930s, Chen was the senior party official concerned with the economy from the inauguration of the PRC, but withdrew from active politics after Mao's return to a leftist path in 1962. During the Cultural Revolution was relieved of all his offices except membership in the CC, but returned to the PSC in 1978.

CHEN ZAIDAO (1909–1993) General and commander of the Wuhan Military Region. Implicated in the "Wuhan Incident" in the summer of 1967, when members of a conservative mass organization together with officers and men under his command kidnapped an emissary from the center. Imprisoned but released soon after the 1971 "Lin Biao incident."

DENG TUO (1912–1966) Member of the Beijing municipal party secretariat. A talented essayist with a knack for the satirical, he was attacked at the very beginning of the Cultural Revolution. Committed suicide in May 1966.

DENG XIAOPING (1904–1997) General secretary of the CCP and vice premier, purged in October 1966 as the "second-biggest party-person in power taking the capitalist road." After a period of internal exile during which he worked in a tractor plant in Jiangxi, he was formally rehabilitated in 1973. After alienating Mao a second time, he again fell from power in 1976. After Mao's death, he went on to become the most powerful man in the CCP and the architect of the party's turn away from the Cultural Revolution.

FU CHONGBI (1916–2003) Major general and commander of the Beijing Garrison. Purged in March 1968 together with Yang Chengwu and Yu Lijin.

GAO YANGYUN (1905–1968) Vice chairman of the Hebei People's Political Consultative Conference and concurrent party secretary of Nankai University. Purged in Cultural Revolution as one of the "Sixty-one Renegades," a group of CCP cadres released from KMT prisons on the eve of the Sino-Japanese War.

GONG XIAOJI (1950–): Student in the middle school attached to Peking University and cofounder of the "conservative" Red Guard United Action Committee.

GUAN FENG (1919–2005) Deputy editor of *Red Flag* and an authority on classical Chinese philosophy. Member of the Central Cultural Revolution Group and Central Case Examination Group. Purged as an "ultra-leftist" in August 1967. Imprisoned for more than fifteen years. Now living in retirement in Beijing.

GUO MORUO (1892–1978) One of China's leading men of letters of the twentieth century, who occupied a number of senior cultural posts in the PRC, including the presidency of the Academy of Sciences, he was employed by the CCP as one of its principal interlocutors with foreigners, including in the Soviet front organization the World Peace Council. Exchanged poems with Mao Zedong, but, sensing the coming storm in 1966, denounced everything he had ever written.

HAN AIJING (1946–) Originally a student at the Beijing Aeronautical Institute, Han rose to national fame as the founder and leader of the Beihang Red Flag Combat Team, a university Red Guard organization with close links to the Central Cultural Revolution Group. Sentenced to fifteen years in prison in 1983.

He Long (1896–1969) Member of CCP Politburo, vice premier, and vice chairman of the Central Military Commission. A PLA marshal who ran afoul of Mao at the beginning of the Cultural Revolution, he was imprisoned and falsely accused of having planned to assassinate Mao. His premature death was brought on by what was almost certainly intentionally botched medical treatment.

Hu Qiaomu (1912–1992) Alternate member of CCP Central Secretariat, editor of Mao's *Selected Works*, and one of Mao's ghostwriters. In semiretirement for health reasons at beginning of Cultural Revolution. Returned to influence in 1975.

Hu Yaobang (1915–1989) Became first secretary of the Communist Youth League in 1957, but at the outset of the Cultural Revolution was party first secretary in Shaanxi province. Dismissed like other party leaders, he returned to head the Academy of Sciences in 1975 and helped Deng Xiaoping in drafting new policy directions. He replaced Hua Guofeng as CCP chairman in 1980, the leading party post, which was transformed into the general secretaryship in 1982. Replaced in January 1987 by Zhao Ziyang after pro-democracy student demonstrations, but maintained his Politburo membership. Hu's death on April 15, 1989, sparked the renewed student demonstrations of the "Beijing spring."

Hua Guofeng (1921–) A deputy governor of Hunan province at the beginning of the Cultural Revolution, Hua rose quickly through the ranks. Elected to the Central Committee at the Ninth Party Congress in 1969; promoted to Politburo membership in 1973; and chosen to succeed Zhou Enlai as premier and Mao as party chairman in 1976. Increasingly powerless after 1978, he went into semiretirement in 1981.

Huang Yongsheng (1910–1983) Headed the Guangzhou Military Region before becoming PLA chief of staff after the purge of Yang Chengwu in 1968. As one of the four senior generals loyal to Lin Biao, he was purged in the aftermath of Lin's flight and death, but it became clear at the trial of these men in 1980–81 that none of them had had a hand in Lin's alleged plot to murder Mao. Remained in custody for the rest of his life.

Ji Dengkui (1923–1988) Catapulted into alternate membership of the Politburo at the Ninth Congress and full membership at the Tenth Congress, having apparently impressed Mao on one of the latter's tours. Was thus a conceivable contender for the succession, but Mao chose Hua Guofeng. Though reelected to the Politburo after the Eleventh Congress in 1977, he lost all his posts in 1980 as a result of Deng Xiaoping's purge of the "whatever faction."

Jiang Qing (1914–1991) Wife of Mao Zedong. Ranking deputy director and de facto head of the Central Cultural Revolution Group. Member of the Central Case Examination Group. Promoted to Politburo at the First Plenum of the ninth CCP Central

Committee. Arrested immediately after her husband's death in 1976 together with Zhang Chunqiao, Yao Wenyuan, and Wang Hongwen (the Gang of Four). Famous for her role in promoting the so-called Revolutionary Beijing Operas. Committed suicide in hospital while serving a commuted death sentence.

KANG SHENG (1898–1975) Alternate member of CCP Politburo and member of Central Secretariat. Appointed leading member of the Central Case Examination Group and adviser to the Central Cultural Revolution Group in May 1966. Promoted to Politburo Standing Committee at Eleventh Plenum. Officially No. 5 in the party hierarchy after Ninth Party Congress. Died of bladder cancer. Posthumously stripped of his party membership and held personally responsible for the persecution of hundreds of leading party cadres in the Cultural Revolution.

KE QINGSHI (1902–1965) Member of CCP Politburo, vice premier, and mayor of Shanghai, leftist ally of Chairman Mao.

KUAI DAFU (1945–) Student at Tsinghua University. Rose to national fame as founder and leader of the Jinggangshan Regiment, a university Red Guard organization with close links to the Central Cultural Revolution Group. Sentenced to seventeen years in 1983. Reportedly now in business in Shenzhen.

LI DESHENG (1916–) Major general who was deputy commander of the Nanjing Military Region, 1968–1970; director of the PLA's General Political Department, 1970–71; commander of the Beijing Military Region, 1971–1973, and Shenyang Military Region, 1973–1975. Became a member of the Politburo at the Ninth Congress and of the PSC at the Tenth Congress. Reappointed to the Politburo at the post–Cultural Revolution Eleventh and Twelfth Congresses, but no longer a member of the PSC.

LI FUCHUN (1900–1975) A leading economic official before the Cultural Revolution as chairman of the State Planning Commission, Li became a member of the Politburo at the Eighth Congress in 1956 and of the enlarged PSC at the Eleventh Plenum in 1966, but was dropped from the Politburo in the Ninth Congress. Played an important role in the February Countercurrent in 1967.

LI NA (1943–) Mao's daughter by Jiang Qing.

LI XIANNIAN (1909–1992) A leading economic official before the Cultural Revolution who served as vice premier and finance minister, and joined the Politburo in 1956, he survived the Cultural Revolution helping Zhou Enlai in those capacities. After the Cultural Revolution, he was promoted to the PSC after the Eleventh and Twelfth congresses and served as state president from 1983 to 1988.

LI XUEFENG (1907–2002) Member of CCP Central Secretariat and first secretary of North China Region. Replaced the disgraced Peng Zhen as first secretary of the

Beijing Party Committee in June 1966. Promoted to alternate membership of Politburo at Eleventh Plenum. Made chairman of the Hebei Revolutionary Committee in 1968. Purged at the end of 1970; rehabilitated in 1982.

Li Zuopeng (1914–) Lieutenant general with historical links to Lin Biao. Appointed first political commissar of the navy in 1967 and promoted to Politburo at the First Plenum of the ninth CCP Central Committee. Arrested soon after the Lin Biao "incident."

Lin Biao (1907–1971) PLA marshal, vice chairman of the CCP, vice premier, minister of defense, and vice chairman of the CCP Central Military Commission. At Mao's insistence promoted to the No. 2 spot in the party hierarchy at the Eleventh Plenum of the eighth Central Committee, replacing the disgraced Liu Shaoqi. Largely a passive figure who did not seek enhanced power for himself and who never challenged Mao politically. Officially designated "Chairman Mao's successor" in the party constitution adopted at the Ninth Party Congress. After 1969, Mao grew increasingly wary of Lin, who died under mysterious circumstances in a plane crash in Mongolia in September 1971.

Lin Liguo (1945–1971) Lin Biao's son, alleged to have planned to assassinate Mao Zedong in 1971. Died in plane crash in Mongolia together with his parents.

Liu Lantao (1910–1997) Alternate member of CCP Central Secretariat and first secretary of the Northwest Region. Purged in Cultural Revolution as one of the "Sixty-one Renegades," a group of CCP cadres released from KMT prisons on the eve of the Sino-Japanese War.

Liu Ningyi (1907–1994) The top official in the All-China Federation of Trade Unions before the Cultural Revolution, he emerged afterward as a deputy secretary general and later a standing committee member of the Chinese People's Political Consultative Conference.

Liu Ren (1909–1973) Alternate member of eighth CCP Central Committee, vice mayor of Beijing, and second secretary of the Beijing municipal party secretariat. Purged together with Peng Zhen at beginning of Cultural Revolution. Formally arrested in January 1968. Died in prison.

Liu Shaoqi (1898–1969) Vice chairman of the CCP and president of the People's Republic of China. Demoted at the Eleventh Plenum and subsequently purged as the "biggest party-person in power taking the capitalist road." Expelled from the CCP by the eighth Central Committee at its Twelfth Plenum. The most senior victim of the Cultural Revolution, Liu died in November 1969 from medical neglect and physical abuse at the hands of Central Case Examination Group staff. Fully rehabilitated in 1980.

LIU XIWU (1904–1970) Vice secretary of the CCP Central Committee's Control Commission. Purged in the Cultural Revolution as one of the "Sixty-one Renegades," a group of CCP cadres released from KMT prisons on the eve of the Sino-Japanese War.

LIU YINGJUN (1945–1966) PLA soldier who died in a car accident while trying to avoid hitting six small children. Hailed as a hero and outstanding pupil of Chairman Mao during Cultural Revolution.

LIU ZHIJIAN (1912–2006) Lieutenant general and deputy director of the PLA General Political Department when the Cultural Revolution started. Appointed deputy director of the Central Cultural Revolution Group in May 1966. Purged at the beginning of 1967.

LU DINGYI (1906–1997) Alternate member of CCP Politburo, member of CCP Central Secretariat, vice premier, minister of culture, and director of the CCP Central Propaganda Department. Purged in May 1966 as member of the "Peng-Luo-Lu-Yang" clique. Survived years in prison and returned to influence after Mao's death in 1976.

LU PING (1914–2002) Appointed president of Peking University in 1957 during the anti-rightist campaign and toppled from that post in the first wave of attacks on university authorities in mid-1966. Reemerged as vice minister of the Seventh Ministry of Machine Building from 1975 to 1982.

LUO RUIQING (1906–1978) PLA general, chief of staff, member of CCP Central Secretariat, and vice premier. Purged at the beginning of the Cultural Revolution, accused of opposing "giving prominence to Mao Zedong Thought" and of trying to "seize power" from Lin Biao. Arrested and sent to prison. Returned to influence after Mao's death in 1976.

MAO YUANXIN (1939?–) The son of Mao's brother, Mao Zemin, who was executed in 1943. After Yuanxin's mother remarried, he moved to Zhongnanhai to be brought up as part of his uncle's family. Before becoming Mao's liaison with the Politburo in 1975, he had been vice chairman of the provincial revolutionary committee in Liaoning province and political commissar of the Shenyang MR.

MAO ZEDONG (1893–1976) Cofounder of CCP and party chairman from 1943 until his death in 1976. Clever, ruthless, and unpredictable politician. Launched the Cultural Revolution in what the party media then described as an attempt to "combat and prevent revisionism," but what is now referred to by his successors as the biggest single political mistake of his political career. Together with Joseph Stalin and Adolf Hitler, Mao appears destined to go down in history as one of the great tyrants of the twentieth century.

NIE RONGZHEN (1899–1992) Appointed one of the ten PLA marshals in 1955, he was put in charge of China's defense industries, including its nuclear and rocket program. Appointed to the Politburo at the Eleventh Plenum in 1966, he was dropped at the Ninth Congress and rejoined the body only after the Cultural Revolution.

NIE YUANZI (1921–) CCP general branch secretary in the Department of Philosophy at Peking University. An influential Red Guard leader, she was made a member of the Central Committee at the Ninth Party Congress, but fell from power thereafter. In 1983 she was sentenced to seventeen years in prison. She published her memoirs in 2005.

NIU WANPING (1947–) Student in the Middle School attached to Peking University and cofounder of the "conservative" Red Guard United Action Committee.

PENG DEHUAI (1898–1974) Outspoken minister of defense and CCP Politburo member, purged in 1959 for implicitly criticizing Mao and the Great Leap Forward. Recalled from Sichuan to Beijing at the end of 1966, he was arrested and eventually died in prison. Rehabilitated in 1978.

PENG XIAOMENG (1948–) Student and Red Guard in the middle school attached to Peking University. Singled out for praise by Mao in his "Letter to the Red Guards of Qinghua University Middle School" in August 1966.

PENG ZHEN (1902–1997) Powerful member of the CCP Central Secretariat, mayor of Beijing, first secretary of the Beijing municipal party committee, and head of the CCP center's ad hoc group of five in charge of culture. Purged in May 1966 as a member of the "Peng-Luo-Lu-Yang" clique and attacked for, among other things, having said (possibly with reference to Mao Zedong) that "everyone is equal in front of the truth." Survived a decade in prison and returned to influence after Mao's death in 1976.

QI BENYU (1931–) Staff member of the Central Committee General Office who replaced Tian Jiaying as Mao's secretary in May 1966. Junior member of the Central Cultural Revolution Group and Central Case Examination Group. Arrested and purged as an "ultra-leftist" in January 1968. Now living in retirement in Shanghai.

QIU HUIZUO (1914–2002) Lieutenant general with historical links to Lin Biao. Appointed director of the PLA General Logistics Department in 1968 and promoted to the Politburo at the First Plenum of the ninth CCP Central Committee. Arrested soon after the Lin Biao "incident."

TAN HOULAN (1940–1982) Originally a student at Beijing Normal University, she rose to national fame as the founder and leader of the Jinggangshan Commune, a university Red Guard organization with close links to the Central Cultural Revolution Group. Arrested after 1968. Died of cancer while in prison.

TAN ZHENLIN (1902–1983) Member of CCP Politburo and vice premier. Purged as a "capitalist roader" in the winter of 1966–67. Played a prominent role in the February Countercurrent. Rehabilitated in 1973.

TAO ZHU (1908–1969) Member of eighth CCP Central Committee, vice premier, and first secretary of Central-South Region. Transferred to Beijing at beginning of Cultural Revolution to replace Lu Dingyi as director of Central Propaganda Department. Promoted to No. 4 position on Politburo at Eleventh Plenum. Adviser to Central Cultural Revolution Group and Central Case Examination Group. Purged in early 1967 and put under house arrest in Zhongnanhai. Died of cancer while in the custody of the Central Case Examination Group. Rehabilitated posthumously in 1978.

TIAN JIAYING (1922–1966) Mao Zedong's personal secretary. Committed suicide in May 1966 after having been accused of "tampering with Mao's works."

WAN LI (1916–) Vice mayor of Beijing, purged in October 1966, rehabilitated in 1973 .

WANG DABIN (1946–) Student at the Beijing Geological Institute and nationally famous Red Guard leader of the Diyuan East Is Red Commune. Arrested after 1969 and sentenced in 1983 to nine years for persecuting Peng Dehuai and others. Now said to be working in business.

WANG DONGXING (1916–) Mao's chief bodyguard, who replaced Yang Shangkun as director of the Central Committee General Office in November 1965. Member of the Central Case Examination Group. Elected alternate member of CCP Politburo at First Plenum of ninth Central Committee. Rose steadily in the ranks to become vice chairman of the CCP. Carried out the arrest of the Gang of Four. Clashed with Deng Xiaoping in 1978 and was forced into semiretirement in early 1980s.

WANG GUANGMEI (1921–2006) Wife of Liu Shaoqi and staff member of CCP Central Committee General Office. Purged along with her husband. Survived the Cultural Revolution in prison. Released and rehabilitated after the Third Plenum of the eleventh Central Committee in 1978.

WANG HONGWEN (1932–1992) Security guard in No. 17 Cotton Mill who rose to fame as "rebel" labor leader during Cultural Revolution. Appointed to Central Committee in 1969, and groomed by Mao as possible successor in early 1970s. Vice chairman of the CCP at the time of his arrest as one of the Gang of Four in 1976. Sentenced to life in prison in 1981.

WANG LI (1922–1996) Deputy director of the CCP International Liaison Department and Politburo ghostwriter. Appointed to Central Cultural Revolution Group in 1966. Was kidnapped by conservatives during the Wuhan Incident. Purged as an "ultra-leftist" in August 1967. Incarcerated for fifteen years.

WANG RENZHONG (1917 1992) Alternate member of eighth Central Committee and second secretary of CCP Central-South Region. Appointed deputy director of the Central Cultural Revolution Group in the summer of 1966. Purged and denounced as a "capitalist roader" in early 1967. Returned to influence after Mao's death in 1976.

WANG ZHEN (1908–1993) A three-star general who commanded the PLA Railway Corps in the mid-1950s, he became minister of state farms and land reclamation in 1956, and was made a full member of the CC the same year. He reemerged in 1975 as a vice premier, was appointed to the Politburo in 1977, serving for ten years, and became PRC vice president in 1988.

WU DE (1913–1995) Alternate member of eighth CCP Central Committee. Transferred from Jilin province to become second party secretary and acting mayor of Beijing in 1966. Elected to Central Committee at Twelfth Plenum in 1968. Succeeded Xie Fuzhi as chairman of Beijing Revolutionary Committee in 1972. Fell from grace after death of Mao, when he clashed with Deng Xiaoping.

WU FAXIAN (1915–2004) Lieutenant general with historical links to Lin Biao. Commander of the PLA air force at the beginning of the Cultural Revolution. Promoted to Politburo membership at the First Plenum of the ninth CCP Central Committee. Arrested soon after the Lin Biao "incident."

WU HAN (1909–1969) Prominent historian and vice mayor of Beijing. The first public target of the Cultural Revolution, Wu died a broken man after being subjected to two and a half years of endless public "struggle" rallies, physical abuse, and severe maltreatment in prison.

WU LENGXI (1919–2002) As head of the Xinhua News Agency and chief editor of the *People's Daily*, Wu was China's top journalist at the outbreak of the Cultural Revolution. He was also a member of Peng Zhen's five-man group in charge of cultural revolution, the dissolution of which was part of the first major purge of the Cultural Revolution. He reemerged as a junior official in 1975 but was made minister of radio and television in 1982.

WU XIUQUAN (1908–1997) Member of the eighth Central Committee and deputy director of the CCP International Liaison Department. Attacked by Red Guards at the beginning of Cultural Revolution. Imprisoned in 1968. Released and rehabilitated in 1974.

XIE FUZHI (1909–1972) Member of eighth CCP Central Committee, vice premier, and minister of public security. Member of Central Case Examination Group and deeply involved in the purge of countless senior party figures. Promoted to alternate membership of the Politburo at the Eleventh Plenum and to full membership at the First Plenum of the ninth Central Committee. Buried with honors after dying of cancer, he was posthumously expelled from the CCP in 1980 for his role in the Cultural Revolution.

XU SHIYOU (1906–1985) A three-star general who was Nanjing MR commander for much of the Cultural Revolution. A Mao loyalist, he served as a member of the Politburo from the Ninth through Eleventh congresses, but was not involved in the post–Lin Biao purge.

XU XIANGQIAN (1901–1990) One of the PLA's ten marshals who was made a member of the Politburo at the Eleventh Plenum in 1966, but whose minor role in the 1967 February Countercurrent and bad health presumably led to his not being reappointed at the Ninth Congress.

YAN HONGYAN (1909–1967) A three-star general and first secretary of Yunnan province, Yan was one of the first senior officials to commit suicide during the Cultural Revolution. Rehabilitated in 1979.

YANG CHENGWU (1914–2004) Alternate member of eighth CCP Central Committee, PLA general, and deputy chief of staff. Became acting PLA chief of staff in 1966, after the fall of Luo Ruiqing. According to Zhou Enlai, instrumental in guaranteeing Mao's personal safety during early stages of the Cultural Revolution. Member of Central Case Examination Group. Purged in March 1968 together with Yu Lijin and Fu Chongbi.

YANG SHANGKUN (1907–1998) Alternate member of CCP Central Secretariat and director of the Central Committee General Office (until November 1965). Purged in May 1966 as member of the "Peng-Luo-Lu-Yang" clique, allegedly for bugging Chairman Mao's quarters. Returned to influence after Mao's death. Made president of the PRC in 1988.

YAO DENGSHAN (1918–1998) A diplomat who attained hero status after being expelled from Indonesia, he had a brief career as a leading rebel in the Foreign Ministry, opposing Chen Yi and allegedly helping to mastermind the sack of the British mission.

YAO WENYUAN (1931–2005) Radical Shanghai literary critic and polemicist who wrote "On the New Historical Play *Hai Rui Dismissed from Office*," commonly referred to as the first salvo of the Cultural Revolution. The youngest member of the Central Cultural Revolution Group. Member of the CCP Politburo after 1969. Arrested as one of the Gang of Four after the death of Mao in 1976. Sentenced to twenty years in prison in 1981.

YE JIANYING (1897–1986) CCP Central Committee member, PLA marshal, and secretary general of the Central Military Affairs Commission. Elected to the Politburo by the eighth Central Committee and to its standing committee by the ninth Central Committee. Remained in power throughout the Cultural Revolution and masterminded the arrest of the Gang of Four soon after Mao's death. Retired for health reasons in early 1980s.

YE QUN (1917–1971) Wife of Lin Biao and his acting representative on the Central Case Examination Group. Elected to CCP Politburo at the First Plenum of the ninth Central Committee. Implicated in her son's alleged plot to assassinate Mao. Died in plane crash in Mongolia together with her husband and son.

YU LIJIN (1913–1978) Lieutenant general and political commissar of the PLA air force. Purged in March 1968 together with Yang Chengwu and Fu Chongbi.

ZHANG CHUNQIAO (1917–2005) Shanghai party newspaper editor and senior propaganda official. Rose to fame as member of Mao's inner circle and deputy director of Central Cultural Revolution Group. Elected to the CCP Politburo in 1969. Arrested as a member of the Gang of Four in 1976, at which point he was chairman of the Shanghai Revolutionary Committee and vice premier of the State Council. Sentenced to death with a two-year reprieve in 1981.

ZHANG PINGHUA (1907–2001) Alternate member of the eighth Central Committee and member of CCP Central-South Region. Promoted to post as executive deputy director of the CCP Central Propaganda Department in summer of 1966. Fell from grace a few months later. Appointed deputy chairman of Shanxi Revolutionary Committee in 1971. Returned to influence after Mao's death in 1976.

ZHANG YUFENG (1944–) Mao's favorite attendant in his later years.

ZHOU ENLAI (1898–1976) China's premier and No. 3 in the party hierarchy, the charming and ruthless Zhou chaired not only the regular meetings of the State Council's "inner cabinet," but also those of the Central Cultural Revolution Group and the Central Case Examination Group. Implicated in the inquisition and purge of thousands of senior leaders. Died of cancer in 1976.

ZHOU YANG (1908–1989) A deputy director of the CC's Propaganda Department, Zhou was the hard man overseeing the literary field before the Cultural Revolution. As a member of Peng Zhen's five-man group, he was one of the first senior officials to fall. After the Cultural Revolution, he regained his deputy directorship and became a full member of the CC. In his later years, Zhou Yang transformed himself into what by CCP standards was a liberal.

ZHOU ZHONGYING (1902–1991) Deputy director of the State Economic Commission. Purged in Cultural Revolution as one of the "Sixty-one Renegades," a group of CCP cadres released from KMT prisons on the eve of the Sino-Japanese War.

Zhu Chengzhao (1942–1998) Student at the Beijing Geological Institute and now largely forgotten Red Guard leader who founded the "3rd HQ," the most important Red Guard umbrella organization in Beijing. Denounced by radicals when he turned against the Central Cultural Revolution Group in 1967.

Zhu De (1886–1976) Joined forces with Mao Zedong in 1928 and was his loyal general from then on, ensuring the prevalence of Mao's dictum that the party must command the gun and not vice versa. He was the senior of ten marshals appointed in 1955, and his loyalty to the Chairman enabled him to survive the Cultural Revolution as a quiescent member of the PSC or, between the Ninth and Tenth congresses, of the Politburo, dying only two months before Mao at the age of eighty-nine.

A Note on Sources

George Bernard Shaw is alleged to have remarked that when a historian had to rely on one document he was safe, but if there were two to be consulted he was in difficulty, and if three were available his position was hopeless. We like to think that Shaw was one-third right and that our position as historians of the Cultural Revolution would indeed be hopeless if we had only three documents to rely on. Here we merely want to say a few words about our far more numerous sources—their provenance, strengths, and weaknesses—and how we have put them to use.

Our starting point, as we began work on this book, was not Mao's famous "blank sheet of paper," but our views and opinions shaped by the events themselves and the existing literature. To test those views and opinions, to refine them with an eye to writing a history of the Cultural Revolution that would make sense not only to ourselves but to our imagined readers, we set about consulting sources of every conceivable kind—and then some. We did this not merely in a search for information, but believing that there is in itself a virtue in using many different kinds of sources, that the inevitable bias in one kind is to some degree offset by the counterbias in another. While texts, as our notes and bibliography suggest, in the end remain our primary sources, we also conducted interviews with members of Mao's inner circle and the CCRG, the speechwriters and assistants of PSC members, and Red Guard leaders of the left and the right. We teased memories out of retired Western diplomats, watched contemporary newsreel footage, pored over old photographs, transcribed tape recordings, and even deciphered inscriptions on the reverse side of Mao-badges.

One source that we have found particularly informative and made much use of is the common (in China) so-called chronology of major events—called a *dashiji* when concerning institutions broadly defined and a *nianpu* when documenting the life of a person. Produced in abundance during the Cultural Revolution and in even greater numbers since, chronologies of major events serve as ideal starting points for a more in-depth pursuit of a "story" elsewhere. Typically, they contain hard information to the effect that on such-and-such a date, someone made an important speech, a decision was taken, an event occurred, or a policy document was issued. Recent chronologies published under the auspices of bodies like the Central Documents Research Office (Zhongyang wenxian yanjiushi) under the CCP Central Committee and contemporary chronologies put out by unofficial "rebel" groups in this or that government organ or university complement each other nicely, the strategic omissions in the former often relating to the very events that are foregrounded in the latter, and vice versa.

More than thirty years having passed since they were first issued, large numbers of once secret party documents from the Cultural Revolution have now been de facto declassified inside China and made available to foreign historians in one form or another. In trying to understand high-level politics in particular, we have made extensive use of original party documents, recent reprints from China (in collections whose editors we have sometimes been able to consult directly when questions about form or content have arisen), and—from the years 1966–1969—the convenient pocket-size collections of Central Documents produced in quantity by the then competent authorities for internal party and government use. These collections can sometimes be found on offer in secondhand bookshops across China today, on the shelves all but indistinguishable in their red plastic covers from the *Quotations from Chairman Mao*.

With respect to official documents, the task we set ourselves was to ascertain that the text we relied upon was a reliable original and not a corrupt copy. In the cases of transcripts of speeches, we faced a different and far more complex situation in that there are—especially for the period before and including the CCP's Ninth National Congress in 1969—numerous variant transcripts "out there." Some are official—that is, records of what the speaker after the event wished he or she had said rather than actually did; others are private and unofficial, hastily scribbled notes of what one or more members of the audience heard, including—and herein lies their value to the historian—what the speaker later dearly regretted ever having said. Comparing and collating such variant texts, assessing their provenance, deciding on which one to cite and why: these are just a few of the practical tasks on which we have spent much time. When, in the first half of this book, we cite a particular source text, it is almost always *one of many* that, on the basis of a combination of criteria, we regard as the most accurate record of the speech in question. In the second half of our book, in the final chapters, we have unfortunately now and then had no choice but to make use of speech transcripts whose accuracy we have not been able to confirm to our own full satisfaction in the same way.

In their analyses of what happened in the first years of the Cultural Revolution, foreign and Chinese historians alike have long made good use of so-called Red Guard tabloids—the popular and highly effective instruments of public information and disinformation campaigns pursued at the time by China's "organizations of the revolutionary masses." We have tried to minimize our reliance on such tabloids, whose information value is small by comparison to the one kind of unofficial serial on which we have relied extensively: the remarkable limited-circulation current information bulletins *(dongtai bao)* produced by the major Red Guard organizations for their own members. Feeding into these daily—sometimes twice or more daily—bulletins were vast, in many cases transprovincial, networks of informants and quasi-journalists. Intended originally to keep young decision-makers and Red Guard leaders informed of rapidly shifting political currents, they now serve as the historian's basic tool in constructing a fuller record of the Cultural Revolution. In dealing with events nationwide in the summer months of 1967, for example, we have consulted well in excess of 500 copies of such newsletters, produced in places as far apart as Beijing and Shenyang, Urümqi and Shanghai.

Our access to Chinese archival material from the Cultural Revolution has been sporadic. Our efforts to understand what was happening in society at large have now and then been made easier by our stumbling across an old cache or dossier of archival material in a Chinese flea market. Often such dossiers from closed-down factories or down-sized institutions document private and uniquely human aspects of the Cultural Revolution not dealt with in other, more conventional, sources (including recently published memoirs). A police interrogation record, a missing-person's notice complete with photograph, a diary, an informer's letter, the angry denunciation of a father by his son, an application to join the CCP, the minutes of a neighborhood meeting called in support of Chairman Mao's latest wise decision, together with the even more ephemeral, such material has permitted us to thicken the texture of the narrative and to unfold it with greater confidence.

Notes

Sources are cited in abridged form after the first occurrence. For complete information, see the Bibliography.

Introduction

Epigraphs: Plato, *The Republic,* trans. Benjamin Jowett, book VI (Mineola, N.Y.: Dover, 2000); Mao Zedong, in Stuart Schram, *The Political Thought of Mao Tse-tung* (New York: Praeger, 1963), p. 352.

1. Notably: Correspondents of *The Economist, Consider Japan* (London: G. Duckworth, 1963).
2. *Resolution on CPC History (1949–1981)* (Beijing: Foreign Languages Press, 1981), p. 32.
3. See Roderick MacFarquhar, *The Origins of the Cultural Revolution,* 3 vols. (New York: Columbia University Press, 1974, 1983, 1997) (hereafter *Origins*).
4. *The Polemic on the General Line of the International Communist Movement* (Peking: Foreign Languages Press, 1965), p. 59.
5. See William Taubman, *Khrushchev: The Man and His Era* (New York: Norton, 2003), pp. 270–289. The secret speech soon found its way to the Central Intelligence Agency, which passed it on to the *New York Times,* which published it on June 4, 1956. In Moscow the Chinese delegation to the CPSU had received only an oral report of its contents; it got the full text from a Xinhua (New China News Agency) translation of the *New York Times* text; Wu Lengxi, *Shinian lunzhan, 1956–1966: Zhong Su guanxi huiyilu* (A Decade of Polemics, 1956–1966: A Memoir of Sino-Soviet Relations), 2 vols. (Beijing: Zhongyang wenxian chubanshe, 1999), 1: 3–4. Wu incorrectly states that the *New York Times* version appeared on March 10; he must be referring to extracts from Khrushchev's speech carried by Western news agencies that were discussed by Mao and senior leaders on March 18 at a meeting that Wu attended; Zhonggong zhongyang wenxian yanjiushi, ed., *Zhou Enlai nianpu, 1949–1976* (Chronicle of the Life of Zhou Enlai, 1949–1976), 3 vols.

(Beijing: Zhongyang wenxian chubanshe, 1997) (hereafter *Zhou Enlai nianpu*), 1: 560.

6. *Origins*, 1: 43–48.

7. Ibid., pp. 42–43. The phrase "ripe for revolution" was used by Zhou Enlai on his African tour in 1963–64, and it proved unpopular among his hosts; ibid., 3: 359–360.

8. *The Polemic on the General Line*, pp. 70–74; Pang Xianzhi and Jin Chongji, *Mao Zedong zhuan, 1949–1976* (The Life of Mao Zedong, 1949–1976), 2 vols. (Beijing: Zhongyang wenxian chubanshe, 2003), 1: 723–761. For the relevant texts, see G. F. Hudson, Richard Lowenthal, and Roderick MacFarquhar, eds., *The Sino-Soviet Dispute* (New York: Praeger, 1961), pp. 39–56.

9. *Jianguo yilai Mao Zedong wengao* (Mao Zedong's Papers since the Founding of the State), 13 vols. (Beijing: Zhongyang wenxian chubanshe, 1987–1998), 6: 635–636; translated in Michael Schoenhals, "Mao Zedong: Speeches at the 1957 Moscow Conference," *Journal of Communist Studies*, 2, no. 2 (1986), 109–126.

10. *Origins*, 2: 92.

11. Taubman, *Khrushchev*, p. 402.

12. Khrushchev's proposals also included a plan for joint communications facilities and for Soviet interceptor aircraft to be based in China; *Origins*, 2: 94–96.

13. Wu Lengxi, *Yi Mao Zhuxi: Wo qinshen jinglide ruogan zhongda lishi shijian pianduan* (Remembering Chairman Mao: Fragments of Certain Major Historical Events Which I Personally Experienced) (Beijing: Xinhua chubanshe, 1995), p. 75.

14. *Origins*, 2: 96–100.

15. Ibid., pp. 225–226, 255–264.

16. For the text, see Hudson, Lowenthal, and MacFarquhar, *The Sino-Soviet Dispute*, pp. 78–112.

17. Ibid., pp. 174–205; *Origins*, 2: 264–292.

18. The nine polemics constitute the main contents of *The Polemic on the General Line*.

19. Except where otherwise indicated, the following discussion is based on the arguments and evidence in *Origins*, vol. 3.

20. Taubman, *Khrushchev*, p. 620.

21. *Origins*, 3: 365.

22. The Shanghai workers' uprising organized by Zhou was meant to take over the city for Chiang Kai-shek's Nationalist (Kuomintang) forces, but after its success, Chiang turned on the Communists and Zhou barely escaped with his life. Those events are dramatized in André Malraux's novel *Man's Fate*.

23. "Zhou zonglide jianghua" (Premier Zhou's Speech), in Xi'an yejin jianzhu xueyuan geming weiyuanhui xuanchuanbu, ed., *Lin Biao wenxuan* (Selected Writings

of Lin Biao), 2 vols. (Xi'an: Yejin jianzhu xueyuan, 1967) (hereafter *Lin Biao wenxuan*), 2: 264.

24. In answer to a question after giving a lecture at Harvard University on October 7, 1994; Dr. Li Zhisui was on a book tour after the publication of his *The Private Life of Chairman Mao* (New York: Random House, 1994). For Zhou's subservience during the GLF, see *Origins*, 2: 57–59, 232–233.

25. The judgment is Stuart Schram's, quoted in *Origins*, 1: 7.

26. See Benjamin I. Schwartz, *Chinese Communism and the Rise of Mao* (Cambridge, Mass.: Harvard University Press, 1951).

27. Quoted comments by Zhang Guotao, once Liu's superior, and a rival of Mao's for the leadership of the CCP in the 1930s; see *Origins*, 2: 5.

28. Ibid., 3: 419–427.

29. Ironically, the Chinese analysis closely resembled that of a famous dissident Yugoslav theoretician who had described the "new class" ruling the Soviet Union. See Milovan Djilas, *The New Class: An Analysis of the Communist System* (New York: Praeger, 1957). This book was certainly known in China, having been translated as early as 1957 and reissued in 1963.

30. Quotations in *Origins*, 3: 363–364.

31. Quoted in ibid., p. 428.

1. The First Salvos

1. For a description of Shanghai before and immediately after the 1949 Communist revolution, see Marie-Claire Bergère, "'The Other China': Shanghai from 1919 to 1949," pp. 1–34; and Richard Gaulton, "Political Mobilization in Shanghai, 1949–1951," pp. 35–65; both in Christopher Howe, ed., *Shanghai: Revolution and Development in an Asian Metropolis* (Cambridge: Cambridge University Press, 1981).

2. Ross Terrill, *Madame Mao: The White-Boned Demon*, rev. ed. (Stanford: Stanford University Press, 1999), pp. 56–59, 130–137, 195–198, 219–226. The exact length of the ban from politics is uncertain.

3. Li Zhisui, *The Private Life of Chairman Mao*, pp. 93–94, 103–105, 311, 356–364, 407–408; Terrill, *Madame Mao*, p. 227.

4. The authorities of *Qinghua daxue* decided after the Cultural Revolution that in translation their institution would again be known by its original name, Tsinghua University.

5. *Origins*, 3: 252–256, 443–447.

6. Later Zhang Chunqiao would send investigators to check if Ke had been murdered. In fact, he died after overindulging at a banquet; *Chen Pixian huiyilu: Zai "Yiyue fengbao" de zhongxin* (The Memoirs of Chen Pixian: In the Center of the "January Storm") (Shanghai: Shanghai renmin chubanshe, 2005), pp. 28, 187–191.

7. Email from Jake Rosen, a founding member of the U.S. Progressive Labor Party (PLP), to MacFarquhar, June 2005. As events developed the PLP leadership concluded regretfully that Zhang had played a major role in suppressing the left. "By 1970, after a long meeting in Beijing with Zhou Enlai, we concluded that the aim of CR had been lost, and China was on the way to inevitable capitalist restoration. We concluded that maintaining relations with these Chinese leaders would undermine any possibility of developing a U.S. revolutionary movement. It seemed to us that, like it or not, starting with the crushing of the Shanghai Commune [see below, Chapter 9], Zhang had played a bad role by helping crush the Left, by not moving to organize a new party and army. We criticized him and them and broke relations with the Chinese leadership (the CCP didn't exist at the time). They and Nixon were a better fit."

8. Zhang Chunqiao showed Yao's article to a number of elderly Shanghai academics shortly before publication and was delighted at their dismay, for it confirmed that the polemic was truly provocative; Shanghai "Wenge" shiliao zhengli bianzuan xiaozu, *Shanghai "Wenhua dageming" shihua* (Telling the History of the "Great Cultural Revolution" in Shanghai), 3 vols. (Shanghai, 1992), typeset manuscript (hereafter *Shanghai "Wenhua dageming" shihua*), 1: 18.

9. Chen was informed after the Cultural Revolution by the former head of the party's Organization Department that Ke had tried at least three times to get him transferred out of Shanghai; *Chen Pixian huiyilu*, p. 191.

10. Ibid., pp. 27–34. Chen's account hints at a guilty conscience. In addition, his memoir contains an unusually large number of pictures of him with other leaders, notably survivors of the Cultural Revolution like Peng Zhen. Were they designed to show that men who might be thought to bear him a grudge had absolved him? The pictures are the only indication of the survivors' views of him; Chen did not publish his story until long after the spate of post–Cultural Revolution biographies and autobiographies of senior party officials, by which time those survivors were dead.

11. *Fangeming xiuzhengzhuyi fenzi Fan Jin de zuixing: Buchong cailiao zhi 1* (Crimes of the Counterrevolutionary Revisionist Element Fan Jin: Supplementary Material 1) (Beijing: Beijing ribao wenhua geming yundong bangongshi, 1967), p. 18.

12. Cheng Qian, "'Wenge' mantan" (Random Commentary on the "Cultural Revolution"), manuscript (Beijing, n.d.), item no. 1; copy in John K. Fairbank Center for East Asian Research Library, Harvard University (hereafter Fairbank Center Library).

13. Peng Zhen was able to take this decision because Deng Xiaoping's absence on an inspection tour in southwest China left him in charge of the CC Secretariat and its Propaganda Department.

14. In Shanghai on November 25, Chen Pixian told his friend Luo Ruiqing about the

genesis of the article, and they agreed that Luo should pass on this information to Zhou at breakfast the next day; *Chen Pixian huiyilu*, p. 34.

15. Peng seems to have first made this arresting statement in a speech to a conference of cultural bureau chiefs on September 23, 1965; *Peng Zhen wenxuan (1941–1990)* (Selected Works of Peng Zhen [1941–1990]) (Beijing: Renmin chubanshe, 1991), pp. 355–357.

16. *Chen Pixian huiyilu*, p. 36.

17. Zhejiang sheng Mao Zedong sixiang yanjiu zhongxin and Zhonggong Zhejiang shengwei dangshi yanjiushi, eds., *Mao Zedong yu Zhejiang* (Mao Zedong and Zhejiang) (Beijing: Zhonggong dangshi chubanshe, 1993), pp. 165–169.

18. See An Jianshe, "'Wenge' shiqi Mao Zedong qici nanxun kaoshu" (An Examination of Mao Zedong's Seven Southern Tours during the "Cultural Revolution" Period), *Dangde wenxian* (Party Documents), no. 1 (2005), 24–30, and no. 2 (2005), 44–49.

19. Yang was informed of his impending dismissal on October 29—a "never-to-be-forgotten day," Yang recorded in his diary—by Zhou Enlai, Deng Xiaoping, and Peng Zhen, a measure of his importance and the seriousness of the decision; *Yang Shangkun riji* (Yang Shangkun's Diary), 2 vols. (Beijing: Zhongyang wenxian chubanshe, 2001).

20. See Kenneth Lieberthal, with the assistance of James Tong and Sai-cheung Yeung, *Central Documents and Politburo Politics in China*, Michigan Papers in Chinese Studies No. 33 (Ann Arbor: Center for Chinese Studies, University of Michigan, 1978); and Michael Schoenhals, *CCP Central Documents from the Cultural Revolution: Index to an Incomplete Data Base* (Stockholm: Center for Pacific Asia Studies, Stockholm University, 1993), pp. vi–xiii.

21. *Origins*, 3: 447–448.

22. *Yang Shangkun riji*, 2: 682–686.

23. For Wang Dongxing's reluctance to take on this job, see Li Zhisui, *The Private Life of Chairman Mao*, pp. 433–434. Commander Zhang Yaoci and political commissar Yang Dezhong of PLA Unit 8341 reported directly to Wang.

24. *Wang Dongxing gongkai Mao Zedong si shenghuo* (Wang Dongxing Reveals Mao Zedong's Private Life) (Hong Kong: Mingliu chubanshe, 1997), pp. 60–61.

25. Li Zhisui, *The Private Life of Chairman Mao*, p. 94.

26. See Lin Biao's cover note to Mao, discussed later in the chapter.

27. Deng Xiaoping was the only other civilian allowed to be a member of this key institution.

28. Guofang daxue dangshi dangjian zhenggong jiaoyanshi, ed., *Zhonggong dangshi jiaoxue cankao ziliao* (CCP History Teaching Reference Materials), 24 vols. (Beijing: Guofang daxue, 1979–1986) (hereafter Guofang daxue, *Cankao ziliao*), 24: 554–557.

29. Huang Yao, *San ci da nan buside: Luo Ruiqing dajiang* (General Luo Ruiqing Who Survived Catastrophes Three Times) (Beijing: Zhonggong dangshi chubanshe, 1994), pp. 238–246.

30. Xinghuo liaoyuan bianjibu, ed., *Jiefangjun jiangling zhuan* (Biographies of PLA Generals), 14 vols. (Beijing: Jiefangjun chubanshe, 1984–1995) (hereafter *Jiefangjun jiangling zhuan*), 7: 258.

31. Wang Nianyi, "Da dongluande niandai" (A Decade of Great Upheaval), manuscript (hereafter Wang Nianyi ms.), revised and amended version of *Da dongluande niandai* (A Decade of Great Upheaval) (Zhengzhou: Henan renmin chubanshe, 1988), pp. 86–87; copy in Fairbank Center Library.

32. Others were Vice Admiral Zhang Xiuchuan, director of the navy's Political Department; and Major General Lei Yingfu, deputy director of the PLA General Staff Operations Department, a former military adviser to Zhou Enlai; Huang Yao, *San ci da nan buside*, pp. 266–273; idem, "Luo Ruiqing zhuanlüe xia" (A Brief Biography of Luo Ruiqing, Part 2), *Zhonggong dangshi ziliao* (Materials on CCP History), no. 37 (1991), 179.

33. *Jiefangjun jiangling zhuan*, 7: 260–261. Huang Yao, *San ci da nan buside*, p. 275, notes the strange coincidence that the heads of the CC and MAC general offices were simultaneously removed.

34. Ma Qibin et al., eds., *Zhongguo gongchandang zhizheng sishinian (1949–1989)* (The CCP's Forty Years in Power [1949–1989]), rev. ed. (Beijing: Zhonggong dangshi ziliao chubanshe, 1991), p. 262.

35. *Jiefangjun jiangling zhuan*, 7: 261.

36. Huang Yao, *San ci da nan buside*, p. 280. Lin Biao's final words to Luo were instructions on how he could relieve his toothaches.

37. Ibid., p. 276.

38. Guan Weixun, *Wo suo zhidaode Ye Qun* (The Ye Qun I Knew) (Beijing: Zhongguo wenxue chubanshe, 1993), p. 54; Zhang Yunsheng, *Maojiawan jishi: Lin Biao mishu huiyilu* (The True Story of Maojiawan: The Memoirs of Lin Biao's Secretary) (Beijing: Chunqiu chubanshe, 1988), p. 252. One of Lin's poems went: "Although the colour of our hair is not the same our hearts share the same temperature, [and] while we were not born on the same day we are prepared to die together"; translated in Frederick C. Teiwes and Warren Sun, *The Tragedy of Lin Biao: Riding the Tiger during the Cultural Revolution, 1966–1971* (London: Hurst, 1996), p. 15.

39. Wang Nianyi ms., pp. 85–86.

40. Luo Diandian, "Luo zongzhang mengnan jishi" (A Record of Chief of Staff Luo Confronted by Dangers), in Cheng Min, ed., *Haojie chuqi* (How the Calamity Began) (Beijing: Tuanjie chubanshe, 1993), p. 210.

41. Huang Yao, *San ci da nan buside*, p. 280; Zhang Yunsheng, *Maojiawan*, passim.

42. Luo allegedly made four points: (1) "Everyone has to leave the political stage sooner or later, whether they like it or not, and that goes for Chief Lin too"; (2) "We should rely on you [Ye Qun] to take good care of Chief Lin's health"; (3) "In the future, Chief Lin should not concern himself too much with the affairs of the armed forces, but let other people handle them"; and (4) "Once Luo is in charge, he should be respected and given a free rein to handle affairs"; Wang Nianyi ms., p. 91. See also "Zhongyang gongzuo xiaozu guanyu Luo Ruiqing cuowu wentide baogao" (Report from the Central Work Group in the Matter of Luo Ruiqing's Errors), April 30, 1966, translated as "Report on the Problem of Lo Jui-ch'ing's Mistakes," in *Chinese Law and Government*, 4, nos. 3–4 (Fall–Winter 1971–72), 287–314.

43. See also Huang Yao, *San ci da nan buside*, pp. 284–285.

44. This point is made in Jing Huang, *Factionalism in Chinese Communist Politics* (New York: Cambridge University Press, 2000), pp. 283–284.

45. Mao Zedong, "Fandui zhezhongzhuyide wenti" (On Opposing Eclecticism), in *Mao Zedong sixiang wan sui (1960–1967)* (Long Live Mao Zedong Thought [1960–1967]) (n.p., n.d.), p. 149.

46. Mao Zedong, "Guanyu Luo Ruiqing de tanhua" (Remarks concerning Luo Ruiqing), ibid., p. 151.

47. The scheme lasted from 1964 to 1980; Wu Li, ed., *Zhonghua renmin gongheguo jingji shi, 1949–1999* (An Economic History of the PRC, 1949–1999), 2 vols. (Beijing: Zhongguo jingji chubanshe, 1999), 1: 680. See also Chapter 18 of this volume. For an assessment of the Third Front, see Barry Naughton, "Industrial Policy during the Cultural Revolution: Military Preparation, Decentralization, and Leaps Forward," in William Joseph, Christine P. W. Wong, and David Zweig, eds., *New Perspectives on the Cultural Revolution* (Cambridge, Mass.: Council on East Asian Studies, Harvard University, 1991), pp. 153–181.

48. Chinese sources disagree on whether or not PSC members other than Mao and Lin were told in advance about the meeting's agenda; cf. Wang Nianyi ms., pp. 87–88; and Huang Yao, *San ci da nan buside*, pp. 285, 288. According to Luo's widow, as reported by one of her children, Liu Shaoqi arrived in Shanghai and asked He Long what the meeting was about, to which the marshal replied that if Liu did not know, how would he; Zhao Jianping, Li Xiaochun, and Kang Xiaofeng, *Fengyun zhongde gongheguo dajiang Luo Ruiqing* (The Great General of the Republic Luo Ruiqing during the Tumultuous Era) (Beijing: Zuojia chubanshe, 1997), p. 321.

49. Wang Nianyi ms., p. 381.

50. Huang Yao, *San ci da nan buside*, p. 288; Liao Gailong, ed., *Xin Zhongguo biannianshi (1949–1989)* (The Annals of New China [1949–1989]) (Beijing: Renmin chubanshe, 1989), p. 251.

51. For an account of the summoning and examination of Luo that unwittingly suggests Mao's hypocritical attempt to distance himself from the proceedings, see *Chen Pixian huiyilu*, pp. 37–42.

52. Huang Yao, *San ci da nan buside*, pp. 290–291.

53. Zhang Guanghua, "Yin fandui 'tuchu zhengzhi' bei pohai zhisi de Xiao Xiangrong" (Xiao Xiangrong, Persecuted to Death for Opposing "Giving Prominence to Politics"), *Yanhuang chunqiu* (Chinese Annals), no. 10 (1997), 22.

54. A hint of this kind of sentiment is to be found in Huang Yao, *San ci da nan buside*, p. 285.

55. Ibid., pp. 292–293; Wang Nianyi ms., p. 94.

56. Zhengxie quanguo weiyuanhui jiguan, Weidong geming zhandoudui, Dongfang-hong zhandoutuan, and Hongweibing zaofanpai, eds., *Chedi cuihui shiqi nian lai Zhengxie gongzuo zhongde Liu, Deng fangeming xiuzhengzhuyi luxian* (Thoroughly Smash the Counterrevolutionary Revisionist Line of Liu and Deng in the Work of the Political Consultative Conference during the Past Seventeen Years) (Beijing, 1967), p. 66.

57. Li Xuefeng, "Wo suo zhidaode 'Wenge' fadong neiqing" (My Inside Knowledge of the Launching of the "Cultural Revolution"), in Zhang Hua and Su Caiqing, eds., *Huishou "Wenge"* (Looking Back on the "Cultural Revolution"), 2 vols. (Beijing: Zhonggong dangshi chubanshe, 2000), 2: 607.

58. Wang Nianyi ms., p. 94; Huang Yao, *San ci da nan buside*, pp. 301–311. For an account of how Luo's purge quickly affected others who had been close to him, see Wang Zhongfang, *Lianyu* (Purgatory) (Beijing: Qunzhong chubanshe, 2004).

59. "Report on the Problem of Lo Jui-ch'ing's Mistakes."

60. Guofang daxue dangshi dangjian zhenggong jiaoyanshi, ed., *"Wenhua dageming" yanjiu ziliao* (Research Materials on the "Great Cultural Revolution"), 3 vols. (Beijing, 1988) (hereafter Guofang daxue, *"Wenhua dageming"*), 1: 6.

61. Li Yunsun, "Du Wu Han wentide dingxing yiwen yougan" (Reaction from Reading the Nature of Wu Han's Problems), *Yanhuang chunqiu*, no. 5 (1998), 79. According to one account, Zhang and Yao were aware that the real trouble with Wu Han's article was "dismissed," but Yao did not say so because so grave a charge required the prestige of the Chairman; *Chen Pixian huiyilu*, p. 44. Another possibility is that Mao did not want to alert Peng Dehuai that his case was still a live issue. Mao had recently had a friendly lunch with Peng in order to persuade him to leave the capital for a post in the Southwest; mention of him in Yao's article would have destroyed the illusion of reconciliation. See *Origins*, 3: 441–443, for a discussion of Mao's prudential reasons for removing Peng from the capital.

62. Guofang daxue, *"Wenhua dageming,"* 1: 5–6.

63. Zheng Qian, "Cong 'Ping xinbian lishiju Hai Rui baguan' dao 'eryue tigang'"

(From Criticism of the Newly Revised Play "Hai Rui Dismissed from Office" to the "February Outline"), in Cheng Min, *Haojie chuqi*, p. 166.

64. Mu Xin, *Ban "Guangming ribao" shinian zishu (1957–1967)* (Personal Account of Running the *Guangming Daily* for a Decade [1957–1967]) (Beijing: Zhonggong dangshi chubanshe, 1994), pp. 245–247.

65. Hebei sheng geming weiyuanhui zhengzhibu, ed., *Mao zhuxi zuixin zhishi ruogan zhongyao wenxian* (Several Important Documents on Chairman Mao's Latest Instructions) (Baoding, 1968), pp. 1057–58.

66. Wang Li, *Wang Li fansi lu: Wang Li yi gao* (Wang Li's Reflections), 2 vols. (Hong Kong: Beixing chubanshe, 2001) (hereafter *Wang Li fansi lu*), 2: 1051–52.

67. Wang Nianyi ms., pp. 50–52.

68. *Shanghae Almanac for 1853 and Miscellany* (Shanghai: "Herald" Office, 1852).

69. Guofang daxue, *Cankao ziliao*, 24: 604–610.

70. Gong Yuzhi, "'Eryue tigang' he donghu zhixing" (The "February Outline" and Travels at East Lake), in Zhang Hua and Su Caiqing, *Huishou "Wenge,"* 1: 300.

71. Guofang daxue, *"Wenhua dageming,"* 1: 9. According to Chen Pixian, Peng Zhen handed him the draft outline in Shanghai on February 10 with instructions to convey it to Jiang Qing; *Chen Pixian huiyilu*, p. 48.

2. The Siege of Beijing

1. *Mao zhuxi Lin fuzhuxi guanyu baokan xuanchuan de zhishi* (Chairman Mao's and Vice Chairman Lin's Instructions on Press and Propaganda) (n.p., 1970), pp. 303–308; Li Xuefeng, "Wo suo zhidaode," p. 606. Li Xuefeng recalled Mao as commenting on the *People's Daily* by saying "you're only half Marxist-Leninist, half [Sun Yat-sen's] 'Three Principles of the People.' You decide for yourselves whether or not you count as Marxist-Leninists!"

2. Jin Chongji, ed., *Zhou Enlai zhuan (1949–1976)* (Biography of Zhou Enlai [1949–1976]), 2 vols. (Beijing: Zhongyang wenxian chubanshe, 1998), 2: 879. One other issue may have increased the Chairman's animosity toward Peng Zhen, though the latter seems not to have been attacked for it. In the previous few weeks, China's leaders had been discussing whether to send a delegation to the CPSU's Twenty-third Congress. Peng Zhen was the only one to have made the case for sending a delegation, a course of action that Mao rejected on this occasion; Wu Lengxi, *Shinian lunzhan*, 2: 933–939.

3. Guofang daxue, *"Wenhua dageming,"* 1: 10–11.

4. For an analysis of Chen Boda's role in the formulation of Mao thought, see Raymond F. Wylie, *The Emergence of Maoism: Mao Tse-tung, Ch'en Po-ta, and the Search for Chinese Theory, 1935–1945* (Stanford: Stanford University Press, 1980).

Chen admitted never to having got beyond chapter 1 of Marx's *Das Kapital; Wang Li fansi lu,* 2: 702.

5. Guofang daxue, *"Wenhua dageming,"* 1: 12.
6. For the time line of these events and the questions that it raises, see Jing Huang, *Factionalism in Chinese Communist Politics,* pp. 279–280; for Peng's early adherence to Liu, see ibid., pp. 86, 129, 143–146.
7. Liu's first stop upon arriving back in China was Kunming, where—so his body-guard recalled many years later—he told his wife Wang Guangmei, "the center wants us to rest for a week before returning to Beijing, while the people from the Ministry of Foreign Affairs go on ahead." But he had barely settled in when he received an urgent phone call from Mao, who ordered him to fly to Hangzhou immediately to participate in the enlarged PSC meeting; Jia Lanxun, "Tie shen weishi yi Shaoqi mengnan" (Memories of a Private Guard: How Liu Shaoqi Met with Disaster), *Bainian chao* (Hundred Year Tide), no. 1 (2000), 9–10.
8. Li Xuefeng, "Wo suo zhidaode," pp. 607–609.
9. *Cankao xiaoxi* (Reference News), May 3, 1966.
10. Zhongguo kexueyuan geming lishi yanjiusuo jindai gemingshi yanjiusuo, eds., *Liu Shaoqi fangeming xiuzhengzhuyi yanlun huibian* (Collected Counterrevolutionary Revisionist Statements by Liu Shaoqi) (Beijing, 1967), p. 183.
11. Guofang daxue, *"Wenhua dageming,"* 1: 25.
12. Qinghai 8.18 geming zaofanpai lianhe weiyuanhui xuanchuanzu, ed., *Ziliao xuanbian: Zhongyang shouzhang jianghua zhuanji* (Selected Material: Special Collection of Central Leaders' Speeches) (Xining, 1967), p. 12.
13. Ibid., p. 7.
14. *Fangeming xiuzhengzhuyi fenzi Lu Dingyi zai wenjiao fangmian de zuixing* (Counterrevolutionary Revisionist Element Lu Dingyi's Crimes in Culture and Education) (Beijing: Dou Peng-Luo-Lu-Yang fangeming xiuzhengzhuyi jituan choubeichu, 1967), p. 5.
15. According to the widely accepted post–Cultural Revolutionary version of events; an earlier, alternative, and more complex chronology has it that China's public security organs had been on to Yan as early as 1962. See Beijing zhengfa xueyuan geming weiyuanhui ziliaozu, ed., *Xingxing sese de anjian* (Cases of Every Shape and Color) (Beijing, 1968), pp. 18–33.
16. Xiao Han and Mia Turner, *789 jizhongying* (Camp 789) (Brampton, Ont.: Mirror Books, 1998), pp. 12–30.
17. Wang Nianyi, *Da dongluande niandai,* p. 19.
18. Guofang daxue, *"Wenhua dageming,"* 1: 25.
19. *Ye Zilong huiyilu* (Ye Zilong's Recollections) (Beijing: Zhongyang wenxian chubanshe, 2000), p. 225.

20. *Hongying* (Red Eagle) (Beijing), September 14, 1967, p. 2.

21. *Yang Shangkun riji*, 1: 716; *Ye Zilong huiyilu*, pp. 223–231; Su Shaozhi, interview by Michael Schoenhals, April 1992. At the beginning of the Cultural Revolution, Su was a member of the Theory Department of the *People's Daily*.

22. *Canyue cailiao* (Reference Reading Materials) (n.p., [1976]), 10: 18.

23. Wang Nianyi ms., p. 84.

24. Ibid.; Shoudu bufen dazhuan yuanxiao zhongdeng zhuanye xuexiao Mao Zedong sixiang xuexiban, ed., *Tianfan difu kaierkang—Wuchanjieji wenhua dageming dashiji* (Moved from Watching Heaven and Earth Turn Upside Down—Record of Major Events in the Great Proletarian Cultural Revolution), rev. ed. (Beijing, 1967), p. 23.

25. *Gaoju Mao Zedong sixiang weida hongqi* (Raise High the Great Red Banner of Mao Zedong Thought) (n.p., April 1967), p. 21.

26. Jin Chongji, *Zhou Enlai zhuan*, p. 883.

27. On June 10, 1966; Su Donghai and Fang Kongmu, eds., *Zhonghua renmin gongheguo fengyun shilu* (A Record of the Major Events of the PRC), 2 vols. (Shijiazhuang: Hebei renmin chubanshe, 1994), 1: 1054.

28. Qinghai 8.18, *Ziliao xuanbian*, p. 11.

29. Zhengxie quanguo weiyuanhui jiguan, Weidong geming zhandoudui, Dongfanghong zhandoutuan, and Hongweibing zaofanpai, *Chedi cuihui shiqi nian lai Zhengxie gongzuo zhong de Liu, Deng fangeming xiuzhengzhuyi luxian*, p. 67.

30. Mu Xin, *Ban "Guangming ribao" shinian zishu*, p. 287.

31. Qinghai 8.18, *Ziliao xuanbian*, pp. 4, 6. On Kang Sheng's involvment in drafting Lin's speech, see Chen Xiaonong, ed., *Chen Boda yigao: Yuzhong zishu ji qita* (Manuscripts by the Late Chen Boda: Accounts from Prison and More) (Hong Kong: Cosmos Books, 1998), p. 93.

32. Mu Xin, *Ban "Guangming ribao" shinian zishu*, p. 287.

33. *Cankao xiaoxi*, June 21, 1966.

34. See "Report on the Problem of Lo Jui-ch'ing's Mistakes," pp. 287–314.

35. Text of the statement in Guofang daxue, *"Wenhua dageming,"* 1: 24–25.

36. Wang Ming, a Comintern-backed rival of Mao's in the late 1930s who lived in voluntary exile in Moscow, symbolized the attempts of the CPSU to control the CCP for revisionist purposes.

37. Li Xuefeng, "Wo suo zhidaode," p. 611.

38. Zhonggong Shanghai shiwei bangongting geming zaofandui, ed., *Liu Shaoqi zai gedi sanbude xiuzhengzhuyi yanlun huibian* (Collected Revisionist Utterances Spread in Various Localities by Liu Shaoqi) (Shanghai, 1967), pp. 210–211.

39. Guofang daxue, *"Wenhua dageming,"* 1: 3; emphasis added.

40. Qinghai 8.18, *Ziliao xuanbian*, pp. 10–11.

41. Dazibao bianjizu, ed., *Jiaoyubu wenhua dageming dazibao xuanji* (Selected Great Cultural Revolution Big-Character Posters from the Ministry of Education) (n.p., n.d.), November 21, 1966, p. 131.

42. Shangyebu jiguan hongse zaofantuan and Beijing shangxueyuan hongfanjun, eds., *Yao Yilin fan dang fan shehuizhuyi fan Mao Zedong sixiang zuixing* (Yao Yilin's Anti-Party, Anti-Socialist, and Anti–Mao Zedong Thought Crimes) (Beijing, 1967), p. 58.

43. Public Record Office, Kew, FO 371/1869/80, Restricted telegram from Donald Hopson, U.K. chargé d'affaires, Beijing, to Foreign Office, London, No. 422 (repeated for distribution as No. 425), "Campaign against anti-Party elements," June 4, 1966.

44. Huang Yao, "Luo Ruiqing zhuanlüe xia," p. 186.

45. Idem, "Luo Ruiqing," in Zhonggong dangshi renwu yanjiuhui, ed., *Zhonggong dangshi renwu zhuan* (Biographies of Personalities in the History of the CCP), 60 vols. (Xi'an: Shaanxi renmin chubanshe, 1980–1996) (hereafter *Zhonggong dangshi renwu xhuan*), 46 (pub. 1991): 65.

46. Chen Qingquan and Song Guangwei, "Yuanan bu ping, ju bu chu yu de Lu Dingyi" (The Case Is Unfair: Lu Dingyi Refuses to Leave Prison), *Yanhuang chunqiu*, no. 6 (2000), 26.

47. "Beijing shi 'Wenhua dageming' dashiji, 1965–1967" (A Chronology of the "Great Cultural Revolution" in Beijing, 1965–1967), in Zhonggong Beijing shiwei dangshi ziliao zhengji weiyuanhui, *Beijing dangshi ziliao tongxun* (Beijing Party History Materials Newsletter) (hereafter *Beijing dangshi ziliao tongxun*), extra issue, no. 17 (May 1987), 23; Zhonggong zhongyang zuzhibu, Zhonggong zhongyang dangshi yanjiushi, and Zhongyang dang'anguan, eds., *Zhongguo gongchandang zuzhishi ziliao, 1921–1997* (Materials on the Organizational History of the CCP, 1921–1997), 19 vols. (Beijing: Zhonggong dangshi chubanshe, 2000) (hereafter *Zhongguo gongchandang zuzhishi ziliao*), 10: 134.

48. *Neimenggu zizhiqu dashiji* (Record of Major Events in the Inner Mongolian Autonomous Region) (Huhehot: Neimenggu renmin chubanshe, 1988), pp. 100–101.

49. "Liu Shaoqi tongzhi tong Wulanfu tongzhi tanhua jilu" (Record of Conversation between Comrades Liu Shaoqi and Ulanfu), July 2, 1966, photocopy of transcript from Cultural Revolution, Fairbank Center Library.

50. Timothy Cheek, *Propaganda and Culture in Mao's China: Deng Tuo and the Intelligentsia* (Oxford: Clarendon Press, 1997), pp. 236–237, 279–283. In an odd reflection of the importance of personal ties in the Chinese Communist system, Deng Tuo had been the only member of the Beijing party to be briefed about Yao's article in advance by Zhang Chunqiao; Deng and Zhang had worked together on the same newspaper during the anti-Japanese war; *Shanghai "Wenhua dageming" shihua*, 1: 17.

51. Cheek, *Propaganda and Culture in Mao's China*, pp. 292–293.

52. Li Xuefeng's position as the North China first secretary had always been somewhat anomalous, since he was in charge of a region that notionally included two province-level units with leaders who, as members of the Politburo, were senior to him, Peng Zhen and Ulanfu (a Politburo alternate member) in Inner Mongolia; Neimenggu Wulanfu yanjiuhui, ed., *Wulanfu nianpu* (A Chronicle of the Life of Ulanfu), 2 vols. (Beijing: Zhonggong dangshi chubanshe, 1996), 2: 9–12.

53. *Hongqi zhanbao* (Red Flag Battle Report) (Beijing: CCP Municipal Committee Policy Research Office), no. 5 (January 21, 1967).

54. Chen Xiaonong, comp., *Chen Boda zuihou koushu huiyi* (Chen Boda's Final Oral Memoir) (Hong Kong: Yangguang huanqiu chuban Xianggang youxian gongsi, 2005), p. 268. When Chen suggested that Kang Sheng would be a better choice, Zhou said he was inappropriate, possibly an indication that Mao felt that Kang Sheng would arouse antagonism because of his background in security work.

55. *Jianguo yilai Mao Zedong wengao*, 12: 64–65, 80–84; Wang Nianyi, *Da dongluande niandai*, p. 56. The importance of the CCRG grew dramatically once Mao had returned to Beijing in mid-July; for a more detailed description of its internal makeup, how it operated, and so on, see Chapter 5 of this volume.

56. Duiwai wenwei Jinggangshan geming zaofan lianluozhan, ed., *Dadao fangeming xiuzhengzhuyi fenzi Li Chang* (Down with the Counterrevolutionary Revisionist Element Li Chang) (Beijing, 1967), p. 49.

57. Shanghai jixie xueyuan geming weiyuanhui "Hongse tingjinjun," ed., *Shede yishen gua, gan ba huangdi laxia ma* (He Who Doesn't Fear Being Cut to Pieces Dares Unseat the Emperor), 8 vols. (Shanghai, 1967), 1: 67.

58. Quoted in "Quarterly Chronicle and Documentation," *China Quarterly* (hereafter *CQ*), no. 27 (July–September 1966), 192.

59. Zhonggong zhongyang tongzhanbu Geming zaofantuan and Hongwuyue bingtuan cailiaozu, eds., *Zhongguo Heluxiaofu Liu Shaoqi zai tongyi zhanxian fangmiande fangeming xiuzhengzhuyi yanlun xuanbian* (Selected Counterrevolutionary Revisionist Statements concerning the United Front by China's Khrushchev Liu Shaoqi) (Beijing, 1967), p. 120.

60. Zhengxie quanguo weiyuanhui jiguan, Weidong geming zhandoudui, Dongfanghong zhandoutuan, and Hongweibing zaofanpai, *Chedi cuihui shiqi nian lai Zhengxie gongzuo zhong de Liu, Deng fangeming xiuzhengzhuyi luxian*, p. 71.

61. Ibid., p. 67.

62. Ibid., p. 68.

63. *Jiefangjun bao* (Liberation Army News), June 7, 1966.

64. Mu Xin, *Ban "Guangming ribao" shinian zishu*, p. 283.

65. Wang Nianyi, *Da dongluande niandai*, p. 10.

66. Guofang daxue, *"Wenhua dageming,"* 1: 4.

67. Beijing boli zongchang hongweibing lianluozhan, ed., *Zhongyang shouzhang jianghua* (Central Leaders' Speeches), 4 vols. (Beijing, 1967), 4: 273.

68. *Neibu ziliao* (Internal Materials) (Beijing: Tsinghua University Jinggangshan Battle Operations Group), no. 173 (1967), 1.

69. Zhonggong Beijing shiwei dangxiao ziliaoshi, ed., *Kang Sheng yanlun xuanbian* (Selected Utterances of Kang Sheng), 3 vols. (Beijing, 1979), 3: 82. One Politburo session participant who most definitely failed to read the subtle signs emanating from Mao was Vice Premier Tan Zhenlin, whose regular State Council portfolio included agriculture, forestry, aquatic products, and the weather. When transmitting the "spirit" of the session to the party leadership of the Ministry of Aquatic Products on June 7, he ended with the following call to arms: "Action, comrades! Forward resolutely and boldly in defense of the party center, in defense of Chairman Mao, in defense of Shaoqi, Enlai, Xiaoping, Lin Biao, and the other comrades. Let us resolutely fight, topple, and wipe out completely whoever dares to oppose them!" See *Dadao Tan Zhenlin cailiao huibian* (Down with Tan Zhenlin, Collected Materials) (Shanghai, 1967), 1: 6; *Guanyu Tan Zhenlin wenti de chubu zonghe cailiao* (Initial Comprehensive Material on Tan Zhenlin's Problems) (Beijing, 1967), 2: 17.

70. The concept of "working toward" a secretive leader is borrowed from Ian Kershaw's biography *Hitler,* 2 vols. (London: Allen Lane, 1998, 2000), in which it is a major theme. The problem also afflicted the Khmer Rouge leadership when attempting to divine the wishes of Pol Pot. According to one colleague: "He would imply things, so that we would have to think about them ourselves . . . [Because of this indirectness], it was sometimes very difficult to figure out what he was getting at. So we were very cautious, because we used to worry about misinterpreting his meaning"; Philip Short, *Pol Pot: Anatomy of a Nightmare* (New York: Henry Holt, 2005), p. 338.

71. Mao's paranoia is attested to by his doctor; see Li Zhisui, *The Private Life of Chairman Mao.*

72. Qinghai 8.18, *Ziliao xuanbian,* pp. 2–13. Peng dismissed the accusation by saying that he had never even dreamed of a coup let alone plotted one, and challenged the CC to discover any improper links between himself, Luo, and Lu; Wang Nianyi, *Da dongluande niandai,* pp. 16–18.

73. In *Mao: The Unknown Story* (London: Jonathan Cape, 2005), p. 528, the authors Jung Chang and Jon Halliday state that Peng Zhen paid a secret visit to Marshal Peng Dehuai in Sichuan in February 1966, and they suggest that the two men may have discussed the feasibility of using the PLA to stop Mao. This intriguing thought is vitiated, however, by the unconvincing nature of the Chinese source they use—Shi Dongbing, *Zuichude kangzheng: Peng Zhen zai wenhua dageming*

qianxi (Resistance at the Beginning: Peng Zhen on the Eve of the Great Cultural Revolution) (Beijing: Zhonggong zhongyang dangxiao chubanshe, 1993)—in which whole conversations between leaders are reproduced without indication of how the author could have learned of them. Corroboration one way or the other might be provided if those in charge of the CCP archives were to issue a post-1949 chronicle *(nianpu)* of Peng Zhen's life. Furthermore, in Yuan Beijing shiwei jiguan Mao Zedong sixiang hongqi bingtuan, ed., *Peng Zhen zuie shi (1925–1966)* (Peng Zhen's Criminal History [1925–1966]) (Beijing, 1967), a chronology that contains entries for almost every day in February 1966, Peng visits Sichuan from the 20th to the 28th. It makes no mention of a meeting with Peng Dehuai, only that Peng met with Li Jingquan. *Dadao Li Jingquan* (Down with Li Jingquan) (Chongqing, 1967) has very specific coverage of Peng's visit to Sichuan, explaining what he did, whom he met, what they talked about, and so on. It has Peng arriving in "late February" and returning to Beijing on March 6. It makes no mention of a meeting with Peng Dehuai. Had the publishers of *Dadao Li Jingquan*, who really have to count as remarkably well informed, albeit politically driven in their writing, had any knowledge of a meeting between the two Pengs, they would have been only too happy to mention it as yet another "sinister" machination by Peng's "sinister" host.

74. *Zhou Enlai nianpu*, 3: 31–32.
75. Ibid.
76. Beijing boli zongchang hongweibing lianluozhan, *Zhongyang shouzhang jianghua*, 1: 72.
77. *Zhou Enlai nianpu*, 3: 33.
78. Ibid., p. 32.
79. Michael Schoenhals, "A Question of Loyalty: China's Public Security Forces in 1967," paper presented at the Association for Asian Studies annual meeting, Chicago, March 14, 1997.
80. *Fu Chongbi huiyilu* (The Memoirs of Fu Chongbi) (Beijing: Zhonggong dangshi chubanshe, 1999), pp. 175–183; Zhonggong Beijing shiwei zuzhibu, Zhonggong Beijing shiwei dangshi ziliao zhengji weiyuanhui, and Beijing shi dang'anju, eds., *Zhongguo gongchandang Beijing shi zuzhi shi ziliao* (Material on the Organizational History of the CCP in Beijing) (Beijing: Renmin chubanshe, 1992), pp. 783–789.
81. Tan Zheng, *Zhongguo renmin zhiyuanjun renwu lu* (Biographies of Members of the Chinese People's Volunteer Army) (Beijing: Zhonggong dangshi chubanshe, 1992), pp. 263–264, 653.
82. *Beijing junqu jiguan wuchanjieji gemingpai jiefa pipan zichanjieji yexinjia, yinmoujia, fangeming liangmianpai Yang Chengwu, Yu Lijin, Fu Chongbi zuixing de*

cailiao (Materials Documenting the Exposure and Denunciation by the Proletarian Revolutionary Faction in Organs of the Beijing Military Region of the Crimes of Bourgeois Careerists, Conspirators, and Double-Dealers Yang Chengwu, Yu Lijin, and Fu Chongbi) (Beijing, 1968), p. 17.

83. Yu Sang, "Renmin dahuitang chuanghu boli qiangji shijian zhenpoji" (Record of Cracking the Case of the Rifle Shot Smashing a Window in the Great Hall of the People), in Zhu Chunlin, ed., *Lishi shunjian* (History Twinkling) (Beijing: Qunzhong chubanshe, 1999), 1: 259–267.

84. Beijing shi geming weiyuanhui di er xuexiban dangwei, "Guanyu Liu Yunfeng wenti de fucha huibao cailiao" (Report Materials on the Reinvestigation of the Problems of Liu Yunfeng), April 27, 1972, p. 6. In 1970 the Beijing Revolutionary Committee reopened the case against the two men and sentenced both to death.

85. Wang Nianyi, "Guanyu He Long yuanande yixie ziliao" (Some Materials on the Case of He Long), *Dangshi yanjiu ziliao* (Party History Research Materials), no. 4 (1992), 3.

86. Beijing caimao xueyuan, ed., *Zai Zhonggong ba jie shier zhong quanhui shang Mao zhuxi, Lin fuzhuxi, Zhou zongli de zhongyao jianghua* (Chairman Mao's, Vice Chairman Lin's, and Premier Zhou Enlai's Important Speeches at the Twelfth Plenum of the Eighth CCP Central Committee) (Beijing, 1969), p. 35.

87. Zhejiang shifan xueyuan Hongdonghai zhandoudui, ed., *Wuchanjieji wenhua dageming bufen ziliao huibian III* (Partial Collection of Material from the Great Proletarian Cultural Revolution III) (Taizhou, 1967), p. 283.

88. *Fu Chongbi huiyilu,* p. 180.

89. See General Xu Shiyou's recollection in 1981 of a conversation he had with Mao Zedong in Hangzhou in the winter of 1965–66; quoted in Wang Nianyi, "Guanyu He Long yuanande yixie ziliao," p. 3.

90. *Dongtai* (Current Intelligence) (Beijing: Tsinghua University Jinggangshan Third Current Intelligence Group), no. 74 (June 13, 1967), 1; *Wuchanjieji wenhua dageming ziliao 6* (Materials on the Great Proletarian Cultural Revolution: June), 2 vols. (Beijing, 1967), 1: 329.

91. Xu Zehao, *Wang Jiaxiang zhuan* (Biography of Wang Jiaxiang) (Beijing: Dangdai Zhongguo chubanshe, 1996), p. 571; *Wang Li fansi lu,* 2: 728.

92. Beijing boli zongchang hongweibing lianluozhan, *Zhongyang shouzhang jianghua,* 4: 68.

93. In the autumn of 1966, Chinese students designed a chart intended to contrast the "proletarian and bourgeois" ways of making revolution against each other. The table defined the proletarian "method" as "mass movements, noisy, and spectacular, and very 'disorderly,'" contrasting it with the bourgeois preference for "turning mass movements into something cold and desolate, and very 'orderly.'"

3. Confusion on Campuses

1. Guofang daxue, *"Wenhua dageming,"* 1: 55.

2. Chinese diary no. 18, in the authors' possession.

3. Chinese diary no. 1, in the authors' possession.

4. Chinese diary no. 2, in the authors' possession.

5. Renmin ribao wuchanjieji gemingpai and Shoudu xinwen pipan lianluozhan, eds., *Xinwen zhanxian liangtiao luxian douzheng dashiji, 1948–1966 (chugao)* (Chronology of the Struggle between the Two Lines on the News Front, 1948–1966 [Preliminary Draft]) (Beijing, n.d.), p. 33.

6. *Jiefangjun bao,* April 18, 1966. In the February Outline, the emphasis had been the very opposite: "Without construction, it is impossible to achieve real and thorough destruction."

7. "Gong nong bing qun zhong canjia xueshu pipan shi hua shidaide da shi" (The Participation of the Worker-Peasant-Soldier Masses in Academic Criticism is a Major Epoch-making Event), *Hongqi* (Red Flag), no. 6 (1966), 20–22.

8. Chinese diary no. 3, in the authors' possession.

9. The authorities of *Beijing daxue* (Beida) decided in the 1980s that in translation their institution would be known as Peking, not Beijing, University.

10. Beida dangshi xiaoshi yanjiushi dangshizu, "Kang Sheng, Cao Yiou yu 'di yi zhang dazibao'" (Kang Sheng, Cao Yiou, and the "First Big-Character Poster"), *Bainian chao,* no. 9 (2001), 33. Cao's team also included a vice minister of higher education; three team members were journalists, two of them from Chen Boda's *Red Flag,* one from *Guangming Daily.* In addition to Beida, the team visited Tsinghua University, China People's University, and Beijing Normal University; Mu Xin, "'Quanguo di yi zhang dazibao' chulong jingguo" (How the "First Big-Character Poster" Came About), *Zhonggong dangshi ziliao,* no. 75 (September 2000), 166.

11. Zhongguo renmin daxue Xin renda gongshe and Mao Zedong sixiang hong-weibing, eds., *Fangeming xiuzhengzhuyi fenzi Guo Yingqiu fan dang fan shehuizhuyi fan Mao Zedong sixiang de zuixing* (Counterrevolutionary Revisionist Element Guo Yingqiu's Anti-Party, Anti-Socialist, Anti–Mao Zedong Thought Crimes) (Beijing, 1967), 1: 76.

12. *Origins,* 3: 637, n. 154; Gao Gao and Yan Jiaqi, *"Wenhua dageming" shinian shi, 1966–1976* (A Ten-Year History of the "Great Cultural Revolution," 1966–1976) (Tianjin: Tianjin renmin chubanshe, 1986), p. 19, translated by D. W. Y. Kwok as *Turbulent Decade: A History of the Cultural Revolution* (Honolulu: University of Hawaii Press, 1996), pp. 39–40; Hao Ping, "Reassessing the Starting Point of the Cultural Revolution," *China International Review,* 3, no. 1 (Spring 1996), 71–74.

13. Nie Yuanzi, interview by Michael Schoenhals, Beijing, July 17, 1994.
14. Mao Mao, *Wode fuqin Deng Xiaoping "Wenge" suiyue* (My Father Deng Xiaoping's "Cultural Revolution" Years) (Beijing: Zhongyang wenxian chubanshe, 2000), p. 16; translated as Deng Rong, *Deng Xiaoping and the Cultural Revolution: A Daughter Recalls the Critical Years* (Beijing: Foreign Languages Press, 2002), p. 11.
15. Beida dangshi xiaoshi yanjiushi dangshizu, "Kang Sheng, Cao Yiou yu 'di yi zhang dazibao,'" p. 36.
16. For an indication of some of the sources available to Nie, see Victor Nee, *The Cultural Revolution at Peking University* (New York: Monthly Review Press, 1969), p. 53.
17. Mu Xin, "'Quanguo di yi zhang dazibao' chulong jingguo," p. 168.
18. Such posters had originated in Yan'an, where they were used by the CCP as a makeshift system for the publication of news and opinion; they were used by critics of the party during the Hundred Flowers period and by the CCP to promote production during the GLF. See David Jim-tat Poon, "*Tatzepao:* Its History and Significance as Communication Medium," in Godwin C. Chu, ed., *Popular Media in China: Shaping New Cultural Patterns* (Honolulu: East-West Center, University of Hawaii, 1978), pp. 184–221.
19. Nie Yuanzi, interview by Schoenhals, Beijing, July 17, 1994.
20. For a thoroughly researched account of this whole episode by a Beida scholar, see Yin Hongbiao, "Wengede 'di yi zhang Ma-Liezhuyi dazibao'" ("The First Big-Character Poster of Marxism-Leninism" of the Cultural Revolution), *Ershiyi shiji shuangyuekan* (Twenty-first Century Bimonthly), no. 36 (August 1996), 37–45. See also Guofang daxue, *"Wenhua dageming,"* 1: 32–36. In the first sentence of the June 2 *People's Daily* commentary on the poster, it is simply described as "comrade Nie Yuanzi's"; ibid., p. 36. Though this poster is customarily called the first big-character poster of the Cultural Revolution, that honor in fact belongs to the product of two senior cadres in the Academy of Sciences Department of Philosophy and Social Sciences (or Xuebu, the predecessor of today's Chinese Academy of Social Sciences) who attacked their director, who was concurrently a senior official of the party's North China Region, two days earlier. The Xuebu, despite its name, was not a mere subunit of the Academy, but an organization led directly by the CC Propaganda Department. See *Zhongguo gongchandang zuzhishi ziliao*, 15: 168.
21. Peng toured the United States in 1998 in her role as state councilor and minister-in-charge of the Ministry of Health.
22. The text of the poster is in Guofang daxue, *"Wenhua dageming,"* 1: 30–31.
23. Quoted in ibid., p. 30. The poster writers' citation of the content of Song's speech is indicative of how widely knowledge of the Beijing party's ongoing upheaval had spread.
24. Beijing daxue wenhua geming weiyuanhui xuanchuanzu, ed., *Beijing daxue*

wuchanjieji wenhua dageming yundong jianjie (Brief Introduction to the Great Proletarian Cultural Revolution at Peking University) (Beijing, 1966), pts. 2 and 3, p. 2.

25. Lin Haoji, "Beida di yi zhang dazibao shi zenyang chulongde" (How the First Big-Character Poster Appeared at Peking University), in Zhou Ming, ed., *Lishi zai zheli chensi* (Here History Is Lost in Thought), 6 vols. (vols. 1–3: Beijing: Huaxia chubanshe, 1986; vols. 4–6: Taiyuan: Beiyue wenyi chubanshe, 1989), 2: 32.

26. Nie Yuanzi, interview by Schoenhals, Beijing, July 17, 1994.

27. Wang Nianyi, *Da dongluande niandai*, p. 18; Hebei Beijing shifan xueyuan Douzheng shenghuo bianjibu, ed., *Wuchanjieji wenhua dageming ziliao huibian* (Collected Documents from the Great Proletarian Cultural Revolution) (Beijing, 1967), p. 667. The visit of the premier's man may have given rise to the dubious later report by a foreign student that Zhou himself paid a secret visit to the campus on the night of May 25 to read with mounting anger the already notorious poster; Sirin Phathanothai with James Peck, *The Dragon's Pearl* (New York: Simon & Schuster, 1994), p. 221. Zhou Enlai stood in loco parentis to this Thai politician's daughter, who had lived in China for many years and was a student at Beida at the time.

28. Wang Nianyi, *Da dongluande niandai*, p. 29.

29. Ai Qun, "Luanshi kuangnü Nie Yuanzi" (Crazy Woman Nie Yuanzi in Troubled Times), in Yang Mu, ed., *"Wenge" chuangjiang fengshenbang* (Pathbreakers and Feudal Gangs of the "Cultural Revolution") (Beijing: Tuanjie chubanshe, 1993), p. 44; in "Eyewitness of the Great Proletarian Cultural Revolution," *CQ*, no. 28 (October–December 1966), 2, an anonymous "foreign expert" who lived in Beijing at the time maintains that "it was torn down the same night."

30. *Qinghua daxue dazibao xuanbian* (Selection of Tsinghua University Big-Character Posters), no. 33 (September 12, 1966).

31. Ibid., no. 29 (September 6, 1966), 25.

32. See Roderick MacFarquhar, ed., *The Hundred Flowers Campaign and the Chinese Intellectuals* (New York: Praeger, 1960).

33. Apparently flouting regulations, Kang did not send copies to the other members of the PSC. See *Zhou Enlai nianpu*, 3: 32.

34. *Jianguo yilai Mao Zedong wengao*, 12: 62; Yin Hongbiao, "Wengede 'di yi zhang Ma-Liezhuyi dazibao,'" p. 43.

35. *Zhou Enlai nianpu*, 3: 33.

36. Li Xuefeng, "Wo suo zhidaode," p. 616.

37. Huang Zheng, *Liu Shaoqide zuihou suiyue* (Liu Shaoqi's Last Years) (Beijing: Zhongyang wenxian chubanshe, 1996), p. 64.

38. The essay by a "Commentator" is reprinted in Guofang daxue, *"Wenhua dageming,"* 1: 36–37; a translation is in *Peking Review*, no. 37 (September 9, 1966), 21–22.

39. *Xin Beida* (New Peking University), no. 20 (November 5, 1966).

40. *Mao Zedong sixiang wan sui (1960–1967),* p. 174.

41. Marianne Bastid, a French student of Chinese history at the time, quoted in Nee, *The Cultural Revolution at Peking University,* p. 58.

42. Communication to MacFarquhar, October 2005, from Dr. Endymion Wilkinson, who became European ambassador to China in the 1990s.

43. *Chedi pipan xiuzhengzhuyi youer jiaoyu luxian jiaocai huibian* (Collection on Thoroughly Criticizing the Revisionist Line in Preschool Education Textbooks) (Beijing: Beijing youshi geming zaofantuan, 1967), p. 16.

44. Chen Yuhua, president of Beijing Elementary School, quoted in *Chunlei* (Spring Thunder) (Beijing: Capital August 1 School Revolutionary Rebel Joint Headquarters), special issue, 1967, p. 28.

45. Guofang daxue, *"Wenhua dageming,"* 1: 44–45; *Mao Zedong sixiang wan sui (1960–1967),* p. 162; Guojia tongjiju zonghesi, ed., *Quanguo ge sheng zizhiqu zhixiashi lishi tongji ziliao huibian, 1949–1989* (Collected Historical Statistics for China's Provinces, Autonomous Regions, and Municipalities under Central Jurisdiction, 1949–1989) (Beijing: Zhongguo tongji chubanshe, 1990), p. 37.

46. Liao Gailong, *Xin Zhongguo biannianshi,* p. 271.

47. Lennart Petri, *Sverige i stora världen: Minnen och reflexioner från 40 års diplomattjänst* (Sweden in the Big World: Remembering and Reflecting upon 40 Years of Diplomatic Service) (Stockholm: Atlantis, 1996), pp. 356–357.

48. D. W. Fokkema, *Report from Peking* (London: Hurst, 1971), p. 6.

49. Original letter in the archive of Sweden's Ministry of Foreign Affairs, Stockholm.

50. Percy Cradock, *Experiences of China* (London: John Murray, 1994), p. 48.

51. Fokkema, *Report from Peking,* p. 8.

52. *Fu Chongbi huiyilu,* pp. 175–183.

53. *Cankao xiaoxi,* June 24, 1966.

54. Eric Gordon, *Freedom Is a Word* (London: Hodder & Stoughton, 1971), p. 69.

55. *Renmin ribao,* June 4, 1966.

56. Yu Luoke, "Riji zhaochao" (Diary Extracts), in Zhang Ming and Luo Qun, eds., *"Wenhua dageming" zhongde mingren zhi si* (Famous People Reflect upon the "Great Cultural Revolution") (Beijing: Zhongyang minzu xueyuan chubanshe, 1993), p. 337. Liu Ren was second secretary of the Beijing CCP Committee under Peng Zhen.

57. "White area" cadres were those who had worked behind the lines in territory controlled by the KMT or the Japanese; "red area" cadres were those who had been stationed in CCP base areas, like Yan'an. There had been some friction between the two groups over the division of the spoils after the revolution; see *Origins,* 1: 334–335, n. 59.

58. Gao Wenhua, "Buchong wo he Liu Shaoqi zai Zhongnanhai mimou de zuixing"

(Additions to the Crimes Plotted by Myself and Liu Shaoqi in Zhongnanhai), written deposition submitted to Ministry of Foreign Trade, February 12, 1971, p. 3, copy in the authors' possession.

59. Liu Pingping, Liu Yuan, and Liu Tingting, "Shengli de xianhua xiangei ni: Huainian women de baba Liu Shaoqi" (Fresh Flowers We Give to You: Cherishing the Memory of Our Father Liu Shaoqi), in Zhou Ming, *Lishi zai zheli chensi*, 1: 2–3.

60. Deng Rong, *Deng Xiaoping and the Cultural Revolution*, p. 11.

61. Huang Zheng, *Liu Shaoqide zuihou suiyue*, p. 66.

62. *Zhongguo gongchandang zuzhishi ziliao*, 14: 996–997.

63. Ibid., p. 1132.

64. Bo Yibo, *Ruogan zhongda juece yu shijiande huigu* (Reflections on Certain Important Decisions and Experiences), 2 vols. (Beijing: Zhonggong zhongyang dangxiao chubanshe, 1991, 1993), 2: 1125. For a discussion of the Socialist Education Movement, sometimes called the "four cleanups," see *Origins*, 3: chaps. 15 and 18.

65. "Beijing shi 'Wenhua dageming' dashiji, 1965–1967," p. 9.

66. *Zhou Enlai nianpu*, 3: 34.

67. Ibid.

68. Huang Zheng, *Liu Shaoqide zuihou suiyue*, pp. 131–132.

69. Ibid., p. 65.

70. *Zhou Enlai nianpu*, 3: 34.

71. Huang Zheng, *Liu Shaoqide zuihou suiyue*, p. 131.

72. Guofang daxue, *"Wenhua dageming,"* 1: 39, 41.

73. Huang Zheng, *Liu Shaoqide zuihou suiyue*, p. 66.

74. Zhonggong zhongyang wenxian yanjiushi, ed., *Liu Shaoqi nianpu, 1898–1969* (Chronicle of the Life of Liu Shaoqi, 1898–1969), 2 vols. (Beijing: Zhongyang wenxian chubanshe, 1996) (hereafter *Liu Shaoqi nianpu*), 2: 641.

75. Ibid.; Huang Zheng, *Liu Shaoqide zuihou suiyue*, p. 132.

76. Liao Gailong, *Xin Zhongguo biannianshi*, p. 271.

77. Quan Yanchi, *Tao Zhu zai "Wenhua dageming" zhong* (Tao Zhu during the "Great Cultural Revolution") (Beijing: Zhongyang dangxiao chubanshe, 1991), pp. 78, 81.

78. *Liu Shaoqi nianpu*, 2: 642.

4. The Fifty Days

1. Zhang Chengxian, "Wenhua dageming chuqide Beida gongzuozu" (Peking University Work Teams at the Beginning of the Great Cultural Revolution), *Zhonggong dangshi ziliao*, no. 70 (June 1999), 17.

2. In 1972 Britain's Granada TV made a docudrama based on the transcript of Wang

Guangmei's "trial" titled *The Subject of Struggle*. Playing the role of Wang Guangmei was the Shanghai-born actress Tsai Chin, whose father, the renowned Beijing Opera star Zhou Xinfang, had played Hai Rui on the Shanghai stage before the Cultural Revolution; Tsai Chin, *Daughter of Shanghai* (New York: St. Martin's, 1988), pp. 163–169.

3. Cheng Chao and Wei Haoben, eds., *Zhejiang "Wenge" jishi* (Factual Record of the "Cultural Revolution" in Zhejiang) (Hangzhou: Zhejiang fangzhi bianjibu, 1989), p. 3.

4. Wang Shaoguang, *Failure of Charisma: The Cultural Revolution in Wuhan* (Hong Kong: Oxford University Press, 1995), pp. 54–59.

5. *Dazibao xuan* (Selected Big-Character Posters) (Beijing: Peking University), extra issue, no. 2 (August 1, 1966), 40.

6. Zhongguo renmin daxue Xin renda gongshe and Mao Zedong sixiang hongweibing, *Fangeming xiuzhengzhuyi fenzi Guo Yingqiu*, 1: 113, 122.

7. Geming zaofan zongbu zhenli zhandoudui, ed., *Youdianbu jiguan wenhua dageming yundong shiliao* (Materials on the History of the Great Cultural Revolution Movement in the Organs of the Ministry of Posts and Telecommunications) (Beijing, 1967), p. 3.

8. Xin shida wenge chouweihui, ed., *Zai wuchanjieji wenhua dageming zhong Cao Diqiu yanlun ji* (Utterances by Cao Diqiu in the Course of the Great Proletarian Cultural Revolution) (Shanghai, 1966), 1: 1, 27.

9. *Shanghai "Wenhua dageming" shihua*, 1: 35–37.

10. *Zhou Enlai nianpu*, 3: 47; Beijing jingji xueyuan wuchanjieji geming zaofantuan et al., eds., *Wuchanjieji wenhua dageming cankao ziliao* (Reference Materials on the Great Proletarian Cultural Revolution), 4 vols. (Beijing, 1967), 4: *fang.*

11. Gao Yuan, *Born Red: A Chronicle of the Cultural Revolution* (Stanford: Stanford University Press, 1987), p. 48; Zhai Zhenhua, *Red Flower of China* (New York: Soho, 1992), p. 71.

12. *Dazibao xuan*, no. 17 (August 8, 1966), 12.

13. Ibid., no. 8 (July 2, 1966), 70–71.

14. *Qinghua daxue dazibao xuanbian*, no. 25 (July 28, 1966), 19.

15. Ibid., no. 27 (August 16, 1966), 23–26.

16. *Dazibao xuan*, no. 6(?) [cover missing] (July 1966), 38.

17. Ibid., p. 32.

18. *Qinghua daxue dazibao xuanbian*, no. ? [cover missing] (August 1966), 21–23.

19. Ibid., p. 25.

20. Ibid., p. 21.

21. *Shehuizhuyi wenhua dageming dazibao xuanbian* (Selection of Big-Character Posters of the Socialist Great Cultural Revolution) (Beijing: Municipal Party Committee Organs), no. 95 (June 2, 1966), 1.

22. Ibid., p. 3.

23. Dazibao bianjizu, ed., *Gaojiaobu wenhua dageming dazibao xuanji* (Selection of Big-Character Posters of the Great Cultural Revolution in the Ministry of Higher Education), no. 13 (1966), 35.

24. *Wuchanjieji wenhua dageming dazibao xuanbian* (Selection of Big-Character Posters of the Great Proletarian Cultural Revolution) (Beijing: Guojia kewei jiguan, 1968), no. 9, 9.

25. Beijing shi geming weiyuanhui di er xuexiban dangwei, "Guanyu dui Wang XX de wenti fucha qingkuang" (On the Situation of the Reinvestigation of the Problems of Wang XX), 1973, Schoenhals collection.

26. *Liu Shaoqi nianpu*, 2: 640; *Dazibao xuan*, no. 2 (1966), 23. Of the countless formal instructions of this kind issued by the central authorities during the Cultural Revolution, the "Eight Points" are exceptional in that no firmly fixed original version of them exists. Every senior and junior official who invoked them over the weeks that followed had his or her own version of them. But clearly the emphasis was on secrecy and control.

27. Bu Weihua, "Beijing hongweibing yundong dashiji" (Record of Important Events in the Beijing Red Guard Movement), *Beijing dangshi yanjiu* (Beijing Party History Research), no. 1 (1994), 56.

28. Qinghua daxue Jinggangshan hongweibing xuanchuandui, ed., *Qinghua daxue Kuai Dafu tongxue dazibao xuan* (Selected Big-Character Posters by Tsinghua University Student Kuai Dafu) (Guiyang, 1967), p. 41.

29. Ibid., p. 4.

30. *Guangxi wenge dashi nianbiao* (Chronological Record of Major Events in the Cultural Revolution in Guangxi) (Nanning: Guangxi renmin chubanshe, 1990), p. 2.

31. Qinghua daxue Jinggangshan bingtuan dazibao bianweihui, ed., *Dadao fangeming xiuzhengzhuyi fenzi Bo Yibo* (Down with the Counterrevolutionary Revisionist Element Bo Yibo) (Beijing, 1967), p. 4.

32. Renmin chubanshe ziliaoshi, ed., *Pipan ziliao: Zhongguo Heluxiaofu Liu Shaoqi fangeming xiuzhengzhuyi yanlun ji* (Collected Counterrevolutionary Revisionist Utterances by China's Khrushchev Liu Shaoqi), 3 vols. (Beijing, 1968), 3: 679.

33. Beijing daxue wenhua geming weiyuanhui xuanchuanzu, *Beijing daxue wuchanjieji wenhua dageming yundong jianjie*, p. 7.

34. Yue Daiyun and Carolyn Wakeman, *To the Storm* (Berkeley: University of California Press, 1985), pp. 156–160.

35. *Selected Works of Mao Tse-tung*, 4 vols. (Peking: Foreign Languages Press, 1965), 1: 28.

36. Renmin chubanshe ziliaoshi, *Pipan ziliao*, 3: 664–665.

37. *Liu Shaoqi nianpu*, 2: 642; Huang Zheng, *Liu Shaoqide zuihou suiyue*, p. 67.

38. *Dazibao xuan,* extra issue, no. 2 (August 1, 1966), 52.

39. Ibid., p. 64.

40. Beijing shi huaxue gongyeju jiguan hongse xuanchuanzhan, ed., *Wuchanjieji wenhua dageming ziliao* (Materials on the Great Proletarian Cultural Revolution), 4 vols. (Beijing, 1966), 1: 21.

41. *Dazibao xuan,* extra issue, no. 2 (August 1, 1966), 58.

42. *Liu Shaoqi nianpu,* 2: 644–645.

43. *Mao Zedong sixiang de guanghui zhaoyaozhe zhongyang guangbo shiyeju* (The Brilliant Rays of Mao Zedong Thought Illuminate the Central Broadcasting Administration) (Beijing: Zhongyang guangbo shiyeju "Wuchanjieji gemingpai lianhe zongbu," 1968), pp. 4–6.

44. Ibid., p. 5.

45. Renmin chubanshe ziliaoshi, *Pipan ziliao,* 3: 694.

46. Shanghai jixie xueyuan geming weiyuanhui "Hongse tingjinjun," *Shede yishen gua,* 1: 27.

47. Huang Zheng, "Liu Shaoqi yu 'Wenge' chuqide gongzuozu shijian" (Liu Shaoqi and the Work Team Incident at the Beginning of the "Cultural Revolution"), in Dangde wenxian bianjibu, ed., *Zhonggong dangshi zhongda shijian shushi* (True Accounts of Important Events in the History of the CCP) (Beijing: Renmin chubanshe, 1993), p. 256.

48. *Jianguo yilai Mao Zedong wengao,* 12: 69.

49. Wang Li, "An Insider's Account of the Cultural Revolution: Wang Li's Memoirs," *Chinese Law and Government,* 27, no. 6 (November–December 1994), 15.

50. Zhou Enlai had attended meetings summoned by Liu on July 1, 2, 4, 5, and 7; *Zhou Enlai nianpu,* 3: 39, 40.

51. Liao Shiyu, "1966 nian, Mao Zedong xiata dishuidong" (Mao Zedong's 1966 Stay in Dishuidong), in Zhonggong Xiangtan shiwei dangshi ziliao zhengji bangongshi, ed., *Mao Zedong yu Xiangtan* (Mao Zedong and Xiangtan) (Beijing: Zhonggong dangshi chubanshe, 1993), p. 346.

52. Luo Diandian, "Luo zongzhang mengnan jishi," p. 207.

53. Qian Mu, quoted in Silas H. L. Wu, *Communication and Imperial Control in China: Evolution of the Palace Memorial System, 1693–1735* (Cambridge, Mass.: Harvard University Press, 1970), p. 6.

54. Frederic Wakeman Jr., *Spymaster: Dai Li and the Chinese Secret Service* (Berkeley: University of California Press, 2003), p. 5.

55. On the CCP's network of "eyes and ears," see Luo Ruiqing, "Zai quanguo jingji baowei gongzuo huiyi shangde zongjie baogao" (Summing-Up Report at the National Economic Protection Work Conference), in *Gongan baowei gongzuo* (Public Security and Protection Work), no. 18 (June 1, 1950), 4–24.

56. Michael Schoenhals, "Elite Information in China," *Problems of Communism*, 34 (September–October 1985), 65–71.

57. See Zhonggong zhongyang wenxian yanjiushi, ed., *Chen Yun nianpu (1905–1995)* (Chronicle of the Life of Chen Yun [1905–1995]), 3 vols. (Beijing: Zhongyang wenxian chubanshe, 2000) (hereafter *Chen Yun nianpu*), 3: 145. Individual readers would all have had their own personal policy preferences and hence reasons to complain about the coverage provided by *Internal Reference*. Deng Xiaoping thought that issues of *Internal Reference* resembled big-character posters: "What's in them counts, and then again doesn't. You may trust what's reported in *Internal Reference*, but you don't have to." Mao criticized *Internal Reference* in 1962 for publishing "so many texts about the rural household responsibility system" and questioned the "orientation" of its publisher; *Mao Zedong sixiang wan sui* (Long Live Mao Zedong Thought) ([Shanghai?], [1968?]), p. 38. Two years later, Peng Zhen praised *Internal Reference* for those very same texts, insisting that they had expressed the "bias [*qingxiangxing*] of the 'sober-minded promoter of progress'"; Beijing ribao wenhua geming yundong bangongshi, ed., *Peng Zhen dui jiu "Beijing ribao" gongzuode hei zhishi* (Peng Zhen's Sinister Instructions on the Work of the Old "Beijing Daily") (Beijing, 1967), p. 7. The expression "sober-minded promoter of progress" was one Mao had coined at the height of the GLF. Whatever their personal views, all members of the CCP leadership continued to read *Internal Reference* regularly.

58. Chengjianju shuini chengpinchang gongren geming zaofandui, ed., *Dadao fangeming xiuzhengzhuyi fenzi Chen Pixian* (Down with Counterrevolutionary Revisionist Element Chen Pixian) (Shanghai, 1967), 1: 21.

59. *Mao Zedong sixiang wan sui (1958–59)* (Long Live Mao Zedong Thought [1958–1959]) (n.p., n.d.), p. 158.

60. Mu Xin, *Ban "Guangming ribao" shinian zishu*, p. 290.

61. Idem, *Jiehou changyi: Shinian dongluan jishi* (Thoughts after the Crisis: A Chronicle of the Decade of Upheaval) (Hong Kong: Xintian chubanshe, 1997), pp. 376–378.

62. Cheng Qian, item no. 2: "Zhongyang wenge xiaozude yi xiang jianyi," in "'Wenge' mantan."

63. *Chen Pixian fandang fanshehuizhuyi zuixing cailiao zhaibian* (Selected Material Documenting Chen Pixian's Anti-Party and Anti-Socialist Crimes) (Shanghai, 1967), p. 36.

64. Li Jinchuan, "Huiyi zhongyang wenge jizhe zhan" (Remembering the Central Cultural Revolution Group's Journalists' Station), *Bainian chao*, no. 5 (2002), 12–17; Michael Schoenhals, "Xinxi, juece he Zhongguo de 'wenhua dageming'" (Information, Decision-Making and China's "Great Cultural Revolution"), in *Paper*

Collection: *International Senior Forum on Contemporary History of China: Contemporary China and Its Outside World* (Beijing: Contemporary China Research Institute, 2004), pp. 40–56.

65. Wuhan is the capital of Hubei province. Hubei zhengfa shizhi bianxuan weiyuanhui, ed., *Hubei zhengfa dashiji, 1838–1986* (A Record of Major Events in Politics and Law in Hubei, 1838–1986) (Wuhan: Hubei zhengfa shizhi bianxuan weiyuanhui, 1987), pp. 112–113. See also James T. Myers, Jürgen Domes, and Erik von Groeling, eds., *Chinese Politics: Documents and Analysis*, 4 vols. (Columbia: University of South Carolina Press, 1986), 1: 250–255. Wang Renzhong used the opportunity of Mao's visit to show him his directive to the Hubei party ordering a counterattack on student "rightists," to which the Chairman vouchsafed no objection; Wang Shaoguang, *Failure of Charisma*, p. 59.

66. See "Quarterly Chronicle and Documentation," *CQ*, no. 28 (October–December 1966), 149–152.

67. *Cankao xiaoxi*, July 26, 1966. The *People's Daily* reported Mao's swim on July 26. In Changsha, the capital of Mao's home province of Hunan, the swimming issue was distributed free, and long lines queued up to get it; Liang Heng and Judith Shapiro, *Son of the Revolution* (New York: Knopf, 1983), p. 43.

68. Mu Xin, *Jiehou changyi*, p. 146.

69. The villas were numbered consecutively, but "out of respect for the customs of the foreign dignitaries" none bore the "unlucky" numbers 1, 4, and 13. Hence our occasional references to villas nos. 16, 17, and 18. See Shu Jun, ed., *Diaoyutai lishi dang'an* (Diaoyutai Historical Archives) (Beijing: Zhonggong zhongyang dangxiao chubanshe, 1999), p. 130.

70. Mu Xin, "Guanyu gongzuozu cunfei wenti" (On the Issue of Maintaining or Withdrawing the Work Teams), in Zhang Hua and Su Caiqing, *Huishou "Wenge,"* 2: 643; Quan Yanchi, *Tao Zhu zai "Wenhua dageming" zhong*, p. 99.

71. Youdianbu wenhua geming bangongshi, ed., *Youdianbu wenhua dageming dashiji* (Record of Major Events during the Great Cultural Revolution in the Ministry of Posts and Telecommunications) (Beijing, 1966), pp. 10–11; Zhang Chengxian, "'Wenhua dageming' chuqide Beida gongzuozu," p. 33.

72. Huang Zheng, "Liu Shaoqi yu 'Wenge' chuqide gongzuozu shijian," p. 256.

73. Ibid., p. 257.

74. *Zhou Enlai nianpu*, 3: 41.

75. No indication is given in ibid.

76. *Liu Shaoqi nianpu*, 2: 645–646; Ma Qibin et al., *Zhongguo gongchandang zhizheng sishinian*, p. 272.

77. *Zhou Enlai nianpu*, 3: 41–42.

78. *Wang Li fansi lu*, 2: 611.

79. Huang Zheng, *Liu Shaoqide zuihou suiyue*, p. 68.

80. There appear to have been four successive meetings: on July 24: (1) Liu Shaoqi's report meeting, attendance at which is unclear; and (2) a meeting with the PSC and the CCRG; (3) on July 25, a meeting with CCP regional bureau leaders and the CCRG; (4) on July 26 with the entire CCRG. See ibid.; Ma Qibin et al., *Zhongguo gongchandang zhizheng sishinian*, p. 272; *Liu Shaoqi nianpu*, 2: 646; Su Donghai and Fang Kongmu, *Zhonghua renmin gongheguo fengyun shilu*, 1: 1059.

81. Mu Xin, "Guanyu gongzuozu cunfei wenti," pp. 642–645.

82. *Mao Zedong sixiang wan sui (1960–1967)*, p. 165.

83. Quan Yanchi, *Tao Zhu zai "Wenhua dageming" zhong*, p. 100.

84. Mu Xin, "Guanyu gongzuozu cunfei wenti," p. 644.

85. Ibid., p. 646; Beijing shi huaxue gongyeju jiguan hongse xuanchuanzhan, *Wuchanjieji wenhua dageming ziliao*, 1: 63–64.

86. Ibid., 2: 22.

87. Less than a month later, at the suggestion of Chen Boda and Kang Sheng, Mao agreed that Li Xuefeng should revert to being simply North China first secretary and cede his concurrent Beijing first secretaryship (though not immediately the title) to the then second secretary, Wu De (who would retain that post throughout the Cultural Revolution). On December 16 Li self-criticized before the North China Region for his leadership during the fifty days. Mao approved his speech, and it was distributed to encourage others to emulate Li; *Jianguo yilai Mao Zedong wengao*, 12: 103–104, 177–179.

88. Renmin chubanshe ziliaoshi, *Pipan ziliao*, 3: 702.

89. Ibid., p. 706.

90. Li Zhisui, *The Private Life of Chairman Mao*, pp. 469–470.

91. On August 7 Mao had the PLA General Political Department issue a telegram withdrawing the work teams that had been sent to military academies and schools; Ma Qibin et al., *Zhongguo gongchandang zhizheng sishinian*, p. 274.

92. In China, at least, the Mensheviks defeated the Bolsheviks.

5. Mao's New Successor

1. Though devoted exclusively to news from foreign sources, the paper had developed a technique of using highly selective translations and its own headlines to allow it to function effectively as a domestic propaganda tool. (China's late-nineteenth-century reformers would have recognized the technique as one of "making foreign things serve China" [*yang wei Zhong yong*].) Mao had naturally always figured prominently in *Reference News* headlines for years, but so too had Liu Shaoqi. For instance, on April 3, 1966, the headline across the top of the paper's front page, accompanying excerpts from an article in a Swiss Leninist journal, had read, in praise of Liu's book: "*How to Be a Good Communist* is the source of

power." The final acknowledgment of Liu in the headline on July 27 referred to his message in support of the North Vietnamese in their war against the United States as read out at a rally of nearly a million people in Tiananmen Square on July 22; it read: "The West regards Chairman Liu's statement as immensely significant."

2. Attendance at "normal" plenums after the Second Session of the Eighth Congress averaged 165.5. Only in the case of the Eighth Plenum in 1959, when, as in 1966, it was clear in advance that top leaders' heads would roll, did the number of attendees drop to 149. Deaths cannot account for the fall in attendance at the Eleventh Plenum from attendance at the Tenth, for only three CC members died between those sessions.

3. Liu Tao, in Shanghai jixie xueyuan geming weiyuanhui "Hongse tingjinjun," *Shede yishen gua*, 1: 35.

4. For a photograph of the proceedings showing the PSC at a table facing the rest of the CC, with Mao placed so that he has Zhou Enlai and Lin Biao (who appears to be chairing the session) between him and Liu Shaoqi, see Yang Kelin, ed., *Wenhua dageming bowuguan* (Museum of the Great Cultural Revolution), 2 vols. (Hong Kong: Dongfang chubanshe and Tiandi tushu, 1995), 1: 210–211.

5. Over previous months that nomenclature had been used along with "Cultural Revolution," "Great Cultural Revolution," and "Great Socialist Cultural Revolution."

6. Ma Qibin et al., *Zhongguo gongchandang zhizheng sishinian*, p. 273.

7. Liao Gailong, *Xin Zhongguo biannianshi*, p. 276.

8. *Hu Qiaomu tan Zhonggong dangshi* (Hu Qiaomu on the History of the CCP) (Beijing: Renmin chubanshe, 1999), p. 135.

9. Mao's letter is translated in Stuart Schram, ed., *Mao Tse-tung Unrehearsed* (Harmondsworth: Penguin, 1974), pp. 260–261; a photograph of its first page in Mao's handwriting is in Pang Xianzhi and Jin Chongji, *Mao Zedong zhuan*, 2: 1435. In the letter, Mao also praised Beida Middle School Red Guards, the "Red Flag Combat Team." The Tsinghua posters are in Guofang daxue, "*Wenhua dageming,*" 1: 63–65.

10. Beijing shi huaxue gongyeju jiguan hongse xuanchuanzhan, *Wuchanjieji wenhua dageming ziliao*, 2: 29.

11. Hongdaihui Beijing jianzhu gongye xueyuan 8.1 zhandoutuan, ed., *Jianjue ba Liu Shaoqi jiuhui Beijing jiangong xueyuan doudao douchou* (Resolve to Drag Liu Shaoqi Back to the Beijing Building College to Topple and Discredit Him) (Beijing, 1967), p. 40.

12. Huang Zheng, *Liu Shaoqide zuihou suiyue*, pp. 69–70; *Liu Shaoqi nianpu*, 2: 647–648. Liu's speeches at the college are translated in *Collected Works of Liu Shao-ch'i, 1958–1967* (Hong Kong: Union Research Institute, 1968), pp. 331–355.

13. Wang Nianyi, *Da dongluande niandai*, p. 52.

14. Ibid., pp. 52–53.

15. Mu Xin, *Jiehou changyi*, p. 56.

16. Wang Nianyi, *Da dongluande niandai*, pp. 52–53.

17. *Jianguo yilai Mao Zedong wengao*, 12: 93.

18. Wang Nianyi, *Da dongluande niandai*, pp. 54–55; Guofang daxue, *"Wenhua dageming,"* 1: 70.

19. So instantly did its contents become known that one Beijing Red Guard mis-remembered it as being broadcast to the whole country on August 5; Zhai Zhenhua, *Red Flower of China*, p. 71. But on December 25 Mao refused to let it be quoted in a New Year's Day editorial; *Jianguo yilai Mao Zedong wengao*, 12: 176.

20. Wang Nianyi, *Da dongluande niandai*, p. 55. Xie had been serving under Deng Xiaoping in the Second Field Army on the eve of the Communist revolution, but he now claimed that after the victory, Deng had "changed."

21. *Zhou Enlai nianpu*, 2: 46. Zhou also instructed his duty secretary to get him at any hour if Mao wanted him.

22. Beijing boli zongchang hongweibing lianluozhan, *Zhongyang shouzhang jianghua*, 4: 273–274.

23. Wang Nianyi ms., p. 86.

24. Tu Men and Kong Di, *Gongheguo zuida yuanan* (The Biggest Unjust Case in the Republic) (Beijing: Falü chubanshe, 1993), pp. 22–25. Niu Dayong, original ms. on Lei Yingfu, p. 11, Schoenhals collection. In the published version (Cheng Hua, *Zhou Enlai he tade mishumen* [Zhou Enlai and His Secretaries] [Beijing: Zhongguo guangbo dianshi chubanshe, 1992]), this information was removed.

25. Wang Nianyi, *Da dongluande niandai*, p. 58.

26. *Jianguo yilai Mao Zedong wengao*, 12: 81.

27. *Decision of the Central Committee of the Chinese Communist Party concerning the Great Proletarian Cultural Revolution* (Peking: Foreign Languages Press, 1966) (hereafter *Decision on the CR*), p. 1.

28. Gao Yuan, *Born Red*, p. 86.

29. *Decision on the CR*, p. 5; emphasis added.

30. Ibid., pp. 4–5.

31. Ibid., p. 42.

32. *Hongri zhao Tianshan: Guanyu Xinjiang wenti Zhonggong zhongyang wenjian ji zhongyang shouzhangde jianghua huibian* (Red Sun Shines on the Tianshan Range: Collected Central Documents and Central Leaders' Speeches on the Xinjiang Issue) (Urümqi: Xinjiang hong er si "Xinjiang hongweibing bao" bianjibu, 1968), p. 1.

33. Beijing shi huaxue gongyeju jiguan hongse xuanchuanzhan, *Wuchanjieji wenhua dageming ziliao*, 3: 226.

34. It is instructive to review his activities for the years 1963–1976 as contained in *Chen Yun nianpu*, vol. 2.

35. Wang Nianyi, interview by Michael Schoenhals, Beijing, January 20, 1993.

36. *Zhou Enlai nianpu*, 3: 46.

37. This strong support for Deng, which presumably included Mao's own vote, may have reflected the fact that the CC members present remembered the extraordinary tribute that Mao had paid to Deng's fairness and ability in 1956 at a preparatory meeting for the Eighth Congress, at which Deng would become general secretary; Shi Zhongquan et al., eds., *Zhonggong ba da shi* (The History of the CCP's Eighth Congress) (Beijing: Renmin chubanshe, 1998), p. 137.

38. *Wang Li fansi lu*, 2: 617.

39. Ibid., pp. 667–668.

40. *Zhongguo gongchandang zuzhishi ziliao*, 9: 63; 10: 68–69.

41. Wang Zongbai, "Zhang Jichun" (Zhang Jichun), in *Zhonggong dangshi renwu zhuan*, 23 (pub. 1985): 337–338.

42. *Zhongguo gongchandang zuzhishi ziliao*, 10: 69.

43. Shanghai shi geming weiyuanhui jiedaizu, ed., *Xuexi ziliao* (Study Materials), no. 18 (December 19, 1967).

44. *Zhongguo gongchandang zuzhishi ziliao*, 9: 61; 10: 70–71.

45. *Dongtai*, no. 140 (September 3, 1967).

46. Nie Yuanzi, interview by Schoenhals, July 17, 1994; *Nie Yuanzi huiyilu* (The Memoirs of Nie Yuanzi) (Hong Kong: Shidai guoji chuban youxian gongsi, 2005), pp. 95–106.

47. *Zhongguo gongchandang zuzhishi ziliao*, 10: 70.

48. Beijing hangkong xueyuan "Hongqi," ed., *Wuchanjieji wenhua dageming shouzhang jianghua huiji (1967.1)* (Collected Speeches Made by Central Leaders in the Great Proletarian Cultural Revolution [January 1967]) (Beijing, 1967), p. 81.

49. Lu Yongdi and Liu Zijian, "Fang Fang" (Fang Fang), in *Zhonggong dangshi renwu zhuan*, 11 (pub. 1983): 367–368; Wang Xitang, "Zhang Jingwu" (Zhang Jingwu), in ibid., 49 (pub. 1991): 358.

50. *Zhongguo gongchandang zuzhishi ziliao*, 10: 72.

51. *Wang Li fansi lu*, 2: 621.

52. *Neibu cankao* (Internal Reference) (Beijing: First Ministry of Machine Building), no. 89 (May 24, 1967). For a review of Wang Jiaxiang's foreign-policy views that incurred Mao's displeasure, see *Origins*, 3: 269–273.

53. Xu Zehao, *Wang Jiaxiang zhuan*, p. 568, gives June 27, 1966, as the date of Liu Ningyi's appointment.

54. *Wang Li fansi lu*, 1: 228–235.

55. Cf. Lanzhou junqu zhengzhibu zuzhibu, ed., *Zuzhi gongzuo wenjian huibian di er*

ji: Dangwu gongzuo bufen (Collected Documents on Organization Work, Vol. 2: Party Work) (Lanzhou, 1980), pp. 398–399.

56. At the time, Kong's status as a senior intelligence official was not known to Western China specialists. Donald W. Klein and Anne B. Clark, *Biographic Dictionary of Chinese Communism, 1921–1965,* 2 vols. (Cambridge, Mass.: Harvard University Press, 1971), 1: 456–458, merely describes him as "one of the most important foreign trade specialists since the establishment of the PRC" and notes that "he is frequently present to entertain or negotiate with the many foreign visitors to Peking."

57. Wang Li, interview by Schoenhals, Beijing, May 1995.

58. *Wenge jianxun* (Cultural Revolution News in Brief) (Beijing: Institute of Politics and Law), no. 38 (February 8, 1967).

59. *Zhou Enlai nianpu,* 3: 138.

60. Li Ke and Hao Shengzhang, *"Wenhua dageming" zhongde renmin jiefangjun* (The PLA during the "Great Cultural Revolution") (Beijing: Zhonggong dangshi ziliao chubanshe, 1989), p. 351.

61. See *Chinese Communist Who's Who,* 2 vols. (Taipei: Institute of International Relations, 1971), 2: 69.

62. *Gaoju Mao Zedong sixiang weida hongqi,* p. 34.

63. Wang Nianyi, *Da dongluande niandai,* p. 62.

64. Record of conversation with former members of Lin staff, p. 4, in the authors' possession.

65. *Wang Li fansi lu,* 2: 941.

66. Record of conversation with former members of Lin staff, p. 10.

67. Guofang daxue, *"Wenhua dageming,"* 1: 26.

68. Beijing shi huaxue gongyeju jiguan hongse xuanchuanzhan, *Wuchanjieji wenhua dageming ziliao,* 1: 33.

69. Kenneth Lieberthal, *Governing China* (New York: Norton, 1995), p. 190.

70. Michael Schoenhals, "New Texts: Speeches at the Ninth National Congress of the Chinese Communist Party," *Stockholm Journal of East Asian Studies,* 2 (1990), 96.

71. Yang Yinlu, "Jiang Qing de 'nü huang' shenghuo (er)" (Jiang Qing's Life as an "Empress" [2]), *Bainian chao,* no. 6 (1998), 65–66; Yang Yinlu, "Chu jian Jiang Qing: Wo gei Jiang Qing dang mishu (yi)" (My First Meeting with Jiang Qing: I was Jiang Qing's Secretary [1]), ibid., no. 5 (1998), 56.

72. Beijing gongye xueyuan yundong bangongshi, ed., *Dazibao xuanbian* (Selected Big-Character Posters) (Beijing, 1976), 2: 16.

73. Mu Xin, *Jiehou changyi,* p. 368.

74. Wang Li, "An Insider's Account of the Cultural Revolution," 40–41.

75. Mu Xin, "Guanyu 'zhongyang wenge xiaozu' de yixie qingkuang" (Some Circum-

stances about the "Central Cultural Revolution Group"), *Zhonggong dangshi ziliao,* no. 69 (1999), 86, 88.

76. *Zhou Enlai nianpu,* 3: 183.

77. Hong Yung Lee, *The Politics of the Chinese Cultural Revolution* (Berkeley: University of California Press, 1978), pp. 4–5.

78. Wang Naiying, "Jiaodai" (Confession), September 1, 1970, p. 10 of original handwritten text, Schoenhals collection.

79. Kang Sheng, who was charged with preparing the plenum's final communiqué, included a sentence in his first draft, delivered on August 5, that Mao excised: "The plenum enthusiastically supported the declaration made by comrade Liu Shaoqi on behalf of our country." Kang was referring to the pledge of support for North Vietnam against the United States made by Liu on July 22 (see above, note 1); see *Jianguo yilai Mao Zedong wengao,* 12: 94–97. At the time of preparation, Kang might not have been sure of Liu's ultimate fate or he may have included the sentence as a way of ascertaining Mao's views.

6. The Red Guards

1. Even in English (and other Western languages) there is a considerable literature on the Red Guard movement. A number of Red Guards and a few of their victims have published memoirs, and some scholars have written analyses. See, for instance, Gordon A. Bennett and Ronald N. Montaperto, *Red Guard: The Political Biography of Dai Hsiao-ai* (London: Allen & Unwin, 1971); Anita Chan, *Children of Mao* (Seattle: University of Washington Press, 1985); Jung Chang, *Wild Swans* (New York: Simon & Schuster, 1991); Nien Cheng, *Life and Death in Shanghai* (New York: Grove, 1986); Feng Jicai, *Voices from the Whirlwind* (New York: Pantheon, 1991); Gao Anhua, *To the Edge of the Sky* (London: Penguin, 2001); Gao Yuan, *Born Red;* Gong Xiaoxia, "Repressive Movements and the Politics of Victimization" (Ph.D. diss., Harvard University, 1995); Harry Harding, "The Chinese State in Crisis," in Roderick MacFarquhar, ed., *The Politics of China: Second Edition, The Eras of Mao and Deng* (New York: Cambridge University Press, 1997), pp. 148–247; William Hinton, *Hundred Day War: The Cultural Revolution at Tsinghua University* (New York: Monthly Review Press, 1972); Hua Linshan, *Les années rouges* (Paris: Seuil, 1987); Julia Kwong, *Cultural Revolution in China's Schools, May 1966–April 1969* (Stanford.: Hoover Institution Press, 1988); Hong Yung Lee, *The Politics of the Chinese Cultural Revolution;* Liang and Shapiro, *Son of the Revolution;* Ken Ling, *Red Guard: From Schoolboy to "Little General" in Mao's China* (London: Macdonald, 1972); Liu Hong, *Startling Moon* (London: Review, 2001); Ruth Earnshaw Lo and Katharine S. Kinderman, *In the Eye of the Typhoon* (New York: Harcourt Brace Jovanovich, 1980); Ma Bo, *Blood*

Red Sunset (New York: Viking, 1995); Anchee Min, *Red Azalea* (New York: Pantheon, 1994); Mu Aiping, *Vermilion Gate* (London: Abacus, 2002); Nee, *The Cultural Revolution at Peking University;* Sidney Rittenberg and Amanda Bennett, *The Man Who Stayed Behind* (New York: Simon & Schuster, 1993); Stanley Rosen, *Red Guard Factionalism and the Cultural Revolution in Guangzhou (Canton)* (Boulder: Westview, 1982); James R. Ross, *Caught in a Tornado* (Boston: Northeastern University Press, 1994); Michael Schoenhals, ed., *China's Cultural Revolution, 1966–1969: Not a Dinner Party* (Armonk, N.Y.: M. E. Sharpe, 1996); Susan L. Shirk, *Competitive Comrades* (Berkeley: University of California Press, 1982); Anne F. Thurston, *A Chinese Odyssey* (New York: Scribners, 1991); idem, *Enemies of the People* (New York: Knopf, 1987); Jonathan Unger, *Education under Mao* (New York: Columbia University Press, 1982); Andrew G. Walder, "The Communist Party and the Red Guards: Beijing 1966," paper presented at the conference "Turning Points: 1919 and 1989," Center for Chinese Studies, University of California, Berkeley, January 1997; Wang Youqin, *Wenge shounanzhe* (Victims of the Cultural Revolution) (Hong Kong: Kaifang zazhi chubanshe, 2004); idem, "Student Attacks against Teachers: The Revolution of 1966," paper presented at the conference "The Cultural Revolution in Retrospect," Hong Kong University of Science and Technology, July 1996; Ye Ting-xing, *A Leaf in the Bitter Wind* (Toronto: Doubleday, 2002); Yue and Wakeman, *To the Storm;* Zhai Zhenhua, *Red Flower of China;* Zhu Xiao Di, *Thirty Years in a Red House* (Amherst: University of Massachusetts Press, 1998). See also fictional accounts such as Chen Jo-hsi, *The Execution of Mayor Yin and Other Stories from the Great Proletarian Cultural Revolution* (Bloomington: Indiana University Press, 1978); Dai Sijie, *Balzac et la Petite Tailleuse chinoise* (Balzac and the Little Chinese Tailoress) (Paris: Gallimard, 2000), translated by Ina Rilke as *Balzac and the Little Chinese Seamstress* (London: Chatto & Windus, 2001); Anchee Min, *Becoming Madame Mao* (Boston: Houghton Mifflin, 2000); Lulu Wang, *The Lily Theater* (New York: Doubleday, 2000).

2. From a very reliable source seen by one of the authors.

3. *Mao Zedong sixiang wan sui,* p. 269.

4. Guofang daxue, *"Wenhua dageming,"* 1: 71–72.

5. *Mao Zedong sixiang wan sui,* p. 262.

6. Shoudu hongweibing di san silingbu Beijing youdian xueyuan "Dongfanghong" gongshe Chongfengdui, ed., *Beijing shi wuchanjieji wenhua dageming dashiji (1965.9–1967.1)* (Chronology of Major Events in the Beijing Municipality Great Proletarian Cultural Revolution [Sept. 1965–Jan. 1967]) (Beijing, 1967), p. 22.

7. *Peng Zhen guanyu siqing yundong de liu pian jianghua* (Six Speeches by Peng Zhen on the Four Cleanups Movement) (Beijing: Zhonggong Beijing shiwei bangongting, 1966), p. 6.

8. Beijing hangkong xueyuan "Hongqi," *Wuchanjieji wenhua dageming shouzhang jianghua huiji*, p. 372.

9. Sending Cao Yiou off to a middle school to foment support for Mao would probably have seemed ridiculous to most CCP leaders, and maybe they would have thought Mao had lost his sanity. As it was, the effort to mobilize on college campuses started in mid-May, whereas Mao endorsed the middle school movement only at the beginning of August.

10. Yu Hui, *Hongweibing mi lu* (Secret Records of the Red Guards) (Beijing: Tuanjie chubanshe, 1993), pp. 8–9, translated in Gong Xiaoxia, "Repressive Movements and the Politics of Victimization," pp. 142–143.

11. Untitled Red Guard poster, Schoenhals collection.

12. For a list of some of the more important dismissals occurring in Nanjing, Wuhan, Xi'an, Jiangsu, Qinghai, Shandong, Zhejiang, Henan, Guizhou, Sichuan, Guangxi, and Jiangxi, see "Quarterly Chronicle and Documentation," *CQ*, no. 27 (July–September 1966), 214.

13. Zhai Zhenhua, *Red Flower of China*, pp. 61–62.

14. X X X, interview by Michael Schoenhals, Cambridge, Mass., April 8, 1992; Schram, *Mao Tse-tung Unrehearsed*, p. 260.

15. Zhai Zhenhua, *Red Flower of China*, pp. 64–66.

16. X X X, interview by Schoenhals, Cambridge, Mass., April 8, 1992.

17. The texts of the first three posters were published in *Hongqi*, no. 11 (1966), and are reproduced in Guofang daxue, *"Wenhua dageming,"* 1: 63–65; the text of the lesser-known fourth and final poster is in *Hongweibing bao* (Red Guard Paper) (Beijing), September 28, 1966.

18. For penetrating analyses of the early Red Guard movement in Beijing, see Andrew G. Walder, "Beijing Red Guard Factionalism: Social Interpretations Reconsidered," *Journal of Asian Studies*, 61, no. 2 (May 2002), 437–471; idem, "Tan Lifu: A 'Reactionary' Red Guard in Historical Perspective," *CQ*, no. 180 (December 2004), 965–989.

19. Mao's remarks were reported by Wang Li. The memorandum is quoted in Cheng Qian, item no. 2: "Zhongyang wenge xiaozude yi xiang jianyi," in "'Wenge' mantan."

20. *Quotations from Chairman Mao Tse-tung* (Peking: Foreign Languages Press, 1966), p. 288; *Mao zhuxi yulu* (Quotations from Chairman Mao) (Beijing, 1966), p. 249.

21. *Mao Zedong sixiang wan sui (1958–59)* (Long Live Mao Zedong Thought [1958–59]) (n.p., n.d.), p. 86.

22. *Chen Boda tongzhi bufen zhuzuo zhuanji* (Special Collection of Selected Writings by Comrade Chen Boda) (n.p., n.d.), 2: 46–47; Chen Po-ta, "Grow Up Braving Storm and Stress," *Peking Review*, no. 35 (August 26, 1966), 10–11.

23. Zhai Zhenhua, *Red Flower of China*, pp. 84–87. Like all other recent memoirs of the Cultural Revolution, this snapshot may have been tinted by intervening developments.

24. "Quarterly Chronicle and Documentation," *CQ*, no. 28 (October–December 1966), 177–178.

25. *Jianguo yilai Mao Zedong wengao*, 12: 107.

26. For a picture of this occasion, see illustration number 1 and Yang Kelin, *Wenhua dageming bowuguan*, 1: 88. Song Binbin, who later got a Ph.D. in geology at the Massachusetts Institute of Technology and then worked for the Commonwealth of Massachusetts, was a student at the middle school attached to Beijing Normal University and the daughter of Song Renqiong, then first secretary of the party's Northeast Region and, as of the Eleventh Plenum, an alternate member of the Politburo. The use of red cloth for armbands and other purposes became so profligate that in February 1967, the State Council tried to restrict its use; *CCP Documents of the Great Proletarian Cultural Revolution, 1966–1967* (Hong Kong: Union Research Institute, 1968) (hereafter *CCP Documents*), pp. 339–340.

27. Zhai Zhenhua, *Red Flower of China*, pp. 88–89. See also Rittenberg and Bennett, *The Man Who Stayed Behind*, pp. 317–319.

28. Shanghai shi gonganju geming zaofan lianhe zhihuibu zhengzhibu zaofandui, ed., *Chedi jielu shi gonganju jiu dangzu yuyong gongju–jiu wenge bangongshi de taotian zuixing* (Thoroughly Expose the Royal Tool of the Municipal Bureau of the Public Security Party Group and the Heinous Crimes of the Old Cultural Revolution Office) (Shanghai, 1967), 2: 16.

29. *Jianguo yilai Mao Zedong wengao*, 12: 133. See also Li Zhisui, *The Private Life of Chairman Mao*, p. 92, where Mao's doctor recalls that on occasions like these the Chairman "was exhilarated by the crowds and their adulation and his energy always carried him through the event, but he often caught cold afterward."

30. Li Zhisui, *The Private Life of Chairman Mao*, p. 471.

31. *Pipan Liu, Deng luxian xin daibiao Tao Zhu dahui fayan* (Speeches at the Mass Rally to Denounce the New Representative of the Liu-Deng Line, Tao Zhu) (Beijing, 1967), pp. 59–60. It was customary to show pictures of two leaders together if they ranked next to each other; after the Eleventh Plenum, Deng ranked sixth, Kang Sheng seventh. The deputy director of the Propaganda Department lost his job over this photographic fiasco.

32. *Wang Li fansi lu*, 2: 709.

33. Ibid., pp. 622–623.

34. *Lin Biao wenxuan*, 2: 378; *Zhongyang fuze tongzhi guanyu wuchanjieji wenhua dagemingde jianghua (xubian)* (Speeches by Responsible Central Comrades concerning the Great Proleterian Cultural Revolution [2]) (n.p., 1967), p. 54. For photos of the Red Guard rallies in Beijing, see Yang Kelin, *Wenhua dageming*

bowuguan, 1: 84–101. For an example of the extreme discomfort of the journey to Beijing, see Ye Ting-xing, *A Leaf in the Bitter Wind*, pp. 93–98.

35. *Beijing shi jiedai lai-Jing chuanliande geming shisheng he hongweibing gongzuo zongjie* (Summary Report on the Reception Work of Beijing Municipality for Revolutionary Teachers, Students, and Red Guards Visiting Beijing to Exchange Revolutionary Experiences) (Beijing, 1967), pp. 1–3.

36. Lü Hong, "Wo ren hongweibing jiedai zongzhan zhanzhang de rizi" (My Days as Director of the Red Guard General Reception Station), *Yanhuang chunqiu*, no. 12 (1998), 44–45. One of Beijing's four stations was assigned exclusively to handling Red Guards, and another had to give them priority; see "Quarterly Chronicle and Documentation," *CQ*, no. 28 (October–December 1966), 185.

37. Ling, *Red Guard*, pp. 155–157. Under the generous assumption that only 10 million of the Red Guards came from out of town and that none stayed more than a week, the cost of food alone could have been 150 million yuan. For how one senior officer coped with his assignment to look after visiting Red Guards, see the account by his daughter, Mu Aiping, *Vermilion Gate*, pp. 338–340.

38. *Lin Biao wenxuan*, 2: 375.

39. Ling, *Red Guard*, pp. 157, 163.

40. The rallies were held on August 18 and 31, September 15, October 1 and 18, and November 3, 10–11, and 25–26; Yu Hui, *Hongweibing mi lu*, p. 393. (The figures are added up incorrectly.)

41. Schoenhals, *China's Cultural Revolution*, pp. 148–149.

42. Ibid., pp. 166–169.

43. Wang Li, "Lishi jiang xuangao wo wuzui" (History Will Pronounce Me Innocent), manuscript, Beijing, 1993, p. 7.

44. *Mao Zedong sixiang wan sui*, p. 278.

45. Jieke Keruyake, *Zai lushang* (On the Road) (Beijing: Zuojia chubanshe, 1962). A highly readable and informative anthology of recollections by participants is Liu Tao, ed., *Da chuanlian* (Great Exchange of Revolutionary Experiences) (Beijing: Zhishi chubanshe, 1993).

46. On Yan'an and the Cultural Revolution, see David E. Apter and Tony Saich, *Revolutionary Discourse in Mao's Republic* (Cambridge, Mass.: Harvard University Press, 1994).

47. Zhonggong Guangzhou shiwei dangshi yanjiushi, ed., *Zhonggong Guangzhou dangshi dashiji* (A Record of Major Events in the History of the CCP in Guangzhou) (Guangzhou: Guangdong renmin chubanshe, 1991), p. 286.

48. Dan Zeng, ed., *Dangdai Xizang jianshi* (A Short History of Contemporary Tibet) (Beijing: Dangdai Zhongguo chubanshe, 1996), pp. 270–271; *Zhonggong Xizang dangshi dashiji* (Record of Major Events in the History of the CCP in Tibet) (Lhasa: Xizang renmin chubanshe, 1995), p. 179.

49. Beijing shi huaxue gongyeju jiguan hongse xuanchuanzhan, *Wuchanjieji wenhua dageming ziliao*, 3: 76. The Beijing Workers' Gymnasium, located next door to the Workers' Stadium in the eastern outskirts of the city, was built in 1961 and had a seating capacity of about 15,000.

50. *Mao Zedong sixiang wan sui*, p. 277.

51. *Shanghai "Wenhua dageming" shihua*, 1: 81.

52. Neale Hunter, *Shanghai Journal: An Eyewitness Account of the Cultural Revolution* (Boston: Beacon, 1971), p. 107.

53. Rae Yang, *Spider Eaters: A Memoir* (Berkeley: University of California Press, 1997), p. 131.

54. Chinese diary no. 1, in the authors' possession. Something as simple and seemingly straightforward as the purchase of a Mao badge involved a number of taboos, including that of avoiding the verb "purchase" *(mai)* and substituting for it the expression "respectfully request" *(jingqing)*. Bargaining was strongly discouraged as lacking in "respect." When Chen Zhenqing—third granddaughter of CCP cofounder Chen Duxiu—set out to purchase a Mao badge at the beginning of the Cultural Revolution, she happened to remark that the price asked (six mao) was on the steep side and was promptly accused of being an "active counterrevolutionary"; Shangfang tongxun bianjishi, ed., *Chunfeng huayu ji* (Spring Wind Can Turn into Rain), 2 vols. (Beijing: Qunzhong chubanshe, 1981), 1: 453.

55. Li Youping, *Douzheng yu shenghuo* (Struggle and Life), 5 vols. (n.p., n.d.), 5: 30.

56. Wang XX, interview by Schoenhals, Stockholm, December 12, 1977.

57. Jin Lei, "Fasheng zai 1966–1976 niande teda ziran zaihai" (Extremely Serious Natural Disasters That Occurred in 1966–1976), *Dangdai Zhongguo shi yanjiu*, no. 4 (1997), 76.

58. Xin shida wenge chouweihui, *Cao Diqiu yanlun ji*, 1: 4.

59. Shoudu dazhuan yuanxiao hongweibing daibiao dahui Zhengfa gongshe, ed., *Zhongyang fuze tongzhi guanyu wuchanjieji wenhua dagemingde jianghua (bayue-shiyue)* (Speeches on the Great Proletarian Cultural Revolution by Responsible Comrades from the Center [August–October]) (Beijing, 1967), p. 22.

60. Zong houqinbu jiguan, *Wuchanjieji wenhua dageming wan sui* (Long Live the Great Proletarian Cultural Revolution) (Beijing, 1967), 1: 55, 148–149.

61. *Tongdie* (Diplomatic Note), August 24, 1966.

62. *Mingling* (Order), handbill, date largely illegible, Schoenhals collection.

63. *Gao quanshi tongxue shu* (Appeal to Fellow Students in All of Beijing), September 13, 1966.

64. *Huyu!! Tehao* (Appeal!! Special Issue), August 23, 1966.

65. *Zhou Enlai nianpu*, 2: 53.

66. *Cankao xiaoxi*, August 31, 1966.

67. Zou Huaxiang and Shi Jinyan, eds., *Zhongguo jinxiandai tushuguan shiye dashiji*

(Chronicle of China's Library Facilities in Modern Times) (Changsha: Hunan renmin chubanshe, 1988), p. 208.

68. "Quarterly Chronicle and Documentation" (October–December 1966), 180.

69. *Cankao xiaoxi,* September 16, 1966; emphasis added.

70. Schoenhals, *China's Cultural Revolution,* pp. 221–222.

71. Hebei Beijing shifan xueyuan Douzheng shenghuo bianjibu, *Wuchanjieji wenhua dageming ziliao huibian,* p. 480.

72. Zhai Zhenhua, *Red Flower of China,* p. 92. For similar activities in Wuhan, see Wang Shaoguang, *Failure of Charisma,* p. 71.

73. Rittenberg and Bennett, *The Man Who Stayed Behind,* pp. 319–322.

7. Red Terror

1. Sometimes the destruction of property was preemptive, proposed by residents' committees and carried out by the property owners themselves; *Zhi quanti ge jiashu* (To All Members of Revolutionary Families) ["Open Letter" from Yangfangdian No. 1 Residential Area Residents' Committee], August 29, 1966, Schoenhals collection.

2. "Beijing shi 'Wenhua dageming' dashiji, 1965–1967," p. 26. For a Red Guard's firsthand account of raids in Beijing, see Zhai Zhenhua, *Red Flower of China,* pp. 92–100.

3. Wang Nianyi, *Da dongluande niandai,* p. 71. For an account of a Shanghai raid by a victim, see Nien Cheng, *Life and Death in Shanghai,* pp. 69–95; see also Dong Zhujun, *Wode yige shiji* (My Century) (Beijing: Sanlian shudian, 1997), pp. 448–461.

4. Wang Nianyi, *Da dongluande niandai,* p. 71.

5. Elizabeth J. Perry and Li Xun, *Proletarian Power: Shanghai in the Cultural Revolution* (Boulder: Westview, 1997), p. 12; the authors note that these figures cover only the items turned over to the Bank of China and probably represented a small fraction of the total confiscated. For Wuhan figures, see Wang Shaoguang, *Failure of Charisma,* p. 72.

6. Wang Nianyi, *Da dongluande niandai,* p. 71.

7. See Nien Cheng, *Life and Death in Shanghai,* pp. 504–513.

8. Quoted in Hongdaihui xin beida fuzhong Jinggangshan bingtuan zongbu, ed., *Dazibao xuan* (Selected Big-Character Posters) (Beijing, 1967), p. 23. The claim that confiscated moneys could be used for genuine Red Guard activities was confirmed by the center in March 1967; Guofang daxue, *"Wenhua dageming,"* 1: 362.

9. Chinese diary no. 10, in the authors' possession.

10. For a description of the incident at Zhang's house, see the account by his daughter, Zhang Hanzhi, *Feng yu qing: Yi fuqin, yi Zhuxi, yi Guanhua* (Emotions in

Hardships: Remembering Father, the Chairman, and [husband Qiao] Guanhua) (Shanghai: Shanghai wenyi chubanshe, 1994), pp. 51–56. Her account of Mao's debt to her father is on p. 45. For Mao's order to Zhou, see *Jianguo yilai Mao Zedong wengao*, 12: 116–117; for the Mao-Zhang relationship see also Lu Haijiang and He Mingzhou, eds., *Mao Zedong he ta tongshidaide ren* (Mao Zedong and His Contemporaries) (Zhengzhou: Henan renmin chubanshe, 1992), pp. 356–361. Three of Mao's letters to Zhang are included in the collection *Mao Zedong shuxin xuanji* (Selection of Mao Zedong's Letters) (Beijing: Renmin chubanshe, 1983), pp. 559–561, 601–603. For Mao's seventieth birthday, see *Origins*, 3: 635, n. 128. For Zhou's actions, see *Zhou Enlai nianpu*, 3: 53–54; *Selected Works of Zhou Enlai*, 2 vols. (Beijing: Foreign Languages Press, 1981, 1989), 2: 470–471. Zhang Shizhao had his house trashed twice by students when serving as minister of education in the Duan Qirui warlord government in 1925; Howard L. Boorman, ed., *Biographical Dictionary of Republican China*, 5 vols. (New York: Columbia University Press, 1967–1979), 1: 107.

11. *Xuexi ziliao* (Study Materials) (Beijing: Tsinghua University Jinggangshan News Agency), no. 857 (December 6, 1967).

12. For photographs of Red Guards destroying cultural artifacts, see Yang Kelin, *Wenhua dageming bowuguan*, 1: 152–165.

13. *Zhou Enlai nianpu*, 3: 50, 52, 54, 57, 70, 91.

14. Beijing jingji xueyuan wuchanjieji geming zaofantuan et al., *Wuchanjieji wenhua dageming cankao ziliao*, 4: 9–10.

15. Thurston, *Enemies of the People*, pp. 102–103; Wang Nianyi, *Da dongluande niandai*, pp. 118–119.

16. Quanguo chedi daohui Kongjiadian shuli Mao Zedong sixiang juedui quanwei geming zaofan lianluozhan, ed., *Gaoju Mao Zedong sixiang weida hongqi, chedi qingsuan zun-Kong fugu de fangeming zuixing—Qufu xian pinxiazhongnong yong jieji douzheng xuelei shi tongchi Kong laoer de tuzi tusun* (Hold Aloft the Great Red Banner of Mao Zedong Thought and Thoroughly Eradicate the Counterrevolutionary Crimes of Confucius-Veneration and Restoration of Ancient Ways—The Poor and Lower-Middle Peasants of Qufu County Use Class Struggle to Bitterly Denounce the Second Son of the Kong Family, His Hangers-on, and Their Spawn) (n.p., [1966]), p. 13.

17. Wang Naiying, "Jiao xitong de jiefa cailiao" (Fairly Systematic Revelations), January 13, 1968, p. 25, manuscript, Schoenhals collection.

18. As part of the campaign against a film on Wu Xun's life, an investigation commission visited his birthplace in 1951, but did not attempt to destroy his grave. Instead, on the basis of interviews, it concluded that Wu Xun was villainous, feudalistic, and anti-people. See Theodore H. E. Chen, *Thought Reform of the Chinese Intellectuals* (Hong Kong: Hong Kong University Press, 1960), pp. 38–42.

19. At the expanded Politburo session in May, Zhou had not only spoken up in favor of having the ashes of one of Mao's predecessors at the helm of the CCP, Qu Qiubai, thrown out of the Babaoshan Revolutionary Cemetery in western Beijing, but also called for the destruction of the Suzhou palace of Li Xiucheng, one of the military leaders of the Taiping Rebellion. Both men, Zhou had insisted, were "shameless" renegades; see Qinghai 8.18 geming zaofanpai lianhe weiyuanhui xuanchuanzu, *Ziliao xuanbian*, p. 13. Yet when Zhou got word that Red Guards had desecrated the family grave of KMT Generalissimo Chiang Kai-shek in Zhejiang, he immediately ordered the provincial leadership to repair and restore the grave. Moreover, Zhou arranged for photographs of the restored grave to be passed on to Chiang himself through Zhang Shizhao, via Hong Kong; see Yang Qinhua, "1978 nianqian haixia liang'an mouhe zuji shilu" (A Memoir of the Reconciliation-Seeking Process across the Taiwan Straits before 1978), *Yanhuang chunqiu*, no. 8 (1997), 23. The CCP still had hopes of some kind of future dealings with Chiang.

20. Foshan shi dang'anju, ed., *Foshan shi dashiji (1949–1989)* (A Record of Major Events in Foshan City [1949–1989]) (Foshan, 1991), p. 116.

21. Thurston, *Enemies of the People*, p. 101; Jung Chang, *Wild Swans*, p. 292.

22. Zou Huaxiang and Shi Jinyan, *Zhongguo jinxiandai tushuguan shiye dashiji*, pp. 212–231.

23. Beijing si zhong geming shisheng, "Tongling: Guanyu quzhu silei fenzide wuxiang mingling" (General Order: Five Orders on the Deportation of Four Kinds of Elements), August 24, 1966. When Zhou had submitted this idea to Mao on behalf of the Capital Work Team in May, the Chairman had rejected this kind of repatriation on the grounds that it was merely exporting the problem downward; Beijing daxue wenhua geming weiyuanhui ziliaozu, ed., *Wuchanjieji wenhua dageming cankao ziliao* (Great Proletarian Cultural Revolution Reference Materials) (Beijing, 1967), 3: 7; *Zhonghua renmin gongheguo zuzhi faze xuanbian* (Selected Organizational Laws and Regulations of the PRC) (Beijing: Jingji kexue chubanshe, 1985), pp. 204–205; "Shoudu hongweibing jiuchadui xicheng fendui zhihuibu di qi hao tongling" (General Order No. 7 of the Western City District Command of the Red Guard Pickets of the Capital), September 9, 1966; Beijing boli zongchang hongweibing lianluozhan, *Zhongyang shouzhang jianghua*, 1: 249; *Zhou Enlai nianpu*, 3: 33.

24. For example, the CC's Central Investigation Department, the Central Propaganda Department, the Ministry of Foreign Affairs, the Ministry of Construction Materials, and the Supreme People's Court.

25. Beijing daxue wenhua geming weiyuanhui ziliaozu, *Wuchanjieji wenhua dageming cankao ziliao*, 3: 7; *Zhonghua renmin gongheguo zuzhi faze xuanbian*, pp. 204–205.

26. Beijing daxue wenhua geming weiyuanhui ziliaozu, *Wuchanjieji wenhua dageming cankao ziliao,* 3: 7; Hongweibing Shanghai silingbu (Hong Shangsi), ed., *Zalan "liandong"* (Smash the "United Action Committee") (Shanghai, 1967), pp. 31–33.

27. *Wenge jianxun,* no. 14 (January 26, 1967).

28. Hebei Beijing shifan xueyuan, Douzheng shenghuo bianjibu, *Wuchanjieji wenhua dageming ziliao huibian,* pp. 146–147.

29. Beijing shi geming weiyuanhui di er xuexiban dangwei, "Guanyu Li Qinyao wentide fucha huibao cailiao" (Report Materials on the Reinvestigation of the Problems of Li Qinyao), April 26, 1972.

30. "Beijing shi 'Wenhua dageming' dashiji, 1965–1967," p. 24.

31. Wang Nianyi, *Da dongluande niandai,* p. 100.

32. "Beijing shi 'Wenhua dageming' dashiji, 1965–1967," p. 48.

33. Hebei Beijing shifan xueyuan, Douzheng shenghuo bianjibu, *Wuchanjieji wenhua dageming ziliao huibian,* p. 546.

34. Chen Donglin and Du Pu, eds., *Gongheguo shiji* (Historical Records of the Republic), 4 vols. (Changchun: Jilin renmin chubanshe, 1996), 3: 165.

35. Tang Shaojie, *Yi ye zhi qiu: Qinghua daxue 1968 nian "Bai ri da wudou"* (The Falling of One Leaf Heralds the Autumn: The "Hundred Days of Great Violence" at Tsinghua University in 1968) (Hong Kong: Zhongwen daxue chubanshe, 2003), pp. 51–53.

36. Wang Youqin, "Student Attacks against Teachers," pp. 2–3; Gao Yuan, *Born Red,* pp. 50–60; Ling, *Red Guard,* pp. 18–21.

37. Wang Jian, "'Wenhua dageming' shiqi Beijing pujiao qingkuang" (The Situation in Regular Education in Beijing during the Phase of the "Great Cultural Revolution"), *Beijing jiaoyu zhi congkan* (Beijing Education Gazetteer), no. 4 (1991), 23.

38. "Beijing shi 'Wenhua dageming' dashiji, 1965–1967," p. 26.

39. Perry and Li, *Proletarian Power,* p. 11.

40. Wang Shaoguang, *Failure of Charisma,* p. 72.

41. Guofang daxue, *"Wenhua dageming,"* 1: 91; see also Schoenhals, *China's Cultural Revolution,* pp. 48–49.

42. Beijing shi huaxue gongyeju jiguan hongse xuanchuanzhan, *Wuchanjieji wenhua dageming ziliao,* 2: 192.

43. Wang Nianyi, *Da dongluande niandai,* p. 69.

44. Zhai Zhenhua, *Red Flower of China,* p. 92.

45. Wang Jian, "'Wenhua dageming' shiqi Beijing pujiao qingkuang," p. 23.

46. Wang Youqin, "Student Attacks against Teachers," pp. 1, 20–22.

47. Liao Yiwu, "The Public Toilet Manager," *Paris Review,* no. 174 (Summer 2005), 186–187.

48. Wang Youqin, "Student Attacks against Teachers," p. 3. Virtually all books and

articles on the Red Guard movement contain examples of barbaric behavior, but this article is particularly horrifying in its meticulous retelling of firsthand accounts of what happened.

49. Beijing gangtie xueyuan geming zaofan zhandou bingtuan tie 66 nanxia fendui, ed., *Pipan Tan Lifu jianghua xuanji* (Collection Denouncing Tan Lifu's Speeches) (Guangzhou, 1966), p. 30.

50. Yang, *Spider Eaters,* p. 138.

51. Slightly older and sexually aggressive female Red Guards were not to be trifled with, as some men learned the hard way. During a confrontation in October 1966 between members of a Red Guard group in the Central Drama Academy, led by the daughter of one of the PLA's marshals, and the guards of an archive to which the Red Guards insisted on being given access, two guards confronting the "female hooligans" had their testicles squeezed so hard, according to a sympathetic contemporary account, that their "future generations were put at risk" as they "suffered such agony [that] drops the size of peas ran down their faces." The guards were unable to prevent the Red Guards from looting the archive. See Zhongyang xiju xueyuan hongse zaofantuan, ed., *Jiekai zhongyang xiju xueyuan "Mao Zedong zhuyi zhandoutuan" ouda wumie renmin jiefangjun de neimu* (Unveiling the Inside Story of How the "Mao Zedong-ism Combat Regiment" in the Central Drama Academy Exchanged Blows with and Vilified the People's Liberation Army) (Beijing, 1967), pp. 4, 9–10.

52. Yang, *Spider Eaters,* p. 38.

53. Zhao Qizheng, ed., *Ganbu renshi gongzuo shouce* (Cadre Personnel Work Manual) (Shanghai: Shanghai renmin chubanshe, 1986), p. 239.

54. The "five kinds of elements" referred to people who before the Cultural Revolution had already carried one of the stigmatizing labels "landlord elements, rich-peasant elements, counterrevolutionary elements, bad elements, or rightist elements." See Michael Schoenhals, *Talk about a Revolution: Red Guards, Government Cadres, and the Language of Political Discourse,* Working Paper Series on Language and Politics in Modern China No. 1 (Bloomington: East Asian Studies Center, Indiana University, 1993).

55. For violence on a far smaller but equally tragic scale in a minority village in Yunnan province, see Erik Mueggler, *The Age of Wild Ghosts: Memory, Violence, and Place in Southwest China* (Berkeley: University of California Press, 2001), pp. 258–264.

56. Shoudu dazhuan yuanxiao hongweibing daibiao dahui Zhengfa gongshe, ed., *Zhongyang fuze tongzhi guanyu wuchanjieji wenhua dagemingde jianghua (shiyiyue–shieryue)* (Speeches on the Great Proletarian Cultural Revolution by Responsible Comrades from the Center [November–December 1966]) (Beijing, 1967), p. 253.

57. Beijing boli zongchang hongweibing lianluozhan, *Zhongyang shouzhang jianghua*, 1: 8.

58. *Dongfeng* (East Wind) (Beijing: Eighth Ministry of Machine Building Joint General Documentation Office), nos. 20–23 (July 10, 1968).

59. Yu Luowen, "Beijing Daxing xian can'an diaocha" (Investigation into the Massacre in Daxing County, Beijing), in Song Yongyi, ed., *Wenge da tusha* (Massacres during the Cultural Revolution) (Hong Kong: Kaifang zazhi she, 2003), p. 16.

8. Confusion Nationwide

1. *The Complete Works of Chuang Tzu*, trans. Burton Watson (New York: Columbia University Press, 1968), p. 29.

2. *Mao Zedong sixiang wan sui (1960–1967)*, p. 167.

3. Shanghai shi gonganju geming zaofan lianhe zhihuibu zhengzhibu zaofandui, *Chedi jielu shi gonganju jiu dangzu yuyong gongju jiu wenge bangongshi de taotian zuixing*, 2: 26.

4. Beijing shi huaxue gongyeju jiguan hongse xuanchuanzhan, *Wuchanjieji wenhua dageming ziliao*, 3: 224.

5. *Lin Biao tongzhi youguan wuchanjieji wenhua dageming de zhishi* (Comrade Lin Biao's Instructions concerning the Great Proletarian Cultural Revolution) (Beijing: Zhongguo kexue yuan, 1967), p. 53.

6. *Wang Li fansi lu*, 2: 625.

7. In 1980 the Fifth Plenum of the Eleventh CCP Central Committee officially announced that the term was to be discarded, since no bourgeois reactionary line had actually ever existed; Zhonggong zhongyang wenxian yanjiushi, ed., *Sanzhong quanhui yilai zhongyao wenxian huibian* (Collection of Important Documents since the Third Plenum), 2 vols. (Beijing: Renmin chubanshe, 1982), 1: 502.

8. *Wang Li fansi lu*, 2: 624.

9. Beijing shi huaxue gongyeju jiguan hongse xuanchuanzhan, *Wuchanjieji wenhua dageming ziliao*, 4: 34.

10. *Zhou Enlai nianpu*, 3: 73–75; Wang Nianyi, *Da dongluande niandai*, p. 101. In many respects the conference was a direct continuation of a brief central work conference convened in the immediate aftermath of the Eleventh Plenum, from August 13 to August 17.

11. *Mao Zedong sixiang wan sui*, p. 275.

12. *Jianguo yilai Mao Zedong wengao*, 12: 140–142.

13. *Wuchanjieji wenhua dageming zhongde liangtiao luxian—Chen Boda 1966 nian 10 yue 16 ri zai zhongyang gongzuo huiyi shangde jianghua* (The Two Lines in the

Great Proletarian Cultural Revolution—Chen Boda's Talk at the Central Work Conference on October 16, 1966) (Beijing: Zhonggong zhongyang bangongting mishuju, [1966]).

14. *Renmin ribao wenhua geming dongtai* (*People's Daily* Cultural Revolution Trends) (Beijing: Renmin ribao), no. 64 (November 1, 1966).

15. Ibid., no. 79 (November 22, 1966).

16. Renmin chubanshe ziliaoshi, *Pipan ziliao*, 3: 721–732.

17. Hebei Beijing shifan xueyuan, Douzheng shenghuo bianjibu, *Wuchanjieji wenhua dageming ziliao huibian*, pp. 684–687.

18. Renmin chubanshe ziliaoshi, *Pipan ziliao*, 3: 733–743.

19. *Tao Zhu fangeming xiuzhengzhuyi yanlun huibian* (A Collection of Tao Zhu's Counterrevolutionary Revisionist Utterances) (Beijing: Mao Zedong sixiang zhexue shehui kexuebu hongweibing liandui, May 1967), p. 142.

20. *Jianguo yilai Mao Zedong wengao*, 12: 141.

21. In the late 1950s the readership had been 400,000 and rising; by 1974, according to Zhu Muzhi, the head of Xinhua, the print run was 7 million, with an estimated readership of ten for each copy. See Helmut Opletal, *Die Informationspolitik der Volksrepublik China* (The Information Policy of the People's Republic of China) (Bochum: Brockmeyer, 1981), pp. 98–99.

22. *Cankao xiaoxi*, no. 3028 (October 26, 1966).

23. The preamble and the texts of Liu's and Deng's self-criticisms are appended to Lin Biao's May 18, 1966, Politburo speech, his October 25 address to the work conference, and Chen Boda's October 16 report as reprinted by the PLA General Political Department in an untitled 141-page volume of February 1967. The quoted passage occurs on p. 109. Schoenhals collection.

24. Pang Xianzhi and Jin Chongji, *Mao Zedong zhuan*, 2: 1451.

25. Translation of Mao's address in Schoenhals, *China's Cultural Revolution*, pp. 5–9.

26. *Lin Biao wenxuan*, 2: 343.

27. "Wang-Guan-Qi fandang jituan yu gonganbu mouxie fuzeren zai Chen Lining fangeming anjian zhong banyan le shenme juese?" (What Role Did the Wang-Guan-Qi Anti-Party Clique and Certain Senior People in the Ministry of Public Security Play in the Counterrevolutionary Case of Chen Lining?), 9-page stenciled document, p. 4, Schoenhals collection; *Tianjin xin wenyi* (New Tianjin Literature and Art) (Tianjin: Municipal Literature and Art Circles Standing Committee), tabloid, no. 18 (March 1968), 2.

28. Tan Zongji et al., eds., *Shinian houde pingshuo: "Wenhua dageming" shilunji* (Evaluation Ten Years Later: A Collection of Historical Discussions of the "Great Cultural Revolution") (Beijing: Zhonggong dangshi ziliao chubanshe, 1987), p. 54.

29. *Cankao xiaoxi*, December 3, 12, and 21, 1966.

30. *Renmin ribao*, editorial, November 10, 1966, translated in *Survey of China Main-land Press*, no. 3825 (November 22, 1966).

31. See, for instance, *Zhou Enlai nianpu*, 3: 63–64, 105; *Selected Works of Zhou Enlai*, 2: 479–480; Zhou Yan, "Gongheguo zongli xin zhongde 'zhua geming cu shengchan'" (The Heart of the Premier of the Republic in "Grasp Revolution, Boost Production"), in An Jianshe, ed., *Zhou Enlaide zuihou suiyue, 1966–1976* (The Last Days of Zhou Enlai, 1966–1976) (Beijing: Zhongyang wenxian chubanshe, 1995), pp. 68–84. According to one account, from November 1966 until his death, Zhou was on cardiac medicines four times a day, "suffering from arrhythmia, shortness of breath, and fainting spells," and indeed in November was "felled by a heart attack after twenty-two hours of being surrounded and shouted at by hordes of Red Guards"; Han Suyin, *Eldest Son* (New York: Kodansha, 1994), pp. 327–329. The chronology of his life, *Zhou Enlai nianpu*, records almost daily activity during November 1966. Han Suyin may be referring to the diagnosis of heart disease, without indication of a heart attack, on February 2, 1967; *Zhou Enlai nianpu*, 3: 122.

32. Tan Zongji et al., *Shinian houde pingshuo*, p. 43.

33. I Peking vid årsskiftet (Beijing at the Start of the New Year), letter from Beijing embassy to Ministry for Foreign Affairs, Stockholm, January 7, 1967, Swedish Ministry of Foreign Affairs archive, Stockholm.

34. Perry and Li, *Proletarian Power*, pp. 32–36; Wang Nianyi, *Da dongluande niandai*, p. 128; *Wang Li fansi lu*, 2: 653–54; *Shanghai "Wenhua dageming" shihua*, 1: 137–159.

35. Wang Nianyi, *Da dongluande niandai*, pp. 129–131; *Wang Li fansi lu*, 2: 654–655; *Shanghai "Wenhua dageming" shihua*, 1: 160–172.

36. Wang Nianyi, *Da dongluande niandai*, p. 134.

37. Ibid., pp. 135–136.

38. Ibid., pp. 138–139.

39. Beijing hongse yeyu wenyi gongzuozhe geming zaofan zongbu, ed., *Wuchanjieji wenhua dageming cankao ziliao* (Great Proletarian Cultural Revolution Reference Materials), 6 vols. (Beijing, 1967), 6: 23.

40. Ibid., p. 22.

41. Guofang daxue, *"Wenhua dageming,"* 1: 182–183.

42. Ibid., pp. 114, 189–190.

43. Nankai daxue "8.18" hongse zaofantuan, ed., *Lishi de tiezheng* (The Iron Proof of History) (Tianjin, 1967), pp. 134–135.

44. Hao Kewei, "28 zhuan'an de faqi guocheng" (How "Special Case 28" Was Launched), March 23, 1970, handwritten confession from Beijing, Schoenhals collection.

45. Ibid.

46. Gao Wenhua, "'Laotou zaofandui' caozong de '5.16' fangeming yinmou jituan de zuixing" (Crimes of the "May 16" Counterrevolutionary Conspiratorial Clique as Masterminded by the "Old Fogeys' Rebel Team"), January 22–March 11, 1971, handwritten confession from Beijing, Schoenhals collection.

47. *Liu Shaoqi shi Zhongguo de Heluxiaofu* (Liu Shaoqi Is China's Khrushchev) (Beijing, 1966), pp. 4–26. Mao's habit of peppering his speeches with expressions lifted from classical Chinese literature is well attested and led in the Cultural Revolution to the production of manuals with titles like *Idioms Explained* and *Literary Quotations in Mao Zedong's Selected Works*. In the case of this particular quotation, editors—who had no way of knowing with certainty where Mao had picked it up—invariably sourced it to chapter 68 of the popular romantic Qing dynasty novel *Dream of the Red Chamber*. Its *locus classicus*, however, is chapter 25 in the erotic Ming dynasty novel *Jin ping mei*.

48. *Dadao Deng Xiaoping* (Down with Deng Xiaoping) (Beijing, 1967), pp. 26–28.

49. *Tao Zhu fangeming xiuzhengzhuyi yanlun huibian*, p. 230.

50. Deng Rong, *Deng Xiaoping and the Cultural Revolution*, p. 30.

51. Jia Lanxun, "Tie shen weishi yi Shaoqi mengnan," pp. 16–18.

52. Idem, "Tie shen weishi yi Shaoqi mengnan, xu" (Memories of a Private Guard: How Liu Shaoqi Met With Disaster, continued), *Bainian chao*, no. 2 (2000), 18–19.

53. Tu Men and Kong Di, *Gongheguo zuida yuanan*, pp. 47–48.

54. Guizhou wuchanjieji geming zaofan zong zhihuibu (reprinter), *Dadao Liu Shaoqi, dadao Deng Xiaoping (zhuan ji)* (Down with Liu Shaoqi, Down with Deng Xiaoping [Special Edition]) (April 1967), p. 161.

55. "Zhai zi Hao Kewei jiaodai cailiao" (Excerpts from Hao Kewei's Confessions), June 10, 1970, p. 2, handwritten confessions, Beijing, Schoenhals collection.

56. *Mao Zedong sixiang wan sui (xu er)* (Long Live Mao Zedong Thought [Supplement II]) (Beijing: Zhongguo renmin daxue, 1967), p. 15.

57. *Dongtai*, no. 73 (June 11, 1967); also in *Wenge jianxun*, no. 280 (June 8, 1967).

58. Yu Guangyuan, *Wenge zhongde wo* (Me in the Cultural Revolution) (Shanghai: Shanghai yuandong chubanshe, 1996), pp. 27–28.

59. For a translation of this poster, see *Contemporary Chinese Thought*, 33, no. 1 (Fall 2001), 27–29.

60. Schoenhals, *China's Cultural Revolution*, pp. 155–162.

61. Shoudu bufen dazhuan yuanxiao zhongdeng zhuanye xuexiao Mao Zedong sixiang xuexiban, *Tianfan difu kaierkang—Wuchanjieji wenhua dageming dashiji*, p. 77.

62. Shoudu hongweibing di san silingbu Beijing youdian xueyuan "Dongfanghong" gongshe Chongfengdui, *Beijing shi wuchanjieji wenhua dageming dashiji (1965.9–1967.1)*, p. 34.

63. *Wenge jianxun,* extra issue, no. 9 (February 4, 1967).
64. *Cankao xiaoxi,* November 15, 1966.
65. *Dongtai,* no. 124 (August 16, 1967).
66. *Dongfanghong bao* (The East Is Red Paper) (Beijing: Beijing Geological Institute East Is Red Commune), August 29, 1967.
67. Letter, 261 A 5.10.66/Nr 7 HP 1, Swedish Ministry for Foreign Affairs archive, Stockholm.

9. Shanghai's "January Storm"

1. According to Chen Boda's recollections, as recorded by a Chinese journalist and quoted in Wang Nianyi, *Da dongluande niandai* (A Decade of Great Upheaval) (Zhengzhou: Henan renmin chubanshe, 1988), p. 164. Xu Jingxian, a Shanghai writer close to Yao Wenyuan, remembers being told about the toast at the end of a long-distance telephone call from Yao on December 27; Xu Jingxian, *Shinian yimeng* (Ten Years a Dream) (Hong Kong: Time International Publishing, 2004), pp. 6–8. According to Wang Li, Mao had on this occasion toasted the unfolding of a "nationwide, all-round class struggle"; Wang Li, *Xianchang lishi: Wenhua dageming jishi* (On the Scene of History: Chronicle of the Great Cultural Revolution) (Hong Kong: Oxford University Press, 1993), pp. 100–110. For Wang Li's explanation of why Kang Sheng was not invited, see idem, "Insider's Account of the Cultural Revolution," p. 32.
2. *Jianguo yilai Mao Zedong wengao,* 12: 176; Guofang daxue, *"Wenhua dageming,"* 1: 196–203; "Carry the Great Proletarian Cultural Revolution Through to the End," *Peking Review,* no. 1 (January 1, 1967), 8–15. On January 18, 1967, in its biweekly report "Internal Press Themes," the office of the British chargé d'affaires in Beijing speculated that the editorial "promised a lively twelve months to come"; Robert L. Jarman, ed., *China Political Reports 1961–1970,* vol. 3: *1965–1970* (Chippenham: Archive Editions, 2003), p. 252.
3. Li Fuchun's status was ambiguous.
4. On April 21 some members of the Secretariat of the Northeast Region made one last attempt to use the formal weight of their institution to influence their region's politics by issuing "Three Opinions of the Northeast Region Secretariat," but critics immediately challenged their authority. The resulting conflict led, on August 6, to the only known formal central decree dissolving one of the regions.
5. Yunnan sheng geming weiyuanhui, ed., *Wuchanjieji wenhua dageming wenjian huibian* (Collected Documents of the Great Proletarian Cultural Revolution), 2 vols. (Kunming, 1969), 2: 801.
6. Beijing hangkong xueyuan "Hongqi," *Wuchanjieji wenhua dageming shouzhang jianghua huiji,* p. 136. In early February Zhou tried to corral the CCRG by insti-

tutionalizing the de facto new national leadership, writing to Chen Boda and Jiang Qing to suggest a regular schedule of almost daily meetings between the State Council and the CCRG. Mao killed the proposal, commenting on Zhou's letter: "This document is no use; send it back to Zhou"; *Zhou Enlai nianpu*, 3: 122.

7. *Origins*, 2: 59–63.

8. *Mao Zedong sixiang wan sui* ([Shanghai?], [1968?]), p. 263.

9. *Wang Li fansi lu*, 2: 769.

10. See Li Zhisui, *The Private Life of Chairman Mao*, p. 573, where Mao's personal physician describes Zhou as "exceptionally energetic, working long hours, sleeping little, managing the affairs of party and state."

11. *Mao Zedong sixiang wan sui*, p. 116.

12. *Zhongguo gongchandang zuzhishi ziliao*, 15: 166–167, 561.

13. Ibid., pp. 164, 560.

14. *Mao Zedong sixiang wan sui*, p. 282.

15. Ibid., p. 285.

16. "Zhou zongli zai junji ganbu huiyi shangde jianghua" (Premier Zhou's Speech at a Conference for Corps-Level Cadres), in *Xuexi wenjian* (Study Documents) (n.p., 1967), p. 13.

17. Translated from original contemporary transcript as produced and circulated by the Ministry of Food, p. 1, Schoenhals collection.

18. *Zhou Enlai nianpu*, 3: 113 (for Mao), 116, 117, 118 (for Zhou).

19. *Wang Baofu de zuie yanxing* (Criminal Words and Deeds of Wang Baofu) (Nanjing, 1967), p. 1.

20. *Wanshan hongbian* (Mountains and Rivers Awash in Red) (Beijing: East City District Department Stores' Management Office), no. 1 (1967), 20. Xiao Wangdong had taken over from Lu Dingyi as acting minister of culture in June 1966.

21. For a discussion of the fate of the ministries, see *Wang Li fansi lu*, 2: 766–776.

22. *Zhongguo gongchandang zuzhishi ziliao*, 15: 504, 518–525, 534–536, 539, 540, 543, 555.

23. *Wenge jianxun*, no. 113 (March 20, 1967).

24. Quoted in Wang Xiuzhen, "Wode di er ci jiefa he jiaodai" (My Second Exposé and Testimony) (Shanghai: Shanghai shi qu, xian, ju dangyuan fuze ganbu huiyi mishuzu, November 1976), p. 13, Schoenhals collection.

25. *Jianguo yilai Mao Zedong wengao*, 12: 574. For descriptions of May 7 Cadre Schools, see Yue and Wakeman, *To the Storm*, pp. 251–273; Yang Jiang, *A Cadre School Life: Six Chapters* (Hong Kong: Joint Publishing, 1982).

26. Quoted in Schram, *The Political Thought of Mao Tse-tung*, p. 209.

27. *Wang Li fansi lu*, 2: 852. For an account of the struggle within the PLA officer corps in Beijing for position and the benefits that accrued therefrom, written by a woman whose family lost out, see Mu Aiping, *Vermilion Gate*.

28. Zhou had indicated in a speech to Red Guards from all over China that they had another four months to "concentrate exclusively" on the Cultural Revolution; Beijing shi huaxue gongyeju jiguan hongse xuanchuanzhan, *Wuchanjieji wenhua dageming ziliao,* 4: 3. Curiously, delegates returned to the provinces after the meeting to tell other Red Guards that the Cultural Revolution "will go on for quite some time yet! This battle will last at least until summer vacation next year"; Beijing jingji xueyuan wuchanjieji geming zaofantuan, *Wuchanjieji wenhua dageming cankao ziliao,* 3: 11.

29. *Gaoju Mao Zedong sixiang weida hongqi,* p. 73. Zhou was speaking at a PSC conference on December 5.

30. *Mao Zedong sixiang wan sui,* p. 282. The most thorough recent account of the Cultural Revolution in Shanghai is Perry and Li, *Proletarian Power,* on which this account draws heavily. Other important scholarly analyses include Andrew G. Walder, *Chang Ch'un-ch'iao and Shanghai's January Revolution* (Ann Arbor: Center for Chinese Studies, University of Michigan, 1978); Lynn T. White III, *Policies of Chaos: The Organizational Causes of Violence in China's Cultural Revolution* (Princeton: Princeton University Press, 1989). For the account of a victim, see Nien Cheng, *Life and Death in Shanghai.* For sympathetic accounts by foreign English-language teachers based in Shanghai, see Hunter, *Shanghai Journal;* and the far less detailed Sophia Knight, *Window on Shanghai: Letters from China, 1965–1967* (London: Andre Deutsch, 1967).

31. Lin Biao, Mao's "best pupil," expanded on Mao's analogy and used it to describe cadre performance in the Cultural Revolution: the best cadres were those who managed with ease to "swim to the other shore"; the mediocre ones included those who "made every effort to stay afloat, but drowned all the same"; the worst, not surprisingly, were those refusing to get into the water in the first place; Beijing boli zongchang hongweibing lianluozhan, *Zhongyang shouzhang jianghua,* 1: 258.

32. Wang Nianyi, *Da dongluande niandai,* p. 164; *Yiyue fengbao congkan* (January Storm) (Shanghai: Workers' General Headquarters), nos. 5–6 (January–February 1968), 67; Xu Jingxian, *Shinian yimeng,* p. 7.

33. For a firsthand account of the impact of the Beijing Red Guards and the futile efforts of the Shanghai party to keep the movement under control, see *Chen Pixian huiyilu,* pp. 65–72. For another firsthand account of the impact of the Beijing Red Guards in Shanghai, see Ye Ting-xing, *A Leaf in the Bitter Wind,* pp. 70–86; for their role in Wuhan, see Wang Shaoguang, *Failure of Charisma,* pp. 76–82.

34. This is a major theme of Perry and Li, *Proletarian Power.*

35. *Shanghai "Wenhua dageming" shihua,* 1: 175–182.

36. Perry and Li, *Proletarian Power,* pp. 12–14.

37. Ibid., pp. 74–82.

38. "Beijing shi 'Wenhua dageming' dashiji, 1965–1967," *Beijing dangshi ziliao tongxun*, p. 17.

39. Perry and Li, *Proletarian Power*, pp. 86–89; *Shanghai "Wenhua dageming" shihua*, 1: 209–222.

40. *Shanghai "Wenhua dageming" shihua*, 1: 214–216, 224–225. Cf. CCP CC Party History Research Centre, ed., *History of the Chinese Communist Party–A Chronology of Events (1919–1990)* (Beijing: Foreign Languages Press, 1991), p. 334.

41. CCP CC Party History Research Centre, *History of the Chinese Communist Party*, p. 334. According to *Dangdai Zhongguode Shanghai* (Contemporary China's Shanghai), 2 vols. (Beijing: Dangdai Zhongguo chubanshe, 1993), 1: 259, only ninety-one Scarlet Guards were wounded, which seems rather a small number.

42. Chen Shijin, *Jiangjun juanjin xuanwo* (General Drawn into the Whirlpool) (Nanjing: Jiangsu wenyi chubanshe, 1987), pp. 1–4, 12–14.

43. *Chen Pixian huiyilu*, pp. 116–119. Despite illness, Chen's account indicates that he followed local events closely. He had missed the Eleventh Plenum, but after a phone call from Ye Qun, he went to Beijing, with a doctor and on a plane specially sent by Lin Biao, to attend the October work conference. During his time in the capital, Jiang Qing tried to win him over to her side; ibid., pp. 72–115.

44. *Shanghai "Wenhua dageming" shihua*, 1: 224–225; *Zhou Enlai nianpu*, 3: 106.

45. *Chen Pixian huiyilu*, pp. 119–120.

46. Wang Li, *Xianchang lishi*, p. 101.

47. *Shanghai "Wenhua dageming" shihua*, 1: 226–227. The organ of Chen's municipal party committee, the *Liberation Daily*, was the scene of a power-seizure on January 6, with no issue appearing that day.

48. Beijing hangkong xueyuan "Hongqi," *Wuchanjieji wenhua dageming shouzhang jianghua huiji*, p. 117.

49. Xu Jingxian, *Shinian yimeng*, p. 25; for Jiang Qing's obsession with military dress, see *Chen Pixian huiyilu*, pp. 45, 79.

50. *Shanghai "Wenhua dageming" shihua*, 1: 236–237.

51. Xu Jingxian, *Shinian yimeng*, pp. 22, 36.

52. Chen remembers this episode as having taken place at a rally on January 12, and a compromise being reached that enabled him to wear his uniform but without its neck insignia or cap badge; *Chen Pixian huiyilu*, pp. 136–138.

53. *Shanghai "Wenhua dageming" shihua*, 1: 237–238.

54. Ibid., p. 239.

55. *Dangdai Zhongguode Shanghai*, 1: 279.

56. Guo Zhenzhi, "Zhongguo dianshi dashiji (1955–1978)" (A Chronicle of Events in Chinese Television [1955–1978]), *Xinwen yanjiu ziliao* (Press Research Materials), no. 46 (1989), 178–179; Xu Jingxian, *Shinian yimeng*, p. 35, remembers telling television camera crews that if the rally got out of hand and there was violence, they

should turn their lenses elsewhere and not air images that would leave a bad impression with foreign viewers, such as foreign diplomats and sailors on shore leave.

57. The notice is reprinted in "Quarterly Chronicle and Documentation," *CQ*, no. 30 (April–June 1967), 203–204.
58. *Jianguo yilai Mao Zedong wengao*, 12: 186–187. For other signs of Mao's keen interest in Shanghai events, see ibid., pp. 185, 188–189.
59. Wang Li, "Insider's Account of the Cultural Revolution," pp. 35–36.
60. *Yiyue fengbao congkan*, nos. 5–6 (January–February 1968), 45. The telegram was published in *Renmin ribao* on January 12, 1967.
61. Wang Nianyi, *Da dongluande niandai*, p. 178.
62. *Wenge jianxun*, no. 16 (January 28, 1967).
63. *Shanghai "Wenhua dageming" shihua*, 1: 260. See also *Yiyue fengbao congkan*, nos. 5–6 (January–February 1968), 50, where the date of the meeting at which the decision was taken is given as January 23 rather than January 19.
64. *Shanghai "Wenhua dageming" shihua*, 1: 262–263.
65. Li Youping, *Douzheng yu shenghuo*, 5: 35–36.
66. Ibid., p. 36.
67. *Wang Li fansi lu*, 2: 764.
68. Schram, *Mao Tse-tung Unrehearsed*, p. 278.
69. *Shanghai "Wenhua dageming" shihua*, 1: 263.
70. *Dangdai Zhongguode Shanghai*, 2: 389–390. Formal ratification of the creation of the Shanghai Revolutionary Committee was not sought from the CCP center until January 23, 1970. It was granted on March 28, 1970. *Zhongguo gongchandang Shanghai shi zuzhi shi ziliao, 1920.8–1987.10* (Materials on the Organizational History of the CCP in Shanghai, August 1920–October 1987) (Shanghai: Shanghai renmin chubanshe, 1991), p. 520.

10. Seizing Power

1. *Wenge jianxun*, no. 39 (February 9, 1967).
2. The Qinghai Revolutionary Committee was established on August 12, the Inner Mongolian on November 1, and the Tianjin one on December 6, 1967. For a chronological table of the formation of the revolutionary committees, along with their founding leaders, see Xi Xuan and Jin Chunming, *"Wenhua dageming" jianshi* (A Short History of the "Great Cultural Revolution") (Beijing: Zhonggong dangshi chubanshe, 1996), pp. 183–186.
3. Minutes of Mao Zedong's conversation with Albanian visitors, transcript in Chinese diary no. 10, in the authors' possession.
4. *Jianguo yilai Mao Zedong wengao*, 12: 179–182.

5. Zhang Xiangling, ed., *Heilongjiang sishinian* (Forty Years of Heilongjiang) (Harbin: Heilongjiang renmin chubanshe, 1986), pp. 345–355.

6. *Wang Li fansi lu*, 2: 750–753.

7. Ma Qibin et al., *Zhongguo gongchandang zhizheng sishinian*, pp. 277, 285.

8. Zhejiang shifan xueyuan, *Wuchanjieji wenhua dageming bufen ziliao huibian III*, 3: 143.

9. Beijing boli zongchang hongweibing lianluozhan, *Zhongyang shouzhang jianghua*, 2: 109.

10. Beijing hangkong xueyuan "Hongqi," *Wuchanjieji wenhua dageming shouzhang jianghua huiji*, p. 254.

11. Beijing boli zongchang hongweibing lianluozhan, *Zhongyang shouzhang jianghua*, 4: 192.

12. *CCP Documents*, pp. 225–229.

13. Ibid., pp. 231–232.

14. Ibid., pp. 233–236, 319–324, 341–345.

15. Ibid., pp. 377–378, 429–430.

16. Ibid., pp. 271–272, 379–381, 277–279.

17. Ibid., pp. 299–302.

18. Ibid., pp. 311–314.

19. Ibid., pp. 303–306. For a description of the sudden influx of contract workers into Beijing and their short-lived period of influence by on-the-spot foreigners, see David Milton and Nancy Milton, *The Wind Will Not Subside* (New York: Pantheon, 1976), pp. 186–190.

20. *CCP Documents*, pp. 369–375.

21. See the thirty-five grievances drawn up by peasants in the environs of Shanghai in January 1967, quoted in "Quarterly Chronicle and Documentation," *CQ*, no. 30 (April–June 1967), 207–209. For an appraisal of the relative deprivation of peasants as compared with that of urban residents by a British Communist resident in Beijing at the outset of the Cultural Revolution, see Gordon, *Freedom Is a Word*, p. 78.

22. *CCP Documents*, pp. 329–333, 347–350.

23. *Zhongyang junwei kuoda huiyi jingshen* (The Spirit of the Enlarged MAC Plenum (Zhengzhou: Henan erqi gongshe Zhengzhou geming zhigong lianluo weiyuanhui wenjiao weisheng fenhui, 1967), p. 3.

24. *Xuexi wenjian* (Study Documents) (n.p., 1967), pp. 31–35; Guojia tongjiju zonghesi, *Quanguo ge sheng zizhiqu zhixiashi lishi tongji ziliao huibian*, p. 10.

25. By June, military control had been imposed on China's sixty-eight centrally managed coal fields; *Wuchanjieji wenhua dageming ziliao 6*, 2: 265.

26. *Xuexi wenjian*, p. 31.

27. *CCP Documents*, pp. 335–338, 361–363.

28. Ibid., pp. 307–310, 365–368.

29. Chen Shijin, *Jiangjun juanjin xuanwo*, pp. 1–4, 12–14.

30. Wang Nianyi, *Da dongluande niandai*, p. 194; *Jianguo yilai Mao Zedong wengao*, 12: 197–199.

31. *Wuchanjieji wenhua dageming wenjian huiji* (Collected Documents from the Great Proletarian Cultural Revolution) (n.p., 1967), pp. 93–94.

32. Schoenhals, *China's Cultural Revolution*, pp. 52–53.

33. Guofang daxue, *"Wenhua dageming,"* 1: 132–133; Zhang Yunsheng, *Maojiawan jishi*, pp. 42–43.

34. Zhang Yunsheng, *Maojiawan jishi*, p. 76.

35. Jiang Bo and Li Qing, eds., *Lin Biao 1959 nian yihou* (Lin Biao after 1959) (Chengdu: Sichuan renmin chubanshe, 1993), pp. 171–187; *Jianguo yilai Mao Zedong wengao*, 12: 190–206.

36. Guofang daxue, *"Wenhua dageming,"* 1: 262.

37. *Zhongyang shouzhang guanyu Henan wentide zhishi ji fu-Jing huibao jiyao huibian* (Collected Transcripts of Central Leaders' Instructions concerning Henan and Summaries of Reports Given in Beijing) (Zhengzhou: Zhongguo renmin jiefangjun zhu zheng budui zhizuo lianhe bangongshi, 1967), p. 112.

38. Ge Chumin, "Xu Xiangqian zai 'Wenge' zhongde er san shi" (Some Stories about Xu Xiangqian during the "Cultural Revolution"), *Bainian chao*, no. 11 (2001), 40.

39. *Dahai hangxing kao duoshou* (The Helmsman Sets the Ocean Course) (n.p., n.d.), p. 110.

40. *Jianguo yilai Mao Zedong wengao*, 12: 218–219.

41. *CCP Documents*, pp. 258–259, 262. For the PLA's role in the formation of revolutionary committees, see Jürgen Domes, *The Internal Politics of China, 1949–1972* (London: Hurst, 1973), pp. 200–205.

42. *CCP Documents*, pp. 237–241, 243–245, 247–269, 273–276, 281–291.

43. "Quarterly Chronicle and Documentation" (April–June 1967), 215.

44. Guofang daxue, *"Wenhua dageming,"* 1: 361.

45. *CCP Documents*, pp. 351–360.

46. Guofang daxue dangshi dangjian zhengzhi gongzuo jiaoyanshi, *Zhongguo gongchandang qishinian dashi jianjie* (A Summary of the Principal Events in the Seventy Years of the CCP) (Beijing: Guofang daxue chubanshe, 1991) (hereafter Guofang daxue, *Qishinian*), p. 550.

47. Alastair Iain Johnston, "Party Rectification in the PLA, 1983–87," *CQ*, no. 112 (December 1987), 591–630.

48. *CCP Documents*, pp. 383–387, 415–419.

49. Huang Yongsheng, commander of the Canton MR, was appointed chairman of the Guangdong Military Commission; Qian Jun, deputy commander of the Nanjing MR, took on the Anhui MR; ibid., pp. 389–395.

50. Ibid., pp. 389–395, 431–438.

51. Ibid., pp. 457–459.

52. W. Woody, *The Cultural Revolution in Inner Mongolia: Extracts from an Unpublished History* (Stockholm: Center for Pacific Asia Studies, Stockholm University, 1993), p. iii; former member of the "Huhehot Third Headquarters," interview by Michael Schoenhals, December 1991.

53. *Zhongyang shouzhang guanyu Henan wentide zhishi ji fu-Jing huibao jiyao huibian*, p. 72.

54. *Dangdai Zhongguode Sichuan* (Contemporary China's Sichuan) (Beijing: Dangdai Zhongguo chubanshe, 1997), pp. 192–193. The text of the MAC telegram sanctioning the arrests is in *Wenge jianxun*, no. 67 (February 22, 1967).

55. *Fandaodi tongxun* (Resist All the Way Bulletin) (Shanghai: Jiaotong University), no. 12 (May 2, 1967).

56. *Jianguo yilai Mao Zedong wengao*, 12: 314–315. An inquiry mentioned by Red Guards claimed that a secret target had been set to arrest around 10 to 15 percent of the population in the province. See *Dongfanghong* (East Is Red) (Chengdu: Beijing Industrial University), extra issue, no. 2 (July 2, 1967).

57. An indication of what kind of orders were "issued verbally [to soldiers] on the very eve of battle, but kept secret until then" is given in *Jianguo yilai Mao Zedong wengao*, 12: 222–223.

58. Beijing boli zongchang hongweibing lianluozhan, *Zhongyang shouzhang jianghua*, 3: 214.

59. Jin Chunming, Huang Yuchong, and Chang Huimin, *"Wenge" shiqi guaishi guaiyu* (Strange Things and Strange Discourse during the Period of the "Cultural Revolution") (Beijing: Qiushi chubanshe, 1989), p. 273.

60. See Harding, "The Chinese State in Crisis," p. 149.

61. Wang Nianyi, *Da dongluande niandai*, p. 204.

62. Zhonggong Qinghai shengwei zuzhibu, Zhonggong Qinghai shengwei dangshi yanjiushi, and Qinghai sheng dang'anju, eds., *Zhongguo gongchandang Qinghai sheng zuzhi shi ziliao* (Materials on the Organizational History of the CCP in Qinghai Province) (Xining, 1995), p. 124.

63. This also occurred in the aftermath of the shooting of demonstrators in central Beijing in June 1989.

64. Beijing boli zongchang hongweibing lianluozhan, *Zhongyang shouzhang jianghua*, 3: 215. Immediately after the event, the MAC congratulated the units involved, saying: "You did the right thing, you fought well!" See Wang Nianyi, *Da dongluande niandai*, p. 204.

65. Zhao Yongfu was later used as a negative example to deter other senior officers from dealing equally roughly with leftists; *CCP Documents*, pp. 383–387, 408, 411.

66. Wang Nianyi, *Da dongluande niandai*, p. 203.

67. Ibid., pp. 202–203. As early as September 1966, Mao had to accept that Xinjiang merited kid-glove treatment; *Jianguo yilai Mao Zedong wengao*, 12: 122–123. On January 27, 1967, Zhou Enlai told Xinjiang rebels that the center had decided that the Cultural Revolution in the Xinjiang MR was over; *Zhou Enlai nianpu*, 3: 117–118, 120.

68. *Jianguo yilai Mao Zedong wengao*, 12: 305; Yunnan sheng geming weiyuanhui, *Wuchanjieji wenhua dageming wenjian huibian*, 1: 317–324.

69. Chen Zaidao, *Haojie zhongde yi mu: Wuhan qi ershi shijian qin liji* (One Act in a Catastrophe: A Personal Record of the Wuhan July 20 Incident) (Beijing: Jiefangjun chubanshe, 1989), p. 38.

70. Zhang Yunsheng, *Maojiawan jishi*, pp. 105–108; see also *Wang Li fansi lu*, 2: 994.

71. *CCP Documents*, pp. 407–411; *Jianguo yilai Mao Zedong wengao*, 12: 306–309.

72. Ibid., pp. 310–313.

73. On the same day that the PLA was adjured to cherish the people, further indignities were heaped on Liu Shaoqi, who was told by a rebel group that thenceforth he would have to cook his own food, clean his own toilet, wash his own clothes, and change his work and rest schedule; Chen Donglin and Du Pu, *Gongheguo shiji*, 3: 238.

74. *Jiang Qing tongzhi jianghua xuanbian* (Selected Speeches by Comrade Jiang Qing) (Beijing: Renmin chubanshe, 1968), p. 49.

75. *Zhongyang guanyu chuli Neimeng wentide jueding he zhongyang fuze tongzhi jianghua huibian* (Center's Decision on Resolving Matters in Inner Mongolia and Collected Central Leaders' Speeches), 2 vols. (Huhehot, 1967), 2: 67.

76. Ma Qibin et al., *Zhongguo gongchandang zhizheng sishinian*, p. 283.

77. Ibid., p. 284. Jiang Qing's appointment was heralded in late November 1966; ibid., p. 280.

78. Xi Xuan and Jin Chunming, *"Wenhua dageming" jianshi*, p. 144.

79. See Yuan Ding, "Xiao Li yu 'Jiefangjun bao' duoquan fengbao" (Xiao Li and the Seizure of Power at the *PLA Daily*), *Bainian chao*, no. 2 (1999), 42–54.

11. The Last Stand of the Old Guard

1. *Zhou Enlai nianpu*, 3: 119, 121.

2. Ibid., pp. 114, 124; for the "thriller movie" version of He Long's flight, see Suo Guoxin, *1967 niande 78 tian: "Eryue niliu" jishi* (78 Days in 1967: The True Story of the "February Countercurrent") (Changsha: Hunan wenyi chubanshe, 1986), pp. 39–41; translated in *Chinese Law and Government*, 22, no. 1 (Spring 1989), 38–40.

3. "Quarterly Chronicle and Documentation," *CQ*, no. 30 (April–June 1967), 210.

4. Zhang was denounced first by Jiang Qing as an ally of Peng Zhen on December 14, and arrested on December 19 after his return from an inspection visit. He was

subjected to questioning under torture fifty times and beaten black and blue. He was fifty-eight. Ma Qibin et al., *Zhongguo gongchandang zhizheng sishinian*, p. 281. Zhou was able to have the case reopened and Zhang cleared in 1970; *Selected Works of Zhou Enlai*, 2: 475–476.

5. *Zhou Enlai nianpu*, 3: 116, 123.
6. Xi Xuan and Jin Chunming, *"Wenhua dageming" jianshi*, pp. 146–147.
7. *Zhou Enlai nianpu*, 3: 110.
8. Qinghua daxue "Guo Da Jiang," "Chen Yi jiancha dahui jilu" (Record of Chen Yi Self-Investigation Mass Rally), 5-page mimeograph, January 31, 1967, Schoenhals collection.
9. Cited in Wang Nianyi, *Da dongluande niandai*, p. 214.
10. Ibid., p. 313; Lin Biao was speaking to the CC's Twelfth Plenum in October 1968.
11. There are numerous references to consultations with Tao Zhu in *Zhou Enlai nianpu*, vol. 3, during this period. For a negative slant on Tao Zhu's activities, see *Tao Zhu fangeming xiuzhengzhuyi yanlun huibian*.
12. See his wife's account of a moment when Tao Zhu, uncharacteristically, unburdened himself to her about how Jiang Qing and her colleagues goaded him; *Biji Tao Zhu* (Memorial for Tao Zhu) (Beijing: Renmin chubanshe, 1990), pp. 586–589. Wang Li claimed that Jiang Qing had lobbied for Tao Zhu's high standing in the PSC on the grounds that Chen Boda would not be able to handle Deng Xiaoping, but that she fell out with him on a number of concrete issues; *Wang Li fansi lu*, 2: 657–673.
13. Ma Qibin et al., *Zhongguo gongchandang zhizheng sishinian*, p. 280.
14. *Biji Tao Zhu*, p. 575.
15. See above, Chapter 1.
16. *Wang Li fansi lu*, 2: 657–673.
17. For a frank admission by a respected Chinese party historian about the divergence of views on various aspects of the February Countercurrent, due in part to the unavailability of primary materials, see Zhou Yan, "He 'da nao Huairentang' de zhanyoumen" (Comrades-in-Arms during the "Commotion in Huairen Hall"), in An Jianshe, *Zhou Enlaide zuihou suiyue*, p. 35.
18. Xi Xuan and Jin Chunming, *"Wenhua dageming" jianshi*, p. 125.
19. Quan Yanchi, *Tao Zhu zai "Wenhua dageming" zhong*, pp. 201–204. For the impact of Wang Renzhong's fall on politics in Hubei, see Wang Shaoguang, *Failure of Charisma*, p. 83.
20. According to Wang Li's account of the birthday party, Mao happened to use one of Tao Zhu's phrases. However, by the time Wang wrote his memoir, it would not have been politic to give evidence of an active role by Mao in toppling Tao; Wang Li, *Xianchang lishi*, pp. 100–104.
21. In fact this discussion was academic, since Wang Renzhong had been brought

back to Wuhan from Guangzhou by rebels on December 25, and at the start of 1967 three big rallies were held in the city to denounce him; Wang Shaoguang, *Failure of Charisma*, pp. 93–94.

22. *Biji Tao Zhu*, pp. 576–578.

23. Ibid., p. 578; *Zhou Enlai nianpu*, 3: 105.

24. *Biji Tao Zhu*, pp. 578–579; Zheng Hui, Shi Zhongquan, and Zhang Hongru, eds., *Zhonghua renmin gongheguo guoshi quanjian (1949–1995)* (A Comprehensive History of the PRC [1949–1995]), 6 vols. (Beijing: Tuanjie chubanshe, 1996), 4: 3847. One writer has suggested that Mao was trying to protect Tao Zhu by getting him out of Beijing; Quan Yanchi, *Tao Zhu zai "Wenhua dageming" zhong*, p. 191.

25. *Biji Tao Zhu*, pp. 579–580.

26. According to Wang Li, the meeting was organized by Jiang Qing, and Chen Boda knew only shortly before it opened that he would be speaking; Wang Li, *Xianchang lishi*, p. 148. Kang Sheng was also present, but there is no record of his denouncing Tao Zhu. Chen Boda later claimed to have been only half awake, having taken a large dose of sleeping pills the night before, and to have misinterpreted Jiang's words to mean that Mao had given the thumbs-up for an attack on Tao: "It was the stupidest thing I ever did. I was taken for a ride by Jiang Qing"; see Chen Xiaonong, *Chen Boda zuihou koushu huiyi*, pp. 324–325.

27. *Zhou Enlai nianpu*, 3: 107; Ma Qibin et al., *Zhongguo gongchandang zhizheng sishinian*, p. 283.

28. For the relationship between Mao and Wang Renzhong, see Zhang Zhong, *Donghu qingshen: Mao Zedong yu Wang Renzhong shisan niande jiaowang* (Emotions Are Deep on East Lake: Thirteen Years of Contacts between Mao Zedong and Wang Renzhong) (Beijing: Zhonggong dangshi chubanshe, 2004).

29. *Zhou Enlai nianpu*, 3: 110; *Biji Tao Zhu*, pp. 580–582.

30. *Mao Zedong wan sui* ([Shanghai?], [1968?]), p. 282. For Mao's knowledge of Tao Zhu, see *Origins*, 2: 141, 144, 156–159, 304; 3: 44–45, 419.

31. See the interview with Wang Li: Yeh Yung-lieh, "Wang Li Who Is Ill Answers His Guest's Questions," *Ta Kung Pao*, January 3–7, 1989, p. 2; translated in Joint Publications Research Service, CAR-89-011, Springfield, Va., February 7, 1989, p. 4.

32. Guofang daxue, *"Wenhua dageming,"* 1: 240–241.

33. Ma Qibin et al., *Zhongguo gongchandang zhizheng sishinian*, p. 284.

34. *Biji Tao Zhu*, pp. 591–592.

35. Wang Li, "Insider's Account of the Cultural Revolution," pp. 40–41.

36. See the observation by Chen Boda's son in Chen Xiaonong, *Chen Boda zuihou koushu huiyi*, p. 326.

37. Ibid., p. 327.

38. Wang Li, *Xianchang lishi*, pp. 29–30.

39. Quan Yanchi, *Tao Zhu zai "Wenhua dageming" zhong,* p. 191. Mao did not want to keep Tao because he was close to him, Quan argues; many people who were close to Mao fell.

40. The aide was his former political secretary, Hu Qiaomu. So precipitately did Mao act that there was no time for his officials to set up the visit, and when he got to the house Mao found that Hu was not at home; "Wang Li tan Mao Zedong" (Wang Li on Mao Zedong), manuscript, 1995, p. 58, Fairbank Center Library.

41. This is also the opinion of Chen Boda's son, who says that Mao was influenced by old cadres grumbling about a PSC member's being brought down in this way; Chen Xiaonong, *Chen Boda zuihou koushu huiyi,* p. 326.

42. See Terrill, *Madame Mao,* pp. 137–138, for a discussion of Mao's attitude toward Jiang Qing's strong personality.

43. Beijing boli zongchang hongweibing lianluozhan, *Zhongyang shouzhang jianghua,* 4: 54.

44. Notably Sun Yat-sen in the early 1920s.

45. Xi Xuan and Jin Chunming, *"Wenhua dageming" jianshi,* p. 148.

46. Ibid.; *Wang Li fansi lu,* 2: 974.

47. *Wang Li fansi lu,* 2: 974.

48. *Dongtai,* no. 62 (May 28, 1967).

49. Guofang daxue, *Qishinian,* pp. 551–552; Zhou Yan, "He 'da nao Huairentang' de zhanyoumen," pp. 36–38; Xi Xuan and Jin Chunming, *"Wenhua dageming" jianshi,* p. 152.

50. Tan Zhenlin, interview, November 29, 1978, and quoted in Ji Xichen, *Shi wuqianliede niandai: Yiwei "Renmin ribao" lao jizhede biji* (A Historically Unprecedented Decade: Notes of a *People's Daily* Reporter), 2 vols. (Beijing: Renmin ribao chubanshe, 2001), 1: 256.

51. Xi Xuan and Jin Chunming, *"Wenhua dageming" jianshi,* p. 148.

52. Jiang Qing pleaded sickness; Zhang Chunqiao and Yao Wenyuan had not yet returned from Shanghai; Guan Feng and Qi Benyu were not invited because the agenda topics did not concern them.

53. Wang Nianyi, *Da dongluande niandai,* p. 208.

54. Ibid.

55. Wang Li, *Xianchang lishi,* p. 30.

56. Wang Li, "Insider's Account of the Cultural Revolution," p. 44; *Wang Li fansi lu,* 2: 977; *Zhou Enlai nianpu,* 3: 126–127.

57. Zhonggong zhongyang wenxian yanjiushi, ed., *"Wenge" shinian ziliao xuanbian* (Selected Materials on the Ten-Year "Cultural Revolution"), 3 vols. (Beijing, 1981), 1: 183.

58. Ibid., pp. 183–185. See also Song Yongyi, Wu Tong, and Zhou Zehao, eds., "The Debate between the Blood Lineage Theory and Yu Luoke's 'On Family Back-

ground' during the Cultural Revolution," *Contemporary Chinese Thought*, 35, no. 4 (Summer 2004).

59. Zhonggong zhongyang wenxian yanjiushi, *"Wenge" shinian ziliao xuanbian*, 1: 184.

60. Quoted in Beijing caimao xueyuan, ed., *Zai Zhonggong ba jie shier zhong quanhui shang Mao zhuxi, Lin fuzhuxi, Zhou zongli de zhongyao jianghua* (Beijing: Maoyi xueyuan, April 1969), p. 35. The remark attributed to Tan Zhenlin is not included in the minutes of the meeting, but was cited in Zhou's Twelfth Plenum speech.

61. Zhonggong zhongyang wenxian yanjiushi, *"Wenge" shinian ziliao xuanbian*, 1: 184.

62. Ibid., pp. 184–185.

63. Ibid., p. 185.

64. Wang Nianyi, *Da dongluande niandai*, pp. 211–215.

65. Zhou Yan, "He 'da nao Huairentang' de zhanyoumen," pp. 39–41.

66. Zhou instructed Wang Li to prepare immediately a document on what had transpired at the meeting, to be shared with other members of the Politburo and the CCRG who had not been present. Wang Li drafted a document titled "Meeting in Huairen Hall on February 16," which underwent some revisions by Zhou and Kang Sheng before being printed.

67. *Wang Li fansi lu*, 1: 242; 2: 980–981.

68. This point is made by Harding, "The Chinese State in Crisis," pp. 209–210.

69. Xi Xuan and Jin Chunming, *"Wenhua dageming" jianshi*, p. 153.

70. Guofang daxue, *"Wenhua dageming,"* 1: 294.

71. *Jianguo yilai Mao Zedong wengao*, 12: 233–234; Chen Yi's comment on the editorial was "Superb! It's how things should be done"; *Wang Li fansi lu*, 2: 982.

72. Wang Nianyi, *Da dongluande niandai*, p. 216; *Zhou Enlai nianpu*, 3: 129.

73. Wang Nianyi, *Da dongluande niandai*, p. 216. This outburst is not included in *Jianguo yilai Mao Zedong wengao*, vol. 12, because it does not satisfy the editors' criteria for inclusion (the existence of a textual record ratified by Mao himself).

74. *Wang Li fansi lu*, 2: 983.

75. Wang Li, "Insider's Account of the Cultural Revolution," p. 53.

76. Wang Nianyi, *Da dongluande niandai*, pp. 216–217. Zhou Enlai reported to Mao on March 21 on how the seven meetings had progressed; *Zhou Enlai nianpu*, 3: 139. Previously Mao had been receiving interim reports from Wang Dongxing; Wang Li, "Insider's Account of the Cultural Revolution," p. 54.

77. All the translations above, unless otherwise indicated, originate with these minutes. Chen Yi subsequently protested at the inclusion of his remarks directly criticizing Mao Zedong by comparing him to Khrushchev, which he insisted he had never made, but Zhou (who together with Kang Sheng finalized the text) refused to remove them, claiming that he had indeed made them; Wang Li, "Insider's Account of the Cultural Revolution," p. 53.

78. Beijing boli zongchang hongweibing lianluozhan, *Zhongyang shouzhang jianghua,* 3: 172.

79. *Jianguo yilai Mao Zedong wengao,* 12: 247.

80. Beijing boli zongchang hongweibing lianluozhan, *Zhongyang shouzhang jianghua,* 3: 43, 110.

81. More than 100 "old" (i.e., joined up before the first Tiananmen Square rally on August 18) Red Guards were arrested on January 25; Ma Qibin et al., *Zhongguo gongchandang zhizheng sishinian,* p. 285.

82. Beijing hangkong xueyuan "Hongqi," *Wuchanjieji wenhua dageming shouzhang jianghua huiji,* p. 219.

83. Ibid.

84. Hongweibing Shanghai silingbu, *Zalan "liandong,"* pp. 125–126.

85. Beijing boli zongchang hongweibing lianluozhan, *Zhongyang shouzhang jianghua,* 4: 216.

86. "Chen Boda, Qi Benyu tongzhi 4.30 lingchen jiejian lianhe jiedaishi quanti renyuan shide jianghua" (Speeches of Comrades Chen Boda and Qi Benyu at a Reception for the Entire Staff of the Joint Reception Office at Dawn on April 30), original transcript (n.p., n.d.), p. 11, Schoenhals collection.

87. Xi Xuan and Jin Chunming, *"Wenhua dageming" jianshi,* p. 158; Rittenberg and Bennett, *The Man Who Stayed Behind,* p. 376.

12. The Wuhan Incident

1. Xi Xuan and Jin Chunming, *"Wenhua dageming" jianshi,* p. 167.

2. Mao, who made the admission when he had the American journalist Edgar Snow (whom he had known since the mid-1930s) to breakfast on December 18, 1970, said "all-round civil war" in English and Chinese *(quanmian neizhan); Jianguo yilai Mao Zedong wengao,* 13: 163. Snow made no mention of this admission in his account of that breakfast; Edgar Snow, *The Long Revolution* (London: Hutchinson, 1973), pp. 167–176.

3. Zhang Yunsheng, *Maojiawan jishi,* p. 108.

4. Zhou's busiest month in 1967 seems to have been January, as a result of the sudden onset of power-seizures, though figures are not available for all months. He met 88 times with responsible officials, civilian and military, and 114 times with mass organizations. In the following few months, he averaged just under 30 meetings a month with mass organizations, but in August the figure jumped to more than 50; *Zhou Enlai nianpu,* 3: 120, 132, 142, 159, 184.

5. The roles of various protagonists in these events have been given by themselves or others: Chen Zaidao, *Haojie zhongde yi mu;* Chen Zaidao, "Wuhan 'qi.er.ling shijian' shimo" (The Wuhan "July 20 Incident" from Start to Finish), in Guofang

daxue, *"Wenhua dageming,"* 1: 508–525; Wang Li, *Xianchang lishi*, pp. 38–46, in which the author is principally concerned to correct misinformation about his role purveyed by Chen Zaidao; Wang Li, "Insider's Account of the Cultural Revolution"; Quan Yanchi, *Weixing: Yang Chengwu zai 1967* (Traveling Incognito: Yang Chengwu in 1967) (Guangzhou: Guangdong lüyou chubanshe, 1997). Extraordinarily, Jin Chongji, *Zhou Enlai zhuan*, the most recent and authoritative biography of the premier, does not deal with the Wuhan incident. The major secondary source in English is Wang Shaoguang, *Failure of Charisma*.

6. Wuhan gang er si, ed., *Qiandao wangua Chen Zaidao* (Cut Chen Zaidao to Pieces), 2 vols. (Wuhan, 1967), 1: 28.

7. Kang Sheng quoted in *Zhongyang shouzhang guanyu Henan wentide zhishi ji fu-Jing huibao jiyao huibian*, p. 119.

8. For instance, when the provincial and Wuhan city party committees came under attack from Beijing Red Guards in late August 1966, Wang Renzhong dispatched a rival Red Guard group from the capital to defend them; Wang Shaoguang, *Failure of Charisma*, pp. 76–82.

9. Ibid., pp. 84–94.

10. "Quarterly Chronicle and Documentation," *CQ*, no. 30 (April–June 1967), 217.

11. Wang Shaoguang, *Failure of Charisma*, pp. 114–119.

12. Chen Zaidao, *Haojie zhongde yi mu*, pp. 29–33.

13. Wang Shaoguang, *Failure of Charisma*, pp. 121–124.

14. The MAC regulations are reproduced in Guofang daxue, *"Wenhua dageming,"* 1: 290–291.

15. Wuhan gang er si, *Qiandao wangua Chen Zaidao*, 1: 1–7.

16. Wang Shaoguang, *Failure of Charisma*, pp. 125–128.

17. Chen Zaidao, *Haojie zhongde yi mu*, pp. 38–39.

18. Ibid., pp. 40–45; Wang Shaoguang, *Failure of Charisma*, pp. 128–132. According to Chen Zaidao's account, he consulted with Zhou sometime during April 16–19 to arrange the meeting, and the premier chaired it; but Zhou went to Canton on April 14, and though he flew back on April 19, there is no record of his doing anything else on that day; *Zhou Enlai nianpu*, 3: 145–146.

19. Chen Zaidao, *Haojie zhongde yi mu*, p. 111.

20. *Wenge fengyun* (Cultural Revolution Storm) (Shanghai: Shanghai Industrial College Red Guard Revolutionary Committee), no. 11 (1967), 10.

21. Chen Zaidao, *Haojie zhongde yi mu*, p. 111.

22. Wang Nianyi, *Da dongluande niandai*, p. 260.

23. Wuhan gang er si, *Qiandao wangua Chen Zaidao*, 1: 1–7.

24. Guofang daxue, *"Wenhua dageming,"* 1: 492.

25. Wang Nianyi, *Da dongluande niandai*, p. 221.

26. Guofang daxue, *"Wenhua dageming,"* 1: 496–497.

27. Mao Zedong sixiang hongweibing Wuhan diqu geming zaofan silingbu, ed., *Yong xianxue he shengming baowei Mao zhuxi* (Defending Chairman Mao with Our Blood and Lives) (Wuhan, 1967), p. 37. The name of the Hongwubing, one of the key groups in this battle, means "Red Armed Forces"; thus somebody altering their name pejoratively, shouting "Down with the Heiwubing [Black Armed Forces]," was clearly an enemy.

28. *Weida de jiaodao guanghui de zhenli: Mao zhuxi shicha Huabei, Zhongnan he Huadong diqu* (Great Teachings and Brilliant Truths: Chairman Mao Inspects the North, Central-South, and East China Regions) (Nanchang: Jiangxi ribao she Jinggangshan hongqi huoju, 1967), p. 23.

29. *Wuchanjieji wenhua dageming zhong xuexi wenjian teji* (Special Collection of Documents Studied in the Great Proletarian Cultural Revolution) (Beijing: Beijing dizhi xueyuan geming weiyuanhui ziliaozu, 1967), pp. 82–84.

30. Wang Shaoguang, *Failure of Charisma*, pp. 133–149.

31. *Wenge fengyun*, no. 11 (1967), 4, 10.

32. Wang Nianyi, *Da dongluande niandai*, p. 260.

33. Wang Shaoguang, *Failure of Charisma*, p. 149.

34. *Zhou Enlai nianpu*, 3: 168–169. Other accounts suggest that Mao's decision to go to Wuhan may not have been revealed until July 13; according to Quan Yanchi, *Weixing*, pp. 22–31, the acting chief of staff who accompanied Mao to Wuhan was told about the trip at a meeting on the afternoon of July 13, although there is no record of such a meeting in *Zhou Enlai nianpu*. A decision taken on July 13 to leave immediately would explain why Zhou phoned Xie Fuzhi only that night to go to Wuhan the following day "on an emergency assignment," as Wang Li puts it; Wang Li, "Insider's Account of the Cultural Revolution," p. 67.

35. *Mao Zedong sixiang wan sui* ([Shanghai?], [1968?]), p. 319.

36. *Dongtai*, no. 125 (August 17, 1967). For comment on coverage of events in Wuhan by journalists working for the *People's Daily, Red Flag, Liberation Army News*, and the Xinhua News Agency, see ibid., no. 100 (July 19, 1967).

37. Gang gongzong "Wuhu sihai" zhandou bingtuan, ed., *Zhenhan quanguo de riri yeye* (Days and Nights That Shook the Entire Nation) (Wuhan: Huazhong fangzhi gongxueyuan, 1967), p. 3.

38. Quan Yanchi, *Weixing*, p. 46; for an account of the PLA's elaborate deployment of land, water, and air units to protect Mao, see ibid., p. 42.

39. Wang Li, "Insider's Account of the Cultural Revolution," pp. 67–68; Chen Zaidao, *Haojie zhongde yi mu*, pp. 54–57, 65–66; Wang Shaoguang, *Failure of Charisma*, p. 149. There are many discrepancies of detail in the various accounts of this period. According to Chen Zaidao, Zhou informed him that Mao might come to swim when he telephoned on July 10; Wang Li's account implies that Zhou did not; Wang Shaoguang, *Failure of Charisma*, says he did not; *Zhou Enlai*

nianpu, 3: 168–169, says only that Zhou told the MR about the change of venue for the negotiations. Chen's claim seems suspect, since he admits that he was not alerted to go to the airport to meet Zhou. The point is important if unresolvable because it could indicate Zhou's view of Chen's reliability. Chen also says that the premier managed to energize the highly factionalized staff at the East Lake Hotel to clean the rooms, which they had been neglecting; Wang Li says that Zhou dismissed the staffers who were adherents of the Million Heroes and replaced them with members of the rebels. There is also disagreement about the date of Mao's arrival: according to Zhonggong Hubei shengwei dangshi ziliao zhengbian weiyuanhui, ed., *Mao Zedong zai Hubei* (Mao Zedong in Hubei) (Beijing: Zhonggong dangshi chubanshe, 1993), p. 337, Chen Zaidao (*Haojie zhongde yi mu*, p. 57), and Yang Chengwu (Quan Yanchi, *Weixing*, p. 59), it was July 14, and the last source (p. 50) says the train left Beijing at 3:00 A.M. earlier the same day; but Wang Shaoguang (*Failure of Charisma*, p. 148) gives the arrival date as July 13, while Wang Li ("Insider's Account of the Cultural Revolution," p. 68) says July 15. Since a normal express train takes eighteen hours from Beijing to Wuhan, Mao's special train could have arrived by the evening of July 14, even if the decision to leave was taken on the afternoon of July 13.

40. Wang Li, "Insider's Account of the Cultural Revolution," p. 68.
41. Wang Shaoguang, *Failure of Charisma*, pp. 149–150.
42. According to Wang Li, the premier originally intended returning to Beijing on July 15, but was persuaded to stay since the Xie-Wang delegation was ignorant about central policy on Wuhan; Wang Li, "Insider's Account of the Cultural Revolution," pp. 68–69.
43. Ibid. For a more elaborate version of these points, see Wang Shaoguang, *Failure of Charisma*, p. 151.
44. Chen Zaidao, *Haojie zhongde yi mu*, pp. 74–79; Wang Li, "Insider's Account of the Cultural Revolution," p. 71; Li Ke and Hao Shengzhang, *Wenhua dageming zhongde renmin jiefangjun*, p. 49; Wang Shaoguang, *Failure of Charisma*, pp. 152–153; according to this last source, Wang Li's lecture lasted from 4:00 until 11:00 P.M. One reason for Wang Li's prominence was that he had leaked Mao's formula for solving the Wuhan problem to the Beijing Red Guards who had come from Chongqing with him and Xie; when the Red Guards had, predictably, leaked the news to the local rebels, they had attributed the formula to Wang.
45. Chen Zaidao, *Haojie zhongde yi mu*, pp. 79–85; Wang Shaoguang, *Failure of Charisma*, pp. 154–155. Chen Zaidao attributes Xie's immunity to his Hubei origins and high rank; Wang attributes it to Xie's discretion relative to Wang Li in his public remarks about the Million Heroes.
46. For the view from Lin Biao's headquarters, see Zhang Yunsheng, *Maojiawan jishi*, pp. 124–132. The urgency of the situation as seen by radicals in Beijing is il-

lustrated by three "urgent telegrams" from Wuhan published by Tsinghua Red Guards on July 21; *Dongtai*, no. 102 (July 21, 1967).

47. For a description of Mao's flight, see Quan Yanchi, *Weixing*, pp. 97–101, 106–111. This account (p. 108) details the elaborate measures then in force governing the use of planes by Politburo members. For instance, neither Mao nor Lin Biao was supposed to fly without a report's being made to the premier. See also Wang Li, "Insider's Account of the Cultural Revolution," pp. 72–73. The quotation is in Li Zhisui, *The Private Life of Chairman Mao*, p. 492.

48. *Dongtai*, no. 103 (July 22, 1967).

49. Wang Li, "Insider's Account of the Cultural Revolution," p. 73. Perhaps the premier was trying to disguise the fact that he had been away, for his absence would have underlined the gravity of the recent crisis; "Quarterly Chronicle and Documentation," *CQ*, no. 32 (October–December 1967), 185.

50. After the Cultural Revolution, Wang Li claimed that Mao's view was that the Wuhan incident was not a counterrevolutionary coup, but simply an attempt to take himself hostage to pressure the center to change its policy on the Wuhan question; Wang Li, "Insider's Account of the Cultural Revolution," p. 72.

51. *Zhou Enlai nianpu*, 3: 171–172; Chen Zaidao, *Haojie zhongde yi mu*, pp. 99–103, 112.

52. Wang Li claims that he successfully opposed a suggestion that he and Xie Fuzhi should tour Tiananmen Square in an open convertible; Wang Li, "Insider's Account of the Cultural Revolution," p. 73. For a description of Chiang Kai-shek's "triumphant return" to his capital, Nanjing, after the Xi'an incident, and his subsequent shifts of policy, see Lloyd E. Eastman, *The Abortive Revolution: China under Nationalist Rule, 1927–1937* (Cambridge, Mass.: Council on East Asian Studies, Harvard University, 1990), pp. 269–270.

53. Chen Zaidao, *Haojie zhongde yi mu*, p. 58.

54. Zhou Enlai did apparently safeguard the Wuhan contingent from being "dragged out" by Beijing Red Guards; *Jianguo yilai Mao Zedong wengao*, 12: 383–384; *Zhou Enlai nianpu*, 3: 173; Chen Zaidao, *Haojie zhongde yi mu*, pp. 119–126.

55. Wang Nianyi, *Da dongluande niandai*, pp. 264–266; Wang Shaoguang, *Failure of Charisma*, pp. 159–160.

56. Ma Qibin et al., *Zhongguo gongchandang zhizheng sishinian*, p. 308.

57. Wang Nianyi, *Da dongluande niandai*, p. 260.

58. *Zhongyang shouzhang guanyu Henan wentide zhishi ji fu-Jing huibao jiyao huibian*, p. 50.

59. *Chedi fouding "Wenhua dageming" jianghua* (Lectures on Thoroughly Repudiating the "Great Cultural Revolution") (Beijing: Zhongguo renmin jiefangjun zhengzhi xueyuan chubanshe, 1985), p. 149.

60. Cf. Michael Schoenhals, "'Why Don't We Arm the Left?': Mao's Culpability for

the Cultural Revolution's 'Great Chaos' of 1967," *CQ*, no. 182 (June 2005), 277–300.

61. *Wang Li fansi lu*, 1: 251; 2: 1012.

62. Shanghai minbing douzhengshi ziliaozu, ed., *Shanghai minbing douzheng shi ziliao* (Documents on the History of the Struggle of the Shanghai Militia), no. 17 (December 1980), 3–4.

63. *Wang Li fansi lu*, 1: 1012.

64. Wang Li, "Insider's Account of the Cultural Revolution," pp. 75–76. Mao's July 18 dictum was not passed on by the premier. Mao's letter to Jiang Qing is not included in *Jianguo yilai Mao Zedong wengao*, vol. 12.

65. Wang Li, "Lishi jiang xuangao wo wuzui," pp. 13, 72.

66. *Jiedai tongxun* (Reception Newsletter) (Shanghai: Shanghai Revolutionary Committee Reception Office), no. 53 (August 29, 1967).

67. Yunnan sheng geming weiyuanhui, *Wuchanjieji wenhua dageming wenjian huibian*, 1: 429.

68. Lin Biao, "Tingqu Zeng Siyu, Liu Feng tongzhi huibao shide chahua yiji ting huibao houde zhishi" (Instructions Issued during and after Reporting and Interjections Made While Listening to Report from Comrades Zeng Siyu and Liu Feng), p. 1, mimeographed anonymous contemporary transcript, copy in Fairbank Center Library.

69. Yunnan sheng geming weiyuanhui, *Wuchanjieji wenhua dageming wenjian huibian*, 1: 435.

70. *Qinghua Jinggangshan tongxunshe* (Tsinghua Jingganshan News Agency) (Beijing), individual transcript, no. 756 (October 26, 1967), 2; *Dangdai Zhongguode Ningxia* (Contemporary China's Ningxia) (Beijing: Zhongguo shehui kexue chubanshe, 1990), pp. 157–158, 799; *Dongfanghong*, no. 66 (September 26, 1967), 6–8; Wang Nianyi, *Da dongluande niandai*, p. 268; Zhong Kan, *Kang Sheng pingzhuan* (A Critical Biography of Kang Sheng) (Beijing: Hongqi chubanshe, 1982), p. 410; Zhonggong zhongyang wenxian yanjiushi, *Sanzhong quanhui yilai zhongyao wenxian huibian*, 1: 689.

71. *Yaowen jianbao* (Important News Bulletin) (Beijing: Beijing Institute of Politics and Law), nos. 47–60 (August 1967).

72. Ibid., no. 47 (August 14, 1967).

73. *Zhongyang bande Mao Zedong sixiang xuexiban Sichuan ban geming dapipan fayan* (Revolutionary Great Criticism: Statements from the Sichuan Class of the Mao Zedong Thought Study Classes Organized by the Center), 21 vols. (n.p., 1970), 21: 15.

74. Ibid., 7: 12.

75. *Chongqing shizhi* (Gazetteer of Chongqing Municipality) (Chengdu: Sichuan daxue chubanshe, 1992), 1: 410.

76. Jin Chunming, Huang Yuchong, and Chang Huimin, *"Wenge" shiqi guaishi guaiyu*, p. 196.

77. *Daqing shizhi* (Daqing Gazetteer) (Nanjing: Nanjing renmin chubanshe, 1988), p. 25.

78. *Yaowen jianbao*, no. 47 (August 14, 1967).

79. Yunnan sheng geming weiyuanhui, *Wuchanjieji wenhua dageming wenjian huibian*, 1: 477–479.

80. For a description of the hostilities between the "Allied Command," the rebel organization based at the Diesel Plant, and Wang Hongwen's Workers' General Headquarters, see also Perry and Li, *Proletarian Power*, pp. 132–141.

81. *Jiedai tongxun*, no. 37 (July 10, 1967). These regulations were drafted because the Reception Group of the Shanghai Revolutionary Committee discovered that "ordinary people" were worried not just about the "civil war" itself but also about care of the injured, medical expenses, and other pressing family matters; ibid., no. 15 (May 17, 1967).

82. Ibid., no. 40 (July 16, 1967); no. 49 (August 14, 1967); no. 55 (September 1, 1967); no. 59 (September 15, 1967).

83. See Andrew G. Walder, "Factional Conflict at Beijing University, 1966–1968," manuscript, Fairbank Center Library. For the autobiograpy of one of Nie's leading opponents, mentioned by Walder, see Yang Xun, *Xinlu: Liangzhide mingyun* (The Way of the Heart: The Fate of a Conscience) (Beijing: Xinhua chubanshe, 2004). Her younger brother, Yang Bingzhang, who was seized along with his sister, described Nie in a wall poster in December as a "political whore" (Walder, "Factional Conflict"); in the 1980s he got a Ph.D. in history at Harvard. His autobiography is *Cong beida dao hafo* (From Peking University to Harvard) (Beijing: Zuojia chubanshe, 1998).

84. See Hong Yung Lee, *Politics of Chinese Cultural Revolution*, pp. 204–243.

85. "Beijingshi 'Wenhua dageming' dashiji, 1965–1967," pp. 44–46.

86. Changchun gongshe 503 zhandoudui, ed., *Chuncheng wuchanjieji wenhua dageming dashiji (1965.11–1968.3)* (Record of Major Events in the Spring City in the Great Proletarian Cultural Revolution [November 1965–March 1968]), 2 vols. (Changchun, 1968), 2: 152–155.

87. Ma Qibin et al., *Zhongguo gongchandang zhizheng sishinian*, p. 303.

13. The May 16 Conspiracy

1. As cited in *Wang Li fansi lu*, 1: 386.

2. Ibid., 2: 1023.

3. Jin Chunming, Huang Yuchong, and Chang Huimin, *"Wenge" shiqi guaishi guaiyu*, p. 313.

4. Ibid., p. 101. Cf. Yan Jiaqi and Gao Gao, *Turbulent Decade*, p. 252; Wang Nianyi, *Da dongluande niandai*, pp. 271–272; Jin Chunming, *"Wenhua dageming" shigao* (Historical Sketch of the "Great Cultural Revolution") (Chengdu: Sichuan renmin chubanshe, 1995), p. 323; Xi Xuan and Jin Chunming, *"Wenhua dageming" jianshi*, p. 223.

5. Wang Nianyi, *Da dongluande niandai*, p. 272.

6. *Dongtai bao* (Current Intelligence Reports) (Beijing: Finance and Trade Liaison Station), no. 105 (August 19, 1967).

7. Bu Weihua, "Beijing hongweibing yundong dashiji," p. 60.

8. Yunnan sheng geming weiyuanhui, *Wuchanjieji wenhua dageming wenjian huibian*, 1: 542.

9. *Dongtai*, no. 154 (September 20, 1967).

10. "Zongli guanyu qingcha '5.16' de zhishi (zhailu)" (Extracts from the Premier's Instructions on Investigating the "May 16"), November 4, 1970, handwritten copy, available in Fairbank Center Library.

11. Barbara Barnouin and Yu Changgen, *Chinese Foreign Policy during the Cultural Revolution* (London: Kegan Paul International, 1998), pp. 12–13.

12. "Quarterly Chronicle and Documentation," *CQ*, no. 30 (April–June 1967), 240–249; ibid., no. 31 (July–September 1967), 212–223; ibid., no. 32 (October–December 1967), 221–227. For a fuller account, see Barnouin and Yu, *Chinese Foreign Policy during the Cultural Revolution*. An older study worth consulting is Melvin Gurtov, "The Foreign Ministry and Foreign Affairs in the Chinese Cultural Revolution," in Thomas W. Robinson, ed., *The Cultural Revolution in China* (Berkeley: University of California Press, 1971), pp. 313–366.

13. Anthony Grey, *Hostage in Peking* (London: Michael Joseph, 1970), pp. 96–97.

14. For an account of the Foreign Ministry during the Cultural Revolution by an insider, see Ma Jisen, *The Cultural Revolution in the Foreign Ministry of China* (Hong Kong: Chinese University Press, 2004). For her account of the events of August 1967, see pp. 191–220.

15. The key to Chinese diplomats' panic was the statement by Mao on September 9, 1966, that embassy staffs needed to be revolutionized; see Barnouin and Yu, *Chinese Foreign Policy during the Cultural Revolution*, pp. 12–13.

16. Cheng Hua, *Zhou Enlai he tade mishumen*, pp. 248–249.

17. FCO 21/33, Confidential draft, Registry no. FCI/14, Public Record Office, Kew (hereafter PRO). We are grateful to Dalena Wright for sharing her findings at the PRO.

18. Grey, *Hostage in Peking*, pp. 83–108; "Quarterly Chronicle and Documentation" (October–December 1967), 221–223.

19. See Mr. Hopson to Mr. Brown, "The Burning of the British Office in Peking," Confidential, September 8, 1967, FC 1/14, FCO 21/34, PRO. This file also con-

tains the personal accounts of all the other British personnel involved; that of Percy Cradock, the counselor and head of the chancery, is largely reproduced in his *Experiences of China*, pp. 58–71.

20. See the copy of the confidential message sent to Hong Kong on August 31, TELNO 1801, FCO 21/84, PRO. A copy of the same message, typed up by the British embassy in Stockholm on September 1, is in the archives of the Swedish Ministry for Foreign Affairs, Stockholm.

21. Top secret, K(69)1, FCO 40/160, PRO.

22. See for instance the Top Secret and Personal Comments by James Murray on a draft paper by Michael Wilford, November 17, 1969, FCO 40/160, PRO.

23. Cradock, *Experiences of China*, p. 72.

24. Barnouin and Yu, *Chinese Foreign Policy during the Cultural Revolution*, p. 71.

25. Ibid., pp. 72–73.

26. *Dongtai*, no. 121 (August 12, 1967).

27. Shoudu hongdaihui Beijing di er waiguoyu xueyuan hongweibing, ed., *Jiu ping Wang Li* (Nine Critiques of Wang Li) (Beijing, 1967), pp. 22–26.

28. Wang Li, "Insider's Account of the Cultural Revolution," pp. 77–79; idem, *Xianchang lishi*, pp. 47–65.

29. Quoted in Barnouin and Yu, *Chinese Foreign Policy during the Cultural Revolution*, pp. 155–159. See also Jin Ge, "Zai waijiaobu 'duoquan' qian hou" (The Background to the "Seizure of Power" in the Foreign Ministry), in An Jianshe, *Zhou Enlaide zuihou suiyue*, pp. 230–234.

30. *Dongtai bao*, no. 111 (August 26, 1967). Yao soon found himself having to admit to Zhou Enlai that he had "misunderstood" Wang Li; *Wenge tongxun* (Cultural Revolution News) ([Tianjin?]: Xinhua fang), no. 58 (September 23, 1967).

31. Wang Li, *Xianchang lishi*, pp. 52–53.

32. Quoted by Gurtov, "The Foreign Ministry and Foreign Affairs in the Cultural Revolution," p. 348; see also Jin Ge, "Zai waijiaobu 'duoquan' qian hou," pp. 235, 239.

33. Barnouin and Yu, *Chinese Foreign Policy during the Cultural Revolution*, pp. 26–27. For a Western report on Wang Li's unsuccessful efforts to achieve rehabilitation, see Patrick E. Tyler, "A Ghost of Maoist Fervor Lives on in Disgrace," *New York Times*, April 10, 1996.

34. Graham told Sidney Rittenberg, but when he tried to confirm the statement with one of Zhou's secretaries, he was told that it was "pure fantasy" on Graham's part; Rittenberg and Bennett, *The Man Who Stayed Behind*, pp. 381–382. For confirmation of the Zhou-Graham meeting, see Zhonghua renmin gongheguo waijiaobu and Waijiao shi yanjiushi, eds., *Zhou Enlai waijiao huadong dashiji, 1949–1975* (A Chronology of Zhou Enlai's Activities in Foreign Affairs, 1949–1975) (Beijing: Shijie zhishi chubanshe, 1993), p. 515.

35. Wang Li, "Lishi jiang xuangao wo wuzui," p. 21.

36. Zhang Zishen, *Zhanjiang yu tongshuai: Yang Chengwu zai Mao Zedong huixiade sishiba nian* (Battle General and Commander-in-Chief: Yang Chengwu's Forty-eight Years under Mao Zedong's Command) (Shenyang: Liaoning renmin chubanshe, 2000), pp. 373–376.

37. According to *Wang Li fansi lu*, 2: 1014, "when Lin Biao noticed that Beijing was becoming increasingly chaotic, he took the train and left."

38. Zhang Zishen, *Zhanjiang yu tongshuai*, p. 378.

39. Cheng Hua, *Zhou Enlai he tade mishumen*, pp. 525–556; Jin Chongji, *Zhou Enlai zhuan*, 2: 972.

40. *Wang Li fansi lu*, 1: 212–220.

41. *Zhou Enlai nianpu*, 3: 183.

42. *Wang Li fansi lu*, 2: 1015; *Zhou Enlai nianpu*, 3: 175; *Dongtai bao*, no. 111 (August 26, 1967).

43. *Baige zhengliu* (One Hundred Boats Battle the Current) (Beijing: Finance and Trade Red Rebels), no. 144 (October 9, 1967). In late July in Shanghai, Mao had also seen a TV broadcast of a mass rally at which Chen Pixian and Cao Diqiu, the former city leaders, were being denounced. He became very excited about such TV rallies as a way of reaching out to and "educating" large numbers of people, and once he had returned to Beijing, he said, he would see to it that Beijing TV followed Shanghai's example; ibid.

44. *Wang Li fansi lu*, 2: 1014.

45. *Wenge jianxun*, no. 414 (August 14, 1967).

46. *Dongtai bao*, no. 111 (August 26, 1967).

47. *Caimao doupigai tongxun* (Finance and Trade Struggle, Criticize, and Transform Bulletin) (Shanghai: Finance and Trade Sector, "Struggle-Criticize-Transform" Liaison Station), no. 4 (September 6, 1967).

48. *Wang Li fansi lu*, 1: 212–220.

49. *Jianguo yilai Mao Zedong wengao*, 12: 412.

50. *Huanxintian* (To Alter the Sky) (Beijing: Eighth Ministry of Machine Building), no. 18 (October 16, 1967), 8.

51. *Wang Li fansi lu*, 1: 11.

52. "Zongli guanyu qingcha '5.16' de zhishi (zhailu)," November 9, 1970.

53. *Dongtai*, no. 141 (September 5, 1967); emphasis added.

54. Wang Naiying, "Yi ri dao qi ri wo dou zuole xie shenme?" (What Did I Do from the 1st to the 7th [of August 1967]?), handwritten 15-page record dated September 15, 1967, Schoenhals collection.

55. Wang Naiying, "Renzuishu" (Admission of Guilt), December 10, 1970.

56. Ibid., December 11, 1970.

57. Ibid., December 12, 1970.

58. *Zhongfa* [1970] 20, March 27, 1970, in Guofang daxue, *"Wenhua dageming,"* 2: 420.

59. Minzu yanjiusuo Jinggangshan bingtuan, ed., *Pan Zinian Wu Chuanqi Lin Yushi Hong Tao Wang Enyu fandang jituan de taotian zuixing dazibao cailiao huibian* (Collected Big-Character Posters and Materials on the Heinous Crimes of the Counterrevolutionary Clique of Pan Zinian, Wu Chuanqi, Lin Yushi, Hong Tao, and Wang Enyu) (Beijing, 1967), p. 7.

60. Hebei sheng geming weiyuanhui zhengzhibu, *Mao zhuxi zuixin zhishi ruogan zhongyao wenxian*, p. 636; Yunnan sheng geming weiyuanhui, *Wuchanjieji wenhua dageming wenjian huibian*, 1: 554–555.

61. Barbara Barnouin and Yu Changgen, *Ten Years of Turbulence: The Chinese Cultural Revolution* (London: Kegan Paul International, 1993), p. 198.

62. Wang Nianyi, *Da dongluande niandai*, p. 273.

63. *Guanyu fangeming jituan zhongyao chengyuan Fu Chonglan deng jianli di er tao banzi* (On How Fu Chonglan and Other Important Members of the Counter-revolutionary Clique Set Up a Second Team) (Beijing: Xuebu Hongweibing zongdui Geming lishisuo Xinghuo bingtuan, 1968), p. 18.

64. Jin Chunming, Huang Yuchong, and Chang Huimin, *"Wenge" shiqi guaishi guaiyu*, p. 313.

65. Jin Chunming, *"Wenhua dageming" shigao*, p. 324.

66. Liu Dinghan, ed., *Dangdai Jiangsu jianshi* (A Short History of Contemporary Jiangsu) (Beijing: Dangdai Zhongguo chubanshe, 1999), p. 235. An unofficial source gives a significantly higher estimate and claims that 270,000 "May 16 elements" were arrested in the provincial capital of Nanjing alone. See Hei Yan'nan (pseud.), *Shinian dongluan* (Ten Years of Turmoil) ([Beijing]: Guoji wenhua chuban gongsi, 1988), p. 198.

67. *Guangxi wenge dashi nianbiao*, p. 154.

68. Guofang daxue, *"Wenhua dageming,"* 2: 512–513.

69. Handwritten transcript of document dated February 28, 1971, in the authors' possession.

70. *Zhongguo renmin gongan shigao* (Draft History of the Chinese People's Public Security) (Beijing: Jingguan jiaoyu chubanshe, 1997), pp. 343–344.

71. Jin Chunming, Huang Yuchong, and Chang Huimin, *"Wenge" shiqi guaishi guaiyu*, p. 314.

14. The End of the Red Guards

1. *Jianguo yilai Mao Zedong wengao*, 12: 424; Ma Qibin et al., *Zhongguo gongchandang zhizheng sishinian*, p. 300.

2. Ma Qibin et al., *Zhongguo gongchandang zhizheng sishinian*, p. 300. See Harry Harding's assessment, "The Chinese State in Crisis," pp. 214–217.

3. Ma Qibin et al., *Zhongguo gongchandang zhizheng sishinian*, p. 307.

4. Renshibu difang jigou bianzhi guanlisi, ed., *Zhonghua renmin gongheguo sheng, zizhiqu, zhixiashi dang sheng qun jiguan zuzhi jigou gaiyao* (Outline of the Organizational Structure of Party, Government, and Mass Organs in Provinces, Autonomous Regions, and Municipalities Directly Subordinate to the Central Government in the PRC) (Beijing: Zhongguo renshi chubanshe, 1989), p. 414.

5. Gao Xingjian, *One Man's Bible,* trans. Mabel Lee (New York: HarperCollins, 2002), p. 298.

6. According to Zhou Enlai, speaking in April 1967, the CCP had 18 million members in 1967, of whom five-sixths had joined since 1949; *Xuexi wenjian*, p. 6.

7. In Heilongjiang, Shandong, Guizhou, Shanghai, Shanxi, Beijing, and Qinghai; Li Ke and Hao Shengzhang, *"Wenhua dageming" zhongde renmin jiefangjun*, pp. 245–246.

8. Ma Qibin et al., *Zhongguo gongchandang zhizheng sishinian*, pp. 299, 302.

9. *Renmin ribao*, March 30, 1968.

10. Ibid., September 7, 1968.

11. Based on a survey of the first eight months of 1968 in *Zhou Enlai nianpu*, vol. 3.

12. Yunnan sheng geming weiyuanhui, *Wuchanjieji wenhua dageming wenjian huibian*, 2: 845–846.

13. The capital of Hebei shifted first to the city of Baoding and then in February 1968 to Shijiazhuang, which became the seat of the provincial RC; see Zhonggong Hebei shengwei dangshi yanjiushi, ed., *Zhongguo gongchandang Hebei lishi dashiji (1949.7–1978.12)* (A Chronicle of the CCP in Hebei History [July 1949–December 1978]) (Beijing: Zhongyang wenxian chubanshe, 1999), pp. 380, 395, 402.

14. Beijing boli zongchang hongweibing lianluozhan, *Zhongyang shouzhang jianghua*, 4: 56.

15. Ibid.

16. Ibid., pp. 68–69.

17. Ibid., p. 73.

18. Li Yifu, late July 1967, quoted in "Hao Kewei jiaodai cailiao" (Hao Kewei's Confessions), p. 1, handwritten confessions from Beijing, Schoenhals collection.

19. *Yejin fenglei* (Metallurgy Tempest) (Tianjin: Municipal Metallurgy Industry Revolutionary Committee), no. 3 (December 21, 1967).

20. In *Zhou Enlai nianpu*, vol. 3, Zhou Enlai is recorded as dealing with Tianjin only in early April, on May 8, and finally on December 2, 1967, when Kang Sheng informed Tianjin's delegates that their revolutionary committee had been approved. In the case of Guangxi, in the same source there are eleven references for 1967 and thirteen for 1968.

21. *Zhou Enlai nianpu*, 3: 135.

22. *Guangxi wenge dashi nianbiao*, pp. 47–48.

23. In Hebei a similar situation existed, with the centrally commanded troops supporting one mass organization and the local troops supporting the other; Zhang Yunsheng, *Maojiawan jishi*, pp. 182–184.

24. *Guangxi wenge dashi nianbiao*, p. 68.

25. Ibid., illustration no. 30.

26. Ma Qibin et al., *Zhongguo gongchandang zhizheng sishinian*, p. 301.

27. Ibid., p. 302.

28. *327 tongxun* (The 327 Newsletter) ([Guangzhou?]: New First Headquarters), no. 2 (1968), 3.

29. Wang Nianyi, *Da dongluande niandai*, p. 306.

30. Li Ke and Hao Shengzhang, *"Wenhua dageming" zhongde renmin jiefangjun*, pp. 244–246.

31. Frederick C. Teiwes, "The Establishment and Consolidation of the New Regime, 1949–57," in MacFarquhar, *The Politics of China: Second Edition*, pp. 28–32.

32. For one semiofficial post–Cultural Revolution explanation of this still obscure episode, see Guofang daxue, *Qishinian*, pp. 555–557. For a careful Western analysis of the complex career ties and personal antagonisms revealed in Chinese sources, see Teiwes and Sun, *The Tragedy of Lin Biao*, pp. 90–102. For a discussion of the military factional politics behind the three dismissals, see Jing Huang, *Factionalism in Chinese Communist Politics*, pp. 311–314. Another source describes the purge as the last major instance of cooperation between the Lin Biao and Jiang Qing factions; Gao Wenqian, *Wannian Zhou Enlai* (Zhou Enlai's Later Years) (New York: Mingjing chubanshe, 2003), p. 265.

33. Zhang Yunsheng, *Maojiawan jishi*, pp. 215–220.

34. Ma Qibin et al., *Zhongguo gongchandang zhizheng sishinian*, p. 299.

35. *Jiaoyu geming* (Revolution in Education) (Beijing: Beijing Normal University), no. 5 (1967), 5.

36. Wang Jian, "'Wenhua dageming' shiqi Beijing pujiao qingkuang," p. 26.

37. *Jiaoyu geming*, no. 5 (1967), 10.

38. Ibid., p. 6.

39. *Baige zhengliu*, no. 151 (October 17, 1967).

40. Schoenhals, *China's Cultural Revolution*, pp. 176–181.

41. Shanghai shi geming weiyuanhui jiedaizu, ed., *Xuexi ziliao*, no. 1 (October 12, 1967), 8.

42. Chinese diary no. 2; emphasis added.

43. Thurston, *A Chinese Odyssey*, p. 229.

44. *Nie Yuanzi huiyilu*, pp. 282–283. Nie at first could not understand why she was being "summoned" *(zhaojian)* rather than simply being invited *(jiejian)* to a "reception." Upon arrival at the Great Hall of the People, the Red Guard leaders were frisked.

45. Ibid., pp. 282–315. The equivalent in the United States in 1968 would have been for the leaders of the Students for a Democratic Society (SDS) and the Weathermen to have been berated at the White House by President Johnson, accompanied by the vice president, congressional leaders, members of the cabinet, and the chairman of the Joint Chiefs. The SDS, incidentally, may have been quite well known to Red Guard activists at the time, its activities having been reported regularly in the Xinhua News Agency's daily *Reference News* for a number of years (see the extended coverage in *Cankao xiaoxi*, January 7 and April 21, 1966).

46. *Nie Yuanzi huiyilu*, p. 304.

47. *Miscellany of Mao Tse-tung Thought (1949–1968)*, 2 vols. (Arlington, Va.: Joint Publications Research Service, 1974), 2: 469–497.

48. The classic study of this movement is Thomas P. Bernstein, *Up to the Mountains and Down to the Villages* (New Haven: Yale University Press, 1977).

49. Wang Jian, "'Wenhua dageming' shiqi Beijing pujiao qingkuang," p. 27.

50. Quoted in Schoenhals, *China's Cultural Revolution*, pp. 77–78.

51. Yunnan sheng geming weiyuanhui, *Wuchanjieji wenhua dageming wenjian huibian*, 2: 1006.

52. Wu Li, *Zhonghua renmin gongheguo jingji shi*, 1: 706–707.

53. Jung Chang, *Wild Swans*, pp. 379–443, describes how she and other family members were sent down from Chengdu to "distant parts of the Sichuan wilderness."

54. For a vivid firsthand account of the life of urban youths, mainly from Beijing and Shanxi, in Inner Mongolia, and the disastrous impact of their "developmental" endeavors on the local economy and ecology, see Ma Bo, *Blood Red Sunset*.

55. Bernstein, *Up to the Mountains, Down to the Villages*, pp. 2, 29, 30. Bernstein also points out (pp. 38–41) that lack of urban employment opportunities increased the urgency of shipping urban youths to the countryside. However, this was probably a more important factor in the 1970 emigration waves rather than in the late 1960s.

56. *Zhishi qingnian shangshan xiaxiang gongzuo youguan wenjian* (Documents Relating to the Work of Educated Youth Going up to the Mountains and down to the Countryside) (Beijing: Quanguo zhishi qingnian shangshan xiaxiang gongzuo xiaotanhui, 1972), p. 41.

57. Ibid., p. 45.

58. See Gao Anhua, *To the Edge of the Sky*, who describes her horror at experiencing rural conditions as a middle school student in 1964 (pp. 106–110) and her desperate (and ultimately successful) efforts to avoid experiencing them again by joining the PLA in 1968 (pp. 181–187).

59. Andrew G. Walder, "Anatomy of an Inquisition: Cleansing the Class Ranks, 1968–1971," paper presented at the conference "The Cultural Revolution in Retro-

spect," Hong Kong University of Science and Technology, July 1996; see Chapter 15.

60. Ma Qibin et al., *Zhongguo gongchandang zhizheng sishinian*, p. 308.

15. Cleansing the Class Ranks

1. Hu Qiaomu, quoted in Xinwen yanjiusuo, ed., *Tantan baozhi gongzuo* (On Newspaper Work) (Beijing, 1978), p. 55.
2. Beijing shi geming weiyuanhui di er xuexiban dangwei, "Guanyu Yuan Lirong tongzhi de fucha qingkuang" (On the Situation of the Reinvestigation of Comrade Yuan Lirong), October 18, 1972, p. 1.
3. *Xuexi ziliao* (Study Materials) (Beijing: Tsinghua University Jinggangshan Struggle-Criticize-Transform Battle Regiment), no. 117 (February 20, 1968), 4. Was it Taiwanese agents entering Zhejiang by boat or parachute that he had in mind?
4. Kunming nonglin xueyuan geming weiyuanhui zhengxuanzu, ed., *Qingli jieji duiwu ziliao huibian* (Collected Materials on Cleansing the Class Ranks) (Kunming, 1969), p. 107; see also *Xuexi ziliao* (Zhantuan), no. 127 (March 2, 1968), 9.
5. Neibu cankao bianjibu, ed., *Guanyu qingli jieji duiwu wenti (cailiao huibian)* (On Cleansing the Class Ranks [Collected Materials]) (n.p., 1968), 2: 77–78.
6. Cf. *Qingli jieji duiwu xuexi ziliao* (Cleansing the Class Ranks Study Materials) ([Shanghai], 1969). "Puppet" could refer to either of two governments set up by the Japanese on Chinese soil: that of the deposed last Chinese emperor, Pu Yi, in "Manchukuo" in the 1930s; or that of Wang Jingwei in Nanjing in 1940 as a rival to Chiang Kai-shek's.
7. "Lun paixing de fandongxing" (On the Reactionary Nature of Factionalism), reprinted in *Renmin ribao*, January 15, 1968.
8. Guofang daxue, *"Wenhua dageming,"* 2: 126.
9. Ibid., pp. 126–130.
10. *Daqing shizhi*, p. 25.
11. Guofang daxue, *"Wenhua dageming,"* 2: 120.
12. Neibu cankao bianjibu, *Guanyu qingli jieji duiwu wenti*, p. 16.
13. See for instance this comment on Nazi Holocaust policy: "Most scholars accept that a simple, linear, top-down model of decision-order-implementation does not capture the amorphous and unstructured nature of the Nazi decision-making process. Rather, Nazi policy evolved through an unsystematic dialectical interaction of mutual radicalization between central and local authorities involving numerous variations of exhortation, legitimization, and support, as well as decisions and orders from above; and intuition, initiative, and experimentation, as well as

obedience from below. The relative weighting of center and periphery, Hitler's precise role, and the timing and context of key turning points in this complex process are still contested issues"; Christopher R. Browning, *The Origins of the Final Solution: The Evolution of Nazi Jewish Policy, September 1939–March 1942* (Lincoln: University of Nebraska Press, 2004), p. 214.

14. This is the argument in Walder, "Anatomy of an Inquisition," which is also the source of the quotation.

15. Guofang daxue, *"Wenhua dageming,"* 2: 18–19.

16. Dangdai Zhongguo shangye bianjibu, ed., *Zhonghua renmin gongheguo shangye dashiji, 1958–1978* (A Record of Major Events in PRC Commerce, 1958–1978) (Beijing: Zhongguo shangye chubanshe, 1990), p. 642.

17. *Dangdai Zhongguode Jilin* (Contemporary China's Jilin), 2 vols. (Beijing: Dangdai Zhongguo chubanshe, 1991), 1: 155.

18. Guofang daxue, *"Wenhua dageming,"* 2: 16.

19. Zhang Xiangling, *Heilongjiang sishinian,* p. 360.

20. Fan Dechang, ed., *Jiayin xianzhi* (Jiayin County Gazetteer) (Harbin: Heilongjiang renmin chubanshe, 1988), p. 23.

21. *Kedong xianzhi* (Kedong County Gazetteer) (Harbin: Heilongjiang renmin chubanshe, 1987), p. 27.

22. The source for the information on Inner Mongolia is W. Woody, *Cultural Revolution in Inner Mongolia,* pp. i–vi, 30–35.

23. Jin Chunming, Huang Yuchong, and Chang Huimin, *"Wenge" shiqi guaishi guaiyu,* pp. 386–387.

24. *Zhongguo gongchandang Yunnan sheng zuzhi shi ziliao Yunnan sheng zheng jun tong qun zuzhi shi ziliao 1926.11–1987.10* (Materials on the History of the CCP Organization, Government, Military, United Front, and Mass Organizations in Yunnan Province, November 1926–October 1987) (Beijing: Zhonggong dangshi chubanshe, 1994), p. 231.

25. "Beijing shi 'Wenhua dageming' dashiji, 1968–1970" (A Chronology of the "Great Cultural Revolution" in Beijing, 1968–1970), in *Beijing dangshi ziliao tongxun,* extra issue, no. 18 (July 1987), 30.

26. Cheng Chao and Wei Haoben, *Zhejiang "Wenge" jishi,* p. 104.

27. Andrew G. Walder and Yang Su, "The Cultural Revolution in the Countryside: Scope, Timing and Human Impact," *CQ,* no. 173 (March 2003), 77.

28. Jin Chunming, *"Wenhua dageming" shigao,* p. 185.

29. Zheng Yi, *Scarlet Memorial: Tales of Cannibalism in Modern China,* trans. T. P. Sym (Boulder: Westview, 1996), p. 190.

30. Ding Longjia, *Kang Sheng yu "Zhao Jianmin yuanan"* (Kang Sheng and the "Unjust Case of Zhao Jianmin") (Beijing: Renmin chubanshe, 1999), p. 179.

31. Zheng Yi, *Scarlet Memorial,* p. 131.

32. Wakeman, *Spymaster,* p. 165.

33. *Jianguo yilai Mao Zedong wengao,* 12: 617–618.

34. *Mao zhuxi zai Zhongguo gongchandang di jiu ci quanguo daibiao dahui shangde zhongyao zhishi* (Chairman Mao's Important Instructions at the CCP's Ninth Congress) (n.p., 1969), p. 3.

35. Beijing shi geming weiyuanhui di er xuexiban dangwei, "Guanyu Heng Yingzhu tongzhi wentide fucha qingkuang" (On the Situation of the Reinvestigation of the Problems of Comrade Heng Yingzhu), October 6, 1972.

36. Ibid.

37. Beijing shi geming weiyuanhui di er xuexiban dangwei, "Guanyu Yang XX de wenti fucha chuli yijian" (Opinion on How to Deal with the Reinvestigation of the Problems of Yang XX), April 14, 1972.

38. Walder and Su, "Cultural Revolution in the Countryside," pp. 95–96.

39. Jin Chunming, Huang Yuchong, and Chang Huimin, *"Wenge" shiqi guaishi guaiyu,* pp. 34–35.

40. Michael Schoenhals, *Saltationist Socialism: Mao Zedong and the Great Leap Forward, 1958* (Stockholm: Foreningen för Orientaliska Studier, 1987), p. 38.

41. Beijing 64 zhong hongweibing zongbu, "Kaizhan 'yiri zhongzihua' huodong de chubu yijian" (Tentative Views on Activities Aimed at the "Loyalty-fication of the Entire Day"), stenciled Red Guard pamphlet, in the authors' possession.

42. Yunnan sheng geming weiyuanhui, *Wuchanjieji wenhua dageming wenjian huibian,* 1: 645–671. Mao's doctor participated in this operation at the Chairman's insistence; Li Zhisui, *The Private Life of Chairman Mao,* pp. 483–487.

43. Gao Xingjian, *One Man's Bible,* pp. 104–105.

44. Gao Anhua, *To the Edge of the Sky,* p. 190.

45. *Beijing ribao* (Beijing Daily), March 4, 1968.

46. Jin Chunming, Huang Yuchong, and Chang Huimin, *"Wenge" shiqi guaishi guaiyu,* p. 260.

47. On the anniversary of Mao's birth on December 26, 2001, Xinhua announced the discovery of the largest-ever Mao badge, made of aluminum, 1.4 meters in diameter, 2.5 centimeters thick, and weighing over 100 kilograms. The continued dependence of the CCP on Mao's image in post-Mao China was illustrated by a report in January 2002 that the People's Bank of China had decided to put Mao on four new currency bills; John Pomfret, "Currency Events: A Great Leap Backward?" at http://www.washingtonpost.com/wp-dyn/articles/A52632–2002Jan28.html.

48. See the PLA General Political Department's compilation, *Zhua huo sixiangde 60 duo ge zenme ban?* (60 Examples of How to Deal with Living Thoughts) (Beijing: Zhonggong zhongyang guofang gongye zhengzhibu, 1966).

49. Shijiazhuang was the only larger than medium-size *(zhongdeng yishang)* industri-

alized city in all of China that had met the targets of the state economic plan in 1967; Chen Xiaonong, *Chen Boda zuihou koushu huiyi*, p. 333.

50. Jiangsu Nanjing shi caimao xitong geming zaofan lianhe weiyuanhui, "Guanyu xuexi Shijiazhuang shi kaizhan 'san zhong yu' huodong qingkuang de huibao" (Report on Learning from the Development of "Three Loyalties" Activities in Shijiazhuang Municipality), mimeograph, Nanjing, June 28, 1968, p. 6.

51. Ibid., p. 8.

52. Ibid., p. 3.

53. Shangfang tongxun bianjishi, *Chunfeng huayu ji*, 1: 436.

54. Zhonggong Hebei shengwei dangshi yanjiushi, *Zhongguo gongchandang Hebei lishi dashiji*, p. 417.

55. Beijing shi geming weiyuanhui di er xuexiban dangwei, "Guanyu Jin Ke wentide fucha huibao cailiao" (Report Materials on the Reinvestigation of the Problems of Jin Ke), April 1972, p. 2.

56. *Jianguo yilai Mao Zedong wengao*, 13: 175.

57. Ma Qibin et al., *Zhongguo gongchandang zhizheng sishinian*, p. 303.

58. *Zhou Enlai nianpu*, 3: 210.

59. Guojia tongjiju, ed., *Zhongguo tongji nianjian, 1983* (China Statistical Yearbook, 1983) (Beijing: Zhongguo tongji chubanshe, 1983), pp. 302, 304.

60. Li Ping'an et al., eds., *Shaanxi jingji dashiji, 1949–1985* (A Chronicle of Major Economic Events in Shaanxi, 1949–1985) (Xi'an: Sanqin chubanshe, 1987), pp. 286–307.

61. Ma Qibin et al., *Zhongguo gongchandang zhizheng sishinian*, p. 317.

62. Based on figures in Guojia tongjiju zonghesi, *Quanguo ge sheng zizhiqu zhixiashi lishi tongji ziliao huibian*.

63. Ma Qibin et al., *Zhongguo gongchandang zhizheng sishinian*, p. 317.

64. See Beijing RC Notification in *Wanshan hongbian*, no. 16 (December 31, 1967).

65. Yunnan sheng geming weiyuanhui, *Wuchanjieji wenhua dageming wenjian huibian*, 2: 747.

66. *Nie Yuanzi huiyilu*, p. 300. It was not always easy to tell what amounted to illicit economic activities: in the summer of 1968, children were caught tearing down big-character posters across Beijing and selling the paper for pulp, prompting the minister of public security to complain that at seven fen per kilogram, "the kids are making a killing!" *(fa dacai)*.

67. Yunnan sheng geming weiyuanhui, *Wuchanjieji wenhua dageming wenjian huibian*, 2: 805–812.

68. Beijing shi geming weiyuanhui di er xuexiban dangwei, "Guanyu Heng Yingzhu tongzhi wentide fucha jielun baogao."

69. Dangdai Zhongguo shangye bianjibu, *Zhonghua renmin gongheguo shangye dashiji*, p. 642.

70. Yunnan sheng geming weiyuanhui, *Wuchanjieji wenhua dageming wenjian huibian,* 2: 1007–11.

71. Beijing shi geming weiyuanhui di er xuexiban dangwei, "Guanyu Guo Buyue wentide fucha qingkuang" (On the Situation of the Reinvestigation of the Problems of Guo Buyue), May 1972.

72. Guowuyuan caimao bangongshi, "Guanyu liangshi gongzuo huiyi de baogao" (Report on the Meeting on Grain Work), p. 4, seven-page transcript, produced in Beijing and dated October 30, 1967, in authors' possession.

73. Guojia tongjiju, *Zhongguo tongji nianjian, 1983,* pp. 158, 438. In the confusion of the final year of the Cultural Revolution, 1976, imports dropped to 2.36 million tons, but rebounded to 7.34 million tons in 1977 and reached 12.35 million tons by 1979. The drops in imports were presumably attributable partly to shortage of foreign exchange and partly to unrest in port cities.

74. Zhonghua renmin gongheguo caizhengbu, ed., *Zhongguo nongmin fudan shi* (A History of the Chinese Peasants' Burden), 4 vols. (Beijing: Zhongguo caizheng jingji chubanshe, 1990–1994), 4: 291.

75. *Zhongyang bande Mao Zedong sixiang xuexiban Sichuan ban geming dapipan fayan* (Revolutionary Great Criticism: Statements from the Sichuan Class of the Mao Zedong Thought Study Classes Organized by the Center), no. 21 (n.p., 1970), 7.

16. Dispatching Liu Shaoqi

1. *Renmin ribao,* May 23, 1967. It had always been Mao's assumption, human nature being what it was, that there would have to be successive cultural revolutions in the future to revive flagging zeal.

2. He Li, ed., *Zhonghua renmin gongheguo shi* (History of the PRC), rev. ed. (Beijing: Zhongguo dang'an chubanshe, 1995), pp. 350–351.

3. Wang Nianyi, *Da dongluande niandai,* p. 311. The agenda had undergone some significant revisions since first discussed by the CCRG caucus on September 19. Earlier, in addition to preparing for the Ninth Congress, it had summarized what had been learned in the course of the Cultural Revolution, paving the way for the creation of a Central (i.e., national) Revolutionary Committee and, in the process, resolving the outstanding issue of the presidency of the People's Republic of China; see Pang Xianzhi and Jin Chongji, *Mao Zedong zhuan,* 2: 1528.

4. "Mao zhuxi zai dangde ba jie kuodade shier zhong quanhui shangde jianghua" (Speech by Chairman Mao at the Enlarged Twelfth Plenum of the Party's Eighth Central Committee), p. 1, copy in Fairbank Center Library.

5. Ibid., pp. 1–2. Square brackets indicate positions on the eve of the Cultural Revolution.

6. Ibid., p. 4.

7. "Lin Biao zai Zhonggong ba jie kuodade shier zhong quanhui di er ci huiyi shangde jianghua" (Lin Biao's Speech at the Second Session of the Enlarged Twelfth Plenum of the Eighth Central Committee of the CCP), in Zhonggong zhongyang bangongting, ed., *Canyue wenjian* (Reference Readings), 12 vols. (Beijing, 1972), 12: 38–39.

8. Beijing caimao xueyuan, "Zai Zhonggong ba jie shier zhong quanhui shang Mao zhuxi, Lin fuzhuxi, Zhou zongli de zhongyao jianghua," pp. 31–34.

9. "Lin Biao zai Zhonggong ba jie kuodade shier zhong quanhui di er ci huiyi shangde jianghua," p. 38.

10. Ibid., p. 2.

11. Kang Sheng, "Zai ba jie shier zhong quanhui di si xiaozu huiyi shang de fayan" (Statement at the Meeting of the Fourth Group at the Twelfth Plenum of the Eighth Central Committee), in Zhonggong Beijing shiwei dangxiao ziliaoshi, ed., *Kang Sheng yanlun xuanbian* (Selected Utterances of Kang Sheng), 3 vols. (Beijing, 1979), 3: 81.

12. "Mao zhuxi zai dangde ba jie kuodade shier zhong quanhui shangde jianghua," p. 8.

13. He Li, *Zhonghua renmin gongheguo shi*, p. 351. Possibly Chen's pre-1949 trade union work and central China organizing had once brought her into close contact with Liu.

14. Lowell Dittmer, "Death and Transfiguration: Liu Shaoqi's Rehabilitation and Contemporary Chinese Politics," *Journal of Asian Studies*, 11, no. 3 (May 1981), 459.

15. Zhonggong Zhejiang shengwei dangxiao dangshi jiaoyanshi, ed., *"Wenhua dageming" shiqi ziliao xuanji* (Selected Materials concerning the "Great Cultural Revolution" Era) (Hangzhou, 1984), p. 177. The Chinese phrase quoted refers to the five creatures regarded as most venomous in traditional lore: the scorpion, the viper, the centipede, the house lizard, and the toad.

16. Personal communication to Michael Schoenhals.

17. Huang Zheng, "Liu Shaoqi yu 'Wenhua dageming'" (Liu Shaoqi and the "Great Cultural Revolution"), *Dangde wenxian*, no. 5 (1988), 10.

18. For a graphic synthesis of Chinese accounts of Liu's last illness and death, see Dittmer, "Death and Transfiguration," pp. 459–460.

19. Zhongguo kexueyuan geming weiyuanhui zhengzhizu, ed., *Zhengdang xuexi ziliao* (Party Rectification Study Materials) (Beijing, 1968) (hereafter *Zhengdang xuexi ziliao*), 4: 38–40.

20. According to Kang Sheng's report to the Ninth Congress; *"Jiuda" ziliao huibian* (Collected Materials from the "Ninth Congress") (Ji'nan: Ji'nan tieluju Ji'nan cheliangduan 5.7 zhongxue, 1969), p. 28.

21. *Zhengdang xuexi ziliao*, 5: 12.

22. "Lin Biao zai Zhonggong ba jie kuodade shier zhong quanhui di er ci huiyi shangde jianghua," p. 63.

23. Zhonggong Beijing shiwei dangxiao ziliaoshi, *Kang Sheng yanlun xuanbian*, 3: 81.

24. Cf. Yunnan sheng geming weiyuanhui, *Wuchanjieji wenhua dageming wenjian huibian*, 2: 1191; Hubei sheng geming weiyuanhui, ed., *Wuchanjieji wenhua dageming wenjian huibian* (Collected Documents from the Great Proletarian Cultural Revolution), 3 vols. (Wuhan: Hubei sheng geming weiyuanhui, 1968–69), 3: 1168.

25. "Lin Biao zai Zhonggong ba jie kuodade shier zhong quanhui di er ci huiyi shangde jianghua," pp. 62–63.

26. "Mao zhuxi zai dangde ba jie kuodade shier zhong quanhui shangde jianghua," p. 14.

27. Deng Rong, *Deng Xiaoping and the Cultural Revolution*, pp. 68–73.

28. Deng Xiaoping, "Wode zishu" (My Own Account), in *Canyue cailiao*, 10: 19.

29. "Mao zhuxi zai dangde ba jie kuodade shier zhong quanhui shangde jianghua," pp. 8–14.

30. Ibid., p. 14.

31. Wang Nianyi, "Guanyu He Long yuanande yixie ziliao," p. 11.

32. "Mao zhuxi zai dangde ba jie kuodade shier zhong quanhui shangde jianghua," p. 8.

33. "Lin Biao zai Zhonggong ba jie kuodade shier zhong quanhui di er ci huiyi shangde jianghua," p. 14.

34. Michael Schoenhals, "The Central Case Examination Group, 1966–1979," *CQ*, no. 145 (March 1996), 87–111.

35. See above, Chapter 2.

36. For his involvement in cases of party leaders' historic "crimes," see *Jianguo yilai Mao Zedong wengao*, 12: 169–171.

37. For an English-language biography of Kang, see John Byron and Robert Pack, *The Claws of the Dragon: Kang Sheng, the Evil Genius behind Mao and His Legacy of Terror in People's China* (New York: Simon & Schuster, 1992).

38. Schoenhals, "Central Case Examination Group, 1966–1979," p. 91.

39. Ibid., pp. 92, 103.

40. Huang Zheng, "The Beginning and End of the 'Liu Shaoqi Case Group,'" in Michael Schoenhals, ed., "Mao's Great Inquisition: The Central Case Examination Group, 1966–1979," *Chinese Law and Government*, 29, no. 3 (May–June 1996), 13.

41. Cf. Hao Kewei, "28 zhuan'an de faqi guocheng." After the Cultural Revolution, Nie Yuanzi defended the services that she and her Peking University Red Guards had rendered the CCEG by maintaining that they had been approved by Zhou Enlai personally; *Nie Yuanzi huiyilu*, pp. 232–233.

42. Doubtless Wu Faxian would have justified this expansion by insisting that prosecutors must follow leads wherever they point, the argument used in the United States by Special Prosecutor Kenneth Starr to explain how over the course of years his investigations took him from the Whitewater land deal to the White House intern Monica Lewinsky.

43. Zhang Songshan, "On the 'He Long Case Group,'" in Schoenhals, "Mao's Great Inquisition," pp. 24–42; For a description of the downfall and investigation by the CCEG of one of He Long's longtime associates, see "Wang Shangrong jiangjun" bianxiezu, *Wang Shangrong jiangjun* (General Wang Shangrong) (Beijing: Dangdai Zhongguo chubanshe, 2000), pp. 523–539.

44. Jin Chunming, Huang Yuchong, and Chang Huimin, *"Wenge" shiqi guaishi guaiyu,* pp. 113–115.

45. Ling Yun, "Kang Sheng weihe zhizao 'mousha Su Mei' an" (Why Did Kang Sheng Fabricate the "Su Mei Murder" Case?), in Zhu Chunlin, *Lishi shunjian,* 1: 95–96.

46. Zhong Kan, *Kang Sheng pingzhuan,* p. 423.

47. Ibid., p. 415.

17. The Congress of Victors

1. *Renmin ribao,* April 2, 1969.

2. Ibid., November 7, 1967.

3. *"Jiuda" ziliao huibian,* p. 4. Already at the Twelfth Plenum in the autumn of 1968, Mao said: "The movement is not yet finished. Even after the Ninth Congress has been held, it won't necessarily be finished right away either, since it involves every factory, every rural village, every school and government organ." See "Mao zhuxi zai dangde ba jie kuodade shi er zhong quanhui shangde jianghua," p. 10; translation amended on the basis of tape recording; the printed Chinese text does not include Mao's reference to "every rural village."

4. Chen Xiaonong, *Chen Boda yigao,* p. 114; Wang Wenyao and Wang Baochun, "Guanyu Chen Boda qicao jiuda baogao de qianqian houhou" (The Ins and Outs of Chen Boda's Drafting of the Report of the Ninth Party Congress), *Zhonggong dangshi yanjiu* (Research on CCP Party History), no. 2 (2003), 88–91.

5. "Kang Sheng tongzhi zai zhongzhi jiguan chuanda 'jiuda' jingshen dahui shangde zhongyao jianghua" (Comrade Kang Sheng's Important Speech Transmitting the Spirit of the "Ninth Congress" to Central Organs), May 23, 1969, p. 13, copy in Fairbank Center Library.

6. See the quantitative study by Walder and Su, "Cultural Revolution in the Countryside."

7. *Wuchanjieji wenhua dageming zhongyao wenjian huiji,* pp. 278–283.

8. Guofang daxue, *"Wenhua dageming,"* 1: 638.

9. *Jianguo yilai Mao Zedong wengao,* 12: 436.

10. Wang Nianyi, *Da dongluande niandai,* p. 310.

11. Ma Qibin et al., *Zhongguo gongchandang zhizheng sishinian,* p. 302.

12. Guofang daxue, *"Wenhua dageming,"* 1: 636–638, 644.

13. *Zhou Enlai nianpu,* 3: 284, 285, 288.

14. Wang Nianyi claims that "one or two" non-CCP members "participated" in the Ninth Congress (*Da dongluande niandai,* p. 320), but does not indicate whether or not they were actual delegates. During the congress, Mao was asked by the commander of the Wuhan MR if one could "make some allowances" and permit three rebel leaders from Hubei who still had not become members of the CCP to attend as delegates; Mao's immediate reply was this would not be possible (*"Jiuda" ziliao huibian,* p. 9). Chen Ada, from Shanghai, was not a CCP member when he was singled out by Zhang Chunqiao et al. to be a delegate, but had become a member by the time the congress began. See Wang Xiuzhen, "Wode jiefa he jiaodai" (My Exposé and Admission) (Shanghai: Shanghai shi qu, xian, ju dangyuan fuze ganbu huiyi mishuzu, November 6, 1976), p. 24.

15. *"Jiuda" ziliao huibian,* p. 44.

16. For a discussion of the degeneration of party life, how delegates were chosen, and the secrecy of the proceedings, see Xi Xuan and Jin Chunming, *"Wenhua dageming" jianshi,* pp. 202–203.

17. *"Jiuda" ziliao huibian,* p. 42. The rules were relaxed after opening day: cf. the record of "a long-distance telephone call from Beijing" in *Doupigai tongxun* (Struggle, Criticize, and Transform Bulletin) (Shanghai: Workers' Mao Zedong Thought Propaganda Team in the Publishing and Press Sector Regimental Headquarters), no. 69 (April 2, 1969); Chi Zehou, "Zhonggong 'jiuda' neimu suoyi" (Random Memories of the Background to the "Ninth Party Congress"), *Yanhuang chunqiu,* no. 3 (2003), 45.

18. "Kang Sheng tongzhi jiejian chuxi zhongyang he quanjun zhengdang jiandang gongzuo zuotanhui quanti tongzhi shide jianghua" (Kang Sheng's Speech at the Reception for Comrades Attending the Work Forum on All-Party and All-Military Consolidation and Rebuilding), April 18, 1970, p. 25, photocopy of original contemporary transcript (lacking information about who produced it), Fairbank Center Library.

19. *"Jiuda" ziliao huibian,* p. 4; "Wang Hongwen tongzhi de fayan" (Comrade Wang Hongwen's Statement), April 14, 1969, p. 2; and "Chen Yonggui tongzhi de fayan" (Comrade Chen Yonggui's Statement), April 14, 1969, p. 2, copies of official transcripts produced by the CC General Office Secretariat, Fairbank Center Library. Zhou's speech is translated in Schoenhals, "New Texts," pp. 93–101.

20. Chen Xiaonong, *Chen Boda yigao,* pp. 113–114.

21. *Zhou Enlai nianpu*, 3: 283–284.

22. Yet according to Mao's official biography, in the aftermath of the congress Mao was paying particular attention to the economy; Pang Xianzhi and Jin Chongji, *Mao Zedong zhuan*, 2: 1559–60.

23. *Zhou Enlai nianpu*, 3: 283–284; Chen Xiaonong, *Chen Boda yigao*, p. 114.

24. *Jianguo yilai Mao Zedong wengao*, 13: 11–18. Mao began seeing portions of the draft on March 16 and continued to revise the text during the congress.

25. Ibid., pp. 11–13.

26. Zhang Yunsheng, *Maojiawan jishi*, pp. 209–215. Since major reports like this were normally read out word for word, with the audience following along with their copies of the text, there was no need for Lin, even had he been so inclined, to practice his delivery for the purpose of gaining oratorical effect.

27. *Jianguo yilai Mao Zedong wengao*, 13: 118.

28. Pang Xianzhi and Jin Chongji, *Mao Zedong zhuan*, 2: 1543.

29. *Renmin ribao*, April 28, 1969.

30. Ibid.

31. *"Jiuda" ziliao huibian*, p. 50.

32. Ibid., p. 12. The definitive version of the report was ratified by Mao on April 25 and published in the *People's Daily* three days later.

33. Wang Nianyi, interview by Michael Schoenhals in Beijing, April 1992.

34. Schoenhals, "New Texts," p. 95.

35. Ibid., p. 98.

36. Talking to local PLA commanders in Jiangxi, of which Nanchang is the capital, Mao asserted that the Nanchang uprising on August 1, 1927, taken by CCP historians as the founding date of the Red Army, was "mainly the work of Vice Chairman Lin and the premier"; "Mao zhuxi 69.8–69.9 shicha da Jiang nanbei de jianghua" (Remarks Made by Chairman Mao during an Inspection Tour North and South of the Yangtze in August–September 1969), copy of handwritten transcript, Fairbank Center Library. Mao would change his tune on this in February 1971 as he was preparing to purge Lin Biao; Wang Nianyi, He Shu, and Chen Zhao, "Mao Zedong bichulaide 'jiu.yisan Lin Biao chutao shijian'" ("The Incident of September 13 When Lin Biao Fled" Which Mao Zedong Brought About), *Dangdai Zhongguo yanjiu* (Modern China Studies), no. 2 (2004), 149.

37. Schoenhals, "New Texts," p. 100.

38. For Lin Biao's reaction to Zhou's statement, see ibid., pp. 101–102.

39. Zhonggong Anhui shengwei dangxiao tushuguan ziliaoshi, ed., *Jiaoxue cankao: Quanguo dangxiao xitong Zhonggong dangshi xueshu taolunhui zhuanti baogao he fayan huibian* (Teaching Reference: Collection of Special Reports and Speeches at the Symposium of the Nationwide Party School System on CCP History), 2 vols. (1980), 2: 63.

40. Deng Rong, *Deng Xiaoping and the Cultural Revolution*, p. 101.
41. Quoted in Xi Xuan and Jin Chunming, *"Wenhua dageming" jianshi*, p. 207.
42. *"Jiuda" ziliao huibian*, p. 30.
43. Cf. Zhongguo geming bowuguan, ed., *Zhongguo gongchandang dangzhang huibian* (Collected Constitutions of the CCP) (Beijing: Renmin chubanshe, 1979), pp. 46, 146, 206.
44. *Zhou Enlai nianpu*, 3: 288–289.
45. *"Jiuda" ziliao huibian*, pp. 14, 38–41, 44; Chi Zehou, "Zhonggong 'jiuda' neimu suoyi," pp. 46–49.
46. Chi Zehou, "Zhonggong 'jiuda' neimu suoyi," pp. 46–49.
47. Chen Boda was the one Politburo Standing Committee member whose wife was not put on the CC. In 1969 she worked as an adviser to the CCEG.
48. *"Jiuda" ziliao huibian*, p. 44. The figures are based on the official classification in use at the congress. After the Cultural Revolution, the definition of a "member" of the military was altered, and as a result the proportion of "military cadres" on the Ninth CC rose to 45 percent; see Li Ke and Hao Shengzhang, *"Wenhua dageming" zhongde renmin jiefangjun*, p. 111. Western estimates range from 38 to 50 percent; see Roderick MacFarquhar, "The Succession to Mao and the End of Maoism, 1969–82," in MacFarquhar, *The Politics of China: Second Edition*, p. 250, n. 5.
49. *"Jiuda" ziliao huibian*, p. 44.
50. Ibid., pp. 14–15. On April 23, Mao asked the conveners of the groups into which delegates were organized for purposes of discussion if the electoral procedure had been "fair." Not receiving an immediate reply, he answered himself, saying it had been "on the whole" fair. See "Zhuxi 69.4.23 xiawu jiejian bufen daibiao" (The Chairman Receives Some Delegates in the Afternoon of April 23, 1969), copy of handwritten transcript, Fairbank Center Library.
51. Chi Zehou, "Zhonggong 'jiuda' neimu suoyi," p. 49. A handful of delegates were pregnant women who gave birth halfway through the congress; this may explain the absence of two delegates on voting day. See *Meizhou wenzhai* (Weekly Extracts), no. 41 (October 7, 1992).
52. Chi Zehou, "Zhonggong 'jiuda' neimu suoyi," p. 48. Lin Biao's wife, Ye Qun, crossed out her husband's name; Zhou's wife, Deng Yingchao, apparently did not.
53. *Zhou Enlai nianpu*, 3: 291; Chi Zehou, "Zhonggong 'jiuda' neimu suoyi," p. 48. Also regarded by Mao as a bona fide member of his own intra-party opposition was the onetime procurator general Zhang Dingcheng, who received 1,099 votes.
54. "Mao zhuxi 69.4.11 jianghua" (Chairman Mao's Speech on April 11, 1969), copy of handwritten transcript, Fairbank Center Library.
55. *"Jiuda" ziliao huibian*, pp. 48–49.
56. *Zhou Enlai nianpu*, 3: 331, 341; *Dangdai Sichuan dashi jiyao* (Main Points con-

cerning Major Events in Contemporary Sichuan) (Chengdu: Sichuan renmin chubanshe, 1991), p. 283.

57. "Mao zhuxi zai 69.4.5 (jiuda) de jianghua" (Chairman Mao's Speech on April 5, 1969 [at the Ninth Congress]), handwritten copy, Fairbank Center Library.

58. *Nie Yuanzi huiyilu*, pp. 320–321, 331–336. Nie was briefly "liberated" in late July 1970 and attended the Second Plenum of the Ninth CC, which met at Lushan in Jiangxi; *Lishide shenpan* (The Verdict of History), 2 vols. (Beijing: Qunzhong chubanshe, 1981), 2: 149.

59. "Mao zhuxi zai 69.4.5 (jiuda) de jianghua."

60. *Lishide shenpan*, 2: 154, 163. Long after the Cultural Revolution, Kuai confessed that he had admired the fortitude of another woman, the one whom he and his schoolmates had humiliated, Liu Shaoqi's wife, Wang Guangmei; Chang and Halliday, *Mao*, p. 550.

61. Mao Zedong, "4.28 jianghua" (Speech on April 28 [1969]), copy of handwritten transcript, Fairbank Center Library.

62. In 1971 Mao told PLA provincial commanders that "comrade Ye Jianying rendered a great service at a crucial moment, so therefore you should respect him." Cf. Zhonggong Zhejiang shengwei dangxiao dangshi jiaoyanshi, *"Wenhua dageming" shiqi ziliao xuanji*, p. 291; "Mao zhuxi 71 nian 8 yue zhi 9 yue shicha nanfang shide jici jianghua" (Chairman Mao's Remarks during His Inspection of the South in August–September 1971), copy of handwritten transcript, Fairbank Center Library.

63. Mao Zedong, "4.28 jianghua."

64. Pang Xianzhi and Jin Chongji, *Mao Zedong zhuan*, 2: 1556.

65. *Jianguo yilai Mao Zedong wengao*, 13: 51; *Zhou Enlai nianpu*, 3: 300.

66. *Zhongguo gongchandang zuzhi shi ziliao*, 10: 61.

67. *Zhou Enlai nianpu*, 3: 328.

68. Ibid., p. 305.

69. Calculated from data in ibid., vol. 3.

70. It is unclear why ibid., 3: 305, does not list Zhang Chunqiao as a regular participant in the "everyday work meetings."

71. Chen Xiaonong, *Chen Boda yigao*, p. 114.

72. *"Jiuda" ziliao huibian*, p. 14. Mao may have been engaging in preemptive distancing. It will be remembered that Mao claimed not to have known much about Tao Zhu after he had been disgraced, though this assertion was manifestly untrue, quite apart from the unlikelihood of his having let Tao rise to be the fourth-ranking member of the PSC on the recommendation of Deng Xiaoping, with whom he was already at odds. In the case of Huang, Mao could have worried that a general occupying a key post such as chief of staff might be more loyal to Lin than to himself. His remark may thus have been designed either to dissociate himself

from Huang in the event of his proving unreliable or to encourage Huang to report to him and become his man. In the summer of 1971, when his confrontation with Lin Biao was reaching a climax, Mao told provincial PLA commanders to whom he felt close: "These [particular] high-ranking officers, I really don't know them well. I'm not clear about Huang Yongsheng's state of mind." See "Mao zhuxi 71 nian 8 yue zhi 9 yue shicha nanfang shide jici jianghua."

73. Yang Yinlu, "Jiang Qing yu Lin Biao: Wo gei Jiang Qing dang mishu (si)" (Jiang Qing and Lin Biao: I was Jiang Qing's Secretary [4]), *Bainian chao*, no. 4 (1999), 72. For a different explanation of Jiang's move, see the memoirs of her chief bodyguard, Wu Jicheng, *Hongse jingwei* (Red Bodyguard) (Beijing: Dangdai Zhongguo chubanshe, 2003), pp. 143–144.

74. Li Naiyin, "'Sirenbang' beishen qijian choutai tu" (Pictures of the Ugly Performance of the "Gang of Four" on Trial), *Yanhuang chunqiu*, no. 7 (1997), 43.

75. Zhong Kan, *Kang Sheng pingzhuan*, p. 434.

76. Zhang Yunsheng, *Maojiawan jishi*, pp. 382–393; Gao Wenqian, *Wannian Zhou Enlai*, pp. 268–269.

77. Domes, *The Internal Politics of China*, p. 215.

78. For a sophisticated argument that Lin Biao was essentially passive during his last years and certainly not striving to form a military dictatorship, see Teiwes and Sun, *The Tragedy of Lin Biao*. The point missed by these authors is that for Mao the issue of Bonapartism probably had far less to do with Lin Biao's subjective intentions than with the objective fact of military dominance of the party and revolutionary committees throughout the country.

79. *Zhou Enlai nianpu*, 3: 305, 333, 335.

80. Wang Nianyi, *Da dongluande niandai*, p. 361.

81. *Zhou Enlai nianpu*, 3: 346.

82. Text in Schoenhals, *China's Cultural Revolution*, pp. 85–89.

83. *Zhonghua renmin gongheguo falü guifanxing jieshi jicheng* (Collection of Normative Explanations of the Laws of the PRC) (Changchun: Jilin renmin chubanshe, 1990), pp. 17–18.

84. Zhongyang dang'anguan, ed., *Gongheguo wushinian zhengui dang'an* (Precious Archives from Fifty Years of the Republic), 2 vols. (Beijing: Zhongguo dang'an chubanshe, 1999), 2: 1000–01.

85. Zhonggong Yinchuan shiwei dangshi yanjiushi, ed., *Zhonggong Yinchuan dangshi dashiji, 1949.9–1996.12* (Record of Major Events in the History of the CCP in Yinchuan, September 1949–December 1996) (Yinchuan: Ningxia renmin chubanshe, 1998), pp. 128–129; Shangfang tongxun bianjishi, *Chunfeng huayu ji*, 2: 63–73, translated as Chen Chuan, "Youths Who Sought the Truth," *Chinese Sociology and Anthropology*, 26, no. 1 (Fall 1993), 59–64.

86. *Chen Yun nianpu*, 3: 158, 172.

87. *Shanghai "Wenhua dageming" shihua*, 2: 523.

88. Cf. *Tianjin shi Heping qu jianjue zhenya fangeming fenzi dahui xuanpanci* (Sentences Read at the Mass Rally to Firmly Suppress Counterrevolutionary Elements in the Heping District of Tianjin Municipality), May 31, 1970, 8-page public announcement put out by the public security authorities, Schoenhals collection.

89. Handwritten record of remarks by Liu Yusheng, Zhang Xiuqing, and other residents of Yangfang District Residential Area, Beijing, during debates organized by the Neighborhood Committee on August 30 and September 9, 1970; untitled, handwritten, and lacking title in Chinese; Schoenhals collection.

90. *Hu Qiaomu tan Zhonggong dangshi*, pp. 200–201.

91. Zhonggong Kunming shiwei Kunming jingbeiqu fu-Hu xuexi xiaozu, ed., *Shanghai minbing gongzuo jingyan xuanbian* (Selected Work Experiences of the Shanghai Militia) (Anshun: Shi minbing zhihuibu, 1974), pp. 7–8; Shanghai minbing douzhengshi ziliaozu, ed., *Shanghai minbing douzhengshi ziliao*, no. 17 (December 1980), 50.

92. *Shanghai "Wenhua dageming" shihua*, 2: 524–525.

93. From original archival material in the authors' possession.

94. Ibid.

95. "Dangdai Guizhou jianshi" bianweihui, ed., *Dangdai Guizhou dashiji, 1949.10–1995.12* (Record of Major Events in Contemporary Guizhou, October 1949–December 1995) (Guiyang: Guizhou renmin chubanshe, 1996), p. 341.

96. "Beijing shi 'Wenhua dageming' dashiji, 1968–1970," pp. 44–45.

97. Zhonggong Heilongjiang shengwei dangshi yanjiushi, ed., *Zhonggong Heilongjiang dangshi dashiji (1949.10–1989.12)* (Record of Major Events in CCP History of Heilongjiang [October 1949–December 1989]) (Harbin: Heilongjiang renmin chubanshe, 1991), p. 436.

98. Zhonggong Guangzhou shiwei dangshi yanjiushi, *Zhonggong Guangzhou dangshi dashiji*, p. 313.

99. Zhonggong Baoding shiwei dangshi yanjiushi, ed., *Zhonggong Baoding dangshi dashiji (1949.10–1978.12)* (Record of Major Events in the History of the CCP in Baoding [October 1949–December 1978]) (Beijing: Zhongyang wenxian chubanshe, 1999), p. 361.

100. *Shanghai "Wenhua dageming" shihua*, 2: 523.

101. Ma Qibin et al., *Zhongguo gongchandang zhizheng sishinian*, p. 330.

18. War Scares

1. See for instance the opinion of Deng Liqun, once secretary to Liu Shaoqi, in Zhonggong Anhui shengwei dangxiao tushuguan ziliaoshi, *Jiaoxue cankao*, 2: 43,

on the importance of having a successor who, unlike Liu Shaoqi, was a military man as well as a politician.

2. For a description of the rushed preparation for Beijing's first major condemnation of the Soviet invasion, made at the Romanian embassy's National Day celebration, see Jiang Benliang, "'Kangke shijian' yu Zhou Enlaide 'liuba' jianghua" (The "Czech Incident" and Zhou Enlai's "'68" Speech), *Zhonggong dangshi ziliao,* no. 72 (December 1999), 36–44.

3. "77 Conversations between Chinese and Foreign Leaders on the Wars in Indochina, 1964–1977," Working Paper No. 22, Woodrow Wilson Center, Cold War International History Project, p. 158.

4. *Origins,* 3: 373–377.

5. For a description and a post-Mao appraisal, see Wu Li, *Zhonghua renmin gongheguo jingji shi,* 1: 680–693.

6. Naughton, "Industrial Policy during the Cultural Revolution," pp. 153–181. The cost was estimated by Deng Liqun in a lecture given on November 11, 1993. See *Deng Liqun guoshi jiangtan lu* (A Record of Deng Liqun's Talks on National History), 5 vols. (Beijing: "Zhonghua renmin gongheguo shigao" bianweihui huibian, 2000), 2: 327; according to this source the loss sustained as a result of the GLF was 500 billion yuan. The relocation of weapons factories to Sichuan—which had taken place both during the anti-Japanese war and as a result of the Third Front—had unintended consequences: the weapons used by Red Guards in their internecine battles in that province were rifles and machine guns rather than sticks and stones.

7. Zheng Qian, "60 niandai mo Zhongguo beizhan miwen" (Secrets of China's War Preparations in the Late 1960s), in Qiu Shi, ed., *Gongheguo zhongda shijian he juece neimu* (The Inside Story of the Major Incidents and Decisions of the [Chinese People's] Republic), 2 vols. (Beijing: Jingji ribao chubanshe, 1997), 2: 625–658.

8. Quoted in James Mann, *About Face: A History of America's Curious Relationship with China from Nixon to Clinton* (New York: Knopf, 1999), p. 21. For a CIA view on the difficulties of interpreting photographic intelligence, see Dino A. Brugioni, "The Unidentifieds," in H. Bradford Westerfield, ed., *Inside CIA's Private World: Declassified Articles from the Agency's Internal Journal, 1955–1992* (New Haven: Yale University Press, 1995), pp. 8–26. For a Chinese assessment of the Soviet advantage in weaponry along the border, see Chen Dunde, *Bai zhan jiang xing: Kong Congzhou* (A Brilliant General in One Hundred Battles: Kong Congzhou) (Beijing: Jiefangjun wenyi chubanshe, 2000), pp. 366–373.

9. *Important Documents on the Great Proletarian Cultural Revolution in China* (Peking: Foreign Languages Press, 1970), pp. 93–94. See also Zong canmoubu zhengzhibu, ed., *Choushi Suxiu maoshi Suxiu bishi Suxiu* (Hate the Soviet Revi-

sionists, Despise the Soviet Revisionists, and Look Down upon the Soviet Revisionists) (Beijing, 1969), pp. 42–65.

10. Lyle J. Goldstein, "Return to Zhenbao Island: Who Started Shooting and Why It Matters?" *CQ*, no. 168 (December 2001), 985–997.

11. "Zhenbaodao qingkuang diandi" (Information Accumulated on Zhenbao Island), in *"Jiuda" ziliao huibian*, pp. 33–34.

12. Ibid., p. 33. The account claims that because they had already reported to Moscow that they had suffered a mere thirty-one fatalities in the first clash, the Soviet troops hesitated to retrieve altogether fifty-nine bodies from the Chinese, since the larger number would "put the government of the Soviet Union on the defensive."

13. From a Soviet report to the leadership of East Germany on March 8, translated as "Soviet Report to GDR Leadership on 2 March 1969," *Bulletin* (Cold War International History Project, Woodrow Wilson Center), nos. 6–7 (Winter 1995–96), 189–190.

14. "Zhenbaodao qingkuang diandi," p. 33. The discrepancy between this version of events and the tale of heroic exploits by PLA soldiers in their teens included in some accounts of the fighting intended for a domestic audience is quite remarkable. Compare Heilongjiang sheng fu Zhenbaodao weiwentuan, "Fanxiu zhanbei jiaoyu baogao" (Report on Teaching Preparation for Anti-Revisionist War), in *"Jiuda" ziliao huibian*, pp. 73–77. For Mao's exact words in their original context, see above, Chapter 5.

15. By 1989, if not earlier, the fact that there had been a third battle on March 17 was public knowledge in China. See Li Ke and Hao Shengzhang, *"Wenhua dageming" zhongde renmin jiefangjun*, p. 323; Ma Qibin et al., *Zhongguo gongchandang zhizheng sishinian*, p. 319; and Heilongjiang sheng difang zhi bianzuan weiyuanhui, ed., *Heilongjiang shengzhi dashiji* (Gazetteer of Heilongjiang Province: Record of Major Events) (Harbin: Heilongjiang renmin chubanshe, 1992), p. 952.

16. See Ma Qibin et al., *Zhongguo gongchandang zhizheng sishinian*, p. 319.

17. Y. M. Galenovich, *Rossia i Kitai v XX Veke: Granitsa* (Russia and China in the Twentieth Century: Frontier) (Moscow: Izograph, 2001), p. 311.

18. "Zhenbaodao qingkuang diandi," pp. 33–34. Zhou made his speech on the night of March 24–25; *"Jiuda" ziliao huibian*, p. 65. For the bitter public Sino-Soviet exchanges on the border clashes, see Richard Wich, *Sino-Soviet Crisis Politics: A Study of Political Change and Communication* (Cambridge, Mass.: Council on East Asian Studies, Harvard University, 1980), pp. 97–112.

19. According to Chen Xilian, the commander of the Shenyang MR at that time, the order to retaliate had been agreed to by the "center," which almost certainly

means Mao, since it would have been unlikely that Lin Biao or Zhou Enlai would agree to so important an initiative without running it by the Chairman; Yang Kuisong, *Mao Zedong yu Mosikede enen yuanyuan* (Mao Zedong's Good and Bad Relations with Moscow) (Nanchang: Jiangxi renmin chubanshe, 1999), p. 492. The account of the preparations for and conduct of the Chinese counterattack is heavily based on this source, pp. 491–494.

20. "Zhou zongli zai 'jiuda' yubeihui jieshu shi chuanda Mao zhuxi zhishi" (Premier Zhou Transmits Chairman Mao's Instructions at the End of the Preparatory Meeting for the "Ninth Congress"), in *'Jiuda' ziliao huibian*, p. 55.
21. Li Danhui, "1969 nian Zhong Su bianjie chongtu: Yuanqi he jieguo" (The Sino-Soviet Border Conflict in 1969: Origins and Consequences), in Zhang Hua and Su Caiqing, *Huishou "Wenge,"* 2: 918.
22. *Zhou Enlai nianpu*, 3: 282–283.
23. Dangdai Guizhou jianshi bianweihui, *Dangdai Guizhou dashiji*, pp. 325–328; "Zhonggong zhongyang pizhuan 'Neimenggu zizhiqu geweihui hexin xiaozu "Jianjue guanche zhixing zhongyang guanyu Neimeng dangqian gongzuo zhishi de jidian yijian"'" (CCP Center Circular with Comment: "Some Opinions of the Nucleus of the Inner Mongolia Autonomous Region Revolutionary Committee on the 'Resolute Implementation of the CCP Center's Instructions on Work in Inner Mongolia at Present'"), August 3, 1981, p. 1, photocopy of original in Fairbank Center Library.
24. Yang Kuisong, *Mao Zedong yu Mosikede enen yuanyuan*, pp. 496–498.
25. Patrick Tyler, *A Great Wall: Six Presidents and China—An Investigative History* (New York: Public Affairs, 1999), pp. 54–71. This account rejects the one given in Kissinger's memoir, *White House Years* (Boston: Little Brown, 1979), p. 184, which sought to suggest that the White House never considered anything but opposition to a Soviet strike against China. Ironically, five years earlier, Nixon's predecessor, Lyndon Johnson, had considered a surgical strike against China and had sounded out the Russians without success; Mann, *About Face*, p. 20. See also Yang Kuisong, *Mao Zedong yu Mosikede enen yuanyuan*, p. 496.
26. *Zhou Enlai nianpu*, 3: 320–321; Chai Chengwen, "Zhou Enlai yu Zhong Su bianjie tanpan" (Zhou Enlai and the Sino-Soviet Border Talks), in Qiu Shi, *Gongheguo zhongda shijian he juece neimu*, 2: 659–671; Yang Kuisong, *Mao Zedong yu Mosikede enen yuanyuan*, p. 499.
27. This account relies heavily on Zheng Qian, "60 niandai mo Zhongguo beizhan miwen."
28. Ye Ting-xing, *A Leaf in the Bitter Wind*, p. 146. MacFarquhar visited the Beijing shelters early on with a group of British journalists in the autumn of 1972. At their height, they boasted a hospital, a cinema, granaries, and public baths. Today those

shelters are empty except for foreign tourists, but around the country they apparently house 3,700 hotels and nearly 4,000 restaurants, shops, and similar facilities; see Craig S. Smith, "Mao's Buried Past: A Strange Subterranean City," *New York Times,* November 26, 2001.

29. Yang Kuisong, *Mao Zedong yu Mosikede enen yuanyuan,* p. 498.

30. Ibid., p. 501; *Jianguo yilai Mao Zedong wengao,* 13: 66.

31. *Zhou Enlai nianpu,* 3: 322.

32. Yang Kuisong, *Mao Zedong yu Mosikede enen yuanyuan,* pp. 501–502.

33. *Zhou Enlai nianpu,* 3: 324.

34. Ibid., p. 301. One suggestion about the origin of this group is that Zhou put it to Mao that it would be a good way to keep the marshals occupied, for despite their positions as vice chairmen of the MAC, Mao and Lin Biao allowed them no role in it; Gao Wenqian, *Wannian Zhou Enlai,* p. 407.

35. *Zhou Enlai nianpu,* 3: 281, 301–302, 305. See also Zhang Baojun, "Dakai Zhong Mei guanxi damen shimo" (The Story of How Sino-American Relations Were Opened Up), in Qiu Shi, *Gongheguo zhongda shijian he juece neimu,* 2: 673–717, for details of the Chen Yi group's activities. Marshal Nie did not mention the group in his memoirs; Nie Rongzhen, *Inside the Red Star* (Beijing: New World Press, 1988).

36. Extracts from the two reports are translated in Barnouin and Yu, *Chinese Foreign Policy during the Cultural Revolution,* pp. 139–144.

37. CCP CC Party History Research Centre, *History of the Chinese Communist Party,* p. 347; Zheng Qian, "60 niandai mo Zhongguo beizhan miwen," p. 634.

38. Wang Nianyi, *Da dongluande niandai,* pp. 361–368.

39. Yang Kuisong, *Mao Zedong yu Mosikede enen yuanyuan,* p. 504.

40. Zheng Qian, "60 niandai mo Zhongguo beizhan miwen," pp. 636–645.

41. Yang Kuisong, *Mao Zedong yu Mosikede enen yuanyuan,* p. 502.

42. Barnouin and Yu, *Chinese Foreign Policy during the Cultural Revolution,* p. 95.

43. CCP CC Party History Research Centre, *History of the Chinese Communist Party,* p. 348; Ma Qibin et al., *Zhongguo gongchandang zhizheng sishinian,* p. 325.

44. Liao Gailong, *Xin Zhongguo biannian shi,* p. 326; Yang Kuisong, *Mao Zedong yu Mosikede enen yuanyuan,* p. 502. *Zhou Enlai nianpu,* 3: 328, states that a Politburo meeting took place on October 12, but this normally very full source does not list emergency defense measures among the topics discussed. Zhou and a group of influential Politburo members met Mao and Lin the following day, and defense could have been discussed then.

45. See *Zhou Enlai nianpu,* 3: 329.

46. Li Zhisui, *The Private Life of Chairman Mao,* p. 518; Yang Kuisong, *Mao Zedong yu Mosikede enen yuanyuan,* p. 502; Wu Jicheng, *Hongse jingwei,* p. 151.

47. See for example the treatment accorded Ye Jianying during his ten-month exile from the capital; Zhang Tingdong, *Wo pei Ye shuai zouwan zuihou shiqinian* (I Was with Marshal Ye during His Last Seventeen Years) (Beijing: Zhonggong dangshi chubanshe, 1999), pp. 53–57.

48. Most sources dealing with Lin's notorious order are understandably reticent about the background to it because of the implications for the Mao-Lin relationship.

49. CCP CC Party History Research Centre, *History of the Chinese Communist Party*, p. 348; Wang Dongxing, *Mao Zedong yu Lin Biao fangeming jituande douzheng* (The Struggle between Mao Zedong and the Lin Biao Counterrevolutionary Clique) (Beijing: Dangdai Zhongguo chubanshe, 1997), p. 15; Zheng Qian, "60 niandai mo Zhongguo beizhan miwen," p. 641.

50. Li Ke and Hao Shengzhang, *"Wenhua dageming" zhongde renmin jiefangjun*, p. 124. While most Chinese sources like this one say the order went out as "Vice Chairman" Lin's, his secretary remembers it as referring to Lin as "Vice Commander-in-Chief" *(futongshuai)*; Zhang Yunsheng, *Maojiawan jishi*, p. 319. In Chinese historical compilations, both forms can be found. According to the recollection of informant P, who was serving in a frontier region, the order was received by telephone at 9:44 P.M. In English translations, Lin's directive *(di yige haoling)* is usually rendered, not quite accurately, as "Order No. 1" (which might be better rendered as *di yi hao mingling*). The latter rendering perhaps sounds more authoritative than "first order," but either translation conveys the implication of a future stream of orders.

51. See for instance Pang Xianzhi and Jin Chongji, *Mao Zedong zhuan*, 2: 1564, where it is claimed more moderately that Lin Biao had no right to decide on such important measures without the prior agreement of the chairman of the MAC, i.e., Mao.

52. Gao Wenqian, *Wannian Zhou Enlai*, p. 280.

53. Wang Dongxing, *Mao Zedong yu Lin Biao fangeming jituande douzheng*, pp. 14–15.

54. Zhang Yunsheng, *Maojiawan jishi*, pp. 316–323.

55. Li Ke and Hao Shengzhang, *"Wenhua dageming" zhongde renmin jiefangjun*, p. 124. The second order was to China's missile forces, the third to the General Staff's second and third departments, and the fourth to various headquarters—service arms, defense industry, and science.

56. Ibid., p. 125; Yang Kuisong, *Mao Zedong yu Mosikede enen yuanyuan*, p. 503. The order even reached May 7 Cadre Schools run by the PLA; Gao Xingjian, *One Man's Bible*, p. 111.

57. There is even a hint in one source that Mao may not have been angry at all; Li Ke and Hao Shengzhang, *"Wenhua dageming" zhongde renmin jiefangjun*, p. 124.

58. Mao's doctor, whose account is replete with examples of the Chairman's paranoia, recounts the latter's grumbling at this time about the growing number of soldiers around him; Li Zhisui, *The Private Life of Chairman Mao*, pp. 517–518.

59. For a Russian description of the negotiations, see Galenovich, *Rossia i Kitai v XX Veke*, pp. 148–179; the author participated in the talks as a technical expert. For his account of the Zhou-Kosygin talks on September 11, 1969, and subsequent exchanges of texts of agreements to remove the danger of further border conflict, see ibid., pp. 125–147.

60. Zheng Qian, "60 niandai mo Zhongguo beizhan miwen," pp. 642–658.

61. The feelers put forward by the Nixon administration have been detailed in *RN: The Memoirs of Richard Nixon* (London: Book Club Associates, 1978); Kissinger, *White House Years*, pp. 163–194, 684–787; and most recently in John H. Holdridge, *Crossing the Divide: An Insider's Account of the Normalization of U.S.-China Relations* (Lanham, Md.: Rowman & Littlefield, 1997); Mann, *About Face;* and Tyler, *A Great Wall.* See also Jonathan D. Pollack, "The Opening to America," in John K. Fairbank and Roderick MacFarquhar, eds., *Cambridge History of China*, vol. 15, pt. 2 (New York: Cambridge University Press, 1991), pp. 402–472; Roderick MacFarquhar, ed., *Sino-American Relations, 1949–1971* (New York: Praeger, 1972), pp. 241–257. For a Chinese view, see Zhang Baojun, "Dakai Zhong Mei guanxi damen shimo," pp. 680–685.

62. Mann, *About Face*, pp. 23–28.

63. Tyler, *A Great Wall*, p. 86.

64. *Zhou Enlai nianpu*, 3: 449–450. Zhou asked the Foreign Ministry and the National Physical Culture and Sports Commission to make a recommendation on whether or not to invite the U.S. team, and was annoyed when they recommended against. However, he forwarded the recommendation to Mao, signifying his endorsement. Mao approved the recommendation but then changed his mind; Pang Xianzhi and Jin Chongji, *Mao Zedong zhuan*, 2: 1629–32; Gao Wenqian, *Wannian Zhou Enlai*, pp. 430–432.

65. Zheng Qian, "Dakai Zhong Mei guanxi damen shimo," pp. 646–649; this conversation is not included in *Jianguo yilai Mao Zedong wengao*, vol. 13.

66. For accounts, see note 61, above.

67. Tyler, *A Great Wall*, p. 61.

68. William Burr, ed., *The Kissinger Transcripts: The Top Secret Talks with Beijing and Moscow* (New York: New Press, 1999), p. 61. The Mao-Nixon exchanges are not included in *Jianguo yilai Mao Zedong wengao*, vol. 13.

69. This point is made forcefully by Teiwes and Sun, *The Tragedy of Lin Biao*, pp. 123–126.

70. Gao Wenqian, *Wannian Zhou Enlai*, p. 427.

71. *RN,* p. 580.
72. Gao Wenqian, *Wannian Zhou Enlai,* p. 427.
73. Ibid., n. 49.

19. The Defection and Death of Lin Biao

1. According to *Wang Li fansi lu,* 2: 940–941, expanded sessions of the PSC were chaired by Mao unless he asked Lin Biao to do so, in which case Lin obeyed. If Mao was chairing, Lin always turned up.
2. Wang Nianyi, *Da dongluande niandai,* pp. 387–388; Liu Zhinan, "Jiuda zhi jiu jie er zhong quanhui qian xi Mao Zedong yu Lin Biaode fenqi he maodun" (The Split and Contradictions between Mao Zedong and Lin Biao from the Ninth Congress to the Eve of the Second Plenum), *Dangdai Zhongguo shi yanjiu,* no. 3 (1997), 38–48.
3. The other was Mme. Song Qingling, the widow of Dr. Sun Yat-sen, who was not a CCP member, it being thought at the highest levels that she was more use to the country's image as a non-Communist; she was allowed to join the party only on her deathbed.
4. Wang Nianyi and He Shu, "1970 niande Lushan huiyi ji Mao Zedong, Lin Biao chongtu zhi qiyuan—zai 'she guojia zhuxi' zhi zhengde beihou" (The Origins of the Clash between Mao Zedong and Lin Biao at the 1970 Lushan Conference—The Background to the Argument over "Establishing [the Post of] Head of State"), *Jilin nongye zengkan* (Jilin Agriculture Supplement), 1999, p. 20.
5. According to Wang Dongxing, Mao's proposal was made in response to a query in a letter from Zhou Enlai, but there is no mention in *Zhou Enlai nianpu,* vol. 3, of any such letter; nor does Wang indicate on whose initiative Zhou had decided to look at the state constitution; Wang Dongxing, *Mao Zedong yu Lin Biao fangeming jituande douzheng,* pp. 18–20.
6. It was not until 1977 that the Soviet party leader, Brezhnev, became concurrently state president, presumably so that he could deal with the U.S. president on formally equal terms. Until then, the role of head of state was played by the chair of the legislature, normally a second-rank politician.
7. In the twelve months between November 1969 and November 1970, only 45 of 2,185 counties set up party committees.
8. Wang Dongxing, *Mao Zedong yu Lin Biao fangeming jituande douzheng,* p. 34.
9. Teiwes and Sun, *The Tragedy of Lin Biao,* p. 136. Contrary to the official line, Wang Nianyi in *Da dongluande niandai,* p. 394, states that there is no way of being sure that Lin Biao was interested in the head-of-state position or that he knew of his wife's activities. Ye Qun allegedly asked Wu Faxian what would become of Lin Biao if there were no state chairmanship, but after the Cultural Revolution

Wu retracted his testimony, stating that he had made it under duress; Jin Qiu, *The Culture of Power: The Lin Biao Incident in the Cultural Revolution* (Stanford: Stanford University Press, 1999), pp. 128, 234, n. 68. Jin Qiu is Wu Faxian's daughter. For Wang Dongxing's message to the Politburo from Mao, see also Gao Wenqian, *Wannian Zhou Enlai*, p. 281.

10. Jin Qiu, *The Culture of Power*, p. 121. Wu Faxian's ms. states that Wang Dongxing conveyed Mao's message in May rather than March, but this date is contradicted in a multitude of Chinese sources.

11. After the Cultural Revolution was over, even in discussions with foreigners, Chinese would commonly hold up four fingers to indicate the Gang of Four while semisurreptitiously waggling their thumbs to indicate that they knew it was a Gang of Five, with Mao as its leader.

12. *Resolution on CPC History (1949–1981)*, p. 38.

13. *Jianguo yilai Mao Zedong wengao*, 13: 244–245, translated in Michael Y. M. Kau, ed., *The Lin Piao Affair: Power Politics and Military Coup* (White Plains, N.Y.: International Arts and Sciences Press, 1975), p. 60.

14. Wang Dongxing, *Mao Zedong yu Lin Biao fangeming jituande douzheng*, pp. 20–21; *Zhou Enlai nianpu*, 3: 353, 361; *Jianguo yilai Mao Zedong wengao*, 13: 94.

15. Teiwes and Sun, *The Tragedy of Lin Biao*, pp. 137–139.

16. Ibid., p. 139.

17. Jin Qiu, *The Culture of Power*, p. 122.

18. Ibid.

19. *Quotations from Chairman Mao Tse-tung*, p. i.

20. Wang Dongxing, *Mao Zedong yu Lin Biao fangeming jituande douzheng*, pp. 26–28; Jin Qiu, *The Culture of Power*, pp. 122–123; *Zhou Enlai nianpu*, 3: 385.

21. *Zhou Enlai nianpu*, 3: 386–387. Curiously, Wang Dongxing's detailed account does not mention this part of the discussion; Wang Dongxing, *Mao Zedong yu Lin Biao fageming jituande douzheng*, pp. 31–35.

22. Kau, *The Lin Piao Affair*, p. 60.

23. Jin Qiu, *The Culture of Power*, p. 123; Teiwes and Sun, *The Tragedy of Lin Biao*, p. 143. Leading Chinese historians of the Cultural Revolution in effect accused Mao of lying on this issue, although their temerity could be aired only in an obscure journal; see Wang Nianyi and He Shu, "1970 niande Lushan huiyi ji Mao Zedong, Lin Biao chongtu zhi qiyuan—zai 'she guojia zhuxi' zhi zhengde beihou," pp. 24–25. This accusation was aired again with a more provocative title in an overseas journal published by exiles; see Wang Nianyi, He Shu, and Chen Zhao, "Mao Zedong bichulaide 'jiu.yisan Lin Biao chutao shijian,'" pp. 137–154. Mao's official biographers can justify Mao's claim only by stating that Lin Biao had not given a formal Notification in advance of his speech; they add that the majority of the PSC knew nothing about what he was going to say, but of course

the key issue is that Mao did know; Pang Xianzhi and Jin Chongji, *Mao Zedong zhuan,* 2: 1572.

24. See above, Chapter 6.

25. This anomalous behavior of Zhou in using two of the three adverbs is stressed in Teiwes and Sun, *The Tragedy of Lin Biao,* p. 138. Possibly Mao had no objection to the adverbs when used orally, but objected to their being written into a major document, which would preserve his immodesty for posterity.

26. Text of Lin Biao's speech available in Fairbank Center Library.

27. *Nie Yuanzi huiyilu,* p. 323.

28. One Chinese source sums up the reasons for the anti–Zhang Chunqiao tide as follows: (1) some wanted to prove their loyalty to Mao by criticizing Zhang's call to drop the reference to genius; (2) some of the military region commanders attributed the assaults they had suffered at the hands of rebels to Zhang's incitement; (3) it was known at the plenum that Zhang was being accused by some in Shanghai of having been a traitor in the past; (4) Zhang was a surrogate for Jiang Qing who could not be touched; Wang Nianyi, He Shu, and Chen Zhao, "Mao Zedong bichulaide 'jiu.yisan Lin Biao chutao shijian,'" pp. 141–142.

29. But see Xu Jingxian, *Shinian yimeng,* pp. 208, 212.

30. *Bulletin,* no. 6, of the North China Group and speech transcripts available in Fairbank Center Library.

31. Wang Dongxing, *Mao Zedong yu Lin Biao fangeming jituande douzheng,* p. 44. Wang insisted that *Bulletin,* no. 6, did not accurately represent what he had actually said at the meetings of the North China Group and that he had not been given an opportunity to review its contents beforehand. For this confusion, he held Wang Liang'en, his deputy as director of the Central Committee General Office, responsible. Wang Liang'en, who had indeed been in charge of everyday logistics, including production of bulletins at Lushan, committed suicide in January 1973, after being charged with illicit contacts with Lin Biao's "sworn followers"; Wu Jicheng, *Hongse jingwei,* pp. 301–311.

32. Wang was not present at the Mao-Lin pre-plenum discussion, but he could have learned about the gist of the discussion from Ye Qun.

33. Wang Dongxing, *Mao Zedong yu Lin Biao fangeming jituande douzheng,* pp. 44–46. Many of the finer points that Chen made in his speech may well have been lost on those members of his audience, who, unlike Wang, were not used to his Fujian accent. A senior political commissar (born in Anhui) from the Beijing MR who also heard him speak admitted years later that "to understand what he said was extremely difficult. But I basically managed to get the main content of his talk"; Chen Xianrui, "Pi-Chen pi-Lin qijian de Beijing junqu" (The Beijing Military Region at the Time of the Criticism of Chen and Lin), *Bainian chao,* no. 5 (2000), 44.

34. Teiwes and Sun, *The Tragedy of Lin Biao,* pp. 148–149.

35. Gao Wenqian, *Wannian Zhou Enlai,* pp. 300, 303, 313. Mao had previously used this tactic with Peng Dehuai (*Origins,* 3: 441–443) and Liu Shaoqi (see above, Chapter 8).

36. Mao learned of this from Jiang Qing; Gao Wenqian, *Wannian Zhou Enlai,* p. 271.

37. For Mao's debt to Chen Boda, see Wylie, *The Emergence of Maoism.*

38. Mao would regularly encourage others to read the Marxist classics. His wedding gift to his own daughter Li Na, who married for the first time shortly after the Lushan meeting, was a set of the *Complete Works of Marx and Engels;* Xu Jingxian, *Shinian yimeng,* p. 111. As a parting gift after meeting him in Zhongnanhai on June 21, 1975, Mao offered Cambodian leader Pol Pot thirty titles by Marx, Engels, Lenin, and Stalin; Short, *Pol Pot,* pp. 299–300.

39. Wang Nianyi, He Shu, and Chen Zhao, "Mao Zedong bichulaide 'jiu.yisan Lin Biao chutao shijian,'" p. 148.

40. Jin Qiu, *The Culture of Power,* p. 132.

41. Gao Wenqian, *Wannian Zhou Enlai,* pp. 324–325.

42. So much did Mao trust Li Desheng that he ensured that he filled numerous important roles: membership of a new central propaganda group; membership of the CC's MAC and of its administrative group; head of the PLA's General Political Department; head of the Anhui Provincial Revolutionary Committee and, from the beginning of 1971, first secretary of the Anhui party; commander of the Beijing Military Region and first secretary of its party organization; Wang Nianyi, He Shu, and Chen Zhao, "Mao Zedong bichulaide 'jiu.yisan Lin Biao chutao shijian,'" p. 147.

43. MacFarquhar, "Succession to Mao and the End of Maoism, 1969–82," pp. 266–268; Chen Xianrui, "Pi-Chen pi-Lin qijian de Beijing junqu," p. 45.

44. Kau, *The Lin Piao Affair,* pp. 89–90.

45. Lin Biao even thrust his dignity aside and went to see Jiang Qing at Diaoyutai Guest House, hoping she could get him in to see Mao, but this device did not work; Wang Nianyi, He Shu, and Chen Zhao, "Mao Zedong bichulaide 'jiu.yisan Lin Biao chutao shijian,'" p. 151; see also Gao Wenqian, *Wannian Zhou Enlai,* pp. 323–326.

46. Kau, *The Lin Piao Affair,* pp. 88–105; MacFarquhar, "Succession to Mao and the End of Maoism, 1969–82," pp. 268–272; *A Great Trial in Chinese History* (Beijing: New World Press, 1981), pp. 89–100.

47. Gao Wenqian, *Wannian Zhou Enlai,* pp. 331–332.

48. Ibid., p. 334.

49. For Mao's suspicion that something might be afoot, see Wang Dongxing, *Mao Zedong yu Lin Biao fangeming jituande douzheng,* pp. 184–185.

50. Gao Wenqian, *Wannian Zhou Enlai,* pp. 342–348.

51. In 1962, discussing Soviet attacks on China with the Soviet ambassador, Mao said: "(1) The heavens won't fall; (2) trees will grow as before; (3) fish will keep on swimming in the rivers; (4) women will go on having children"; Wu Lengxi, *Shinian lunzhan,* 2: 914.

52. For extended accounts of these events, see Wang Nianyi, *Da dongluande niandai,* pp. 415–434; Wang Dongxing, *Mao Zedong yu Lin Biao fangeming jituande douzheng,* pp. 196–219; Jin Qiu, *The Culture of Power,* pp. 163–199; MacFarquhar, "Succession to Mao and the End of Maoism, 1969–82," pp. 268–275; Kau, *The Lin Piao Affair,* pp. 102–105.

53. The most revisionist version appeared in the pseudonymous Yao Ming-le's *The Conspiracy and Murder of Mao's Heir* (London: Collins, 1983), supposedly based on the diary of an official who participated in the investigation of the Lin Biao affair. This account concluded even more dramatically, if that were possible, than the official version, with Lin Biao and Ye Qun being blown up by rockets as they were driving away from a dinner with Mao and Zhou in the Western Hills. In an earlier version of events, MacFarquhar noted: "The following account of Lin Biao's plot has been put together from a number of sources, but virtually all are official or semi-official versions, written by the victors or based on their evidence. In events so momentous as the demise of an heir-apparent, there are many reasons why evidence should be doctored, and there can be no guarantee that if the CC's innermost archives are one day opened, another version will not emerge. It still seems worthwhile to spell out in detail the currently most believable version of the Lin Biao affair in order to depict the nature of Chinese politics of the time. Any revised version is likely only to underline the way in which the fate of China was settled by the ambitions and intrigues of a very small group of desperate leaders and their families"; MacFarquhar, "Succesion to Mao and the End of Maoism, 1969–82," p. 268, n. 76. More recent revisionist accounts are Teiwes and Sun, *The Tragedy of Lin Biao;* and Jin Qiu, *The Culture of Power,* though the former has little to say about the details of the plot, only to argue that Lin Biao was unlikely to have played any role in whatever Lin Liguo was up to.

54. Wang Dongxing, *Mao Zedong yu Lin Biao fangeming jituande douzheng,* pp. 87–176.

55. Kau, *The Lin Piao Affair,* p. 112.

20. Mao Becalmed

1. Pang Xianzhi and Jin Chongji, *Mao Zedong zhuan,* 2: 1605.

2. Chen Donglin and Du Pu, *Gongheguo shiji,* 3: 689–691.

3. Zhonggong zhongyang bangongting, *Canyue wenjian,* 1: 2, 6, 19–20, 22.

4. You Lin, Zheng Xinli, and Wang Ruipu, eds., *Zhonghua renmin gongheguo guoshi*

tongjian (A Comprehensive Mirror of National History of the PRC), 4 vols. (Beijing: Hongqi chubanshe, 1993), 3: 905, n. 1. Some signals were rather more subtle, such as Zhang Chunqiao's ceasing to wear in public the PLA uniform that had been his trademark since the autumn of 1966 and reverting to civilian attire in the form of a light gray "Mao jacket"; Xu Jingxian, *Shinian yimeng*, p. 271.

5. This is the figure for the total number of copies printed on the back of a copy held in the Fairbank Center Library.

6. A CC document stated: "the working people have permission to discuss the [Lin Biao] matter among themselves," but "the matter is not to be mentioned in the press or on the radio, nor are big-character posters or slogans to be written . . . Vigilance must be raised, and secrets must not be revealed to the class enemy"; Zhonggong zhongyang wenjian, *Zhongfa* [1971] 67, p. 4. See also Kau, *The Lin Piao Affair*, p. lxvi.

7. Yue and Wakeman, *To the Storm*, p. 309.

8. This judgment is based on numerous conversations between the authors and Chinese.

9. Li Zhisui, *The Private Life of Chairman Mao*, p. 542.

10. *Mao zhuxi yulu suoyin* (Index to Chairman Mao's Quotations) (n.p., 1970), p. 1677.

11. *Renmin ribao*, April 24, 1972.

12. This was only the third time since the founding of the PRC that Mao had attended a memorial service of this kind: the first was for Ren Bishi, the fifth-ranking Politburo member when he died in 1950; the second was for Stalin in 1953; Zhonggong Zhejiang shengwei dangxiao dangshi jiaoyanshi, *"Wenhua dageming" shiqi ziliao xuanji*, p. 35.

13. Li Zhisui, *The Private Life of Chairman Mao*, p. 545; *Zhou Enlai nianpu*, 3: 508.

14. Li Zhisui, *The Private Life of Chairman Mao*, pp. 545–546.

15. *Zhou Enlai nianpu*, 3: 507–508.

16. Liu Shunhui, "Zeng Shan" (Zeng Shan), in *Zhonggong dangshi renwu zhuan*, 25 (pub. 1985): 258–259; Gong Zhong, You Sheng, and Sheng Yang, "Chen Zhengren" (Chen Zhengren), ibid., 40 (pub. 1989): 267; *Deng Liqun guoshi jiangtan lu*, 3: 161. See also Li Yong, ed., *Wenge mingrenzhi si* (The Deaths of Well-Known People during the Cultural Revolution) (Taipei: Paise chubanshe, 1994).

17. Beijing shi geming weiyuanhui di er xuexiban dangwei, "Guanyu Yang Zizheng wentide fucha qingkuang" (On the Situation of the Reinvestigation of the Problems of Yang Zizheng), July 4, 1972, Schoenhals collection.

18. Beijing shi geming weiyuanhui di er xuexiban dangwei, "Guanyu Han Guang tongzhi wentide fucha qingkuang" (On the Situation of the Reinvestigation of the Problems of Comrade Han Guang), December 9, 1972, Schoenhals collection.

19. Beijing shi geming weiyuanhui di er xuexiban dangwei, "Guanyu dui Zhu Qiming tongzhi wentide fucha qingkuang baogao" (Report on the Situation of the Reinvestigation of the Problems of Comrade Zhu Qiming), November 1972, Schoenhals collection.

20. Zhou Yixing, ed., *Dangdai Beijing jianshi* (A Short History of Contemporary Beijing) (Beijing: Dangdai Zhongguo chubanshe, 1999), p. 229.

21. In Beijing in October 1972, MacFarquhar handed an up-and-coming Chinese Foreign Ministry official a copy of his edited volume *Sino-American Relations, 1949–1971*, published only a few months earlier. The following day, having read overnight the essay in the book that described the purge of his ministry, the official averred that it was already out of date and predicted that within a year the ministry would be back to full strength.

22. See for instance Jung Chang, *Wild Swans*, pp. 444–445.

23. Michael Schoenhals, "Editor's Introduction: Guan Feng Is Back," *Chinese Studies in Philosophy*, 26, nos. 1–2 (Fall–Winter 1994–95), 5.

24. Schoenhals, "The Central Case Examination Group, 1966–79," pp. 106–107.

25. Tu Men and Kong Di, *Gongheguo zuida yuanan*, p. 89; Xiao Sike (in *Chaoji shenpan: Tu Men jiangjun canyu shenli Lin Biao fangeming jituan qinli ji* [Super Trial: General Tu Men's Personal Experience of Participating in the Trial of the Lin Biao Counterrevolutionary Clique] [Ji'nan: Ji'nan chubanshe, 1992], p. 43) cites a former Qincheng warden who gave the number of prisoners who went insane as "more than thirty."

26. For an interesting contemporary account by Rittenberg, as told to a Chinese audience in the Jinjiang Hotel in Shanghai on June 13, 1967, of his own involvement in the early Cultural Revolution, see *Wuchanjieji wenhua dageming ziliao* 6, 1: 384–401.

27. Rittenberg and Bennett, *The Man Who Stayed Behind*, pp. 414–415. Despite his desperate years of solitary confinement, Rittenberg was resilient, retaining his sense of humor and his chutzpah. When MacFarquhar asked him after the Cultural Revolution how it had felt to have had the reputation of having briefly been, as head of Beijing Radio's Broadcast Administration, the most powerful foreigner in China since Marco Polo, he replied: "Why talk of Marco Polo!"

28. *Jianguo yilai Mao Zedong wengao*, 13: 334; *Zhou Enlai xuanji* (Selected Works of Zhou Enlai), 2 vols. (Beijing: Renmin chubanshe, 1980, 1984), 2: 456–457. The wife had finally been allowed to visit her husband.

29. *Zhongguo renmin gongan shigao*, p. 341.

30. Quoted by Schoenhals, "The Central Case Examination Group, 1966–79," p. 107.

31. *Zhou Enlai nianpu*, 3: 697.

32. The figure 670 did not include cadres investigated because of presumed links to Lin Biao. See ibid., p. 699, n. 1.

33. Deng Rong, *Deng Xiaoping and the Cultural Revolution*, p. 311. According to Deng Xiaoping's daughter, her father and Zhou Enlai were actively involved in pushing for these releases.

34. *Zhongguo renmin gongan shigao*, pp. 346–347.

35. Interestingly, it was Deng who chose to dwell specifically on the case of the so-called May 16 "conspirators" when pushing for a speedy resolution of all outstanding cases in 1975: "In the campaign to ferret out members of the 'May Sixteenth Group,' over 6,000 persons in Xuzhou came under attack. This figure is quite shocking . . . The treatment of [them] . . . affects tens of thousands of others, if we count an average of five members in each of their families, plus other relatives, friends and social connections. Measures must be taken to help them shed their mental burden as soon as possible"; "Some Problems Outstanding in the Iron and Steel Industry," in *Selected Works of Deng Xiaoping (1975–82)* (Beijing: Foreign Languages Press, 1984), pp. 20–21. It was, of course, alleged opposition to Zhou Enlai, rather than to Deng or Liu Shaoqi, that defined the members of the "May 16" group, and so it is not surprising that before Deng's return to power, Zhou is not known to have made any particular effort to push for the speedy resolution of cases relating to this group.

36. *Wang Li fansi lu*, 2: 922.

37. Laszlo Ladany, *The Communist Party of China and Marxism, 1921–1985: A Self-Portrait* (Stanford.: Hoover Institution Press, 1988), p. 355.

38. Wang Nianyi, *Da dongluande niandai*, pp. 442–443; Zhonggong zhongyang wenxian yanjiushi, *"Wenge" shinian ziliao xuanbian*, 2: 178.

39. See above, Chapter 3 and Chapter 4. Jiang Qing's speech is in *Zhongyang pi Lin zhengfeng houbaohuiyi shi ge wenjian huibian* (Ten Documents from the Criticize Lin and Rectify Work-Style Report-Back Conference) (Hefei: Zhonggong Anhui shengwei, 1972), pp. 5–10.

40. Xu Jingxian, *Shinian yimeng*, p. 266.

41. *Guanyu dui yexinjia, yinmoujia, pantu, maiguozei Lin Biao zuixing de jiefa pipan* (Exposing and Denouncing the Crimes of Careerist, Conspirator, Renegade, and Traitor Lin Biao) (n.p., [1972]), p. 3.

42. Ibid., pp. 7, 24, 27.

43. Wang Nianyi, He Shu, and Chen Zhao, "Mao Zedong bichulaide 'jiu.yisan Lin Biao chutao shijian,'" pp. 147–148.

44. *Guanyu dui yexinjia, yinmoujia, pantu, maiguozei Lin Biao zuixing de jiefa pipan*, p. 8.

45. *Shanghai "Wenhua dageming" shihua*, 3: 639–640.

46. Robert S. Ross, *Negotiating Cooperation: The United States and China, 1969–1989* (Stanford: Stanford University Press, 1995), pp. 42–43; Tyler, *A Great Wall*, pp. 116–117.

47. *Zhou Enlai nianpu*, 3: 438 439.

48. Wolf Mendl, *Issues in Japan's China Policy* (London: Macmillan for RIIA, 1978), pp. 57–68. It is a historical curiosity that all three national leaders who made breakthroughs with China in 1972 lost office soon thereafter, two (Nixon and Tanaka) in disgrace, the third (Heath) never to return to power. President Jimmy Carter, who negotiated the second breakthrough in Sino-U.S. relations, the 1979 normalization of diplomatic relations, suffered electoral defeat in 1980.

49. *RN*, p. 570.

50. Mann, *About Face*, pp. 63–64; a similar later request was for the film *Z*.

51. See Roxane Witke, *Comrade Chiang Ch'ing* (Boston: Little, Brown, 1977). For a Chinese version, with a full record of the Jiang-Witke conversations by the Foreign Ministry official deputed to accompany Witke, as well as the repercussions of the visit within the ministry, see Zhang Ying, *Waijiao fengyun: Qinli ji* (Storms in Foreign Relations: A Personal Account) (Wuhan: Hubei renmin chubanshe, 2005), pp. 177–330.

52. Liu Gao and Shi Feng, eds., *Xin Zhongguo chu ban wushinian jishi* (A Record of Fifty Years of Publishing in New China) (Beijing: Xinhua chubanshe, 1999), pp. 139–140.

53. For instance on Japan.

54. *Tuopai ziliao xuanyi* (Selected Translations of Trotskyite Material) (Shanghai: Fudan daxue, 1972), 1: 19, translation of "The Worldwide Youth Radicalization and the Tasks of the Fourth International," *International Socialist Review* (July–August 1969), 48–69. The authors include Ernest Mandel, Jack Barnes, and Joseph Hansen.

55. *Zhou Rongxin tongzhi de jianghua huibian* (Collected Speeches of Comrade Zhou Rongxin) (n.p., December 1975), pp. 14–18.

56. Jan Wong, *Red China Blues: My Long March from Mao to Now* (Toronto: Doubleday/Anchor, 1997), p. 74.

57. Many of the parents were officials who were either in prison or at May 7 Cadre Schools.

58. At the time there was no "forum for opposition" recognizable as such to a foreign observer. At a U.S. Senate Committee on Foreign Relations hearing in 1972, John S. Service, a member of the American "Dixie Mission" to Yan'an in 1945, one of those foreign service officers who had been excoriated during the debate over "Who lost China?," admitted that "we don't know of any intellectual ferment going on . . . In China generally only one view is expressed. There is no forum for opposition." Nonetheless, Service concluded, "I don't think we should say it is a completely dead society; it is not that, I think"; Schoenhals, *China's Cultural Revolution*, pp. 281–284.

59. Sebastian Heilmann, *Sozialer Protest in der VR China: Die Bewegung vom 5. April 1976 und die Gegen-Kulturrevolution der siebziger Jahre* (Social Protest in the People's Republic of China: The April 5 Movement of 1976 and the Counter-Cultural Revolution of the Seventies) (Hamburg: Institut für Asienkunde, 1994), pp. 33–37.

60. Shangfang tongxun bianjishi, *Chunfeng huayu ji,* 2: 5.

61. Ibid., p. 2.

62. Ibid., p. 5.

63. Ibid., pp. 393–394.

64. *Dangdai Zhongguode Jilin,* 1: 156.

65. Shangfang tongxun bianjishi, *Chunfeng huayu ji,* 2: 392–406.

66. Li-I-Che, "On Socialist Democracy and the Legal System," *Chinese Law and Government,* 10, no. 3 (Fall 1977), 42–43.

67. Ibid., pp. 49–50.

68. Zhonggong Guangzhou shiwei dangshi yanjiushi, *Zhonggong Guangzhou dangshi dashiji,* p. 328.

69. For an account of the Li-Yi-Zhe phenomenon by the principal protagonist, see Wang Xizhe, *Wang Xizhe zizhuan: Zou xiang heian* (The Autobiography of Wang Xizhe: Toward the Darkness) (Hong Kong: Minzhu daxue, 1996).

70. Song Yongyi and Sun Dajin, eds., *Wenhua dageming he tade yiduan sichao* (Heterodox Thoughts during the Cultural Revolution) (Hong Kong: Tianyuan shuwu, 1997), p. 447.

71. Ibid., p. 453.

72. *Baokan ziliao* (Newspaper Materials), no. 25 (October 12, 1972).

73. Wang Nianyi, *Da dongluande niandai,* p. 450.

74. Wang Ruoshui, *Zhihui de tongku* (The Pain of Wisdom) (Hong Kong: Sanlian shudian, 1989), p. 331.

75. *Zhou Enlai nianpu,* 3: 567.

76. Though this is implied by some Chinese historians; see Wang Nianyi, *Da dongluande niandai,* p. 451.

77. An Jianshe, "'Jiu yi san' hou Zhou Enlai lingdao de pipan jizuo sichao de douzheng" (After "September 13": How Zhou Enlai Led the Struggle to Criticize Ultra-Leftism), in Zhang Hua and Su Caiqing, *Huishou "Wenge,"* 2: 1084.

78. See William A. Joseph, *The Critique of Ultra-Leftism in China, 1958–1981* (Stanford: Stanford University Press, 1984), pp. 120–150.

79. *Bianji yewu* (The Editor's Profession), no. 7 (June 8, 1973).

80. Ibid., no. 1 (March 13, 1973).

81. Li Zhisui, *The Private Life of Chairman Mao,* pp. 549–572; Guofang daxue, *"Wenhua dageming,"* 2: 706. In 1982 Chen was visited in prison by an old colleague

and friend who told him that no other high-level victim of the Cultural Revolution seemed to have managed to become the target of quite the same ridiculous number of charges; Chen Xiaonong, *Chen Boda zuihou koushu huiyi*, p. 271.

82. *Polemic on General Line of the International Communist Movement*, pp. 477–478.

83. *Chen Yun nianpu*, 3: 175.

21. Zhou under Pressure

1. From one of the hundreds of poems memorializing Zhou Enlai or denigrating the Gang of Four in April 1976; Xiao Lan, ed., *The Tiananmen Poems* (Beijing: Foreign Languages Press, 1979), p. 31. See above, Chapter 19.

2. Deng Rong, *Deng Xiaoping and the Cultural Revolution*, pp. 106–155.

3. Ibid., pp. 184–187, 198, 208–210.

4. *Jianguo yilai Mao Zedong wengao*, 13: 308.

5. *Zhou Enlai nianpu*, 3: 583–585; Deng Rong, *Deng Xiaoping and the Cultural Revolution*, pp. 244–245. The former source does not mention the presence of Jiang Qing at Zhou's meeting with Deng.

6. Deng Rong, *Deng Xiaoping and the Cultural Revolution*, pp. 264–269.

7. See *Origins*, 3: 424–425.

8. All party constitutions under Mao laid down that congresses were quinquennial affairs, but there had been eleven years between the Seventh and Eighth and thirteen years between the Eighth and Ninth. Between the Ninth and the Tenth there was only a little over four years.

9. *Zhou Enlai nianpu*, 3: 585–586.

10. Zhang Chunqiao and Wang Hongwen (who supervised the screening of delegates) selected a delegate from Hebei province who was not a CCP member but had impeccable "rebel" credentials. Their justification was that though this rebel had not joined the party in organizational terms, he certainly had already joined it ideologically and in his actions; Tan Zongji, "Shida pingshu" (Comments on the Tenth Party Congress), in Zhang Hua and Su Caiqing, *Huishou "Wenge,"* 2: 1096. In the past this line of reasoning had been employed in the opposite direction, e.g., in 1959, when Chen Boda described Peng Dehuai and his colleagues, in a favorite Maoist phrase, as being party members organizationally but not ideologically.

11. Li Zhisui, *The Private Life of Chairman Mao*, pp. 576–577.

12. Tan Zongji, "Shida pingshu," p. 1093. Mao is also known to CCP historians to have nodded his head repeatedly while Zhou Enlai read out the following passage in the report: "It should be emphatically pointed out that quite a few party committees are engrossed in daily routines and minor matters, paying no attention to

major issues. This is very dangerous. If they do not change, they will inevitably step on to the road of revisionism"; ibid., p. 1100.

13. See the analysis by Richard Wich, "The Tenth Party Congress: The Power Structure and the Succession Question," *CQ*, no. 58 (April–June 1974), 231–248.

14. *Zhou Enlai nianpu*, 3: 614; *Jianguo yilai Mao Zedong wengao*, 13: 358.

15. Ma Tianshui, "Wode jiefa jiaodai" (My Exposé and Testimony) (Shanghai: Shanghai shi qu, xian, ju dangyuan fuze ganbu huiyi mishuzu, November 5, 1976), pp. 4–5.

16. *Zhou Enlai nianpu*, 3: 614–615. Deng set up an advisory commission when he became the effective party leader after Mao's death.

17. *The Tenth National Congress of the Communist Party of China (Documents)* (Peking: Foreign Languages Press, 1973), p. 48. Mao had spelled out these standards in 1958 when exhorting his colleagues to emulate Hai Rui, the Ming dynasty official who was dismissed by the emperor for his boldness; see *Origins*, 2: 207. For Hai Rui, see above, Chapter 1.

18. *Tenth National Congress*, pp. 4, 42, 45, 47, 48, 50, 52, 55.

19. *Zhou Enlai nianpu*, 3: 595; *Shanghai "Wenhua dageming" shihua*, 3: 654.

20. Tan Zongji, "Shida pingshu," p. 1096.

21. CCP CC Party History Research Centre, *History of the Chinese Communist Party*, p. 360.

22. Xu Jingxian, *Shinian yimeng*, p. 291.

23. *Shanghai "Wenhua dageming" shihua*, 3: 652–653; Xu Jingxian, *Shinian yimeng*, pp. 272–274.

24. Tan Zhenlin, like Deng, was a longtime follower of Mao, having participated in the Autumn Harvest Uprising in 1927 and loyally followed him thereafter; Klein and Clark, *Biographic Dictionary of Chinese Communism*, 2: 796.

25. *Zhou Enlai nianpu*, 3: 616–617.

26. Ibid., pp. 617–618; Li Ke and Hao Shengzhang, *"Wenhua dageming" zhongde renmin jiefangjun*, pp. 145–146.

27. *Zhou Enlai nianpu*, 3: 616.

28. When the CCP does not wish to rank its officials, it states that it is listing them according to the number of strokes in their surname, the character equivalent of alphabetical order; see *Tenth National Congress*, p. 97.

29. All of them were dismissed by Deng after the Cultural Revolution.

30. See above, Chapter 9.

31. Roderick MacFarquhar, "China after the 10th Congress," *World Today*, 29, no. 12 (December 1973), 524–526.

32. Gao Wenqian, *Wannian Zhou Enlai*, p. 451.

33. For the Mao-Kissinger meeting, see Burr, *The Kissinger Transcripts*, pp. 179–200;

for the Politburo meeting, see *Zhou Enlai nianpu,* 3: 634–635; for Deng's criticism, see Deng Rong, *Deng Xiaoping and the Cultural Revolution,* pp. 255–256. Zhou's dismay at Deng's role was reported to MacFarquhar by an eyewitness at the meeting; in conversation with MacFarquhar, Chinese foreign service officers expressed the view that Deng had been brought back to check Zhou.

34. The characterization of *How to Be a Good Communist* as "Confucianist" *(Kongfuzizhuyide)* was Sidney Rittenberg's. See Beijing waiguo yu xueyuan Hongqi zhandou dadui, ed., *Liu Shaoqi zuixing lu* (Record of Liu Shaoqi's Crimes) (Beijing, 1967), 5: 30.

35. "Liu Shaoqi Kong miao chao sheng" (Liu Shaoqi's Pilgrimage to the Confucius Temple), p. 2, essay denouncing Liu (pp. 1–4) included in 137-page collection published in Shanghai in 1967 but with cover page and hence title missing.

36. "Mao zhuxi zai dangde ba jie kuodade shi er zhong quanhui shangde jianghua," p. 11.

37. See Jiang Qing's speech, quoted in the previous chapter, in *Zhongyang pi Lin zhengfeng houbaohuiyi shi ge wenjian huibian,* p. 7; see also *Xuexi "Mao zhuxi zhi Jiang Qing tongzhi de xin" de tihui* (Insights Gained from Studying "Chairman Mao's Letter to Comrade Jiang Qing") (n.p., [1974?]), p. 6, typed study document, Schoenhals collection.

38. The very same people who formulated this charge also insisted that Lin was someone who read neither books nor newspapers, and that the books he was known *not* to have read included the entire Confucian canon, namely the *Four Books* and the *Five Classics;* "Jiang Qing, Yao Wenyuan, Chi Qun, Xie Jingyi zai zhongyang zhishu jiguan he guojia jiguan pi-Lin pi-Kong dongyuan dahui shangde jianghua" (Speeches by Jiang Qing, Yao Wenyuan, Chi Qun, and Xie Jingyi at a Criticize-Lin Criticize-Confucius Mobilization Rally for Staff of Organs Directly under the Party Center and Central Government), January 25, 1974, p. 24, Fairbank Center Library. Jiang Qing had not read the *Four Books* and *Five Classics* either, but she said that Zhou had.

39. Wang Nianyi, *Da dongluande niandai,* p. 469.

40. Guan Weixun, *Wo suo zhidaode Ye Qun,* pp. 28–29.

41. Yang Rongguo, *Pipan Kongzi baogao* (Report Denouncing Confucius) (Baoding: Zhonggong Baoding diwei xuanchuanbu, 1974), p. 2.

42. Ibid., pp. 6–8.

43. Beijing daxue Liang Xiao zhuan'anzu, ed., *Liang Xiao zuizheng cailiao* (Documentation on Liang Xiao's Crimes) (Beijing, 1978), p. 5.

44. Ibid., p. 115.

45. See ibid., pp. 65–68; see also Wang Nianyi, *Da dongluande niandai,* p. 474.

46. *Jianguo yilai Mao Zedong wengao,* 13: 371.

47. Preface to Beijing daxue and Qinghua daxue, eds., *Lin Biao yu Kong Meng zhi dao*

(cailiao zhi 1) (Lin Biao and Confucius and Mencius' Way [Materials 1]) (Beijing, 1973), p. iii.

48. James Legge, *The Chinese Classics: With a Translation, Critical and Exegetical Notes, Prolegomena, and Copious Indexes,* 7 vols. (Oxford: Clarendon Press, 1893), 1: 250.

49. The other major theme was an unconvincing attempt to take a comment by Lin Biao out of context in order to suggest that the marshal had been critical of Qin Shi Huangdi, the founding Chinese emperor, to whom Mao was often compared, both by himself, complacently, and by his colleagues, fearfully.

50. *Yang Shangkun riji,* 1: 184.

51. MacFarquhar, "China after the 10th Congress," pp. 523–524.

52. Beijing daxue Liang Xiao zhuan'anzu, *Liang Xiao zuizheng cailiao,* p. 50.

53. Ibid., pp. 65–68.

54. "Jiang Qing, Yao Wenyuan, Chi Qun, Xie Jingyi zai zhongyang zhishu jiguan he guojia jiguan pi-Lin pi-Kong dongyuan dahui shangde jianghua," p. 42.

55. Wang Nianyi, *Da dongluande niandai,* pp. 488–489.

56. *Shanghai "Wenhua dageming" shihua,* 3: 673.

57. Ibid., p. 671; *Zhou Enlai nianpu,* 3: 659.

58. Guofang daxue, *"Wenhua dageming,"* 3: 140–141.

59. "Jiang Qing, Yao Wenyuan, Chi Qun, Xie Jingyi zai zhongyang zhishu jiguan he guojia jiguan pi-Lin pi-Kong dongyuan dahui shangde jianghua," p. 2.

60. See Jing Jun, *The Temple of Memories: History, Power, and Morality in a Chinese Village* (Stanford: Stanford University Press, 1996), pp. 52–55.

61. *Chen Yun nianpu,* 3: 176.

62. Zhonghua renmin gongheguo caizhengbu, *Zhongguo nongmin fudan shi,* 4: 282– 283, 293, 308. Some 8.3 percent of the figure for grain income was *fanxiaoliang,* foodstuffs returned to the place of production because of hardship.

63. Zhonggong Heilongjiang shengwei dangshi yanjiushi, *Zhonggong Heilongjiang dangshi dashiji,* p. 458; Heilongjiang sheng difang zhi bianzuan weiyuanhui, *Heilongjiang shengzhi dashiji,* p. 985.

64. Zhonggong Hebei shengwei dangshi yanjiushi, *Zhongguo gongchandang Hebei lishi dashiji,* p. 518.

65. Ibid., p. 467; Heilongjiang sheng difang zhi bianzuan weiyuanhui, *Heilongjiang shengzhi dashiji,* p. 985.

66. *Zhou Enlai nianpu,* 3: 530.

67. Zhonggong Hebei shengwei dangshi yanjiushi, *Zhongguo gongchandang Hebei lishi dashiji,* p. 478; Zhonggong Baoding shiwei dangshi yanjiushi, *Zhonggong Baoding dangshi dashiji,* pp. 385–386.

68. Shanxi sheng gongye xue Daqing jingyan jiaoliu huiyi, ed., *Xuexi wenjian* (Study Documents) (Taiyuan, 1971), pp. 40–45.

69. *Dangdai Zhongguode laodong buohu* (Labor Protection in Contemporary China) (Beijing: Dangdai Zhongguo chubanshe, 1992), p. 23.

70. Ibid., pp. 146–147.

71. *Chedi pipan Lin Chen fandang jituan fangeming zuixing—da pipan fayan cailiao xuanbian zhi er* (Thoroughly Denounce the Counterrevolutionary Crimes of the Lin and Chen Anti-Party Clique—A Second Selection of Great Denunciation Materials) ([Chengdu]: Sichuan sheng geming weiyuanhui shengchan jianshe bangongshi zhenggongzu, April 1972), p. 52.

72. Ibid., p. 53; *Chongqing shizhi*, pp. 432–433. One rumor circulating in China at the time had it that during his visit to Beijing in February President Richard Nixon had consumed 2,000 jin of fish; another rumor had it that he had eaten fifty prawns. In the words of one Chinese writer, "ordinary people were resentful toward the Americans and really did not want 'the Yankees' to eat too well in China"; Shu Jun, *Diaoyutai lishi dang'an*, p. 139.

73. Heilongjiang sheng difang zhi bianzuan weiyuanhui, *Heilongjiang shengzhi dashiji*, p. 978.

74. He Jinming and Zhao Bingzhang, eds., *Dangdai Shaanxi jianshi* (A Short History of Contemporary Shaanxi) (Beijing: Dangdai Zhongguo chubanshe, 1996), p. 174.

75. Dangdai Zhongguo shangye bianjibu, *Zhonghua renmin gongheguo shangye dashiji*, p. 726.

76. *Chongqing shizhi*, p. 448.

77. *Zhou Enlai nianpu*, 3: 562; *Zhongguo renmin gongan shigao*, pp. 341, 449.

78. Dangdai Zhongguo shangye bianjibu, *Zhonghua renmin gongheguo shangye dashiji*, pp. 675, 690–691, 698.

79. *Chongqing shizhi*, 1: 435.

80. Zhonggong Heilongjiang shengwei dangshi yanjiushi, *Zhonggong Heilongjiang dangshi dashiji*, p. 438.

81. Ibid., p. 454.

82. Zhonggong zhongyang wenxian yanjiushi, *"Wenge" shinian ziliao xuanbian*, 3: 1–15.

22. Deng Xiaoping Takes Over

1. From a big-character poster at Fudan University, Shanghai, copied by Michael Schoenhals, who was a student there at the time. Imre Nagy was the Communist leader who attempted to take Hungary out of the Soviet-dominated Warsaw Pact in 1956. After the Hungarian revolt was suppressed, he took refuge in the Yugoslav embassy, but was handed over to the Soviets and executed.

2. Wang Nianyi, *Da dongluande niandai*, p. 533.

3. *Zhou Enlai nianpu,* 3: 636–639; Deng Rong, *Deng Xiaoping and the Cultural Revolution,* pp. 258–261; *Selected Works of Deng Xiaoping (1975–1982),* p. 97.

4. Deng Rong, *Deng Xiaoping and the Cultural Revolution,* p. 286; *Zhou Enlai nianpu,* 3: 687.

5. Deng Rong, *Deng Xiaoping and the Cultural Revolution,* p. 293; Ma Qibin et al., *Zhongguo gongchandang zhizheng sishinian,* p. 386.

6. Wang may well not have understood the subtle signals of disappointment that Mao issued now and then. One day Mao suggested to Wang—without explaining why—that he read the biography of Emperor Liu Penzi in the *History of the Later Han* (A.D. 25–220). His classical erudition being nil, Wang was incapable of doing so on his own and called on a Shanghai historian who had assisted Yao Wenyuan in producing "On the New Historical Play *Hai Rui Dismissed from Office*" to help him with the classical grammar and terminology. While the historian soon realized as he guided Wang through the text that Mao was allegorically implying that Wang—like Liu Penzi—would not last long in office if he did not make a serious effort at moral cultivation, this point never actually dawned on Wang; Zhu Yongjia, interview by Michael Schoenhals, Shanghai, December 2003; Xu Jingxian, *Shinian yimeng,* pp. 293–300. By early 1975, even some of his old friends from Shanghai were informing on Wang, revealing his bad habits and "decadent ways"; ibid., pp. 424–428.

7. Pang Xianzhi and Jin Chongji, *Mao Zedong zhuan,* 2: 1693, 1729.

8. *Zhou Enlai nianpu,* 3: 679.

9. Wang Nianyi, *Da dongluande niandai,* p. 511.

10. According to a transcript made by Tang Wensheng and Wang Hairong, who were present, as published in Zhonggong zhongyang wenxian yanjiushi, *"Wenge" shinian ziliao xuanbian,* 3: 63–64. The deterioration in Mao's ability to write is glaringly obvious in the collection of Mao's post-1949 manuscripts, *Jianguo yilai Mao Zedong wengao:* the cover of each volume bears his name in his calligraphy from the period dealt with by the volume. His signature on the cover of vol. 13, 1969–1976, is notably shakier than that on vol. 12.

11. Wang Nianyi, *Da dongluande niandai,* p. 513.

12. Ibid.

13. Mao Zedong laid this down very firmly on May 19, 1953; *Jianguo yilai Mao Zedong wengao,* 4: 229.

14. *Zhou Enlai nianpu,* 3: 709; Pang Xianzhi and Jin Chongji, *Mao Zedong zhuan,* 2: 1739. According to the latter source, Mao's decision on Deng's new role was made on the basis of a suggestion from Ye Jianying on July 1.

15. Wang Xiuzhen, "Wode jiefa he jiaodai" (My Exposé and Testimony), November 6, 1976, p. 2, Schoenhals collection.

16. *"Sirenbang" zuixing cailiao* (Materials on the Crimes of the "Gang of Four") (n.p., 1976), p. 74.

17. *Zhou Rongxin tongzhi jianghua huibian*, p. 16.

18. "Oppose Bookism" (May 1930), translated in Stuart R. Schram, ed., *Mao's Road to Power: Revolutionary Writings, 1912–1949*, vol. 3: *July 1927–December 1930* (Armonk, N.Y.: M. E. Sharpe, 1995), p. 425.

19. *Selected Works of Deng Xiaoping (1975–1982)*, p. 4.

20. See Guofang daxue, *"Wenhua dageming,"* 3: 235.

21. *Jianguo yilai Mao Zedong wengao*, 13: 413–414.

22. Ibid., p. 402.

23. Ibid., p. 410.

24. Zhang Tuosheng, "Deng Xiaoping yu 1975 niande quanmian zhengdun" (Deng Xiaoping and the All-Round Readjustment in 1975), in Zhang Hua and Su Caiqing, *Huishou "Wenge,"* 2: 1163.

25. *Selected Works of Deng Xiaoping (1975–1982)*, pp. 16–17.

26. Ibid., p. 18.

27. *Zhongguo renmin gongan shigao*, p. 345.

28. Zhang Tuosheng, "Deng Xiaoping yu 1975 niande quanmian zhengdun," p. 1162.

29. *Selected Works of Deng Xiaoping (1975–1982)*, p. 19.

30. Guofang daxue, *"Wenhua dageming,"* 3: 265.

31. *Selected Works of Deng Xiaoping (1975–1982)*, p. 20.

32. Guofang daxue, *"Wenhua dageming,"* 3: 264.

33. Ibid., pp. 278–280.

34. Zhu Chuan and Shen Xianhui, eds., *Dangdai Liaoning jianshi* (A Short History of Contemporary Liaoning) (Beijing: Dangdai Zhongguo chubanshe, 1999), pp. 269–271.

35. "Deng Xiaoping tongzhi zai Guowuyuan bangong huiyshangde jianghua zhailu" (Excerpts from Comrade Deng Xiaoping's Talk at a State Council Office Meeting), May 21, 1975, p. 1, typed transcript circulated in China in the winter of 1975–76, Fairbank Center Library.

36. Nie Yuanzi, interview by Michael Schoenhals, Beijing, July 1994.

37. *Jianguo yilai Mao Zedong wengao*, 13: 504.

38. "Quarterly Chronicle and Documentation," *CQ*, no. 65 (March 1976), 181. The Chinese first tested their DF-5 missile at almost its full 13,000-kilometer range in May 1980; John Wilson Lewis and Xue Litai, *China Builds the Bomb* (Stanford: Stanford University Press, 1988), pp. 213–214.

39. Guofang daxue, *"Wenhua dageming,"* 3: 279.

40. Deng Rong, *Deng Xiaoping and the Cultural Revolution*, p. 259.

41. According to Pang Xianzhi and Jin Chongji, *Mao Zedong zhuan*, 2: 1739. Wang

Hongwen was sent to Zhejiang and Shanghai in late June to help with work there at Mao's suggestion.

42. Weng had for some time attended the meetings of the Standing Committee of the provincial party committee as a "nonvoting member," in a local variation of a precedent set by Mao himself in enlarged meetings of the PSC, where, in order to groom successors of the revolution, a small number of people had recently been allowed to attend, watch, and learn; interview with a Chinese informant in a position to know.

43. "Quarterly Chronicle and Documentation," *CQ*, no. 64 (December 1975), 786–788.

44. Cheng Chao and Wei Haoben, *Zhejiang "Wenge" jishi*, pp. 238–240.

45. *Dangdai Yunnan jianshi* (A Short History of Contemporary Yunnan) (Beijing: Dangdai Zhongguo chubanshe, 2004), pp. 306–308; *Dangdai Yunnan dashi jiyao (1949–1995)* (Summary Record of Major Events in Contemporary Yunnan [1949–1995]) (Beijing: Dangdai Zhongguo chubanshe, 1996), pp. 533–534. Schoenhals interview with former militiaman who took part in the operation, October 1991; Dru C. Gladney, *Muslim Chinese: Ethnic Nationalism in the People's Republic* (Cambridge, Mass.: Harvard University Press, 1996), pp. 137–140.

46. Li Ke and Hao Shengzhang, *"Wenhua dageming" zhongde renmin jiefangjun*, p. 145.

47. Ibid., pp. 148–152.

48. "Xu Jingxian de buchong jiefa jiaodai" (Xu Jingxian's Supplementary Exposé and Testimony) (Shanghai: Shanghai shi qu, xian, ju dangyuan fuze ganbu huiyi mishuzu, November 21, 1976), p. 1. This abrupt reversal aroused fevered speculation among foreign China watchers.

49. Li Ke and Hao Shengzhang, *"Wenhua dageming" zhongde renmin jiefangjun*, p. 148.

50. *Selected Works of Deng Xiaoping (1975–1982)*, p. 13.

51. Li Ke and Hao Shengzhang, *"Wenhua dageming" zhongde renmin jiefangjun*, pp. 143–156.

52. *Selected Works of Deng Xiaoping (1975–1982)*, pp. 28–29.

53. Ibid., p. 30.

54. Ibid., pp. 30–31.

55. A handwritten transcript available in the Fairbank Center Library is a fuller version of *Jianguo yilai Mao Zedong wengao*, 13: 249–250.

56. *Selected Works of Deng Xiaoping (1975–1982)*, p. 31.

57. For an extensive account of the impact of the Cultural Revolution on education, see Suzanne Pepper, *Radicalism and Education Reform in 20th-Century China: The Search for an Ideal Development Model* (New York: Cambridge University Press, 1996), pp. 352–477.

58. *Zhou Enlai nianpu*, 3: 686.

59. *Lishide shenpan,* 2: 36–46.
60. *Zhou Rongxin tongzhi de jianghua huibian,* p. 4.
61. Guofang daxue, *"Wenhua dageming,"* 2: 540–547.
62. *Zhou Rongxin tongzhi de jianghua huibian,* pp. 28–30.
63. Wang Nianyi, *Da dongluande niandai,* p. 511.
64. Ibid., pp. 534–535.
65. At Peking University on October 1, 1976; Beijing gongye xueyuan yundong bangongshi, *Dazibao xuanbian,* p. 17.
66. *Jianguo yilai Mao Zedong wengao,* 8: 446.
67. *"Sirenbang" zuixing cailiao,* pp. 9–10.
68. Beijing daxue Liang Xiao zhuan'anzu, *Liang Xiao zuizheng cailiao,* p. 63.
69. Wang Nianyi, *Da dongluande niandai,* p. 544.
70. Deng Rong, *Deng Xiaoping and the Cultural Revolution,* p. 300.
71. *"Deng Xiaoping tongzhi zai Guowuyuan bangong huiyishangde jianghua zhailu,"* p. 1.
72. *Jianguo yilai Mao Zedong wengao,* 13: 426.
73. *"Sirenbang" zuixing cailiao,* pp. 68–69.

23. The Gang of Four Emerges

1. *Jianguo yilai Mao Zedong wengao,* 13: 394–399.
2. Wang Nianyi, *Da dongluande niandai,* p. 545.
3. *Deng Liqun guoshi jiangtan lu,* 3: 89.
4. *Jianguo yilai Mao Zedong wengao,* 13: 396.
5. Wang Nianyi, *Da dongluande niandai,* p. 545; Shen Baoxiang, *Zhenli biaozhun wenti taolun shimo* (The Whole Story of the Truth Criterion Debate) (Beijing: Zhongguo qingnian chubanshe, 1997), p. 10. Mao need not have blamed himself, since the reference occurred not in Zhang's but in Yao's article.
6. *Jianguo yilai Mao Zedong wengao,* 13: 396; Pang Xianzhi and Jin Chongji, *Mao Zedong zhuan,* 2: 1731–33.
7. Zhang Chunqiao remarked as early as August 1973, in the context of preparations for the Tenth Congress, that the label "Shanghai gang" was being thrown at himself and others. In conversation with colleagues from Shanghai who had just arrived to talk inter alia about promotions onto central bodies, Zhang remarked: "To begin with, I am not too eager to transfer cadres in from Shanghai [to the center], because if too many are transferred [here], people will again begin talking about a 'Shanghai gang'"; *Shanghai "Wenhua dageming" shihua,* 3: 648.
8. Pang Xianzhi and Jin Chongji, *Mao Zedong zhuan,* 2: 1693.
9. Zhonggong zhongyang wenxian yanjiushi, *"Wenge" shinian ziliao xuanbian,* 3: 55.
10. *"Sirenbang" zuixing cailiao,* p. 69.

11. Leng Rong and Wang Zuoling, eds., *Deng Xiaoping nianpu, 1975–1997* (Chronicle of the Life of Deng Xiaoping, 1975–1997), 2 vols. (Beijing: Zhongyang wenxian chubanshe, 2004), 1: 41.

12. Mao Mao, *Wode fuqin Deng Xiaoping "Wenge" suiyue*, p. 362.

13. Zhonggong zhangyang wenxian yanjiushi, *"Wenge" shinian ziliao xuanbian*, 3: 108.

14. Ibid., p. 109.

15. Wang Nianyi, *Da dongluande niandai*, pp. 545–546.

16. *Zhou Enlai nianpu*, 3: 705.

17. Wang-Zhang-Jiang-Yao zhuan'anzu, ed., *Wang Hongwen, Zhang Chunqiao, Jiang Qing, Yao Wenyuan fandang jituan zuizheng (cailiao zhi 1)* (Record of the Crimes of the Wang Hongwen, Zhang Chunqiao, Jiang Qing, Yao Wenyuan Anti-Party Group [1st set of materials]) (Beijing: Zhonggong zhongyang bangongting, 1976) (hereafter Wang-Zhang-Jiang-Yao zhuan'anzu), pp. 18, 24, 25.

18. Deng Rong, *Deng Xiaoping and the Cultural Revolution*, p. 307.

19. "Xu Jingxian de chubu jiefa jiaodai" (Xu Jingxian's Initial Exposé and Testimony) (Shanghai: Shanghai shi qu, xian, ju dangyuan fuze ganbu huiyi mishuzu, November 1976), p. 1, original in Schoenhals collection.

20. *"Sirenbang" zuixing cailiao*, pp. 52, 68.

21. *Deng Liqun guoshi jiangtan lu*, 5: 172.

22. Cheng Zhongyuan, "1975 nian zhengdun zhongde sange zhuming wenjian" (Three Famous Documents during the 1975 Rectification), in Zhang Hua and Su Caiqing, *Huishou "Wenge,"* 2: 1195–1212.

23. Guofang daxue, *"Wenhua dageming,"* 3: 487–498.

24. Ibid., pp. 528–531.

25. "Guowuyuan tingqu Hu Yaobang tongzhi huibao shi Xiaoping tongzhi deng zhongyang lingdao tongzhi zhuyao chahua jiyao" (Transcript of Main Interjections by Comrade Xiaoping and Other Leading Comrades from the Center during Comrade Hu Yaobang's Report to the State Council), p. 5, typed original transcript from Beijing during the anti-Deng campaign in the spring of 1976, Fairbank Center Library.

26. *Deng Liqun wenji* (Collected Works of Deng Liqun), 4 vols. (Beijing: Dangdai Zhongguo chubanshe, 1998), 1: 1–28.

27. Ibid., p. 16, as translated in Andrew Watson, *Mao Zedong and the Political Economy of the Border Region: A Translation of Mao's Economic and Financial Problems* (Cambridge: Cambridge University Press, 1980), p. 198.

28. *Deng Liqun wenji*, 1: 17, as translated in *Selected Works of Mao Tse-tung*, 4 vols. (Peking: Foreign Languages Press, 1967), 3: 250.

29. Guofang daxue, *"Wenhua dageming,"* 3: 525.

30. Xing Fangqun, "Deng Xiaoping shouyi chuangban 'Sixiang zhanxian' bei 'sirenbang' e sha jingguo" (How the "Gang of Four" Strangled Deng Xiaoping's

Instruction on Creating the Magazine *Ideological Battle Lines*), *Yanhuang chunqiu,* no. 9 (1997), 18–19.

31. Zhongguo banben tushuguan, ed., *Quanguo neibu faxing tushu zongmu* (National Bibliography of Internally Distributed Books) (Beijing: Zhonghua shuju, 1988), p. 98; Guofang daxue, *"Wenhua dageming,"* 3: 518; Beijing daxue yundong bangongshi, ed., *Wang-Wei-Guo-Lin zuixing cailiao* (Material on the Crimes of Wang [Lianlong], Wei [Yinqiu], Guo [Zonglin], and Lin [Jiakuan]), 4 vols. (Beijing, 1977), 2: 12; Liu Gao and Shi Feng, *Xin Zhongguo chuban wushinian jishi,* pp. 161–162. The three documents are included as an appendix in a record of conversations between Deng and Hu Qiaomu from January 1975 to January 1976; Hu Qiaomu bianxiezu, ed., *Deng Xiaopingde ershisi ci tanhua* (Deng Xiaoping's Chats on Twenty-four Occasions) (Beijing: Renmin chubanshe, 2004), pp. 117–180.

32. From big-character posters at Fudan University, Shanghai, copied by Michael Schoenhals, who was a student there at the time.

33. Known to Western readers under the title of Pearl Buck's translation, *All Men Are Brothers.*

34. *"Sirenbang" zuixing cailiao,* p. 20.

35. Jiang Qing was one of an estimated 10 million-plus visitors from China and abroad who visited Dazhai during the Cultural Revolution after Mao's call to "Learn from Dazhai." For a discussion of the rise and post-Mao fall of the Dazhai model, see David Zweig, *Agrarian Radicalism in China, 1968–1981* (Cambridge, Mass.: Harvard University Press, 1989). For Dazhai's later reinvention as a new kind of model, the Dazhai Economic Development Company, see Sun Xiaohua, "Agriculture Ex-Model Grapples for 'New Spirit,'" *China Daily,* July 26, 2005, p. 2.

36. *"Sirenbang" zuixing cailiao,* pp. 63, 66.

37. *Zhou Enlai nianpu,* 3: 721.

38. "Jiang Weiqing tongzhi chuanda zhongyang lingdao tongzhi jianghua jingshen" (Comrade Jiang Weiqing Transmits the Spirit of a Central Leading Comrade's Speech), October 26, 1976, p. 3, typed original transcript from Beijing during the anti-Deng campaign in the spring of 1976, Fairbank Center Library.

39. *Jianguo yilai Mao Zedong wengao,* 13: 487.

40. Jin Chunming, *"Wenhua dageming" shigao,* p. 400.

41. Wang Nianyi, *Da dongluande niandai,* pp. 551–552.

42. Ibid., p. 552.

43. Beijing daxue yundong bangongshi, *Wang-Wei-Guo-Lin zuixing cailiao,* 2: 1.

44. Ibid., pp. 1, 10.

45. Zhang Hua, "1975 nian jiaoyujiede douzheng" (The 1975 Struggle on the Educational Front), *Zhonggong dangshi ziliao,* no. 70 (June 1999), 159.

46. Copy of contemporary transcript of letter from Liu Bing et al. to Mao Zedong dated August 13, 1975, Fairbank Center Library. See also partially different transcript in Yu Xiguang, ed., *Weibei weigan wangyouguo: "Wenhua dageming" shangshuji* (Of Inferior Position but Concerned about the Fate of the Country: Memorials from the "Great Cultural Revolution") (Changsha: Hunan renmin chubanshe, 1989), pp. 425–426.

47. Copy of contemporary transcript of letter from Liu Bing et al. to Mao Zedong dated October 13, 1975, Fairbank Center Library. See also partially different transcript in Yu Xiguang, *Weibei weigan wangyouguo*, pp. 431–434.

48. Beijing gongye xueyuan yundong bangongshi, *Dazibao xuanbian*, 2: 14.

49. "Beijing shi 'Wenhua dageming' dashiji, 1975–1976" (A Chronology of the "Great Cultural Revolution" in Beijing, 1975–1976), *Beijing dangshi ziliao tongxun*, extra issue, no. 20 (August 1987), 28.

50. Ibid., p. 32. Mao's reference to cats was an allusion to Deng's 1962 remark, made when espousing allegedly capitalist policies during the recovery from the Great Leap famine, to the effect that it "doesn't matter if a cat is black or white; so long as it catches the mouse, it's a good cat"; see *Origins*, 3: 233.

51. "Beijing shi 'Wenhua dageming' dashiji, 1975–1976," p. 32.

52. Deng Rong, *Deng Xiaoping and the Cultural Revolution*, p. 355.

53. *Jianguo yilai Mao Zedong wengao*, 13: 504. Of the twenty-one members of the Politburo, those either known or highly likely to have been absent for health reasons included Mao, Zhu De, Zhou Enlai, Kang Sheng, and Liu Bocheng.

54. See *The Poetry of T'ao Ch'ien*, trans. and ed. James Robert Hightower (Oxford: Clarendon Press, 1970), p. 255; Mao Mao, *Wode fuqin Deng Xiaoping*, p. 427. Mao referred to the same quotation in his final coherent utterances; *Jianguo yilai Mao Zedong wengao*, 13: 488.

55. "Xu Jingxian de chubu jiefa jiaodai," p. 21.

56. "Beijing shi 'Wenhua dageming' dashiji, 1975–1976," pp. 16–21.

57. *Shanghai "Wenhua dageming" shihua*, 3: 767.

58. "Xu Jingxian de chubu jiefa jiaodai," p. 18.

59. Ma Tianshui, "Wode jiefa jiaodai," p. 2.

60. *"Sirenbang" zuixing cailiao*, p. 124.

61. Deng Rong, *Deng Xiaoping and the Cultural Revolution*, p. 364.

62. *Shanghai "Wenhua dageming" shihua*, 3: 765.

63. Guofang daxue, *"Wenhua dageming,"* 3: 309–310.

64. Deng Rong, *Deng Xiaoping and the Cultural Revolution*, pp. 367–372; *Jianguo yilai Mao Zedong wengao*, 13: 513.

65. "Beijing shi 'Wenhua dageming' dashiji, 1975–1976," pp. 19–20.

66. Wang Nianyi, *Da dongluande niandai*, pp. 556–557.

67. Ma Tianshui, "Wode buchong jiefa jiaodai" (My Supplementary Exposé and Testimony) (Shanghai: Shanghai shi qu, xian, ju dangyuan fuze ganbu huiyi mishuzu, November 1976), p. 5, original in Schoenhals collection.

24. The Tiananmen Incident of 1976

1. Wang Nianyi, *Da dongluande niandai*, pp. 600–601; Chen and Du, *Gongheguo shiji*, 3: 1239.
2. Li Zhisui, *The Private Life of Chairman Mao*, p. 592.
3. Ibid., p. 581.
4. In the summer of 2003, when there was still "not one effective treatment for this uniformly fatal disease," gene therapy on mice with artificially induced ALS was reported successful enough for trials on humans to start within a year. The disease got its colloquial name when the baseball star Lou Gehrig died of the disease in 1941, aged thirty-seven. A rare exception to the normal fatality rate is the British physicist Stephen Hawking, who got the disease in college but still survives at the age of sixty-four, and is living proof that the disease does not impair mental functions. See Carey Goldberg, "With Gene Therapy in Mice a Success, Researchers See Hope for ALS Patients," *Boston Globe*, August 8, 2003, p. A3.
5. Li Zhisui, *The Private Life of Chairman Mao*, pp. 581–608; *Zhou Enlai nianpu*, 3: 696–697. We have accepted the latter source for the dating of the February 1975 meeting.
6. His last visitor on that date was Premier Bhutto of Pakistan; Chen and Du, *Gongheguo shiji*, 3: 1234.
7. Li Zhisui, *The Private Life of Chairman Mao*, pp. 406–411, 593–596, 602–603.
8. *Zhou Enlai nianpu*, 3: 723–724; Byron and Pack, *The Claws of the Dragon*, pp. 93–95; Frederic Wakeman Jr., *Policing Shanghai: 1927–1937* (Berkeley: University of California Press, 1995), pp. 137–140.
9. Schoenhals' recording of Chinese roommate's words, diary entry, January 9, 1976.
10. Li Zhisui, *The Private Life of Chairman Mao*, pp. 609–610.
11. "Quarterly Chronicle and Documentation," *CQ*, no. 66 (June 1976), 423–424; the speech is not included in Deng's *Selected Works*.
12. *Selected Works of Deng Xiaoping (1975–1982)*, pp. 329–330.
13. *Zhou Enlai nianpu*, 3: 727; Roger Garside, *Coming Alive: China after Mao* (London: Andre Deutsch, 1981), pp. 7–8.
14. Rittenberg and Bennett, *The Man Who Stayed Behind*, p. 424.
15. Guofang daxue, *"Wenhua dageming,"* 3: 361.
16. Qing Ye and Fang Lei, *Deng Xiaoping zai 1976* (Deng Xiaoping in 1976), 2 vols. (Shenyang: Chunfeng wenyi chubanshe, 1993), 1: 57.
17. Wang-Zhang-Jiang-Yao zhuan'anzu, 1: 39.

18. "Xu Jingxian de chubu jiefa jiaodai," p. 27.

19. Ma Tianshui, "Wode buchong jiefa jiaodai," p. 7.

20. "Xu Jingxian de chubu jiefa jiaodai," p. 28.

21. Deng Rong, *Deng Xiaoping and the Cultural Revolution,* p. 384.

22. Xu Jingxian, *Shinian yimeng,* p. 381.

23. Guofang daxue, *"Wenhua dageming,"* 3: 361.

24. *Wang-Wei-Guo-Lin zuixing cailiao,* 2: 9–10.

25. Here as quoted/translated in Barnouin and Yu, *Ten Years of Turbulence,* p. 290.

26. Li Zhisui, *The Private Life of Chairman Mao,* p. 610.

27. Guofang daxue, *"Wenhua dageming,"* 3: 385.

28. *"Sirenbang" zuixing cailiao,* p. 74.

29. "Beijing shi 'Wenhua dageming' dashiji, 1975–1976," pp. 29, 32; *Jianguo yilai Mao Zedong wengao,* 13: 486–490.

30. *Wang-Wei-Guo-Lin zuixing cailiao,* 2: 6.

31. Yu Huanchun, "'Renmin ribao' yu 1976 nian Tiananmen shijian" (The *People's Daily* and the 1976 Tiananmen Events), *Bainian chao,* no. 2 (1998), 43.

32. *"Sirenbang" zuixing cailiao,* p. 75.

33. *Chongqing shizhi,* 1: 453; see also Yu Xiguang, *Weibei weigan wangyouguo,* pp. 212–220.

34. Ibid., pp. 214–215, 220–228. For an extended discussion of Zhang Chunqiao's article in its original 1958 context, see Schoenhals, *Saltationist Socialism,* pp. 128–150.

35. *Chongqing shizhi,* 1: 454; Zhonggong Chengdu shiwei dangshi yanjiushi, ed., *Zhonggong Chengdu difangshi dashiji (1949–1989)* (Record of Major Events in the Local History of Chengdu [1949–1989]) (Chengdu: Chengdu chubanshe, 1995), pp. 176, 209; Heilmann, *Sozialer Protest in der VR China,* p. 86.

36. Jin Yanfeng, ed., *Dangdai Zhejiang jianshi (1949–1998)* (A Short History of Contemporary Zhejiang [1949–1998]) (Beijing: Dangdai Zhongguo chubanshe, 2000), p. 283; *Zhongguo renmin gongan shigao,* p. 349.

37. Shen Kui, ed., *Dangdai Anhui jianshi* (A Short History of Contemporary Anhui) (Beijing: Dangdai Zhongguo chubanshe, 2001), p. 345.

38. *Zhongyang shouzhang fenbie jiejian dazhuan yuanxiao daibiaode jianghua* (Central Leaders Speak at Separate Receptions for University Delegates) (n.p., September 1967), p. 8.

39. Not all readers of the *Wenhui bao* shared the students' sentiment. A fifty-one-year-old worker in the Jiangsu First Provincial Construction Company by the name of Wang Yilin insisted that the "central leaders Zhang Chunqiao, Jiang Qing, and Yao Wenyuan" had in actuality been "entirely correct" in deleting Zhou's inscription from March 1963, given that it called on people to emulate "the fighting will of the propertyless class that defies personal danger." Wang maintained that the only "propertyless class" on whose behalf Zhou could possi-

bly have been speaking was that of the onetime exploiters, who by 1963 had lost all their property during land reform and the socialist transformation of industry and commerce in 1956. Zhou's "fighting will" was hence a will to fight *against* "our great leader and great teacher Chairman Mao, the socialist revolutionaries, and the working class that controls the means of production." See Wang Yilin's big-character poster "Xiang chongyang zhijing" (Saluting the Double Ninth Festival), handwritten 9-page copy, in the authors' possession.

40. *Wenhui bao* staffer, interview by Michael Schoenhals, Washington, D.C., September 1990.

41. "Xu Jingxian de buchong jiefa jiaodai," p. 13; Xu was a member of the Shanghai Party Committee.

42. *Jing'aide Zhou zongli yongyuan huo zai women xinzhong* (Respected and Beloved Premier Zhou Lives Forever in Our Hearts) (Beijing: Shoudu jixiechang, 1978), p. 80. Xu Jingxian subsequently ("Xu Jingxian de buchong jiefa jiaodai," p. 13) admitted that it was an ambiguous passage, and one "extremely easy for people to misinterpret," but claimed, again unconvincingly, that it had not been meant as an attack on Zhou.

43. Wang Nianyi, *Da dongluande niandai*, p. 575.

44. Wei Renzhen, ed., *Dangdai Jiangsu jianshi* (A Short History of Contemporary Jiangsu) (Beijing: Dangdai Zhongguo chubanshe, 2002), pp. 239–243. For an extended discussion of conflict and popular resistance in Jiangsu in the spring of 1976, see Sebastian Heilmann, *Nanking 1976 Spontane Massenbewegungen im Gefolge der Kulturrevolution: Eine Regionalstudie* (Spontaneous Mass Movements in the Wake of the Cultural Revolution: A Regional Study) (Bochum: Brockmeyer, 1990).

45. Schoenhals, *China's Cultural Revolution*, p. 228. In fact this redirection of the Qingming Festival had been encouraged by the CCP long before the Cultural Revolution.

46. Wang Nianyi, *Da dongluande niandai*, pp. 573–574; Gao Gao and Yan Jiaqi, *"Wenhua dageming" shinian shi*, pp. 582–586.

47. Garside, *Coming Alive*, pp. 115–116.

48. Xiao Lan, *The Tiananmen Poems*, p. 28.

49. Ibid., p. 34.

50. This was the immediate reaction of Roderick MacFarquhar, who was in Beijing on April 1–4. Nor was this an isolated reaction among those brought up on *Macbeth;* see the evocative account of these events by a diplomatic eyewitness in Garside, *Coming Alive*, chap. 6, esp. p. 128. Garside relies partly upon the revisionist account published by the Xinhua News Agency in November 1978, when the April 5 "incident" was stripped of its counterrevolutionary label at Deng's orders. For another eyewitness Western account, see Lois Fisher, *Go Gently through Pe-*

king: A Westerner's Life in China (London: Souvenir Press, 1979), chap. 8. There is also a detailed account in Gao Gao and Yan Jiaqi, *"Wenhua dageming" shinian shi,* pp. 598–637, on which, along with MacFarquhar's experiences, our description is partly based.

51. Xiao Lan, *The Tiananmen Poems,* p. 29.

52. "Beijing shi 'Wenhua dageming' dashiji, 1975–1976," p. 35. Roderick MacFarquhar was one of the 2 million, but left on the night train for Nanjing and was but dimly aware of the stirring developments in the square until the official verdict was announced days later.

53. Deng Rong, *Deng Xiaoping and the Cultural Revolution,* p. 397.

54. Chen and Du, *Gongheguo shiji,* 3: 1214–15.

55. Fan Shuo, *Ye Jianying zai 1976* (Ye Jianying in 1976) (Beijing: Zhonggong zhongyang dangxiao chubanshe, 1992), pp. 95–96.

56. The characterization of a funerary event as a politically motivated use of the dead to exert pressure on the living was Mao Zedong's. In October 1966, Mao had spoken in these same terms of the funeral of the first party secretary of Tianjin, Wan Xiaotang, who had died under tragic circumstances that month and whose funeral was attended by 500,000 people "actually protesting against the party." See *Mao Zedong sixiang wan sui* ([Shanghai?], [1968?]), p. 277.

57. Fan Shuo, *Ye Jianying zai 1976,* pp. 96–97. The Petőfi Club played a big role in stirring up the Hungarian revolt against the Soviet Union in 1956; after the blooming of the Hundred Flowers in 1957 was suppressed, for Mao the club became a symbol of how intellectuals could stir up trouble.

58. Deng Rong, *Deng Xiaoping and the Cultural Revolution,* p. 397.

59. Fisher, *Go Gently through Peking,* pp. 202–211, esp. 206; Garside, *Coming Alive,* p. 131.

60. Jin Chunming, "Siwu yundong shuping" (Critical Account of the April 5 Movement), in Zhang Hua and Su Caiqing, *Huishou "Wenge,"* 2: 1241.

61. Zhonggong Zhejiang shengwei dangxiao dangshi jiaoyanshi, *"Wenhua dageming" shiqi ziliao xuanji,* p. 281.

62. Ibid.

63. Qing Ye and Fang Lei, *Deng Xiaoping zai 1976,* 1: 203–204. Deng's daughter mentions the absence of Ye Jianying and Li Xiannian from this meeting, but does not mention the presence of her father, perhaps because it was a humiliating experience for him; Deng Rong, *Deng Xiaoping and the Cultural Revolution,* p. 397.

64. After the arrest of the Gang of Four, Liu Chuanxin came under investigation for his role in "performing numerous evil deeds at their orders, including at the time of the Qingming Festival in early April 1976." He committed suicide shortly thereafter, in the words of an official history of the PRC public security apparat, "in order to escape punishment." See *Zhongguo renmin gongan shigao,* p. 353.

65. Qing Ye and Fang Lei, *Deng Xiaoping zai 1976,* 1: 228–231.

66. In the transcript of his speech published in the *People's Daily* on April 8, 1976, Wu De criticized Deng Xiaoping by name, but foreigners who had heard the original broadcast in the square say that it had not referred to Deng by name. See Jay Mathews, "China's '76 Riot," *Washington Post Foreign Service,* January 31, 1978.

67. Zhonggong Zhejiang shengwei dangxiao dangshi jiaoyanshi, *"Wenhua dageming" shiqi ziliao xuanji,* p. 282. There were differences among the Gang of Four about how much force should be used, with Jiang Qing being the most hawkish; Frederick C. Teiwes and Warren Sun, "The First Tiananmen Incident Revisited: Elite Politics and Crisis Management at the End of the Maoist Era," *Pacific Affairs,* 77, no. 2 (Summer 2004), 211–235.

68. Shanghai minbing douzhengshi ziliaozu, ed., *Shanghai minbing douzheng shi ziliao,* no. 18 (December 1980), 61.

69. "Beijing shi 'Wenhua dageming' dashiji, 1975–1976," p. 37.

70. Xi Xuan and Jin Chunming, *"Wenhua dageming" jianshi,* p. 329.

71. Jin Chunming, "Siwu yundong shuping," p. 1246.

72. Wang Nianyi, *Da dongluande niandai,* p. 583.

73. Yu Huanchun, "'Renmin ribao' yu 1976 Tiananmen shijian," p. 44.

74. Pang Xianzhi and Jin Chongji, *Mao Zedong zhuan,* 2: 1777; Zhonggong zhongyang wenxian yanjiushi, *"Wenge" shinian ziliao xuanbian,* 3: 202–204.

75. John Gardner, *Chinese Politics and the Succession to Mao* (London: Macmillan, 1982), p. 85.

76. From the night of April 4, Roderick MacFarquhar was traveling with a parliamentary colleague in central China with Foreign Ministry escorts. On April 6, braving the static of an ancient radio in a Wuxi guest house, he got an inkling from a BBC broadcast of some big disturbance in Beijing, but when he questioned the Foreign Ministry officials, they professed ignorance of any such event.

77. "Quarterly Chronicle and Documentation," *CQ,* no. 67 (September 1976), 663–666.

78. In an interview in Beijing just before the Tiananmen incident, Roderick MacFarquhar somewhat disingenuously asked Foreign Minister Qiao Guanhua why three months had passed since Zhou Enlai's death without the naming of an official premier, when at that very moment in the U.K. the succession to Prime Minister Harold Wilson was being decided within three weeks (March 16–April 5).

79. "Quarterly Chronicle and Documentation" (September 1976), 663.

80. Beijing gongye xueyuan yundong bangongshi, *Dazibao xuanbian,* 2: 33.

81. Li Zhisui, *The Private Life of Chairman Mao,* p. 610.

82. Ibid., p. 621.

83. Ji Xichen, *Shi wuqianliede niandai,* 2: 751.

84. Li Naiyin, "Cong Yao Wenyuan de zhaji an 'sirenbang' fumie qian de zuie xintai" (The Criminal State of Mind of the "Gang of Four" Prior to Their Demise as Reflected in Yao Wenyuan's Reading Notes), *Yanhuang chunqiu,* no. 9 (1997), 38–39.

85. Deng Rong, *Deng Xiaoping and the Cultural Revolution,* pp. 400–404. At the time, Deng's disappearance from view was attributed in the West to his being spirited out of the capital to Guangzhou by a friendly general.

25. The Last Days of Chairman Mao

1. *Zhongguo renmin gongan shigao,* p. 349.

2. Zhu Chuan and Shen Xianhui, *Dangdai Liaoning jianshi,* p. 273.

3. Zhonggong Hebei shengwei dangshi yanjiushi, *Zhongguo gongchandang Hebei lishi dashiji,* p. 568.

4. *Zhongguo renmin gongan shigao,* p. 451.

5. Heilmann, *Sozialer Protest in der VR China,* pp. 180–183.

6. Jin Chunming, in Zhonggong Zhejiang shengwei dangxiao dangshi jiaoyanshi, *"Wenhua dageming" shiqi ziliao xuanji,* p. 282.

7. Shanghai minbing douzhengshi ziliaozu, ed., *Shanghai minbing douzheng shi ziliao,* no. 16 (December 1980), 27; Xu Jingxian, *Shinian yimeng,* p. 419.

8. "Beijing shi 'Wenhua dageming' dashiji, 1975–1976," p. 39.

9. Fisher, *Go Gently through Peking,* pp. 211–212.

10. "Beijing shi 'Wenhua dageming' dashiji, 1975–1976," p. 41.

11. *Di san ci lilun taolunhuide wuge fayan cailiao* (Five Oral Presentations at the Third Theory Conference) (Beijing: Beijing renmin chubanshe, 1976), pp. 1–7.

12. Shanghai shi wenhuaju yundong bangongshi cailiaozu, ed., *"Sirenbang" jiqi yudang zai Shanghai wenhua xitongde fangeming xiuzhengzhuyi yanlun zhaibian (chugao)* (Collected Examples of the Counterrevolutionary Revisionist Utterances in the Shanghai Cultural Sector Made by the "Gang of Four" and Their Ilk [First Draft]) (Shanghai, 1977), p. 14.

13. Ibid., p. 17.

14. Chen and Du, *Gongheguo shiji,* 3: 1229–30; interview by MacFarquhar with a close colleague of Foreign Minister Qiao, Cambridge, Mass., February 4, 1991; *Jianguo yilai Mao Zedong wengao,* 13: 538.

15. *Jianguo yilai Mao Zedong wengao,* 13: 538.

16. Lian Zhixiang, ed., *Dangdai Shanxi jianshi* (A Short History of Contemporary Shanxi) (Beijing: Dangdai Zhongguo chubanshe, 1999), p. 373.

17. Zhonggong Baoding shiwei dangshi yanjiushi, *Zhonggong Baoding dangshi dashiji,* pp. 430–436.

18. Yu Shun, ed., *Dangdai Hunan jianshi (1949–1995)* (A Short History of Contem-

porary Hunan [1949–1995]) (Beijing: Dangdai Zhongguo chubanshe, 1997), p. 304.

19. *Zhongguo renmin gongan shigao,* pp. 349–350.

20. Li Zhisui, *The Private Life of Chairman Mao,* p. 614.

21. "Quarterly Chronicle and Documentation," *CQ,* no. 67 (September 1976), 676.

22. Shanghai minbing douzhengshi ziliaozu, ed., *Shanghai minbing douzheng shi ziliao,* no. 22 (January 1981), 84.

23. *Shanghai "Wenhua dageming" shihua,* 3: 909.

24. Chen and Du, *Gongheguo shiji,* 3: 1244.

25. Ibid., pp. 1253–56.

26. Li Zhisui, *The Private Life of Chairman Mao,* p. 622.

27. Deng Rong, *Deng Xiaoping and the Cultural Revolution,* pp. 422–423.

28. Wang Nianyi, *Da dongluande niandai,* pp. 599–600.

29. Wu De, "Guanyu fensui 'sirenbang' de douzheng" (The Struggle to Smash the "Gang of Four"), *Dangdai Zhongguo shi yanjiu,* no. 5 (2000), 53; Wang-Zhang-Jiang-Yao zhuan'anzu, 1: 95.

30. *Zhongguo renmin gongan shigao,* pp. 349–351; "Beijing shi 'Wenhua dageming' dashiji, 1975–1976," p. 42.

31. "Beijing shi 'Wenhua dageming' dashiji, 1975–1976," p. 42.

32. Wang Xiuzhen, "Wode di er ci jiefa he jiaodai," p. 5.

33. Shanghai minbing douzhengshi ziliaozu, ed., *Shanghai minbing douzheng shi ziliao,* no. 16 (December 1980), 25; ibid., no. 18 (December 1980), 61.

34. Wang Xiuzhen, "Wode di er ci jiefa he jiaodai," p. 19; Shanghai minbing douzhengshi ziliaozu, ed., *Shanghai minbing douzheng shi ziliao,* no. 18 (December 1980), 61.

35. Shanghai minbing douzhengshi ziliaozu, ed., *Shanghai minbing douzheng shi ziliao,* no. 22 (January 1981), 83–88.

36. Chen and Du, *Gongheguo shiji,* 3: 1259–60.

37. Zhang vouchsafed his thoughts to one of Wang Hongwen's secretaries, Xiao Mu, later in April; "Xu Jingxian de buchong jiefa jiaodai," p. 2.

38. Li Ke and Hao Shengzhang, *"Wenhua dageming" zhongde renmin jiefangjun,* p. 180; Chen and Du, *Gongheguo shiji,* 3: 1238.

39. *Liang Biye jiangjun zishu* (General Liang Biye's Account) (Shenyang: Liaoning renmin chubanshe, 1997), pp. 186–191.

40. Wang-Zhang-Jiang-Yao zhuan'anzu, 1: 106–107.

41. Li Zhisui, *The Private Life of Chairman Mao,* p. 13.

42. Qing Ye and Fang Lei, *Deng Xiaoping zai 1976,* 2: 5.

43. Li Zhisui, *The Private Life of Chairman Mao,* p. 5.

44. Qing Ye and Fang Lei, *Deng Xiaoping zai 1976,* 2: 12.

45. "Quarterly Chronicle and Documentation," *CQ*, no. 68 (December 1976), 874–877.

46. Li Zhisui, *The Private Life of Chairman Mao*, p. 9.

47. "Xu Jingxian de chubu jiefa jiaodai," p. 5.

48. *"Sirenbang" zuixing cailiao*, p. 148.

49. Beijing daxue Liang Xiao zhuan'anzu, *Liang Xiao zuizheng cailiao*, p. 125.

50. Wang-Zhang-Jiang-Yao zhuan'anzu, 1: 97.

51. Beijing gongye xueyuan yundong bangongshi, *Dazibao xuanbian*, 2: 11.

52. "Quarterly Chronicle and Documentation" (December 1976), 886.

53. Beijing gongye xueyuan yundong bangongshi, *Dazibao xuanbian*, 2: 15.

54. "Beijing shi 'Wenhua dageming' dashiji, 1975–1976," pp. 42–43.

55. Shanghai minbing douzhengshi ziliaozu, ed., *Shanghai minbing douzheng shi ziliao*, no. 19 (December 1980), 33; ibid., no. 22 (January 1981), 88.

56. Garside, *Coming Alive*, p. 139; Fisher, *Go Gently through Peking*, p. 231; Edoarda Masi, *China Winter: Workers, Mandarins, and the Purge of the Gang of Four* (New York: Dutton, 1982), p. 98.

57. Jung Chang, *Wild Swans*, p. 495.

58. *Wang Li fansi lu*, 1: 30.

59. Rittenberg and Bennett, *The Man Who Stayed Behind*, p. 427.

60. Qing Ye and Fang Lei, *Deng Xiaoping zai 1976*, 2: 90.

61. Wang-Zhang-Jiang-Yao zhuan'anzu, 1: 106–107.

62. "Xu Jingxian de chubu jiefa jiaodai," p. 14.

63. Beijing daxue Liang Xiao zhuan'anzu, *Liang Xiao zuizheng cailiao*, p. 88.

64. Guofang daxue, *"Wenhua dageming,"* 3: 564.

65. "Xu Jingxian de chubu jiefa jiaodai," p. 34.

66. Wu De, "Guanyu fensui 'sirenbang' de douzheng," p. 55.

67. Ibid., pp. 56–57.

68. One member of the Politburo in Beijing at the time who was kept in the dark by Hua Guofeng was Ji Dengkui. This, apparently, after a probing informal question from Hua Guofeng in mid-September about "How should we solve the 'Gang of Four' issue raised by Chairman Mao?" had elicited the "wrong" answer (that distinctions had to be made and that it would not be appropriate to dispose of them as a group). Hua may also have heard of Jiang Qing's claim in mid-1974 that Ji was moving to the Gang's side; see ibid., pp. 57–58; and Chapter 18, above.

69. Wu De, "Guanyu fensui 'sirenbang' de douzheng," p. 57. That savvy survivor Chen Yun, informed by Wang Zhen about plans to deal with the Gang, initially favored voting, but after a prolonged study of the CC membership roster, he concluded that the result was not predictable; *Chen Yun nianpu*, 3: 204.

70. Wu De, "Guanyu fensui 'sirenbang' de douzheng," p. 54; Fan Shuo, *Ye Jianying*

zhuan (Biography of Ye Jianying) (Beijing: Dangdai Zhongguo chubanshe, 1995), pp. 646–647.

71. Wu De, "Guanyu fensui 'sirenbang' de douzheng," p. 54.

72. Ibid., p. 58.

73. Ibid.

74. Ibid., pp. 58–59. Apparently, despite the putatively superior numbers of a division over a battalion, the garrison's force would actually outnumber and outgun the Beijing MR's.

75. Zhang Zishen, *Zhanjiang yu tongshuai*, pp. 472–473. Yang Chengwu was among the generals rehabilitated after the Lin Biao affair on the grounds that the late heir apparent had misled Mao about his committing crimes. Jiang Qing asked to see Yang to find out if the military were plotting anything, or so Ye Jianying and others believed, and Yang was told to see her but not to give anything away. Yang was deputy chief of staff reporting directly to Ye. By late 1976 he should not have been reporting to Deng, since the latter had been deprived of all his posts, including that of chief of staff.

76. Wu De, "Guanyu fensui 'sirenbang' de douzheng," p. 61.

77. According to one senior member of Liang Xiao, Peking University professor Fan Daren, the group had no interest in writing this article; the *Guangming Daily* was an unimportant paper, while Fan himself was frantically studying English preparatory to accompanying his diplomat wife to Warsaw. However, the paper was importunate, an article was dashed off, but it had no hidden agenda. Professor Fan was interrogated about the article after the Cultural Revolution, and since he was later permitted to go abroad, his account was presumably accepted. See Fan Daren, *Wen ze: "Liang Xiao" wangshi* (Literary Responsibility: Past Events concerning "Liang Xiao") (Privately published), pp. 123–131.

78. Fan Shuo, *Ye Jianying zhuan*, p. 652.

79. *Wang Dongxing gongkai Mao Zedong si shenghuo*, p. 169.

80. Fan Shuo, *Ye Jianying zhuan*, p. 653. Li Desheng was not in Beijing at the time and was therefore not called to the meeting.

81. Fan Shuo, *Ye Jianying zhuan*, p. 654.

82. Ibid., pp. 654–657.

83. "Xu Jingxian de chubu jiefa jiaodai," pp. 36–41; *Shanghai "Wenhua dageming" shihua,* 3: 912.

84. Ma Tianshui, "Wode buchong jiefa jiaodai," p. 13.

85. *Shanghai "Wenhua dageming" shihua,* 3: 912; "Xu Jingxian de chubu jiefa jiaodai," pp. 36–41.

86. Ma Tianshui, "Wode buchong jiefa jiaodai," p. 14.

87. "Xu Jingxian de chubu jiefa jiaodai," pp. 36–41.

Conclusion

Epigraphs: Gao Xingjian, *One Man's Bible*, trans. Mabel Lee (New York: HarperCollins, 2002), pp. 151, 195.

1. The photograph is reproduced in Richard Baum, *Burying Mao: Chinese Politics in the Age of Deng Xiaoping* (Princeton: Princeton University Press, 1994), p. 28.

2. MacFarquhar, "The Succession to Mao and the End of Maoism, 1969–82," p. 313.

3. The Politburo called for Hua's appointments to be confirmed by the CC as was formally necessary, and this was duly done at the latter's Third Plenum in July 1977; Chen and Du, *Gongheguo shiji*, 3: 1279–81. A volume of Mao's works covering 1949–1957 was published in 1977, but it was quickly remaindered as unsatisfactory after Hua fell.

4. MacFarquhar, "The Succession to Mao and the End of Maoism, 1969–82," pp. 311–327.

5. *The Eleventh National Congress of the Communist Party of China (Documents)* (Peking: Foreign Languages Press, 1977), pp. 52–53.

6. See Michael Schoenhals, "The 1978 Truth Criterion Controversy," *CQ*, no. 126 (June 1991), 243–268.

7. The term "paramount leader" was employed by the media, first in Hong Kong, to get round the fact that Deng was supreme but did not hold the top offices of party or state.

8. This account is based on Dittmer, "Death and Transfiguration," p. 467. For Deng Xiaoping's confirmation that there was argument about Liu's rehabilitation, see *Selected Works of Deng Xiaoping (1975–1982)*, pp. 276–277.

9. This is not to say that the proceedings in Beijing adhered as punctiliously to rule-of-law judicial procedures as did those at Nuremberg, but rather that the procedures were effectively irrelevant. On Chinese failure to adhere to their own legal norms, see Hungdah Chiu, "Certain Legal Aspects of the Recent Peking Trials of the 'Gang of Four' and Others," in James C. Hsiung, ed., *Symposium: The Trial of the "Gang of Four" and Its Implication in China* (Baltimore: School of Law, University of Maryland, 1989), pp. 27–39; and Baum, *Burying Mao*, pp. 113–114.

10. This account of Jiang Qing's trial and prison behavior draws on Terrill, *Madame Mao*, pp. 330–359.

11. Xu Jingxian, *Shinian yimeng*, p. 409.

12. Xiao Sike, *Chaoji shenpan*, 2: 613–614.

13. The official record of the trial is in Zuigao renmin fayuan yanjiushi, ed., *Zhonghua renmin fayuan tebie fating shenpan Lin Biao Jiang Qing fangeming jituan an zhufan jishi* (A Record of the Trial by the Special Tribunal of the PRC's Su-

preme People's Court of the Principal Criminals of the Lin Biao and Jiang Qing Counterrevolutionary Cliques) (Beijing: Falü chubanshe, 1982).

14. For an account of a mother's attempt to bring her daughter's murderer to justice and how he was eventually treated leniently, see Nien Cheng, *Life and Death in Shanghai*, pp. 477–522. Nien Cheng was told by a public security official that 10,000 people had died "unnaturally" in Shanghai (p. 488).

15. *Resolution on CPC History (1949–81)*, p. 32. Of course, that description is not accurate. The Cultural Revolution was indeed an all-round disaster, particularly for the party and the state, but for the people greater losses occurred during the post-GLF famine, when something like 30 million more died than should have.

16. *Selected Works of Deng Xiaoping (1975–1982)*, pp. 276–296.

17. Ibid., p. 287.

18. *Resolution on CPC History (1949–81)*, pp. 32–44, quotation on p. 33; emphasis added.

19. *Selected Works of Deng Xiaoping (1975–1982)*, p. 277. In 1988, after Roderick MacFarquhar gave his first course on the Cultural Revolution in Harvard's Core program, a brief description of it appeared in the restricted Chinese newssheet, *Cankao xiaoxi,* ending with a query to the effect "Why can't we have such a course here?" As late as 1997, when he had to give a formal lecture at Peking University in his capacity as a guest professor, no official notices were sent out in case his topic was the Cultural Revolution. In the academic year 2003–04, a course on the Cultural Revolution was offered at Fudan University, Shanghai; in the academic year 2004–05, courses were given in the history departments of Peking and Xiamen universities, and reportedly in the CCP History Department of China People's University as well.

20. *Resolution on CPC History (1949–81)*, pp. 44–46.

21. Ibid., pp. 46–47.

22. The relevant passage, in Chinese and English, can be found in James Legge, *The Chinese Classics*, vol. 2: *The Works of Mencius* (reprint, Taipei: Southern Materials Center, 1983), p. 167.

23. Mary Clabaugh Wright devised this phrase in *The Last Stand of Chinese Conservatism: The T'ung-Chih Restoration, 1862–1874* (Stanford: Stanford University Press, 1957) to describe mid-nineteenth-century reactions to the onset of the West.

24. The loss is estimated at 279.3 billion yuan; Wu Li, *Zhonghua renmin gongheguo jingji shi,* 1: 741. At the exchange rate prevailing in mid-2006, the loss amounted to about $34 billion. The two best years for China's national income during the Cultural Revolution were 1975 (250.3 billion yuan) and 1976 (242.7 billion yuan); Guojia tongjiju, *Zhongguo tongji nianjian, 1983,* p. 22.

25. Charles O. Hucker, *China's Imperial Past: An Introduction to Chinese History and Culture* (Stanford: Stanford University Press, 1975), p. 187.

26. Patricia Buckley Ebrey, ed., *Chinese Civilization and Society: A Source Book* (New York: Free Press, 1981), pp. 23–26.

27. Hucker, *China's Imperial Past*.

28. John King Fairbank and Merle Goldman, *China: A New History*, enl. ed. (Cambridge, Mass.: The Belknap Press of Harvard University Press, 1998), pp. 179–182.

29. See the description of the "three-antis" and "five-antis" campaigns in Teiwes, "The Establishment and Consolidation of the New Regime, 1949–1957," pp. 37–40.

30. *Selected Works of Deng Xiaoping (1982–92): III* (Beijing: Foreign Languages Press, 1994), p. 33.

31. Geremie R. Barmé, *In the Red: On Contemporary Chinese Culture* (New York: Columbia University Press, 1999), pp. 181–182.

32. http://www.forbes.com/2003/10/29/Chinaland.html.

33. Xinhua announced on June 1, 2004, that China's reputedly eleventh-richest tycoon, Zhou Zhengyi, had been sentenced to three years in prison for stock market fraud. In October 2002, Yang Bin, worth $900 million according to *Forbes* magazine and by now a Dutch citizen, was arrested on suspicion of tax evasion.

34. *Selected Works of Deng Xiaoping (1982–92): III*, p. 279.

35. Ibid., pp. 172–181.

36. *South China Morning Post,* July 7, 2005. The Chinese People's Political Consultative Conference, which normally meets directly before the NPC, is a "united front" institution that includes non-party worthies as well as CCP officials. See also Edward Cody, "China Growing More Wary amid Rash of Protests," *Washington Post,* August 10, 2005, p. A11; Richard McGregor, "China's Official Data Confirm Rise in Social Unrest," *Financial Times* (Asia Edition), January 20, 2006, p. 2. For an example of a protest, see Edward Cody, "Chinese City's Rage at the Rich and Powerful; Beating of Student Sparks Riot, Looting," *Washington Post,* August 1, 2005, p. A1.

37. For the most recent expression of an optimistic political scenario for China, see Bruce Gilley, *China's Democratic Future: How It Will Happen and Where It Will Lead* (New York: Columbia University Press, 2004).

Bibliography

Ai Qun. "Luanshi kuangnü Nie Yuanzi" (Crazy Woman Nie Yuanzi in Troubled Times). In Yang Mu, ed., *"Wenge" chuangjiang fengshenbang*, pp. 36–66.

An Jianshe. "'Jiu yi san' hou Zhou Enlai lingdao de pipan jizuo sichao de douzheng" (After "September 13": How Zhou Enlai Led the Struggle to Criticize Ultra-Leftism). In Zhang Hua and Su Caiqing, eds., *Huishou "Wenge,"* 2: 1073–88.

———— "'Wenge' shiqi Mao Zedong qici nanxun kaoshu" (An Examination of Mao Zedong's Seven Southern Tours during the "Cultural Revolution" Period). *Dangde wenxian*, nos. 1 (2005), 24–30; 2 (2005), 44–49.

————, ed. *Zhou Enlaide zuihou suiyue, 1966–1976* (The Last Days of Zhou Enlai, 1966–1976). Beijing: Zhongyang wenxian chubanshe, 1995.

Apter, David E., and Tony Saich. *Revolutionary Discourse in Mao's Republic.* Cambridge, Mass.: Harvard University Press, 1994.

Baige zhengliu (One Hundred Boats Battle the Current). Beijing: Finance and Trade Red Rebels.

Bainian chao (Hundred Year Tide). Beijing: Zhonggong zhongyang dangshi yanjiushi.

Baokan ziliao (Newspaper Materials). Beijing: Beijing ribao ziliaoshi.

Barmé, Geremie R. *In the Red: On Contemporary Chinese Culture.* New York: Columbia University Press, 1999.

Barnouin, Barbara, and Yu Changgen. *Chinese Foreign Policy during the Cultural Revolution.* London: Kegan Paul International, 1998.

———— *Ten Years of Turbulence: The Chinese Cultural Revolution.* London: Kegan Paul International, 1993.

Baum, Richard. *Burying Mao: Chinese Politics in the Age of Deng Xiaoping.* Princeton: Princeton University Press, 1994.

Beida dangshi xiaoshi yanjiushi dangshizu. "Kang Sheng, Cao Yiou yu 'di yi zhang dazibao'" (Kang Sheng, Cao Yiou, and the "First Big-Character Poster"). *Bainian chao*, no. 9 (2001), 32–38.

Beijing boli zongchang hongweibing lianluozhan, ed. *Zhongyang shouzhang jianghua* (Central Leaders' Speeches). 4 vols. Beijing, 1967.

Beijing caimao xueyuan, ed. *Zai Zhonggong ba jie shier zhong quanhui shang Mao zhuxi, Lin fuzhuxi, Zhou zongli de zhongyao jianghua* (Chairman Mao's, Vice Chairman Lin's, and Premier Zhou Enlai's Important Speeches at the Twelfth Plenum of the Eighth CCP Central Committee). Beijing: Maoyi xueyuan, April 1969.

Beijing dangshi yanjiu (Beijing Party History Research). Beijing: Zhonggong Beijing shiwei dangshi yanjiushi.Bimonthly, 1989–1998.

Beijing dangshi ziliao tongxun. See Zhonggong Beijing shiwei dangshi ziliao zhengji weiyuanhui.

Beijing daxue Liang Xiao zhuan'anzu, ed. *Liang Xiao zuizheng cailiao* (Documentation of Liang Xiao's Crimes). Beijing, 1978.

Beijing daxue and Qinghua daxue, eds. *Lin Biao yu Kong Meng zhi dao (cailiao zhi 1)* (Lin Biao and Confucius and Mencius' Way [Materials 1]). Beijing, 1973.

Beijing daxue wenhua geming weiyuanhui xuanchuanzu, ed. *Beijing daxue wuchanjieji wenhua dageming yundong jianjie* (Brief Introduction to the Great Proletarian Cultural Revolution at Peking University). Beijing, 1966.

Beijing daxue wenhua geming weiyuanhui ziliaozu, ed. *Wuchanjieji wenhua dageming cankao ziliao* (Great Proletarian Cultural Revolution Reference Materials). Beijing, 1967.

Beijing daxue yundong bangongshi, ed. *Wang-Wei-Guo-Lin zuixing cailiao* (Material on the Crimes of Wang [Lianlong], Wei [Yinqiu], Guo [Zonglin], and Lin [Jiakuan]). 4 vols. Beijing, 1977.

Beijing gangtie xueyuan geming zaofan zhandou bingtuan tie 66 nanxia fendui, ed. *Pipan Tan Lifu jianghua xuanji* (Collection Denouncing Tan Lifu's Speeches). Guangzhou, 1966.

Beijing gongye xueyuan yundong bangongshi, ed. *Dazibao xuanbian* (Selected Big-Character Posters). Beijing, 1976.

Beijing hangkong xueyuan "Hongqi," ed. *Wuchanjieji wenhua dageming shouzhang jianghua huiji (1967.1)* (Collected Speeches Made by Central Leaders in the Great Proletarian Cultural Revolution [January 1967]). Beijing, 1967.

Beijing hongse yeyu wenyi gongzuozhe geming zaofan zongbu, ed. *Wuchanjieji wenhua dageming cankao ziliao* (Great Proletarian Cultural Revolution Reference Materials). 6 vols. Beijing, 1967.

Beijing jiaoyu zhi congkan (Beijing Education Gazetteer), comp. Beijing Municipal History of Education. Beijing.

Beijing jingji xueyuan wuchanjieji geming zaofantuan et al., eds. *Wuchanjieji wenhua dageming cankao ziliao* (Reference Materials on the Great Proletarian Cultural Revolution). 4 vols. Beijing, 1967.

Beijing junqu jiguan wuchanjieji gemingpai jiefa pipan zichanjieji yexinjia, yinmoujia, fangeming liangmianpai Yang Chengwu, Yu Lijin, Fu Chongbi zuixing de cailiao (Materials Documenting the Exposure and Denunciation by the Proletarian

Revolutionary Faction in Organs of the Beijing Military Region of the Crimes of Bourgeois Careerists, Conspirators, and Double-Dealers Yang Chengwu, Yu Lijin, and Fu Chongbi). Beijing, 1968.

Beijing 64 zhong hongweibing zongbu. "Kaizhan 'yiri zhongzihua' huodong de chubu yijian" (Tentative Views on Activities Aimed at the "Loyalty-fication of the Entire Day"). Stenciled Red Guard pamphlet. In authors' possession.

Beijing ribao (Beijing Daily). Beijing: Beijing ribao she.

Beijing ribao wenhua geming yundong bangongshi, ed. *Peng Zhen dui jiu "Beijing ribao" gongzuode hei zhishi* (Peng Zhen's Sinister Instructions on the Work of the Old *Beijing Daily*). Beijing, 1967.

Beijing shi geming weiyuanhui di er xuexiban dangwei. "Guanyu dui Wang XX de wenti fucha qingkuang" (On the Situation of the Reinvestigation of the Problems of Wang XX). 1973. Schoenhals collection.

—— "Guanyu dui Zhu Qiming tongzhi wentide fucha qingkuang baogao" (Report on the Situation of the Reinvestigation of the Problems of Comrade Zhu Qiming). November 1972. Schoenhals collection.

—— "Guanyu Guo Buyue wentide fucha qingkuang" (On the Situation of the Reinvestigation of the Problems of Guo Buyue). May 1972. Schoenhals collection.

—— "Guanyu Han Guang tongzhi wentide fucha qingkuang" (On the Situation of the Reinvestigation of the Problems of Comrade Han Guang). December 9, 1972. Schoenhals collection.

—— "Guanyu Heng Yingzhu tongzhi wentide fucha qingkuang" (On the Situation of the Reinvestigation of the Problems of Comrade Heng Yingzhu). October 6, 1972. Schoenhals collection.

—— "Guanyu Jin Ke wentide fucha huibao cailiao" (Report Materials on the Reinvestigation of the Problems of Jin Ke). April 1972. Schoenhals collection.

—— "Guanyu Li Qinyao wentide fucha huibao cailiao" (Report Materials on the Reinvestigation of the Problems of Li Qinyao). April 26, 1972. Schoenhals collection.

—— "Guanyu Liu Yunfeng wenti de fucha huibao cailiao" (Report Materials on the Reinvestigation of the Problems of Liu Yunfeng). April 27, 1972. Schoenhals collection.

—— "Guanyu Yang XX de wenti fucha chuli yijian" (Opinion on How to Deal with the Reinvestigation of the Problems of Yang XX). April 14, 1972. Schoenhals collection.

—— "Guanyu Yang Zizheng wentide fucha qingkuang" (On the Situation of the Reinvestigation of the Problems of Yang Zizheng). July 4, 1972. Schoenhals collection.

—— "Guanyu Yuan Lirong tongzhi de fucha qingkuang" (On the Situation of the

Reinvestigation of the Problems of Comrade Yuan Lirong). October 18, 1972. Schoenhals collection.

Beijing shi huaxue gongyeju jiguan hongse xuanchuanzhan, ed. *Wuchanjieji wenhua dageming ziliao* (Materials on the Great Proletarian Cultural Revolution). 4 vols. Beijing, 1966.

Beijing shi jiedai lai-Jing chuanliande geming shisheng he hongweibing gongzuo zongjie (Summary Report on the Reception Work of Beijing Municipality for Revolutionary Teachers, Students, and Red Guards Visiting Beijing to Exchange Revolutionary Experiences). Beijing, 1967.

"Beijing shi 'Wenhua dageming' dashiji, 1965–1967" (A Chronology of the "Great Cultural Revolution" in Beijing, 1965–1967). In Zhonggong Beijing shiwei dangshi ziliao zhengji weiyuanhui, *Beijing dangshi ziliao tongxun,* extra issue, no. 17 (May 1987).

"Beijing shi 'Wenhua dageming' dashiji, 1968–1970" (A Chronology of the "Great Cultural Revolution" in Beijing, 1968–1970). In Zhonggong Beijing shiwei dangshi ziliao zhengji weiyuanhui, *Beijing dangshi ziliao tongxun,* extra issue, no. 18 (July 1987).

"Beijing shi 'Wenhua dageming' dashiji, 1975–1976" (A Chronology of the "Great Cultural Revolution" in Beijing, 1975–1976). In Zhonggong Beijing shiwei dangshi ziliao zhengji weiyuanhui, *Beijing dangshi ziliao tongxun,* extra issue, no. 20 (August 1987).

Beijing si zhong geming shisheng. "Tongling: Guanyu quzhu silei fenzide wuxiang mingling" (General Order: Five Orders on the Deportation of Four Kinds of Elements). August 24, 1966.

Beijing waiguo yu xueyuan Hongqi zhandou dadui, ed. *Liu Shaoqi zuixing lu* (Record of Liu Shaoqi's Crimes). Beijing, 1967.

Beijing zhengfa xueyuan geming weiyuanhui ziliaozu, ed. *Xingxing sese de anjian* (Cases of Every Shape and Color). Beijing, 1968.

Bennett, Gordon A., and Ronald N. Montaperto. *Red Guard: The Political Biography of Dai Hsiao-ai.* London: Allen & Unwin, 1971.

Bergère, Marie-Claire. "'The Other China': Shanghai from 1919 to 1949." In Howe, ed., *Shanghai,* pp. 1–34.

Bernstein, Thomas P. *Up to the Mountains and Down to the Villages.* New Haven: Yale University Press, 1977.

Bianji yewu (The Editor's Profession). Beijing: Beijing Daily Editorial Office, n.d.

Biji Tao Zhu (Memorial for Tao Zhu). Beijing: Renmin chubanshe, 1990.

Bo Yibo. *Ruogan zhongda juece yu shijiande huigu* (Reflections on Certain Important Decisions and Experiences). 2 vols. Beijing: Zhonggong zhongyang dangxiao chubanshe, 1991, 1993.

Boorman, Howard L., ed. *Biographical Dictionary of Republican China.* 5 vols. New York: Columbia University Press, 1967–1979.

Brugioni, Dino A. "The Unidentifieds." In Westerfield, ed., *Inside CIA's Private World*, pp. 8–26.

Bu Weihua. "Beijing hongweibing yundong dashiji" (Record of Important Events in the Beijing Red Guard Movement). *Beijing dangshi yanjiu*, no. 1 (1994), 56–61.

Bulletin, No. 6, of the North China Group and speech transcripts. Available at Fairbank Center Library.

Burr, William, ed. *The Kissinger Transcripts: The Top Secret Talks with Beijing and Moscow*. New York: New Press, 1999.

Byron, John, and Robert Pack. *The Claws of the Dragon: Kang Sheng, the Evil Genius behind Mao and His Legacy of Terror in People's China*. New York: Simon & Schuster, 1992.

Caimao doupigai tongxun (Finance and Trade Struggle, Criticize, and Transform Bulletin). Shanghai: Finance and Trade Sector, "Struggle-Criticize-Transform" Liaison Station.

Cankao xiaoxi (Reference News). Beijing: Xinhua News Agency.

Canyue cailiao (Reference Reading Materials). N.p., [1976].

"Carry the Great Proletarian Cultural Revolution Through to the End." *Peking Review*, no. 1 (January 1, 1967), 8–15.

CCP CC Party History Research Centre, ed. *History of the Chinese Communist Party—A Chronology of Events (1919–1990)*. Beijing: Foreign Languages Press, 1991.

CCP Documents of the Great Proletarian Cultural Revolution, 1966–1967. Hong Kong: Union Research Institute, 1968.

Chai Chengwen. "Zhou Enlai yu Zhong Su bianjie tanpan" (Zhou Enlai and the Sino-Soviet Border Talks). In Qiu Shi, ed., *Gongheguo zhongda shijian he juece neimu*, 2: 659–671.

Chan, Anita. *Children of Mao*. Seattle: University of Washington Press, 1985.

Chang Jung. *Wild Swans*. New York: Simon & Schuster, 1991.

Chang Jung and Jon Halliday. *Mao: The Unknown Story*. London: Jonathan Cape, 2005.

Changchun gongshe 503 zhandoudui, ed. *Chuncheng wuchanjieji wenhua dageming dashiji (1965.11–1968.3)* (Record of Major Events in the Spring City in the Great Proletarian Cultural Revolution [November 1965–March 1968]). 2 vols. Changchun, 1968.

Chedi fouding "Wenhua dageming" jianghua (Lectures on Thoroughly Repudiating the "Great Cultural Revolution"). Beijing: Zhongguo renmin jiefangjun zhengzhi xueyuan chubanshe, 1985.

Chedi pipan Lin Chen fandang jituan fangeming zuixing—da pipan fayan cailiao xuanbian zhi er (Thoroughly Denounce the Counterrevolutionary Crimes of the Lin and Chen Anti-Party Clique—A Second Selection of Great Denunciation Materials). [Chengdu]: Sichuan sheng geming weiyuanhui shengchan jianshe bangongshi zhenggongzu, April 1972.

Chedi pipan xiuzhengzhuyi youer jiaoyu luxian jiaocai huibian (Collection on Thoroughly Criticizing the Revisionist Line in Preschool Education Textbooks). Beijing: Beijing youshi geming zaofantuan, 1967.

Cheek, Timothy. *Propaganda and Culture in Mao's China: Deng Tuo and the Intelligentsia.* Oxford: Clarendon Press, 1997.

"Chen Boda, Qi Benyu tongzhi 4.30 lingchen jiejian lianhe jiedaishi quanti renyuan shide jianghua" (Speeches of Comrades Chen Boda and Qi Benyu at a Reception for the Entire Staff of the Joint Reception Office at Dawn on April 30). Original transcript. N.p., [1967]. Schoenhals collection.

Chen Boda tongzhi bufen zhuzuo zhuanji (Special Collection of Selected Writings by Comrade Chen Boda). N.p., n.d.

Chen Chuan. "Youths Who Sought the Truth." *Chinese Sociology and Anthropology,* 26, no. 1 (Fall 1993), 59–64.

Chen Donglin and Du Pu, eds. *Gongheguo shiji* (Historical Records of the Republic). 4 vols. Changchun: Jilin renmin chubanshe, 1996.

Chen Dunde. *Bai zhan jiang xing: Kong Congzhou* (A Brilliant General in One Hundred Battles: Kong Congzhou). Beijing: Jiefangjun wenyi chubanshe, 2000.

Chen Jo-hsi. *The Execution of Mayor Yin and Other Stories from the Great Proletarian Cultural Revolution.* Bloomington: Indiana University Press, 1978.

Chen Pixian fandang fanshehuizhuyi zuixing cailiao zhaibian (Selected Material Documenting Chen Pixian's Anti-Party and Anti-Socialist Crimes). Shanghai, 1967.

Chen Pixian huiyilu: Zai "Yiyue fengbao" de zhongxin (The Memoirs of Chen Pixian: In the Center of the "January Storm"). Shanghai: Shanghai renmin chubanshe, 2005.

Chen Po-ta. "Grow Up Braving Storm and Stress." *Peking Review,* no. 35 (August 26, 1966), 10–11.

Chen Qingquan and Song Guangwei. "Yuanan bu ping, ju bu chu yu de Lu Dingyi" (The Case Is Unfair: Lu Dingyi Refuses to Leave Prison). *Yanhuang chunqiu,* no. 6 (2000), 26–31.

Chen Shijin. *Jiangjun juanjin xuanwo* (General Drawn into the Whirlpool). Nanjing: Jiangsu wenyi chubanshe, 1987.

Chen, Theodore H. E. *Thought Reform of the Chinese Intellectuals.* Hong Kong: Hong Kong University Press, 1960.

Chen Xianrui. "Pi-Chen pi-Lin qijian de Beijing junqu" (The Beijing Military Region at the Time of the Criticism of Chen and Lin). *Bainian chao,* no. 5 (2000), 42–49.

Chen Xiaonong, comp. *Chen Boda zuihou koushu huiyi* (Chen Boda's Final Oral Memoir). Hong Kong: Yangguang huanqiu chuban Xianggang youxian gongsi, 2005.

Chen Xiaonong, ed. *Chen Boda yigao: Yuzhong zishu ji qita* (Manuscripts by the Late

Chen Boda: Accounts from Prison and More). Hong Kong: Cosmos Books, 1998.

"Chen Yonggui tongzhi de fayan" (Comrade Chen Yonggui's Statement). April 14, 1969. Official transcript. Beijing: CC General Office Secretariat. Available at Fairbank Center Library.

Chen Yun. See Zhonggong zhongyang wenxian yanjiushi, ed., *Chen Yun nianpu (1905–1995)*.

Chen Zaidao. *Haojie zhongde yi mu: Wuhan qi ershi shijian qin liji* (One Act in a Catastrophe: A Personal Record of the Wuhan July 20 Incident). Beijing: Jiefangjun chubanshe, 1989.

——— "Wuhan 'qi.er.ling shijian' shimo" (The Wuhan "July 20 Incident" from Start to Finish). In Guofang daxue dangshi dangjian zhenggong jiaoyanshi, ed., *"Wenhua dageming" yanjiu ziliao*, 1: 508–525.

Cheng Chao and Wei Haoben, eds. *Zhejiang "Wenge" jishi* (Factual Record of the "Cultural Revolution" in Zhejiang). Hangzhou: Zhejiang fangzhi bianjibu, 1989.

Cheng Hua. *Zhou Enlai he tade mishumen* (Zhou Enlai and His Secretaries). Beijing: Zhongguo guangbo dianshi chubanshe, 1992.

Cheng Min, ed. *Haojie chuqi* (How the Calamity Began). Beijing: Tuanjie chubanshe, 1993.

Cheng Nien. *Life and Death in Shanghai*. New York: Grove Press, 1986.

Cheng Qian. "'Wenge' mantan" (Random Commentary on the "Cultural Revolution"). Manuscript. Beijing, n.d. Copy in Fairbank Center Library.

Cheng Zhongyuan. "1975 nian zhengdun zhongde sange zhuming wenjian" (Three Famous Documents during the 1975 Rectification). In Zhang Hua and Su Caiqing, eds., *Huishou "Wenge,"* 2: 1195–1212.

Chengjianju shuini chengpinchang gongren geming zaofandui, ed. *Dadao fangeming xiuzhengzhuyi fenzi Chen Pixian* (Down with Counterrevolutionary Revisionist Element Chen Pixian). Shanghai, 1967.

Chi Zehou. "Zhonggong 'jiuda' neimu suoyi" (Random Memories of the Background to the "Ninth Party Congress"). *Yanhuang chunqiu*, no. 3 (2003), 42–49.

China Daily. Beijing: China Daily Distribution Corp.

China Quarterly. London: Contemporary China Institute, School of Oriental and African Studies.

Chinese Communist Who's Who. 2 vols. Taipei: Institute of International Relations, 1971.

Chinese Law and Government. Armonk, N.Y.: M. E. Sharpe.

Chinese Sociology and Anthropology. Armonk, N.Y.: M. E. Sharpe.

Chinese Studies in Philosophy. White Plains, N.Y.: International Arts and Sciences Press.

Chiu Hungdah. "Certain Legal Aspects of the Recent Peking Trials of the 'Gang of Four' and Others." In Hsiung, ed., *Symposium*, pp. 27–39.

Chongqing shizhi (Gazetteer of Chongqing Municipality). Chengdu: Sichuan daxue chubanshe, 1992.

Chu, Godwin C., ed. *Popular Media in China: Shaping New Cultural Patterns.* Honolulu: East-West Center, University of Hawaii, 1978.

Chuang Tzu. *The Complete Works of Chuang Tzu,* trans. Burton Watson. New York: Columbia University Press, 1968.

Chunlei (Spring Thunder). Beijing: Capital August 1 School Revolutionary Rebel Joint Headquarters.

Cody, Edward. "China Growing More Wary amid Rash of Protests." *Washington Post,* August 10, 2005, p. A11.

——— "Chinese City's Rage at the Rich and Powerful; Beating of Student Sparks Riot, Looting." *Washington Post,* August 1, 2005, p. A1.

Contemporary Chinese Thought. Armonk, N.Y.: M. E. Sharpe.

Correspondents of *The Economist. Consider Japan.* London: G. Duckworth, 1963.

CQ. China Quarterly.

Cradock, Percy. *Experiences of China.* London: John Murray, 1994.

Dadao Deng Xiaoping (Down with Deng Xiaoping). Beijing, 1967.

Dadao Li Jingquan (Down with Li Jingquan). Chongqing, 1967.

Dadao Tan Zhenlin cailiao huibian (Down with Tan Zhenlin, Collected Materials). Shanghai, 1967.

Dahai hangxing kao duoshou (The Helmsman Sets the Ocean Course). N.p., n.d.

Dai Sijie. *Balzac et la Petite Tailleuse chinoise* (Balzac and the Little Chinese Tailoress). Paris: Gallimard, 2000. Translated by Ina Rilke as *Balzac and the Little Chinese Seamstress.* New York: Knopf, 2001.

Dan Zeng, ed. *Dangdai Xizang jianshi* (A Short History of Contemporary Tibet). Beijing: Dangdai Zhongguo chubanshe, 1996.

"Dangdai Guizhou jianshi" bianweihui, ed. *Dangdai Guizhou dashiji, 1949.10–1995.12* (Record of Major Events in Contemporary Guizhou, October 1949–December 1995). Guiyang: Guizhou renmin chubanshe, 1996.

Dangdai Sichuan dashi jiyao (Main Points concerning Major Events in Contemporary Sichuan). Chengdu: Sichuan renmin chubanshe, 1991.

Dangdai Yunnan dashi jiyao (1949–1995) (Summary Record of Major Events in Contemporary Yunnan [1949–1995]). Beijing: Dangdai Zhongguo chubanshe, 1996.

Dangdai Yunnan jianshi (A Short History of Contemporary Yunnan). Beijing: Dangdai Zhongguo chubanshe, 2004.

Dangdai Zhongguo shangye bianjibu, ed. *Zhonghua renmin gongheguo shangye dashiji, 1958–1978* (A Record of Major Events in PRC Commerce, 1958–1978). Beijing: Zhongguo shangye chubanshe, 1990.

Dangdai Zhongguo shi yanjiu (Research on Contemporary Chinese History). Beijing: Dangdai Zhongguo shi yanjiu zazhi she.

Dangdai Zhongguo yanjiu (Modern China Studies). Princeton: Center for Modern China.

Dangdai Zhongguode Jilin (Contemporary China's Jilin). 2 vols. Beijing: Dangdai Zhongguo chubanshe, 1991.

Dangdai Zhongguode laodong baohu (Labor Protection in Contemporary China). Beijing: Dangdai Zhongguo chubanshe, 1992.

Dangdai Zhongguode Ningxia (Contemporary China's Ningxia). Beijing: Zhongguo shehui kexue chubanshe, 1990.

Dangdai Zhongguode Shanghai (Contemporary China's Shanghai). 2 vols. Beijing: Dangdai Zhongguo chubanshe, 1993.

Dangdai Zhongguode Sichuan (Contemporary China's Sichuan). Beijing: Dangdai Zhongguo chubanshe, 1997.

Dangde wenxian (Party Documents). Beijing: Zhongyang wenxian chubanshe.

Dangde wenxian bianjibu, ed. *Zhonggong dangshi zhongda shijian shushi* (True Accounts of Important Events in the History of the CCP). Beijing: Renmin chubanshe, 1993.

Dangshi yanjiu ziliao (Party History Research Materials). Beijing: Zhongguo geming bowuguan dangshi yanjiushi.

Daqing shizhi (Daqing Gazetteer). Nanjing: Nanjing renmin chubanshe, 1988.

Dazibao bianjizu, ed. *Gaojiaobu wenhua dageming dazibao xuanji* (Selection of Big-Character Posters of the Great Cultural Revolution in the Ministry of Higher Education). N.p., n.d.

——— *Jiaoyubu wenhua dageming dazibao xuanji* (Selected Great Cultural Revolution Big-Character Posters from the Ministry of Education).

Dazibao xuan (Selected Big-Character Posters). Beijing: Peking University.

Decision of the Central Committee of the Chinese Communist Party concerning the Great Proletarian Cultural Revolution. Peking: Foreign Languages Press, 1966.

Deng Liqun guoshi jiangtan lu (A Record of Deng Liqun's Talks on National History). 5 vols. Beijing: "Zhonghua renmin gongheguo shigao" bianweihui huibian, 2000.

Deng Liqun wenji (Collected Works of Deng Liqun). 4 vols. Beijing: Dangdai Zhongguo chubanshe, 1998.

Deng Rong. *Deng Xiaoping and the Cultural Revolution: A Daughter Recalls the Critical Years.* Beijing: Foreign Languages Press, 2002.

Deng Xiaoping. *Selected Works of Deng Xiaoping (1975–1982).* Beijing: Foreign Languages Press, 1984.

——— *Selected Works of Deng Xiaoping (1982–92): III.* Beijing: Foreign Languages Press, 1994.

——— "Some Problems Outstanding in the Iron and Steel Industry." In *Selected Works (1975–1982),* pp. 18–22.

——— "Wode zishu" (My Own Account). In *Canyue cailiao,* p. 10.

"Deng Xiaoping tongzhi zai Guowuyuan bangong huiyshangde jianghua zhailu" (Excerpts from Comrade Deng Xiaoping's Talk at a State Council Office Meeting), p. 1. May 21, 1975. Typed transcript circulated in China in winter 1975–76. Available at Fairbank Center Library.

Di san ci lilun taolunhuide wuge fayan cailiao (Five Oral Presentations at the Third Theory Conference). Beijing: Beijing renmin chubanshe, 1976.

Ding Longjia. *Kang Sheng yu "Zhao Jianmin yuanan"* (Kang Sheng and the "Unjust Case of Zhao Jianmin"). Beijing: Renmin chubanshe, 1999.

Dittmer, Lowell. "Death and Transfiguration: Liu Shaoqi's Rehabilitation and Contemporary Chinese Politics." *Journal of Asian Studies*, 11, no. 3 (May 1981), 455–479.

Djilas, Milovan. *The New Class: An Analysis of the Communist System.* New York: Praeger, 1957.

Domes, Jürgen. *The Internal Politics of China, 1949–1972.* London: Hurst, 1973.

Dong Zhujun. *Wode yige shiji* (My Century). Beijing: Sanlian shudian, 1997.

Dongfanghong (East Is Red). Chengdu: Beijing Industrial University.

Dongfanghong bao (The East Is Red Paper). Beijing: Beijing Geological Institute East Is Red Commune.

Dongfeng (East Wind). Beijing: Eighth Ministry of Machine Building Joint General Documentation Office.

Dongtai (Current Intelligence). Beijing: Tsinghua University Jinggangshan Third Current Intelligence Group.

Dongtai bao (Current Intelligence Reports). Beijing: Finance and Trade Liaison Station.

Doupigai tongxun (Struggle, Criticize, and Transform Bulletin). Shanghai: Workers' Mao Zedong Thought Propaganda Team in the Publishing and Press Sector Regimental Headquarters.

Duiwai wenwei Jinggangshan geming zaofan lianluozhan, ed. *Dadao fangeming xiuzhengzhuyi fenzi Li Chang* (Down with the Counterrevolutionary Revisionist Element Li Chang). Beijing, 1967.

Eastman, Lloyd E. *The Abortive Revolution: China under Nationalist Rule, 1927–1937.* Cambridge, Mass.: Council on East Asian Studies, Harvard University, 1990.

Ebrey, Patricia Buckley, ed. *Chinese Civilization and Society: A Source Book.* New York: Free Press, 1981.

The Eleventh National Congress of the Communist Party of China (Documents). Peking: Foreign Languages Press, 1977.

Ershiyi shiji shuangyuekan (Twenty-first Century Bimonthly). Hong Kong: Institute of Chinese Studies, Chinese University.

"Eyewitness of the Great Proletarian Cultural Revolution." *CQ*, no. 28 (October–December 1966), 1–7.

Fairbank, John King, and Merle Goldman. *China: A New History.* Enl. ed. Cambridge, Mass.: The Belknap Press of Harvard University Press, 1998.

Fairbank, John K., and Roderick MacFarquhar, eds. *Cambridge History of China.* Vol. 15, pt. 2. New York: Cambridge University Press, 1991.

Fan Daren. *Wen ze: "Liang Xiao" wangshi* (Literary Responsibility: Past Events concerning "Liang Xiao"). Privately published, n.d.

Fan Dechang, ed. *Jiayin xianzhi* (Jiayin County Gazetteer). Harbin: Heilongjiang renmin chubanshe, 1988.

Fan Shuo. *Ye Jianying zai 1976* (Ye Jianying in 1976). Beijing: Zhonggong zhongyang dangxiao chubanshe, 1992.

—— *Ye Jianying zhuan* (Biography of Ye Jianying). Beijing: Dangdai Zhongguo chubanshe, 1995.

Fandaodi tongxun (Resist All the Way Bulletin). Shanghai: Jiaotong University.

Fangeming xiuzhengzhuyi fenzi Fan Jin de zuixing: Buchong cailiao zhi 1 (Crimes of the Counterrevolutionary Revisionist Element Fan Jin: Supplementary Material 1). Beijing: Beijing ribao wenhua geming yundong bangongshi, 1967.

Fangeming xiuzhengzhuyi fenzi Lu Dingyi zai wenjiao fangmian de zuixing (Counterrevolutionary Revisionist Element Lu Dingyi's Crimes in Culture and Education). Beijing: Dou Peng-Luo-Lu-Yang fangeming xiuzhengzhuyi jituan choubeichu, 1967.

Feng Jicai. *Voices from the Whirlwind.* New York: Pantheon, 1991.

Fisher, Lois. *Go Gently through Peking: A Westerner's Life in China.* London: Souvenir Press, 1979.

Fokkema, D. W. *Report from Peking.* London: Hurst, 1971.

Foshan shi dang'anju, ed. *Foshan shi dashiji (1949–1989)* (Chronology of Major Events in Foshan City [1949–1989]). Foshan, 1991.

Fu Chongbi huiyilu (The Memoirs of Fu Chongbi). Beijing: Zhonggong dangshi chubanshe, 1999.

Galenovich, Y. M. *Rossia i Kitai v XX Veke: Granitsa* (Russia and China in the Twentieth Century: Frontier). Moscow: Izograph, 2001.

Gang gongzong "Wuhu sihai" zhandou bingtuan, ed. *Zhenhan quanguo de riri yeye* (Days and Nights That Shook the Entire Nation). Wuhan: Huazhong fangzhi gongxueyuan, 1967.

Gao Anhua. *To the Edge of the Sky.* London: Penguin, 2001.

Gao Gao and Yan Jiaqi. *"Wenhua dageming" shinian shi, 1966–1976* (A Ten-Year History of the "Great Cultural Revolution," 1966–1976). Tianjin: Tianjin renmin chubanshe, 1986.

Gao quanshi tongxue shu (Appeal to Fellow Students in All of Beijing). September 13, 1966. Schoenhals collection.

Gao Wenhua. "Buchong wo he Liu Shaoqi zai Zhongnanhai mimou de zuixing" (Additions to the Crimes Plotted by Myself and Liu Shaoqi in Zhongnanhai). February 12, 1971. Written deposition submitted to Ministry of Foreign Trade. Copy in authors' possession.

———. "'Laotou zaofandui' caozong de '5.16' fangeming yinmou jituan de zuixing" (Crimes of the "May 16" Counterrevolutionary Conspiratorial Clique as Masterminded by the "Old Fogeys' Rebel Team"). January 22–March 11, 1971. Handwritten confession from Beijing. Schoenhals collection.

Gao Wenqian. *Wannian Zhou Enlai* (Zhou Enlai's Later Years). New York: Mingjing chubanshe, 2003.

Gao Xingjian. *One Man's Bible,* trans. Mabel Lee. New York: HarperCollins, 2002.

Gao Yuan. *Born Red: A Chronicle of the Cultural Revolution.* Stanford: Stanford University Press, 1987.

Gaoju Mao Zedong sixiang weida hongqi (Raise High the Great Red Banner of Mao Zedong Thought). N.p., April 1967.

Gardner, John. *Chinese Politics and the Succession to Mao.* London: Macmillan, 1982.

Garside, Roger. *Coming Alive: China after Mao.* London: Andre Deutsch, 1981.

Gaulton, Richard. "Political Mobilization in Shanghai, 1949–1951." In Howe, ed., *Shanghai,* pp. 35–65.

Ge Chumin. "Xu Xiangqian zai 'Wenge' zhongde er san shi" (Some Stories about Xu Xiangqian during the "Cultural Revolution"). *Bainian chao,* no. 11 (2001), 39–40.

Geming zaofan zongbu zhenli zhandoudui, ed. *Youdianbu jiguan wenhua dageming yundong shiliao* (Materials on the History of the Great Cultural Revolution Movement in the Organs of the Ministry of Posts and Telecommunications). Beijing, 1967.

Gilley, Bruce. *China's Democratic Future: How It Will Happen and Where It Will Lead.* New York: Columbia University Press, 2004.

Gladney, Dru C. *Muslim Chinese: Ethnic Nationalism in the People's Republic.* Cambridge, Mass.: Harvard University Press, 1996.

Goldman, Merle. *China's Intellectuals: Advise and Dissent.* Cambridge, Mass.: Harvard University Press, 1981.

Goldstein, Lyle J. "Return to Zhenbao Island: Who Started Shooting and Why It Matters?" *CQ,* no. 168 (December 2001), 985–997.

"Gong nong bing qun zhong canjia xueshu pipan shi hua shidaide da shi" (The Participation of the Worker-Peasant-Soldier Masses in Academic Criticism Is a Major Epoch-making Event). *Hongqi,* no. 6 (1966), 20–22.

Gong Xiaoxia. "Repressive Movements and the Politics of Victimization." Ph.D. diss., Harvard University, 1995.

Gong Yuzhi. "'Eryue tigang' he donghu zhixing" (The "February Outline" and Travels at East Lake). In Zhang Hua and Su Caiqing, eds., *Huishou "Wenge,"* 1: 289–320.

Gong Zhong, You Sheng, and Sheng Yang. "Chen Zhengren" (Chen Zhengren). In Zhonggong dangshi renwu yanjiuhui, ed., *Zhonggong dangshi renwu zhuan*, 40 (published 1989): 211–260.

Gongan baowei gongzuo (Public Security and Protection Work). Harbin: Northeast People's Government Ministry of Public Security.

Gordon, Eric. *Freedom Is a Word.* London: Hodder & Stoughton, 1971.

A Great Trial in Chinese History. Beijing: New World Press, 1981.

Grey, Anthony. *Hostage in Peking.* London: Michael Joseph, 1970.

Guan Weixun. *Wo suo zhidaode Ye Qun* (The Ye Qun I Knew). Beijing: Zhongguo wenxue chubanshe, 1993.

Guangxi wenge dashi nianbiao (Chronological Record of Major Events in the Cultural Revolution in Guangxi). Nanning: Guangxi renmin chubanshe, 1990.

Guanyu dui yexinjia, yinmoujia, pantu, maiguozei Lin Biao zuixing de jiefa pipan (Exposing and Denouncing the Crimes of Careerist, Conspirator, Renegade, and Traitor Lin Biao). N.p., [1972].

Guanyu fangeming jituan zhongyao chengyuan Fu Chonglan deng jianli di er tao banzi (On How Fu Chonglan and Other Important Members of the Counterrevolutionary Clique Set Up a Second Team). Beijing: Xuebu Hongweibing zongdui Geming lishisuo Xinghuo bingtuan, 1968.

Guanyu Tan Zhenlin wenti de chubu zonghe cailiao (Initial Comprehensive Material on Tan Zhenlin's Problems). Beijing, 1967.

Guizhou wuchanjieji geming zaofan zong zhihuibu (reprinter). *Dadao Liu Shaoqi, dadao Deng Xiaoping (zhuan ji)* (Down with Liu Shaoqi, Down with Deng Xiaoping [Special Edition]). April 1967. Available at Fairbank Center Library.

Guo Zhenzhi. "Zhongguo dianshi dashiji (1955–1978)" (A Chronicle of Events in Chinese Television [1955–1978]). *Xinwen yanjiu ziliao*, no. 46 (1989), 169–184.

Guofang daxue, *Cankao ziliao.* See Guofang daxue dangshi dangjian zhenggong jiaoyanshi, ed., *Zhonggong dangshi jiaoxue cankao ziliao.*

Guofang daxue, *Qishinian.* See Guofang daxue dangshi dangjian zhengzhi gongzuo jiaoyanshi, *Zhongguo gongchandang qishinian dashi jianjie.*

Guofang daxue, *"Wenhua dageming."* See Guofang daxue dangshi dangjian zhenggong jiaoyanshi, ed., *"Wenhua dageming" yanjiu ziliao.*

Guofang daxue dangshi dangjian zhenggong jiaoyanshi, ed. *"Wenhua dageming" yanjiu ziliao* (Research Materials on the "Great Cultural Revolution"). 3 vols. Beijing, 1988.

—— *Zhonggong dangshi jiaoxue cankao ziliao* (CCP History Teaching Reference Materials). 24 vols. Beijing: Guofang daxue, 1979–1986.

Guofang daxue dangshi dangjian zhengzhi gongzuo jiaoyanshi. *Zhongguo gongchandang qishinian dashi jianjie* (A Summary of the Principal Events in the Seventy Years of the CCP). Beijing: Guofang daxue chubanshe, 1991.

Guojia tongjiju, ed. *Zhongguo tongji nianjian, 1983* (China Statistical Yearbook, 1983). Beijing: Zhongguo tongji chubanshe, 1983.

Guojia tongjiju zonghesi, ed. *Quanguo ge sheng zizhiqu zhixiashi lishi tongji ziliao huibian, 1949–1989* (Collected Historical Statistics for China's Provinces, Autonomous Regions, and Municipalities under Central Jurisdiction, 1949–1989). Beijing: Zhongguo tongji chubanshe, 1990.

Guowuyuan caimao bangongshi. "Guanyu liangshi gongzuo huiyi de baogao" (Report on the Meeting on Grain Work). October 30, 1967. Beijing. Original seven-page transcript. In authors' possession.

"Guowuyuan tingqu Hu Yaobang tongzhi huibao shi Xiaoping tongzhi deng zhongyang lingdao tongzhi zhuyao chahua jiyao" (Transcript of Main Interjections by Comrade Xiaoping and Other Leading Comrades from the Center during Comrade Hu Yaobang's Report to the State Council). Typed original transcript from Beijing during anti-Deng campaign in spring 1976. Available at Fairbank Center Library.

Gurtov, Melvin. "The Foreign Ministry and Foreign Affairs in the Chinese Cultural Revolution." In Robinson, ed., *The Cultural Revolution in China*, pp. 313–366.

Han Suyin. *Eldest Son.* New York: Kodansha, 1994.

Hao Kewei. "28 zhuan'an de faqi guocheng" (How "Special Case 28" Was Launched). March 23, 1970. Beijing. Handwritten confession. Schoenhals collection.

"Hao Kewei jiaodai cailiao" (Hao Kewei's Confessions). Beijing. Handwritten confessions. Schoenhals collection.

Hao Ping. "Reassessing the Starting Point of the Cultural Revolution." *China International Review,* 3, no. 1 (Spring 1996), 66–86.

Harding, Harry. "The Chinese State in Crisis." In MacFarquhar, ed., *The Politics of China: Second Edition,* pp. 148–247.

He Jinming and Zhao Bingzhang, eds. *Dangdai Shaanxi jianshi* (A Short History of Contemporary Shaanxi). Beijing: Dangdai Zhongguo chubanshe, 1996.

He Li, ed. *Zhonghua renmin gongheguo shi* (History of the PRC). Rev. ed. Beijing: Zhongguo dang'an chubanshe, 1995.

Hebei Beijing shifan xueyuan, Douzheng shenghuo bianjibu, ed. *Wuchanjieji wenhua dageming ziliao huibian* (Collected Documents from the Great Proletarian Cultural Revolution). Beijing, 1967.

Hebei sheng geming weiyuanhui zhengzhibu, ed. *Mao zhuxi zuixin zhishi ruogan zhongyao wenxian* (Several Important Documents on Chairman Mao's Latest Instructions). Baoding, 1968.

Hei Yan'nan (pseud.). *Shinian dongluan* (Ten Years of Turmoil). [Beijing]: Guoji wenhua chuban gongsi, 1988.

Heilmann, Sebastian. *Nanking 1976 Spontane Massenbewegungen im Gefolge der Kulturrevolution: Eine Regionalstudie* (Spontaneous Mass Movements in the

Wake of the Cultural Revolution: A Regional Study). Bochum: Brockmeyer, 1990.

———— *Sozialer Protest in der VR China: Die Bewegung vom 5. April 1976 und die Gegen-Kulturrevolution der siebziger Jahre* (Social Protest in the People's Republic of China: The April 5 Movement of 1976 and the Counter–Cultural Revolution of the Seventies). Hamburg: Institut für Asienkunde, 1994.

Heilongjiang sheng difang zhi bianzuan weiyuanhui, ed. *Heilongjiang shengzhi dashiji* (Gazetteer of Heilongjiang Province: Record of Major Events). Harbin: Heilongjiang renmin chubanshe, 1992.

Heilongjiang sheng fu Zhenbaodao weiwentuan. "Fanxiu zhanbei jiaoyu baogao" (Report on Teaching Preparation for Antirevisionist War). In *"Jiuda" ziliao huibian*.

Hinton, William. *Hundred Day War: The Cultural Revolution at Tsinghua University*. New York: Monthly Review Press, 1972.

Holdridge, John H. *Crossing the Divide: An Insider's Account of the Normalization of U.S.-China Relations*. Lanham, Md.: Rowman & Littlefield, 1997.

Hongdaihui Beijing jianzhu gongye xueyuan 8.1 zhandoutuan, ed. *Jianjue ba Liu Shaoqi jiuhui Beijing jiangong xueyuan doudao douchou* (Resolve to Drag Liu Shaoqi Back to the Beijing Building Institute to Topple and Discredit Him). Beijing, 1967.

Hongdaihui xin beida fuzhong Jinggangshan bingtuan zongbu, ed. *Dazibao xuan* (Selected Big-Character Posters). Beijing, 1967.

Hongqi (Red Flag). Beijing: Hongqi zazhi she.

Hongqi zhanbao (Red Flag Battle Report). Beijing: CCP Municipal Committee Policy Research Office.

Hongri zhao Tianshan: Guanyu Xinjiang wenti Zhonggong zhongyang wenjian ji zhongyang shouzhangde jianghua huibian (Red Sun Shines on the Tianshan Range: Collected Central Documents and Central Leaders' Speeches on the Xinjiang Issue). Urümqi: Xinjiang hong er si "Xinjiang hongweibing bao" bianjibu, 1968.

Hongweibing bao (Red Guard Paper). Beijing.

Hongweibing Shanghai silingbu (Hong Shangsi), ed. *Zalan "liandong"* (Smash the "United Action Committee"). Shanghai, 1967.

Hongying (Red Eagle). Beijing.

Howe, Christopher, ed. *Shanghai: Revolution and Development in an Asian Metropolis*. Cambridge: Cambridge University Press, 1981.

Hsiung, James C., ed. *Symposium: The Trial of the "Gang of Four" and Its Implication in China*. Baltimore: School of Law, University of Maryland, 1989.

Hu Qiaomu bianxiezu, ed. *Deng Xiaopingde ershisi ci tanhua* (Deng Xiaoping's Chats on Twenty-four Occasions). Beijing: Renmin chubanshe, 2004.

Hu Qiaomu tan Zhonggong dangshi (Hu Qiaomu on the History of the CCP). Beijing: Renmin chubanshe, 1999.

Hua Linshan. *Les années rouges* (The Red Years). Paris: Seuil, 1987.

Huang Jing. *Factionalism in Chinese Communist Politics*. New York: Cambridge University Press, 2000.

Huang Yao. "Luo Ruiqing" (Luo Ruiqing). In Zhonggong dangshi renwu yanjiuhui, ed., *Zhonggong dangshi renwu zhuan*, 46 (published 1991): 1–78.

——— "Luo Ruiqing zhuanlüe xia" (A Brief Biography of Luo Ruiqing, Part 2). *Zhonggong dangshi ziliao*, no. 37 (1991), 154–204.

——— *San ci da nan buside: Luo Ruiqing dajiang* (General Luo Ruiqing Who Survived Catastrophes Three Times). Beijing: Zhonggong dangshi chubanshe, 1994.

Huang Zheng. "The Beginning and End of the 'Liu Shaoqi Case Group.'" In Schoenhals, ed., "Mao's Great Inquisition," pp. 7–23.

——— "Liu Shaoqi yu 'Wenge' chuqide gongzuozu shijian" (Liu Shaoqi and the Work Team Incident at the Beginning of the "Cultural Revolution"). In Dangde wenxian bianjibu, ed., *Zhonggong dangshi zhongda shijian shushi*, pp. 252–260.

——— "Liu Shaoqi yu 'Wenhua dageming'" (Liu Shaoqi and the "Great Cultural Revolution"). *Dangde wenxian*, no. 5 (1988), 4–10.

——— *Liu Shaoqide zuihou suiyue* (Liu Shaoqi's Last Years). Beijing: Zhongyang wenxian chubanshe, 1996.

Huanxintian (To Alter the Sky). Beijing: Eighth Ministry of Machine Building.

Hubei sheng geming weiyuanhui, ed. *Wuchanjieji wenhua dageming wenjian huibian* (Collected Documents from the Great Proletarian Cultural Revolution). 3 vols. Wuhan: Hubei sheng geming weiyuanhui, 1968–69.

Hubei zhengfa shizhi bianxuan weiyuanhui, ed. *Hubei zhengfa dashiji, 1838–1986* (A Record of Major Events in Politics and Law in Hubei, 1838–1986). Wuhan: Hubei zhengfa shizhi bianxuan weiyuanhui, 1987.

Hucker, Charles O. *China's Imperial Past: An Introduction to Chinese History and Culture*. Stanford: Stanford University Press, 1975.

Hudson, G. F., Richard Lowenthal, and Roderick MacFarquhar, eds. *The Sino-Soviet Dispute*. New York: Praeger, 1961.

Hunter, Neale. *Shanghai Journal: An Eyewitness Account of the Cultural Revolution*. Boston: Beacon, 1971.

Huyu!! Tehao (Appeal!!). Handbill. Schoenhals collection.

I Peking vid årsskiftet (Beijing at the Start of the New Year). Letter from Swedish embassy in Beijing to ministry in Stockholm. January 7, 1967. Swedish Ministry for Foreign Affairs archive, Stockholm.

Important Documents on the Great Proletarian Cultural Revolution in China. Peking: Foreign Languages Press, 1970.

Janis, Irving L. *Victims of Groupthink: A Psychological Study of Foreign-Policy Decisions and Fiascoes.* Boston: Houghton Mifflin, 1972.

Jarman, Robert L., ed. *China Political Reports 1961–1970.* Vol. 3: *1965–1970.* Chippenham: Archive Editions, 2003.

Ji Xichen. *Shi wuqianliede niandai: Yiwei "Renmin ribao" lao jizhede biji* (A Historically Unprecedented Decade: Notes of a *People's Daily* Reporter). 2 vols. Beijing: Renmin ribao chubanshe, 2001.

Jia Lanxun. "Tie shen weishi yi Shaoqi mengnan" (Memories of a Private Guard: How Liu Shaoqi Met with Disaster). *Bainian chao,* no. 1 (2000), 9–18.

———— "Tie shen weishi yi Shaoqi mengnan, xu" (Memories of a Private Guard: How Liu Shaoqi Met with Disaster, continued). *Bainian chao,* no. 2 (2000), 16–29, 55.

Jiang Benliang. "'Kangke shijian' yu Zhou Enlaide 'liuba' jianghua" (The "Czech Incident" and Zhou Enlai's "'68" Speech). *Zhonggong dangshi ziliao,* no. 72 (December 1999), 36–44.

Jiang Bo and Li Qing, eds. *Lin Biao 1959 nian yihou* (Lin Biao after 1959). Chengdu: Sichuan renmin chubanshe, 1993.

Jiang Qing tongzhi jianghua xuanbian (Selected Speeches by Comrade Jiang Qing). Beijing: Renmin chubanshe, 1968.

"Jiang Qing, Yao Wenyuan, Chi Qun, Xie Jingyi zai zhongyang zhishu jiguan he guojia jiguan pi-Lin pi-Kong dongyuan dahui shangde jianghua" (Speeches by Jiang Qing, Yao Wenyuan, Chi Qun, and Xie Jingyi at a Criticize-Lin Criticize-Confucius Mobilization Rally for Staff of Organs Directly under the Party Center and Central Government). January 25, 1974. Available at Fairbank Center Library.

"Jiang Weiqing tongzhi chuanda zhongyang lingdao tongzhi jianghua jingshen" (Comrade Jiang Weiqing Transmits the Spirit of a Central Leading Comrade's Speech). October 26, 1975. Beijing. Typed original transcript from anti-Deng campaign in spring 1976. Available at Fairbank Center Library.

Jiangsu Nanjing shi caimao xitong geming zaofan lianhe weiyuanhui. "Guanyu xuexi Shijiazhuang shi kaizhan 'san zhong yu' huodong qingkuang de huibao" (Report on Learning from the Development of "Three Loyalties" Activities in Shijiazhuang Municipality). Mimeograph. Nanjing, June 28, 1968.

Jianguo yilai Mao Zedong wengao (Mao Zedong's Papers since the Founding of the State). 13 vols. Beijing: Zhongyang wenxian chubanshe, 1987–1998.

Jiaoyu geming (Revolution in Education). Beijing: Beijing Normal University.

Jiedai tongxun (Reception Newsletter). Shanghai: Shanghai Revolutionary Committee Reception Office.

Jiefangjun bao (Liberation Army News).

Jiefangjun jiangling zhuan. See Xinghuo liaoyuan bianjibu.

Jieke Keruyake. *Zai lushang* (On the Road). Beijing: Zuojia chubanshe, 1962.

Jin Chongji, ed. *Zhou Enlai zhuan (1949–1976)* (Biography of Zhou Enlai [1949–1976]). 2 vols. Beijing: Zhongyang wenxian chubanshe, 1998.

Jin Chunming. "Siwu yundong shuping" (Critical Account of the April 5 Movement). In Zhang Hua and Su Caiqing, eds., *Huishou "Wenge,"* 2: 1231–49.

——— *"Wenhua dageming" shigao* (Historical Sketch of the "Great Cultural Revolution"). Chengdu: Sichuan renmin chubanshe, 1995.

Jin Chunming, Huang Yuchong, and Chang Huimin. *"Wenge" shiqi guaishi guaiyu* (Strange Things and Strange Discourse during the Period of the "Cultural Revolution"). Beijing: Qiushi chubanshe, 1989.

Jin Ge. "Zai waijiaobu 'duoquan' qian hou" (The Background to the "Seizure of Power" in the Foreign Ministry). In An Jianshe, ed., *Zhou Enlaide zuihou suiyue*, pp. 207–243.

Jin Lei. "Fasheng zai 1966–1976 niande teda ziran zaihai" (Extremely Serious Natural Disasters That Occurred in 1966–1976). *Dangdai Zhongguo shi yanjiu*, no. 4 (1997), 75–77.

Jin Qiu. *The Culture of Power: The Lin Biao Incident in the Cultural Revolution.* Stanford: Stanford University Press, 1999.

Jin Yanfeng, ed. *Dangdai Zhejiang jianshi (1949–1998)* (A Short History of Contemporary Zhejiang [1949–1998]). Beijing: Dangdai Zhongguo chubanshe, 2000.

Jing Jun. *The Temple of Memories: History, Power, and Morality in a Chinese Village.* Stanford: Stanford University Press, 1996.

Jing'aide Zhou zongli yongyuan huo zai women xinzhong (Respected and Beloved Premier Zhou Lives Forever in Our Hearts). Beijing: Shoudu jixiechang, 1978.

"Jiuda" ziliao huibian (Collected Materials from the "Ninth Congress"). Ji'nan: Ji'nan tieluju Ji'nan cheliangduan 5.7 zhongxue, 1969.

Johnston, Alastair Iain. "Party Rectification in the PLA, 1983–87." *CQ*, no. 112 (December 1987), 591–630.

Joint Publications Research Service (JPRS). Springfield, Va.: National Technical Information Service.

Joseph, William A. *The Critique of Ultra-Leftism in China, 1958–1981.* Stanford: Stanford University Press, 1984.

Joseph, William, Christine P. W. Wong, and David Zweig, eds. *New Perspectives on the Cultural Revolution.* Cambridge, Mass.: Council on East Asian Studies, Harvard University, 1991.

Kang Sheng. "Zai ba jie shier zhong quanhui di si xiaozu huiyi shang de fayan" (Statement at the Meeting of the Fourth Group at the Twelfth Plenum of the Eighth Central Committee). In Zhonggong Beijing shiwei dangxiao ziliaoshi, ed., *Kang Sheng yanlun xuanbian*, 3: 81–85.

"Kang Sheng tongzhi jiejian chuxi zhongyang he quanjun zhengdang jiandang gongzuo zuotanhui quanti tongzhi shide jianghua" (Kang Sheng's Speech at the Reception for Comrades Attending the Work Forum on All-Party and All-Military Consolidation and Rebuilding). April 18, 1970. Photocopy of an original contemporary transcript. Available at Fairbank Center Library.

"Kang Sheng tongzhi zai zhongzhi jiguan chuanda 'jiuda' jingshen dahui shangde zhongyao jianghua" (Comrade Kang Sheng's Important Speech Transmitting the Spirit of the "Ninth Congress" to Central Organs). May 23, 1969. Copy in Fairbank Center Library.

Kang Sheng yanlun xuanbian. See Zhonggong Beijing shiwei dangxiao ziliaoshi, ed., *Kang Sheng yanlun xuanbian.*

Kau, Michael Y. M., ed. *The Lin Piao Affair: Power Politics and Military Coup.* White Plains, N.Y.: International Arts and Sciences Press, 1975.

Kedong xianzhi (Kedong County Gazetteer). Harbin: Heilongjiang renmin chubanshe, 1987.

Kershaw, Ian. *Hitler.* 2 vols. London: Allen Lane, 1998, 2000.

Kissinger, Henry. *White House Years.* Boston: Little Brown, 1979.

Klein, Donald W., and Anne B. Clark. *Biographic Dictionary of Chinese Communism, 1921–1965.* 2 vols. Cambridge, Mass.: Harvard University Press, 1971.

Knight, Sophia. *Window on Shanghai: Letters from China, 1965–1967.* London: Andre Deutsch, 1967.

Kunming nonglin xueyuan geming weiyuanhui zhengxuanzu, ed. *Qingli jieji duiwu ziliao huibian* (Collected Materials on Cleansing the Class Ranks). Kunming, 1969.

Kwong, Julia. *Cultural Revolution in China's Schools, May 1966–April 1969.* Stanford: Hoover Institution Press, 1988.

Ladany, Laszlo. *The Communist Party of China and Marxism, 1921–1985: A Self-Portrait.* Stanford: Hoover Institution Press, 1988.

Lanzhou junqu zhengzhibu zuzhibu, ed. *Zuzhi gongzuo wenjian huibian di er ji: Dangwu gongzuo bufen* (Collected Documents on Organization Work, Vol. 2: Party Work). Lanzhou, 1980.

Lee Hong Yung. *The Politics of the Chinese Cultural Revolution.* Berkeley: University of California Press, 1978.

Legge, James. *The Chinese Classics.* Vol. 2: *The Works of Mencius.* Reprint, Taipei: Southern Materials Center, 1983.

——— *The Chinese Classics: With a Translation, Critical and Exegetical Notes, Prolegomena, and Copious Indexes.* 7 vols. Oxford: Clarendon Press, 1893.

Leng Rong and Wang Zuoling, eds. *Deng Xiaoping nianpu, 1975–1997* (Chronicle of the Life of Deng Xiaoping, 1975–1997). 2 vols. Beijing: Zhongyang wenxian chubanshe, 2004.

Letter from Liu Bing et al. to Mao Zedong. August 13, 1975. Copy of contemporary transcript at Fairbank Center Library.

———— October 13, 1975. Copy of contemporary transcript at Fairbank Center Library.

Lewis, John Wilson, and Xue Litai. *China Builds the Bomb.* Stanford: Stanford University Press, 1988.

Li Danhui. "1969 nian Zhong Su bianjie chongtu: Yuanqi he jieguo" (The Sino-Soviet Border Conflict in 1969: Origins and Consequences). In Zhang Hua and Su Caiqing, eds., *Huishou "Wenge,"* 2: 903–923.

Li Jinchuan. "Huiyi zhongyang wenge jizhe zhan" (Remembering the Central Cultural Revolution Group's Journalists' Station). *Bainian chao,* no. 5 (2002), 12–17.

Li Ke and Hao Shengzhang. *"Wenhua dageming" zhongde renmin jiefangjun* (The PLA during the "Great Cultural Revolution"). Beijing: Zhonggong dangshi ziliao chubanshe, 1989.

Li Naiyin. "Cong Yao Wenyuan de zhaji an 'sirenbang' fumie qian de zuie xintai" (The Criminal State of Mind of the "Gang of Four" Prior to Their Demise as Reflected in Yao Wenyuan's Reading Notes). *Yanhuang chunqiu,* no. 9 (1997), 36–40.

———— "'Sirenbang' beishen qijian choutai tu" (Pictures of the Ugly Performance of the "Gang of Four" on Trial). *Yanhuang chunqiu,* no. 7 (1997), 42–46.

Li Ping'an et al., eds. *Shaanxi jingji dashiji, 1949–1985* (A Chronicle of Major Economic Events in Shaanxi, 1949–1985). Xi'an: Sanqin chubanshe, 1987.

Li Xuefeng. "Wo suo zhidaode 'Wenge' fadong neiqing" (My Inside Knowledge of the Launching of the "Cultural Revolution"). In Zhang Hua and Su Caiqing, eds., *Huishou "Wenge,"* 2: 603–616.

Li Yong, ed. *Wenge mingrenzhi si* (The Deaths of Well-Known People during the Cultural Revolution). Taipei: Paise chubanshe, 1994.

Li Youping. *Douzheng yu shenghuo* (Struggle and Life). 5 vols. N.p., n.d.

Li Yunsun. "Du Wu Han wentide dingxing yiwen yougan" (Reaction from Reading the Nature of Wu Han's Problems). *Yanhuang chunqiu,* no. 5 (1998), 79.

Li Zhisui. *The Private Life of Chairman Mao,* trans. Tai Hung-chao. New York: Random House, 1994.

Lian Zhixiang, ed. *Dangdai Shanxi jianshi* (A Short History of Contemporary Shanxi). Beijing: Dangdai Zhongguo chubanshe, 1999.

Liang Biye jiangjun zishu (General Liang Biye's Account). Shenyang: Liaoning renmin chubanshe, 1997.

Liang Heng and Judith Shapiro. *Son of the Revolution.* New York: Knopf, 1983.

Liao Gailong, ed. *Xin Zhongguo biannianshi (1949–1989)* (The Annals of New China [1949–1989]). Beijing: Renmin chubanshe, 1989.

Liao Shiyu. "1966 nian, Mao Zedong xiata dishuidong" (Mao Zedong's 1966 Stay in Dishuidong). In Zhonggong Xiangtan shiwei dangshi ziliao zhengji bangongshi, ed., *Mao Zedong yu Xiangtan,* pp. 346–352.

Liao Yiwu. "The Public Toilet Manager." *Paris Review*, no. 174 (Summer 2005), 181–189.

Lieberthal, Kenneth. *Governing China*. New York: Norton, 1995.

Lieberthal, Kenneth, with the assistance of James Tong and Sai-cheung Yeung. *Central Documents and Politburo Politics in China*. Michigan Papers in Chinese Studies No. 33. Ann Arbor: Center for Chinese Studies, University of Michigan, 1978.

Li-I-Che. "On Socialist Democracy and the Legal System." *Chinese Law and Government*, 10, no. 3 (Fall 1977), 40–61.

Lin Biao. "Tingqu Zeng Siyu, Liu Feng tongzhi huibao shide chahua yiji ting huibao houde zhishi" (Instructions Issued during and after Reporting and Interjections Made While Listening to Report from Comrades Zeng Siyu and Liu Feng). Mimeographed anonymous contemporary transcript. August(?) 1967. Copy in Fairbank Center Library.

Lin Biao tongzhi youguan wuchanjieji wenhua dageming de zhishi (Comrade Lin Biao's Instructions concerning the Great Proletarian Cultural Revolution). Beijing: Zhongguo kexue yuan, 1967.

Lin Biao wenxuan (Selected Writings of Lin Biao), ed. Xi'an yejin jianzhu xueyuan geming weiyuanhui xuanchuanbu. 2 vols. Xi'an: Yejin jianzhu xueyuan, 1967.

"Lin Biao zai Zhonggong ba jie kuodade shier zhong quanhui di er ci huiyi shangde jianghua" (Lin Biao's Speech at the Second Session of the Enlarged Twelfth Plenum of the Eighth Central Committee of the CCP). In Zhonggong zhongyang bangongting, ed., *Canyue wenjian*, 12: 38–39.

Lin Haoji. "Beida di yi zhang dazibao shi zenyang chulongde" (How the First Big-Character Poster Appeared at Peking University). In Zhou Ming, ed., *Lishi zai zheli chensi*, 2: 27–35.

Ling, Ken. *Red Guard: From Schoolboy to "Little General" in Mao's China*. London: Macdonald, 1972.

Ling Yun. "Kang Sheng weihe zhizao 'mousha Su Mei' an" (Why Did Kang Sheng Fabricate the "Su Mei Murder" Case?). In Zhu Chunlin, ed., *Lishi shunjian*, 1: 90–105.

Lishide shenpan (The Verdict of History). 2 vols. Beijing: Qunzhong chubanshe, 1981.

Liu Dinghan, ed. *Dangdai Jiangsu jianshi* (A Short History of Contemporary Jiangsu). Beijing: Dangdai Zhongguo chubanshe, 1999.

Liu Gao and Shi Feng, eds. *Xin Zhongguo chu ban wushinian jishi* (A Record of Fifty Years of Publishing in New China). Beijing: Xinhua chubanshe, 1999.

Liu Hong. *Startling Moon*. London: Review, 2001.

Liu Pingping, Liu Yuan, and Liu Tingting. "Shengli de xianhua xiangei ni: Huainian women de baba Liu Shaoqi" (Fresh Flowers We Give to You: Cherishing the Memory of Our Father Liu Shaoqi). In Zhou Ming, ed., *Lishi zai zheli chensi*, 1: 1–48.

Liu Shaoqi. *Collected Works of Liu Shao-ch'i, 1958–1967.* Hong Kong: Union Research Institute, 1968.

—— See Zhonggong zhongyang tongzhanbu Geming zaofantuan and Hongwuyue bingtuan cailiaozu, eds., *Zhongguo Heluxiaofu Liu Shaoqi zai tongyi zhanxian fangmiande fangeming xiuzhengzhuyi yanlun xuanbian.*

Liu Shaoqi fangeming xiuzhengzhuyi yanlun huibian. See Zhongguo kexueyuan geming lishi yanjiusuo jindai gemingshi yanjiusuo, eds., *Liu Shaoqi fangeming xiuzhengzhuyi yanlun huibian.*

"Liu Shaoqi Kong miao chao sheng" (Liu Shaoqi's Pilgrimage to the Confucius Temple). Essay denouncing Liu (pp. 1–4) in a 137-page collection with cover page and hence title missing. Shanghai, 1967. Schoenhals collection.

Liu Shaoqi nianpu. See Zhonggong zhongyang wenxian yanjiushi, ed., *Liu Shaoqi nianpu, 1898–1969.*

Liu Shaoqi shi Zhongguo de Heluxiaofu (Liu Shaoqi Is China's Khrushchev). Beijing, 1966.

"Liu Shaoqi tongzhi tong Wulanfu tongzhi tanhua jilu" (Record of Conversation between Comrades Liu Shaoqi and Ulanfu). July 2, 1966. Photocopy of transcript from Cultural Revolution. Available at Fairbank Center Library.

Liu Shaoqi zai gedi sanbude xiuzhengzhuyi yanlun huibian. See Zhonggong Shanghai shiwei bangongting geming zaofandui, ed., *Liu Shaoqi zai gedi sanbude xiuzhengzhuyi yanlun huibian.*

Liu Shunhui. "Zeng Shan" (Zeng Shan). In Zhonggong dangshi renwu yanjiuhui, ed., *Zhonggong dangshi renwu zhuan*, 25 (published 1985): 239–268.

Liu Tao, ed. *Da chuanlian* (Great Exchange of Revolutionary Experiences). Beijing: Zhishi chubanshe, 1993.

Liu Zhinan. "Jiuda zhi jiu jie er zhong quanhui qian xi Mao Zedong yu Lin Biaode fenqi he maodun" (The Split and Contradictions between Mao Zedong and Lin Biao from the Ninth Congress to the Eve of the Second Plenum). *Dangdai Zhongguo shi yanjiu*, no. 3 (1997), 38–48.

Lo, Ruth Earnshaw, and Katharine S. Kinderman. *In the Eye of the Typhoon.* New York: Harcourt Brace Jovanovich, 1980.

Lu Haijiang and He Mingzhou, eds. *Mao Zedong he ta tongshidaide ren* (Mao Zedong and His Contemporaries). Zhengzhou: Henan renmin chubanshe, 1992.

Lü Hong. "Wo ren hongweibing jiedai zongzhan zhanzhang de rizi" (My Days as Director of the Red Guard General Reception Station). *Yanhuang chunqiu*, no. 12 (1998), 44–48.

Lu Yongdi and Liu Zijian. "Fang Fang" (Fang Fang). In Zhonggong dangshi renwu yanjiuhui, ed., *Zhonggong dangshi renwu zhuan*, 11 (published 1983): 323–368.

"Lun paixing de fandongxing" (On the Reactionary Nature of Factionalism). Reprinted in *Renmin ribao*, January 15, 1968.

Luo Diandian. "Luo zongzhang mengnan jishi" (A Record of Chief of Staff Luo Confronted by Dangers). In Cheng Min, ed., *Haojie chuqi*, pp. 204–248.

Luo Ruiqing. "Zai quanguo jingji baowei gongzuo huiyi shangde zongjie baogao" (Summing-Up Report at the National Economic Protection Work Conference). *Gongan baowei gongzuo*, no. 18 (June 1, 1950), 4–24.

Ma Bo. *Blood Red Sunset*. New York: Viking, 1995.

Ma Jisen. *The Cultural Revolution in the Foreign Ministry of China*. Hong Kong: Chinese University Press, 2004.

Ma Qibin et al., eds. *Zhongguo gongchandang zhizheng sishinian (1949–1989)* (The CCP's Forty Years in Power [1949–1989]). Rev. ed. Beijing: Zhonggong dangshi ziliao chubanshe, 1991.

Ma Tianshui. "Wode buchong jiefa jiaodai" (My Supplementary Exposé and Testimony). Shanghai: Shanghai shi qu, xian, ju dangyuan fuze ganbu huiyi mishuzu, November 1976. Original in Schoenhals collection.

—— "Wode jiefa jiaodai" (My Exposé and Testimony). Shanghai: Shanghai shi qu, xian, ju dangyuan fuze ganbu huiyi mishuzu, November 5, 1976. Original in Schoenhals collection.

MacFarquhar, Roderick. "China after the 10th Congress." *World Today*, 29, no. 12 (December 1973), 514–526.

—— *The Origins of the Cultural Revolution*. 3 vols. New York: Columbia University Press, 1974, 1983, 1997.

—— *Sino-American Relations, 1949–1971*. New York: Praeger, 1972.

—— "The Succession to Mao and the End of Maoism, 1969–82." In MacFarquhar, ed., *The Politics of China: Second Edition*, pp. 248–339.

——, ed. *The Hundred Flowers Campaign and the Chinese Intellectuals*. New York: Praeger, 1960.

——, ed. *The Politics of China: Second Edition, The Eras of Mao and Deng*. New York: Cambridge University Press, 1997.

Mann, James. *About Face: A History of America's Curious Relationship with China from Nixon to Clinton*. New York: Knopf, 1999.

Mao Mao. *Wode fuqin Deng Xiaoping "Wenge" suiyue* (My Father Deng Xiaoping's "Cultural Revolution" Years). Beijing: Zhongyang wenxian chubanshe, 2000.

Mao Zedong. "Fandui zhezhongzhuyide wenti" (On Opposing Eclecticism). In *Mao Zedong sixiang wan sui (1960–1967)*.

—— "Guanyu Luo Ruiqing de tanhua" (Remarks concerning Luo Ruiqing). In *Mao Zedong sixiang wan sui (1960–1967)*.

—— "Oppose Bookism." May 1930. Translated in Schram, ed., *Mao's Road to Power*, 3: 425.

—— *Selected Works of Mao Tse-tung*. 4 vols. Peking: Foreign Languages Press, 1965.

—— *Selected Works of Mao Tse-tung*. 4 vols. Peking: Foreign Languages Press, 1967.

———— "4.28 jianghua" (Speech on April 28 [1969]). Copy of handwritten transcript available at Fairbank Center Library.

Mao Zedong shuxin xuanji (Selection of Mao Zedong's Letters). Beijing: Renmin chubanshe, 1983.

Mao Zedong sixiang de guanghui zhaoyaozhe zhongyang guangbo shiyeju (The Brilliant Rays of Mao Zedong Thought Illuminate the Central Broadcasting Administration). Beijing: Zhongyang guangbo shiyeju "Wuchanjieji gemingpai lianhe zongbu," 1968.

Mao Zedong sixiang hongweibing Wuhan diqu geming zaofan silingbu, ed. *Yong xianxue he shengming baowei Mao zhuxi* (Defending Chairman Mao with Our Blood and Lives). Wuhan, 1967.

Mao Zedong sixiang wan sui (Long Live Mao Zedong Thought). [Shanghai?], [1968?].

Mao Zedong sixiang wan sui (1958–59) (Long Live Mao Zedong Thought [1958–59]). N.p., n.d.

Mao Zedong sixiang wan sui (1960–1967) (Long Live Mao Zedong Thought [1960–1967]). N.p., n.d.

Mao Zedong sixiang wan sui (xu er) (Long Live Mao Zedong Thought [Supplement II]). Beijing: Zhongguo renmin daxue, 1967.

Mao zhuxi Lin fuzhuxi guanyu baokan xuanchuan de zhishi (Chairman Mao's and Vice Chairman Lin's Instructions on Press and Propaganda). N.p., 1970.

"Mao zhuxi 69.8–69.9 shicha da Jiang nanbei de jianghua" (Remarks Made by Chairman Mao during an Inspection Tour North and South of the Yangtze in August–September 1969). Copy of handwritten transcript in Fairbank Center Library.

"Mao zhuxi 69.4.11 jianghua" (Chairman Mao's Speech on April 11, 1969). Copy of handwritten transcript in Fairbank Center Library.

"Mao zhuxi 71 nian 8 yue zhi 9 yue shicha nanfang shide jici jianghua" (Chairman Mao's Remarks during His Inspection of the South in August–September 1971). Copy of handwritten transcript in Fairbank Center Library.

Mao zhuxi yulu (Quotations from Chairman Mao). Beijing, 1966.

Mao zhuxi yulu suoyin (Index to Chairman Mao's Quotations). N.p., 1970.

"Mao zhuxi zai dangde ba jie kuodade shier zhong quanhui shangde jianghua" (Speech by Chairman Mao at the Enlarged Twelfth Plenum of the Party's Eighth Central Committee). Copy in Fairbank Center Library.

"Mao zhuxi zai 69.4.5 (jiuda) de jianghua" (Chairman Mao's Speech on April 5, 1969 [at the Ninth Congress]). Handwritten copy in Fairbank Center Library.

Mao zhuxi zai Zhongguo gongchandang di jiu ci quanguo daibiao dahui shangde zhongyao zhishi (Chairman Mao's Important Instructions at the CCP's Ninth Congress). N.p., 1969.

Masi, Edoarda. *China Winter: Workers, Mandarins, and the Purge of the Gang of Four.* New York: Dutton, 1982.

Mathews, Jay. "China's '76 Riot." *Washington Post Foreign Service,* January 31, 1978.

McGregor, Richard. "China's Official Data Confirm Rise in Social Unrest." *Financial Times* (Asia Edition), January 20, 2006, p. 2.

Meizhou wenzhai (Weekly Extracts). Shanghai[?]: Liberation Daily[?].

Mendl, Wolf. *Issues in Japan's China Policy.* London: Macmillan for RIIA, 1978.

Milton, David, and Nancy Milton. *The Wind Will Not Subside.* New York: Pantheon, 1976.

Min, Anchee. *Becoming Madame Mao.* Boston: Houghton Mifflin, 2000.

——— *Red Azalea.* New York: Pantheon, 1994.

Mingling (Order). Handbill. Schoenhals collection.

Minzu yanjiusuo Jinggangshan bingtuan, ed. *Pan Zinian Wu Chuanqi Lin Yushi Hong Tao Wang Enyu fandang jituan de taotian zuixing dazibao cailiao huibian* (Collected Big-Character Posters and Materials on the Heinous Crimes of the Counterrevolutionary Clique of Pan Zinian, Wu Chuanqi, Lin Yushi, Hong Tao, and Wang Enyu). Beijing, 1967.

Miscellany of Mao Tse-tung Thought (1949–1968). 2 vols. Arlington, Va.: Joint Publications Research Service, 1974.

Mu Aiping. *Vermilion Gate.* London: Abacus, 2002.

Mu Xin. *Ban "Guangming ribao" shinian zishu (1957–1967)* (Personal Account of Running the *Guangming Daily* for a Decade [1957–1967]). Beijing: Zhonggong dangshi chubanshe, 1994.

——— "Guanyu gongzuozu cunfei wenti" (On the Issue of Maintaining or Withdrawing the Work Teams). *Dangdai Zhongguo shi yanjiu,* no. 2 (1997), 55–64. Reprinted in Zhang Hua and Su Caiqing, eds., *Huishou "Wenge,"* 2: 637–651.

——— "Guanyu 'zhongyang wenge xiaozu' de yixie qingkuang" (Some Circumstances about the "Central Cultural Revolution Group"). *Zhonggong dangshi ziliao,* no. 69 (1999), 63–94.

——— *Jiehou changyi: Shinian dongluan jishi* (Thoughts after the Crisis: A Chronicle of the Decade of Upheaval). Hong Kong: Xintian chubanshe, 1997.

——— "'Quanguo di yi zhang dazibao' chulong jingguo" (How the "First Big-Character Poster" Came About). *Zhonggong dangshi ziliao,* no. 75 (September 2000), 166–173.

Mueggler, Erik. *The Age of Wild Ghosts: Memory, Violence, and Place in Southwest China.* Berkeley: University of California Press, 2001.

Myers, James T., Jürgen Domes, and Erik von Groeling, eds. *Chinese Politics: Documents and Analysis.* 4 vols. Columbia: University of South Carolina Press, 1986.

Nankai daxue "8.18" hongse zaofantuan, ed. *Lishi de tiezheng* (The Iron Proof of History). Tianjin, 1967.

Naughton. Barry. "Industrial Policy during the Cultural Revolution: Military Preparation, Decentralization, and Leaps Forward." In Joseph, Wong, and Zweig, eds., *New Perspectives on the Cultural Revolution*, pp. 153–181.

Nee, Victor. *The Cultural Revolution at Peking University*. New York: Monthly Review Press, 1969.

Neibu cankao (Internal Reference). Beijing: First Ministry of Machine Building.

Neibu cankao bianjibu, ed. *Guanyu qingli jieji duiwu wenti (cailiao huibian)* (On Cleansing the Class Ranks [Collected Materials]). N.p., 1968.

Neibu ziliao (Internal Materials). Beijing: Tsinghua University Jinggangshan Battle Operations Group.

Neimenggu Wulanfu yanjiuhui, ed. *Wulanfu nianpu* (A Chronicle of the Life of Ulanfu). 2 vols. Beijing: Zhonggong dangshi chubanshe, 1996.

Neimenggu zizhiqu dashiji (Record of Major Events in the Inner Mongolian Autonomous Region). Huhehot: Neimenggu renmin chubanshe, 1988.

Nie Rongzhen. *Inside the Red Star*. Beijing: New World Press, 1988.

Nie Yuanzi huiyilu (The Memoirs of Nie Yuanzi). Hong Kong: Shidai guoji chuban youxian gongsi, 2005.

Niu Dayong. Original ms. on Lei Yingfu. Schoenhals collection.

Nixon, Richard. *RN: The Memoirs of Richard Nixon*. London: Book Club Associates, 1978.

Opletal, Helmut. *Die Informationspolitik der Volksrepublik China* (The Information Policy of the People's Republic of China). Bochum: Brockmeyer, 1981.

Origins. See MacFarquhar, Roderick, *Origins of the Cultural Revolution*.

Pang Xianzhi and Jin Chongji. *Mao Zedong zhuan, 1949–1976* (The Life of Mao Zedong, 1949–1976). 2 vols. Beijing: Zhongyang wenxian chubanshe, 2003.

Paper Collection: International Senior Forum on Contemporary History of China: Contemporary China and Its Outside World. Beijing: Contemporary China Research Institute, 2004.

Peking Review. Beijing.

Peng Zhen guanyu siqing yundong de liu pian jianghua (Six Speeches by Peng Zhen on the Four Clean-ups Movement). Beijing: Zhonggong Beijing shiwei bangongting, 1966.

Peng Zhen wenxuan (1941–1990) (Selected Works of Peng Zhen [1941–1990]). Beijing: Renmin chubanshe, 1991.

Pepper, Suzanne. *Radicalism and Education Reform in 20th-Century China: The Search for an Ideal Development Model*. New York: Cambridge University Press, 1996.

Perry, Elizabeth, and Li Xun. *Proletarian Power: Shanghai in the Cultural Revolution*. Boulder: Westview, 1997.

Petri, Lennart. *Sverige i stora världen: Minnen och reflexioner från 40 års diplomattjänst*

(Sweden in the Big World: Remembering and Reflecting upon 40 Years of Diplomatic Service). Stockholm: Atlantis, 1996.

Phathanothai, Sirin, with James Peck. *The Dragon's Pearl*. New York: Simon & Schuster, 1994.

Pipan Liu, Deng luxian xin daibiao Tao Zhu dahui fayan (Speeches at the Mass Rally to Denounce the New Representative of the Liu-Deng Line, Tao Zhu). Beijing, 1967.

PLA General Political Department, comp. *Zhua huo sixiangde 60 duo ge zenme ban?* (60 Examples of How to Deal with Living Thoughts). Beijing: Zhonggong zhongyang guofang gongye zhengzhibu, 1966.

Plato. *The Republic,* trans. Benjamin Jowett. Mineola, N.Y.: Dover, 2000.

The Polemic on the General Line of the International Communist Movement. Peking: Foreign Languages Press, 1965.

Pollack, Jonathan D. "The Opening to America." In Fairbank and MacFarquhar, eds., *Cambridge History of China,* pp. 402–472.

Pomfret, John. "Currency Events: A Great Leap Backward?" http://www.washingtonpost.com/wp-dyn/articles/A52632-2002Jan28.html.

Poon, David Jim-tat. "*Tatzepao:* Its History and Significance as Communication Medium." In Chu, ed., *Popular Media in China,* pp. 184–221.

Public Record Office. Kew. FCO 21/33. Confidential draft. Registry No. FCI/14.

———— FCO 21/34. "The Burning of the British Office in Peking." Mr. Hopson to Mr. Brown. Confidential. September 8, 1967. FC 1/14.

———— FCO 21/84, TELNO 1801. Confidential message to Government of Hong Kong. August 31.

———— FCO 40/160. Top secret, K(69)1.

———— FCO 40/160. Top Secret and Personal Comments by James Murray on a draft paper by Michael Wilford. November 17, 1969.

———— FO 371/186/80. Restricted telegram from Donald Hopson, U.K. chargé d'affaires, Beijing, to Foreign Office, London, No. 422 (repeated for distribution as No. 425). "Campaign against anti-Party elements." June 4, 1966.

Qing Ye and Fang Lei. *Deng Xiaoping zai 1976* (Deng Xiaoping in 1976). 2 vols. Shenyang: Chunfeng wenyi chubanshe, 1993.

Qinghai 8.18 geming zaofanpai lianhe weiyuanhui xuanchuanzu, ed. *Ziliao xuanbian: Zhongyang shouzhang jianghua zhuanji* (Selected Material: Special Collection of Central Leaders' Speeches). Xining, 1967.

Qinghua daxue dazibao xuanbian (Selection of Tsinghua University Big-Character Posters). N.p., n.d.

Qinghua daxue "Guo Da Jiang." "Chen Yi jiancha dahui jilu" (Record of Chen Yi Self-investigation Mass Rally). Mimeograph, 5 pp. January 31, 1967. Schoenhals collection.

Qinghua daxue Jinggangshan bingtuan dazibao bianweihui, ed. *Dadao fangeming xiuzhengzhuyi fenzi Bo Yibo* (Down with the Counterrevolutionary Revisionist Element Bo Yibo). Beijing, 1967.

Qinghua daxue Jinggangshan hongweibing xuanchuandui, ed. *Qinghua daxue Kuai Dafu tongxue dazibao xuan* (Selected Big-Character Posters by Tsinghua University Student Kuai Dafu). Guiyang, 1967.

Qinghua Jinggangshan tongxunshe (Tsinghua Jingganshan News Agency). Individual transcripts. Beijing, n.d.

Qingli jieji duiwu xuexi ziliao (Cleansing the Class Ranks Study Materials). [Shanghai], 1969.

Qiu Shi, ed. *Gongheguo zhongda shijian he juece neimu* (The Inside Story of the Major Incidents and Decisions of the [Chinese People's] Republic). 2 vols. Beijing: Jingji ribao chubanshe, 1997.

Quan Yanchi. *Tao Zhu zai "Wenhua dageming" zhong* (Tao Zhu during the "Great Cultural Revolution"). Beijing: Zhongyang dangxiao chubanshe, 1991.

———— *Weixing: Yang Chengwu zai 1967* (Traveling Incognito: Yang Chengwu in 1967). Guangzhou: Guangdong lüyou chubanshe, 1997.

Quanguo chedi daohui Kongjiadian shuli Mao Zedong sixiang juedui quanwei geming zaofan lianluozhan, ed. *Gaoju Mao Zedong sixiang weida hongqi, chedi qingsuan zun-Kong fugu de fangeming zuixing—Qufu xian pinxiazhongnong yong jieji douzheng xuelei shi tongchi Kong laoer de tuzi tusun* (Hold Aloft the Great Red Banner of Mao Zedong Thought and Thoroughly Eradicate the Counterrevolutionary Crimes of Confucius-Veneration and Restoration of Ancient Ways— The Poor and Lower-Middle Peasants of Qufu County Use Class Struggle to Bitterly Denounce the Second Son of the Kong Family, His Hangers-on, and Their Spawn). N.p., [1966].

"Quarterly Chronicle and Documentation." *CQ*, nos. 27 (July–September 1966), 191– 226; 28 (October–December 1966), 146–194; 30 (April–June 1967), 195–249; 31 (July–September 1967), 176–223; 32 (October–December 1967), 184–227; 64 (December 1975), 784–819; 65 (March 1976), 162–209; 66 (June 1976), 409–454; 67 (September 1976), 661–694; 68 (December 1976), 873–907.

Quotations from Chairman Mao Tse-tung. Peking: Foreign Languages Press, 1966.

Remarks by Liu Yusheng, Zhang Xiuqing, and other residents of Yangfang District Residential Area, Beijing, during debates organized by the Neighborhood Committee on August 30 and September 9, 1970. Untitled, handwritten. Schoenhals collection.

Renmin chubanshe ziliaoshi, ed. *Pipan ziliao: Zhongguo Heluxiaofu Liu Shaoqi fangeming xiuzhengzhuyi yanlun ji* (Collected Counterrevolutionary Revisionist Utterances by China's Khrushchev Liu Shaoqi). 3 vols. Beijing, 1968.

Renmin ribao (People's Daily).

Renmin ribao wenhua geming dongtai (*People's Daily* Cultural Revolution Trends). Beijing: Renmin ribao.

Renmin ribao wuchanjieji gemingpai and Shoudu xinwen pipan lianluozhan, eds. *Xinwen zhanxian liangtiao luxian douzheng dashiji, 1948–1966 (chugao)* (Chronology of the Struggle between the Two Lines on the News Front, 1948–1966 [Preliminary Draft]). Beijing, n.d.

Renshibu difang jigou bianzhi guanlisi, ed. *Zhonghua renmin gongheguo sheng, zizhiqu, zhixiashi dang sheng qun jiguan zuzhi jigou gaiyao* (Outline of the Organizational Structure of Party, Government, and Mass Organs in Provinces, Autonomous Regions, and Municipalities Directly Subordinate to the Central Government in the PRC). Beijing: Zhongguo renshi chubanshe, 1989.

"Report on the Problem of Lo Jui-ch'ing's Mistakes." *Chinese Law and Government*, 4, nos. 3–4 (Fall–Winter 1971–72), 287–314.

Resolution on CPC History (1949–1981). Beijing: Foreign Languages Press, 1981.

Rittenberg, Sidney, and Amanda Bennett. *The Man Who Stayed Behind*. New York: Simon & Schuster, 1993.

Robinson, Thomas W., ed. *The Cultural Revolution in China*. Berkeley: University of California Press, 1971.

Rosen, Stanley. *Red Guard Factionalism and the Cultural Revolution in Guangzhou (Canton)*. Boulder: Westview, 1982.

Ross, James R. *Caught in a Tornado*. Boston: Northeastern University Press, 1994.

Ross, Robert S. *Negotiating Cooperation: The United States and China, 1969–1989*. Stanford: Stanford University Press, 1995.

327 tongxun (The 327 Newsletter). [Guangzhou?]: New First Headquarters.

Schoenhals, Michael. "The Central Case Examination Group, 1966–1979." *CQ*, no. 145 (March 1996), 87–111.

——— *CCP Central Documents from the Cultural Revolution: Index to an Incomplete Data Base*. Stockholm: Center for Pacific Asia Studies, Stockholm University, 1993.

——— "Editor's Introduction: Guan Feng Is Back." *Chinese Studies in Philosophy*, 26, nos. 1–2 (Fall–Winter 1994–95), 3–10.

——— "Elite Information in China." *Problems of Communism*, 34 (September–October 1985), 65–71.

——— "Information, Decision-Making and China's 'Great Cultural Revolution'" (Xinxi, juece he Zhongguo de "wenhua dageming"). In *Paper Collection*, pp. 40–56.

——— "Mao Zedong: Speeches at the 1957 Moscow Conference." *Journal of Communist Studies*, 2, no. 2 (1986), 109–126.

——— "New Texts: Speeches at the Ninth National Congress of the Chinese Communist Party." *Stockholm Journal of East Asian Studies*, 2 (1990), 91–102.

——— "The 1978 Truth Criterion Controversy." *CQ*, no. 126 (June 1991), 243–268.

——— "A Question of Loyalty: China's Public Security Forces in 1967." Paper presented at the Association for Asian Studies annual meeting, Chicago, March 14, 1997.

———— *Saltationist Socialism: Mao Zedong and the Great Leap Forward, 1958.* Stockholm: Foreningen för Orientaliska Studier, 1987.

———— *Talk about a Revolution: Red Guards, Government Cadres and the Language of Political Discourse.* Working Paper Series on Language and Politics in Modern China No. 1. Bloomington: East Asian Studies Center, Indiana University, 1993.

———— "'Why Don't We Arm the Left?' Mao's Culpability for the Cultural Revolution's 'Great Chaos' of 1967." *CQ,* no. 182 (June 2005), 277–300.

————, ed. *China's Cultural Revolution, 1966–1969: Not a Dinner Party.* Armonk, N.Y.: M. E. Sharpe, 1996.

———— "Mao's Great Inquisition: The Central Case Examination Group, 1966–1979." *Chinese Law and Government,* 29, no. 3 (May–June 1996), 3–95.

Schram, Stuart R. *The Political Thought of Mao Tse-tung.* New York: Praeger, 1963.

————, ed. *Mao Tse-tung Unrehearsed.* Harmondsworth: Penguin, 1974.

———— *Mao's Road to Power: Revolutionary Writings, 1912–1949.* Vol. 3: *July 1927–December 1930.* Armonk, N.Y.: M. E. Sharpe, 1995.

Schwartz, Benjamin I. *Chinese Communism and the Rise of Mao.* Cambridge, Mass.: Harvard University Press, 1951.

"77 Conversations between Chinese and Foreign Leaders on the Wars in Indochina, 1964–1977." Working Paper No. 22, Woodrow Wilson Center, Cold War International History Project. Washington, D.C., May 1998.

Shangfang tongxun bianjishi, ed. *Chunfeng huayu ji* (Spring Wind Can Turn into Rain). 2 vols. Beijing: Qunzhong chubanshe, 1981.

Shanghae Almanac for 1853 and Miscellany. Shanghai: "Herald" Office, 1852.

Shanghai jixie xueyuan geming weiyuanhui "Hongse tingjinjun," ed. *Shede yishen gua, gan ba huangdi laxia ma* (He Who Doesn't Fear Being Cut to Pieces Dares Unseat the Emperor). 8 vols. Shanghai, 1967.

Shanghai minbing douzhengshi ziliaozu, ed. *Shanghai minbing douzheng shi ziliao* (Documents on the History of the Struggle of the Shanghai Militia). Shanghai, n.d.

Shanghai shi geming weiyuanhui jiedaizu, ed. *Xuexi ziliao* (Study Materials). Shanghai, n.d.

Shanghai shi gonganju geming zaofan lianhe zhihuibu zhengzhibu zaofandui, ed. *Chedi jielu shi gonganju jiu dangzu yuyong gongju–jiu wenge bangongshi de taotian zuixing* (Thoroughly Expose the Royal Tool of the Municipal Bureau of the Public Security Party Group and the Heinous Crimes of the Old Cultural Revolution Office). Shanghai, 1967.

Shanghai shi wenhuaju yundong bangongshi cailiaozu, ed. *"Sirenbang" jiqi yudang zai Shanghai wenhua xitongde fangeming xiuzhengzhuyi yanlun zhaibian (chugao)* (Collected Examples of the Counterrevolutionary Revisionist Utterances in the

Shanghai Cultural Sector Made by the "Gang of Four" and Their Ilk [First Draft]). Shanghai, 1977.

Shanghai "Wenge" shiliao zhengli bianzuan xiaozu. *Shanghai "Wenhua dageming" shihua* (Telling the History of the "Great Cultural Revolution" in Shanghai). 3 vols. Typeset manuscript. Shanghai, 1992.

Shangyebu jiguan hongse zaofantuan and Beijing shangxueyuan hongfanjun, eds. *Yao Yilin fan dang fan shehuizhuyi fan Mao Zedong sixiang zuixing* (Yao Yilin's Anti-Party, Anti-Socialist, and Anti–Mao Zedong Thought Crimes). Beijing, 1967.

Shanxi sheng gongye xue Daqing jingyan jiaoliu huiyi, ed. *Xuexi wenjian* (Study Documents). Taiyuan, 1971.

Shehuizhuyi wenhua dageming dazibao xuanbian (Selection of Big-Character Posters of the Socialist Great Cultural Revolution). Beijing: Municipal Party Committee Organs, n.d.

Shen Baoxiang. *Zhenli biaozhun wenti taolun shimo* (The Whole Story of the Truth Criterion Debate). Beijing: Zhongguo qingnian chubanshe, 1997.

Shen Kui, ed. *Dangdai Anhui jianshi* (A Short History of Contemporary Anhui). Beijing: Dangdai Zhongguo chubanshe, 2001.

Shi Dongbing. *Zuichude kangzheng: Peng Zhen zai wenhua dageming qianxi* (Resistance at the Beginning: Peng Zhen on the Eve of the Great Cultural Revolution). Beijing: Zhonggong zhongyang dangxiao chubanshe, 1993.

Shi Zhongquan et al., eds. *Zhonggong ba da shi* (The History of the CCP's Eighth Congress). Beijing: Renmin chubanshe, 1998.

Shirk, Susan L. *Competitive Comrades.* Berkeley: University of California Press, 1982.

Shoudu bufen dazhuan yuanxiao zhongdeng zhuanye xuexiao Mao Zedong sixiang xuexiban, ed. *Tianfan difu kaierkang—Wuchanjieji wenhua dageming dashiji* (Moved from Watching Heaven and Earth Turn Upside Down—Record of Major Events in the Great Proletarian Cultural Revolution). Rev. ed. Beijing, 1967.

Shoudu dazhuan yuanxiao hongweibing daibiao dahui Zhengfa gongshe, ed. *Zhongyang fuze tongzhi guanyu wuchanjieji wenhua dagemingde jianghua (bayue–shiyue)* (Speeches on the Great Proletarian Cultural Revolution by Responsible Comrades from the Center [August–October]). Beijing, 1967.

———— *Zhongyang fuze tongzhi guanyu wuchanjieji wenhua dagemingde jianghua (shiyiyue–shieryue)* (Speeches on the Great Proletarian Cultural Revolution by Responsible Comrades from the Center [November–December 1966]). Beijing, 1967.

Shoudu hongdaihui Beijing di er waiguoyu xueyuan hongweibing, ed. *Jiu ping Wang Li* (Nine Critiques of Wang Li). Beijing, 1967.

Shoudu hongweibing di san silingbu Beijing youdian xueyuan "Dongfanghong" gongshe Chongfengdui, ed. *Beijing shi wuchanjieji wenhua dageming dashiji (1965.9–*

1967.1) (Chronology of Major Events in the Beijing Municipality Great Proletarian Cultural Revolution [September 1965–January 1967]). Beijing, 1967.

"Shoudu hongweibing jiuchadui xicheng fendui zhihuibu di qi hao tongling" (General Order No. 7 of the Western City District Command of the Red Guard Pickets of the Capital). September 9, 1966. Schoenhals collection.

Shu Jun, ed. *Diaoyutai lishi dang'an* (Diaoyutai Historical Archives). Beijing: Zhonggong zhongyang dangxiao chubanshe, 1999.

"Sirenbang" zuixing cailiao (Materials on the Crimes of the "Gang of Four"). N.p., 1976.

Smith, Craig S. "Mao's Buried Past: A Strange Subterranean City." *New York Times,* November 26, 2001.

Snow, Edgar. *The Long Revolution.* London: Hutchinson, 1973.

Song Yongyi, ed. *Wenge da tusha* (Massacres during the Cultural Revolution). Hong Kong: Kaifang zazhi she, 2003.

Song Yongyi and Sun Dajin, eds. *Wenhua dageming he tade yiduan sichao* (Heterodox Thoughts during the Great Cultural Revolution). Hong Kong: Tianyuan shuwu, 1997.

Song Yongyi, Wu Tong, and Zhou Zehao, eds. "The Debate between the Blood Lineage Theory and Yu Luoke's 'On Family Background' during the Cultural Revolution." *Contemporary Chinese Thought,* 35, no. 4 (Summer 2004), 3–108.

"Soviet Report to GDR Leadership on 2 March 1969." *Bulletin* (Cold War International History Project, Woodrow Wilson Center), nos. 6–7 (Winter 1995–96), 189–190.

Su Donghai and Fang Kongmu, eds. *Zhonghua renmin gongheguo fengyun shilu* (A Record of the Major Events of the PRC). 2 vols. Shijiazhuang: Hebei renmin chubanshe, 1994.

Sun Xiaohua. "Agriculture Ex-Model Grapples for 'New Spirit.'" *China Daily,* July 26, 2005, p. 2.

Suo Guoxin. *1967 niande 78 tian: "Eryue niliu" jishi* (78 Days in 1967: The True Story of the "February Countercurrent"). Changsha: Hunan wenyi chubanshe, 1986. Translated in *Chinese Law and Government,* 22, no. 1 (Spring 1989), 16–96.

Survey of China Mainland Press. Hong Kong: American Consulate General.

Tan Zheng. *Zhongguo renmin zhiyuanjun renwu lu* (Biographies of Members of the Chinese People's Volunteer Army). Beijing: Zhonggong dangshi chubanshe, 1992.

Tan Zongji. "Shida pingshu" (Comments on the Tenth Party Congress). In Zhang Hua and Su Caiqing, eds., *Huishou "Wenge,"* 2: 1091–1103.

Tan Zongji et al., eds. *Shinian houde pingshuo: "Wenhua dageming" shilunji* (Evaluation Ten Years Later: A Collection of Historical Discussions of the "Great Cultural Revolution"). Beijing: Zhonggong dangshi ziliao chubanshe, 1987.

Tang Shaojie. *Yi ye zhi qiu: Qinghua daxue 1968 nian "Bai ri da wudou"* (The Falling of

One Leaf Heralds the Autumn: The "Hundred Days of Great Violence" at Tsinghua University in 1968). Hong Kong: Zhongwen daxue chubanshe, 2003.

T'ao Ch'ien. *The Poetry of T'ao Ch'ien,* trans. and ed. James Robert Hightower. Oxford: Clarendon Press, 1970.

Tao Zhu fangeming xiuzhengzhuyi yanlun huibian (A Collection of Tao Zhu's Counter-revolutionary Revisionist Utterances). Beijing: Mao Zedong sixiang zhexue shehui kexuebu hongweibing liandui, May 1967.

Taubman, William. *Khrushchev: The Man and His Era.* New York: Norton, 2003.

Teiwes, Frederick C. "The Establishment and Consolidation of the New Regime, 1949–57." In MacFarquhar, ed., *The Politics of China: Second Edition,* pp. 5–86.

Teiwes, Frederick C., and Warren Sun. "The First Tiananmen Incident Revisited: Elite Politics and Crisis Management at the End of the Maoist Era." *Pacific Affairs,* 77, no. 2 (Summer 2004), 211–235.

———— *The Tragedy of Lin Biao: Riding the Tiger during the Cultural Revolution, 1966–1971.* London: Hurst, 1996.

The Tenth National Congress of the Communist Party of China (Documents). Peking: Foreign Languages Press, 1973.

Terrill, Ross. *Madame Mao: The White-Boned Demon.* Rev. ed. Stanford: Stanford University Press, 1999.

Thurston, Anne F. *A Chinese Odyssey.* New York: Scribners, 1991.

———— *Enemies of the People.* New York: Knopf, 1987.

Tianjin shi Heping qu jianjue zhenya fangeming fenzi dahui xuanpanci (Sentences Read at the Mass Rally to Firmly Suppress Counterrevolutionary Elements in the Heping District of Tianjin Municipality). May 31, 1970. 8 pp. Public announcement put out by public security authorities. Schoenhals collection.

Tianjin xin wenyi (New Tianjin Literature and Art). Tianjin: Municipal Literature and Art Circles Standing Committee.

Tongdie (Diplomatic Note).

Tsai Chin. *Daughter of Shanghai.* New York: St. Martin's, 1988.

Tu Men and Kong Di. *Gongheguo zuida yuanan* (The Biggest Unjust Case in the Republic). Beijing: Falü chubanshe, 1993.

Tuopai ziliao xuanyi (Selected Translations of Trotskyite Material). Shanghai: Fudan daxue, 1972.

Tyler, Patrick E. "A Ghost of Maoist Fervor Lives on in Disgrace." *New York Times,* April 10, 1996.

———— *A Great Wall: Six Presidents and China—An Investigative History.* New York: Public Affairs, 1999.

Unger, Jonathan. *Education under Mao.* New York: Columbia University Press, 1982.

Wakeman, Frederic, Jr. *Policing Shanghai: 1927–1937.* Berkeley: University of California Press, 1995.

——— *Spymaster: Dai Li and the Chinese Secret Service.* Berkeley: University of California Press, 2003.

Walder, Andrew G. "Anatomy of an Inquisition: Cleansing the Class Ranks, 1968–1971." Paper presented at the conference "The Cultural Revolution in Retrospect," Hong Kong University of Science and Technology, July 1996.

——— "Beijing Red Guard Factionalism: Social Interpretations Reconsidered." *Journal of Asian Studies,* 61, no. 2 (May 2002), 437–471.

——— *Chang Ch'un-ch'iao and Shanghai's January Revolution.* Ann Arbor: Center for Chinese Studies, University of Michigan, 1978.

——— "The Communist Party and the Red Guards: Beijing 1966." Paper presented at the conference "Turning Points: 1919 and 1989," Center for Chinese Studies, University of California, Berkeley, January 1997.

——— "Factional Conflict at Beijing University, 1966–1968." Manuscript. Available at Fairbank Center Library.

——— "Tan Lifu: A 'Reactionary' Red Guard in Historical Perspective." *CQ,* no. 180 (December 2004), 965–989.

Walder, Andrew G., and Yang Su. "The Cultural Revolution in the Countryside: Scope, Timing and Human Impact." *CQ,* no. 173 (March 2003), 74–99.

Wang Baofu de zuie yanxing (Criminal Words and Deeds of Wang Baofu). Nanjing, 1967.

Wang Dongxing. *Mao Zedong yu Lin Biao fangeming jituande douzheng* (The Struggle between Mao Zedong and the Lin Biao Counterrevolutionary Clique). Beijing: Dangdai Zhongguo chubanshe, 1997.

Wang Dongxing gongkai Mao Zedong si shenghuo (Wang Dongxing Reveals Mao Zedong's Private Life). Hong Kong: Mingliu chubanshe, 1997.

"Wang-Guan-Qi fandang jituan yu gonganbu mouxie fuzeren zai Chen Lining fangeming anjian zhong banyan le shenme juese?" (What Role Did the Wang-Guan-Qi Anti-Party Clique and Certain Senior People in the Ministry of Public Security Play in the Counterrevolutionary Case of Chen Lining?). 9 pp. Stenciled document. Schoenhals collection.

"Wang Hongwen tongzhi de fayan" (Comrade Wang Hongwen's Statement). April 14, 1969. Official transcript. Beijing: CC General Office Secretariat. Available at Fairbank Center Library.

Wang Jian. "'Wenhua dageming' shiqi Beijing pujiao qingkuang" (The Situation in Regular Education in Beijing during the Phase of the "Great Cultural Revolution"). *Beijing jiaoyu zhi congkan,* no. 4 (1991), 22–31.

Wang Li. "An Insider's Account of the Cultural Revolution: Wang Li's Memoirs." *Chinese Law and Government,* 27, no. 6 (November–December 1994), 5–89.

———. "Lishi jiang xuangao wo wuzui" (History Will Pronounce Me Innocent). Manuscript. Beijing, 1993.

———— "Memoirs of a Year and Two Months." *Chinese Law and Government*, 27, no. 6 (November–December 1994), 5–89.

———— *Wang Li fansi lu: Wang Li yi gao* (Wang Li's Reflections). 2 vols. Hong Kong: Beixing chubanshe, 2001.

———— "Wang Li tan Mao Zedong" (Wang Li on Mao Zedong). Manuscript. 1995. Available at Fairbank Center Library.

———— *Xianchang lishi: Wenhua dageming jishi* (On the Scene of History: Chronicle of the Great Cultural Revolution). Hong Kong: Oxford University Press, 1993.

Wang, Lulu. *The Lily Theater*. New York: Doubleday, 2000.

Wang Naiying. "Jiao xitong de jiefa cailiao" (Fairly Systematic Revelations). January 13, 1968. Handwritten text. Available at Fairbank Center Library.

———— "Jiaodai" (Confession). September 1, 1970. Page 10 of original handwritten text. Available at Fairbank Center Library.

———— "Renzuishu" (Admission of Guilt). Handwritten document. December 10–12, 1970. Available at Fairbank Center Library.

———— "Yi ri dao qi ri wo dou zuole xie shenme?" (What Did I Do from the First to the Seventh [of August 1967]?). September 15, 1967. 15 pp. Handwritten record. Available at Fairbank Center Library.

Wang Nianyi. *Da dongluande niandai* (A Decade of Great Upheaval). Zhengzhou: Henan renmin chubanshe, 1988.

———— "Da dongluande niandai" (A Decade of Great Upheaval). Manuscript (revised and amended version). Copy in Fairbank Center Library.

———— "Guanyu He Long yuanande yixie ziliao" (Some Materials on the Case of He Long). *Dangshi yanjiu ziliao*, no. 4 (1992), 2–13.

Wang Nianyi and He Shu. "1970 niande Lushan huiyi ji Mao Zedong, Lin Biao chongtu zhi qiyuan—zai 'she guojia zhuxi' zhi zhengde beihou" (The Origins of the Clash between Mao Zedong and Lin Biao at the 1970 Lushan Conference—The Background to the Argument over "Establishing [the Post of] Head of State"). *Jilin nongye zengkan* (Jilin Agriculture Supplement [*sic*]), 1999, pp. 18–34.

Wang Nianyi, He Shu, and Chen Zhao. "Mao Zedong bichulaide 'jiu.yisan Lin Biao chutao shijian'" ("The Incident of September 13 When Lin Biao Fled" Which Mao Zedong Brought About). *Dangdai Zhongguo yanjiu*, no. 2 (2004), 137–154.

Wang Ruoshui. *Zhihui de tongku* (The Pain of Wisdom). Hong Kong: Sanlian shudian, 1989.

"Wang Shangrong jiangjun" bianxiezu. *Wang Shangrong jiangjun* (General Wang Shangrong). Beijing: Dangdai Zhongguo chubanshe, 2000.

Wang Shaoguang. *Failure of Charisma: The Cultural Revolution in Wuhan*. Hong Kong: Oxford University Press, 1995.

Wang Wenyao and Wang Baochun. "Guanyu Chen Boda qicao jiuda baogao de qianqian houhou" (The Ins and Outs of Chen Boda's Drafting of the Report of the Ninth Party Congress). *Zhonggong dangshi yanjiu*, no. 2 (2003), 88–91.

Wang Xitang. "Zhang Jingwu" (Zhang Jingwu). In Zhonggong dangshi renwu yanjiuhui, ed., *Zhonggong dangshi renwu zhuan*, 49 (published 1991): 328–359.

Wang Xiuzhen. "Wode di er ci jiefa he jiaodai" (My Second Exposé and Testimony). Shanghai: Shanghai shi qu, xian, ju dangyuan fuze ganbu huiyi mishuzu, November 1976. Original in Schoenhals collection.

——— "Wode jiefa he jiaodai" (My Exposé and Testimony). Shanghai: Shanghai shi qu, xian, ju dangyuan fuze ganbu huiyi mishuzu, November 6, 1976. Original in Schoenhals collection.

Wang Xizhe. *Wang Xizhe zizhuan: Zou xiang heian* (The Autobiography of Wang Xizhe: Toward the Darkness). Hong Kong: Minzhu daxue, 1996.

Wang Yilin's big-character poster "Xiang chongyang zhijing" (Saluting the Double Ninth Festival). Handwritten copy. 9 pp. Schoenhals collection.

Wang Youqin. "Student Attacks against Teachers: The Revolution of 1966." Paper presented at the conference "The Cultural Revolution in Retrospect," Hong Kong University of Science and Technology, July 1996.

——— *Wenge shounanzhe* (Victims of the Cultural Revolution). Hong Kong: Kaifang zazhi chubanshe, 2004.

Wang-Zhang-Jiang-Yao zhuan'anzu, ed. *Wang Hongwen, Zhang Chunqiao, Jiang Qing, Yao Wenyuan fandang jituan zuizheng (cailiao zhi 1)* (Record of the Crimes of the Wang Hongwen, Zhang Chunqiao, Jiang Qing, Yao Wenyuan Anti-Party Group [1st set of materials]). Beijing: Zhonggong zhongyang bangongting, 1976.

Wang Zhongfang. *Lianyu* (Purgatory). Beijing: Qunzhong chubanshe, 2004.

Wang Zongbai. "Zhang Jichun" (Zhang Jichun). In Zhonggong dangshi renwu yanjiuhui, ed., *Zhonggong dangshi renwu zhuan*, 23 (published 1985), 307–339.

Wanshan hongbian (Mountains and Rivers Awash in Red). Beijing: East City District Department Stores' Management Office.

Watson, Andrew. *Mao Zedong and the Political Economy of the Border Region: A Translation of Mao's Economic and Financial Problems.* Cambridge: Cambridge University Press, 1980.

Wei Renzhen, ed. *Dangdai Jiangsu jianshi* (A Short History of Contemporary Jiangsu). Beijing: Dangdai Zhongguo chubanshe, 2002.

Weida de jiaodao guanghui de zhenli: Mao zhuxi shicha Huabei, Zhongnan he Huadong diqu (Great Teachings and Brilliant Truths: Chairman Mao Inspects the North, Central-South, and East China Regions). Nanchang: Jiangxi ribao she Jinggangshan hongqi huoju, 1967.

Wenge fengyun (Cultural Revolution Storm). Shanghai: Shanghai Industrial College Red Guard Revolutionary Committee.

Wenge jianxun (Cultural Revolution News in Brief). Beijing: Institute of Politics and Law.

Wenge tongxun (Cultural Revolution News). [Tianjin?]: Xinhua fang.

Westerfield, H. Bradford, ed. *Inside CIA's Private World: Declassified Articles from the Agency's Internal Journal, 1955–1992.* New Haven: Yale University Press, 1995.

White, Lynn T., III. *Policies of Chaos: The Organizational Causes of Violence in China's Cultural Revolution.* Princeton: Princeton University Press, 1989.

Whitney, Ray M. P. "When the Red Guards Stormed Our Embassy." *Sunday Telegraph,* November 23, 1980.

Wich, Richard. *Sino-Soviet Crisis Politics: A Study of Political Change and Communication.* Cambridge, Mass.: Council on East Asian Studies, Harvard University, 1980.

———— "The Tenth Party Congress: The Power Structure and the Succession Question." *CQ,* no. 58 (April–June 1974), 231–248.

Witke, Roxane. *Comrade Chiang Ch'ing.* Boston: Little, Brown, 1977.

Wong, Jan. *Red China Blues: My Long March from Mao to Now.* Toronto: Doubleday/Anchor, 1997.

Woody, W. *The Cultural Revolution in Inner Mongolia: Extracts from an Unpublished History.* Stockholm: Center for Pacific Asia Studies, Stockholm University, 1993.

Wright, Mary Clabaugh. *The Last Stand of Chinese Conservatism: The T'ung-Chih Restoration, 1862–1874.* Stanford: Stanford University Press, 1957.

Wu De. "Guanyu fensui 'sirenbang' de douzheng" (The Struggle to Smash the "Gang of Four"). *Dangdai Zhongguo shi yanjiu,* no. 5 (2000), 51–64.

Wu Jicheng. *Hongse jingwei* (Red Bodyguard). Beijing: Dangdai Zhongguo chubanshe, 2003.

Wu Lengxi. *Shinian lunzhan, 1956–1966: Zhong Su guanxi huiyilu* (A Decade of Polemics, 1956–1966: A Memoir of Sino-Soviet Relations). 2 vols. Beijing: Zhongyang wenxian chubanshe, 1999.

———— *Yi Mao Zhuxi: Wo qinshen jinglide ruogan zhongda lishi shijian pianduan* (Remembering Chairman Mao: Fragments of Certain Major Historical Events Which I Personally Experienced). Beijing: Xinhua chubanshe, 1995.

Wu Li, ed. *Zhonghua renmin gongheguo jingji shi, 1949–1999* (An Economic History of the PRC, 1949–1999). 2 vols. Beijing: Zhongguo jingji chubanshe, 1999.

Wu, Silas H. L. *Communication and Imperial Control in China: Evolution of the Palace Memorial System, 1693–1735.* Cambridge, Mass.: Harvard University Press, 1970.

Wuchanjieji wenhua dageming dazibao xuanbian (Selection of Big-Character Posters of the Great Proletarian Cultural Revolution). Beijing: Guojia kewei jiguan, 1968.

Wuchanjieji wenhua dageming wenjian huiji (Collected Documents from the Great Proletarian Cultural Revolution). N.p., 1967.

Wuchanjieji wenhua dageming zhong xuexi wenjian teji (Special Collection of Documents Studied in the Great Proletarian Cultural Revolution). Beijing: Beijing dizhi xueyuan geming weiyuanhui ziliaozu, 1967.

Wuchanjieji wenhua dageming zhongde liangtiao luxian—Chen Boda 1966 nian 10 yue 16 ri zai zhongyang gongzuo huiyi shangde jianghua (The Two Lines in the Great Proletarian Cultural Revolution—Chen Boda's Talk at the Central Work Conference on October 16, 1966). Beijing: Zhonggong zhongyang bangongting mishuju, [1966].

Wuchanjieji wenhua dageming ziliao 6 (Great Proletarian Cultural Revolution Materials: June). 2 vols. Beijing, 1967.

Wuhan gang er si, ed. *Qiandao wangua Chen Zaidao* (Cut Chen Zaidao to Pieces). 2 vols. Wuhan, 1967.

Wylie, Raymond F. *The Emergence of Maoism: Mao Tse-tung, Ch'en Po-ta, and the Search for Chinese Theory, 1935–1945.* Stanford: Stanford University Press, 1980.

Xi Xuan and Jin Chunming. *"Wenhua dageming" jianshi* (A Short History of the "Great Cultural Revolution"). Beijing: Zhonggong dangshi chubanshe, 1996.

Xiao Han and Mia Turner. *789 jizhongying* (Camp 789). Brampton, Ont.: Mirror Books, 1998.

Xiao Lan, ed. *The Tiananmen Poems.* Beijing: Foreign Languages Press, 1979.

Xiao Sike. *Chaoji shenpan: Tu Men jiangjun canyu shenli Lin Biao fangeming jituan qinli ji* (Super Trial: General Tu Men's Personal Experience of Participating in the Trial of the Lin Biao Counterrevolutionary Clique). Ji'nan: Ji'nan chubanshe, 1992.

Xin shida wenge chouweihui, ed. *Zai wuchanjieji wenhua dageming zhong Cao Diqiu yanlun ji* (Utterances by Cao Diqiu in the Course of the Great Proletarian Cultural Revolution). Shanghai, 1966.

Xing Fangqun. "Deng Xiaoping shouyi chuangban 'Sixiang zhanxian' bei 'sirenbang' e sha jingguo" (How the "Gang of Four" Strangled Deng Xiaoping's Instruction on Creating the Magazine "Ideological Battle Lines"). *Yanhuang chunqiu,* no. 9 (1997), 18–19.

Xinghuo liaoyuan bianjibu, ed. *Jiefangjun jiangling zhuan* (Biographies of PLA Generals). 14 vols. Beijing: Jiefangjun chubanshe, 1984–1995.

Xinwen yanjiu ziliao (Press Research Materials). Beijing: Zhongguo shehui kexue yuan, Xinwen yanjiusuo.

Xinwen yanjiusuo, ed. *Tantan baozhi gongzuo* (On Newspaper Work). Beijing, 1978.

Xu Jingxian. *Shinian yimeng* (Ten Years a Dream). Hong Kong: Time International, 2004.

"Xu Jingxian de buchong jiefa jiaodai" (Xu Jingxian's Supplementary Exposé and Testimony). Shanghai: Shanghai shi qu, xian, ju dangyuan fuze ganbu huiyi mishuzu, November 21, 1976. Original in Schoenhals collection.

"Xu Jingxian de chubu jiefa jiaodai" (Xu Jingxian's Initial Exposé and Testimony). Shanghai: Shanghai shi qu, xian, ju dangyuan fuze ganbu huiyi mishuzu, November 1976. Original in Schoenhals collection.

Xu Zehao. *Wang Jiaxiang zhuan* (Biography of Wang Jiaxiang). Beijing: Dangdai Zhongguo chubanshe, 1996.

Xuexi "Mao zhuxi zhi Jiang Qing tongzhi de xin" de tihui (Insights Gained from Studying "Chairman Mao's Letter to Comrade Jiang Qing"). N.p., [1974?]. Typed study document. Original in Schoenhals collection.

Xuexi wenjian (Study Documents). N.p., 1967.

Xuexi ziliao (Study Materials). Beijing: Tsinghua University Jinggangshan News Agency.

Xuexi ziliao (Study Materials). Beijing: Tsinghua University Jinggangshan Struggle-Criticize-Transform Battle Regiment.

Yan Jiaqi and Gao Gao. *Turbulent Decade: A History of the Cultural Revolution*, trans. D. W. Y. Kwok. Honolulu: University of Hawaii Press, 1996.

Yang Bingzhang. *Cong beida dao hafo* (From Peking University to Harvard). Beijing: Zuojia chubanshe, 1998.

Yang Jiang. *A Cadre School Life: Six Chapters*. Hong Kong: Joint Publishing, 1982.

Yang Kelin, ed. *Wenhua dageming bowuguan* (Museum of the Great Cultural Revolution). 2 vols. Hong Kong: Dongfang chubanshe and Tiandi tushu, 1995.

Yang Kuisong. *Mao Zedong yu Mosikede enen yuanyuan* (Mao Zedong's Good and Bad Relations with Moscow). Nanchang: Jiangxi renmin chubanshe, 1999.

Yang Mu, ed. *"Wenge" chuangjiang fengshenbang* (Pathbreakers and Feudal Gangs of the "Cultural Revolution"). Beijing: Tuanjie chubanshe, 1993.

Yang Qinhua. "1978 nianqian haixia liang'an mouhe zuji shilu" (A Memoir of the Reconciliation-seeking Process across the Taiwan Straits before 1978). *Yanhuang chunqiu*, no. 8 (1997), 19–23.

Yang, Rae. *Spider Eaters: A Memoir*. Berkeley: University of California Press, 1997.

Yang Rongguo. *Pipan Kongzi baogao* (Report Denouncing Confucius). Baoding: Zhonggong Baoding diwei xuanchuanbu, 1974.

Yang Shangkun riji (Yang Shangkun's Diary). 2 vols. Beijing: Zhongyang wenxian chubanshe, 2001.

Yang Xun. *Xinlu: Liangzhide mingyun* (The Way of the Heart: The Fate of a Conscience). Beijing: Xinhua chubanshe, 2004.

Yang Yinlu. "Chu jian Jiang Qing: Wo gei Jiang Qing dang mishu (yi)" (My First Meeting with Jiang Qing: I was Jiang Qing's Secretary [1]). *Bainian chao*, no. 5 (1998), 54–59.

——— "Jiang Qing de 'nü huang' shenghuo (er)" (Jiang Qing's Life as an "Empress" [2]). *Bainian chao*, no. 6 (1998), 65–69.

——— "Jiang Qing yu Lin Biao: Wo gei Jiang Qing dang mishu (si)" (Jiang Qing and Lin Biao: I was Jiang Qing's Secretary [4]). *Bainian chao*, no. 4 (1999), 69–73.

Yanhuang chunqiu (Chinese Annals). Beijing: Zhonghua yanhuang wenhua yanjiuhui.

Yao Ming-le. *The Conspiracy and Murder of Mao's Heir*. London: Collins, 1983.

Yaowen jianbao (Important News Bulletin). Beijing: Beijing Institute of Politics and Law.

Ye Ting-xing. *A Leaf in the Bitter Wind*. Toronto: Doubleday, 2002.

Ye Zilong huiyilu (Ye Zilong's Recollections). Beijing: Zhongyang wenxian chubanshe, 2000.

Yeh Yung-lieh. "Wang Li Who Is Ill Answers His Guest's Questions." *Ta Kung Pao,* January 3–7, 1989, p. 2. Translated in Joint Publications Research Service. CAR-89–011. Springfield, Va., February 7, 1989, pp. 1–7.

Yejin fenglei (Metallurgy Tempest). Tianjin: Municipal Metallurgy Industry Revolutionary Committee.

Yin Hongbiao. "Wengede 'di yi zhang Ma-Liezhuyi dazibao'" ("The First Big-Character Poster of Marxism-Leninism" of the Cultural Revolution). *Ershiyi shiji shuangyuekan,* no. 36 (August 1996), 37–45.

Yiyue fengbao congkan (January Storm). Shanghai: Workers' General Headquarters.

You Lin, Zheng Xinli, and Wang Ruipu, eds. *Zhonghua renmin gongheguo guoshi tongjian* (A Comprehensive Mirror of National History of the PRC). 4 vols. Beijing: Hongqi chubanshe, 1993.

Youdianbu wenhua geming bangongshi, ed. *Youdianbu wenhua dageming dashiji* (Record of Major Events during the Great Cultural Revolution in the Ministry of Posts and Telecommunications). Beijing, 1966.

Yu Guangyuan. *Wenge zhongde wo* (Me in the Cultural Revolution). Shanghai: Shanghai yuandong chubanshe, 1996.

Yu Huanchun. "'Renmin ribao' yu 1976 nian Tiananmen shijian" (The *People's Daily* and the 1976 Tiananmen Events). *Bainian chao,* no. 2 (1998), 41–48.

Yu Hui. *Hongweibing mi lu* (Secret Records of the Red Guards). Beijing: Tuanjie chubanshe, 1993.

Yu Luoke. "Riji zhaochao" (Diary Extracts). In Zhang Ming and Luo Qun, eds., *"Wenhua dageming" zhongde mingren zhi si,* pp. 334–339.

Yu Luowen. "Beijing Daxing xian can'an diaocha" (Investigation into the Massacre in Daxing County, Beijing). In Song Yongyi, ed., *Wenge da tusha,* pp. 13–36.

Yu Sang. "Renmin dahuitang chuanghu boli qiangji shijian zhenpoji" (Record of Cracking the Case of the Rifle Shot Smashing a Window in the Great Hall of the People). In Zhu Chunlin, ed., *Lishi shunjian,* 1: 259–267.

Yu Shun, ed. *Dangdai Hunan jianshi (1949–1995)* (A Short History of Contemporary Hunan [1949–1995]). Beijing: Dangdai Zhongguo chubanshe, 1997.

Yu Xiguang, ed. *Weibei weigan wangyouguo: "Wenhua dageming" shangshuji* (Of Inferior Position but Concerned about the Fate of the Country: Memorials from the "Great Cultural Revolution"). Changsha: Hunan renmin chubanshe, 1989.

Yuan Beijing shiwei jiguan Mao Zedong sixiang hongqi bingtuan, ed. *Peng Zhen zuie shi (1925–1966)* (Peng Zhen's Criminal History [1925–1966]). Beijing, 1967.

Yuan Ding. "Xiao Li yu 'Jiefangjun bao' duoquan fengbao" (Xiao Li and the Seizure of Power at the *PLA Daily*). *Bainian chao,* no. 2 (1999), 42–54.

Yue Daiyun and Carolyn Wakeman. *To the Storm.* Berkeley: University of California Press, 1985.

Yunnan sheng geming weiyuanhui, ed. *Wuchanjieji wenhua dageming wenjian huibian* (Collected Documents of the Great Proletarian Cultural Revolution). 2 vols. Kunming, 1969.

Zhai Zhenhua. *Red Flower of China.* New York: Soho, 1992.

"Zhai zi Hao Kewei jiaodai cailiao" (Excerpts from Hao Kewei's Confessions). June 10, 1970. Handwritten confessions. Beijing. Schoenhals collection.

Zhang Baojun. "Dakai Zhong Mei guanxi damen shimo" (The Story of How Sino-American Relations Were Opened Up). In Qiu Shi, ed., *Gongheguo zhongda shijian he juece neimu*, 2: 673–717.

Zhang Chengxian. "Wenhua dageming chuqide beida gongzuozu" (Peking University Work Teams at the Beginning of the Cultural Revolution). *Zhonggong dangshi ziliao*, no. 70 (June 1999), 16–44.

Zhang Guanghua. "Yin fandui 'tuchu zhengzhi' bei pohai zhisi de Xiao Xiangrong" (Xiao Xiangrong, Persecuted to Death for Opposing "Giving Prominence to Politics"). *Yanhuang chunqiu*, no. 10 (1997), 21–24.

Zhang Hanzhi. *Feng yu qing: Yi fuqin, yi Zhuxi, yi Guanhua* (Emotions in Hardships: Remembering Father, the Chairman, and [husband Qiao] Guanhua). Shanghai: Shanghai wenyi chubanshe, 1994.

Zhang Hua. "1975 nian jiaoyujiede douzheng" (The 1975 Struggle on the Educational Front). *Zhonggong dangshi ziliao*, no. 70 (June 1999), 132–160.

Zhang Hua and Su Caiqing, eds. *Huishou "Wenge"* (Looking Back on the "Cultural Revolution"). 2 vols. Beijing: Zhonggong dangshi chubanshe, 2000.

Zhang Ming and Luo Qun, eds. *"Wenhua dageming" zhongde mingren zhi si* (Famous People Reflect upon the "Great Cultural Revolution"). Beijing: Zhongyang minzu xueyuan chubanshe, 1993.

Zhang Songshan. "On the 'He Long Case Group.'" In Schoenhals, ed., "Mao's Great Inquisition," pp. 24–42.

Zhang Tingdong. *Wo pei Ye shuai zouwan zuihou shiqinian* (I Was with Marshal Ye during his Last Seventeen Years). Beijing: Zhonggong dangshi chubanshe, 1999.

Zhang Tuosheng. "Deng Xiaoping yu 1975 niande quanmian zhengdun" (Deng Xiaoping and the All-Round Readjustment in 1975). In Zhang Hua and Su Caiqing, eds., *Huishou "Wenge,"* 2: 1161–74.

Zhang Xiangling, ed. *Heilongjiang sishinian* (Forty Years of Heilongjiang). Harbin: Heilongjiang renmin chubanshe, 1986.

Zhang Ying. *Waijiao fengyun: Qinli ji* (Storms in Foreign Relations: A Personal Account). Wuhan: Hubei renmin chubanshe, 2005.

Zhang Yunsheng. *Maojiawan jishi: Lin Biao mishu huiyilu* (The True Story of Maojiawan: The Memoirs of Lin Biao's Secretary). Beijing: Chunqiu chubanshe, 1988.

Zhang Zhong. *Donghu qingshen: Mao Zedong yu Wang Renzhong shisan niande jiaowang* (Emotions Are Deep on East Lake: Thirteen Years of Contacts between Mao Zedong and Wang Renzhong). Beijing: Zhonggong dangshi chubanshe, 2004.

Zhang Zishen. *Zhanjiang yu tongshuai: Yang Chengwu zai Mao Zedong huixiade sishiba nian* (Battle General and Commander-in-Chief: Yang Chengwu's Forty-eight Years under Mao Zedong's Command). Shenyang: Liaoning renmin chubanshe, 2000.

Zhao Jianping, Li Xiaochun, and Kang Xiaofeng. *Fengyun zhongde gongheguo dajiang Luo Ruiqing* (The Great General of the Republic Luo Ruiqing during the Tumultuous Era). Beijing: Zuojia chubanshe, 1997.

Zhao Qizheng, ed. *Ganbu renshi gongzuo shouce* (Cadre Personnel Work Manual). Shanghai: Shanghai renmin chubanshe, 1986.

Zhejiang sheng Mao Zedong sixiang yanjiu zhongxin and Zhonggong Zhejiang shengwei dangshi yanjiushi, eds. *Mao Zedong yu Zhejiang* (Mao Zedong and Zhejiang). Beijing: Zhonggong dangshi chubanshe, 1993.

Zhejiang shifan xueyuan Hongdonghai zhandoudui, ed. *Wuchanjieji wenhua dageming bufen ziliao huibian III* (Partial Collection of Material from the Great Proletarian Cultural Revolution III). Taizhou, 1967.

"Zhenbaodao qingkuang diandi" (Information Accumulated on Zhenbao Island). In *"Jiuda" ziliao huibian.*

Zheng Hui, Shi Zhongquan, and Zhang Hongru, eds. *Zhonghua renmin gongheguo guoshi quanjian (1949–1995)* (A Comprehensive History of the PRC [1949–1995]). 6 vols. Beijing: Tuanjie chubanshe, 1996.

Zheng Qian. "Cong 'Ping xinbian lishiju Hai Rui baguan' dao 'eryue tigang'" (From Criticism of the Newly Revised Play "Hai Rui Dismissed from Office" to the "February Outline"). In Cheng Min, ed., *Haojie chuqi*, pp. 161–182.

——— "60 niandai mo Zhongguo beizhan miwen" (Secrets of China's War Preparations in the Late 1960s). In Qiu Shi, ed., *Gongheguo zhongda shijian he juece neimu*, 2: 625–658.

Zheng Yi. *Scarlet Memorial: Tales of Cannibalism in Modern China*, trans. T. P. Sym. Boulder: Westview, 1996.

Zhengdang xuexi ziliao. See Zhongguo kexueyuan geming weiyuanhui zhengzhizu, ed., *Zhengdang xuexi ziliao.*

Zhengxie quanguo weiyuanhui jiguan, Weidong geming zhandoudui, Dongfanghong zhandoutuan, and Hongweibing zaofanpai, eds. *Chedi cuihui shiqi nian lai Zhengxie gongzuo zhongde Liu, Deng fangeming xiuzhengzhuyi luxian* (Thoroughly Smash the Counterrevolutionary Revisionist Line of Liu and Deng in the Work of the Political Consultative Conference during the Past Seventeen Years). Beijing, 1967.

Zhi quanti ge jiashu (To All Members of Revolutionary Families ["Open Letter" from

Yangfangdian No. 1 Residential Area Residents' Committee]). August 29, 1966. Schoenhals collection.

Zhishi qingnian shangshan xiaxiang gongzuo youguan wenjian (Documents Relating to the Work of Educated Youth Going Up to the Mountains and Down to the Countryside). Beijing: Quanguo zhishi qingnian shangshan xiaxiang gongzuo xiaotanhui, 1972.

Zhong Kan. *Kang Sheng pingzhuan* (A Critical Biography of Kang Sheng). Beijing: Hongqi chubanshe, 1982.

Zhonggong Anhui shengwei dangxiao tushuguan ziliaoshi, ed. *Jiaoxue cankao: Quanguo dangxiao xitong Zhonggong dangshi xueshu taolunhui zhuanti baogao he fayan huibian* (Teaching Reference: Collection of Special Reports and Speeches at the Symposium of the Nationwide Party School System on CCP History). 2 vols. Anhui province, 1980.

Zhonggong Baoding shiwei dangshi yanjiushi, ed. *Zhonggong Baoding dangshi dashiji (1949.10–1978.12)* (Record of Major Events in the History of the CCP in Baoding [October 1949–December 1978]). Beijing: Zhongyang wenxian chubanshe, 1999.

Zhonggong Beijing shiwei dangshi ziliao zhengji weiyuanhui. *Beijing dangshi ziliao tongxun* (Beijing Party History Materials Newsletter).

Zhonggong Beijing shiwei dangxiao ziliaoshi, ed. *Kang Sheng yanlun xuanbian* (Selected Utterances of Kang Sheng). 3 vols. Beijing, 1979.

Zhonggong Beijing shiwei zuzhibu, Zhonggong Beijing shiwei dangshi ziliao zhengji weiyuanhui, and Beijing shi dang'anju, eds. *Zhongguo gongchandang Beijing shi zuzhi shi ziliao* (Material on the Organizational History of the CCP in Beijing). Beijing: Renmin chubanshe, 1992.

Zhonggong Chengdu shiwei dangshi yanjiushi, ed. *Zhonggong Chengdu difangshi dashiji (1949–1989)* (Record of Major Events in the Local History of Chengdu [1949–1989]). Chengdu: Chengdu chubanshe, 1995.

Zhonggong dangshi renwu yanjiuhui, ed. *Zhonggong dangshi renwu zhuan* (Biographies of Personalities in the History of the CCP). 60 vols. Xi'an: Shaanxi renmin chubanshe, 1980–1996.

Zhonggong dangshi renwu zhuan. See Zhonggong dangshi renwu yanjiuhui, ed.

Zhonggong dangshi yanjiu (Research on CCP History). Beijing: Zhonggong dangshi yanjiu bianjibu.

Zhonggong dangshi ziliao (Materials on CCP History). Beijing: Zhonggong zhongyang dangxiao chubanshe.

Zhonggong Guangzhou shiwei dangshi yanjiushi, ed. *Zhonggong Guangzhou dangshi dashiji* (A Record of Major Events in the History of the CCP in Guangzhou). Guangzhou: Guangdong renmin chubanshe, 1991.

Zhonggong Hebei shengwei dangshi yanjiushi, ed. *Zhongguo gongchandang Hebei lishi dashiji (1949.7–1978.12)* (A Chronicle of the CCP in Hebei History [July 1949–December 1978]). Beijing: Zhongyang wenxian chubanshe, 1999.

Zhonggong Heilongjiang shengwei dangshi yanjiushi, ed. *Zhonggong Heilongjiang dangshi dashiji (1949.10–1989.12)* (Record of Major Events in CCP History of Heilongjiang [October 1949–December 1989]). Harbin: Heilongjiang renmin chubanshe, 1991.

Zhonggong Hubei shengwei dangshi ziliao zhengbian weiyuanhui, ed. *Mao Zedong zai Hubei* (Mao Zedong in Hubei). Beijing: Zhonggong dangshi chubanshe, 1993.

Zhonggong Kunming shiwei Kunming jingbeiqu fu-Hu xuexi xiaozu, ed. *Shanghai minbing gongzuo jingyan xuanbian* (Selected Work Experiences of the Shanghai Militia). Anshun: Shi minbing zhihuibu, 1974.

Zhonggong Qinghai shengwei zuzhibu, Zhonggong Qinghai shengwei dangshi yanjiushi, and Qinghai sheng dang'anju, eds. *Zhongguo gongchandang Qinghai sheng zuzhi shi ziliao* (Materials on the Organizational History of the CCP in Qinghai Province). Xining, 1995.

Zhonggong Shanghai shiwei bangongting geming zaofandui, ed. *Liu Shaoqi zai gedi sanbude xiuzhengzhuyi yanlun huibian* (Collected Revisionist Utterances Spread in Various Localities by Liu Shaoqi). Shanghai, 1967.

Zhonggong Xiangtan shiwei dangshi ziliao zhengji bangongshi, ed. *Mao Zedong yu Xiangtan* (Mao Zedong and Xiangtan). Beijing: Zhonggong dangshi chubanshe, 1993.

Zhonggong Xizang dangshi dashiji (Record of Major Events in the History of the CCP in Tibet). Lhasa: Xizang renmin chubanshe, 1995.

Zhonggong Yinchuan shiwei dangshi yanjiushi, ed. *Zhonggong Yinchuan dangshi dashiji, 1949.9–1996.12* (Record of Major Events in the History of the CCP in Yinchuan, September 1949–December 1996). Yinchuan: Ningxia renmin chubanshe, 1998.

Zhonggong Zhejiang shengwei dangxiao dangshi jiaoyanshi, ed. *"Wenhua dageming" shiqi ziliao xuanji* (Selected Materials Concerning the "Great Cultural Revolution" Era). Hangzhou, 1984.

Zhonggong zhongyang bangongting, ed. *Canyue wenjian* (Reference Readings). 12 vols. Beijing, 1972.

"Zhonggong zhongyang pizhuan 'Neimenggu zizhiqu geweihui hexin xiaozu "Jianjue guanche zhixing zhongyang guanyu Neimeng dangqian gongzuo zhishi de jidian yijian"'" (CCP Center Circular with Comment: "Some Opinions of the Nucleus of the Inner Mongolia Autonomous Region Revolutionary Committee on the 'Resolute Implementation of the CCP Center's Instructions on Work in Inner Mongolia at Present'"). August 3, 1981. Photocopy of original. Available at Fairbank Center Library.

Zhonggong zhongyang tongzhanbu Geming zaofantuan and Hongwuyue bingtuan cailiaozu, eds. *Zhongguo Heluxiaofu Liu Shaoqi zai tongyi zhanxian fangmiande fangeming xiuzhengzhuyi yanlun xuanbian* (Selected Counterrevolutionary Revisionist Statements concerning the United Front by China's Khrushchev, Liu Shaoqi). Beijing, 1967.

Zhonggong zhongyang wenxian yanjiushi, ed. *Chen Yun nianpu (1905–1995)* (Chronicle of the Life of Chen Yun [1905–1995]). 3 vols. Beijing: Zhongyang wenxian chubanshe, 2000.

———— *Liu Shaoqi nianpu, 1898–1969* (Chronicle of the Life of Liu Shaoqi, 1898–1969). 2 vols. Beijing: Zhongyang wenxian chubanshe, 1996.

———— *Sanzhong quanhui yilai zhongyao wenxian huibian* (Collection of Important Documents since the Third Plenum). 2 vols. Beijing: Renmin chubanshe, 1982.

———— *"Wenge" shinian ziliao xuanbian* (Selected Materials on the Ten-Year "Cultural Revolution"). 3 vols. Beijing, 1981.

———— *Zhou Enlai nianpu, 1949–1976* (Chronicle of the Life of Zhou Enlai, 1949–1976). 3 vols. Beijing: Zhongyang wenxian chubanshe, 1997.

Zhonggong zhongyang zuzhibu, Zhonggong zhongyang dangshi yanjiushi, and Zhongyang dang'anguan, eds. *Zhongguo gongchandang zuzhishi ziliao, 1921–1997* (Materials on the Organizational History of the CCP, 1921–1997). 19 vols. Beijing: Zhonggong dangshi chubanshe, 2000.

Zhongguo banben tushuguan, ed. *Quanguo neibu faxing tushu zongmu* (National Bibliography of Internally Distributed Books). Beijing: Zhonghua shuju, 1988.

Zhongguo geming bowuguan, ed. *Zhongguo gongchandang dangzhang huibian* (Collected Constitutions of the CCP). Beijing: Renmin chubanshe, 1979.

Zhongguo gongchandang Shanghai shi zuzhi shi ziliao, 1920.8–1987.10 (Materials on the Organizational History of the CCP in Shanghai, August 1920–October 1987). Shanghai: Shanghai renmin chubanshe, 1991.

Zhongguo gongchandang Yunnan sheng zuzhi shi ziliao Yunnan sheng zheng jun tong qun zuzhi shi ziliao, 1926.11–1987.10 (Materials on the History of the CCP Organization, Government, Military, United Front, and Mass Organizations in Yunnan Province, November 1926–October 1987). Beijing: Zhonggong dangshi chubanshe, 1994.

Zhongguo gongchandang zuzhishi ziliao. See Zhonggong zhongyang zuzhibu, Zhonggong zhongyang dangshi yanjiushi, and Zhongyang dang'anguan, eds.

Zhongguo kexueyuan geming lishi yanjiusuo jindai gemingshi yanjiusuo, eds. *Liu Shaoqi fangeming xiuzhengzhuyi yanlun huibian* (Collected Counterrevolutionary Revisionist Statements by Liu Shaoqi). Beijing, 1967.

Zhongguo kexueyuan geming weiyuanhui zhengzhizu, ed. *Zhengdang xuexi ziliao* (Party Rectification Study Materials). Beijing, 1968.

Zhongguo renmin daxue, Xin renda gongshe, and Mao Zedong sixiang hongweibing, eds. *Fangeming xiuzhengzhuyi fenzi Guo Yingqiu fan dang fan shehuizhuyi fan*

Mao Zedong sixiang de zuixing (Counterrevolutionary Revisionist Element Guo Yingqiu's Anti-Party, Anti-Socialist, Anti–Mao Zedong Thought Crimes). Beijing, 1967.

Zhongguo renmin gongan shigao (Draft History of the Chinese People's Public Security). Beijing: Jingguan jiaoyu chubanshe, 1997.

Zhonghua renmin gongheguo caizhengbu, ed. *Zhongguo nongmin fudan shi* (A History of the Chinese Peasants' Burden). 4 vols. Beijing: Zhongguo caizheng jingji chubanshe, 1990–1994.

Zhonghua renmin gongheguo falü guifanxing jieshi jicheng (Collection of Normative Explanations of the Laws of the PRC). Changchun: Jilin renmin chubanshe, 1990.

Zhonghua renmin gongheguo waijiaobu and Waijiao shi yanjiushi, eds. *Zhou Enlai waijiao huadong dashiji, 1949–1975* (A Chronology of Zhou Enlai's Activities in Foreign Affairs, 1949–1975). Beijing: Shijie zhishi chubanshe, 1993.

Zhonghua renmin gongheguo zuzhi faze xuanbian (Selected Organizational Laws and Regulations of the PRC). Beijing: Jingji kexue chubanshe, 1985.

Zhongyang bande Mao Zedong sixiang xuexiban Sichuan ban geming dapipan fayan (Revolutionary Great Criticism: Statements from the Sichuan Class of the Mao Zedong Thought Study Classes Organized by the Center). N.p., 1970.

Zhongyang dang'anguan, ed. *Gongheguo wushinian zhengui dang'an* (Precious Archives from Fifty Years of the Republic). 2 vols. Beijing: Zhongguo dang'an chubanshe, 1999.

Zhongyang fuze tongzhi guanyu wuchanjieji wenhua dagemingde jianghua (xubian) (Speeches by Responsible Central Comrades concerning the Great Proleterian Cultural Revolution [2]). N.p., 1967.

Zhongyang guanyu chuli Neimeng wentide jueding he zhongyang fuze tongzhi jianghua huibian (Center's Decision on Resolving Matters in Inner Mongolia and Collected Central Leaders' Speeches). 2 vols. Huhehot, 1967.

Zhongyang junwei kuoda huiyi jingshen (The Spirit of the Enlarged MAC Plenum). Zhengzhou: Henan erqi gongshe Zhengzhou geming zhigong lianluo weiyuanhui wenjiao weisheng fenhui, 1967.

Zhongyang pi Lin zhengfeng houbaohuiyi shi ge wenjian huibian (Ten Documents from the Criticize Lin and Rectify Work-Style Report-Back Conference). Hefei: Zhonggong Anhui shengwei, 1972.

Zhongyang renmin gongan xueyuan, ed. *"Teqing gongzuo" jiangyi* (Teaching Material on "Special Intelligence Work"). N.p., 1957.

Zhongyang shouzhang fenbie jiejian dazhuan yuanxiao daibiaode jianghua (Central Leaders Speak at Separate Receptions for University Delegates). N.p., September 1967.

Zhongyang shouzhang guanyu Henan wentide zhishi ji fu-Jing huibao jiyao huibian (Collected Transcripts of Central Leaders' Instructions concerning Henan and Summaries of Reports Given in Beijing). Zhengzhou: Zhongguo renmin jiefangjun zhu zheng budui zhizuo lianhe bangongshi, 1967.

Zhongyang xiju xueyuan hongse zaofantuan, ed. *Jiekai zhongyang xiju xueyuan "Mao Zedong zhuyi zhandoutuan" ouda wumie renmin jiefangjun de neimu* (Unveiling the Inside Story of How the "Mao Zedong-ism Combat Regiment" in the Central Drama Academy Exchanged Blows with and Vilified the People's Liberation Army). Beijing, 1967.

Zhou Enlai. *Selected Works of Zhou Enlai.* 2 vols. Beijing: Foreign Languages Press, 1981, 1989.

Zhou Enlai nianpu. See Zhonggong zhongyang wenxian yanjiushi, ed.

Zhou Enlai xuanji (Selected Works of Zhou Enlai). 2 vols. Beijing: Renmin chubanshe, 1980, 1984.

Zhou Ming, ed. *Lishi zai zheli chensi* (Here History Is Lost in Thought). Vols. 1–3: Beijing: Huaxia chubanshe, 1986; vols. 4–6: Taiyuan: Beiyue wenyi chubanshe, 1989.

Zhou Rongxin tongzhi de jianghua huibian (Collected Speeches of Comrade Zhou Rongxin). N.p., December 1975.

Zhou Yan. "Gongheguo zongli xin zhongde 'zhua geming cu shengchan'" (The Heart of the Premier of the Republic in "Grasp Revolution, Boost Production"). In An Jianshe, ed., *Zhou Enlaide zuihou suiyue*, pp. 68–84.

——— "He 'da nao Huairentang' de zhanyoumen" (Comrades-in-Arms during the "Commotion in Huairen Hall"). In An Jianshe, ed., *Zhou Enlaide zuihou suiyue*, pp. 31–49.

Zhou Yixing, ed. *Dangdai Beijing jianshi* (A Short History of Contemporary Beijing). Beijing: Dangdai Zhongguo chubanshe, 1999.

"Zhou zongli zai 'jiuda' yubeihui jieshu shi chuanda Mao zhuxi zhishi" (Premier Zhou Transmits Chairman Mao's Instructions at the End of the Preparatory Meeting for the "Ninth Congress"). In *"Jiuda" ziliao huibian.*

"Zhou zongli zai junji ganbu huiyi shangde jianghua" (Premier Zhou's Speech at a Conference for Corps-Level Cadres). In *Xuexi wenjian.*

"Zhou zonglide jianghua" (Premier Zhou's Speech). In *Lin Biao wenxuan*, 2: 257–264.

Zhu Chuan and Shen Xianhui, eds. *Dangdai Liaoning jianshi* (A Short History of Contemporary Liaoning). Beijing: Dangdai Zhongguo chubanshe, 1999.

Zhu Chunlin, ed. *Lishi shunjian* (History Twinkling). Beijing: Qunzhong chubanshe, 1999.

Zhu Xiao Di. *Thirty Years in a Red House.* Amherst: University of Massachusetts Press, 1998.

"Zhuxi 69.4.23 xiawu jiejian bufen daibiao" (The Chairman Receives Some Delegates in the Afternoon of April 23, 1969). Copy of handwritten transcript. Available at Fairbank Center Library.

Zong canmoubu zhengzhibu, ed. *Choushi Suxiu muoshi Suxiu bishi Suxiu* (Hate the Soviet Revisionists, Despise the Soviet Revisionists, and Look Down Upon the Soviet Revisionists). Beijing, 1969.

Zong houqinbu jiguan. *Wuchanjieji wenhua dageming wan sui* (Long Live the Great Proletarian Cultural Revolution). Beijing, 1967.

"Zongli guanyu qingcha '5.16' de zhishi (zhailu)" (Instruction by the Premier about Ferreting Out the "5.16" Clique [Abstract]). November 4, 1970. Handwritten copy. Available at Fairbank Center Library.

"Zongli guanyu qingcha '5.16' de zhishi (zhailu)" (Instruction by the Premier about Ferreting Out the "5.16" Clique [Abstract]). November 9, 1970. Handwritten copy. Available at Fairbank Center Library.

Zou Huaxiang and Shi Jinyan, eds. *Zhongguo jinxiandai tushuguan shiye dashiji* (Chronicle of China's Library Facilities in Modern Times). Changsha: Hunan renmin chubanshe, 1988.

Zuigao renmin fayuan yanjiushi, ed. *Zhonghua renmin fayuan tebie fating shenpan Lin Biao Jiang Qing fangeming jituan an zhufan jishi* (A Record of the Trial by the Special Tribunal of the PRC's Supreme People's Court of the Principal Criminals of the Lin Biao and Jiang Qing Counterrevolutionary Cliques). Beijing: Falü chubanshe, 1982.

Zweig, David. *Agrarian Radicalism in China, 1968–1981.* Cambridge, Mass.: Harvard University Press, 1989.

Illustration Credits

The photographs in this book come from three works. We are particularly grateful to Li Zhensheng, the author of and photographer for *Red-Color News Soldier: A Chinese Photographer's Odyssey through the Cultural Revolution,* edited by Robert Pledge with text adapted and augmented by Jacques Menasche and introduction by Jonathan D. Spence (New York and London: Phaidon Press, 2003), for permission to reproduce photographs from pages 103 (our photo number 21), 106 (26), 111 (25), 125 (16), 126 (19), 128 (20), 189 (18), 224 (38), 265 (43), and 269 (39), all © Li Zhensheng/Contact Press Images. Our photographs number 16, 44, 47, 48, and 56 are from the excellent collection *The Unforgettable Days (Yongheng zhi ri),* edited by the Photographic Department of the Xinhua News Agency and Jilin Education Publishing House, executive editor Wang Baohua (Changchun, Jilin: Jilin Education Publishing House, 1989), their pages 128 (ill. 1, photographer Chu Ying), 145 (ill. 3, Du Xiuxian), 150 (ill. 2, Du Xiuxian), 152 (ill. 3, Bao Naiyong), 161 (Li Xiaobin). Except for numbers 32 (Schoenhals collection) and 54 (MacFarquhar collection), the remaining photographs are all from the invaluable two-volume *Wenhua dageming bowuguan* (Museum of the Great Cultural Revolution), edited by Yang Kelin, 2 vols. (Hong Kong: Dongfang chubanshe and Tiandi tushu, 1995), 1:88 (our ill. 1), 91–ill. 4 (our ill. 4), 93 (5), 143 (31), 144 (28), 145 (29), 152 (30), 177 (22), 183 (27), 207–ill. 3 (37), 215 (36), 220 (24); 2:400–401 (10, 11), 402–ill. 2 (3), 403–ill. 1 (2), 408–ill. 1 (33), 410 (7), 411–ill. 1 (7), 417 (6), 422–ill. 3 (40), 430 (42), 438 (45), 441–ill. 2 (46), 449–second ill. (41), 460 (row 1, both ills. [our 23, 14]; row 2, both ills. [13, 12]), 461 (row 1, second ill. [15]), 469–ills. 2, 4 (34, 35), 531–ill. 2 (49), 537–ill. 1 (9), 568–ills. 1–2 (50–51), 579–ill. 3 (52), 584–ill. 3 (57), 590 (53), 597–ill. 2 (55). The poster of caricatures on pages 152–153 in Chapter 8 was presented to the authors by Dr. Ronald Suleski.

Index

187, 359, 460; three-in-one alliance and, 202; travels of, 110–113, 132, 151; violence and, 74, 102–103, 117–131, 219, 249, 286, 373; weapons of, 570n6; vs. workers, 161–163; in Wuhan Incident, 199, 200–201, 207, 213, 543n8, 545n44

Red Rebel Regiment (Nankai University), 144–145

red terror, 103, 117–131; attempts to control, 130–131

red vs. expert debate, 21–22, 24

Reference News (internal publication), 86, 115, 121, 139, 140, 509n1, 526n21, 555n45

refugees, 217, 218–219

Ren Bishi, 581n12

Renmin huabao. See *People's Pictorial*

Renmin ribao. See *People's Daily*

repatriation, 122–123

"Report on an Investigation of the Peasant Movement in Hunan" (Mao), 74

The Republic (Plato), 1

Republican revolution (1911), 200

Resistance University (Yan'an), 105

Resolution on Party History (CC), 3, 456–458

revolution, 498n93; uninterrupted, 290–291

revolutionary committees (RCs), 158, 171–173, 238, 239–242, 273, 300; bureaucracy and, 239–240, 243; CCP constitution and, 278; CCRG and, 241, 242–243; "cleansing the class ranks" and, 253, 254, 256, 257; PLA and, 241, 242, 243, 244, 245–246, 568n78; provincial, 239–242, 241, 246, 309, 533n2; students on, 251; "three-in-one" alliances in, 245; Ussuri River incident and, 313; violence and, 240, 243, 244–245, 286; Zhou Enlai and, 241, 242, 244, 553n20

revolutionary successors, 12–13, 137, 171, 247, 250, 356, 362, 593n42

right-deviationist wind, 409–412, 420, 427, 432, 433

Rittenberg, Sidney, 550n34, 582nn26,27, 588n34; on Qincheng Prison, 342–343

Romance of the Three Kingdoms (Luo Guanzhong), 349

Romania, 77

Rong Guotuan, 252

Rosen, Jake, 486n7

rural areas. *See* agriculture; countryside

Rural Work Department, 32

rustication, 173, 251–252, 304, 350, 555nn53,54,55

satellites, 385–386

Scarlet Guards (Shanghai), 162–163, 165, 532n41

Schoenhals, Michael, 590n1, 596n32

schools: CCRG and, 99; closing of, 59–60, 105; discipline in, 248; elementary, 104, 124, 126, 173, 247, 251; military, 176, 201, 245, 509n91; Red Guards in, 201, 251; reopening of, 247–248; work teams in, 66, 67, 82, 84, 105. *See also* colleges and universities; education; middle schools; students; teachers

SDS. *See* Students for a Democratic Society

2nd Headquarters (Mao Zedong Thought Red Guards; Wuhan), 200, 203

Secretariat (CC), 24, 32, 49, 64, 296; CCRG and, 100, 156, 189; demise of, 94; Deng Xiaoping and, 94, 156; reorganization of, 44, 45; role of, 156–157

Selected Essential Letters (CC General Office), 354

Selected Works of Mao Zedong, 240, 445, 447, 451

SEM. *See* Socialist Education Movement

September 13 incident (Lin Biao), 335–336; aftermath of, 337–339. *See also* Lin Biao

Service, John S., 584n58

Seventh Ministry of Machine Building, 385–386

sexuality, 70–71, 74

Shaanxi province, 241, 264, 268, 376

Shadian incident, 387–388

Shandong province, 170, 178, 218, 269, 301

shang shan, xia xiang (up to the mountains and down to the villages), 173, 251–252, 304, 350, 555nn53,54,55

Shanghai, 18, 298, 299, 394; Beijing Red Guards in, 161–162; big-character posters in, 67; "cleansing the class ranks" in, 253, 254, 256; Deng Xiaoping and, 410, 412, 420; economic decline and, 269; February Countercurrent and, 191, 192, 193; Gang of Four and, 189, 357, 439, 448, 449, 594n7;

United Front Work Department (CC), 46, 96
United Kingdom (UK), 5, 7
United Nations (UN), 5, 347, 360
United States: Chinese relations with, 4, 298, 316, 320–323, 350, 365, 584n48; Communists from, 16; Deng's visit to, 453; imperialism of, 222, 305; looting and, 121; partial test-ban treaty (1963) and, 7; Sino-Soviet relations and, 313, 321–322, 572n25; Soviet relations with, 316, 321–322; in students' diaries, 52; Taiwan Straits crisis (1958) and, 6; as threat, 315–316
universities. *See* colleges and universities
up to the mountains and down to the villages. See *shang shan, xia xiang*
"Urgent Instruction" (*Zhongfa* [1966] 515), 135
Ussuri River incident, 309–312

Van Roosbroeck, 225
Vietnam, 313
Vietnam War, 52, 237, 244, 308, 313; Liu Shaoqi on, 510n1, 514n79; opening to U.S. and, 320, 322
violence, 124–131, 199, 252; arms seizures and, 214–216; attempts to control, 239; at Beida, 73–74, 219; in biochemical research facilities, 218; cannibalism and, 259; "cleansing the class ranks" and, 254, 256–259, 261–262; in colleges and universities, 102, 126, 249; in early demonstrations, 71, 73–74; economy and, 205, 218, 220, 268; factionalism and, 216–220; in factories, 217–218, 219, 231; filming of, 121; foreign relations and, 222–224; Mao and, 74, 102–103, 124, 125, 131, 132, 205, 215, 216, 217; media and, 532n56; in middle schools, 102, 103, 104, 126; murder and, 124, 126, 128, 184; "One Strike, Three Anti" campaign and, 301, 306–307; payment for, 204–205; *Pi-Lin pi-Kong* campaign and, 373; by PLA, 178–180; post-Tiananmen (1976) crackdown and, 432; in provinces, 124, 207, 216–220, 262, 316–317, 434; RCs and, 238, 240, 243, 244–245, 286; Red Guards and, 74, 102–103, 117–131, 219, 249, 251, 286, 373; rusticated youth and, 252;

in Shanghai, 161–163; student, 102–103, 124–131, 248–249, 251; tax collection and, 271; women and, 126, 127–128; Wuhan Incident and, 204–205, 208, 210, 212, 214; *Zhongfa* on, 124–125, 130, 204, 317

Wan Li, 43, 124, 473
Wan Xiaotang, 172, 601n56
Wang Baidan, 293
Wang Dabin, 250, 473
Wang Dongxing, 20, 45, 51, 98, 403, 473, 487n23, 576n5; arrest of Gang of Four and, 443, 445, 446, 447, 449; CCEG and, 282, 283; daughter of, 119; death of Mao and, 440; economy and, 383; end of CR and, 450; genius issue and, 331; head-of-state issue and, 325, 326, 327, 329, 331; Politburo and, 296; on political prisoners, 344; roles of, 359; Tenth Party Congress and, 364; verdict on CR and, 409; work teams and, 64; in Wuhan, 207
Wang Dongxing, relations with: Deng Xiaoping, 408, 430; Hua Guofeng, 452, 453; Lin Biao, 318, 319, 336, 577n10, 578n31; Mao, 541n76; Mao Yuanxin, 444; Zhou Enlai, 404
Wang Enmao, 181
Wang Guangmei, 66, 124, 250, 278, 454, 473, 492n7, 567n60; caricature of, 151; CCEG and, 282–283; docudrama about trial of, 503n2; work teams and, 64, 76
Wang Hongwen, 141–142, 160, 162, 351, 473, 586n10; arrest of, 447, 448; attempted power-seizure by, 443; on foreign policy, 365; Gang of Four and, 396–400; genius issue and, 330; May 16 Conspiracy and, 238; Ninth Party Congress and, 288–289; "One Strike, Three Anti" campaign and, 304; *Pi-Lin pi-Kong* campaign and, 369; Politburo factions and, 300; preparations for Mao's death and, 437, 438, 439; readjustment in Zhejiang and, 386; rectification of PLA and, 388, 390; self-criticism by, 399; Shanghai power-seizure and, 164, 166, 169; Tenth Party Congress and, 361, 362, 363, 364; Tiananmen Incident (1976) and, 424; trial of, 455, 456; verdict on CR and,